Violence Against Children in the Family and the Community

Violence Against Children in the Family and the Community

Edited by

Penelope K. Trickett

Cynthia J. Schellenbach

American Psychological Association
Washington, DC

First printing February 1998
Second printing September 1998

Published by
American Psychological Association
750 First Street, NE
Washington, DC 20002

Copies may be ordered from
APA Order Department
P.O. Box 92984
Washington, DC 20090-2984

In the UK and Europe, copies may be ordered from
American Psychological Association
3 Henrietta Street
Covent Garden, London
WC2E 8LU England

Typeset in Goudy by EPS Group Inc., Easton, MD

Printer: Braun-Brumfield, Ann Arbor, MI
Cover Designer: Minker Design, Bethesda, MD
Technical/Production Editor: Catherine R. W. Hudson

Library of Congress Cataloging-in-Publication Data
Violence against children in the family and the community / edited by Penelope K.
    Trickett and Cynthia J. Schellenbach.—1st ed.
        p.   cm.
    Includes bibliographical references and index.
    ISBN 1-55798-480-8
    1. Children and violence—United States.   2. Child development—United
States.   3. Child abuse—United States.   4. Family violence—United
States.   5. Violence—United States—Prevention.   I. Trickett, Penelope K.
II. Schellenbach, Cynthia J.
HQ784.V55V48   1998
362.76—dc21   97-48347
                                                                                             CIP

British Library Cataloguing-in-Publication Data
A CIP record is available from the British Library.

Printed in the United States of America

CONTENTS

CONTRIBUTORS

LaRue Allen, New York University, NY

Frank Barry, Cornell University, Ithaca, NY

C. Hendricks Brown, University of South Florida, Tampa

Patricia McKinsey Crittenden, Family Relations Institute, Miami, FL

Norma D. Feshbach, University of California, Los Angeles

Seymour Feshbach, University of California, Los Angeles

James Garbarino, Cornell University, Ithaca, NY

Nancy Guerra, University of Illinois, Chicago

Jeffrey J. Haugaard, Cornell University, Ithaca, NY

John L. Horn, University of Southern California, Los Angeles

David Kolko, University of Pittsburgh Medical Center, PA

Kathleen Kostelny, Erikson Institute, Chicago, IL

Deborah Land, University of Virginia, Charlottesville

Susan P. Limber, University of South Carolina, Columbia

Gayla Margolin, University of Southern California, Los Angeles

Judith C. Meyers, Consulting Services, Geneva, NY

Joel S. Milner, Northern Illinois University, Dekalb

Maury A. Nation, University of South Carolina, Columbia

Frank W. Putnam, National Institute of Mental Health, Bethesda, MD

N. Dickon Reppucci, University of Virginia, Charlottesville

Jane Silovsky, University of Oklahoma Health Sciences Center, Oklahoma City

Ronald G. Slaby, Education Development Center, Newton, MA

Cynthia J. Schellenbach, Oakland University, Rochester, MI

Penelope K. Trickett, University of Southern California, Los Angeles

Patrick H. Tolan, University of Illinois, Chicago

Christine Wekerle, York University, Ontario, Canada

Brian L. Wilcox, University of Nebraska, Lincoln

Diane J. Willis, University of Oklahoma Health Sciences Center, Oklahoma City

David A. Wolfe, The University of Western Ontario, Canada

Edward F. Zigler, Yale University, New Haven, CT

ACKNOWLEDGMENTS

The springboard for this book was a conference held at the University of Southern California in 1995, which brought together researchers from all over the United States interested in the causes and developmental consequences of violence experienced by children and the issues of prevention, early intervention, and public policy. This conference, planned by the American Psychological Association's Committee on Children, Youth, and Families, was supported by APA's Board for the Advancement of Psychology in the Public Interest, several APA divisions, and the University of Southern California. The interest and excitement generated by this conference resulted in the decision to develop this book.

We would especially like to thank Mary Campbell and Henry Tomes of APA's Public Interest Directorate for their support of this process all along the way, and Peggy Schlegel, Judy Nemes, and Catherine Hudson of APA Books for wonderful assistance in bringing the book to completion. We are also very grateful to our many colleagues who aided in the editorial process by reviewing manuscripts and to Lorena Duran who, starting as a work study student at USC, has provided supremely competent clerical and research assistance. We are ever grateful for the help and support of our families—Colon, Nikki, Troy, and Jonathon Brown (CJS); and John Horn, and Jennifer and Kate Trickett (PKT).

Violence Against Children in the Family and the Community

1

INTRODUCTION

PENELOPE K. TRICKETT AND CYNTHIA J. SCHELLENBACH

Children in the United States experience violence in many forms. They are the victims of physical and sexual abuse within their families; they witness battering of and by their parents; and they experience or witness physical or sexual violence in their schools or day care centers, on the playground, or in their neighborhoods. U.S. society has been aware of the frequency of this exposure to violence for only about 30 years. In the late 1960s, doctors "discovered" that children were being physically injured by parents and coined the term *battered-child syndrome* (Kempe, Silverman, Steele, Droegemueller, & Silver, 1962). About a decade later, awareness arose of the alarming frequency of sexual abuse, which had previously been considered an extremely rare phenomenon. It is only in the last decade that professionals have considered the impact on children of two other forms of violence, domestic violence and community violence.

Recent studies have indicated that the incidence of physical and sexual abuse in the United States is extremely high and apparently still increasing. The third national incidence study by the National Center of Child Abuse and Neglect (NCCAN, 1996) indicated that the annual incidence of child physical abuse doubled from 1986 to 1993, with the number of children known to be physically abused in 1993 totaling over 600,000. During this same interval, the number of children who were seriously injured from all forms of child maltreatment, including physical abuse, sexual abuse, and neglect, nearly quadrupled to more than 572,000 yearly. The same study documented that approximately 300,000 children were recognized to have been sexually abused in 1993. This figure represents an increase in recognized cases of child sexual abuse of about 125% from 1986 (NCCAN, 1988) and an increase of more than 600% from 1980 to 1993 (Burgdorf, 1980; NCCAN, 1996). A number of prevalence studies have suggested even higher rates of sexual abuse than are indicated by this work on annual incidence. In separate studies, for example, Russell (1986) and Finkelhor, Hotaling, Lewis, and Smith (1990) reported childhood prevalence rates between 27% and 38%.

Although there are no national incidence studies of the number of children who witness domestic violence, there are studies of the incidence of domestic violence in the United States, and there is information on the proportion of such families in which there are children. From these figures, estimates have been made that each year between 3 and 10 million children are at risk of exposure to interparental violence (i.e., are residing in homes where such violence occurs (Carlson, 1984; Straus, 1992)). Even less is known about the number of children who witness community violence each year. We do know that such violence is frequent, especially in many urban areas, and that it often occurs in neighborhoods in which children reside. Researchers of studies with delimited samples have suggested the high frequency of such exposure, at least for urban children. For example, Shakoor and Chalmers (1991) found that nearly three fourths of a sample of 1,000 urban African American elementary and high school students reported witnessing at least one robbery, stabbing, shooting, or murder. In another study, every child in a sample of children living in public housing in Chicago had witnessed a shooting by age 5 (Garbarino, Dubrow, Kostelny, & Pardo, 1992). Jenkins and Bell (1997) reviewed a number of other studies of exposure to community violence that also indicate high rates, especially for adolescents in poor inner-city communities.

Although there is some uncertainty about how often these different forms of violence are experienced by children in the United States, it is clear that it is a disturbingly frequent occurrence for many, and thus there is an urgent need to understand the impact of these different forms of violence on children's development and to determine the best ways to ameliorate adverse effects or to prevent them entirely. The research needed to address some of the issues has been proliferating recently, paralleling the awareness of these different phenomena: First, there was research on the causes and developmental consequences of child physical abuse, then of child sexual abuse, and most recently of children's exposure to domestic violence and community violence. Over the same decades, the quality of the research has improved, and a lot has been learned; however, there is a lack of integration in this research. For the most part, the researchers who study the causes or developmental consequences of one form of violence are different individuals (not infrequently from different disciplines or with different perspectives) from those who research other forms of violence. As a result, it has been difficult to answer questions such as the following: Are the adverse effects of maltreatment or violence experienced by a child the result of a general stress reaction common to all types of violence experiences or exposure, or are there specific effects of, for example, physical versus sexual violence? Do chronic or long-lasting experiences (e.g., physical abuse over many years) have the same impact as acute or one-time-only experiences (e.g., witnessing a murder)? What difference does it make if the parent, rather than some other individual, is the perpetrator of the violence? What difference does it make at what age or developmental stage different forms of violence are experienced by children?

It has been equally difficult to answer integrating questions concerning the degree to which the causal factors of different forms of violence experienced by children overlap and the degree to which they are distinct. Cicchetti and Lynch (1993) described a transactional–ecological model of community violence and child maltreatment: "A question to be addressed, then, is to what extent do violent communities and maltreating families find each other? It is possible that the same type of psychological factors within parents that are associated with maltreatment draw families to communities where there is extensive violence" (p. 101). Until questions such as these are answered, the design and efficacy of efforts toward intervention and prevention targeting these different forms of violence will be compromised. Integration, therefore, is the focus of this book: to establish integrated theory and knowledge about (a) the impact of these varied forms of violence on children's development, (b) the causes of these forms of violence, and (c) effective prevention and intervention strategies.

The book is organized into five parts. The first part consists of four chapters on the consequences of these varied forms of violence for children's well-being and development. The book begins with the consequences of violence for children's development; our purpose is to make explicit and emphasize that the focus of the book is the children and how violence affects their lives. This part begins with a chapter by Crittenden in which she reviews 35 years of research on physical abuse of children, presenting a unique perspective on how the physical abuse of children can be understood in terms of parent–child attachment. Next, Trickett and Putnam examine research on the consequences of sexual abuse within an explicitly developmental framework. Margolin reviews considerable research on the impact of domestic violence on the children who witness it. Finally, Horn and Trickett review the much smaller body of research on how community violence affects children, emphasizing the methodological complexities of this "first-generation" research and suggesting directions for advancing the field.

To understand how violence affects children and how one can ameliorate these effects or prevent the violence, it is essential to understand the complex, multiple causes of these forms of violence. The three chapters of the second part consider causes within an ecological framework. The first chapter, by Milner, reviews research on causes of violence within children's most critical microsystem—the family. Limber and Nation then examine causes at the level of the larger systems of the neighborhood and community; Tolan and Guerra focus on causes at the societal level.

The third and fourth parts of the book examine the state of knowledge about effective intervention and prevention strategies, that is, efforts to ameliorate the adverse developmental consequences of violence, to prevent recurrences of these varied forms of violence, and to prevent such violence from taking place at all. The third part summarizes the knowledge base on intervention and treatment programs for these forms of violence. In the first chapter, Kolko summarizes recent research on treatment of children who have experienced various forms of abuse, especially sexual abuse and physical abuse. In the next chapter, Schellenbach examines the research on treatment for abusive families. This chapter underscores the emphasis to date on changing the parenting of physically abusive parents, especially mothers, recognizing that little research has focused on the parent–child relationship in intervention for sexual abuse, domestic violence, or community violence. Feshbach and Feshbach examine violence in schools and describe ongoing research on school-based intervention programs. Garbarino, Kostelny, and Barry describe the state of research on child abuse intervention at the neighborhood and community level.

The fourth part of the book focuses on prevention of all forms of violence toward children. Reppucci, Land, and Haugaard open this part with a summary of prevention research that targets children; essentially all of this research has examined whether children can prevent their own sexual victimization. Wekerle and Wolfe follow with a presentation of theory and research on efforts at prevention directed toward parents and potential parents. In this area, the emphasis has been on the prevention of physical abuse. In the next chapter, Slaby summarizes the state of knowledge on prevention of violence at the neighborhood level. The part closes with a broadly defined view by Willis and Silovsky of efforts at prevention at the societal level.

Finally, in the fifth and concluding part, the focus is on how to address gaps in knowledge about violence that affects children and about effective intervention and prevention strategies. Trickett, Allen, Schellenbach, and Zigler integrate the research reviewed in the earlier chapters on the consequences and causes of these different forms of violence and discuss how this knowledge can be used to advance intervention and prevention approaches. Tolan and Brown provide a practical approach to conducting evaluations of intervention and prevention programs to enhance the knowledge of effectiveness. Meyers and Wilcox describe the public policy implications of the research reviewed in previous chapters, indicate how the value of this research for policy can be enhanced, and caution about the limitations of research knowledge in influencing the policy process.

The chapters included in this book show that research knowledge about violence that affects the lives of children is extensive and that such knowledge has aided the development of appropriate intervention and prevention programs. It is also clear that there are considerable gaps in knowledge that need to be filled and that there are even greater gaps in how this knowledge has been used to develop ways to prevent the violence from occurring or at least ameliorating its negative consequences for children. The hope and promise of this book is that it can provide the background and the impetus for future advances.

REFERENCES

Burgdorf, K. (1980). *Recognition and reporting of child maltreatment: Summary findings from the national study of the incidence and severity of child abuse and neglect.* Washington, DC: National Center for Child Abuse and Neglect, U.S. Department of Health and Human Services.

Carlson, B. E. (1984). Children's observations of interparental violence. In A. R. Roberts (Ed.), *Battered women and their families* (pp. 147–167). New York: Springer.

Cicchetti, D., & Lynch, M. (1993). Toward an ecological/transactional model of community violence and child maltreatment: Consequences for children's development. In D. Reiss, J. E. Richters, M. Radke-Yarrow, & D. Scharff (Eds.), *Children and violence* (pp. 96–118). New York: Guilford Press.

Finkelhor, D., Hotaling, G., Lewis, I. A., & Smith, C. (1990). Sexual abuse in a national survey of adult men and women: Prevalence, characteristics and risk factors. *Child Abuse and Neglect, 14,* 19–28.

Garbarino, J., Dubrow, N., Kostelny, K., & Pardo, C. (1992). *Children in danger: Coping with the consequences of community violence.* San Francisco: Jossey-Bass.

Jenkins, E. J., & Bell, C. C. (1997). Exposure and response to community violence among children and adolescents. In J. E. Osofsky (Ed.), *Children in a violent society* (pp. 9–31). New York: Guilford Press.

Kempe, C., Silverman, F., Steele, B., Droegemueller, W., & Silver, H. (1962). The battered child syndrome. *Journal of the American Medical Association, 181,* 17–24.

National Center for Child Abuse and Neglect (NCCAN). (1988). *Study of national* incidence and prevalence of child abuse and neglect. Washington DC: U.S. Department of Health and Human Services.

National Center for Child Abuse and Neglect (NCCAN). (1996). *Third study of national incidence and prevalence of child abuse and neglect*. Washington, DC: U.S. Department of Health and Human Services.

Russell, D. E. H. (1986). *The secret trauma: Incest in the lives of girls and women*. New York: Basic Books.

Shakoor, B. H., & Chalmers, D. (1991). Co-victimization of African American children who witness violence and the theoretical implications of its effects on their cognitive, emotional, and behavioral development. *Journal of the National Medical Association, 83*, 233–238.

Straus, M. A. (1992). Children as witnesses to marital violence: A risk factor for lifelong problems among a nationally representative sample of American men and women. In D. Schwarz (Ed.), *Children and violence: Report of the twenty-third Ross roundtable on critical approaches to common pediatric problems* (pp. 98–109). Columbus, OH: Ross Laboratories.

I

THE DEVELOPMENTAL CONSEQUENCES OF VIOLENCE AGAINST CHILDREN

2

DANGEROUS BEHAVIOR AND DANGEROUS CONTEXTS: A 35-YEAR PERSPECTIVE ON RESEARCH ON THE DEVELOPMENTAL EFFECTS OF CHILD PHYSICAL ABUSE

PATRICIA McKINSEY CRITTENDEN

In 1962, professionals were appalled to "discover" that some parents battered their children (Kempe, Silverman, Steele, Droegemueller, & Silver, 1962). The task at that time seemed to be to learn how to differentiate these severe and life-threatening injuries from accidental injuries and to protect children from such dangerous parents. Back then, it was thought that there were only a few such parents and that "they" were recognizably different from "us." It also was presumed that members of society could protect the innocent children so that they could grow up to live happy and normal lives.

Thirty-five years of research have yielded a different picture of child abuse. First, researchers have found more child abuse than anyone expected; the few have become many. In addition, the definition of acceptable parental discipline of children has narrowed to the point that most parents at some time treat their children in ways that some would call abusive. "They" have become "us." Furthermore, it has become clear that abuse and accidental injury are not clearly differentiable—that they have more shared than unique features (Newberger, Hampton, Marx, & White, 1986; Peterson & Brown, 1994). Possibly even more unsettling is the growing awareness that everyone helps to create and maintain the social conditions that increase the probability that some parents will harm their children. Such conditions include poverty, single-parent and divorced families, overwhelmed service systems, and the glorification of violence in the media and entertainment industry. Finally, social scientists are coming to realize that child abuse is not simply an event between two people. To the contrary, there is an underlying psychological process between individuals, among family members, and within communities that reflects predictable patterns in the way the individuals process information about danger and safety. In this chapter, I explore these observations and suggest areas for future work. Because the emerging understanding of the interpersonal nature of abuse implies a developmental process, I focus on the developmental impact of growing up in dangerous environments.

THE STATE OF RESEARCH ON PHYSICAL ABUSE OF CHILDREN

Research on child abuse,[1] in contrast to research on most other forms of maltreatment, is rapidly becoming a mature field of study. An emerging focus on any clinical condition passes through a predictable series of transitions, and research on child abuse exemplifies this process well.

Initial Work

Early on, research focused on proving that abuse, that is, the "battered-child syndrome," existed. Following publication of an article by Kempe et al. in 1962, clinical case studies were published, which were followed by incidence studies and later by epidemiological studies. Once abuse was shown to be real and prevalent, studies of its correlates became the focus of research activity. Researchers reported on the demographic and personality characteristics of abused children and the adults who abused them. As a result, child abuse came to be viewed as a problem associated primarily with minority and disadvantaged groups.

Causal Theories

Identification of the correlates of child abuse led to causal attributions regarding risk for abuse. A variety of myths were publicized: Abuse was

---

[1]In this chapter, the term *abuse* refers to physical rather than sexual abuse.

more common in minority-group cultures; teenaged parents and single parents were more likely to commit abuse; there was a "scapegoat child" in abusive families; children who were abused would become abusers. Although there were data to lend some credence to each of these conclusions, the data were insufficient to validate them.

At the same time, the range of conditions associated with abuse increased with each new study. It began to appear that all bad things were interconnected both laterally across many domains of personal functioning and also hierarchically across many levels of social interaction, from social policy to neighborhood and family functioning to interpersonal and intrapersonal functioning. By the late 1970s, professionals knew a lot about child abuse, enough, in fact, to be overwhelmed by its multiple causes and the multiple relations among the causal conditions. It was as though a Pandora's box had been opened that made careful viewing of any segment of the problem simply magnify the awareness of the complexity and interconnectedness of the rest of the problem.

Identifying the Unique and Shared Aspects of Child Abuse

During the 1980s, researchers began refining knowledge with better designed studies that had increasingly carefully selected comparison groups and sophisticated, multimethod procedures. Psychologists, particularly those working at the intersection of developmental and clinical psychology, brought the methodological rigor and skeptical inquiry typical of academic research to the politically sensitive and highly clinical field of child abuse. With these studies, researchers were able to differentiate the effects of correlated sets of variables. For example, socioeconomic status was identified as more important than minority-group membership (Wauchope & Straus, 1990). Also, it was found that a history of abuse as a child was common among identified adult abusers, but that abused children did not necessarily become abusers (Kaufman & Zigler, 1988). In addition, groups of researchers began series of studies that were bound together by the application of one or another theoretical perspective. These perspectives were drawn from sociology (Straus & Gelles, 1990), behaviorism (Wolfe, Sandler, & Kaufman, 1981), sociobiology (Daly & Wilson, 1981), attachment theory (Aber & Allen, 1988; Carlson, Cicchetti, Barnett, & Braunwald, 1989; Crittenden & Ainsworth, 1989; Egeland & Sroufe, 1981), and social ecology (Belsky, 1980; Garbarino, 1977). Possibly even more important were attempts to combine several psychological theories, for example, cognitive–behaviorial–developmental (Azar, 1986), or several systems theories, such as communication, attachment, family systems, social ecology (Crittenden, 1992b), and ecological–transactional (Cicchetti & Lynch, 1993), to create complex, hierarchical understandings of the influences on maltreating families.

The evidence indicated that families in which children are injured, whether intentionally or accidentally, (a) live in low-income neighborhoods characterized by high rates of crime and violence, (b) have large numbers of children relative to the number of protective and supervising adults, (c) are isolated from nonfamilial supportive networks, (d) move frequently (and thus often are in unfamiliar settings and surrounded by unknown people), and (e) have relatively young and, often, single parents. All of these conditions increase stress and reduce the safety of children. It is not surprising, therefore, that parents of injured children are often found to be stressed, emotionally disturbed, and substance abusing (possibly as a self-medicating form of anxiety reduction). In addition, their children are often irritable and difficult as infants and anxious and hard to supervise when older.

These attempts at integrative theory acknowledged the complexity and breadth of child abuse but did not explain its occurrence. Although the components can be organized hierarchically, by community, family, and person, there is no evidence of a *causal* hierarchy. To the contrary, the common components seem to be simply *danger* and *response to danger*. After 35 years of research, the clearest findings are that bad things are highly correlated and that interventions to change sets of these components yield some effects, but that no intervention lowers the incidence of injury to children or prevents the long-term effects of living in dangerous environments on children (and on the adults they become). If danger is, indeed, the unifying component, the question becomes how environmental danger is translated into higher rates of dangerous behavior among both children and their caregivers.

Critical Causes

In a chapter written by Mary Ainsworth and myself (Crittenden & Ainsworth, 1989), we suggested that the plethora of "causes" of child abuse needed to be reduced to a small number that were "critical causes," that is, aspects of functioning that, if changed, would lead to a concatenating set of changes throughout the set of factors supporting abusive behavior. One critical cause, we thought, was the availability to the family of at least one trustworthy, supportive, and protective attachment figure. More recently, I suggested that information processing may be a critical variable that can explain why attachment figures behave as they do, particularly when their behavior endangers the children they claim to love and protect (Crittenden, 1993). In this chapter, I describe the search for a "critical cause" by noting that danger itself may change the way people process information about safety and danger and that awareness of this process might lead to improved intervention strategies.

Integrating Child Abuse Research With Research on Normative Development and Psychopathology

The influx of theoretically focused researchers into the study of child abuse created the potential for bridges of communication between those studying normal development and those concerned with child abuse and between researchers in the fields of psychopathology and child abuse (Cicchetti & Toth, 1991). The flow of information has gone both ways: An understanding of abuse has enriched the understanding of normal developmental processes and psychopathology, and work in those areas has enlightened the perspective with regard to abuse. As a result, researchers have begun to focus on normative developmental processes as they affect children and families in varying circumstances, including a range of threatening circumstances. As a further result, fewer researchers work solely on child abuse, and more researchers do some work on abuse, with the outcome of greater integration of findings among otherwise disparate and specialized areas.

This change reflects a maturing of the field; interactive processes (rather than events, social conditions, or traits) have become the fundamental constructs used to organize meaning about development. In such research, abuse is defined primarily as a person–environment interaction that has characteristics that affect individuals' mental and behavioral functioning in specifiable, but probabilistic, ways. In particular, the recognition of the near universality of violence in the ontogenesis of psychopathology and in the history of abusive parents has focused attention on the effects of danger on human development. This is, I think, the single most powerful and meaningful outcome of 35 years of research on child abuse.

IMPORTANT FINDINGS ON THE EFFECTS OF DANGER ON CHILDREN

Among the hundreds of conclusions about child abuse that can be drawn from the research, I focus on several that are supported by mounting evidence, that lend themselves to integration into a unifying theory, and that may be critical to designing effective interventions. My phrasing of these findings reflects a focus on processes and organizations of behavior, as well as the focus of attachment theory on functional outcomes. Furthermore, it reflects a conscious attempt to avoid the evaluative moral–ethical framework in which most child abuse research has been cast and to focus instead on describing the phenomena.

Physical Abuse Reflects an Extreme of Normative Parenting

Although for political reasons child abuse is often identified with heinous incidents of injury to children, in fact most abuse is not spectacular, not life threatening, not an isolated occurrence, and not limited to a small number of children. To the contrary, most often it is minor, recurrent, accompanied by other forms of danger such as neglect and psychological maltreatment, and in the form of physical punishment directed toward most children in the family (Briere & Runtz, 1988; Claussen & Crittenden, 1991; Crittenden, Claussen, & Sugarman, 1994; Herrenkohl, Herrenkohl, Egolf, & Seech, 1980; Straus, 1994; USDHHS, 1994, 1996; Wauchope & Straus, 1990). Moreover, there is evidence that many of the effects of child abuse are attributable to neglect and psychological maltreatment (Brassard, Germain, & Hart, 1987; Claussen & Crittenden, 1991; Crittenden et al., 1994; Jean-Gilles & Crittenden, 1990). These findings suggest that much of the developmental impact of abuse results from something other than the injury itself. Similarly, a number of researchers have pointed out the similarity of abuse to physical punishment (Straus, 1994), other distortions of parenting behavior (Trickett, 1993; Wolfe, 1993a, 1993b), and accidental injury (Peterson & Brown, 1994). This observation suggests that abuse is not a discrete category of event and that abusive parents are not categorically different from other parents. To the contrary, abuse appears to be one outcome among many of the system of conditions affecting parental behavior. Understanding this requires an understanding of the motivation underlying parental behavior. Instead of asking what is wrong with adults who are violent to children, one might ask why so many humans do this. How can this behavior serve our species? What differentiates minor violence against children, such as spanking, from child abuse? At least one obvious answer is that parents at the dangerous extremes of otherwise common child-rearing practices are those who live in the most dangerous circumstances and have themselves experienced the most danger in the past. One focus of inquiry, therefore, might be the role of danger in human development.

Child Abuse May Be Related to Protection

Child abuse reflects a familial and interpersonal process that may be tied to the function of protection from danger. More children are harmed by parents than by people with any other relationship to children. Apparently, love not only fails to protect children, but could be considered a risk factor. Moreover, although there is little evidence of particular personality traits typifying abusers, there is ample evidence that individuals who abuse their children have trouble managing anger in other committed relationships (Averill, 1982). These include spousal relationships: Abusive adults often are in violent marriages; frequently find it difficult to maintain adult partnerships; and are often unmarried, separated, or divorced. Furthermore, abuse of one child often indicates that other children in the family have been or will be mistreated (Jean-Gilles & Crittenden, 1990). Abusive adults were often maltreated when they were children. In addition, the distorted interpersonal styles of endangering familial relationships have been shown to pervade more distal relationships such as friendships, professional relationships, and peer relationships, which are characterized by angry displays and threats of dissolution (Crittenden, 1985, 1988; Garbarino & Sherman, 1980; George & Main, 1979). In other words, abuse has something to do with love, anger, and fear in the process of human interaction, particularly familial interaction.

Explaining the presence of so much violence among people who love one another is difficult. I suggest the possibility that fear of danger is often expressed as anger and underlies much family violence. For example, although spousal violence appears to involve anger, there is evidence that it also reflects fear of abandonment. Both the accusations of infidelity that are used by men to explain their violence and women's increased vulnerability to spousal violence when they plan to leave abusive men suggest that men's fear of abandonment leads to angry displays that function to maintain the partnership.[2] In this way, adult anger functions like the anger of children toward insufficiently available attachment figures: Anger both attracts the parent's attention and, by its unpleasantness, reduces the probability that the attachment figure will repeat the anger-eliciting behavior.[3]

A similar motivation may underlie many instances of child abuse. In this case, parents' fear that vulnerable children will not be safe may elicit angry displays aimed at keeping children from doing dangerous things, such as putting objects in their mouth or in electrical sockets or running into the street. With older children, parents' punishment of lack of respect (Peterson, Ewigman, & Vandiver, 1994) highlights the importance of respect as a measure of children's likelihood of following parental directives when parents are absent. The rationale, in both spousal and parental violence, is that interpersonal behavior is organized to promote the safety of self, children, and partners; this includes both children's activities when unsupervised and the long-term maintenance of relationships that have a protective function. When necessary, the function of protection may be promoted through angry feelings that motivate violent behavior. Punishment can lead to inhibition of the danger-eliciting behavior that preceded it and, therefore, can reduce the probability of danger in the future. Of course, the inhibitory effect is achieved only if the punishment is specific

---

[2]The argument is not that this is the only cause of spousal abuse, but that it is one important precipitant of violence.
[3]See Bowlby (1973) for a discussion of anger as an attachment behavior.

and predictable. Similarly, the protective effect is achieved only if the punishment is not injurious itself.

As a corollary to the notion of the protective function of anger, it is hypothesized that the more fearful parents are about their children's safety, the greater is the likelihood of their experiencing angry feelings and behaving violently. Because children are more vulnerable than adults and are in dangerous circumstances more often than adults (Finkelhor & Dzuiba-Leatherman, 1994), more angry and violent behavior would be expected to be displayed toward children than toward adults. Furthermore, parents living in dangerous neighborhoods would be expected to fear for the safety of their children more often than parents in safe contexts and thus to display violent behavior more often (Kelley, 1992). One risk is that fear, combined with high demands for supervision, will result in inconsistent use of physical punishment; because it is motivated by intense affect, it may also be dangerously harsh.

In conclusion, it appears that violence toward children is not an isolated behavior but reflects a pattern across time and other familial relationships. I propose that familial violence often reflects the use of anger in response to concern for children's safety and that its function is protection. In cases of abuse, the risk is that the cure may be more dangerous than the original danger. The issue is probabilistic, analogous to giving a toxic medicine to a person with a life-threatening disease; if, overall, more people are protected, society accepts the risk to the few. Intrafamilial violence may function similarly, differing primarily in the lack of conscious awareness of the evolved motive for the behavior.

Child Abuse Affects Mental Processing

Child abuse is dangerous. It affects the way information is mentally processed and used to organize behavior. Attachment theory is concerned with how parents protect children from danger until children can protect themselves. The conflict between these two statements explains in part the reason so many researchers have sought explanations for abuse and its effects in distortions of attachment relationships between parent and child. Although this line of research has produced the universal finding of distorted attachment relationships in maltreating families (Carlson et al., 1989; Crittenden, 1985, 1988; Egeland & Sroufe, 1981; Gaensbauer & Harmon, 1982; Lyons-Ruth, Connell, & Zoll, 1989), anxious attachment is not specific to cases of abuse or even to injury or maltreatment. Furthermore, the underlying process that yields anxious attachment, as well as the effects of anxious attachment on caregiver behavior, needs exploration. Differences in the way information about danger is processed may inform these issues.

The Neurobiology of Response to Danger

Researchers have begun to focus on biological explanations for human behavior. I offer a biological explanation for some violence, but it depends on the universal genetic heritage of the human species interacting with individuals' experiences, which are unique. Evolutionary and learning theory provide much of the explanatory process, whereas attachment theory points to the function of that process, that is, to the essential roles of safety and danger in organizing mental and behavioral functioning of both parents and children. The argument is that learning about safety and danger is an innate, preconscious priority that organizes mental and behavioral functioning for all humans. Exactly what is learned and how that learning is expressed vary as a function of life circumstances.

Privileged information. I propose that the human brain has evolved to identify dangerous circumstances in several ways.[4] One is a predisposition to focus perception and attention on circumstances relevant to danger and safety. One way that this occurs is through the functioning of sensory neurons that respond differentially to unfamiliar (novel) or intense stimuli (Le Doux, 1994). Because most dangerous conditions are either unfamiliar or intense, this innate perceptual–attentional bias promotes preferential attention to potential dangers. Although individuals differ by temperament in their innate thresholds of response to novelty and intensity, experience resets these thresholds to fit actual conditions. Thus, if novelty has not been associated with danger, neuronal functioning changes to permit higher tolerance of novelty before defensive processes begin. Similarly, if danger has been associated with subtle changes in intensity, individuals become more alert to these; that is, they become hypervigilant. With experience, individuals become neurologically attuned to their unique context.

Temporally ordered, cognitive information. A second way that danger is identified is through the tendency of humans to organize events temporally, such that events that have often preceded danger become learned stimuli that predict danger. In the presence of such stimuli, according to the principles of learning theory (Pavlov, 1928; Skinner, 1976), humans modify their behavior in protective ways, either by inhibiting danger-eliciting behavior or by exhibiting danger-preventing behavior. The neurological processing of temporally ordered information occurs simultaneously through several neural pathways that differ in (a) the number of synapses, (b) the portions of the brain included in the pathway, and (c) the time it takes to complete the pathway and initiate action. The shortest route involves only the afferent sensory neurons, brain stem, mediating nuclei, cerebellum, and efferent nerves to the muscles (Thompson, 1991). This route yields extremely rapid, preconscious, and maximally protective sensorimotor behav-

---

[4]See Crittenden (in press) for a fuller discussion of neurological functioning.

ior. It is not, however, well attuned to (a) subtle differences among eliciting stimuli, (b) conditional relations among stimuli, or (c) contextual variables that affect the probability of specific outcomes. For example, in response to an angry face, a child may learn to inhibit crying. However, without cortical processing that involves more synapses and additional time, the child cannot differentiate conditions in which he or she is the source of parental anger (and therefore truly in danger) from circumstances in which other conditions are responsible for the anger (and therefore the child may not be in danger). Thus, subcortical processing provides rapid, protective action, but at the cost of accuracy. Depending on the probability of severe danger (as assessed by heuristics such as novelty and intensity), either immediate action is undertaken or cortical processing continues.

Needless to say, the greater the prior experience of self-threatening danger (particularly danger from which one was not protected), the more likely it is that the shorter route of rapid, preconscious, precortical responding will be used. Furthermore, in infancy full cortical processing is not possible because substantial portions of the cortex mature only after birth (Mrzljak, Uylings, van Eden, & Judas, 1990; Uylings & van Eden, 1990). This circumstance imposes precortical defensive responding on infants and may account for some of the enduring effects of exposure to danger early in life. Functionally, temporal ordering of incoming sensory information is treated as evidence of a causal relation between preceding and subsequent events. Without advanced cortical processing (possible only in mature humans), errors of causal attribution may be made and may influence behavior, such that the behavior appears irrational (Crittenden, 1995, 1997a, in press).

I label the transformation of sensory input on the basis of predictable temporal order *cognitive* information. Cognitive information regulates behavior when events have a predictable temporal relation. It is used by all infants and by older people whenever circumstances are familiar (and thus do not require cortical processing) or when circumstances are perceived to be extremely dangerous (and thus there is insufficient time for cortical processing). This analysis has implications for children whose parents behave in predictably harsh ways to enforce rules of (safe) behavior.

Contextually sensitive, affective information. The third way of identifying danger is on the basis of feelings of anxiety that are elicited by contextual stimuli, for example, darkness, loud noises, and being alone. These stimuli function as natural cues to an increased probability of danger (Bowlby, 1973; Le Doux, 1986; Seligman, 1971). Of these stimuli, being alone is especially important because one person is more vulnerable than two. Moreover, people are safest when the second person is stronger and wiser than they are and committed to their welfare; that is, one is safest with an attachment figure (Bowlby, 1982). Information about universally risky contexts is encoded genetically and permits response to dangers that have not yet been experienced; the advantage is that defensive action can be taken prior to risk of injury or death (during the first opportunity for experiential learning). In addition, experience with danger or anxiety can become associated with contextual conditions, thus expanding (both accurately and erroneously) the conditions that, in the future, will elicit feelings of anxiety (Pavlov, 1928). Feelings of anxiety motivate individuals to defend themselves through preparing to fight, flee, or freeze (Lang, 1995; Selye, 1976), whereas a display of feelings elicits protective caregiving from others, especially attachment figures.[5] Finally, generalized, "free-floating" anxiety is composed of at least three separate feelings states: fear, anger, and desire for comfort. Depending on immediate circumstances, one or another may be the perceived feeling. For example, a mother whose child is missing feels intense fear, but when the child is found, her former fear may be expressed to the child as anger.

Information about cues to danger is processed through the limbic system, particularly through the amygdala. As in temporally ordered information, there are several parallel processing routes that differ in time and specificity. The shortest route is through the thalamus to the limbic system to the brain stem for reflexive responding. The addition of the cerebellum to the output pathway permits variation in the motor response (but takes possibly precious time). Inclusion of the sensory cortices in the early processing of the stimulus permits differentiation of similar stimuli that may have different implications for safety. This takes longer but prevents over-inclusive responding. Further processing through the prefrontal cortices permits inhibition of inappropriate responses, whereas an additional pathway from the prefrontal cortex to the hippocampus results in relational processing, that is, conditional and contextual variations on the probability of danger (Eichenbaum, 1994). Because these pathways take longer, they are suspended if early processing suggests high probabilities of danger or the probability of severe danger. These facts lead to the observation that, under stress (i.e., threat of danger), "primitive" fears are elicited and regulate behavior (Jacobs & Nadel, 1985). Moreover, the prefrontal cortex and hippocampus are not mature at birth (Nadel, Wilson, & Kurz, 1993). Patterns of preconscious, affect-laden, protective response are influenced by intensity and novelty of stimuli as well as by maturation. Furthermore, recent experience with fear-eliciting stimuli leads to potentiated response states in which the individual is hypervigilant with regard to stimuli indicative of danger, responds more rapidly to such stimuli, and responds with greater amplitude. In such cases, the defensive response is said to be *primed* (Brown, Chapman, Kairiss, & Keenan, 1988; Brown, Kalish, & Farber, 1951). The more intense and frequent the danger that is experienced

---

[5]See Campos, Campos, and Barrett (1989) and Gut (1989) for examples of the interpersonal, communicative function of affect.

early in life and throughout life, the more rapid, protective, affect laden, and preconscious will be the response. When the relation among events is unpredictable, affect (indicative of dangerous contexts) is particularly likely to organize behavior. This has implications for children of unpredictable, chaotic, overwhelmed, or affectively labile parents.

Cortical integration. Cortical functioning, which does not develop fully until late adolescence, takes longer and enables the mind to make finer distinctions and construct more adaptive responses. Furthermore, cortical functioning includes integration of cognitively transformed information with affectively transformed information. Depending on which source of information has been more reliable in the past in predicting danger and organizing protective responses, the mind will weight the inputs accordingly. Cortical processing also permits correction of processing errors of cognition and affect. In addition, through recall of previous experiences, it makes possible reconsideration of past responses to danger (or misattributions of danger) and mental construction of more adaptive responses. Thus, cortical processing during and after danger improves the quality of response. If danger is perceived to be highly likely or imminent, however, such processing is unlikely to take place. Cortical processing is most frequent and thorough under conditions of relative safety. When parents and children live in dangerous conditions (or believe that they do), they are less likely to delay responding to engage in cortical problem solving.

Experience-dependent organization of brain structure and function. Current knowledge of the experience-dependent organization of the brain (Edelman, 1987) indicates that these processes are even more significant. The human brain is highly plastic at birth, and repeated patterns of processing influence brain development. The human brain adapts to the constraints of its developmental context. When that context contains substantial danger, the outcome is exquisite sensitivity to cues to danger, rapid and precortical response patterns, and overidentification of dangerous conditions. These patterns begin to develop early in life and promote safety under conditions of danger. The cost is risk for certain kinds of mental disturbance, including inhibition and compulsion, paranoia, violence,[6] and posttraumatic stress disorder (PTSD).[7]

Applications of neurological development to conditions of danger. If my line of thinking is correct, individuals who have experienced abuse should (a) be particularly vigilant to stimuli indicative of possible dangerous outcomes, (b) display behavior that, in the past, has prevented parental anger and violence; and (c) use affect in ways that have been reinforced by a reduction in danger. If affective displays have led to dangerous outcomes, evidence of anxiety (e.g., fear, anger, and desire for comfort) should be

---

[6]Violence is likely to be aimed at *attachment figures*, who might abandon one, and at *attached children*, who might do something dangerous or fail to respect parental advice.
[7]See Crittenden (1995, 1997b) for a more complete discussion of these ideas.

inhibited. If affective displays have tended to elicit protective caregiving, displays of anxiety should be heightened and exaggerated. Parents who were abused as children should be less likely to use cortical reasoning and more likely to respond quickly and intensively to aspects of children's safety, including disrespectful behavior, than nonabused parents.

Supporting Evidence in Maltreated Children's Behavior

In fact, there are data relevant to the perspective described. Rieder and Cicchetti (1989) and Dodge and his colleagues (Dodge & Frame, 1982; Dodge & Steinberg, 1983) have shown that abused children are hypervigilant to stimuli tied to danger and violence, even in nonthreatening circumstances, particularly with regard to interadult anger (Hennessy, Rabideau, & Cicchetti, 1994). Similarly, aggressive boys consistently interpret ambiguous stimuli as threatening (Nasby, Hayden, & De Paulo, 1979). In addition, Hill, Bleichfeld, Brunstetter, Herbert, and Steckler (1989) found that abused children have more negative feelings than nonabused children in response to observing violence, as well as have decreases in heart rate and lower resting heart rate patterns indicative of hypervigilance.[8] Furthermore, it is consistent with this hypothesis of vigilance directed toward sources of potential danger that both anxious children and abused children (a) attend less than other children to athletic interests, creative challenges, academic tasks, and peer relationships; (b) appear distractible and inflexible to adults; and (c) are often diagnosed as attention-deficit-disordered and hyperactive (Egeland, Sroufe, & Erickson, 1983; Erickson & Egeland, 1987; Famularo, Kinscherff, & Fenton, 1992; Hoffman-Plotkin & Twentyman, 1984; Howes & Eldredge, 1985; Kolko, Moser, & Weldy, 1990; Oates, Peacock, & Forrest, 1984; Vondra, Barnett, & Cicchetti, 1990; Wodarski, Kurtz, Gaudin, & Howing, 1990; Wolfe & Mosk, 1983). One explanation is that anxious and abused children attend preferentially to issues of safety and danger and that they interpret ambiguous information as indicative of danger, thus inflating their estimate of danger.

Supporting Evidence in Maltreating Parents' Behavior

A similar process has been observed in abusive parents in response to infant signals such that abusive parents identify negative affect when other parents do not (Frodi & Lamb, 1988). Although this finding is usually interpreted as indicating that such parents have skewed interpretations that lead to increased parental anger, it should be noted that negative affect is the means by which infants alert caregivers to their need for care, that is,

---

[8]The gender-specific findings of this study are not considered here, although the topic of gender effects in child abuse deserves both thorough review and systematic research.

that they are in danger. It may be that, like abused children, abusive parents are hypervigilant to signals of danger. Certainly their fairly uniform history of abuse as children would support this interpretation. There are also data indicating that abusive parents are more punitive, less flexible, less likely to use reasoning, less willing to permit their children to be autonomous (in dangerous contexts), less satisfied with child behavior, and more angry than parents who have not been abused and who do not live in dangerous contexts (Burgess & Conger, 1978; Reid, 1986; Trickett & Kuczynski, 1986; Wolfe, 1993a). These findings are consistent with theory regarding acquired neurological biases based on prior experience with danger.

Patterns of Children's Response to Predictable Parental Violence

In addition to the preceding general evidence, there are some specific patterns of children's responses to parental violence. Children who have been seriously abused are often exceedingly compliant with adults' demands; this behavior has the obvious effect of satisfying adults and reducing the probability of punishment. Children who are quiet and withdrawn are unlikely to elicit parental anger (Garbarino, Sebes, & Schellenbach, 1984; Kaufman & Cicchetti, 1989; Trickett, Aber, Carlson, & Cicchetti, 1991; Wodarski et al., 1990; Wolfe & Mosk, 1983). Others have noted that many abused children engage in stereotypical, ritualized, or compulsive behavior that seems essential to the child but appears meaningless to observers. Possibly, on some earlier occasion, the behavior coincided with a perceived threat of violence that did not, in fact, occur. To the preconscious mind of the child, the behavior may have seemed to cause the abuse not to happen; in repeating, exaggerating, and elaborating the compelled behavior, the child may be attempting to exploit its protective power. Ironically, such superstitious learning is reinforced by every instance of nonabuse that follows its display. A particularly powerful preventive behavior is positive affect; Crittenden (1992a) reported that abused children learn to falsify the display of affect to please parents. This mechanism could account for the occasional reported finding of securely attached maltreated children (Carlson et al., 1989).

Crittenden and DiLalla (1988) suggested that these behaviors reflect an organized pattern, labeled *compulsive compliance*, which includes vigilant attention to parents' cues, inhibition of affect that could elicit parental anger or violence, falsification of positive affect, compulsive (stereotypical) behavior, and compliance with parental directives. This pattern may be the result of learning to discern subtle cues to danger and organizing behavior to prevent is recurrence. Mental and behavioral processes are modified to increase the probability of safety, even when the source of danger is the parent. This strategy works well, but only if parental violence is predictable.

Patterns of Children's Response to Unpredictable Parental Violence

What happens to the many children whose parents are unpredictable? It appears that, in infancy, many become increasingly distressed and angry; their experience is one of not knowing when parental protection will be available or how to elicit it (Crittenden, 1992a). By toddlerhood, their displays of anger elicit both more attention and more parental aggression; evidence for this can be found in descriptions of toddler-aged (and older) abused children as aggressive, noncompliant, negative, demanding, and having an external locus of control (Barahal, Waterman, & Martin, 1981; Erickson & Egeland, 1987; Hoffman-Plotkin & Twentyman, 1984; Reid, 1986; Reidy, 1977; Trickett, 1993).

Elsewhere I have proposed that with the competencies associated with preoperational functioning, children are able to (a) organize new and complex affective displays of coy behavior that terminate aggression and elicit nurturance, (b) exaggerate both positive (coy) and negative (angry) affective displays to increase the probability of eliciting a parental response, and (c) alternate angry and coy displays to increase the probability of a caregiving response (Crittenden, 1992a, 1995). Although angrily threatening and coyly disarming behavior appear different on the surface, both depend on provocation or risk taking to focus parents' attention on the child's need for protection. This complex strategy of splitting, exaggerating, and alternating affective displays creates a *coercive* pattern of behavior that maintains parental attention and regulates the nature of that attention (Crittenden, 1992a). The coercive strategy is particularly suited to parents whose behavior is unpredictable because it escalates the issue of protection by pitting the danger of parental failure to protect their children against the danger of eliciting parental anger. Use of this strategy appears as a range of externalizing problems to observers who focus on the child alone or who use parental reports of child behavior, including oppositional and conduct disorders; personality, social, and adjustment disorders; and even psychotic symptoms. All these behaviors have been associated with abused children, particularly children over 3 years of age (Famularo et al., 1992; Garbarino et al., 1984; Kaufman & Cicchetti, 1989; Kolko et al., 1990; Wodarski et al., 1990; Youngblade & Belsky, 1990), as well as with anxiously attached children (Erickson, Sroufe, & Egeland, 1985; Lyons-Ruth, Repacholi, McLeod, & Silva, 1991; Waters, Posada, Crowell, & Kengling, 1993). For coercive children, therefore, such as compulsively compliant children, mental processing of information has been distorted, and although the distortion is different from that of children whose parents were predictably punitive, the functional outcome—promotion of protection—is the same.

Maltreated Children's Behavior Is Both Organized and Adaptive

Given their circumstances, abused children behave in ways that reflect age-related changes in danger. People like to believe that human society is safe and that the recipients of violence are innocent victims whose lives have been disrupted unjustly from their expectable course. As a consequence of these beliefs, behavioral changes that result from violence are viewed as detrimental interruptions to the victim's "normal" course of development. I think this perspective is questionable in three ways. First, there is no evidence that human life has ever been sufficiently safe that parental protection of children was not essential. Indeed, the central goal of child rearing is to keep the child alive; an ancillary goal is to assist children in learning to protect themselves. Moreover, evolution itself can be conceptualized as a series of progressive enhancements to functioning that resolve problems of danger, thus promoting survival. Danger is the one universal threat. Second, the source and extent of danger vary over the course of childhood (Finkelhor & Dzuiba-Leatherman, 1994). Some dangers increase with age; for example, toddlers can run into streets, whereas infants cannot. The same danger may decrease later: School-aged children can safely cross streets. Children's adaptation to experienced danger, including danger from parents, can make them less vulnerable in the future. This is true in the evolutionary sense, if not in the sense of personal happiness; compulsive compliance does not make a child happy, although it is associated with a reduced risk of eliciting parental violence. Third, it is entirely possible, even probable, that the behavior of children universally elicits parental restriction. Sometimes this restriction is in the form of physical punishment and, therefore, in some cases, abusive. Parents who have experienced early, continuing, and present danger would be maximally likely to respond with intensity to child behavior that might be endangering. Child behavior that reduces this threat can be considered adaptive, at least in terms of survival.

This discussion of behavioral strategies suggests that behavior associated with maltreatment may be organized, context-specific adaptations that reduce children's risk of future abuse or danger. It is my observation that many of the children of predictably violent parents who learn the strategy of compulsive compliance not only reduce their risk of future abuse but also increase the probability of occurrence of supportive interactions with their parents (Crittenden, 1992a). Furthermore, this adaptation begins in the first year of life, and by the time the child is 2 or 3 years old, it produces smooth parent–child interactions that maximize the potential of the parent to engage the child in learning activities and of the child to feel safe enough to engage in other aspects of life. Of course, it is true that these exchanges are affectively limited and often have a restricted, non-spontaneous, and inhibited quality; nevertheless, they are much improved over the distressed and distressing exchanges of infancy.

Similarly, children of inconsistently available parents who, as preschoolers, adopt a coercive strategy increase the probability of parental protection from external threats and regulate the use of parental violence against themselves. It is not surprising that this strategy of attention getting and maintenance of physical proximity develops just as children gain the motoric competence to leave the parent's protective range. Although children who use a coercive strategy are often disruptive and unpleasant to be around, they are, in fact, resilient in the face of adults' anger (Patterson & Forgatch, 1990).

Danger appears in different forms in different families, with different sorts of child behavior eliciting parental violence at different ages and promoting the organization of varied strategies to resolve the threat. In infancy, the message from many violence-prone parents is that infants need to learn to stay alone and quiet to be safe; certainly, there are other mammalian species in which this is the case, as well as instances in human experience when crying infants have endangered entire communities. In toddlerhood, violence-prone parents often use abusive punishment to protect children by teaching self-protective rules (e.g., stay in the yard) and respect (e.g., do what I say even when I'm not there). If this developmental conceptualization is reasonably accurate, it should produce a rise in abuse at about 18 months, when language and memory are relatively delayed compared to locomotion.[9] Parents of adolescents assess their children's values to determine whether the children are likely to follow safe pathways to adulthood. In adolescence, therefore, parental anger may be triggered by a conflict in values (i.e., the construct by which the adults and adolescents organize their behavior).

Confirming these observations will require longitudinal evidence of changes in children's behavior across time, tied to age at maltreatment, the dangerousness of contexts, variation in parental predictability, and changes in parental behavior in the months and years after the early incidents of abuse.

The Perception of Danger Varies

What parents perceive as dangerous reflects what they learned as children, their particular child-rearing context, and the behavior of their child.

---

[9]Current data on age of abuse indicate that the highest rate of abuse is to children below age 1 and that half of all abuse occurs to children at or below 6 years of age (USDHHS, 1994). These data do not indicate whether it is the same children who are reabused across time or whether the same sorts of behavior elicit abuse at different ages. The hypothesis offered here is that children abused at one age learn strategies that reduce risk of abuse and that it is, for the most part, other children using different sorts of eliciting behavior who are abused at later ages.

There is nothing new in this precept, although it can be noted that when preconscious adaptations have been made concerning what is perceived as dangerous and safe, these may affect parents' processing of information and may do so out of awareness. Parents may be able to state one set of values and to demonstrate appropriate learned parenting behaviors, but when *they* perceive danger, they may respond with fear, anger, and violence to those they love the most. This may be especially true when the parent experienced great fear as a child. Indeed, some of the most violent individuals are those who perceive themselves to be victims. In this regard, it is important to recognize that children's behavior can elicit abuse and that it does so under conditions that would elicit fear and anger in many parents. Child abuse is an interactive process (a) in each instance, (b) across the childhood of each child, and (c) across generations as children mature and become parents. Viewed from this perspective, the concepts of victim and perpetrator become distortions of reality that create false dichotomies.

Another consequence of the argument presented here is that higher levels of familial violence would be expected in societies and neighborhoods that are, in fact, more dangerous, that is, where vigilance and strategies for protecting oneself are needed (Kelley, 1992). Of course, there is ample evidence that community violence and familial violence are related (Garbarino & Sherman, 1980). What is unclear is the causal relation between them. At the individual level, it becomes important to know whether behavior changes when the dangerousness of circumstances changes.

CONCLUSIONS

Four conclusions can be drawn from this review of the research on child abuse and children's development. It should be emphasized, however, that whereas the behaviors described have strong empirical support, the methods of organization that I offer and their function reflect a theoretical integration that awaits empirical testing.

First, parent–child behavior may be organized in ways that function to protect children. Parents themselves usually explain actions that result in injury as attempts to protect children, to teach them safe behavior, or to teach them respect. Although these explanations are often treated as "cover-ups," they may, in fact, reflect parental motivations that operate at a preconscious level under the perception of imminent danger.

In addition, I have offered two patterns of child organization—compulsive compliance and coercion—each of which is tied to particular types of parental behavior and to the competencies of children at particular ages. I have no reason to believe that these are the only methods of organization possible. To the contrary, humans constantly refine their behavior to maximize safety. Nevertheless, I offer these two to demonstrate that what professionals consider to be maladaptive and deficient aspects of abused children's behavior may be strategic patterns that function to reduce danger. These patterns suggest the adaptability of humans, even at very young ages, to the dangerousness of their circumstances. I suggest that researchers seek evidence of other such strategic organizations.

According to this model, abused children learn from caregivers what the cues to danger are, how to prevent dangerous outcomes, and how to elicit caregiving that promotes safety. From this perspective, evaluation of the behavior of maltreated children should consider not only children's deficits with regard to common childhood activities but also their conditioned attention to cues to danger and their expertise in eliciting caregiving from parents who can also be a source of danger. Similarly, parents who abuse children are applying what they learned in childhood to the rearing of their own children, for the benefit of those children. Although one might wish to argue that such parents have failed to adjust their behavior to changed circumstances, the fact that child abuse is highest in communities that are the most dangerous leaves open the possibility that abusive parents have both correctly evaluated their circumstances and contributed to the maintenance of those conditions. This suggestion points out the irony of blaming and punishing the abused child who becomes an abusive parent, particularly in the context of dangerous communities. Viewed from the parents' perspective, one is punishing their attempts to cope with, and protect their children from, danger. In other words, family misery has been criminalized. It may be that under dangerous conditions, parents do dangerous things to protect their children, and children do dangerous things to elicit protection from their parents.

Second, I have argued that the processes that underlie abusive parents' behavior are the same as those that underlie other parents' behavior. If this statement is accurate, one must ask why a species would evolve to be violent. I think the answer is that the perceptual and response biases that underlie abuse are the same as those that more often result in protection. That is, *species* evolve in ways that promote the good of the many, whereas *individuals* adapt to promote individual well-being within the constraints of specific contexts. It may be that injury of children is an unfortunate outcome of evolved processes selected because they more often promote safety.

Of course, these child and parental adaptations function adaptively only if future contexts resemble past contexts in terms of their dangerousness. The sad truth is that for our most at-risk families, this condition is usually met both through parents' own contributions and through the social conditions associated with poverty.

Third, my argument seems to imply that physical punishment of children is typical of humans and, in moderation, may have benefits. This outlook conflicts with current views of desirable parenting strategies and the negative effects of punishment. Is punishment necessary and does it work? Ask any parent: Parents *know* that punishment, both physical and psychological, works. For example, a toddler running thoughtlessly toward a street filled with fast-moving cars is unable to predict the outcome of his behavior without first experiencing it. Better that his mother grab him back and spank him, an outcome that he will remember, than that he be injured or killed by his first experience with traffic. Of course, she could clutch him back and gently explain the consequences of being near the street. However, this is wasted effort (and therefore dangerous) because toddlers have a limited capacity to process verbal information, especially when it is not preceded by concrete experience. The spanking, combined with the mother's intensely fearful or angry affect, is a far more memorable consequence.

In this discussion, I have tried to explain why punishment is used by so many parents in terms of its protective function. Again, one's perspective is critical. Psychologists consider inhibition and withdrawal to be evidence of emotional problems, whereas parents, faced with dangerous circumstances, consider them to be desirable characteristics of children who are unlikely to engage in dangerous or danger-eliciting behavior. Similarly, conduct disorders, hyperactivity, and anxiety are evidence of disturbance to professionals, but they may function to elicit attention, with its potential for protection, from inconsistent parents. In such cases, academic success may be a luxury that endangered children cannot afford. Therefore, the dangerousness of the daily context may provide one means for evaluating the adaptiveness of parent and child behavior. In the role of middle-class experts, professionals may overlook the reality and pervasiveness of danger in the low-income environments that produce the highest rates of child abuse.

Fourth, although research is becoming more systemic, social policy continues to focus on the innocence of victims and the need to identify and punish perpetrators. Pity and anger may be poor, even futile, bases on which to organize interpersonal relationships, individual therapy, or social policy. A more effective approach might be to describe with some accuracy the reciprocal contributions of parent, child, and environment to violent behavior, without presuming that participation in a process implies responsibility for it.

This perspective does not imply that physical punishment is to be encouraged or that its use is without danger. Injury to children cannot be tolerated, especially when there is no reason to believe that parents have learned nonabusive ways to protect and discipline their children. It should be remembered, however, that the frequent parental complaint that children will become dangerously out of control has merit, especially for young, preschool-aged children. Changes, including changes in disciplinary techniques, usually have multiple effects, some of which may be unintended. This may be the case with physical punishment that leads to abuse and inconsistent parental response that leads to accidents. A truism captures the essence of the issue: Few things are always right or always wrong. In most cases, a judicial balance is needed. This is particularly true with a complex function like parental caregiving.

If the notion of experience-dependent brain development is accurate, a central issue becomes the extent to which adults who have developed in dangerous contexts can adapt to safety in ways that protect their children. Certainly, there is strong evidence that the human brain remains plastic even into old age (Stein, Brailowsky, & Will, 1995). The conditions under which one can access that plasticity to change adult caregiving behavior are at present unknown. In all probability, change depends on the functioning and history of adults, the current safety of their context, and the sophistication of the technology for intervention. Moreover, children's developmental needs constrain greatly the time frame within which change must be accomplished. Therefore, there remain cases in which professionals must protect children from their parents.

Under both flexible and unchanging conditions, the current moralistic approach is counterproductive and indefensible. It is counterproductive because accusations and moral–ethical censure create an unsafe environment for the parent; by creating such conditions, one reduces the probability that parents will be able to trust professionals enough to make the necessary changes in their patterns of caregiving. It is indefensible because (a) the conditions from which one wishes to protect innocent children are the conditions that were experienced by their parents and (b) the causes of violence extend beyond the parent to a complex web of interlocking conditions, some of which are maintained or even exacerbated by policies that serve the interests of more advantaged people. The causes of maltreatment are complex, and everyone has some complicity. It may be time to respond to parents of injured children with greater understanding and compassion. As with children, we must find ways to limit their dangerous behavior without attacking them.

The theory that I offer regarding the protective function of parental behavior, including physical punishment, under conditions of danger has the advantage of integrating knowledge across many domains and levels of detail. Specifically, the neurological information indicates that the brain has evolved to be structurally and functionally responsive to variations in developmental contexts. The particular aspect of the context that is most influential in organizing patterns of neural development is the extent and nature of danger. Innate biases for responding to dangerous circumstances predict the very sorts of behavior that are, in fact, observed by psychologists and other professionals who work with violent families. Furthermore, learned response patterns fit the evidence regarding the social ecology of child injury. A set of interlocking systems, all organized in terms of the evolved human capacity for coping with dangerous circumstances, protects humans and, in cases of early, intense, and pervasive danger, sometimes functions to maintain both the danger and the patterns of adaptation to it. The outcome is a complex model in which individuals' behavior is one factor that affects the functioning of a hierarchy of overlapping systems, but it is not the sole factor. Indeed, each individual's behavior can also be seen as the outcome of the contextually adapted functioning of the system. This suggests the limitation of a moral code and a legal system that ignore complexity and assign blame on the basis of actions taken. Under such conditions, it must be expected that violent families will perceive and respond to social authorities as a source of danger.

A nonevaluative, systemic approach to understanding child abuse might free both the members of society and the victim-perpetrators of familial violence to contemplate and modify their own behavior in ways that reflect the dangerousness of their circumstances. For parents, this implies more conscious preparation for parental responsibilities. For professionals, it means caring for parents more compassionately and using that compassion to develop interventions that help parents to function more effectively and to be freed of the limitations imposed by their own experience of danger. For the remainder of society, it implies creating (and paying for) an actual and a perceptible reduction in the dangerousness of low-income neighborhoods.

In suggesting this perspective, I attempt to reduce the complex, multicausal environment of child abuse to one or a few critical causes. In a rephrasing of my earlier thinking regarding distorted interpersonal relationships, I now suggest that *previously experienced and currently perceived danger* is the critical cause of child abuse, of distorted interpersonal relationships, and of abnormalities in the development of abused children. To prevent risk of injury to children will require (a) reducing the actual danger, (b) helping parents to modify their mental processing of information so that lack of danger in nonthreatening situations is accurately assessed, and (c) teaching parents behavioral responses that more effectively reduce danger without concurrently creating danger. Finally, I think these interventions must be made in a developmental context that reflects the changing pattern of dangers to children, respects children's abilities to respond to those dangers, and acknowledges parents' intentions accurately.

REFERENCES

Aber, J. L., & Allen, J. P. (1988). The effects of maltreatment on young children's socioemotional development: An attachment theory perspective. *Developmental Psychology, 23,* 406–414.

Averill, J. R. (1982). *Anger and aggression: An essay on emotion.* New York: Springer-Verlag.

Azar, S. T. (1986). A framework for understanding child maltreatment: An integration of cognitive-behavioural and developmental perspectives. *Canadian Journal of Behavioural Science, 18,* 340–355.

Barahal, R. M., Waterman, J., & Martin, H. P. (1981). The social cognitive development of abused children. *Journal of Consulting and Clinical Psychology, 49,* 508–516.

Belsky, J. (1980). Child maltreatment: An ecological integration. *American Psychologist, 35,* 320–335.

Bowlby, J. (1973). *Attachment and loss: Vol. II. Separation.* New York: Basic Books.

Bowlby, J. (1982). *Attachment and loss: Vol. I. Attachment.* New York: Basic Books. (Original work published 1969)

Brassard, M. R., Germain, R. B., & Hart, S. N. (1987). *Psychological maltreatment of children and youth.* New York: Pergamon Press.

Briere, J., & Runtz, M. (1988). Multivariate correlates of childhood psychological and physical maltreatment among university women. *Child Abuse and Neglect, 12,* 331–341.

Brown, J. S. , Kalish, H. I., & Farber, I. E. (1951). Conditioned fear as revealed by magnitude of startle response to an auditory stimulus. *Journal of Experimental Psychology, 32,* 317–328.

Brown, T. H., Chapman, P. F., Kairiss, E. W., & Keenan, C. L. (1988). Long-term synaptic potentiation. *Science, 242,* 724–728.

Burgess, R. L., & Conger, R. C. (1978). Family interactions in abusive, neglectful, and normal families. *Child Development, 49,* 1163–1173.

Campos, J. J., Campos, R. G., & Barrett, K. C. (1989). Emergent themes in the study of emotional development and emotion regulation. *Developmental Psychology, 25,* 394–402.

Carlson, V., Cicchetti, D., Barnett, D., & Braunwald, K. (1989). Disorganized/disoriented attachment relationships in maltreated infants. *Developmental Psychology, 25,* 525–531.

Cicchetti, D., & Lynch, M. (1993). Toward an ecological/transactional model of community violence and child maltreatment. *Psychiatry, 56,* 96–118.

Cicchetti, D., & Toth, S. (1991). The making of a developmental psychopathologist. In J. Cantor, C. Spieker, & L. Lipsitt (Eds.), *Child behavior and development: Training for diversity* (pp. 34–72). Norwood, NJ: Ablex.

Claussen, A. H., & Crittenden, P. M. (1991). Physical and psychological maltreatment: Relations among types of maltreatment. *Journal of Child Abuse and Neglect, 15,* 5–18.

Crittenden, P. M. (1985). Social networks, quality of parenting, and child development. *Child Development, 56,* 1299–1313.

Crittenden, P. M. (1988). Distorted patterns of relationship in maltreating families:

The role of internal representational models. *Journal of Reproductive and Infant Psychology, 6*, 183–199.

Crittenden, P. M. (1992a). Children's strategies for coping with adverse home environments. *International Journal of Child Abuse and Neglect, 16*, 329–343.

Crittenden, P. M. (1992b). The social ecology of treatment: Case study of a service system for maltreated children. *American Journal of Orthopsychiatry, 62*, 22–34.

Crittenden, P. M. (1993). Characteristics of neglectful parents: An information processing approach. *Criminal Justice and Behavior, 20*, 27–48.

Crittenden, P. M. (1995). Attachment and psychopathology. In S. Goldberg, R. Muir, & J. Kerr (Eds.), *Attachment theory: Social, developmental, and clinical perspectives* (pp. 367–406). Hillsdale, NJ: Analytic Press.

Crittenden, P. M. (1997a). Patterns of attachment and sexuality: Risk of dysfunction versus opportunity for creative integration. In L. Atkinson & K. J. Zuckerman (Eds.), *Attachment and psychopathology* (pp. 47–93). New York: Guilford Press.

Crittenden, P. M. (1997b). Toward in integrative theory of trauma: A dynamic-maturation approach. In D. Cicchetti & S. Toth (Eds.), *Rochester Symposium on Developmental Psychopathology: Trauma*. Rochester, NY: University of Rochester Press.

Crittenden, P. M. (in press). Truth, error, omission, distortion, and deception: The application of attachment theory to the assessment and treatment of psychological disorder. In S. M. C. Dollinger & L. F. DiLalla (Eds.), *Assessment and intervention across the lifespan* (pp. 35–76). Hillsdale, NJ: Erlbaum.

Crittenden, P. M., & Ainsworth, M. D. S. (1989). Child maltreatment and attachment theory. In D. Cicchetti & V. Carlson (Eds.), *Child maltreatment: Theory and research on the causes and consequences of child abuse and neglect* (pp. 432–463). New York: Cambridge University Press.

Crittenden, P. M., Claussen, A. H., & Sugarman, D. B. (1994). Physical and psychological maltreatment in middle childhood and adolescence. *Development and Psychopathology, 6*, 145–164.

Crittenden, P. M., & DiLalla, D. L. (1988). Compulsive compliance: The development of an inhibitory coping strategy in infancy. *Journal of Abnormal Child Psychology, 5*, 585–599.

Daly, M., & Wilson, M. (1981). Child maltreatment from a sociobiological perspective. *New Directions for Child Development, 11*, 93–112.

Dodge, K. A., & Frame, C. L. (1982). Social cognitive biases and deficits in aggressive boys. *Child Development, 53*, 620–635.

Dodge, K. A., & Steinberg, M. S. (1983). Attributional bias in aggressive adolescent boys and girls. *Journal of Social and Clinical Psychiatry, 1*, 312–321.

Edelman, G. (1987). *Neural Darwinism: The theory of neuronal group selection.* New York: Basic Books.

Egeland, B., & Sroufe, L. A. (1981). Attachment and early maltreatment. *Child Development, 52*, 44–52.

Egeland, B., Sroufe, L. A., & Erickson, M. (1983). The developmental consequences of different patterns of maltreatment. *Child Abuse and Neglect, 7,* 459–469.

Eichenbaum, H. (1994). The hippocampal system and declarative memory in humans and animals: Experimental analysis and historical origins. In D. L. Schacter & E. Tulving (Eds.), *Memory systems 1994* (pp. 147–201). Cambridge, MA: Bradford/MIT Press.

Erickson, M., & Egeland, B. (1987). A developmental view of the psychological consequences of maltreatment. *School Psychology Review, 16,* 156–168.

Erickson, M., Sroufe, A., & Egeland, B. (1985). The relationship between quality of attachment and behavior problems in preschool in a high-risk sample. *Monographs of the Society for Research in Child Development, 50,* 147–166.

Famularo, R., Kinscherff, R., & Fenton, T. (1992). Psychiatric diagnoses of maltreated children: Preliminary findings: *Journal of the American Academy of Child and Adolescent Psychiatry, 31,* 863–867.

Finkelhor, D., & Dzuiba-Leatherman, J. (1994). Victimization of children. *American Psychologist, 49,* 138–173.

Frodi, A. M., & Lamb, M. E. (1988). Child abusers' responses to infant smiles and cries. *Child Development, 51,* 238–241.

Gaensbauer, T. J., & Harmon, R. J. (1982). Attachment behavior in abused/neglected and premature infants: Implications for the concept of attachment. In R. N. Emde & R. J. Harmon (Eds.), *The development of attachment and affiliative systems* (pp. 263–280). New York: Plenum Press.

Garbarino, J. (1977). The human ecology of maltreatment: A conceptual model for research. *Journal of Marriage and the Family, 39,* 721–736.

Garbarino, J., Sebes, J., & Schellenbach, C. (1984). Families at risk for destructive parent-child relations in adolescence. *Child Development, 55,* 174–183.

Garbarino, J., & Sherman, D. (1980). High-risk neighborhoods and high-risk families: The human ecology of child maltreatment. *Child Development, 51,* 188–198.

George, C., & Main, M. (1979). Social interactions of young abused children: Approach, avoidance, and aggression. *Child Development, 50,* 306–318.

Gut, E. (1989). *Productive and unproductive depression: Success or failure of a vital process.* New York: Basic Books.

Hennessy, K. D., Rabideau, G. J., & Cicchetti, D. (1994). Responses of physically abused and nonabused children to different forms of interadult anger. *Child Development, 65,* 815–828.

Herrenkohl, R. C., Herrenkohl, E. C., Egolf, B., & Seech, M. (1980). The repetition of child abuse: How frequently does it occur? In H. C. Kempe, A. W. Franklin, & C. Cooper (Eds.), *The abused child in the family and community: Selected papers from the second international Congress on Child Abuse and Neglect, London 1978* (Vol. 1, pp. 67–72). Elmsford, NY: Pergamon Press.

Hill, S. D., Bleichfeld, B., Brunstetter, R. D., Herbert, J. M., & Steckler, S. (1989). Cognitive and physiological responsiveness of abused children. *Journal of the American Academy of Child and Adolescent Psychiatry, 28,* 219–224.

Hoffman-Plotkin, D., & Twentyman, C. (1984). A multimodal assessment of behavioral and cognitive deficits in abused and neglected preschoolers. *Child Development, 55,* 794–802.

Howes, C., & Eldredge, R. (1985). Responses of abused, neglected, and non-maltreated children to the behaviors of their peers. *Journal of Applied Developmental Psychology, 6,* 261–270.

Jacobs, W. J., & Nadel, L. (1985). Stress-induced recovery of fears and phobias. *Psychological Review, 92,* 512–531.

Jean-Gilles, M., & Crittenden, P. M. (1990). Maltreating families: A look at siblings. *Family Relations, 39,* 323–329.

Kaufman, J., & Cicchetti, D. (1989). Effects of maltreatment on school-aged children's socioemotional development: Assessment in a day camp setting. *Developmental Psychology, 25,* 516–524.

Kaufman, J., & Zigler, E. F. (1988). Do abused children become abusive parents? *American Journal of Orthopsychiatry, 57,* 186–192.

Kelley, M. (1992). Determinants of disciplinary practices in low-income black families. *Child Development, 63,* 573–582.

Kempe, C., Silverman, F., Steele, B., Droegemueller, W., & Silver, H. (1962). The battered child syndrome. *Journal of the American Medical Association, 181,* 17–24.

Kolko, D. J., Moser, J. T., & Weldy, S. R. (1990). Medical/health histories and physical evaluation of physically and sexually abused child psychiatric patients: A controlled study. *Journal of Family Violence, 5,* 249–267.

Lang, P. J. (1995). The emotion probe: Studies of motivation and attention. *American Psychologist, 50,* 372–385.

Le Doux, J. E. (1994, June). Emotion, memory, and the brain. *Scientific American,* pp. 50–57.

Le Doux, J. E. (1986). The neurobiology of emotion. In J. E. Le Doux & W. Hirst (Eds.), *Mind and brain: Dialogues in cognitive neuroscience* (pp. 301–354). Cambridge, England: Cambridge University Press.

Lyons-Ruth, K., Connell, D. B., & Zoll, D. (1989). Patterns of maternal behavior among infants at risk for abuse: Relations with infant attachment behavior and infant development at 12 months of age. In D. Cicchetti & V. Carlson (Eds.), *Child maltreatment: Theory and research on the causes and consequences of child abuse and neglect* (pp. 464–493). New York: Cambridge University Press.

Lyons-Ruth, K., Repacholi, B., McLeod, S., & Silva, E. (1991). Disorganized attachment behavior in infancy: Short-term stability, maternal and infant correlates, and risk-related subtypes. *Development & Psychopathology, 3,* 377–396.

Mrzljak, L., Uylings, H. B. M., van Eden, C. G., & Judas, M. (1990). Neuronal development in human prefrontal cortex in prenatal and postnatal stages. *Progress in Brain Research, 85,* 185–222.

Nadel, L., Wilson, L., & Kurz, E. M. (1993). Hippocampus: Effects of alterations in timing of development. In G. Turkowitz & D. A. Devenny (Eds.), *Developmental time and timing* (pp. 233–252). Hillsdale, NJ: Erlbaum.

Nasby, W., Hayden, B., & De Paulo, B. M. (1979). Attributional bias among aggressive boys to interpret unambiguous social stimuli as displays of hostility. *Journal of Abnormal Psychology, 89,* 459–468.

Newberger, E. H., Hampton, R. L., Marx, T. J., & White, K. M. (1986). Child abuse and pediatric social illness: An epidemiological analysis and ecological formulation, *American Journal of Orthopsychiatry, 56,* 589–601.

Oates, R. K., Peacock, A., & Forrest, D. (1984). The development of abused children. *Developmental Medicine and Child Neurology, 26,* 649–656.

Patterson, G. R., & Forgatch, M. S. (1990). Initiation and maintenance of processes disrupting single-parent families. In G. R. Patterson (Ed.), *Depression and aggression in family interaction* (pp. 209–245). Hillsdale, NJ: Erlbaum.

Pavlov, I. P. (1928). *Lectures on conditioned reflexes: The higher nervous activity of animals* (Vol. 1, H. Ganett, Trans.). London: Lawrence & Wishart.

Peterson, L., & Brown, D. (1994). Integrating child injury and abuse-neglect research: Common histories, etiologies, and solutions. *Psychological Bulletin, 116,* 293–315.

Peterson, L., Ewigman, B., & Vandiver, T. (1994). Role of parental anger in low-income women: Discipline strategy, perceptions of behavior problems, and need for control. *Journal of Clinical Child Psychology, 23,* 435–443.

Reid, J. B. (1986). Social interaction patterns in families of abused and non-abused children. In C. Zahn-Waxler, E. M. Cummings, & R. Iannotti (Eds.), *Altruism and aggression: Social and biological origins* (pp. 238–255). Cambridge, England: Cambridge University Press.

Reidy, T. (1977). The aggressive characteristics of abused and neglected children. *Journal of Clinical Psychology, 33,* 1140–1145.

Rieder, C., & Cicchetti, D. (1989). Organizational perspective on cognitive control functioning and cognitive-affective balance in maltreated children. *Developmental Psychology, 25,* 382–393.

Seligman, M. (1971). Preparedness and phobias. *Behavior Therapy, 2,* 307–320.

Selye, H. (1976). *The stress of life.* New York: McGraw-Hill.

Skinner, B. F. (1976). *About behaviorism.* New York: Vintage Books.

Stein, D. G., Brailowsky, S., & Will, B. (1995). *Brain repair.* New York: Oxford University Press.

Straus, M. A. (1994). *Beating the devil out of them: Corporal punishment in America.* New York: Lexington Books.

Straus, M. A., & Gelles, R. J. (Eds.). (1990). *Physical violence in American families: Risk factors and adaptation to violence in 8,145 families.* Brunswick, NJ: Transaction Publishers.

Thompson, R. F. (1991). Are memory traces localized or distributed? *Neuropsychologia, 29,* 571–582.

Trickett, P. K. (1993). Maladaptive development of school-aged, physically abused children: Relationships with the child-rearing context. *Journal of Family Psychology, 7,* 134–147.

Trickett, P. K., Aber, J. L., Carlson, V., & Cicchetti, D. (1991). Relationship of socioeconomic status to the etiology and developmental sequelae of physical child abuse. *Development Psychology, 27,* 148–158.

Trickett, P. K., & Kuczynski, L. (1986). Children's misbehaviors and parental discipline strategies in abusive and non-abusive families. *Developmental Psychology, 22,* 115–23.

U. S. Department of Health and Human Services. National Center on Child Abuse and Neglect. (1994). *Child maltreatment 1992: Reports from the states to the National Center on Child Abuse and Neglect.* Washington, DC: U.S. Government Printing Office.

U.S. Department of Health and Human Services. National Center on Child Abuse and Neglect. (1996). *Child maltreatment 1994: Reports from the states to the National Center on Child Abuse and Neglect.* Washington, DC: U.S. Government Printing Office.

Uylings, H. B. M., & van Eden, C. G. (1990). Quantitative and qualitative comparison of the prefrontal cortex in rat and primates, including humans. *Progress in Brain Research, 85,* 31–62.

Vondra, J. I., Barnett, D., & Cicchetti, D. (1990). Self-concept, motivation, and competence among preschoolers from maltreating and comparison families. *Child Abuse and Neglect, 14,* 525–540.

Waters, E., Posada, G., Crowell, J., & Kengling, L. (1993). Is attachment theory ready to contribute to our understanding of disruptive behavior problems? *Development and Psychopathology, 5,* 215–224.

Wauchope, B. A., & Straus, M. A. (1990). Physical punishment and physical abuse of American children: Incidence rates by age, gender, and occupational class. In M. A. Straus & R. J. Gelles (Eds.), *Physical violence in American families: Risk factors and adaptation to violence in 8,145 families* (pp. 133–148). Brunswick, NJ: Transaction Publishers.

Wodarski, J.S., Kurtz, P. D., Gaudin, J. M., & Howing, P. T. (1990). Maltreatment and the school-aged child: Major academic, socioemotional, and adaptive outcomes. *Social Work, 35,* 506–513.

Wolfe, D. A. (1993a). Prevention of child physical abuse and neglect: Promising new directions. *Clinical Psychology Review, 13,* 501–540.

Wolfe, D. A. (1993b). Treatment strategies for physical abuse and neglect: A critical progress report. *Clinical Psychology Review, 13,* 473–500.

Wolfe, D. A., & Mosk, M. D. (1983). Behavioral comparisons of children from abusive and distressed families. *Journal of Consulting and Clinical Psychology, 51,* 702–708.

Wolfe, D. A., Sandler, J., & Kaufman, K. (1981). A competency-based parent training program for child abusers. *Journal of Consulting and Clinical Child Psychology, 49,* 633–640.

Youngblade, L. M., & Belsky, J. (1990). The social and emotional consequences of child maltreatment. In R. Ammerman & M. Hersen (Eds.), *Children at risk: An evaluation of factors contributing to child abuse and neglect.* New York: Plenum Press.

3

DEVELOPMENTAL CONSEQUENCES OF CHILD SEXUAL ABUSE

PENELOPE K. TRICKETT AND FRANK W. PUTNAM

In the last 2 decades it has become clear that the sexual abuse of children is much more prevalent than previously was realized. The third national incidence and prevalence study, supported by the National Center of Child Abuse and Neglect (NCCAN, 1996), has documented that each year approximately 300,000 children are recognized (by public officials such as those in protective service and mental health agencies and the schools) as being sexually abused. This figure represents an increase in recognized cases of child sexual abuse of more than 100% from 1988 (NCCAN, 1988) and of more than 600% from 1980 (Burgdorf, 1980; NCCAN, 1996). A number of prevalence studies have suggested even higher rates than are reported in work. In separate studies, for example, Russell (1986) and Finkelhor, Hotaling, Lewis, and Smith (1990) reported prevalence rates between 27% and 38%. Prevalence rates are expected to be higher than annual incidence rates because they represent cumulative childhood experiences and because they are not limited to the cases recognized by official agencies. Usually, retrospective prevalence studies indicate that in most cases the abuse was never reported to authorities. The conclusion thus is clear: Sexual abuse occurs more frequently than previously realized, although it cannot be stated with certainty how frequently it occurs.

These incidence and prevalence studies have also identified other important characteristics of sexual abuse. In almost all studies, females have been found to be the victims more often than males, the ratio being approximately 4:1. For female victims, as compared with males, the abuser is more likely to be a relative or family friend. Abuse occurs from infancy through adolescence. For females, the peak age at onset is between 7 and 8 years, and the mean duration is about 2 years. For male victims, the peak age at onset is prior to puberty, as for females, but the duration of the abuse tends to be shorter (Burgdorf, 1980; NCCAN, 1988). For both males and females, it is important to consider sexual abuse as a *repeated* trauma, rather than a one-time event (Putnam & Trickett, 1993). Poverty is associated with the likelihood of sexual abuse. Poor victims are thus vulnerable to the pernicious effects of both poverty and abuse (NCCAN, 1996). Little is known about ethnic differences in the incidence of sexual abuse (Cupoli & Sewell, 1988; Lindholm & Willey, 1995), although it is clear that sexual abuse is experienced by children of all ethnic groups.

The purpose of this chapter is to examine what is known about the developmental consequences of sexual abuse. We review the research on the effects of sexual abuse, which has proliferated in recent years. (For recent reviews, see Beitchman, Zucker, Hood, daCosta, & Akman, 1991; Beitchman et al., 1992; Kendall-Tackett, Williams, & Finkelhor, 1993; and Trickett & McBride-Chang, 1995.) First, however, we discuss some shortcomings of the research.

LIMITATIONS OF EXISTING RESEARCH

With a few notable exceptions, research on sexual abuse has consisted of two basic designs, each of which has some inherent limitations. First, short-term, or acute, impact has been assessed using cross-sectional designs in samples of children and adolescents in whom sexual abuse has been officially identified or disclosed. Second, long-term impact has been assessed using retrospective designs in samples of adults who report that they were abused as children; that is, their studies rely on self-report of abuse rather than confirmed reports by official agencies. There are few longitudinal studies, and no studies have followed sexually abused children for longer than 1 or 2 years. Although carefully designed cross-sectional studies can provide knowledge about developmental processes and change, most of the cross-sectional studies concerning child abuse have not been well designed. In fact, a number of investigators did not consider age or developmental stage as a variable even when samples included children who ranged widely in age (e.g., from 6 to 17 years of age).

There are particular difficulties with cross-sectional designs in the area of child sexual abuse, because aspects of the abuse can easily be confounded with the age or developmental stage of the research participants. For example, the type of abuse, its frequency or duration, and many other characteristics are likely to differ depending on whether the child is 3 or 8 or 12 years, and a cross-sectional design usually does not allow one to disentangle these factors.

Retrospective designs also have inherent limitations. The most serious problem concerns the distortions of memory that can occur with the passage of time and with experience (see Brewin, Andrews, & Gotlib, 1993). This is particularly problematic in the area of child sexual abuse for two reasons. First, sexual abuse has been shown to affect memory under certain circumstances that are not yet fully understood. In some cases it has been shown to be associated with amnesias and other types of forgetting (e.g., Feldman-Summers & Pope, 1994; Putnam & Carlson, 1993; Williams, 1994). There is also the concern, currently, that "false memories" of sexual abuse experiences can be induced under certain circumstances (e.g., Loftus, 1994). A second problem with the use of retrospective designs in studies of the impact of child sexual abuse on adults is that the sources of the information used to classify a research participant as abused are the memory and perceptions of the adult, which is quite different from the way this classification is made in studies involving children. In studies of children, samples almost always come from an agency (such as a county child protective services agency), which determines the presence of abuse on the basis of a number of sources of evidence, including, but not limited to, self-report.

Although these characteristics of the adult studies can be viewed as problematic, it is important to review the research because it contains the only existing evidence concerning the long-term effects of child sexual abuse. These studies have several strengths, as well. They are quite varied when it comes to sampling strategy; there are large and not-so-large community samples, university samples, and samples from organizations of professionals such as nurses. Also, the samples are generally larger than in the child studies, most often in the hundreds, so these studies do not share the power problems that some of the smaller child studies have.

Besides the limitations coming from the research designs employed, the extant research on child sexual abuse has other shortcomings. Although detailing many of these is beyond the scope of this chapter (see the reviews previously cited or the recent National Research Council, 1993, publication), a few need to be described, because they affected how the review was conducted and how the conclusions can be interpreted. First, many studies on abuse, especially early ones, did not include an appropriate control or comparison group. Given the clear research evidence that many of the outcome measures of interest in child abuse research are adversely influenced by poverty or low socioeconomic status (SES), without an appropriate comparison group, one cannot distinguish between abuse effects and poverty effects (Trickett, Aber, Carlson, & Cicchetti, 1991). For the present review, only studies with an appropriate comparison group have been considered; we do not include studies that compare groups of abused children to test norms or those that have a clinical comparison group only (e.g., studies that compare abused psychiatric patients with non-abused psychiatric patients only). A further requirement for inclusion was evidence that the groups are comparable on relevant demographic characteristics, especially SES, or that statistical methods were used to control for differences.

Another problem with the extant research is that the definition and description of the sexual abuse experienced by the research participants has been inconsistent and, in some cases, too sketchy to allow the reader to understand what it is, exactly, that the child experienced. Sexual abuse differs from other forms of child maltreatment in that persons other than parents or parent figures often are the perpetrators. In some research, samples are limited to intrafamilial abuse, which includes perpetrators who are parents, as well as nonparental figures such as uncles or siblings. In other studies, extrafamilial cases are also included. In some studies, it is unclear who the perpetrators are.

A third limitation of extant research is that, despite what is known about the different forms of behavior problems that predominate in boys versus girls (Zahn-Waxler, 1993), little attention has been paid to potential sex differences in the impact of sexual abuse. More is said about this issue later in the chapter.

REVIEW OF THE LITERATURE

The research reviewed is summarized in Tables 1 and 2, which are organized developmentally. Table 1 includes infancy and early childhood (roughly, birth to age 6) and middle childhood (the elementary school years, roughly age 6 to 11 or 12). Table 2 includes adolescence (the secondary school years) and adulthood. It is important to note that occasionally samples overlap the age groupings listed here; for example, samples may include ages 4 to 11 or 6 to 17. In these cases, if age differences were not examined but a significant group effect was found for the sample as a whole, the result was entered in both of the appropriate columns or tables.

Within the tables, the findings are organized into three general domains: (a) physical and motor status or development, which includes chronic effects of the sexual abuse, such as illness, physiological or other biological effects, and somatic complaints (e.g., headaches or stomachaches), but excludes immediate, acute injuries associated with the maltreat-

TABLE 1

Research Findings on the Impact of Sexual Abuse: Infancy and Early and Middle Childhood

Developmental period	Domain	Finding
Infancy and Early Childhood	Physical–motor development	Enuresis (especially in girls)[a] Somatic complaints (especially in boys)[a]
	Social–emotional development	Inappropriate sexual behavior[a,b] Internalizing problems such as anxiety or social withdrawal[a,b]
	Cognitive–academic development	Developmental delay in girls[a]
Middle Childhood	Physical–motor development	Genital abnormalities;[c] enuresis;[d] dysregulated cortisol[e,f] Increased catecholamine levels[g] Possible immunological dysfunction[h] No increase in somatic complaints[b]
	Social–emotional development	Inappropriate sexual behavior and sexual activity[c,i,j,k] Internalizing (especially depression) and externalizing (especially aggression and conduct disorder)[b,d,l] Dissociation;[m] anxiety higher initially but not at follow-up[n] No greater levels of anxiety or posttraumatic stress disorder[d] Small and unsatisfactory peer networks;[o] low self esteem[p]
	Cognitive–academic development	No lower grades, but lower overall academic performance and more learning problems (teacher ratings)[q] Low overall academic performance[r] No lower grades and test scores (school records)[s] Attention deficit hyperactivity disorder[d]

[a] White, Halpin, Strom, & Santilli, 1988; [b] Friedrich, Beilke, & Urquiza, 1987; [c] Kolko, Moser, & Weldy, 1990; [d] Trickett & Putnam, 1991; [e] DeBellis, Chrousos, et al., 1994; [f] Putnam & Trickett, 1991; [g] DeBellis, Lefter, Trickett, & Putnam, 1994; [h] DeBellis, Burke, Trickett, & Putnam, 1996; [i] Deblinger, McLeer, Atkins, Ralphe, & Foa, 1989; [j] Einbender & Friedrich, 1989; [k] Goldston, Turnquist, & Knutson, 1989; [l] McBride-Chang, Trickett, Horn, & Putnam, 1992; [m] Putnam, Helmers, Trickett, 1993; [n] Mannarino, Cohen, Smith, & Moore-Motily, 1991; [o] Helmers, Everett, & Trickett, 1991; [p] Grayston, De Luca, & Boyes, 1992; [q] Trickett, McBride-Chang, & Putnam, 1994; [r] Tong, Oates, & McDowell, 1987; [s] Eckenrode, Laird, & Doris, 1993.

ment (e.g., bruises, anal tears); (b) social and emotional development, which includes findings concerned with personality and social relationships as well as behavior problems, psychopathology, and social deviancy; and (c) cognitive and academic development and, for adults, work satisfaction and attainment.

Entries in the table indicate that significant differences were found

TABLE 2
Research Findings on the Impact of Sexual Abuse:
Adolescence and Adulthood

Developmental period	Domain	Finding
Adolescence	Physical–motor development	Dysregulated cortisol;[a,b] increased catecholamine levels[c]
		Possible immunological dysfunction[d]
	Social–emotional development	Internalizing and externalizing problems[e,f,g]
		Suicidal or self-injurious behavior[h]
		More male peers in social networks of girls[i]
		Earlier sexual activity, including coitus, and more sexual partners[j]
		Illegal acts, running away;[h] classroom behavior problems[k]
	Cognitive–academic development	No lower grades, but lower overall academic performance, learning problems[k]
		No lower grades and test scores (school records)[l]
		Lower IQ and school achievement;[f] lower overall academic performance[m]
Adulthood	Physical–motor development	Somatic complaints;[n] low hippocampal density[o]
	Social–emotional development	Alcohol or drug abuse (men and women);[p,q] depression;[r,s] anxiety[s,t,u]
		DSM-III diagnoses of antisocial personality disorder (men and women) and affective and anxiety disorders (women)[q]
		High scores on Global Severity Index and increased symptoms of depression, anxiety, and psychosis[n,v]
		Poor social adjustment and more social isolation[w]
		More marriage disruption and dissatisfaction with sex (men and women)[x]
		Maladaptive sexual adjustment relative to physical abuse victims (women)[y]
		No difference in sexual dysfunction or dissatisfaction (women)[v]
		Little difference in sexual adjustment (men)[v]
		Revictimization (e.g., rape, battering);[t,z] child-rearing problems[aa,bb]
	Cognitive–academic development and work	Poor short-term memory[cc]

[a] DeBellis, Chrousos, et al., 1994; [b] Putnam, & Trickett, 1991; [c] DeBellis, Lefter, Trickett, & Putnam, 1994; [d] DeBellis, Burke, Trickett, & Putnam, 1996; [e] Trickett, & Putnam, 1991; [f] Einbender & Friedrich, 1989; [g] McBride-Chang, Trickett, Horn, & Putnam, 1992; [h] Kendall-Tackett, Williams, & Finkelhor, 1993; [i] Helmers, Everett, & Trickett, 1991; [j] Wyatt, 1988; [k] Trickett, McBride-Chang, & Putnam, 1994; [l] Eckenrode, Laird, & Doris, 1993; [m] Tong, Oates, & McDowell, 1987; [n] Greenwald, Leitenberg, Cado, & Tarran, 1990; [o] Bremner, Randall, Vermetten, et al., 1995; [p] Peters, 1988; [q] Stein, Golding, Siegel, Burnam, & Sorenson, 1988; [r] Mullen, Romans-Clarkson, Walton, & Herbison, 1988; [s] Sedney & Brooks, 1984; [t] Fromuth, 1986; [u] Murphy, et al., 1988; [v] Fromuth & Burkhart, 1989; [w] Harter, Alexander, & Neimeyer, 1988; [x] Finkelhor, Hotaling, Lewis, & Smith, 1989; [y] Briere & Runtz, 1990; [z] Russell, 1986; [aa] Cole, Woolger, Power, & Smith, 1992; [bb] Burkett, 1991; [cc] Bremner, Randall, Scott, et al., 1995.

between the abused group and the comparison group. For example, in Table 1 the entry "enuresis" in Column 1 indicates that sexually abused children were found to have a significantly higher frequency of this problem than were children in a nonmaltreated comparison group.

It is important to note that 70% of the studies included in Tables 1 and 2 used samples that were entirely female. For the child studies, almost all of the remaining 30% had considerably more females than males in the sample, and the researchers only rarely analyzed the data for sex differences. Two of the adult studies had samples with both males and females; in each of these cases, the samples were large and sex differences were analyzed. In both tables, gender is indicated if gender differences were established.

Developmental Stages

Infancy and Early Childhood

Little research exists for this age group. Only two studies were found that met the criteria for inclusion in this review (Table 1). Neither included infants in their samples; one had toddlers and preschoolers; and the other included children who were 4 years and older. The major effects seem to be somatic problems (e.g., enuresis, stomachaches, and headaches); inappropriate sexual behavior (e.g., masturbating excessively or in public); internalizing problems (especially anxiety and withdrawal); and developmental delays (Friedrich, Beilke, & Urquiza, 1987; White, Halpin, Strom, & Santilli, 1988).

Middle Childhood

There is considerably more research involving school-aged children than younger children. Some new findings emerged for this age group, and some findings are consistent with the research on younger children. Also, some inconsistencies exist; for example, in the physical–motor domain, although enuresis was reported as a problem in one study (Trickett & Putnam, 1991), another study found no increase in somatic complaints (Friedrich et al., 1987). The genital abnormalities referred to in Table 1 are lasting physical anomalies resulting from injury (Kolko, Moser, & Weldy, 1990). There is also, at this age, evidence of some psychobiological effects similar to those that have been associated with high levels of stress, such as dysregulated cortisol, elevated catecholamine levels, and suggestions of immunological problems (DeBellis, Burke, Trickett, & Putnam, 1996; DeBellis, Lefter, Trickett, & Putnam, 1994; DeBellis et al., 1993).

In the social–emotional realm, inappropriate sexual behaviors and internalizing problems were found, as in younger children (e.g., Deblinger, McLeer, Atkins, Ralphe, & Foa, 1989; Friedrich et al., 1987; Kolko et al., 1990; McBride-Chang, Trickett, Horn, & Putnam, 1992). There is inconsistency, however, in findings concerning anxiety: Some researchers found it to be elevated, as in younger children (Mannarino, Cohen, Smith, & Moore-Motily, 1991), but some did not (Grayston, De Luca, & Boyes, 1992; Trickett & Putnam, 1991). Some different problems seem to emerge in middle childhood: Evidence exists of externalizing problems (e.g., aggression and conduct problems), elevated dissociation, and difficulties with peer relationships (Friedrich et al., 1987; Helmers, Everett, & Trickett, 1991; Putnam, Helmers, & Trickett, 1993; Trickett & Putnam, 1991).

In the cognitive–academic domain, there is some inconsistency, although for the most part there is evidence of poor school performance. The poor school performance may not be reflected in grades, however, but rather in teachers' ratings or achievement test scores (Tong, Oates, & McDowell, 1987; Trickett, McBride-Chang, & Putnam, 1994). There is also evidence from one study of increased diagnoses of attention deficit hyperactivity disorder (ADHD; Trickett & Putnam, 1991). This finding may be particularly important because the study had an all-female sample, and the diagnosis of ADHD is rare in females.

Adolescence

The findings for adolescents are similar to those for school-aged children. Studies with adolescent samples have found cortisol dysregulation and other psychobiological problems, internalizing and externalizing problems, increased dissociation, and school performance problems. The difference between the age groups, in most cases, is in how behaviors are manifested. Adolescents were more likely than younger children to be actively delinquent, sexually active, and exhibiting suicidal behaviors (Kendall-Tackett et al., 1993; Wyatt, 1988).

Adulthood

It is important to remember that all the adult studies reflect retrospective designs and self-reported abuse. What is most notable is that almost all of these studies focused on the social–emotional domain, emphasizing psychopathology; only a few studies considered the physical–motor or cognitive–academic–work domain. One study found somatization to be elevated in a sample of women who were abused as children. In two recent studies, a finding of low hippocampal density was reported in samples of adults with a history of abuse (Bremner, Randall, Scott, et al., 1995; Bremner, Randall, Vermetten, et al., 1995). Except for one study, which found poor short-term memory in a sample of physically and sexually abused adults (Bremner, Randall, Scott, et al., 1995), no adult studies have looked at cognitive abilities or educational or occupational attainment or satisfaction.

Within the social–emotional domain, the adult studies indicate an elevated incidence of alcohol or drug abuse and of externalizing problems (e.g., diagnoses of antisocial personality) in both men and women (Peters, 1988; Stein, Golding, Siegel, Burnam, & Sorenson, 1988). There are also findings of increased depression and anxiety, especially among women (Fromuth, 1986; Mullen, Romans-Clarkson, Walton, & Herbison, 1988; Murphy et al., 1988; Sedney & Brooks, 1984; Stein et al., 1988). There is inconsistency among the studies with regard to marital and other interpersonal relationship problems and concerning sexual adjustment or dysfunction (Briere & Runtz, 1990; Finkelhor, Hotaling, Lewis, & Smith, 1989; Fromuth & Burkhardt, 1989; Greenwald, Leitenberg, Cado, & Tarran, 1990; Harter, Alexander, & Neimeyer, 1988). Studies of women have found greater revictimization rates (i.e., greater likelihood of being raped or battered later in life; Fromuth, 1986; Russell, 1986) and increased problems with child rearing (Burkett, 1991; Cole, Woolger, Power, & Smith, 1992).

In summary, in the physical–motor domain somatic complaints are common in both early childhood and adulthood. In childhood, enuresis and complaints such as headaches and stomachaches are common; in adulthood, similar somatic complaints were found. There is inconsistency in the research concerning school-aged children, and the research is scant. The issue apparently has not been studied in adolescents. Evidence is beginning to emerge of psychobiological disturbance in sexual abuse victims. To date, cortisol dysregulation has been examined directly in school-aged children and adolescents only. A few new studies have suggested the possibility of hippocampal damage in adults who were abused both physically and sexually as children. Prolonged exposure to elevated levels of cortisol is hypothesized to be, at least in part, the cause of this damage.

In the social–emotional domain, internalizing problems are found in sexual abuse victims of all ages. These generally take the form of depression, anxiety, or both. There also seems to be an enhanced risk of suicide from adolescence onward. Externalizing problems such as aggression, conduct problems, and delinquency are found from middle childhood on. In some cases, the form of these problems changes with development (e.g., delinquency emerges in adolescence). There is no evidence of these problems in early childhood, but there are few studies. Levels of dissociation are increased in sexual abuse victims from middle childhood onward; the subject has not been examined among younger children. Sexual behavior problems are apparent from early childhood through adolescence. In younger children, sexualized behavior occurs, such as excessive masturbation. In older children and adolescents, there may be early onset of sexual activity (e.g., coitus). Studies are inconsistent concerning the persistence of sexual problems into adulthood. Of all the problems associated with sexual abuse, sexual problems seem to be associated most strongly with sexual abuse; they are rarely associated with other forms of abuse or violence (Trickett & McBride-Chang, 1995).

In the cognitive–academic–work domain, there is consistent evidence of poor school performance in sexually abused children and adolescents. The nature of these problems is not clear; there has been no research on basic cognitive abilities or memory with this population, although the findings of higher rates of ADHD and of elevated dissociation suggest that there may be attentional problems in these children. With the exception of one study indicating poor short-term memory in adults abused as children, neither cognitive abilities nor educational and occupational attainment in adulthood has been investigated.

Mediators

Possible mediators or moderators of the impact of sexual abuse on development include gender, ethnic group, and social class. As noted, most of the research to date concerns females; little is known conclusively about male victims of sexual abuse. Most of what is known comes from the few adult studies previously reviewed, which suggest that adult males abused as children are less likely to exhibit depression and anxiety than are females but are equally or more likely to be diagnosed with antisocial personality disorder and to have substance abuse problems. As noted, the studies concerned with marital and sexual relationships tend to be inconsistent for both males and females. None of the studies reviewed here investigated whether there is a connection between being sexually abused as a child and becoming a perpetrator of abuse as an adult. Clearly, this and other gender-related issues are important areas for further research.

Also, almost no research has focused on ethnic group or social class differences and developmental outcomes. One exception is the research of Wyatt (e.g., 1988), who studied sexually abused and nonabused African-American and Caucasian women in terms of their adolescent sexual histories and other aspects of adjustment. For the most part, ethnic group differences were minimal. There is beginning to be evidence, however, that there are ethnic differences in the nature of sexual abuse experiences (Huston, Parra, Prihoda, & Foulds, 1995; Mennen, 1994, 1995; Pierce & Pierce, 1984; Trickett, Horowitz, Reiffman, & Putnam, 1997). For example, in the study by Trickett and colleagues, African-American females were more likely to be abused at an older age and for a shorter duration than were Caucasian females. To the degree that differences in sexual abuse experiences predict different developmental outcomes (see the following discussion), understanding such ethnic differences may be critical. Again, this is an area that needs further research.

Some research has been conducted on the importance of various characteristics of the abuse as mediators of impact, for example, the severity of the abuse (often defined in terms of penetration), the age at which the abuse began, its duration and frequency, the relationship of the victim to the perpetrator, and whether the sexual abuse was accompanied by violence. The findings of these studies have been inconsistent. Although a number of studies have found an association between abuse perpetrated by a father or father figure and severity of negative impact (Adams-Tucker, 1982; Briere & Runtz, 1988; McLeer, Deblinger, Atkins, Foa, & Ralphe, 1988; Sirles, Smith, & Kusama, 1989; Tsai, Feldman-Summers, & Edger, 1979), other studies have not shown this association (Einbender & Friedrich, 1989; Kiser et al., 1988; Mennen, 1993). In terms of the impact of duration or frequency of abuse, a number of studies have indicated that abuse that takes place over a longer period of time (Bagley & Ramsey, 1986; Sirles et al., 1989; Tsai et al., 1979) or more frequently (Friedrich, Urquiza, & Beilke, 1986) results in more severe negative outcomes. Other studies do not show this association (Einbender & Friedrich, 1989; Tufts, 1984). Other characteristics of abuse have shown even more inconsistency.

The variables most consistently associated with more adverse impact are longer duration of the abuse, force or violence accompanying the abuse, and father or father figure as perpetrator. It is important to realize that this research has for the most part considered one variable at a time and has been concerned with *severity* of impact rather than differences in impact (i.e., the emergence of different types of problems associated with different types of abuse). There is reason to believe that these characteristics of abuse may covary in ways that are important to understand. For example, in one study, abuse perpetrated by a biological father was found to begin at an earlier age and last longer than abuse by a stepfather or other father figure (Trickett et al., 1997). To understand fully the impact of these different characteristics of abuse, it is important to consider them simultaneously. Two studies so far have used a multivariate approach to investigate this area (Mennen & Meadow, 1995; Trickett et al., 1997). Mennen and Meadow (1995) conducted a study in which several characteristics of abuse were considered simultaneously as predictors of adverse developmental outcomes in a sample of 134 girls up to the age of adolescence. They found that severity of abuse, as indicated by penetration, predicted seriousness of outcome on a variety of measures indicating depression and self-esteem. There was also an interaction effect between force and the perpetrator's identity (father or father figure vs. non-father figure): Girls abused with force by a non-father figure had much higher levels of distress than those abused without force by a non-father figure. Force did not predict a more serious outcome in girls abused by father figures. There was not a "main effect" for identity of perpetrator, and neither age at onset of abuse nor duration of abuse were predictive of symptom levels.

In the study by Trickett and colleagues (1997) of about 80 sexually abused girls and female adolescents, multiple regression analyses were used to investigate the relationship between early onset of abuse, severity, duration, use of force, and identity of perpetrator. When the predictive power of each of these variables was considered, while the others were controlled for, abuse severity (essentially, whether there was penetration) and abuse by a biological father were found to be the most important mediators of impact. Abuse severity predicted amount of depression and hallucinatory symptoms. Abuse by a biological father (but not by father figures, such as stepfathers) was predictive of aggression, delinquency, and other acting-out, externalizing behavior problems. When these variables were controlled for, age at onset of abuse, duration, and use of force were not significant predictors of developmental outcomes. Although there is more to be learned in this area, it seems that for female victims of sexual abuse, the nature of the abusive acts and the identity of the perpetrator, perhaps in conjunction with use of force, are especially important.

CONCLUSION

In many cases, only one or two studies support the findings reported here. The need for further research is clear, and one should be cautious in drawing any conclusions concerning the long-term impact of child sexual abuse on development. The most important findings include the suggestion that there are psychobiological effects of child sexual abuse. The few studies in this area implicate cortisol elevation and dysregulation. Cortisol dysregulation also has been associated with low social competence in preschoolers (Hart, Gunnar, & Cicchetti, 1995), with diagnoses of posttraumatic stress disorder and major depression in adults, and (perhaps as a result of associated hippocampal damage) with short-term memory problems and dissociation among women (Bremner, Randall, Scott, et al., 1995; Bremner, Randall, Vermetten, et al., 1995). An intriguing and disturbing possibility is that such hormonal dysregulation may be related to other findings of long-term impact of sexual abuse on physical health including gynecological problems in women (Loewenstein, 1990), immunological dysfunction (DeBellis et al., 1996), and somatization symptoms (Greenwald et al., 1990).

A second important finding, supported by a number of studies, is the association between sexual abuse and acting-out and externalizing problems in females as well as males, especially in adolescence and adulthood. These problems include delinquency, conduct disorders, antisocial personality, alcohol and substance abuse, and sexual acting out. It now seems clear that maladaptation resulting from sexual abuse takes many more forms than was previously thought, including social deviancies of several types.

Finally, it seems important to consider the impact of sexual abuse on educational attainment and occupational attainment and satisfaction.

Here, the empirical evidence for childhood and adolescence is strong: School performance and achievement and certain cognitive abilities are low among sexual abuse victims compared with nonabused children of comparable SES. This finding suggests that a major long-term effect of sexual abuse is lower educational attainment and, as a result, lower occupational attainment in adulthood. It is striking that no studies of adults have examined outcome variables in this domain. The only study bordering on this domain is one that investigated short-term memory in adults (Bremner, Randall, Scott, et al., 1995). Because occupational attainment and satisfaction are so central to well-being during adulthood, this area demands more research. The notion that sexual abuse may have long-term consequences for educational and occupational attainment also has implications for the selection of adult samples. A university sample would be problematic for studying the long-term effects of sexual abuse because of a likely overselection of adults with less severe impact of abuse. Also, this notion should be taken into account in adult research when matching abuse and comparison groups on SES, because one may be matching on one of the outcomes of the abuse.

Research to date has sketched out the impact of sexual abuse on the development of children. Especially important is a developmental framework; there is much yet to learn about how the experience of sexual abuse in childhood interferes with development at the time of the abuse or how it may affect the resolution of later developmental processes or tasks as the individual goes through adolescence and then adulthood. Such research needs to focus on long-term effects; it should include either longitudinal and long-term data or follow-up studies of individuals documented to have been sexually abused as children. Finally, a multivariate perspective is required, necessitating larger samples than are found in much of the extant research so that the impact of different forms of abuse—experienced by males as well as females, at different ages, by members of different ethnic groups or social classes—can be teased apart. Only then can the complexities of this phenomenon be understood.

REFERENCES

Adams-Tucker, C. (1982). Proximate effects of sexual abuse in children: A report on 28 children. *American Journal of Psychiatry, 139,* 1252–1256.

Bagley, C., & Ramsey, R. (1986). Sexual abuse in childhood: Psychosocial outcomes and implications for social work practice. *Journal of Social Work and Human Sexuality, 4,* 33–47.

Beitchman, J. H., Zucker, K. J., Hood, J. E., daCosta, G. A., & Akman, D. (1991).

A review of the short-term effects of child sexual abuse. *Child Abuse and Neglect, 15,* 537–556.

Beitchman, J. H., Zucker, K. J., Hood, J. E., daCosta, G. A., Akman, D., & Cassavia, E. (1992). A review of the long-term effects of child sexual abuse. *Child Abuse and Neglect, 16,* 101–118.

Bremner, J. D., Randall, P., Scott, S., Capelli, S., Delaney, R., McCarthy, G., & Charney, D. S. (1995). *Deficits in short-term memory in adult survivors of childhood abuse.* Unpublished manuscript, Yale University, New Haven, CT.

Bremner, J. D., Randall, P., Vermetten, E., Staib, L., Bronen, R. A., Capelli, S., McCarthy, G., Innis, R. B., & Charney, D. S. (1995, May). *MRI-based measurement of hippocampal volume in posttraumatic stress disorder related to childhood physical and sexual abuse.* Paper presented at the annual meeting of the American Psychiatric Association, Miami, FL.

Brewin, C. R., Andrews, B., & Gotlib, L. H. (1993). Psychopathology and early experience: A reappraisal of retrospective reports. *Psychological Bulletin, 113,* 82–98.

Briere, J., & Runtz, M. (1988). Multivariate correlates of childhood psychological and physical maltreatment among university women. *Child Abuse and Neglect, 12,* 331–341.

Briere, J., & Runtz, M. (1990). Differential adult symptomatology associated with three types of child abuse histories. *Child Abuse and Neglect, 14,* 357–364.

Burgdorf, K. (1980). *Recognition and reporting of child maltreatment: Summary findings from the National Study of the Incidence and Severity of Child Abuse and Neglect.* Washington, DC: National Center for Child Abuse and Neglect, U.S. Department of Health and Human Services.

Burkett, L. P. (1991). Parenting behaviors of women who were sexually abused as children in their families of origin. *Family Process, 30,* 421–434.

Cole, P. M., Woolger, C., Power, T. G., & Smith, K. D. (1992). Parenting difficulties among adult survivors of father–daughter incest. *Child Abuse and Neglect, 16,* 239–249.

Cupoli, J. M., & Sewell, P. M. (1988). One thousand and fifty-nine children with a chief complaint of sexual abuse. *Child Abuse and Neglect, 12,* 151–162.

DeBellis, M. D., Burke, L., Trickett, T. K., & Putnam, F. W. (1996). Antinuclear antibodies and thyroid function in sexually abused girls. *Journal of Traumatic Stress, 9,* 369–378.

DeBellis, M. D., Chrousos, G. P., Dorn, L. D., Burke, L., Helmers, K., Kling, M. A., Trickett, P. K., & Putnam, F. W. (1994). Hypothalamic-pituitary-adrenal axis dysregulation in sexually abused girls. *Journal of Clinical Endocrinology and Metabolism, 78,* 249–255.

DeBellis, M. D., Lefter, L., Trickett, P. K., & Putnam, F. W. (1994). Urinary catecholamine excretion in sexually abused girls. *Journal of the American Academy of Child and Adolescent Psychiatry, 33,* 320–327.

Deblinger, E., McLeer, S. V., Atkins, M. S., Ralphe, D., & Foa, E. (1989). Posttraumatic stress in sexually abused, physically abused, and nonabused children. *Child Abuse and Neglect, 13,* 403–408.

Eckenrode, J., Laird, M., & Doris, J. (1993). The school performance of abused and neglected children. *Developmental Psychology, 29,* 53–62.

Einbender, A. J., & Friedrich, W. N. (1989). Psychological functioning and behavior of sexually abused girls. *Journal of Consulting and Clinical Psychology, 57,* 155–157.

Feldman-Summers, S., & Pope, K. S. (1994). The experience of "forgetting" childhood abuse: A national survey of psychologists. *Journal of Consulting and Clinical Psychology, 62,* 636–639.

Finkelhor, D., Hotaling, G. T., Lewis, I. A., & Smith, C. (1989). Sexual abuse and its relationship to later sexual satisfaction, marital status, religion, and attitudes. *Journal of Interpersonal Violence, 4,* 379–399.

Finkelhor, D., Hotaling, G., Lewis, I. A., & Smith, C. (1990). Sexual abuse in a national survey of adult men and women: Prevalence, characteristics, and risk factors. *Child Abuse and Neglect, 14,* 19–28.

Friedrich, W. N., Beilke, R. L., & Urquiza, A. J. (1987). Children from sexually abusive families: A behavioral comparison. *Journal of Interpersonal Violence, 2,* 391–402.

Friedrich, W., Urquiza, A., & Beilke, R. (1986). Behavior problems in young, sexually abused children. *Journal of Pediatric Psychology, 19,* 155–164.

Fromuth, M. E. (1986). The relationship of childhood sexual abuse with later psychological and sexual adjustment in a sample of college women. *Child Abuse and Neglect, 10,* 5–15.

Fromuth, M. E., & Burkhart, B. R. (1989). Long-term psychological correlates of childhood sexual abuse in two samples of college men. *Child Abuse and Neglect, 13,* 533–542.

Goldston, D., Turnquist, D. C., & Knutson, J. F. (1989). Presenting problems of sexually abused girls receiving psychiatric services. *Journal of Abnormal Psychology, 98,* 314–317.

Grayston, A. D., De Luca, R. V., & Boyes, D. A. (1992). Self-esteem, anxiety, and loneliness in preadolescent girls who have experienced sexual abuse. *Child Psychiatry and Human Development, 22,* 277–286.

Greenwald, E., Leitenberg, H., Cado, S., & Tarran, M. J. (1990). Childhood sexual abuse: Long-term effects on psychological and sexual functioning in a nonclinical and nonstudent sample of adult women. *Child Abuse and Neglect, 14,* 503–513.

Hart, J., Gunnar, M., & Cicchetti, D. (1995). Salivary cortisol in maltreated children: Evidence of relations between neuroendocrine activity and social competence. *Development and Psychopathology, 7,* 11–26.

Harter, S., Alexander, P. C., & Neimeyer, R. A. (1988). Long-term effects of incestuous child abuse in college women: Social adjustment, social cognition, and family characteristics. *Journal of Consulting and Clinical Psychology, 56,* 5–8.

Helmers, K., Everett, B. A., & Trickett, P. K. (1991, April). *Social support of sexually abused girls and their mothers.* Paper presented at the biennial meeting of the Society for Research in Development, Seattle, WA.

Huston, R. L., Parra, J. M., Prihoda, T. J., & Foulds, D. M. (1995). Characteristics of childhood sexual abuse in a predominantly Mexican-American population. *Child Abuse and Neglect, 19,* 165–176.

Kendall-Tackett, K. A., Williams, L. M., & Finkelhor, D. (1993). Impact of sexual abuse on children: A review and synthesis of recent empirical studies. *Psychological Bulletin, 113,* 164–180.

Kiser, L. J., Ackerman, B. J., Brown, E., Edwards, N. B., McColgan, E., Pugh, R., & Pruitt, D. B. (1988). Post-traumatic stress disorder in young children: A reaction to purported sexual abuse. *Journal of the American Academy of Child and Adolescent Psychiatry, 27,* 645–649.

Kolko, D. J., Moser, J. T., & Weldy, S. R. (1990). Medical/health histories and physical evaluation of physically and sexually abused child psychiatric patients: A controlled study. *Journal of Family Violence, 5,* 249–267.

Lindholm, K. J., & Willey, R. (1995). Ethnic differences in child abuse and sexual abuse. *Journal of Behavioral Sciences, 8,* 111–125.

Loewenstein, R. J. (1990). Somatoform disorders in victims of incest and child abuse. In R. P. Kluft (Ed.), *Incest-related syndromes of adult psychopathology* (pp. 75–112). Washington, DC: American Psychiatric Press.

Loftus, E. (1994). Memories of child sexual abuse. *Psychology of Women Quarterly, 18,* 67–84.

Mannarino, A. P., Cohen, J. A., Smith, J. A., & Moore-Motily, S. (1991). Six- and twelve-month follow-up of sexually abused girls. *Journal of Interpersonal Violence, 6,* 494–511.

McBride-Chang, C., Trickett, P. K., Horn, J. L., & Putnam, F. W. (1992, August). *The CBCL and behavior problems in sexually abused girls.* Paper presented at the annual meeting of the American Psychological Association, Washington, DC.

McLeer, S. V., Deblinger, E., Atkins, M. S., Foa, E. B., & Ralphe, D. L. (1988). Post-traumatic stress disorder in sexually abused children. *Journal of the American Academy of Child and Adolescent Psychiatry, 27,* 650–654.

Mennen, F. E. (1993). Evaluation of risk factors in childhood sexual abuse. *Journal of the American Academy of Child and Adolescent Psychiatry, 32,* 934–939.

Mennen, F. E. (1994). Sexual abuse in Latina girls: Their functioning and a comparison with white and African American girls. *Hispanic Journal of Behavioral Sciences, 16,* 475–486.

Mennen, F. E. (1995). The relationship of race/ethnicity to symptoms in childhood sexual abuse. *Child Abuse and Neglect, 19,* 115–124.

Mennen, F. E., & Meadow, D. (1995). The relationship of abuse characteristics to symptoms in sexually abused girls. *Journal of Interpersonal Violence, 10,* 259–274.

Mullen, P. E., Romans-Clarkson, S. E., Walton, V. A., & Herbison, G. P. (1988).

Impact of sexual and physical abuse on women's mental health. *Lancet, 1,* 841–845.

Murphy, S. M., Kilpatrick, D. G., Amick-McMullen, A., Veronen, L. J., Paduhovich, J., Best, C. L., Villeponteaux, L. A., & Saunders, B. E. (1988). Current psychological functioning of child sexual abuse survivors. *Journal of Interpersonal Violence, 3,* 55–79.

National Center of Child Abuse and Neglect (NCCAN). (1988). *Study of national incidence and prevalence of child abuse and neglect, 1988.* Washington, DC: U.S. Department of Health and Human Services.

National Center of Child Abuse and Neglect (NCCAN). (1996). *Third study of national incidence and prevalence of child abuse and neglect (preliminary findings).* Washington, DC: U.S. Department of Health and Human Services.

National Research Council. (1993). *Understanding child abuse and neglect.* Washington, DC: National Academy Press.

Peters, S. D. (1988). Child sexual abuse and later psychological problems. In G. E. Wyatt & G. J Powell (Eds.), *Lasting effects of child sexual abuse.* Newbury Park, CA: Sage.

Pierce, L. H., & Pierce, R. L. (1984). Race as a factor in the sexual abuse of children. *Social Work Research and Abstracts, 20,* 9–14.

Putnam, F. W., & Carlson, E. B. (1993). *Hypnosis, dissociation and trauma: Myths, metaphors and mechanisms.* Unpublished manuscript.

Putnam, F. W., Helmers, K., & Trickett, P. K. (1993). Development, reliability, and validation of a child dissociation scale. *Child Abuse and Neglect, 17,* 731–740.

Putnam, F. W., & Trickett, P. K. (1991, June). *Cortisol abnormalities in sexually abused girls.* Paper presented at the annual meeting of the American Psychological Society, Washington, DC.

Putnam, F. W., & Trickett, P. K. (1993). Child sexual abuse: A model of chronic trauma. *Psychiatry, 58,* 82–95.

Russell, D. E. H. (1986). *The secret trauma: Incest in the lives of girls and women.* New York: Basic Books.

Sedney, M. A., & Brooks, B. (1984). Factors associated with a history of childhood sexual experience in a nonclinical female population. *Journal of the American Academy of Child Psychiatry, 23,* 215–218.

Sirles, E. A., Smith, J. A., & Kusama, H. (1989). Psychiatric status of intrafamilial child sexual abuse victims. *Journal of the American Academy of Child and Adolescent Psychiatry, 28,* 225–229.

Stein, J. A., Golding, J. M., Siegel, J. M., Burnam, M. A., & Sorenson, S. B. (1988). Long-term psychological sequelae of child sexual abuse: The Los Angeles Epidemiologic Catchment Area Study. In G. E. Wyatt & G. J. Powell (Eds.), *Lasting effects of child sexual abuse.* Newbury Park, CA: Sage.

Tong, L., Oates, K., & McDowell, M. (1987). Personality development following sexual abuse. *Child Abuse and Neglect, 11,* 371–383.

Trickett, P. K., Aber, J. L., Carlson, V., & Cicchetti, D. (1991). Relationship of socioeconomic status to the etiology and developmental sequelae of physical child abuse. *Developmental Psychology, 27,* 148–158.

Trickett, P. K., Horowitz, L. A., Reiffman, A., & Putnam, F. W. (1997). Characteristics of sexual abuse in a sample of girls and female adolescents. In D. Cicchetti & S. L. Toth (Eds.), *Rochester Symposium on Developmental Psychopathology, Volume VIII: The Effects of Trauma on the Developmental Process* (pp. 289–314). Rochester, NY: University of Rochester Press.

Trickett, P. K., & McBride-Chang, C. (1995). The developmental impact of different forms of child abuse and neglect. *Developmental Review, 15,* 311–337.

Trickett, P. K., McBride-Chang, C., & Putnam, F. W. (1994). The classroom performance and behavior of sexually abused females. *Development and Psychopathology, 6,* 183–194.

Trickett, P. K., & Putnam, F. W. (1991, August). *Patterns of symptoms in prepubertal and pubertal sexually abused girls.* Paper presented at the annual meeting of the American Psychological Association, San Francisco, CA.

Tsai, M., Feldman-Summers, S., & Edger, M. (1979). Childhood molestation: Variables related to differential impacts on psychosocial functioning in adult women. *Journal of Abnormal Psychology, 88,* 407–417.

Tufts New England Medical Center, Division of Child Psychiatry. (1984). *Sexually exploited children: Service and research project* (final report for the Office of Juvenile Justice and Delinquency Prevention). Washington, DC: U.S. Department of Justice.

White, S., Halpin, B. M., Strom, G. A., & Santilli, G. (1988). Behavioral comparisons of young sexually abused, neglected, and nonreferred children. *Journal of Clinical Child Psychology, 17,* 53–61.

Williams, L. M. (1994). Recall of childhood trauma: A prospective study of women's memories of child sexual abuse. *Journal of Consulting and Clinical Psychology, 62,* 1167–1176.

Wyatt, G. E. (1988). The relationship between child sexual abuse and adolescent sexual functioning in Afro-American and white American women. *Annals of the New York Academy of Sciences, 528,* 111–122.

4

EFFECTS OF DOMESTIC VIOLENCE ON CHILDREN

GAYLA MARGOLIN

In the last decade there has been a burgeoning of attention directed at the problem of domestic violence and its consequences. Initially the study of domestic violence was limited to a focus within the two-person adult system: the female victims and the male perpetrators. It has become increasingly evident, however, that the consequences of domestic violence involve all family members, with children being the *unintended victims* in this system. Evidence is becoming available regarding the immediate and short-term consequences of witnessing violence, as well as the long-term consequences. However, because of the difficulty identifying children who are exposed to violence (other than those who accompany their mothers to shelters) and because of the multitude of variables that either exacerbate or buffer the effects of exposure, relatively little is known regarding why some children are intensely affected by exposure to marital violence whereas others survive relatively unscathed.

Witnessing violence, in general, has been associated with emotional, behavior, and learning problems in children, with children's susceptibility

Preparation of this manuscript was supported by National Institute of Mental Health Grant 1RO1 36595.

affected by developmental level, chronicity of exposure, physical closeness to the incident, and emotional closeness to the victim (Bell & Jenkins, 1993; Garbarino, Dubrow, Kostelny, & Pardo, 1992; Martinez & Richters, 1993). On the basis of those parameters, one may conclude that witnessing violence between one's own parents is a particularly insidious event. Violence between parents often is recurring and chronic. It is most likely to occur in the home—the one environment generally associated with safety and protection of the child. Moreover, the aggressor and the victim are the persons with whom the child is most likely to identify and to whom the child would wish to turn to for support. The effects of exposure are not limited to the commission of the violent act; they also involve acts of parental omission, in terms of typical supportive and nurturing functions that may be disrupted as a consequence of the domestic violence. It is not surprising, therefore, that exposure to marital violence has been associated with a variety of problems in children. However, the literature examining these developmental risks still is in a beginning phase in terms of identifying processes that render children at greater or lesser risk. In attempting to understand these mechanisms, one must grapple with issues such as (a) the co-occurrence of marital violence with other forms of abuse and exposure to violence, (b) the definition of domestic violence and its differentiation from other forms of marital conflict, and (c) direct versus indirect effects of exposure to domestic violence.

INCIDENCE AND PREVALENCE OF CHILDREN'S EXPOSURE TO MARITAL VIOLENCE

Nationwide surveys indicate that nearly one eighth of husbands in the United States carry out one or more acts of physical aggression against their wives each year and one fifth to one third of all women are assaulted by a partner or ex-partner during their lifetime (Frieze & Browne, 1989; Straus & Gelles, 1990). Determining how much of that violence occurs in the presence of children proves to be difficult. Using original survey data by Straus, Gelles, and Steinmetz (1980), Carlson (1984) estimated that at least 3.3 million children in the United States between the ages of 3 and 17 are at risk each year for exposure to interparental violence. This estimate is based on an average of two children in 55% of violent households. On the basis of both his 1975 and 1985 national surveys, Straus (1992) more recently estimated that more than 10 million children in the United States witness physical abuse between their parents each year, with childhood prevalence rates being at least triple the annual rates. He further projected that, in two thirds of the cases, children are exposed to repeated violence between their parents.

Data that directly address the issue of children's witnessing of interparental aggression are available from several sources. Straus (1974) collected college students' anonymous reports of interparental physical aggression during the last year they were in high school. Sixteen percent of students living in two-parent homes reported physical aggression between their parents during that year. O'Brien, John, Margolin, and Erel (1994) directly interviewed 181 children between 8 and 11 years, inquiring about the occurrence of marital physical aggression at any point in their memories. Data from children in this nonreferred two-parent community sample indicated that approximately 25% had witnessed husband-to-wife aggression and a similar number had witnessed wife-to-husband aggression. McCloskey, Figueredo, and Koss (1995) reported that 20% of the children in their community sample had seen their father slap their mother within the past year. Incidence and prevalence data have been limited, however, by restriction to specific ages as well as by the use of volunteer or convenience samples. Moreover, the data on marital violence consistently show an inverse relationship with age (Suitor, Pillemer, & Straus, 1990), indicating that rates of marital violence are particularly high during the early stages of marriage, when young children are likely to be in the home (Fantuzzo & Lindquist, 1989). Other than the large number of pre–elementary school children who accompany their mothers to battered-women's shelters, few sources are available to provide information about young children's exposure to marital violence. Data from random samples on the extent of overall exposure to marital violence, exposure at specific developmental stages, and exposure to specific types of marital violence are still needed.

Whereas there are obvious problems in collecting this type of sensitive data directly from children, there also are reliability problems in collecting such data from parents. Parents' agreement with one another simply about the occurrence of spousal violence is low (Jouriles & O'Leary, 1985; Margolin, 1987). Furthermore, parents' agreement rates drop even lower in response to the more complicated question of whether their child has been a witness to marital physical aggression compared to the question of whether physical aggression has ever occurred in the marriage (O'Brien et al., 1994). There are similar problems with interrater agreement between parents and children on whether the child has witnessed aggression in the marriage. When children of violent parents are interviewed, they generally can give detailed information about the violence that the parents assumed went unnoticed (Jaffe, Wolfe, & Wilson, 1990; Rosenberg, 1987). Parents tend to underreport the extent to which children are knowledgeable about the marital violence, mistakenly reporting that the children were asleep or otherwise preoccupied when the violence occurred. O'Brien et al. (1994) stated that approximately 10% of the children in their community sample reported witnessing interparental physical aggression when neither parent even acknowledged the occurrence of physical aggression in the marriage. It generally is concluded that most children who live in homes with chronic violence have directly seen or heard the violence, despite parents' intentions to shield the children from this darker side of their marriage (Jaffe et al., 1990). Children's adjustment is said to be related to their actual exposure and their perceptions of the marital violence, rather than simply to the amount of violence occurring in the relationship (Grych, Seid, & Fincham, 1992; Hershorn & Rosenbaum, 1985; O'Brien et al., 1994). It has been suggested, therefore, that children's reports or some combination of parents' and children's reports be used to evaluate children's exposure to marital violence.

CO-OCCURRENCE OF EXPOSURE TO MARITAL VIOLENCE AND TO OTHER FORMS OF VIOLENCE

To understand the effects of marital violence on children requires disentangling the marital violence from exposure to other forms of violence as well as from other sources of severe family stress. Other forms of exposure to violence, namely, direct victimization experiences as a result of child abuse and the witnessing of community violence, tend to co-occur with exposure to interparental abuse. Hughes, Parkinson, and Vargo (1989) suggested that this combination creates a "double-whammy" effect. Because the likelihood of developmental problems tends to be greater when multiple risks are present (Rutter, 1987), it is essential to control for other risks when attempting to understand the effects of exposure to marital violence. Studies have indicated that children who witness marital violence have an increased likelihood of being the target of child abuse (Owens & Straus, 1975; Wolfe, Jaffe, Wilson, & Zak, 1985), with estimates that between 45% and 70% of children exposed to marital violence also are victims of physical child abuse (Layzer, Goodson, & deLange, 1986; Prescott & Letko, 1977; Straus et al., 1980). Conversely, it has been estimated that as many as 40% of the children victimized by physical child abuse also are exposed to interparental aggression (Straus et al., 1980). Jouriles, Barling, and O'Leary (1987) reported a correlation of .56 between interspousal aggression and parent-to-child physical aggression. O'Keefe (1994) reported a significant correlation of .34 between husband-to-wife violence witnessed by the child and father-to-child physical aggression, but a nonsignificant correlation between husband-to-wife violence and mother-to-child aggression. Children living with an abused mother also are at serious risk for sexual abuse; they are 12 to 14 times more likely to experience sexual abuse by the mother's partner as well as 7 times more likely to report sexual abuse occurring outside the home (McCloskey et al., 1995).

Community violence, which can be a stressor to the parents as well as to the child, has shown strong relationships with intrafamilial violence (Bell & Jenkins, 1993; Garbarino et al., 1992). Although they did not differentiate marital violence from other forms of familial violence, Richters and Martinez (1993) reported that children growing up in violent neighborhoods tend to have families with high levels of family violence. Osofsky, Wewers, Hann, and Fick (1993) reported that physically aggressive forms of family conflict were significantly correlated with victimization from community violence (.44) and witnessing of community violence (.37). Furthermore, children's witnessing of family violence and their exposure to physically aggressive forms of conflict in the family each were associated with higher levels of stress symptoms in the children.

Families in which there is interparental violence also often experience other mental health risks, such as separation of children from a parent owing to divorce or incarceration of the parent, parental drinking problems, unemployment, school and home relocation, and overall family stress (Emery, 1989; Jaffe, Wolfe, Wilson, & Zak, 1986b; Spaccarelli, Sandler, & Roosa, 1994). These variables, alone or in conjunction with the exposure to violence may be responsible for the negative outcomes attributed to the exposure.

FEATURES OF EXPOSURE TO MARITAL VIOLENCE

Exposure to marital violence not only tends to co-occur with child abuse and community violence but also shares some common features with these other types of childhood stressors, as shown in Table 1. Although the evidence is clearer for child abuse, exposure to marital violence has been shown to occur at critical developmental phases. Marital abuse of pregnant women, for example, can be particularly deleterious to the health of the unborn child. Exposure to marital violence tends to be chronic. Children have no power to remove themselves from the situation, although in some cases the mother decides to separate from or divorce her abusive partner. According to Finkelhor and Dzuiba-Leatherman (1994), a key characteristic of childhood victimization is the violation of dependency

TABLE 1
Children's Exposure to Violence

| | Type of exposure | | |
Features of exposure	Marital violence	Child abuse	Community violence
Likely to occur at critical developmental phases	X	X	
Chronic stressor	X	X	?
Violation of dependency needs	X	X	
Parents less available for emotional support	X	X	?
Violation of home as safe haven	X	X	X
Threat to personal safety	X	X	X

needs; that is, as a consequence of the victimization, the child is not cared for in terms of her or his basic biological and psychological needs. In both child abuse and exposure to marital violence, the victimization may reflect a compromise of the caretaking functions. The issue with respect to witnessing abuse is the special status of the child vis-à-vis both the perpetrator and the victim. The child watches one caretaker injure and frighten the other caretaker. The abuse makes each caretaker less available to the child, one being overbearing, frightening, and untrustworthy, and the other being vulnerable and perhaps requiring caretaking herself. In a related vein, children who are exposed to marital violence may experience less emotional support from their parents. Evidence is beginning to emerge that parents who experience marital discord—not even as extreme as marital violence—are less emotionally attuned and less attentive to their children, with social, emotional, and academic consequences for the children. Whereas the trauma of exposure makes children more needy of emotional support, the parents' personal struggles may make the parents less available for such support. In addition, such parents, particularly if they have problems managing their own emotions, frequently are inept socialization agents for their children. Violation of the home as a safe haven is one of the negative consequences of exposure to marital violence, child abuse, and, possibly, community violence, depending on the location of the community violence relative to the child's residence. Each of the three types of exposure also poses a threat to the child's personal safety. A common reaction of children, particularly as they approach adolescence, is to attempt to intervene in their parents' battles, with clear risk of injury to themselves. Thus, children exposed to marital violence may be victimized on several levels.

OUTCOMES ASSOCIATED WITH EXPOSURE TO MARITAL VIOLENCE

There is a rapidly expanding literature that supports the impression that exposure to marital abuse is associated with maladjustment in children. Despite theoretical notions that the most direct risk of exposure to violence is that the child will exhibit aggression toward others (Parke & Slaby, 1983; Patterson, 1982), the sequelae of exposure to marital abuse are multifaceted and diverse, leading to the conclusion that the disruptive effects of this stressor do not follow a common pathway. Virtually all types of childhood symptoms have been associated with exposure to marital abuse. Exposure to parents' violence has both immediate effects, as seen in transient distress symptoms, and chronic effects, such as major symptoms of psychopathology and the extension of relationship patterns into the next generation. As indicated later in this chapter, results are mixed concerning which characteristics of the abuse, as well as which characteristics of the child, mediate the effects. Despite the widespread conclusion that marital violence is associated with negative consequences for children, however, there is evidence of considerable resiliency in children, many of whom remain asymptomatic.

The effects of exposure to marital violence have been documented through a number of different research paradigms: (a) retrospective reports by adults on their history of exposure and its relationship to current functioning; (b) current assessments of children's exposure to marital violence and its relationship to behavioral, emotional, social, and academic functioning of the children; and (c) assessments of children's immediate reactions to observing real or simulated versions of marital aggression. The key question pertinent to all the studies examining the effects of exposure to marital aggression is whether the results are specific to marital violence, as opposed to other forms of abuse, and to marital discord. As discussed subsequently, the negative outcomes associated with marital violence sometimes are expressed in terms of elevated levels of dysfunctional child behaviors and sometimes through formal diagnoses of child psychopathology.

Adults' and Older Adolescents' Retrospective Reports of Interparental Violence

Research with perpetrators and victims of wife abuse reveals an association between violence in one generation and exposure to violence in the previous generation. Exposure to marital violence as a child has been associated with involvement in an aggressive relationship and aggression toward one's children one generation later (Cappell & Heiner, 1990; Kalmuss, 1984). According to Hotaling and Sugarman (1986), witnessing interparental violence as a child or adolescent is the most consistent risk for perpetrators and victims of husband-to-wife violence. Fourteen out of 16 studies these authors reviewed indicated that exposure to interparental violence was a characteristic of male batterers, and 11 out of 15 studies indicated that exposure to interparental violence also was a characteristic of female victims. Examining the unique variance contributed by exposure to child abuse versus exposure to marital aggression, Doumas, Margolin, and John (1994) reported that witnessing marital aggression was a significant predictor for husbands' next-generation abuse of their wives and abuse potential of their children. For wives, witnessing marital abuse in the family of origin was a significant predictor of being victimized by their own husband. The intergenerational data, taken as a whole, indicate that the childhood experience of witnessing interparental violence can lay the foundation for an aggressively oriented behavioral repertoire as well as different expectations regarding aggression in adult intimate relationships. For the most part, however, these data are based on identified samples, thereby eliminating persons who may have witnessed interparental aggression but have not gone on to exhibit such behavior themselves. These studies also are based on retrospective data. It is known from the literature on other types of exposure, such as child abuse (e.g., Kaufman & Zigler, 1987; Widom, 1989), that persons victimized as children may have a higher likelihood of becoming adult perpetrators of violence but that the majority of those victimized do not become perpetrators. Ultimately, an improved understanding of the perpetuation of aggression across generations requires prospective examinations of the effects on children of the witnessed aggression.

The effects of witnessing violence also have been studied in adolescent and college-aged samples, with particular attention given to aggression in dating relationships. Some studies have indicated that exposure to interparental violence is related to dating aggression, particularly for males (Foo & Margolin, 1995; O'Keefe, Brockopp, & Chew, 1986), whereas others have shown that both interparental violence and child abuse are related to dating aggression (Bernard & Bernard, 1983; Marshall & Rose, 1988; Riggs, O'Leary, & Breslin, 1990). Besides exhibiting aggression in early-adult relationships, there are additional risks of exposure to interparental aggression. For instance, Carlson (1990) found that, for males only, exposure to spousal abuse as a child was related to running away, experiencing suicidal ideation, and behaving aggressively toward parents. Forsstrom-Cohen and Rosenbaum (1985), in contrast, reported significant findings for females but not males: Females exposed to interparental violence reported more depression and more aggression compared to females whose parents had nonviolent discordant marriages or satisfactory marriages.

Effects on Children of Current Exposure to Marital Violence

The immediate effects of exposure to marital violence have been assessed in children currently living in maritally violent homes. Data on such children have been derived from a variety of samples, such as children accompanying their mothers to shelters, children coming to the attention of social service agencies other than battered-women's shelters, and community samples of children from both violent and nonviolent homes. The literature has evolved, over the past decade, from uncontrolled case studies to studies that control for different types of abuse and to studies that control for exposure to marital discord versus abuse. Sampling from identified or treatment samples, as opposed to community samples, has been associated with different outcomes, which indicates that the distinction is important.

Attention to the plight of children subjected to their parents' violent arguments initially was sparked by clinical and anecdotal reports regarding symptoms in children who were seeking refuge with their mothers in shelters for battered women or were identified through social service or medical networks. A series of uncontrolled studies indicated that such children exhibit a high level of stress-related disorders, including physical health problems; externalizing, or acting-out problems; problems with the law; school problems; and a wide range of internalizing disorders, reflecting low self-concept, fear and anxiety, and social isolation (Carlson, 1984; Hilberman & Munson, 1978; Hughes & Barad, 1983; Levine, 1975; Westra & Martin, 1981). Describing children in six shelters, Layzer et al. (1986) reported health problems in more than half of the infants, including weight and eating problems in 15% and sleep problems or reduced responsiveness in nearly 20%. Of children older than 18 months, nearly 70% exhibited mood problems and 40% had problems interacting with other children or adults. The question repeatedly raised regarding these uncontrolled case studies, however, was whether the children's symptoms were due to the relocation to an unfamiliar surrounding, to the marital violence, or to other forms of abuse occurring in the family.

A second wave of studies, summarized in Table 2, focused on identified samples but controlled for one or more risk factors other than the exposure to marital violence. The table shows the broad range of possible outcomes of exposure to marital violence that were studied. Although most of the studies examined the effects on children in terms of diagnostic categories (e.g., depression, conduct disorders) or of broadband clinical phenomena (e.g., internalizing, externalizing), some studies focused on the more subtle dimensions of children's social skills, interpersonal problem solving, and empathy.

Studies of children who accompany their mother to shelters for battered women provide strong evidence of the detrimental effects of exposure to marital violence, even when other risk factors are taken into account. Witnessing marital violence has been associated with internalizing only (Christopoulos et al., 1987; Holden & Ritchie, 1991) and with both internalizing and externalizing problems (Fantuzzo et al., 1991; Holden & Ritchie, 1991; Hughes, Vargo, Ito, & Skinner, 1991; Jaffe, Wolfe, Wilson, & Zak, 1986a, 1986b; McCloskey et al., 1995; O'Keefe, 1994; Wolfe et al., 1985). Exposure also has been associated with problems with social competence (Wolfe, Zak, Wilson, & Jaffe, 1986), aggression and difficult temperaments (Holden & Ritchie, 1991), extreme approaches to problem solving (Rosenberg, 1987), and impaired empathic abilities (Hinchey & Gavelek, 1982). In some instances, these effects of exposure to marital violence hold even after controlling for parent–child aggression (O'Keefe, 1994). In other instances, the parent–child aggression is associated with more severe consequences than the marital violence alone (Jaffe et al., 1986b), or else it is the combination of exposure to spousal abuse and child abuse that is associated with the most problems (Davis & Carlson, 1987; Hughes, 1988; Hughes et al., 1989). Exposure to physical abuse results in more negative outcomes than exposure to verbal abuse (Fantuzzo et al., 1991; Rossman & Rosenberg, 1992). The effects of marital violence also

TABLE 2

Studies Examining Global Effects of Exposure to Marital Violence

Study	Sample	Groups	Results
Christopoulos et al. (1987)	$n = 80$ Age = 5–13	a. Spousal abuse in battered-women's shelter sample b. Community comparison with no severe spousal abuse	Spousal abuse group had more internalizing but not more externalizing problems than comparison group. No differences on social competence scales.
Davis & Carlson (1987)	$n = 67$ Age = 4–11	a. Spousal abuse only b. Spousal abuse and parent–child abuse Both groups recruited from five domestic violence shelters	Witnessing violence and being the victim of child abuse related to lower social competence scores and higher internalizing and externalizing scores than witnessing only.
Doumas, Margolin, & John (1994)	$n = 181$ Age = 8–11	Community sample recruited through announcements or direct mailings	Parents' marital aggression and child abuse potential together predicted boys', but not girls', aggression and hostility. Child abuse potential contributed unique variance; marital aggression did not.
Fantuzzo et al. (1991)	$n = 107$ Age = 3.5–6.4	a. Physical and verbal spousal abuse in battered-women's shelter sample b. Physical and verbal spousal abuse in Head Start sample c. Verbal spousal abuse in Head Start sample d. No physical or verbal abuse in Head Start sample	Both groups exposed to physical abuse had more problems than the verbal-abuse-only, or control, group. Shelter residence was associated with greater internalizing and social competency problems than nonshelter violence and verbal abuse groups.
Hershorn & Rosenbaum (1985)	$n = 45$ Age range unknown	a. Spousal abuse in mental health clinic sample b. Marital discord in mental health clinic sample c. Satisfactory marriages, from telephone directory	Children exposed to spousal abuse and to marital discord had more severe conduct and personality problems than children of parents in satisfactory marriages. No differences between spousal abuse and marital discord groups.

Study		Sample	Results
Hinchey & Gavelek (1982)	n = 32 Age = 4–5	a. Spousal abuse in battered-women's shelter sample b. No spousal abuse Both groups used same child care facility	Children exposed to spousal abuse showed poorer empathic abilities (role enactment, role taking, and social inference) than nonexposed group.
Holden & Ritchie (1991)	n = 74 Age = 2–8	a. Spousal abuse from battered-women's shelter sample b. Community comparison	Children exposed to spousal abuse had higher scores on internalizing than comparison group; no differences on externalizing. Exposed group rated as having more difficult temperaments and being more aggressive.
Hughes (1988)	n = 178 Age = 3–12	a. Spousal abuse only, in battered-women's shelter sample b. Spousal abuse plus physical child abuse in battered-women's shelter sample c. Community comparison	Children exposed to spousal abuse and child abuse showed the most problems and were significantly different from the comparison children. Nonabused witnesses showed a level of distress between the other two groups.
Hughes, Parkinson, & Vargo (1989)	n = 150 Age = 4–12	a. Spousal abuse only, in battered-women's shelter sample b. Spousal abuse plus physical child abuse in battered-women's shelter sample c. Community comparison	Witness-and-abuse group scored higher than comparison children on internalizing and externalizing. Witness-only group scored midway between the other two groups. Witness-and-abuse group scored higher than witness-only group on total problems; both groups scored higher than the comparison group.
Hughes, Vargo, Ito, & Skinner (1991)	n = 154 Age = 4–12	a. Spousal abuse only, in battered-women's shelter sample b. Spousal abuse and physical abuse c. Community comparison	Spousal-abuse-only and combined spousal-and-physical-abuse groups had problem scores significantly higher than those in the comparison group. No differences between the two abuse groups.
Jaffe, Wolfe, Wilson, & Zak (1986a)	n = 126 Age = 6–11	a. Spousal abuse in past 6 weeks in battered-women's shelter sample b. Nonviolent families recruited through newspapers	Boys and girls exposed to spousal abuse showed more problems related to internalizing and social competence; boys showed more externalizing behaviors. Amount of violence was related to amount of behavior problems for boys but not girls.

Table continues

TABLE 2 *(Continued)*

Study	Sample	Groups	Results
Jaffe, Wolfe, Wilson, & Zak (1986b)	*n* = 65 Age = 4–16 (some group variation)	a. Spousal abuse in battered-women's shelter sample b. Child abuse in child welfare agency sample c. Community comparison	Both spousal abuse group and child abuse group showed more internalizing and externalizing problems than community group. Child abuse group, compared to spousal abuse group, showed more externalizing.
Jouriles, Barling, & O'Leary (1987)	*n* = 45 Age = 5–13	One group, but separate measurements of spousal aggression and parent–child aggression Recruited from social service agency	Witnessing spousal abuse was not related to child problems, but parent–child aggression was related to conduct problems, attention problems, anxiety-withdrawal, and motor excess.
Jouriles, Murphy, & O'Leary (1989)	*n* = 87 Age = 5–12	One group, but separate measures for spousal aggression and marital discord Recruited from marital therapy clinic	Marital aggression contributed unique variance to the prediction of conduct disorder, personality disorder, inadequacy-immaturity, and clinical levels after marital discord controlled.
Kempton, Thomas, & Forehand (1989)	*n* = 48 Age = 11.4– 15.0	Community sample recruited through ads, announcements, and schools	Fathers', but not mothers', physical aggression was related to all four measures of adolescent functioning: conduct problems, anxiety-withdrawal, cognitive functioning, prosocial functioning.
McCloskey, Figueredo, & Koss (1995)	*n* = 367 Age = 6–12	a. Spousal abuse in battered-women's shelter sample b. Spousal abuse in community sample c. Community comparison	Few differences between children in two spousal abuse groups. Both spousal abuse groups showed more attention deficit/hyperactivity disorder, separation anxiety, obsessive–compulsive disorder, and conduct disorder than comparison group. No differences in depression.

Study	Sample size/Age	Sample description	Findings
O'Keefe (1994)	$n = 185$ Age = 7–13	All recruited through battered-women's shelters	Marital violence witnessed was significantly related to internalizing and externalizing, after demographic variables and parent–child aggression controlled for. For boys, violence witnessed was a better predictor of child behavior problems than parent–child aggression. For girls, violence witnessed and mother–child aggression predicted internalizing, but not externalizing, behaviors.
Rosenbaum & O'Leary (1981)	$n = 52$ Age mean = 10.0	a. Spousal abuse in social services sample b. Nonviolent, discordant behavior in clinic–social services sample c. Community sample from phone book	Children exposed to spousal abuse were higher in behavior problems than community group but not statistically different from either of other two groups.
Rosenberg (1986, 1987)	Age = 5–8	a. Spousal abuse in battered-women's shelter sample b. No spousal abuse, medical care facility sample	Children who witnessed high rather than low levels of violence performed less well on a measure of interpersonal sensitivity. Children from violent homes tended to choose either passive or aggressive strategies to resolve interpersonal conflict.
Rossman & Rosenberg (1992)	$n = 94$ Age = 6–12	a. Spousal abuse in battered-women's shelter sample b. Intact violent families c. Verbally discordant, but not physically violent, families d. Nondiscordant and nonviolent families For b–d, recruitment through flyers, media, community contacts, and agencies	Children in violent-shelter families were higher on CBCL externalizing, social activity, and social competence and lower on self-acceptance than children in other three groups. Children in violent-home group had higher scores on somatic complaints than other groups, but post hoc comparisons did not achieve significance.
Spaccarelli, Sandler, & Roosa (1994)	$n = 303$ Age = 10–12	Community sample recruited through schools, door-to-door canvassing	In 30% of sample, at least one incident of abuse reported within child's lifetime. Spousal abuse accounted for unique variance in girls' self-reported conduct, with significant risk and demographic factors controlled for. Marital violence did not account for boys' symptoms.

Table continues

TABLE 2 (Continued)

Study	Sample	Groups	Results
Sternberg et al. (1993)	$n = 110$ Age = 8–12	a. Child abuse only b. Spousal abuse only c. Child abuse and spousal abuse d. Comparison All recruited through social services	According to children's reports, those exposed only to spousal abuse did not differ significantly on childhood depression from the child-abuse-only and the combined child abuse and spousal abuse groups; all three abused groups differed from the comparison group. On self-reported internalizing and externalizing, those exposed only to spousal abuse did not show significant differences from the comparison group; the other abuse groups were different from the comparison group. According to mother's reports, the spousal-abuse-only group was significantly higher on externalizing problems than the child abuse group. The abused witnesses were higher on externalizing than the spousal-abuse-only and child-abuse-only groups.
Wolfe, Zak, Wilson, & Jaffe (1986)	$n = 63$ Age = 4–13	a. Previous residents at battered-women's shelters b. Current residents at battered-women's shelters c. Nonviolent community comparison	Children in the current resident group had the lowest social competence rating. Former shelter residents reported highest family disadvantage ratings. No differences on internalizing or externalizing behaviors.
Wolfe, Jaffe, Wilson, & Zak (1985)	$n = 198$ Age = 4–16	a. Spousal abuse in battered-women's shelter sample b. Nonviolent community comparison	Children exposed to abuse rated higher in behavior problems and lower in social competence than comparison groups. Exposed group had 26.5% in clinical range, compared to 10.4% of comparison group.

Note. CBCL = Child Behavior Checklist.

have been demonstrated after controlling for demographic variables that have been shown to put children at risk, such as father status and minority status (O'Keefe, 1994).

Finally, it has been shown that children residing in shelters for battered women may experience somewhat greater problems, particularly with regard to social competency and internalizing, than exposed children in the community or previously sheltered children (Fantuzzo et al., 1991; Wolfe et al., 1986). In a comparison of sheltered and nonsheltered exposed children, Rossman and Rosenberg (1992) reported higher levels of externalizing problems in the sheltered children but also, contrary to the other studies, higher social competency and higher social activity. Moreover, the distinctive characteristics of the sheltered children are not totally attributable to being removed from a familiar environment. The comparison of McCloskey et al. (1995) between children from battered-women's shelters and children witnessing marital violence abuse in the community showed few differences between these groups; both exposed groups showed more conduct disorders, attention deficit and hyperactivity, separation anxiety, and obsessive–compulsive disorder than did children in a nonexposed control group.

The results of exposure also have been examined in groups of children identified through social service or clinical facilities who still reside in their homes, thereby circumventing the added problems of relocation. According to Jouriles, Murphy, and O'Leary (1989), marital violence contributes unique variance, above that of general marital discord, to the prediction of conduct disorder and inadequacy-immaturity for boys and of inadequacy-immaturity for girls. Other studies, however, failed to find significant differences between exposure to spousal abuse and exposure to nonviolent conflict (Hershorn & Rosenbaum, 1985; Rosenbaum & O'Leary, 1981). A study by Sternberg et al. (1993) showed the complexity of attempting to separate the effects of exposure to marital abuse only, child abuse only, and the combination of these factors. On the basis of children's reports, those exposed only to spousal abuse did not significantly differ in terms of childhood depression from those exposed only to child abuse or those exposed to both; all three groups differed from the comparison group. With respect to self-reported internalizing and externalizing, those exposed to spousal abuse did not show significant differences from the comparison group, whereas the two other abuse groups were significantly different from the comparison group on these measures. On the basis of mothers' reports, the spousal-abuse-only group was significantly higher on externalizing problems than was the child abuse group; the group experiencing both types of abuse was significantly higher on externalizing than were the spousal abuse or child abuse groups. Overall, on the basis of children's reports, child abuse was associated with more negative outcomes, whereas on the basis of mothers' reports, exposure to marital violence showed a stronger association with externalizing problems.

There are a number of ways of examining the significance of exposure to marital violence. Some studies have compared symptoms in the exposed and the nonexposed children, regardless of whether or not either group mean was in the clinically significant range. In other studies, the mean score of the exposed group was in the clinical range, whereas the mean score of the nonexposed group was below the clinical cutoff point (e.g., Fantuzzo et al., 1991; Jaffe et al., 1986a). Still other studies have provided data on the percentage of children in the exposed group, compared to that of control groups, who were in the clinical range. Table 3 summarizes studies that offer percentile data on children who fall into the clinical range on commonly used scales such as the Child Behavior Checklist (Achenbach & Edelbrock, 1983) and the Behavior Problem Checklist (Quay, 1977). With the exception of the child reports from Sternberg et al. (1993), 26%–75% of children exposed to spousal abuse were rated as showing clinical problems in percentages that are higher than those found for community controls. The study by Sternberg et al. (1993) stands out owing to the dramatic comparison between children's reports and mothers' reports. Almost no children in the group exposed to marital violence revealed clinically significant problems in their self-reports (6% and 0% for internalizing and externalizing). Mothers of those children, however, reported high levels of clinically significant problems (75% for both internalizing and externalizing). The impact of child abuse is readily seen in the children's self-reports in the Sternberg et al. (1993) sample, as well as in parents' reports in the Jaffe et al. (1986b) sample.

The effects of exposure to marital violence are somewhat less pronounced when examined in nonreferred, community samples, perhaps because of the better controlled nature of the studies or perhaps because the violence that the children witness is less severe. Compared to the previously reviewed studies, in which either it was assumed that nonidentified community children were nonviolent or community children who were violent were eliminated, these studies have attempted to identify the extent to which exposure to interparental violence within a community sample affects children's adjustment. Whereas it is reasonable to assume that the physical aggression in these studies is of lower frequency and intensity than that found in shelter samples (Straus, 1990), the range of persons experiencing at least some physical aggression tends to be high, upward of 25%–30% (Pan, Neidig, & O'Leary, 1994; Margolin, John, & Foo, in press). Kempton, Thomas, and Forehand (1989) pointed to the greater impact of fathers', as opposed to mothers', marital aggression on the functioning of their adolescent children. Doumas et al. (1994) raised questions about the impact of exposure to marital aggression contrasted with parents' potential for child abuse. Together, parents' marital aggression and their child abuse

TABLE 3

Studies Examining Percentage of Children Showing Problems in the Clinical Range

Study	Dimension	Group Spousal abuse (%)	Group Other (%)				Definition of other groups
Christopoulos et al. (1987)	Internalizing	32.5	10.0				Community control
	Externalizing	32.5	17.5				
Holden & Ritchie (1991)	Total behavior problems	27.0	8.0				Community control
Jaffe, Wolfe, Wilson, & Zak (1986b)	Total behavior problems	75.0	90.0[a]	13.0[b]			[a]Child abuse [a]Control
Jouriles, Murphy, & O'Leary (1989)	Conduct disorder, personality disorder, inadequacy-immaturity	48.2	12.9				Marital discord
O'Keefe (1994)	Internalizing	31.0					No control
	Externalizing	21.0					
Rosenbaum & O'Leary (1981)	Conduct disorder	26.0	23.0[a]	11.0[b]			[a]Marital discord [b]Community
Sternberg et al. (1993)	Internalizing (child report)	6.0	27.0[a]	27.0[b]	3.0[c]		[a]Child abuse [b]Abuse and witness [c]Control
	Externalizing (child report)	0.0	15.0[a]	10.0[b]	3.0[c]		
	Internalizing (mother report)	75.0	61.0[a]	77.0[b]	58.0[c]		
	Externalizing (mother report)	75.0	49.0[a]	77.0[b]	36.0[c]		
Wolfe, Jaffe, Wilson, & Zak (1985)	Total behavior problems	26.5	10.4				Nonviolent control

Note. Cutoffs for inclusion in the clinic sample are as follows: For Christopoulos et al., $T > 70$ on Child Behavior Checklist (CBCL); for Holden & Ritchie, $T > 65$ on CBCL; for Jaffe, Wolfe, Wilson, and Zak, $T >$ one standard deviation above the norm on CBCL; for Jouriles, Murphy, and O'Leary, $T > 10$ and 8 for boys and girls on conduct disorder, >6 and 7 on personality disorder, >3 and 3 on inadequacy-immaturity on Peterson-Quay Behavior Problem Checklist; for O'Keefe, $T > 98$th percentile on CBCL; for Rosenbaum & O'Leary, $T >$ clinic mean on Peterson-Quay Behavior Problem Checklist; for Sternberg et al., $T > 63$ (10th percentile) on Youth Self-Report for child report and on CBCL for mother report; for Wolfe, Jaffe, Wilson, and Zak, $T > 70$ on CBCL.

potential were predictive of boys', but not girls', aggression, but unique variance came only from the parents' child abuse potential. Spaccarelli et al. (1994), in contrast, found unique effects of marital violence for girls', but not boys', conduct disorders. Although these effects for girls are found even after controlling for other, correlated risks, such as maternal alcohol problems and parental divorce, the exposure to violence accounts for only a limited amount of the unique variance, for example, 3% of unique variance in girls' depression and conduct problems.

Effect of Exposure to Violence on Children's Immediate Reactions to Conflict

A body of research recently has emerged examining children's specific reactions to the different component processes of interparental anger, with an emphasis on characteristics of the anger, the content of the discussion, and the final resolution of the discussion (Table 4). These studies are designed to monitor children's immediate reactions to interparental or interadult anger, either as they respond in real life to spontaneous occurrences of interparental anger or as they respond in analogous situations when exposed to audiotaped or videotaped samples of interadult anger. The studies have provided information on two questions pertaining to children's exposure to marital violence: Are discussions containing physical aggression, compared to other components of anger, more upsetting for children? Are children's immediate reactions to interparental conflict influenced by their personal histories of exposure to interparental violence? Children perceive disagreements as more negative (Cummings, Vogel, Cummings, & El-Sheikh, 1989) and perceive the actors as more negative (El-Sheikh & Cheskes, 1995) when the conflict includes physical aggression, contrasted with verbal aggression or nonviolent conflict. Children also report more negative emotions and more negative evaluations in response to tapes involving physical aggression as opposed to negative voice tones and name-calling (Laumakis, Margolin, & John, in press). Although interactions involving physical aggression, compared to nonphysical aggression, also tend to elicit more distress reactions in young children (Cummings, Zahn-Waxler, & Radke-Yarrow, 1981), they do not consistently induce more negative emotional reactions in older children (E. M. Cummings et al., 1989). Despite the predictions of a modeling hypothesis, children are not more likely to display physical anger after observing episodes involving hitting (Cummings et al., 1981). Moreover, according to El-Sheikh & Cheskes (1995), boys are more likely to report aggressive impulses during exposure to verbal than to physical arguments.

Four studies examined the question of whether prior exposure to marital violence influences the way children respond to current episodes of marital conflict, either between their own parents or in simulated video-

TABLE 4
Studies Examining Relation Between Immediate Distress Reactions to Conflict and Marital Violence

Study	Sample	Groups	Results
Cummings, Pellegrini, Notarius, & Cummings (1989)	$n = 48$ Age = 2–6	Not described	Children of parents with a history of physical hostility showed heightened preoccupation, concern, support seeking, and social responsibility in response to play-acted angry scenarios involving the mother.
Cummings, Vogel, Cummings, & El-Sheikh (1989)	$n = 63$ Age = 4–9	Not described	Children exposed to interparental physical conflict were more distressed than children from families without physical conflict when watching videotapes of marital conflict.
Cummings, Zahn-Waxler, & Radke-Yarrow (1981)	$n = 24$ Age = 10–20 months	Not described	Exposure to interparental physical fights was marginally related to responding to fights with anger, distress, or affectionate, prosocial behavior. Children who observed the most physical fights were the only ones to comfort, distract, or reconcile angry parents.
El-Sheikh & Cheskes (1995)	$n = 64$ Age = 6–7 and 9–10	Community sample recruited through ads, newspapers, and flyers	Actors in adult–adult physical conflict were perceived as more angry than actors in verbal conflict. Boys reported more aggressive impulses during physical than during verbal conflict.
Garcia, O'Hearn, Margolin, & John (1997)	$n = 110$ Age = 8–11	a. Severe physical abuse b. Moderate conflict c. Low conflict All three groups recruited through mailings, ads, announcements in the community	On the basis of parents' daily report data for 6 weeks, children with exposure to severe abuse were more likely to respond to daily interparental conflict with aggression or withdrawal.
Laumakis, Margolin, & John (in press)	$n = 75$ Age = 9–12	a. High conflict b. Low conflict Both groups recruited through mailings, ads, announcement in the community	For both groups, audiotaped conflicts involving physical aggression elicited more negative affect than audiotapes with negative voice tones or name-calling. Physical aggression was not distinguished from threats to leave the marriage.
O'Brien, Margolin, John, & Krueger (1991)	$n = 35$ Age = 8–11	a. Physical aggression b. Verbal aggression c. Low conflict All three groups recruited through general ads and announcements in newspapers	In response to audiotaped conflicts, boys exposed to physical aggression were more likely to suggest self-distraction than boys in the other two groups. Boys exposed to physical aggression also made more comments suggesting efforts to interfere in parents' conflicts.

taped interactions. In general, children of families with interparental physical aggression showed more extreme reactions when faced with additional
episodes of conflict. Studies have shown that exposed, compared to nonexposed, children are more likely to distract themselves or their parents
from conflict (O'Brien, Margolin, John, & Krueger, 1991); to interfere or
become actively involved in the parents' conflict (Cummings et al., 1981;
O'Brien et al., 1991); to become angry, to appear sad or frightened, or to
leave the room (Garcia, O'Hearn, Margolin, & John, 1997); to be more
distressed (E. M. Cummings et al., 1989); or to be more preoccupied, so-
licitous, and support seeking (Cummings, Pellegrini, Notarius, & Cummings, 1989). In general, these data suggest that exposure to parental aggression is likely to sensitize children to further episodes of conflict, such
that they are likely to show a wide range of emotions indicative of distress,
as well as diverse and sometimes extreme efforts to cope, including the
opposing strategies of intervening and distancing themselves.

SUMMARY OF OUTCOMES

Anecdotal reports based on observations of children in shelters support the impression of a connection between marital violence and behavior
problems. Authors of controlled studies and studies based on community
samples have revealed less pronounced differences between exposed and
nonexposed children or differences specific to one age group or one gender
(Goodman & Rosenberg, 1987; McDonald & Jouriles, 1991). Recent research has brought some clarity to the distinction between children who
are witnesses to abuse and those who are directly victimized. It generally
has been found that children who observe interparental violence exhibit
a level of adjustment that is somewhat "in between"; that is, their adjustment tends to be better than that of children who are physically abused
or who are physically abused *and* witness interparental abuse, but it is worse
than that of children in comparison or control groups (Hughes et al., 1989;
Jaffe et al., 1986b; Sternberg et al., 1993). To further the understanding of
the sequelae of multiple forms of abuse, more information is needed concerning the magnitude of each type of abuse as well as concerning other
variables that might exacerbate or buffer the effects of abuse. To improve
understanding of children's overall reactions, it is important to examine
how one type of abuse renders children more vulnerable to other types of
abuse.

The other important distinction is between the role of marital violence and that of marital conflict. There is a large body of literature documenting the association between marital discord and childhood adjustment (e.g., Cummings & Davies, 1994; Emery, 1982; Fincham & Osborne,
1993; Grych & Fincham, 1990; Margolin, 1981; Reid & Crisafulli, 1990).

Moreover, the incidence of marital violence among those seeking marital therapy is reported to be over 50% (O'Leary, Vivian, & Malone, 1992). Because the majority of studies examining the effects of marital conflict did not specifically assess the participants for marital violence, it is not known to what extent effects in the marital conflict studies can be attributed to violent as opposed to nonviolent forms of marital discord. The recent well-controlled studies that have attempted to separate the effects of marital violence from those of nonviolent discord illustrate the serious long-term consequences of violence per se. Violent, compared to nonviolent, conflict has been shown to predict more extensive long-term problems (Fantuzzo et al., 1991; Jenkins & Smith, 1991; Jouriles et al., 1989; Rossman & Rosenberg, 1992), as well as more negative immediate reactions (E. M. Cummings et al., 1989; J. S. Cummings et al., 1989; El-Sheikh & Cheskes, 1995; Garcia et al., 1997; Laumakis et al., in press; O'Brien et al., 1991). Only two studies failed to find a distinction between children's reactions to violent and nonviolent forms of conflict (Hershorn & Rosenbaum, 1985; Rosenbaum & O'Leary, 1981). There is a methodological problem, however, in that children exposed to marital violence also tend to experience other forms of marital conflict more frequently than do nonexposed children (McDonald & Jouriles, 1991). Moreover, the nature of the nonviolent conflict may be more threatening and serious than that found in nonviolent homes. Laumakis et al. (in press) reported that physical aggression is more upsetting than verbal aggression and comparable to verbal threats to end the marriage. In general, little has been learned directly from children concerning what dimensions of the marital conflict, either violent or nonviolent, are most threatening to them. Moreover, both marital conflict and marital violence are ill-defined constructs. The definitions can be sufficiently broad to encompass almost all marriages at some point in time or can be sufficiently narrow to capture only the extreme, extraordinarily destructive marriages. Ultimately, from the perspective of identifying directions that will lead to protection of children, the goal is to identify which dimensions of nonviolent marriages are distressing to children and what increases children's vulnerability to those dimensions.

FACTORS MEDIATING THE EFFECTS OF EXPOSURE TO INTERPARENTAL VIOLENCE

Developmental Effects

There have been several recent attempts to examine age-related changes and developmental trajectories related to exposure to interparental violence. Three questions are pertinent to this issue: (a) Are children differentially affected at different developmental stages by exposure to marital violence? (b) Does exposure to violence at specific stages interrupt the stage-salient issues of the stages? (c) Is the child's developmental stage related to increases in interparental violence?

Scant attention has been paid to the fundamental question of whether children's reactions to marital violence vary with developmental stage. The data that exist, however, are consistent with the idea of developmental trends in emotional responding in that children at different ages show different types of problems (Cummings & Cummings, 1988). Younger children, such as preschoolers, were more likely to exhibit emotional distress, immature behavior, and somatic complaints (Jaffe et al., 1990). The combination of witnessing violence and being physically abused clearly differentiated the distress levels of preschool children but was less of a factor in 6- to 8- or 9- to 12-year-olds (Hughes, 1988). School-aged children were more likely to evaluate the violence negatively and to attempt purposive behavioral interventions (Cummings, Zahn-Waxler, & Radke-Yarrow, 1984). Adolescents were shown to exhibit anxiety and high levels of aggression as well as to act out in typical adolescent fashion, for example, by running away (Carlson, 1990; Jaffe et al., 1990).

Although there is evidence that developmental level and abuse experiences interact to influence the child's level of adjustment, there are no clear patterns as to specific effects for specific ages (e.g., Hughes et al., 1989). Whereas some studies show that school-aged children have more behavior problems than preschool children (Holden & Ritchie, 1991; Hughes et al., 1989), other studies show the reverse (Hughes, 1988; O'Keefe, 1994). Davis and Carlson (1987) reported that more preschool-aged boys exhibited problems than school-aged boys, but more school-aged girls exhibited problems than preschool-aged girls. At younger ages, negative outcomes are more likely to be exhibited in behavior. It is hypothesized that younger children, who are less able to understand violence or to mobilize resources to cope with violence, are more likely to act out and exhibit behavior problems. Older children, in contrast, are more likely to apply negative evaluations and judgments to abusive interactions and less likely to display distress reactions.

Unfortunately, once developmental stage is considered, the number of children per group is so small as to render interpretation of these data quite tentative. Moreover, the effects of age and developmental stage generally are confounded with the effects of repeated exposure and time of initial exposure. Although the literature suggests that children become sensitized to conflict with repeated exposure (Cummings & Cummings, 1988; J. S. Cummings et al., 1989), that variable has not been studied in conjunction with developmental stage. Thus, it is not clear whether the differences noted across developmental stages are a function of developmental stage, of amount of total exposure, of age at initial exposure, or of a combination of these factors.

In general, the outcomes of exposure to interparental aggression are expressed in the language and concepts of psychopathology, with little attention paid to the accomplishment of typical developmental tasks. As children develop, they face a number of important age- and stage-appropriate tasks (Cicchetti, 1989). Successive progression through these tasks within general chronological periods is critical to the child's adaptation. From a developmental psychology perspective, it would be useful to know to what extent age-salient tasks are disrupted by exposure to interparental violence. For example, there is preliminary evidence that exposure to marital violence disrupts stage-salient tasks for preschoolers, as exhibited in poor empathic abilities (Hinchey & Gavelek, 1982) and compromised interpersonal sensitivity and problem-solving strategies (Rosenberg, 1987).

The other issue is whether exposure to violence peaks in relation to children's developmental phases. It is possible that children's transitions between developmental phases, which can be sources of parental stress, are linked to higher levels of spousal aggression. For example, pregnancy has been identified as a time when women living with a violent partner are at particular risk for abuse. The 1985 National Violence Survey indicated that 154 of every 1,000 pregnant women were assaulted by their partners during the first 4 months of pregnancy and 170 per 1,000 were assaulted during the 5th through 9th months (Gelles, 1988). Assaults often are directed toward the back or abdomen, resulting in injury to the fetus and preterm labor (Goodman, Koss, & Russo, 1993). Interparental violence also may increase at later transition phases during childhood and adolescence, at times when the child requires more parental attention and at times when the child's behavior may create stress and uncertainty for the parents. Rather than implying that the child is responsible for or has any control over the violence, this speculation merely suggests that violence may escalate at the very time that the child is at a particularly vulnerable phase in his or her own development.

Gender Effects

The study of gender effects has produced mixed findings. Several studies failed to find differences between boys and girls (Fantuzzo et al., 1991) or reported similar effects across gender with respect to internalizing and social competence (Jaffe et al., 1986a) and with respect to children's self-reports of depression (Spaccarelli et al., 1994). Moreover, contrary to earlier suppositions that girls are more shielded from family violence than are boys (Emery, 1982), recent data suggest that boys and girls are exposed to similar levels of marital violence (O'Keefe, 1994). There has been evidence on both sides, however, concerning whether boys or girls are more vulnerable to the effects of marital violence.

Supporting the notion of greater vulnerability in boys than girls, a number of researchers have reported significant findings for effects on boys exposed to marital conflict but nonsignificant findings for girls in similar situations. The exposed boys, but not the girls, showed significantly higher levels of aggression (Doumas et al., 1994), externalizing behaviors (Jaffe et al., 1986a), total behavior problems (Wolfe et al., 1985), adolescent acting-out behaviors, such as running away and suicidal thoughts (Carlson, 1990). The overall impression regarding boys' vulnerability may be due in part to the existence of several studies that included only boys (e.g., Jaffe et al., 1986b; O'Brien et al., 1991; Rosenbaum & O'Leary, 1981). It also may reflect the co-occurrence of marital violence and parent–child aggression; boys, overall, are more likely to be recipients of father–child aggression (O'Keefe, 1994). Moreover, more frequent and severe levels of husbands' marital aggression toward their wives covaries with higher levels of both mothers' and fathers' aggression toward boys but not toward girls (Jouriles & LeCompte, 1991).

For girls, compared to boys, exposure to violence has been linked with less empathy (Hinchey & Gavelek, 1982), more anxiety (Hughes & Barad, 1983), and more internalizing problems (Holden & Ritchie, 1991). O'Keefe (1994) reported that violence witnessed and amount of mother–child aggression both are better predictors of girls' than of boys' behavior problem scores, particularly for externalizing behavior problems. Spaccarelli et al. (1994) reported that exposure to spousal abuse accounts for unique variance in self-reported conduct problems and self-esteem of girls but not of boys. According to Sternberg et al. (1993), mothers of girls in each of the family violence groups reported more externalizing behavior problems than did mothers of boys in these groups, whereas the opposite gender pattern was found for mothers in the comparison group. Similar patterns were found for children's reports, with girls in the spousal and child abuse groups reporting more externalizing problems than did boys.

Conclusions about gender differences have been complicated by the small number of studies examining gender effects on any one dependent variable, the differences in gender findings across age levels (Peled & Davis, 1995), the finding of gender differences as a main effect rather than as an interaction with the exposure variable, and the finding that the observed gender differences are partially a function of differences between boys and girls in control samples rather than differences in exposure samples (Christopoulos et al., 1987; Sternberg et al., 1993). Gender effects also may extend to effects of parents' gender, as mediated through the parent–child relationship and in terms of the differential impact of violence by the mother versus the father. Kempton et al. (1989), for example, reported that fathers', but not mothers', physical marital abuse was related to adolescent problems.

Effects of Reporter

Studies based on identified samples that use multiple reporters have produced a fairly consistent picture of parents, particularly mothers, reporting more distress in the children than do the children themselves (Hughes et al., 1989; McCloskey et al., 1995; Sternberg et al., 1993). McCloskey et al. (1995), for example, reported that total family violence (both experiencing violence from either of the parents and witnessing interparental violence) accounts for about 12% of the variance in child psychopathology in children's reports and 56% of the variance in mothers' reports. Possible explanations for the greater distress reported by mothers than by children include the children's defensiveness and unwillingness to report problems, mothers' generalizing their high emotional turmoil to children, and mothers' sensitivity to the possibility that their children are at psychological risk as well as their attentiveness to children's symptoms (Hughes et al., 1989; McCloskey et al., 1995). In the Spaccarelli et al. (1994) community sample, however, correlations between violence against mothers and children's adjustment were found only for reports by children, not for those by parents. Reporter effects also are observed with respect to the question of whether children are more negatively affected by child abuse or by spousal abuse. Regarding children's reports, being a victim of child abuse, compared to observing spousal abuse, accounts for more variance in their adjustment (McCloskey et al., 1995) and is associated with lower adjustment levels (Sternberg et al., 1993). Regarding parents' reports in the Sternberg et al. (1993) study, witnessing spousal abuse is associated with poorer outcomes than children's direct experiencing of abuse.

Although most studies have relied heavily on data from mothers, Sternberg et al. (1993) also provide data from fathers. In contrast to the significant group differences for mothers, fathers of children who were victims or witnesses of abuse were no more likely to report problem behavior in their children than fathers of children in the comparison group. Implying that the fathers were not sensitive reporters, Sternberg et al. (1993) attributed the nonsignificant findings for fathers to lack of statistical power owing to the smaller number of fathers, fathers' unfamiliarity with their children's problems, fathers' lack of experience in describing their children's development and functioning, fathers' difficulty completing standardized measures, and fathers' mislabeling of children's maladaptive behaviors. Errors in reporting can, of course, occur in either direction: Whereas it is possible that fathers, as the perpetrators of spousal abuse, may wish to minimize negative outcomes, mothers, as victims themselves, may wish to call particular attention to the negative consequences.

In general, this body of literature has been restricted greatly by reliance on single reporters, most often the mother. Although reports and data from persons outside the family—school records, teachers' reports, and peer ratings—have been used to examine the effects of marital conflict on children (Grych et al., 1992; Jaycox & Repetti, 1993; Katz & Gottman, 1993) and the effects of child abuse on children (e.g., Eckenrode, Laird, & Doris, 1993; Vondra, Barnett, & Cicchetti, 1989), only Kempton et al. (1989) have provided teacher data to examine the effects of exposure to interparental aggression. The Kempton et al. (1989) data indicate that fathers', but not mothers', verbal and physical aggression was related to teachers' measures of internalizing and externalizing problems and prosocial and cognitive functioning.

Effects of Ethnicity

The handful of studies examining ethnic influences have shed little light on the important question of how race or ethnicity interacts with family violence and affects children's adjustment. One question examined is whether children from different racial backgrounds are exposed to different levels of interparental abuse. Out of five demographic variables examined (i.e., minority status, marital status, income, maternal education, and family size) by Spaccarelli et al. (1994), minority status was the only one that was not significantly related to abuse of mothers. Another question examined is whether children of different ethnic backgrounds report different levels of symptoms. O'Keefe (1994) reported that race was a significant predictor of externalizing behavior problems for boys, with Caucasian boys scoring significantly higher than African American boys. A similar finding was reported by Stagg, Wills, and Howell (1989) on the basis of a sample of children accompanying their mothers to battered-women's shelters; white male children had the highest mean T scores on the Child Behavior Checklist and the highest percentage falling into the clinically significant range. McCloskey et al. (1995) found that Hispanic children reported significantly higher numbers of symptoms, particularly symptoms of phobia and anxiety, than children from all other ethnic groups. These data suggest the importance of controlling for ethnicity, as did O'Keefe (1994), who then was able to conclude that violence witnessed was significantly related to boys' externalizing behavior scores even after the variable of race was taken account of.

Effects of Parental Stress, Psychopathology, and Alcoholism

In light of data indicating that mothers victimized by spousal abuse experience high levels of stress, psychopathology, and alcoholism (e.g., Walker, 1984), the question has been asked whether children's outcomes are a function of exposure to these maternal characteristics rather than to the abuse. In addition, the research has shown male batterers to have a high incidence of problem drinking, incarceration, and personality problems (Rosenbaum & O'Leary, 1981), all of which may have an impact on children's adjustment. Wolfe et al. (1985) examined the variance in child adjustment as a function of family violence and of maternal stress, defined as maternal health problems, negative life events, and family crises. Family violence did not predict children's outcomes after controlling for maternal stress, but maternal stress contributed unique variance after controlling for family violence. Although McCloskey et al. (1995) found that abused mothers were more likely than nonabused mothers to experience mental health problems, that variable failed to mediate children's negative responses to family violence. Similarly, although Spaccarelli et al. (1994) found maternal and paternal alcohol problems and paternal incarceration to be related to children's outcomes, violence against mothers still accounted for unique variance in girls' self-reported depression and conduct problems. In summary, these studies illustrate the coexistence of risk factors, indicate that there may be considerable shared variance across risk factors, and suggest that the combination of these risk factors may account for greater variance in children's outcomes than does any one variable alone.

Effects of Severity and Chronicity of Abuse

One impression that emerges across the different research paradigms is that of vastly different outcomes: relatively serious symptoms reported by mothers and social service personnel in women's shelters, compared to small effects found on the basis of reports by parents and children in community samples. According to Straus (1990), women in shelters report 65–68 assaults per year, which is about 11 times greater than the 6 assaults per year reported by abused women in a national survey. In addition to frequency, the types of assault may vary greatly in seriousness, ranging from pushing and slapping to attacking with a weapon. Therefore, one interpretation of the difference between studies of exposed children who come to shelters versus studies of exposed children who remain in the community is that the level of children's symptoms reflects a difference in the nature and extent of the marital violence. Unfortunately, there are few studies on which to base this conclusion. Only a handful of studies have examined whether the severity of violence is related to the extent of children's problems (e.g., Jaffe et al., 1986a; Rosenberg, 1987). To determine whether frequency and severity of exposure to violence is associated with seriousness of outcomes, it would be necessary to have precise descriptions of the violence to which the children were exposed, which generally is lacking in this literature (Fantuzzo & Lindquist, 1989). Equally important is knowing the length of time that the child has been exposed to violence, although that, too, has been ignored as an explanatory variable.

Summary of Mediating Factors

A number of variables have been presented that help to clarify and explain the relationship between marital violence and children's adjustment. It is hypothesized, for example, that various child characteristics—developmental stage, gender, ethnicity—interact with the exposure to violence and render children more or less vulnerable. Exposure to marital abuse, for example, seems to have different psychological significance for boys and girls, and this may be particularly true at different developmental stages. Unfortunately, small sample sizes have made it difficult to examine these variables separately, let alone in combination. Characteristics of the parents, such as their own emotional adjustment, and characteristics of the abuse, such as its severity and chronicity, are important in defining the nature of the risk that children face. Children's experience with marital violence ranges from highly sporadic to ever present, with this dimension rarely accounted for in determining the child outcomes. Similarly, parents' own psychopathology may present an additional source of stress for the children. In light of these mediating factors and the difficulty in adequately assessing each of them, it is not surprising to find large variability across children's reactions to exposure to marital violence.

EXPLANATORY FACTORS AND MECHANISMS

The growing body of research documenting the association between exposure to marital violence and child adjustment problems has focused mainly on identifying risk indicators, that is, variables that are statistically associated with a risk of problem behaviors. Little is known, however, regarding the mechanisms by which marital violence affects children. Rutter (1994) suggested that the identification of mechanisms involves the questions, Wherein lies the risk? and How do the risk mechanisms operate? What is known about risk mechanisms specific to marital violence is quite limited; however, the mechanisms can be surmised, in part, from the rapidly growing literature on risk mechanisms in general marital discord. Additionally, it is important to identify and understand protective mechanisms.

Indirect Effects Mediated Through the Parent–Child Relationship

The key debate in the literature on the association between marital conflict and child adjustment is whether the effects are direct or are mediated through the parent–child relationship (Emery, Fincham, & Cummings, 1992; Fauber & Long, 1991). Proponents of the indirect model argue that impaired parent–child relations are the critical mechanism by which marital conflict affects children. Fincham, Grych, and Osborne (1994) stated that "marital and parent–child relationships are so tightly interwoven that one cannot draw valid inferences about the effects of marital conflict without simultaneously considering the nature of parent–child relations" (p. 132). This issue is equally pertinent to the understanding of how marital violence affects children. Recent reviews have summarized the link between marital relations and the parenting relationship (Easterbrooks & Emde, 1988; Engfer, 1988; Erel & Burman, 1995). Specifically, parents experiencing marital discord may disagree over child rearing (e.g., Block, Block, & Morrison, 1981); may be unavailable emotionally or may withdraw from their children (Dickstein & Parke, 1988; Howes & Markman, 1989); may provide inconsistent or punitive discipline (Fauber, Forehand, Thomas, & Wierson, 1990; Jouriles, Pfiffner, & O'Leary, 1988); may have a cold, unresponsive, angry parenting style (Gottman & Katz, 1989); or may engage in triangulation, whereby the child is drawn into the marital conflict through pressure by one parent to side against the other parent (Minuchin, Rosman, & Baker, 1978; Westerman, 1987).

Regarding marital violence, there is evidence that some husbands who batter treat their children in a nonoptimal fashion. Despite early reports that both perpetrators and victims of spousal abuse are more abusive to their children than are other parents, recent data suggest that it is the men, in particular, who tend to be physically aggressive with their children (O'Keefe, 1994), mostly toward their sons (Jouriles & LeCompte, 1991). Margolin, John, Ghosh, and Gordis (1996) found, through the direct observation of family process, that men's physical and emotional marital aggression toward their wives was linked to their authoritarian and controlling behaviors with their sons. Holden and Ritchie (1991) provided a comprehensive evaluation of parenting in abusive couples, using both maternal reports and mother–child observations to compare abusive and nonabusive couples. Batterers, compared to nonbatterers, were portrayed by their wives as more irritable, less involved in child rearing, less physically affectionate, less likely to use inductive reasoning in response to misbehavior, and more likely to use negative control techniques such as physical punishment and power-assertive responses. The abused wives, although reporting higher levels of parenting stress, did not differ from control wives in their approaches to discipline. However, 34% of the battered women, compared to 5% of the control sample, reported frequently changing their child-rearing behavior in the husband's presence, presumably to avoid inciting the father's anger.

There are many parenting roles that could be undermined by marital violence, although empirical evidence is needed to support most of these linkages. Parents serve as providers of emotional support; as models of emotional regulation; as instructors; as providers of opportunities; as facilitators of relationships outside the family with peers, teachers, and the larger social network; and as disciplinarians. Any of these roles may be disrupted in victims of abuse who are distracted by concerns of basic safety for themselves or their children, who live with fear in their own homes, who may not have the energy to monitor or discipline their children adequately, and who may be isolated from community resources. These parenting roles likewise tend to be disrupted in male perpetrators of abuse who demonstrate negative models of emotional regulation; tend to exhibit harsh, authoritarian interpersonal and disciplinary styles with their children; and may have a dysfunctional interpersonal style impeding their ability to help their children become involved in larger social networks.

Marital Violence as a Form of Child Psychological Abuse

Simply stated, marital violence is a form of child psychological abuse. Hart and Brassard (1987) include in the definition of psychological abuse of children acts such as rejection, coercive punitive, and erratic discipline; a chaotic family environment; poor socializing; and terrorizing. Marital abuse creates a chaotic, dangerous, and frightening family environment. Allowing a child to live in a dangerous environment and to be exposed to acts of violence constitutes child endangerment and neglect. Although directly witnessing any type of violence is traumatic, witnessing violence against one's parent and at the hands of the other parent is even worse (Pynoos & Eth, 1985). Seeing one parent treat another parent with contempt raises questions about who can be trusted, respected, admired, and loved. Children are further confused by the fact that their life is different from that of others, is not to be discussed with others, and lacks someone to protect them from this situation. The child also may experience shame for being part of such a family, for having to maintain the family secret, and for not being able to bring friends to the house or celebrate typical family rituals (Davidson, 1978). "The major negative effects of child maltreatment are generally psychological in nature, affecting the victim's view of self, other, human relationships, goals, and strategies for living" (Hart & Brassard, 1987, p. 161). Even if children growing up with marital violence do not experience obvious psychopathology, they still may be psychologically affected by this experience in terms of their self-respect and self-esteem and the extent to which they can trust and care for others.

Marital Violence as a Traumatic Stressor

The direct-effects model suggests that witnessing the physical threats of one parent against another may be traumatic and personally threatening, creating reactions akin to other traumatic stressors (Pynoos & Eth, 1985). Recent attention to posttraumatic stress disorder (PTSD) in abused women has led to the suggestion that children who witness severe wife battering also may be at risk for PTSD, as are children who are victims of, or witnesses to, any life-threatening incident (Silvern, Karyl, & Landis, 1995). The primary symptom involves intense fear, helplessness, or horror, although young children may instead exhibit disorganized or agitated behavior. Other symptoms of PTSD are categorized into three clusters: (a) avoidance or numbing (lapses of attention, avoiding things that stimulate memories of the event, developmental regression, withdrawal); (b) reexperiencing the event (preoccupying, intrusive recollections; recurrent nightmares; repetitive, compulsive play surrounding impressions of the event); and (c) autonomic hyperarousal (sleep problems, irritability, distractibility, hyper-alertness, nervousness, and somatic complaints). Outcome studies on exposure to interparental violence are only beginning to assess the participants for diagnoses of PTSD, although some of the reactions previously noted can be viewed as responses to trauma, for example, outbursts of anger, reductions in normal routine activities, and somatic and emotional complaints (Jaffe et al., 1990).

Evidence from the literature on marital conflict suggests that even nonviolent interparental conflict is a significant stressor for children. According to teacher, pediatrician, and mental health worker ratings, an increase in the number of conflicts between parents is stressful for children (Coddington, 1972). Children themselves rated "having parents argue in front of you" as the third worst event in a list of 20 events that made them feel bad (Lewis, Siegel, & Lewis, 1984). Gottman and Katz (1989) recently provided evidence that children living in families with marital distress may be under chronic stress, as indexed by their high levels of urinary catecholamines. Remaining in a high affective state may make it hard for the child to regulate affect or may cause the child to become hypervigiliant, both of which could explain these investigators' findings that children from highly conflictual homes play at a low level with peers, display negative peer interactions, and have health problems. This pattern of results converges with some of the trauma responses related to PTSD.

Sensitization to Conflict

Data suggest that with repeated exposures to marital conflict and marital violence, children become more reactive to conflict. Children from high-conflict homes respond to conflict with greater distress and anger (O'Brien et al., 1991). According to Davies and Cummings' (1994) recent model, repeated exposure to marital conflict increases children's feeling of emotional insecurity, which impairs their capacity for regulating their emotions and results in greater behavioral reactivity. This leaves them more prone to feelings of fear, distress, and anger. This model further proposes that the emotional and behavioral symptoms reflecting emotional insecurity predict adjustment problems. For example, O'Brien, Margolin, and

John (1995) reported that behaviorally reactive strategies that involve children in parents' marital conflict are predictive of greater child maladjustment, whereas strategies that distance the child from the marital conflict are predictive of lesser child maladjustment. Other forms of abuse also appear to sensitize children to interparental conflict. Hennessy, Rabideau, Cicchetti, and Cummings (1994), for example, found that physically abused boys reported greater fear than nonabused boys when faced with a standardized presentation of interadult conflict.

Modeling of Violence

According to modeling and social interaction theories, the most direct risk of exposure to aggression is that the child will exhibit aggression toward others (Parke & Slaby, 1983; Patterson, 1982; Widom, 1989). Although the exposure to marital violence does not manifest itself only, or even primarily, in violent behavior, the evidence does point to an increased risk for aggression in a number of arenas: with parents, siblings, dating partners, and, at a future time, one's own spouse or children. It is not that children are learning the execution of specific aggressive behaviors—these they learn on the playground by age 5 (Patterson, 1982). More significantly, the children are learning about the conditions under which aggression may be applied in intimate relationships. Children absorb many negative and dysfunctional messages about the acceptability of violence as a way to resolve conflict, about rationalizing the use of violence as essential under stressful conditions, and about the devaluation of women (Carlson, 1990; Wolfe, Wekerle, Reitzel, & Gough, 1995). These are known to be the subtle consequences of growing up with interparental violence (Jaffe et al., 1990; Straus et al., 1980).

Control Beliefs

Studies suggest that children's beliefs as to whether they can or cannot control stressor events play a role in their response to stressors. With regard to coping with marital conflict, two types of control beliefs are posited to be important: children's beliefs in their control of parental conflict through intervention and children's beliefs in their control of arousal or distress when faced with interparental conflict (Rossman & Rosenberg, 1992). Whereas it is considered positive for children's mental health to believe in their ability to soothe themselves and regulate their emotions, it is considered negative for them to believe in their ability to affect their parents' relationship or conflict. As predicted by Rossman and Rosenberg (1992), self-calming conflict-control beliefs acted as compensatory moderators of the negative relationship between marital conflict and other stressors, on the one hand, and children's problem behaviors on the other.

Intervention control beliefs acted as vulnerability moderators of the relationship between stress and perceived competence. Children's beliefs that they can intervene in their parents' conflict are likely to be met with failure, which may negatively affect their sense of competency.

Protective Factors

In light of the clear finding that not all children exposed to marital violence display negative outcomes, there have been some recent attempts to identify protective factors. The psychological literature on resilience (e.g., Garmezy, 1983) has identified three categories of protective factors: (a) support within the family system, such as a good relationship with one parent or a parenting figure; (b) support from outside the family system, such as a person outside the family or strong involvement in community activities and structures; and (c) attributes of the child, such as high intelligence, physical attractiveness, or strong self-esteem. Emery (1982), for example, suggested that a particularly supportive relationship with one parent can mitigate the effects of marital discord on the child. Neighbors, Forehand, and McVicar (1993) reported that adolescents' relationship with their mother, as well as self-esteem, buffered the effects of high interparental conflict. Jenkins and Smith (1991) identified several protective factors that interacted with the quality of the parental marriage, namely, a relationship with an adult outside the family, an activity for which the child received much positive recognition, good sibling relationships, good parent–child relationships, and relationships with friends.

In an exciting new direction of research, Katz and Gottman (1995) found that vagal tone, a physiological measure of parasympathetic nervous system activity, moderates the negative impact of marital hostility. According to their data, high rates of marital hostility lead to increased likelihood of externalizing problems for children (Katz & Gottman, 1993). However, for children with high vagal tone, marital hostility does not lead to as high a level of antisocial behavior as it does for children with low vagal tone. The explanation is that children with high vagal tone may be better able to modulate their internal state of physiological arousal, which may be related to their ability to self-soothe and to regulate their emotions when faced with interparental conflict.

Summary of Mechanisms

Despite the considerable debate about the relative importance of direct effects from the marital relationship versus indirect effects mediated through the parent–child relationship, there is evidence for both points of view. To understand the effects of marital conflict on children, one must focus on the crucial role of all family relationships—marital and parent–

child—and how they interact with characteristics of the child. The emotional tone of the marital relationship and the parent–child relationships sets the stage for the child's ability to develop relationships beyond the family. Hostility in any of these family relationships creates an overall negative affective family tone and deprives the child of positive roles for relationships based on love, trust, respect, and constructive problem solving. Outright violence in these relationships creates an atmosphere of danger, fear, and unpredictability, and it deprives the child of normal family functions and typical nurturing relationships. Parents who expose their children to marital violence are compromising their caretaking responsibilities even if they strive to maintain an optimal parent–child relationship. The effects of these relationships, however, interact with characteristics of the child, such as their unique talents, abilities to establish supportive relationships outside the family, abilities to regulate emotions, and interpretations and beliefs about the violence. Whereas some of these child variables are modifiable characteristics that could serve as focal points for therapeutic interventions, others, such as vagal tone, may reflect the physiologically based emotional wiring of the child.

QUESTIONS FOR FURTHER RESEARCH

Are There Continuities and Discontinuities in Children's Reactions to Marital Violence?

The child victimization literature in general suffers from lack of information about how abuse alters developmental trajectories over time (Cicchetti, 1994; Dodge, Pettit, & Bates, 1994; Kendall-Tackett, Williams, & Finkelhor, 1993), and the literature on exposure to marital violence is no exception. Despite a handful of longitudinal studies on the association between marital discord and child adjustment (e.g., Easterbrooks, Cummings, & Emde, 1994; Howes & Markman, 1989; Katz & Gottman, 1993), the research on children's reactions to marital violence has been strictly cross sectional. One-time measurements of children's adjustment and of marital violence provide little information about the developmental course of this association. Is children's adjustment related to the current level of exposure, or is it a function of cumulative exposure? What variables influence children's capacity to recover from the exposure if it ceases? Are the effects of exposure more likely at a particular developmental stage? What are the long-term consequences with respect to the intergenerational transmission of violence? Marital violence tends to be a shifting rather than constant phenomenon in a child's life, owing to marital separation, divorce, and other changes in the child's life. By monitoring these changes and their effects on children, researchers can learn a great deal about children's vulnerabilities at different stages and about immediate versus delayed reactions in children's responses to marital violence.

Are There Alternatives to a Simple, Cause–Effect Linear Model of the Relationship Between Interparental Abuse and Child Outcomes?

Although bidirectional effects have been considered in the relationship between marital conflict and child outcomes (Margolin, 1981), the concept has not been applied to interparental violence. Characteristics of the child, or even of the wife, do not *cause* a man to strike out against his wife. However, for individuals who have chosen to include physical spousal abuse as part of their behavioral repertoire in intimate relationships, the child's behavior may be a factor in the likelihood of abuse at particular points in time. Is an abusive husband likely to strike out against his wife for her inability to quiet an unusually fussy, irritable infant or for her failure to straighten out the house when the child's toys are strewn about? Is a woman who is unskilled at and unprepared for parenting and faced with a child with significant behavior or health problems likely to blame the abuse she receives on the child? Jaffe et al. (1990) speculated that a child's behavioral reactions to marital violence can put additional stress on the marital relationship, perhaps aggravating a volatile situation.

It is also possible to consider that the child may influence positive coping responses on the part of a parent. A woman may seek shelter for the sake of her children as much as for herself. Appreciation for the emotional and physical health of her children may impel a woman to leave an abusive relationship. Concern for the child also may positively influence the male partner. One man attributed his cessation of violence toward his wife to his preadolescent daughters' growing awareness of the violence, their recent attempts to intervene in the violence, and his concern for their future. He simply stated, "I would hate for my children to grow up and, when I'm gone, to remember their father as someone who was a mean person. I really don't want them to have those thoughts. I always remember my parents with love and care, and that's what I want them to have for me. . . . When they marry, I want them to look for a decent man—not someone who is violent" (Margolin & Fernandez, 1987).

According to family systems theory, children are not simply the passive recipients of their parents' behavior. Not only may they become involved in the marital violence, but they may also influence the violence. The simple presence of a child in the home, reflected in changes from preparenting to parenting status, may affect the topography of the marital violence. Moreover, the specific behavior of the child at a given point in time may serve as a protective factor, reducing the likelihood of interparental abuse, or it may serve as a stressor, potentiating the likelihood of abuse.

CONCLUSION

Exposure to marital violence is a problem affecting a significant number of children. Like other stress reactions, children's responses to the stress of marital violence vary greatly. The picture is further complicated by the fact that there is a great deal of variability in what is meant by marital violence. Although additional research is needed to document the extent and nature of children's reactions, a more productive direction would be to explore intervening variables that mediate children's reactions to marital violence. Incorporating a developmental perspective that examines children's vulnerabilities at specific stages, as well as their adjustment over time, would help explain the mechanisms by which marital abuse affects children. More attention to cognitive and affective variables of the child that interact with exposure would help identify which children are at greatest risk. As in other forms of childhood traumatization, the empirical literature in this area has been directed toward documenting the existence of symptoms and some of their obvious correlates (e.g., Kendall-Tackett et al., 1993). These data have served as the stimulus for the recent burgeoning of treatment perspectives for such children (Harway & Hansen, 1994; Peled & Davis, 1995). It is time now to turn attention to the empirical investigation of the mechanisms through which children are affected by marital violence for the purpose of improving intervention efforts.

REFERENCES

Achenbach, T. M., & Edelbrock, C. (1983). *Manual for the Child Behavior Checklist and Revised Child Behavior Profile*. Burlington, VT: Author.

Bell, C. C., & Jenkins, E. J. (1993). Community violence and children on Chicago's southside. In D. Reiss, J. E. Richters, M. Radke-Yarrow, & D. Scharff (Eds.), *Children and violence* (pp. 46–54). New York: Guilford Press.

Bernard, M. L., & Bernard, J. L. (1983). Violent intimacy: The family as model for love relationships. *Family Relations, 32*, 283–286.

Block, J. H., Block, J., & Morrison, A. (1981). Parental agreement-disagreement in child-rearing orientations and gender-related personality correlates in children. *Child Development, 49*, 1163–1173.

Cappell, C., & Heiner, R. B. (1990). The intergenerational transmission of family aggression. *Journal of Family Violence, 5*, 135–152.

Carlson, B. E. (1984). Children's observations of interparental violence. In A. R. Roberts (Ed.), *Battered women and their families* (pp. 147–167). New York: Springer.

Carlson, B. E. (1990). Adolescent observers of marital violence. *Journal of Family Violence, 5*, 285–299.

Christopoulos, C., Cohn, D. A., Shaw, D. S., Joyce, S., Sullivan-Hanson, J., Kraft,

S. P., & Emery, R. E. (1987). Children of abused women: I. Adjustment at time of shelter residence. *Journal of Marriage and the Family, 49*, 611–619.

Cicchetti, D. (1989). How research on child maltreatment has informed the study of child development: Perspectives from developmental psychology. In D. Cicchetti & V. Carlson (Eds.), *Child maltreatment: Theory and research on the causes and consequences of child abuse and neglect* (pp. 377–431). Cambridge, England: Cambridge University Press.

Cicchetti, D. (1994). Advances and challenges in the study of the sequelae of child maltreatment. *Development and Psychopathology, 6*, 1–3.

Coddington, R. D. (1972). The significance of life events as etiological factors in the diseases of children: A study of a normal population. *Journal of Psychosomatic Research, 16*, 205–213.

Cummings, E. M., & Cummings, J. L. (1988). A process-oriented approach to children's coping with adults' angry behavior. *Developmental Review, 8*, 296–321.

Cummings, E. M., & Davies, P. (1994). *Children and marital conflict: The impact of family dispute and resolution*. New York: Guilford Press.

Cummings, E. M., Vogel, D., Cummings, J. S., & El-Sheikh, M. (1989). Children's responses to different forms of expression of anger between adults. *Child Development, 60*, 1392–1404.

Cummings, E. M., Zahn-Waxler, C., & Radke-Yarrow, M. (1981). Young children's responses to expressions of anger and affection by others in the family. *Child Development, 52*, 1274–1282.

Cummings, E. M., Zahn-Waxler, C., & Radke-Yarrow, M. (1984). Developmental changes in children's reactions to anger in the home. *Journal of Child Psychology and Psychiatry, 25*, 63–74.

Cummings, J. S., Pellegrini, D., Notarius, C., & Cummings, E. M. (1989). Children's responses to angry adult behavior as a function of marital distress and history of interparent hostility. *Child Development, 60*, 1035–1043.

Davidson, T. (1978). *Conjugal crime: Understanding and changing the wifebeating pattern*. New York: Hawthorn.

Davies, P. T., & Cummings, E. M. (1994). Marital conflict and child adjustment: An emotional security hypothesis. *Psychological Bulletin, 116*, 387–411.

Davis, L. V., & Carlson, B. E. (1987). Observation of spouse abuse: What happens to the children? *Journal of Interpersonal Violence, 2*, 278–291.

Dickstein, S., & Parke, R. (1988). Social referencing in infancy: A glance at fathers and marriage. *Child Development, 59*, 506–511.

Dodge, K. A., Pettit, G. S., & Bates, J. E. (1994). Effects of physical maltreatment on the development of peer relations. *Development and Psychopathology, 6*, 43–56.

Doumas, D., Margolin, G., & John, R. S. (1994). The intergenerational transmission of aggression across three generations. *Journal of Family Violence, 9*, 157–175.

Easterbrooks, M. A., Cummings, E. M., & Emde, R. N. (1994). Young children's responses to constructive marital disputes. *Journal of Family Psychology, 8,* 160–169.

Easterbrooks, M. A., & Emde, R. N. (1988). Marital and parent–child relationships: The role of affect in the family system. In R. A. Hinde & J. Stevenson-Hinde (Eds.), *Relationships within families: Mutual influences* (pp. 83–103). Oxford, England: Clarendon.

Eckenrode, J., Laird, M., & Doris, J. (1993). School performance and disciplinary problems among abused and neglected children. *Developmental Psychology, 29,* 53–62.

El-Sheikh, M., & Cheskes, J. (1995). Background verbal and physical anger: A comparison of children's responses to adult–adult and adult–child arguments. *Child Development, 66,* 446–458.

Emery, R. E. (1982). Interparental conflict and the children of discord and divorce. *Psychological Bulletin, 92,* 310–330.

Emery, R. E. (1989). Family violence. *American Psychologist, 44,* 321–328.

Emery, R. E., Fincham, F. D., & Cummings, E. M. (1992). Parenting in context: Systemic thinking about parental conflict and its influence on children. *Journal of Consulting and Clinical Psychology, 60,* 909–912.

Engfer, S. (1988). The interrelatedness of marriage and the mother–child relationship. In R. A. Hinde & J. Stevenson-Hinde (Eds.), *Relationships within families: Mutual influences* (pp. 104–118). Oxford, England: Clarendon.

Erel, O., & Burman, B. (1995). The linkage between marital quality and the parent–child relationship: A meta-analysis. *Psychological Bulletin, 118,* 108–132.

Fantuzzo, J. W., DePaola, L. M., Lambert, L., Martino, T., Anderson, G., & Sutton, S. (1991). Effects of interparental violence on the psychological adjustment and competencies of young children. *Journal of Consulting and Clinical Psychology, 59,* 258–265.

Fantuzzo, J. W., & Lindquist, C. V. (1989). The effects of observing conjugal violence on children: A review and analysis of research methodology. *Journal of Family Violence, 4,* 77–93.

Fauber, R., Forehand, R., Thomas, A. M., & Wierson, M. (1990). A mediational model of the impact of marital conflict on adolescent adjustment in intact and divorced families: The role of disrupted parenting. *Child Development, 61,* 1112–1123.

Fauber, R. L., & Long, N. (1991). Children in context: The role of the family in child psychotherapy. *Journal of Consulting and Clinical Psychology, 59,* 813–820.

Fincham, F., Grych, J., & Osborne, L. (1994). Does marital conflict cause child maladjustment? Directions and challenges for longitudinal research. *Journal of Family Psychology, 8,* 128–140.

Fincham, F. D., & Osborne, L. N. (1993). Marital conflict and children: Retrospect and prospect. *Clinical Psychology Review, 13,* 75–88.

Finkelhor, D., & Dziuba-Leatherman, J. (1994). Victimization of children. *American Psychologist, 49,* 173–183.

Foo, L., & Margolin, G. (1995). A multivariate investigation of dating aggression. *Journal of Family Violence, 10,* 351–378.

Forsstrom-Cohen, B., & Rosenbaum, A. (1985). The effects of parental marital violence on young adults: An exploratory investigation. *Journal of Marriage and the Family, 47,* 467–471.

Frieze, I. H., & Browne, A. (1989). Violence in marriage. In L. Ohlin & M. Tonry (Eds.), *Family violence* (pp. 163–218). Chicago: University of Chicago Press.

Garbarino, J., Dubrow, N., Kostelny, K., & Pardo, C. (1992). *Children in danger.* San Francisco: Jossey-Bass.

Garcia, H., O'Hearn, H., Margolin, G., & John, R. S. (1997). Mothers' and fathers' reports of children's reactions to naturalistic marital conflict. *Journal of the American Academy of Child and Adolescent Psychiatry, 36,* 1366–1373.

Garmezy, N. (1983). Stressors of childhood. In N. Garmezy & M. Rutter (Eds.), *Stress, coping, and development in children* (pp. 43–84). New York: McGraw-Hill.

Gelles, R. J. (1988). Violence and pregnancy: Are pregnant women at greater risk of abuse? *Journal of Marriage and the Family, 50,* 841–847.

Goodman, G. S., & Rosenberg, M. S. (1987). The child witness to family violence: Clinical and legal considerations. In D. J. Sonkin (Ed.), *Domestic violence on trial: Psychological and legal dimensions of family violence* (pp. 97–126). New York: Springer.

Goodman, L. A., Koss, M. P., & Russo, N. F. (1993). Violence against women: Physical and mental health effects. *Applied and Preventive Psychology, 2,* 79–89.

Gottman, J. M., & Katz, L. F. (1989). Effects of marital discord on young children's peer interaction and health. *Developmental Psychology, 25,* 373–381.

Grych, J. H., & Fincham, F. D. (1990). Marital conflict and children's adjustment: A cognitive-contextual framework. *Psychological Bulletin, 108,* 267–290.

Grych, J. H., Seid, M., & Fincham, F. D. (1992). Assessing marital conflict from the child's perspective: The Children's Perception of Interparental Conflict Scale. *Child Development, 63,* 558–572.

Hart, S. N., & Brassard, M. R. (1987). A major threat to children's mental health: Psychological maltreatment. *American Psychologist, 42,* 160–165.

Harway, M., & Hansen, M. (1994). *Spouse abuse: Assessing and treating battered women, batterers, and their children.* Sarasota, FL: Professional Resource Press.

Hennessy, K. D., Rabideau, G. J., Cicchetti, D., & Cummings, E. M. (1994). Responses of physically abused and nonabused children to different forms of interadult anger. *Child Development, 65,* 815–828.

Hershorn, M., & Rosenbaum, A. (1985). Children of marital violence: A closer look at the unintended victims. *American Journal of Orthopsychiatry, 55,* 260–266.

Hilberman, E., & Munson, K. (1978). Sixty battered women. *Victimology, 2,* 460–470.

Hinchey, F. S., & Gavelek, J. R. (1982). Empathic responding in children of battered mothers. *Child Abuse and Neglect, 6,* 395–401.

Holden, G. W., & Ritchie, K. L. (1991). Linking extreme marital discord, child rearing, and child behavior problems: Evidence from battered women. *Child Development, 62,* 311–327.

Hotaling, G. T., & Sugarman, D. B. (1986). Analysis of risk markers in husband to wife violence: The current state of knowledge. *Violence and Victims, 1,* 101–122.

Howes, P., & Markman, H. J. (1989). Marital quality and child functioning: A longitudinal investigation. *Child Development, 60,* 1044–1051.

Hughes, H. M. (1988). Psychological and behavioral correlates of family violence in child witnesses and victims. *American Journal of Orthopsychiatry, 18,* 77–90.

Hughes, H. M., & Barad, S. J. (1983). Psychological functioning of children in a battered women's shelter: A preliminary investigation. *American Journal of Orthopsychiatry, 53,* 525–531.

Hughes, H. M., Parkinson, D., & Vargo, M. (1989). Witnessing spouse abuse and experiencing physical abuse: A "double whammy"? *Journal of Family Violence, 4,* 197–210.

Hughes, H. M., Vargo, M. C., Ito, E. S., & Skinner, S. K. (1991). Psychological adjustment of children of battered women: Influences of gender. *Family Violence Bulletin, 7*(1), 15–17.

Jaffe, P. G., Wolfe, D. A., & Wilson, S. K. (1990). *Children of battered women.* Newbury Park, CA: Sage.

Jaffe, P. G., Wolfe, D. A., Wilson, S. K., & Zak, L. (1986a). Family violence and child adjustment: A comparative analysis of girls' and boys' behavioral symptoms. *American Journal of Psychiatry, 143,* 74–76.

Jaffe, P. G., Wolfe, D. A., Wilson, S., & Zak, L. (1986b). Similarities in behavioral and social maladjustment among child victims and witnesses to family violence. *American Journal of Orthopsychiatry, 56,* 142–146.

Jaycox, L. H., & Repetti, R. L. (1993). Conflict in families and the psychological adjustment of preadolescent children. *Journal of Family Psychology, 7,* 344–355.

Jenkins, J. M., & Smith, M. A. (1991). Marital disharmony and children's behavior problems: Aspects of poor marriage that affect children adversely. *Journal of Child Psychology and Psychiatry, 32,* 793–810.

Jouriles, E. N., Barling, J., & O'Leary, K. D. (1987). Predicting child behavior problems in maritally violent families. *Journal of Abnormal Psychology, 15,* 165–173.

Jouriles, E. N., & LeCompte, S. H. (1991). Husbands' aggression toward wives and mothers' and fathers' aggression toward children: Moderating effects of child gender. *Journal of Consulting and Clinical Psychology, 59,* 190–192.

Jouriles, E. N., Murphy, C. M., & O'Leary, K. D. (1989). Interspousal aggression, marital discord, and child problems. *Journal of Consulting and Clinical Psychology, 57*, 453–455.

Jouriles, E. N., & O'Leary, K. D. (1985). Interspousal reliability of reports of marital violence. *Journal of Consulting and Clinical Psychology, 53*, 419–421.

Jouriles, E. N., Pfiffner, L. J., & O'Leary, S. G. (1988). Marital conflict, parenting, and toddler conduct problems. *Journal of Abnormal Child Psychology, 16*, 197–206.

Kalmuss, D. (1984). The intergenerational transmission of marital aggression. *Journal of Marriage and the Family, 46*, 11–19.

Katz, L. F., & Gottman, J. M. (1993). Patterns of marital conflict predict children's internalizing and externalizing behaviors. *Developmental Psychology, 29*, 940–950.

Katz, L. F., & Gottman, J. M. (1995). Vagal tone protects children from marital conflict. *Development and Psychopathology, 7*, 83–92.

Kaufman, J., & Zigler, E. (1987). Do abused children become abusive parents? *American Journal of Orthopsychiatry, 57*, 186–192.

Kempton, T., Thomas, A. M., & Forehand, R. (1989). Dimensions of interparental conflict and adolescent functioning. *Journal of Family Violence, 4*, 297–307.

Kendall-Tackett, K. A., Williams, L. M., & Finkelhor, D. (1993). Impact of sexual abuse on children: A review and synthesis of recent empirical studies. *Psychological Bulletin, 115*, 164–180.

Laumakis, M. A., Margolin, G., & John, R. S. (in press). The emotional, cognitive, and coping responses of preadolescent children to different dimensions of marital conflict. In G. W. Holden, R. Geffner, & E. N. Jouriles (Eds.), *Children exposed to marital violence*. Washington, DC: American Psychological Association. Manuscript submitted for review.

Layzer, J. I., Goodson, B. D., & deLange, C. (1986). Children in shelters. *Response, 9*, 2–5.

Levine, M. B. (1975). Interparental violence and its effect on the children: A study of 50 families in general practice. *Medicine, Science, and the Law, 15*, 172–176.

Lewis, C. E., Siegel, J. M., & Lewis, M. A. (1984). Feeling bad: Exploring sources of distress among pre-adolescent children. *American Journal of Public Health, 74*, 117–122.

Margolin, G. (1981). The reciprocal relationship between marital and child problems. In J. P. Vincent (Ed.), *Advances in family intervention, assessment and theory* (Vol. 2, pp. 131–182). Greenwich, CT: JAI Press.

Margolin, G. (1987). The multiple forms of aggressiveness between marital partners: How do we identify them? *Journal of Marital and Family Therapy, 13*, 77–84.

Margolin, G., & Fernandez, V. (1987). The "spontaneous" cessation of marital violence: Three case examples. *Journal of Marital and Family Therapy, 13*, 241–250.

Margolin, G., John, R. S., & Foo, L. (in press). Interactive and unique risk factors for husbands' emotional and physical abuse of their wives. *Journal of Family Violence*.

Margolin, G., John, R. S., Ghosh, C. M., & Gordis, E. B. (1996). Family interaction process: An essential tool for exploring abusive relations. In D. D. Cahn & S. A. Lloyd (Eds.), *Family violence from a communication perspective* (pp. 37–58). Thousand Oaks, CA: Sage.

Marshall, L. L., & Rose, P. (1988). Family of origin violence and courtship abuse. *Journal of Counseling and Development, 66,* 414–418.

Martinez, P., & Richters, J. E. (1993). The NIMH Community Violence Project: II. Children's distress symptoms associated with violence exposure. In D. Reiss, J. E. Richters, M. Radke-Yarrow, & D. Scharff (Eds.), *Children and violence* (pp. 22–35). New York: Guilford Press.

McCloskey, L. A., Figueredo, A. J., & Koss, M. P. (1995). The effects of systemic family violence on children's mental health. *Child Development, 66,* 1239–1261.

McDonald, R., & Jouriles, E. N. (1991). Marital aggression and child behavior problems: Research findings, mechanisms, and intervention strategies. *Behavior Therapist, 14,* 189–192.

Minuchin, S., Rosman, B. L., & Baker, L. (1978). *Psychosomatic families.* Cambridge, MA: Harvard University Press.

Neighbors, B., Forehand, R., & McVicar, D. (1993). Resilient adolescents and interparental conflict. *American Journal of Orthopsychiatry, 63,* 462–471.

O'Brien, M., John, R. S., Margolin, G., & Erel, O. (1994). Reliability and diagnostic efficacy of parents' reports regarding children's exposure to marital aggression. *Violence and Victims, 9,* 45–62.

O'Brien, M., Margolin, G., & John, R. S. (1995). Relation among marital conflict, child coping, and child adjustment. *Journal of Clinical Child Psychology, 24,* 346–360.

O'Brien, M., Margolin, G., John, R. S., & Krueger, L. (1991). Mothers' and sons' cognitive and emotional reactions to simulated marital and family conflict. *Journal of Consulting and Clinical Psychology, 59,* 692–703.

O'Keefe, M. (1994). Linking marital violence, mother–child/father–child aggression, and child behavior problems. *Journal of Family Violence, 9,* 63–78.

O'Keeffe, N. K., Brockopp, K., & Chew, E. (1986). Teen dating violence. *Social Work, 31,* 465–468.

O'Leary, K. D., Vivian, D., & Malone, J. (1992). Assessment of physical aggression against women in marriage: The need for multimodal assessment. *Behavioral Assessment, 14,* 5–14.

Osofsky, J. D., Wewers, S., Hann, D. M., & Fick, A. C. (1993). Chronic community violence: What is happening to our children? In D. Reiss, J. E. Richters, M. Radke-Yarrow, & D. Scharff (Eds.), *Children and violence* (pp. 36–45). New York: Guilford Press.

Owens, D. M., & Straus, M. A. (1975). The societal structure of violence in childhood and approval of violence as an adult. *Aggressive Behavior, 1,* 193–211.

Pan, H. S., Neidig, P. H., & O'Leary, K. D. (1994). Mild and severe husband-to-wife physical aggression. *Journal of Consulting and Clinical Psychology, 62,* 975–981.

Parke, R. D., & Slaby, R. G. (1983). The development of aggression. In E. M. Hetherington (Ed.), *Socialization, personality and social development: Handbook of Child Psychology* (pp. 548–641). New York: Wiley.

Patterson, G. R. (1982). *Coercive family process.* Eugene, OR: Castalia.

Peled, E., & Davis, D. (1995). *Groupwork with children of battered women: A Practitioner's Guide.* Thousand Oaks, CA: Sage.

Prescott, S., & Letko, C. (1977). Battered women: A social psychological perspective. In M. Roy (Ed.), *Battered women: A psychosocial study of domestic violence* (pp. 72–96). New York: Van Nostrand Reinhold.

Pynoos, R. S., & Eth, S. (1985). Children traumatized by witnessing acts of personal violence: Homicide, rape, or suicide behavior. In S. Eth & R. S. Pynoos (Eds.), *Post-traumatic stress disorder in children* (pp. 19–46). Washington, DC: American Psychiatric Press.

Quay, H. (1977). Measuring dimensions of deviant behavior: The Behavior Problem Checklist. *Journal of Abnormal Child Psychology, 5,* 277–289.

Reid, W. J., & Crisafulli, A. (1990). Marital discord and child behavior problems: A meta-analysis. *Journal of Abnormal Child Psychology, 18,* 105–117.

Richters, J. E., & Martinez, P. (1993). The NIMH Community Violence Project: I. Children as victims of and witnesses to violence. *Psychiatry, 56,* 7–21.

Riggs, D., O'Leary, K. D., & Breslin, F. C. (1990). Theoretical model of courtship aggression. In M. A. Pirog-Good & J. E. Stets (Eds.), *Violence in dating relationships: Emerging social issues* (pp. 53–71). New York: Praeger.

Rosenbaum, A., & O'Leary, K. D. (1981). Children: The unintended victims of marital violence. *American Journal of Orthopsychiatry, 51,* 692–699.

Rosenberg, M. S. (1984). The impact of witnessing interparental violence on children's behavior, perceived competence, and social problem solving abilities. *Dissertation Abstracts International, 46,* 4413–4414.

Rosenberg, M. S. (1987). The children of battered women: The effects of witnessing violence on their social problem-solving abilities. *Behavior Therapist, 4,* 85–89.

Rossman, B. B., & Rosenberg, M. S. (1992). Family stress and functioning in children: The moderating effects of children's beliefs about their control over parental conflict. *Journal of Child Psychology and Psychiatry, 33,* 699–715.

Rutter, M. (1987). Psychosocial resilience and protective mechanisms. *American Journal of Orthopsychiatry, 57,* 316–331.

Rutter, M. (1994). Family discord and conduct disorder: Cause, consequence, or correlate? *Journal of Family Psychology, 8,* 170–186.

Silvern, L., Karyl, J., & Landis, T. Y. (1995). Individual psychotherapy for the traumatized children of abused women. In E. Peled, P. G. Jaffe, & J. L. Edleson (Eds.), *Ending the cycle of violence: Community responses to children of battered women* (pp. 43–76). Thousand Oaks, CA: Sage.

Spaccarelli, S., Sandler, I. N., & Roosa, M. (1994). History of spouse violence against mother: Correlated risks and unique effects in child mental health. *Journal of Family Violence, 9,* 79–98.

Stagg, V., Wills, G. D., & Howell, M. (1989). Psychopathology in early childhood witnesses of family violence. *Topics in Early Childhood Special Education, 9,* 73–87.

Sternberg, K. J., Lamb, M. E., Greenbaum, C., Cicchetti, D., Dawud, S., Cortes, R. M., Krispin, O., & Lorey, F. (1993). Effects of domestic violence on children's behavior problems and depression. *Developmental Psychology, 29,* 44–52.

Straus, M. A. (1974). Leveling, civility, and violence in the family. *Journal of Marriage and the Family, 36,* 13–29.

Straus, M. A. (1990). Injury and frequency of assault and the "representative sample fallacy" in measuring wife beating and child abuse. In M. A. Straus & R. J. Gelles (Eds.), *Physical violence in American families* (pp. 75–94). New Brunswick, NJ: Transaction.

Straus, M. A. (1992). Children as witnesses to marital violence: A risk factor for lifelong problems among a nationally representative sample of American men and women. In D. F. Schwarz (Ed.), *Children and violence: Report of the Twenty-Third Ross Roundtable on Critical Approaches to Common Pediatric Problems* (pp. 98–109). Columbus, OH: Ross Laboratories.

Straus, M. A., & Gelles, R. J. (1990). How violent are American families? Estimates from the National Violence Survey and other studies. In M. A. Straus & R. J. Gelles (Eds.), *Physical violence in American families* (pp. 95–112). New Brunswick, NJ: Transaction.

Straus, M., Gelles, R. J., & Steinmetz, S. K. (1980). *Behind closed doors: Violence in the American family.* Garden City, NY: Anchor Books.

Suitor, J. J., Pillemer, K., & Straus, M. A. (1990). Marital violence in a life course perspective. In M. A. Straus & R. J. Gelles (Eds.), *Physical violence in American families* (pp. 305–320). New Brunswick, NJ: Transaction.

Vondra, J., Barnett, D., & Cicchetti, D. (1989). Perceived and actual competence among maltreated and comparison school children. *Development and Psychopathology, 1,* 237–255.

Walker, L. E. (1984). *The battered woman syndrome.* New York: Springer.

Westerman, M. A. (1987). "Triangulation," marital discord and child behavior problems. *Journal of Social and Personal Relationships, 4,* 87–106.

Westra, B. L., & Martin, H. P. (1981). Children of battered women. *Maternity and Child Nursing Journal, 10,* 41–51.

Widom, C. S. (1989). Does violence beget violence? A critical examination of the literature. *Psychological Bulletin, 106,* 3–28.

Wolfe, D. A., Jaffe, P., Wilson, S. K., & Zak, L. (1985). Children of battered women: The relation of child behavior to family violence and maternal stress. *Journal of Consulting and Clinical Psychology, 53,* 657–665.

Wolfe, D. A., Wekerle, C., Reitzel, D., & Gough, R. (1995). Strategies to address violence in the lives of high-risk youths. In E. Peled, P. G. Jaffe, & J. L. Edelson (Eds.), *Ending the cycle of violence: Community responses to children of battered women* (pp. 255–275). Thousand Oaks, CA: Sage.

Wolfe, D. A., Zak, L., Wilson, S., & Jaffe, P. (1986). Child witnesses to violence between parents: Critical issues in behavioral and social adjustment. *Journal of Abnormal Child Psychology, 14,* 95–104.

5

COMMUNITY VIOLENCE AND CHILD DEVELOPMENT: A REVIEW OF RESEARCH

JOHN L. HORN AND PENELOPE K. TRICKETT

THE PROBLEM AREA

The mass media regularly report on violence occurring in U.S. communities—murders, drive-by shootings, battles between gangs, shootouts with police, high-speed chases, spousal beatings. Children who witness this violence or are themselves victims experience community violence directly. Studies indicate that such experiences are not rare for children in some communities. Shakoor and Chalmers (1991) found that nearly three fourths of a sample of 1,000 African American elementary and high school students reported witnessing at least one robbery, stabbing, shooting, or murder. Richters and Martinez (1993b) found that in an elementary school of southeast Washington, DC, 61% of first and second graders and 72% of fifth and sixth graders reported witnessing at least one act of community violence. Bell and Jenkins (1993) found, in African American children living on the south side of Chicago, that 26% and 30% of 536 7- to 15-year-olds reported witnessing a stabbing or shooting, respectively; that 35% and 39% of 997 10- to 19-year-olds witnessed those acts, respectively; and that 23% of the group of older children reported witnessing a killing.

Children also experience community violence indirectly through knowing people who have been assaulted and through accounts of violence given by family members, peers, and others of their neighborhood. In the Bell–Jenkins sample of 10- to 19-year-olds, over 50% of the children reported that they knew someone who had been robbed; 29% said they knew someone who had been shot; and 26% reported that they knew someone who had been stabbed. In addition, children learn about violence committed in their neighborhoods through watching television and reading their local newspaper. Such exposures add to direct experiences, both within individuals and in terms of the numbers of children exposed.

As increasing attention has been paid to the occurrence of violence in U.S. society, researchers and scholars have considered the effects it may have on children's development. The research is recent and, so far, scant, but it provides some indications of how exposure to violence may influence a child's adjustment and adaptation. In this chapter we examine this research and attempt to draw from it directions for further research that can advance the understanding of factors affecting child development.

EXCLUSIONS

There have been a number of studies of children living through the experiences of war that we do not review in any detail (Bodman, 1941; Brenitz, 1983; Freud & Burlingham, 1943; Glover, 1942; Lyons, 1973, 1979; McAuley & Troy, 1983; McWhirter, 1982, 1983; McWhirter & Trew, 1981; Milgram & Milgram, 1976; Ziv & Israel, 1973). Although wartime violence is a form of community violence and can be expected to have effects on child development that are similar to those found in other types of community violence, we did not systematically review studies of wartime violence, partly because they have been well reviewed previously (Garmezy & Rutter, 1985) and partly because of difficulties in equating these studies with those in which war was not a principal instrument of violence, difficulties pertaining to differences in culture and in the kinds of variables that were studied (evacuation, external forces, patriotism, bombing, mass hunger).

From their review of studies of wartime violence, Garmezy and Rutter (1985) concluded that children exposed to such violence develop serious psychological problems—not always, and not all children, but commonly. Symptoms commonly found were fears of recurrence, free-floating anxieties, depression, difficulties in concentrating, sleep disturbances, and psychosomatic complaints—symptoms of the kind that characterize posttraumatic stress disorder (PTSD), as described in, for example, the *Diagnostic and*

Statistical Manual of Mental Disorders (DSM-III-R; American Psychiatric Association, 1987). The reviewers concluded, however, that the studies did not provide a basis for estimating the extent to which wartime violence produced psychiatric illness. Estimates of the prevalence of extremely serious psychological conditions ranged from 10% to 50% of the exposed children. The studies also did not indicate the extent to which symptoms were reactions to particular kinds of stressful experiences, such as witnessing the killing of a person or persons close at hand, loss of a parent or parents, experiencing a direct threat to one's own life, the unpredictability of conditions, loss of sleep or food, discomforts of cold, bombing, evacuation, or any of the many other kinds of stress-producing conditions that can accompany war. The review by Garmezy and Rutter delineated the kinds of effects that might be associated with community violence and pointed to some of the difficulties likely to be encountered in interpreting results from studies of community violence.

OVERVIEW OF THE LITERATURE CONSIDERED

In all, nine studies could be found that report on correlates of children's exposure to community violence. These studies are described in summary form in Table 1, listed in the order in which they are discussed in the text. For conciseness in subsequent discussion, the studies often are referred to simply in terms of the last name of the first author.

It can be seen in Table 1 that the research is recent: None of the studies was published prior to 1985. Usually the studies are of urban children of low socioeconomic status (SES), although the children of the Terr study were rural. Generally, too, the age range was that of elementary school—6–10 years—although in the Fitzpatrick study the age range was 7–14 years. All studies included African American children, and in six of the studies the entire sample was black. Attar and Pynoos also sampled Hispanics, but no differences associated with ethnicity were found; in the Freeman and Terr studies, Caucasian and Hispanic children, as well as African American children, made up the sample, but no analyses of ethnic differences were conducted.

The samples of all studies included boys and girls, usually in approximately equal numbers. Gender differences were analyzed and found to be nonsignificant in the Attar study. In the Fitzpatrick study, girls who reported being a victim of violence scored significantly higher on a measure of depression than did boys who reported being a victim.

Two studies concerned a one-time traumatic event: a school-yard sniper attack in the Pynoos study and a school bus kidnapping in the Terr study. These events provided the indication that the child was exposed to violence. Variation in such exposure was estimated from the children's

TABLE 1

Research on the Impact of Community Violence on Children

Study	Sample characteristics	Community violence exposure	Outcome measures	Results
Terr (1983)	N = 25 rural California male and female schoolchildren aged 7–13	School bus commandeered at gunpoint by three kidnappers, who loaded victims in blackened vans, drove them around for 11 hours, and then buried them alive in a truck-trailer, where they remained for 16 hours.	Interviews 4 years after events focus on cognitive restrictions, memories, misperceptions, disruptions in sense of time, and repetitive phenomena	Event-related anxiety and fear, other fears, thought suppression, future pessimism, repetitive dreams of the events, episodic reenactments, omen formation.
Pynoos, Frederick, Nader, & Arroyo (1987)	N = 159 elementary school students (K–6), approximately 50% black, 50% Hispanic; 50.3% male, mean age 9.2 years	Sniper fired 57 rounds on the school playground, killing one student and a passerby and injuring 13 other children. Four levels of exposure to this violence: on playground, at school, not at school, on vacation.	Interviews of children to assess PTSD symptoms (Reaction Index), life stresses, other disturbing events, whereabouts during the shooting, degree of acquaintance with deceased girl	PTSD increased with level of exposure to violence. No significant PTSD differences associated with age, sex, or ethnicity, or in interaction of exposure level and age, sex, or ethnicity.
Fitzpatrick (1993); Fitzpatrick & Boldizar (1993)	N = 221 low-income, inner-city African American 7- to 14-year-old males (102) and females (119)	Victim scale: sum of nine items (chased, beaten, mugged, sexually assaulted, attacked with a knife, seriously wounded, shot, shot at, at home during break-in), alpha = .55; Witness scale: 12 items (witnessed preceding, plus witnessed serious accident, homicide, suicide), alpha = .65.	Children's Depression Inventory,[1] 27 items. Purdue PTSD[2] revised, 12 items, alpha = .76	Both victimization and witnessing violence associated with heightened PTSD; victimization also associated with depression, but witnessing associated with lower depression. Victimized females reported more PTSD and depression than males. PTSD and depression increased for children in mother-absent homes and homes with few supportive males.

Study	Sample	Measures	Findings
Attar, Guerra, & Tolan (1994)	N = 384 first, second, and fourth graders; urban, poor, African American, and Hispanic, about one half male, one half female.	Exposure-to-violence scale (ECV). Child report, 6 items: family member robbed, attacked; nonfamily member beaten, attacked, hurt; seen anyone beaten, shot, hurt; seen people shooting guns; afraid to go outside (e.g., because of gangs); had to hide because of shootings. Neighborhoods classified as highly (HND) or moderately (MND) disadvantaged	Peer-nominated aggression; CBCL—Teacher Form,[3] aggression and depression–anxiety; academic achievement:[4] average percentile scores in reading and math	Peer-nominated aggression higher for those with higher ECV and living in HND. ECV predicted teacher-rated aggression Year 2, controlling for Year 1; did not predict depression–anxiety or academic achievement Year 1 or 2. Sex, grade, ethnicity differences in ECV not predictive of outcome variables.
Freeman, Mokros, & Poznanski (1993)	N = 223 Midwestern inner-city children; 6–12 years of age, 39% white, 33% African American, 19% Hispanic; 118 males, 105 females	Spontaneous description of violent traumatic event (suicide and suicide attempts, murders, accidental deaths, other accidents) occurring to self, relative, or friend.	Children's Depression Rating Scale,[5] Revised, 17-item interview form	Higher depression scores for those who witnessed or knew of a violent traumatic event, particularly morbid thoughts, excessive weeping, low self-esteem. No age, gender, or ethnicity analysis reported.
Hill & Madhere (1996)	N = 150 inner-city, African American, fourth- to sixth-grade males (72) and females (78)	Children's Perception of Environmental Violence Scale,[6] 29 questions about violence in home, neighborhood, school; factoring indicated three subscales: Apprehension, Witnessing, and Retaliation; Global ECV from mother rating of number, child rating of number, and census track number of violent incidents.	Revised Behavior Problem Scale:[7] oppositional behavior; State Anxiety;[8] Stress,[9] Family-, Peer-, and Teacher-Support;[10] School Competence;[11] Mother Coping Strategies (none, one, multiple)	Global ECV positively associated with Witnessing Violence (but negatively with Apprehension of Violence) and with State Anxiety and Stressful Life Events. Witnessing and Readiness to Retaliate to Violence also negatively associated with State Anxiety but positively associated with oppositional behavior. Violence exposure indicators correlated near zero with teacher-rated School Competence.

Table continues

TABLE 1 *(Continued)*

Study	Sample characteristics	Community violence exposure	Outcome measures	Results
Martinez & Richters (1993)	$N = 165$ low-income, inner-city children, 6–10 years old; $n = 111$ younger (first and second grade), $n = 54$ older (fifth and sixth grade); 97% African American, 51% male	Mother-based Survey of Children's Exposure to Community Violence (SCECV);[12] 20 kinds of violence, e.g., stabbings, shootings, muggings); child-based Things I Have Seen and Heard,[13] 15-item structured interview on exposure to violence administered to first and second graders.	Mother based: Checklist of Child Distress Symptoms, Parent Form (CCDSP,[14] 28 symptom descriptions); child based: Levonn,[15] cartoon-based interview of distress symptoms; Child Depression Inventory (CDI)[16]	Child-based measures of stress, fear, and depression correlated .25–.50 with child-based measures of exposure to violence, particularly violence to self, friends, relatives, acquaintances (compared to strangers), but these measures of exposure to violence were not correlated with parent-based measures of child's stress and problems (CCDSP and CBCL). Mother not having high school education added to multiple regression estimation of stress (child based) in both younger and older samples. Mother-based and child-based measures of child's stress lowly correlated. Means for mother-based lower than for child-based measures.

Osofsky, Wewers, Hann, & Fick (1993)	N = 53 mothers of fifth-grade, low-income, African-American children living in a housing project	SCECV (20 kinds of violence, e.g., stabbings, shootings); Conflict Tactics Scale[13] (CTS), 19-item mother ratings of extent and severity of conflict among family members.	CBCL; CCDSP	Mother-based measures of child Witnessing or Hearing About Violence correlate .21–.51 with mother-based child's Stress (CCDSP), .07–.30 with mother-based child's Behavior Problems (CBCL), and .16–.44 with CTS. Severity subscale of CTS correlates .67 with CBCL.
Richters & Martinez (1993)	N = 72; no-missing-data sample of first and second graders of Martinez & Richters (1993) study; 60% single-parent homes	SCECV (20 kinds of violence); CTS (extent and severity of conflict among family members); teacher ratings of violence in the home and family stability.	Adaptation Failure if teachers rated child as "doing poorly or failing" and parent ratings on CBCL put child in clinical range	Neither mother nor child ratings of children's overall exposure to violence in the community were associated with Adaptation Failure, but Adaptation Failure correlated with teacher ratings of family home as unsafe and unstable and with children's reports of guns and drugs in the home.

Note. From Pynoos, R. S., Frederick, C., Nader, K., & Arroya, W. (1987). Life threat and posttraumatic stress disorder in school age children. *Archives of General Psychiatry, 44,* p. 1060. Copyright 1987 American Medical Association. Reprinted with permission.

[1] Kovacs, 1985; [2] Figley, 1989; [3] CBCL = Child Behavior Checklist (Achenbach & Edelbrock, 1983); [4] Iowa Test of Basic Skills; [5] Poznanski, Freeman, & Mokrus, 1984; [6] Hill & Noblin, 1991; [7] Quai & Peterson, 1983; [8] Spielberger, 1973; [9] Pryor-Brown & Cowen, 1989; [10] Dubow & Ulman, 1989; [11] Hightower, 1986; [12] Richters & Saltzman, 1990; [13] Richters & Martinez, 1990a; [14] Richters & Martinez, 1990b; [15] Richters, Martinez, & Valla, 1990; [16] Kovaks, 1981; [17] Straus, 1979; [18] Richters, 1990.

accounts of how close they were to particular violent events. In six of the other seven studies, a child's exposure to violence was based on the child's answers to several questions about classes of violent events; variations in exposure were estimated by a count of the number of kinds of events to which the child reported being exposed. In the seventh (Osofsky) study, a measure of the child's exposure to violence was obtained from the mother, who answered questions about whether her child had been a victim of, had witnessed, or had heard about each of several kinds of violent events. In the Martinez study, this kind of parental measure was used in addition to a measure based on questions asked of the child. The child-report measure of the Freeman study was a spontaneous description of violence made in an interview aimed at assessing depression. Direct exposure to violence (as victim or witness) was a part of at least one measure in all the studies, but direct exposure was confounded with indirect exposure in the measures of the Attar and Hill studies.

In all the studies, a form of stress theory appeared to direct the choice of variables to analyze, although often such theory was not explicitly stated. In each study community violence was regarded as a stressor or collection of stressors, and measured variations in exposure to such violence were assumed to be monotonically indicative of variations in the stress a child experienced. Most of the variables regarded as dependent—referred to as "outcome variables" in Table 1—are commonly accepted indicators of the effects of stress. In each study at least one of the outcome variables was a putative indicator of PTSD, and in most studies several variables were such indicators. The measure referred to as depression in the Attar, Fitzpatrick, Freeman, and Martinez studies was based partly on responses said to be indicative of PTSD, such as fears, anxieties, and mood changes. Additionally, in the Martinez study and the Richter study, the Child Behavior Checklist (CBCL), with several indicators of PTSD, and counts of symptoms of stress were outcome variables. State anxiety measures were used in the Hill study, and measures of PTSD symptoms were obtained in the Fitzpatrick, Pynoos, and Terr studies.

The Attar, Hill, Richter, and Terr studies explored hypotheses that exposure to community violence (stress) would affect the expression or development of cognitive capabilities, as measured by academic achievement, competence, and cognitive restrictions. Among other outcome variables, Hill looked at oppositional behavior and Attar considered children's aggressiveness.

Although the studies are similar along some dimensions, they are different in respect of many others. They differ concerning such factors as consideration of variables that might alter effects, particular features of samples, number of outcome variables, and specific nature of both independent and dependent variables. It is not possible, therefore, to collate across the findings of the different studies variable by variable, unit by unit.

Rather, the findings can be compared with respect to broad concepts indicating exposure to violence, on the one hand, and deleterious outcomes, on the other.

PARTICULAR STUDIES

Violence on One Occasion

The Terr and Pynoos studies are similar in that both describe behavior of children following a specific episode of violence to which the children were exposed. The children of the Terr study were kidnapped from their school bus. They were loaded into two blackened vans and driven around for 11 hours. Then, they were buried alive in a truck-trailer, where they remained for 16 hours before rescuers were able to free them. Terr provided a narrative description of symptoms found through psychiatric interview in 25 (of 26) of these children 4 years after the events. There was no effort to put the children's responses within a normative context of children not exposed to violence. The principal results of the study are summarized in Table 2.

It can be seen from the table that a number of what are regarded as clinical indicators of PTSD were evinced by the children exposed to the kidnapping violence—thought suppression, fears, repetitive terror dreams, omen formation, reenactments in thoughts about the event, and time distortions—in each case associated with the events of the violence. Also seen are general symptoms not expressed specifically in terms of the violence events: free-floating fears and pessimism about the future.

The 159 children of the Pynoos study were students at an inner-city elementary school in south-central Los Angeles. "Just after the dismissal bell on Feb. 24, 1984, a sniper began firing from a second-story window across the street from this school. He shot repeated rounds of high-powered ammunition at children on the playground. One child and a passerby were killed, 13 other children were injured, and scores were pinned on the playground under gunfire. Some ran screaming across the yard . . . ; others hid behind playground trees or trash cans. . . . The bullets pierced . . . school doors [and] shattered school windows. . . . The siege was not declared over until several hours later, when [police] stormed the sniper's apartment and found that he had killed himself" (Pynoos, Frederick, Nader, & Arroyo, 1987, p. 1058). Approximately 1 month after this event, a stratified (by ethnicity) random sample of 5–8 children from the approximately 25 children in each classroom was selected, and the children were interviewed using a structured form that included 16 questions concerning PTSD, called the Reaction Index, based on *DSM-III* diagnostic criteria. After completing the Reaction Index, the interviewers inquired about the child's whereabouts

TABLE 2
Symptoms in 25 Children Who Were Kidnapped and Buried Alive

Symptom label	Description	Number displaying symptom
Fear (anxiety)	Event focused	
	Fear another kidnapping	15
	Fear kidnapper still at large	13
	Other	
	Fearful of strangers	19
	Afraid of the dark	15
	Fear vehicles	7
	Afraid to be alone	5
Thought suppression	Conscious avoidance of thoughts about the event	25
	Attempt to block resurgence of anxiety, shame, fear	—
Foreshortened future	Belief that life will be short, future is limited	23
Repetitive behavior	Terror dreams	13
	Modified playback dreams	7
	Disguised dreams	12
	Event-related game played again and again over 4 years	5
	Reenactment in thoughts about the event	—
School performance	School problems such as daydreaming, hiding from school bus, missing school	4
Physiological sensations	Feel physical reactions, such as chills, when think of event	2
Time disruptions	Event seemed shorter than it was	3
	Confused day and night in parts of recollection of the event	2
	Event that came after traumatic event interpreted as coming before	—
	Led to false sense that dreams, symptoms, unrelated events had been predictive	—
Omen formation	Sense that sign before the event indicated that the experience was coming	19
Displacement of affect	Memories of event shifted to another time, another person	—
Shame at vulnerability	Embarrassment over event; prefer that no one find out; feel loss of autonomy	—

Note. Dashes indicate the frequency was not reported. Data from Chowchilla Revisited: The Effects of Psychic Trauma Four Years After a School-Bus Kidnapping, by L. C. Terr, 1983, *American Journal of Psychiatry, 140.*

during the shooting. This information was then used to form four categories of nearness to the event. Table 3 provides a summary of the principal results of the study.

A factor analysis of the Reaction Index items suggested three simple-structure factors. As can be seen in the table, all three of these factors and all but two of the items of the Reaction Index were found to be significantly elevated for the children most directly exposed to the sniper violence. For most items of the Reaction Index, the percentage of children reporting the symptom increased monotonically with the child's proximity to the stressful events. Exceptions are Guilt, a symptom expressed by fewer than 12% of all children, and Fears of Recurrence. Approximately 70% of all children attending this inner-city school expressed fears that there would be another sniper attack, and the children who had been directly exposed to the attack were more likely to express such fears than children who had not been so exposed.

Studies Examining Depression and Correlates of PTSD

There were no significant differences in Reaction Index scores by age or sex, or in the Age × Exposure, Sex × Exposure, or Ethnicity × Exposure interactions. In analyses of responses to questions asked after the Reaction Index questions had been asked, it was found that children who knew the child who had been killed reported significantly more PTSD symptoms than children who did not know her.

Fitzpatrick (1993; Fitzpatrick & Boldizar, 1993) studied relationships between self-report measures of being a victim of violence and witnessing violence, on the one hand, and measures of PTSD and depression, on the other hand. The data were collected from 221 low-income African American youth, aged 7–14 years, who participated in a summer camp program organized for eight central-city housing communities in Birmingham, Alabama. Approximately one half of the youth were male.

The victim scale, based on nine items developed by the researchers in which the child was asked to answer yes or no to questions about whether he or she had been beaten, mugged, sexually assaulted, attacked with a knife, shot or shot at, seriously wounded in an incident of violence, chased, hit by a family member, or hit by a nonfamily member or had his or her residence broken into while at home. The yes responses were summed to provide the measure, which was found to have internal consistency (alpha) reliability of .55. The witnessing measure was obtained with items of the victim scale, reworded to indicate witnessing in contrast to being a victim, plus six yes-or-no items in which children indicated whether they had witnessed such violence as murder, attempted murder, suicide, and serious accidents. The internal consistency of this measure was found to be .64. The mean for males on the victim scale was about 0.62 standard de-

TABLE 3
PTSD Symptoms Evinced by Children Following a Sniper Attack at Their School

PTSD Reaction Index item	On playground (n = 35)	At school (n = 18)	Not at school (n = 43)	Off track (n = 63)	Significant at .01 level[b]	F1	F2	F3
Factor 1								
Intrusive thoughts	97.1	70.6	44.2	33.3	y	.76		
Interpersonal distance	58.8	33.3	16.7	9.5	y	.70		
Wish to avoid feelings	94.1	83.3	40.0	43.5	y	.65	.41	
Intrusive imagery and sounds	97.1	70.6	44.2	33.3	y	.64		.28
Loss of interest in activities	65.7	50.0	23.3	17.5	y	.60	.31	
Avoid reminders	88.6	83.3	55.8	52.4	y	.50		.26
Factor 2								
Fears of recurrence	71.4	83.3	70.7	68.3	n		.76	
Jumpy, nervous, startles easily	91.4	77.8	61.9	44.9	y	.34	.66	
Upset when thinks of event	97.1	100	69.8	61.9	y	.43	.64	
Afraid when thinks of event	88.6	88.9	62.8	58.7	y		.57	.30
Factor 3								
Bad dreams	62.9	55.6	41.5	33.3	y			.80
Difficulty paying attention	65.7	23.5	20.9	19.6	y			.60
Thoughts interfere with learning	42.9	35.3	16.3	17.5	y	.40		.59
Sleep disturbance	77.1	55.6	48.8	23.8	y	.26	.38	.57
Other								
Identifies event as stressor	91.7	94.4	79.1	77.9	y	.37	.30	
Guilt	17.1	27.8	7.0	7.9	n	.28		.37

The four columns represent where the child was at the time of the attack above "Percentage endorsing item[a]"; the F1, F2, F3 columns are under "Varimax loadings".

Note. Data from "Life Threat and Posttraumatic Stress in School-age Children," by R. S. Pynoos, C. Frederick, K. Nader, and W. Arroyo, 1987, *Archives of General Psychiatry, 44.*

[a] The four columns represent where the child was at the time of the attack.

[b] y = yes; n = no.

viations (SD) larger than the mean for females, significant at the .05 level. On the witness scale, the mean for males was approximately 0.25 SD larger than the mean for females, also significant at the .05 level.

It was hypothesized that having the mother present in the home, in particular, and the presence of other possible support figures, including the father or a sibling, would tend to reduce the effects of victimization and witnessing violence. A females-present variable was obtained by scoring 2 if both the mother and a sister were in the home, scoring 1 if either the mother or a sister was in the home, and scoring 0 if neither mother nor a sister was present. A males-present variable was obtained in the same way by scoring for father and a brother in the home.

Among the outcome variables, the Children's Depression Inventory (CDI; Kovacs, 1981) was used to provide a self-report measure of the depression component of PTSD. The 26 three-choice items of this scale deal with disturbed mood, self-valuation, withdrawal, and somatization. The internal consistency of the measure was found to be .84.

Self-report measures were also obtained with a revision of the Purdue PTSD scale (Figley, 1989). This test was designed to represent the three diagnostic categories of PTSD symptoms proposed in *DSM-III-R* (American Psychiatric Association, 1987). These categories, the items that represent them, and the percentages of children reporting the symptoms are shown in Table 4.

Using the items of the Purdue scale, the *DSM-III-R* system was applied to provide a basis for estimating the proportion of youths in the sample who were at levels of PTSD regarded as diagnostic of need for therapy. To meet the DSM criterion for recurrence, a respondent would need to report at least one symptom in this category; for classification in the avoidance or physiological arousal category, a respondent would need to report at least three or at least two symptoms, respectively, in these categories. Approximately 27% (n = 54) of the youths of the sample met all three of these PTSD diagnostic criteria; 68 youths (34%) met at least two of the criteria, 54 youths (27%) met one criterion, and 23 youths (12%) met none of the criteria. The results thus indicate that a substantial number of the youths were evincing PTSD symptoms.

Only an overall measure of PTSD was used in statistical analyses. This measure was obtained by summing over all 12 items of Table 4. The resulting linear composite was found to have an internal consistency reliability of .76.

Age differences and presence or absence of father, mother, brother, or sister in the home were not significantly related to either form of exposure to violence. When these variables and gender differences were held constant in multiple regression analysis, both the victim scale and the witness scale were found to be significant predictors of PTSD. A Victim scale × Gender interaction and an interaction for Victim scale × Presence

TABLE 4
Items Indicating PTSD Symptoms by *DSM-III-R* Categories,
and Percentage of African-American Youth Endorsing
Each Symptom (*N* = 199)

DSM-III-R category	Symptom	Percentage	Number
Recurrence, reexperiencing			
	Intrusive thoughts	60.8	121
	Bad dreams, nightmares	53.3	106
	Reliving events	29.6	59
Avoidance, numbing			
	Estrangement from others	34.2	68
	Limited affect	37.2	74
	Possible danger, shortened future	50.8	101
	Avoidance activities	54.3	108
	Loss of interest in usual activities	37.2	74
Physiological arousal			
	Difficulty sleeping	37.2	74
	Difficulty concentrating	35.7	71
	Hypervigilance	46.2	92
	Upset a lot, irritability	44.7	89

Note. Data from "The Prevalence and Consequences of Exposure to Violence Among African American Youth," by K. M. Fitzpatrick and J. P. Boldizar (1993). *Journal of the American Academy of Child and Adolescent Psychiatry, 32,* p. 426. Reprinted with permission.

of male in the household also contributed to the prediction of PTSD (at the .01 level). The first of these interactions suggested that although females may be victims of violence less often, those who are victims report more PTSD symptoms than others. The second interaction suggested that children who have been victims and are living in homes in which there are few or no males are more likely than others to report PTSD symptoms.

In analyses of the depression measure, again holding variables constant as indicated previously, the victim scale was found to be a significant predictor whether or not interaction terms were considered. Presence of the mother in the home was associated with significantly reduced depression in the child. The difference between the depression-score means for mother present and mother absent was approximately 0.8 *SD*, and in the multiple regression analysis the mother-present variable was the strongest single predictor of (absence of) depression.

The results for the relationship between depression and the witness scale are anomalous. The witness scale was found to be significantly related to depression when significant Age × Witnessing and Gender × Victimization interactions were considered, but the relationship was negative: The more witnessing, the lower was the depression. This is probably a suppressor effect resulting from the fact that depression was notably high in the youngest children, although older youths had witnessed more violence. The Age × Witnessing interaction indicated that older youths who had witnessed considerable violence had depression scores above the main-effect trend. This tendency, plus the negative relationship for age and depression, suppressed the small positive relationship between witnessing and depression.

The findings of the Fitzpatrick study, in which both information on exposure to violence and outcome measures were obtained through self-reports, are consistent with hypotheses that community violence brings about symptoms of PTSD and depression. The findings add a suggestion that depression under such circumstances may be reduced for children who live with their mothers but that both depression and PTSD may be particularly high for girls who experience violence. There is a suggestion, too, that both boys and girls in homes in which there are few supportive males (father or brother) are likely to show particularly heightened levels of PTSD.

The Attar, Guerra, and Tolan (1994) study was based on a sample of 384 first-, second-, and fourth-grade children in Chicago schools that serve poor Hispanic and African American families. About half the sample was male. A child-report measure of exposure to community violence (ECV) was obtained from six items constructed by the researchers: Has a family member been robbed or attacked? Has someone else you know been beaten, shot, or really hurt by someone? Have you been around people shooting guns? Have you been afraid to go outside, or have your parents made you stay inside, because of gangs or drugs in your neighborhood? Have you had to hide because of shootings in your neighborhood? The sum of "yes" responses to these six items provided the measure. No information about reliability was presented.

The 6 items constructed to indicate exposure to violence were included with 10 other items in a stress index in which 6 items were designed to measure life transition stress and 4 items were intended to indicate stress response to particular putative stressors (family property wrecked; family member died; other relative or close friend died; family member seriously ill, injured, or in hospital). ECV was found to correlate at .39 and .46 with life transition stress and the particular putative stressors, respectively.

The neighborhoods in which the children attended school were classified as highly disadvantaged (HND) or moderately disadvantaged (MND). This classification was based on whether poverty, unemployment, substandard housing, and crime were high or moderate in the community. The classification was treated as a measure of chronic stress.

Teacher-rated outcome measures were obtained with the 17-item Depression scale, the 25-item Anxiety scale, and the 23-item Aggression scale of the Child Behavior Checklist–Teacher Report Form (CBCL-TRF; Achenbach & Edelbrock, 1986). Because the Anxiety and Depression scales were found to correlate at .87, the two were averaged and added together to form a new instrument, the Teacher-Rated Anxiety–Depression (TAD)

Scale. A second measure of the child's aggressiveness was obtained with a 10-item instrument, the Peer-Nominated Aggression Scale (Eron, Walder, & Lefkowitz, 1972). Objective test measures of academic achievement were obtained by combining scores on the Reading and Math scales of the Iowa Test of Basic Skills.

Descriptively, mean ECV was larger for girls than for boys and larger for blacks than for Hispanics, and it decreased monotonically from first to second to fourth grade. These main-effect differences were not statistically significant, however. With ECV as the dependent variable in an analysis of variance of the classifications for neighborhood disadvantage (HND or MND), gender, ethnicity (African American or Hispanic), and grade (first, second, or fourth), significant Sex × Grade and Sex × Neighborhood disadvantage interactions were found. The first- and second-grade girls reported more exposure to violence than the fourth-grade boys, and boys in MND schools reported less exposure to violence than girls in MND schools and both boys and girls in HND schools.

With ECV treated as a predictor of peer-nominated aggression and teacher-rated anxiety and depression at the time of initial measurement (Time 1), it was found that exposure to violence was significantly related to peer-nominated aggression but not to teacher-rated anxiety and depression. An ECV × Neighborhood disadvantage interaction term also contributed to the estimation of peer-nominated aggression but not to teacher-rated anxiety and depression. Controlling for Time-1 teacher-rated aggression (TRA) in TRA measured a year after the initial measurements (Time 2), the researchers found a low (.14) but statistically significant (.05 level) correlation between ECV and the residual aggression measure. In similar kinds of analyses, ECV did not predict academic achievement or anxiety and depression. None of the other initial indicators of stress predicted achievement a year later.

The results of the Attar study thus indicate no strong main-effect relationships between neighborhood disadvantage and child-report measures of exposure to violence and no substantial relationship between the child-report measures and the teacher-rated measures of anxiety and depression symptoms of PTSD or the objective test measures of disruptions in academic achievement. Although there were gender and grade-level interactions with reported amount of exposure to violence, neither these interactions, the main-effect differences between boys and girls, nor the grade-level differences in reported exposure to violence were predictive of anxiety or depression (or aggression). The results do suggest, however, relationships between child-report measures of exposure to violence and other-based (both teacher and peer) measures of aggression. This effect was more marked for children living in particularly disadvantaged neighborhoods, and it appeared to increase (for the residualized teacher-based measure) over a period of a year.

The sample for the Freeman study included 223 children, ages 6 to 12 years, from a Midwestern city. The children were classified as Hispanic (n = 43), black (n = 74), white (n = 84), and other (n = 18). About 53 percent (n = 118) were male. Indication of exposure to violence was obtained from self-reports of the children during a semistructured interview designed to assess depression; 57 of the children (34 boys, 23 girls) spontaneously described at least one violent event occurring to themselves, a relative, or a friend. In most instances, the violent events were reported in the context of the child being asked about morbid or suicidal thoughts. Of the 57 children, 23 reported exposure to suicides that were contemplated or attempted, 19 reported murders, 12 reported accidental deaths, 12 reported violent acts of intentional harm that did not result in death, and 16 reported multiple events. Seven of the children reported that they were the victim of the violent event; for 5 children, the victim was a first-degree relative; for 14 children, the victim was a second- or third-degree relative; and for 17 children, the victim was a friend.

The principal outcome variable, depression, was obtained with the Children's Depression Rating Scale–Revised (CDRS–R); (Poznanski, Freeman, & Mokros, 1985): A child's responses to each of 17 questions were rated along a 7-point scale for symptoms of depression, and the ratings were summed to provide the measure. The mean CDRS-R score for the 57 children who reported violence was approximately 0.4 SD larger than the mean for 166 children who did not report violence (30.25 compared with 26.98), a difference reported to be significant at the .02 level. Separate items for which there were significant differences were morbid thoughts, depressed feelings, excessive weeping, and low self-esteem. No significant differences were found in analyses for types of violence, number of violent events reported, and type of victim. No analyses examining age, gender, or ethnic differences were reported.

Hill and Madhere (1995) studied a sample of 150 inner-city black fourth, fifth, and sixth graders (78 girls and 72 boys). Canonical analyses and multiple regression analyses were used to describe relationships among 3 variables classified as outcomes and 11 variables regarded as predictors. The outcome measures were (a) State Anxiety, a child self-report measure obtained with the Spielberger (1973) questionnaire; (b) Confrontation (acting-out behavior), obtained with the Revised Behavior Problem Checklist (Quay & Peterson, 1983), filled out by the mother; and (c) Social Competence in a School Setting, measured with the Teacher–Child Rating Scales (TCRS; Hightower, 1986).

Variables classified as predictors included the child's gender and seven measures based on responses obtained from the children, namely, (a) stress, assessed with the 21 items of the Life Events & Circumstances Scale (Pryor-Brown & Cowen, 1989); (b) family support; (c) peer support; and (d) teacher support, measured with Dubow and Ulman's (1989) Social

Support Appraisal Scale, as well as separate indicators of (e) apprehension of violence, (f) witnessing of violence, and (g) retaliation to violence, each derived from a factoring of the Children's Perception of Environmental Violence Scale (CPEVS; Hill & Noblin, 1991).

The CPEVS is a set of 29 statements with which the child indicates agreement or disagreement along a 3-point scale. Separate common factors led to construction of the Apprehension and Witnessing scales. The Apprehension factor was marked by the items "I feel a lot of people are being hurt in this neighborhood," "I hear about people being shot," "I see people being beaten," "I could be killed in this neighborhood," and "People get hurt for no reason." The Witnessing factor was defined by "I see people being shot," "I see people being stabbed," "I see violence in my home," "Because I live in this neighborhood, I get hurt," and "Because I live in this home, I get hurt." Retaliation was clearly separate from these two factors. It was indicated by affirmative responses to "It is ok to carry a weapon," "It is ok to hurt people," "People get killed at school," "I could be killed at school," and "I can kill somebody if I am mad."

Other variables classified as predictors included the mother's flexibility in coping, measured as the number of strategies the mother reported using when she or her child faced violence (no clear strategy, one preferred strategy, or multiple strategies); the mother's report of the family income; and a global measure of the child's exposure to community violence, obtained as a linear combination of standard scores of three variables: (a) mother reports (along a 0–9 scale) of the number of different kinds of violent incidents her children had witnessed, (b) child reports along the same kind of scale, and (c) rating of the census tract of the child's residence as either low crime (score = 1) or high crime (score = 2). The census tract rating was based on police statistics from the 1993 census.

Three canonical dimensions were indicated. The first correlated .99 with the child-report measure of State Anxiety; the second correlated 1.00 with the parent-based measure of Confrontation; and the third correlated .95 with the teacher-based measure of Competence. The three canonical dimensions thus were virtually identical to particular measures—State Anxiety, Confrontation, and Competence—on the outcome side of the equation. The relationships between the canonical dimensions and the variables on the predictor side of the equation, therefore, can be seen most directly in the correlations of these three variables with the other variables.

Child-report predictors correlated most highly with the child-report measure of State Anxiety. The principal correlates were Apprehension of Violence (.50) and the following negative correlates: Retaliation to Violence (−.28, the negative indicating disinclination to retaliate), witnessing (−.21, i.e., not witnessing), and Family Support (−.20, the negative indicating low support). Counterintuitively, State Anxiety also correlated negatively with the broad indicator of exposure to community violence

(−.27, the negative indicating high anxiety going together with low exposure to violence) and positively with the mother-report measure of Flexibility in Coping (.35), Family Income (.35), and Parent Education (.26); that is, indicators of high social status were associated with high anxiety.

Consistent with results from studies of acting-out behavior, the confrontation measure (mothers rating their child as obstreperous, rebellious, intractable) correlated with low family income (−.29), the child-report measure of stress (.24), and teacher ratings of low social competence (−.30). Rather paradoxically, however, the correlation of Confrontation with gender was positive (.23), suggesting that the mothers in this sample saw more acting-out behavior in girls than in boys. Confrontation correlated .20 with Witnessing Violence and .21 with readiness to Retaliate to Violence but only .09 with Apprehending Violence, thus again indicating the factorial distinction between Apprehension and Witnessing.

Teacher ratings of Social Competence were mainly associated with Family Income (.30), Parent Education (.27), the child-report measures of Teacher Support (.26) and Peer Support (.26), and, as indicated previously, the parent ratings indicating acting-out behavior.

The global indicator of exposure to community violence, which contained child and parent estimates of the amount of violence to which the child had been exposed, as well as an objective census indicator of this exposure, thus appears to be positively indicative of the child reports of witnessing violence but negatively indicative of the child measure of apprehending violence and the child measures of State Anxiety and stress.

Studies Based on the Checklist of Child Distress Symptoms

Several variables were operationally the same in the Martinez, Osofsky, and Richters studies. In particular, the same parent-based (almost always mother-based) measures of stress and behavior problems were used in all three studies. The stress measures were obtained with the 28-item, four-choice Checklist of Child Distress Symptoms, Parent Form (CCDSP; Richters & Martinez, 1990a). These items are modeled on *DSM-III-R* (American Psychiatric Association, 1987) criteria for indicating PTSD. In the Martinez study, the items were used with a subsample of older children to obtain self-report measures (CCDSC) of distress. In both the mother and child responses to the CCDS items, two components were identified, depression and anxiety. Each had an alpha reliability of approximately .70, but the two components were correlated at approximately the same level as the reliabilities. In most of the analyses of all three studies, the depression and anxiety components were combined to provide the principal dependent variable, usually labeled Distress.

Other measures common to the Martinez, Osofsky, and Richters studies were obtained from the Child Behavior Checklist (Achenbach & Edelbrock, 1983). In this instrument, a parent estimates on a 3-point a priori scale the extent to which his or her child evinces a wide variety of behaviors usually regarded as problematic. Some of the behaviors are regarded as indicating internalization, others as indicating externalization, and separate scores may be obtained to represent this distinction. The two scores are highly correlated, however, and usually are combined in one total score to indicate behavior problems.

The same items for estimating exposure to violence were used in all three studies, namely, the items of a scheduled interview titled Survey of Children's Exposure to Community Violence (SCECV; Richters & Saltzman, 1990). With these items, one estimates the frequencies of a child's exposure to 20 kinds of violence (e.g., muggings, shootings, drug sales) with respect to three categories of closeness to the violence: (a) being a victim, (b) witnessing the violence in the community, and (c) witnessing it in the home. In the Martinez study a measure based on older children's responses to these items was used, whereas in the other two studies the measure of exposure was based on parent responses. In the Osofsky and Richters studies, the 19-item Conflict Tactics Scale (Straus, 1979) was used to obtain mother-based measures of the extent and severity of conflict among family members during the previous year.

The subjects of the Martinez study were 165 black children aged 6–10 years attending a school located in—according to police statistics—a moderately violent ward of southeast Washington, DC. Of the 165 children, 111 were in the first or second grade, and 54 were in the fifth or sixth grade. The younger and older children did not differ significantly on any of the demographic characteristics that were assessed. About half the children in the two samples were male. Most of the analyses were carried out separately on the two samples or on subsamples of these samples.

In the sample of younger (first and second grade) children, measures of exposure were obtained with a 15-item structured interview (Things I Have Seen and Heard; Richters & Martinez, 1990b) in which the child indicated frequency of exposure to each example of violence for each of three categories of closeness: (a) being a victim, (b) witnessing the violence in the community, and (c) witnessing it in the home.

In this sample, also, the Levonn test (Richters, Martinez, & Valla, 1990) was used to obtain child-based measures of distress and fear. Four subscales of this device were described: Depression (10 items, alpha = .78), Anxiety/Intrusive Thoughts (14 items, alpha = .84), Sleep Problems (7 items, alpha = .71), and Impulsiveness (number of items and alpha not indicated). Girls scored significantly higher than boys on the first three subscales. High intercorrelations among the subscales led the investigators to combine them into a single measure, the alpha reliability of which was reported to be .81.

In the sample of older (fifth- and sixth-grade) children, the items of the SCECV were used to obtain child-based measures of the child's exposure to community violence. Similarly, the CCDSC was used to obtain child-based measures of stress and the Child Depression Inventory (Kovacs, 1985) was used to provide a measure of depression (a component of PTSD).

Results for analyses of relationships between exposure to violence and outcome variables are summarized in Table 5. It can be seen from the table that mother-based estimates of the child's stress and behavior problems correlated near zero with children's self-reports of being a victim of violence and witnessing violence, either in the home or the community. On the other hand, the correlations between child-based measures of stress, fear, and depression were generally correlated between .25 and .50 with child-

TABLE 5
Correlations Between Child Measures of Exposure to Violence and Mother-Based Measures of Child's Stress Symptoms and Behavior Problems, and Child Measures of Stress, Depression, and Fear

	Mother ratings		Child self-ratings	
	CCDSP[a]	CBCL[b]	CCDSC[c]	
Exposure to violence	stress	total	stress	CDI[d]
Fifth- and sixth-grade children's report of	$n = 35$	$n = 36$	$n = 37$	$n = 37$
Being a victim of violence	.06/.05[e]	.13/.09	.37/.08	.42/.01
Witnessing community violence	.01/−.22	.03/−.20	.39/−.05	.35/.01
Witnessing home violence	.11	.04	.33	.24

	CCDSP stress	CBCL total	Levonn[f] stress	Child fear at school	Child fear at home
First- and second-grade children's report of	$n = 76$	$n = 77$	$n = 84$	$n = 82$	$n = 81$
Being a victim of violence	.12	.10	.28	.50	.43
Witnessing community violence	−.22	−.04	.30	.07	.09
Witnessing guns and drugs in home	.13	.13	.30	.36	.25

Note. With a sample of 35, a correlation of .33 or larger is significantly different from zero at the .05 level. For a sample of 84, the correlation needs to be at least .22 to be significant at .05 level. From "The NIMH Community Violence Project: Children's Distress Symptoms Associated With Violence Exposure," by P. Martinez and J. E. Richters, in D. Reiss et al. (Eds.), *Children and Violence*. New York: Guilford Press. Copyright 1993. Reprinted with permission.
[a]Checklist of Child Distress Symptoms, Parent Form (Richters & Martinez, 1990a).
[b]Child Behavior Checklist (Achenbach & Edelbrock, 1983).
[c]Checklist of Child Distress Symptoms, Self-Report (child) Form (Richters & Martinez, 1990a).
[d]Child Depression Inventory (Kovacs, 1985).
[e]Correlations before the slash are for violence involving family, friends, and acquaintances; correlations after the slash are for violence involving strangers.
[f]Cartoon-based interview of children's distress symptoms (Richters, Martinez, & Valla, 1990), also yields measure of fear at school and at home.

based measures of being a victim of violence and witnessing violence in the home and community. Moreover, when a distinction was made between violence associated with strangers and violence associated with friends, relatives, or acquaintances, the latter was found to be the component that produced the significant correlations. The findings were similar for both the younger and the older children.

For both younger and older children, multiple regression estimation of child-based measures of stress from child-based measures of being a victim of violence, witnessing violence in the community, and witnessing violence in the home indicated that only one of these predictors had a significant beta weight; the different exposure variables did not make significant incremental contributions to the estimation. In analyses to determine whether variables such as unemployment of parents, family on public assistance, absence of mother, absence of father, family income, gender, and parents' graduation from high school would add to the estimation of stress, it was found, again in both samples, that only one variable significantly added to the multiple correlation: Parents not having graduated from high school was associated with high levels of stress. Families with less educated parents were also characterized by higher levels of unemployment and public assistance, but these variables alone, when entered with only the exposure variables in multiple regression analyses, did not significantly correlate with or contribute to the multiple correlation of distress.

The correlation between parent-based and child-based measures of the child's distress correlated at .32 over a sample of 76 of the younger children. The comparable correlation was only .19 (not significant) within a group of 38 girls from this sample, although when 9 girls with the most extreme scores were eliminated from the sample, a correlation of .34 was found, which is significantly greater than zero at the .05 level. The correlation was .41 for a group of 38 boys from this sample. For the sample of older children, the correlation between parents' and daughters' estimates of the daughters' distress symptoms was near zero (.06), and the similar correlation for sons was negative ($-.56$, significant at the .01 level). A correlation of .32 ($p < .01$) was found between teacher ratings of the violence within the child's home and the mother's indication of such violence in responses of the Conflict Tactics Scale.

In the sample of older children, comparison of the mean levels of estimates of the child's distress symptoms obtained from 35 parents, on the one hand, and from their children, on the other hand, indicated parental underestimation of the child's expression of symptoms. The mean rating for 22 of the 28 symptoms was significantly smaller for the parent estimates than for the child estimates. For example, "49% of the parents reported that their children never worried about being safe, whereas none of their children said they never worried; only 16% of the parents reported that their children worried about being safe a lot of the time, compared to 50%

of their children" (Martinez & Richters, 1993, p. 29). Other items for which there were such differences between child and parent estimates were intrusive thoughts about upsetting events; hard time getting/staying asleep; difficult time avoiding fear; feel nervous, scared, upset; afraid might not live long; and bad dreams/nightmares. Analysis aimed at checking several possible explanations for these relationships reinforced a conclusion that the parents of this sample generally underestimated their children's symptoms of distress.

The Martinez study suggests, therefore, that in samples of both younger and older children, a child's expressions of symptoms of distress, depression, and fear, both at home and in school, are related to the child's reports of being a victim of violence, witnessing violence, and witnessing violence in the home but that the child-based measures of distress and fear are not related to mother-based estimates of the child's exposure to violence. There was some suggestion that low positive relationships between child-based and mother-based measures of the child's distress obtained when the children were young but not when they became older. It appears, too, that children whose mothers are relatively well educated express fewer distress and depression symptoms than children of less educated mothers.

In the Osofsky study, all the measures were mother based, as described previously. The participants were low-income, African American mothers of fifth graders in New Orleans. Fifty-three of the 83 mothers contacted provided information about the extent of conflict in their home and their child's stress, behavior problems, and exposure to violence. The mothers' responses to the questions of the SCECV suggested that their children were exposed to high levels of violence: Over 98% of their children had heard about violence in the community, 91% had witnessed such violence, and 51% had been victims. The principal relationships between estimates of a child's exposure to violence and the other variables are summarized in Table 6.

It can be seen in the table that a mother's estimate of her child's exposure to violence correlated about .2–.5 with her ratings of the child's level of stress and behavior problems (with virtually no distinction between internalizing and externalizing problems). Moreover, the stress and behavior problem measures correlated almost at the level of their reliabilities (estimated to be about .70) with mother ratings of severe conflicts within the family.

The results indicate that mothers who reported that their child had many behavior problems and symptoms of stress also reported that there was severe conflict in their home. The overlap proportions were nearly as large as they could be, given the fallible nature of the measures. A substantial proportion of those mothers also reported that their child had witnessed severe violence (the stronger relationship) and had been a victim of violence (the weaker relationship). It seems likely that a reasonable

TABLE 6
Correlations Among Mother-Based Measures of Child's Exposure to Violence, Child's Stress Symptoms, Conflict Within the Family, and Child's Behavior Problems

Type of violence	Stress symptoms (CCDSP)[a]	Mother ratings of family conflict		Child Behavior Checklist[b]		
		Moderate	Severe	Total	Internal	External
Community violence[c]						
Victim of violence	.21	.34	.44	.25	.25	.24
Witness to violence	.42	.35	.37	.25	.30	.20
Severe	.51	.29	.30	.07	.14	.02
Less severe	.29	.34	.36	.26	.26	.24
Moderate	.35	.37	.31	.19	.21	.14
Hear about violence	.48	.22	.20	.16	.15	.15
Severe	.34	.24	.16	.12	.10	.10
Less severe	.31	.30	.16	.07	.04	.07
Moderate	.32	.23	.16	.07	.08	.04
Family Conflict						
Moderate	.39	1.00		.37	.34	.41
Severe	.61		1.00	.67	.68	.64

Note. Correlations larger than .28 are significant at the .05 level in this sample. From "Chronic Community Violence: What Is Happening to Our Children? by S. Wewers, D. M. Hann, and A. C. Fick, in D. Reiss, J. E. Richters, M. Radke-Yarrow, and D. Scharff (Eds.), *Children and Violence.* New York: Guilford Press. Copyright 1993. Reprinted with permission.
[a] Checklist of Child Distress Symptoms, Parent Form (Richters & Martinez, 1990).
[b] Derived from parent responses in Child Behavior Checklist (Achenbach & Edelbrock, 1983).
[c] Derived from parent responses in Survey of Children's Exposure to Community Violence (SCECV; Richters & Saltzman, 1990).

proportion of these mothers were saying, in effect, that the severe violence their child witnessed was an aspect of severe conflict that had gone on in the family and that in some cases the violence the child experienced was violence occurring in the family.

The Richters study was based on 72 of the first- and second-grade children of the Martinez study for whom complete information was obtained with the child-based, mother-based, and teacher-based measurement devices. The results for comparable analyses in the two studies were essentially the same and thus are not reported. However, some of the information gathered was used in a different way in the Richters study than in the Martinez study. In particular, an "adaptation failure score" was created to provide the principal dependent variable of the Richters study. Children were classified as adaptation failures if they were graded overall by their teachers as doing poorly or failing and if, on the basis of parent-rated CBCL scores, their behavior problems were in the clinical range. "On the basis of these ratings, [the investigators] created an adaptational failure score for each child, reflecting the number of domains in which he or she was failing (range 0–2)" (Richters & Martinez, 1993b, p. 617).

Neither the mother-based nor the child-based measure of the child's exposure to violence was associated with the teacher- and parent-based adaptation failure scores, but the correlation squared between adaptation failure and teacher ratings of family stability was found to be .11. Children's self-reports with respect to the specific "guns and drugs in the home" dimension of exposure to violence also correlated at the .33 level with adaptation failure. Together, these two variables accounted for an adjusted 21% of the variance ($r = .45$) of the adaptation failure score.

Detailed analysis of the teacher ratings indicated that adaptation failure was associated mainly with the rating that homes were both unstable and unsafe; both the unstable and unsafe ratings, considered separately, indicated some of the criterion variance. It was found, also, that child reports of seeing guns in the house correlated with parent reports of having seen ($r = .24$, $p < .05$) and heard about ($r = .29$) others carrying illegal weapons and with how often the child had heard about people carrying illegal weapons ($r = .29$).

The Richter findings add to the Martinez results, therefore, in suggesting that exposure to violence, whether estimated through mother-based or child-based measures, is generally not robustly related to the child's adaptation in school, although evidence of drugs and guns in the home does adversely relate to such adaptation.

SUMMARY, EVALUATION, AND INTEGRATION

Results from the early studies of Pynoos and Terr are clear in suggesting that when it is known that a child has been close to an episode of considerable violence—a single episode in these two studies—it is likely that he or she will evince symptoms commonly accepted as indicating PTSD. Such a result is indicated also in the studies in which the child's exposure to violence was determined from the child's responses in interviews. The results are more equivocal, however, in studies in which the child's exposure, or the child's symptoms, or both were estimated from interviews with persons other than the child (i.e., mother or teacher).

When both the child's exposure to violence and the measures of the child's distress were obtained from the child, as in the Fitzpatrick, Freeman, and Martinez studies, the correlations between exposure and symptoms were significantly different from zero and positive. The results from the Martinez study exemplify the findings: In the sample of older children in that study, the correlations between child-based measures of distress, on the one hand, and child reports of having been a victim of violence, having witnessed violence in the community, and having witnessed violence in the home, on the other hand, were .37, .39, and .33, respectively, in each case significantly different from zero. The comparable correlations for child-based measures of depression symptoms (the CDI) were .42, .35, and .24. Moreover, the correlations were larger for child reports indicating violence directed against oneself or, to a lesser degree, against a relative, friend, or acquaintance than when the measures of exposure did not discriminate in this manner or indicated violence directed at strangers. It is consistent with the results of Pynoos that the findings suggested that the closer the child is to an incident, or incidents, of violence, the more likely he or she is to evince PTSD-like symptoms.

In the same Martinez study in which child-based measures of exposure and symptoms were correlated .24–.42, the child-based measures of both exposure and symptoms correlated near zero with parent-based measures of distress and behavior problems. In the samples of both the younger and older children, neither the mother's ratings of the child's distress (obtained with the CCDS) nor the measures based on the mother's ratings on the CBCL correlated at a significant level with any of the child-based indicators of the child's exposure to community violence. The averages for the mothers' ratings of the child's PTSD symptoms were substantially lower than the averages for the children's self-ascriptions of these same symptoms, and the mother-based and child-based estimates of the child's symptoms were correlated at a low level only, nonsignificantly different from zero in some samples. Similarly, the correlations between mother-based and child-based measures of the child's exposure to violence were found to be small, bordering on nonsignificant (a finding seen also in Hill's work). In the work of Attar et al. (1994), the child-based measure of exposure to violence correlated near zero with a teacher-based measure of anxiety and depression based on the CBCL.

It might seem, therefore, that mother-based and, perhaps, teacher-based measures of a child's exposure to violence or of a child's symptoms simply do not tap relevant domains of violence and symptoms. Questioning this conclusion, however, are the results from the Osofsky study. Those findings indicate that mother-based measures of the child's exposure to violence correlate positively with mother-based measures of the child's distress, and the correlations are not notably smaller than the correlations between child-based measures of exposure to violence and distress.

The mother-based measures of the child's exposure to violence in the Osofsky study also correlated positively with mother-based measures of the child's behavior problems, based on the CBCL. It is consistent with this finding that Hill and Madhere found that a child-based measure of witnessing violence correlated positively with a mother-based measure (the CBCL) of the child's acting-out behavior problems and that Attar et al. found a small positive correlation between a child-based measure of exposure to violence and estimates of the child's aggressiveness obtained through peer nominations and through a rather abstract teacher-rating measure (namely, the teacher ratings in Year 2 after control for these ratings in Year 1). These results suggest that the child's exposure to violence, whether seen through the eyes of the child or of the mother, is associated with the child's acting-out, aggressive behavior. The mother-based measure of the child's acting-out behavior in the Osofsky study correlated .67 with the mother-based measure of conflict within the family. This finding suggests that the exposure to violence that produces acting-out behavior may often be violence occurring in the home, in some cases directed at the child.

The two relationships—between exposure to violence and acting-out behavior and between exposure to violence and PTSD-like symptoms—need not be contradictory; both can be true. The findings do raise questions about whether or not both relationships are true for the same children, that is, whether elevated exposure to violence produces both acting out and PTSD symptoms in the same child or produces acting out in one child and PTSD symptoms in another. The extant evidence does not speak clearly to the possibilities in this respect. Further research could be designed to deal with these questions.

Some of the results from the Hill study are not consistent with a conclusion that child-based indicators of exposure to violence are indicative of PTSD symptoms. A child-based measure of witnessing violence correlated *negatively* with a child-based measure of state anxiety. Some of the responses in the state anxiety measure (Spielberger, 1973) seem to indicate PTSD-like symptoms, and a high score on this test appears to represent at least a component of PTSD. Hence, the puzzle: Why should witnessing violence be associated with few PTSD-like symptoms? Are the acting-out children (affected by exposure to violence) defending against the expression of PTSD-like symptoms?

related positively with a global measure of exposure to violence: the sum of an objective (census-based) indicator of violence in the child's neighborhood and mother and child ratings of this violence. However, this global measure also correlated negatively with the child-based measure of state anxiety as well as with a child-based assessment of stressful life events.

Overall, the results from the Hill study suggest that exposure to community violence, as assessed objectively and through the self-reports of children, produces acting-out behavior problems and, perhaps in these same children, defenses against expressing PTSD symptoms. Again, however, the results do not indicate whether the same or different children are acting out and expressing defenses against expressions of PTSD. Further research is needed to address this question. It is necessary to replicate the finding of a negative relationship between exposure to violence and PTSD symptoms and, given that confirmation, to establish the conditions under which such a relationship obtains.

Generally speaking, the results from the studies reviewed suggest that when information about exposure to violence and expression of symptoms of PTSD are obtained from the same source—the child or the child's mother—the relationship between the number of exposures and the number of symptoms is positive (a correlation of approximately .30, significantly different from zero). If the measures of exposure and of symptoms are obtained from different sources, however—one from the child, the other from the mother—the relationship is at best substantially smaller than .30 and may be (most parsimoniously, is) no larger than a correlation expected by chance. This conclusion appears to be warranted whether the outcome measure is calculated over an entire set of symptoms regarded as indicative of PTSD or over a particular set, such as that of depression or another component.

Such findings need not indicate bias or artifact in either the parent-based or the child-based measures, although these are possibilities. It is also possible that both sets of measures are accurate but indicate that different phenomena are observed through the different modes of observation. The child, for example, can be quite aware of the violence he or she has witnessed even when the mother is not so aware, and the child's measure of stress may be accurate when the parent does not observe stress. On the other hand, the mother may be aware of violence to which her child has been exposed and the distress that child has experienced when the child is not aware and does not—perhaps cannot—acknowledge the violence or report the distress. In general, the correlations between child–child and mother–mother measures may indicate valid relationships even when child–mother measures correlate near zero. The sets of children identified as affected by violence under such conditions are different, but this means simply that different dynamics—different mechanisms—are at work for the two sets of children.

means simply that different dynamics—different mechanisms—are at work for the two sets of children.

This kind of theory was lacking in the studies reviewed. The studies were not designed, and data were not analyzed, in ways that could reveal separate groups in which exposure to violence or the effects of violence are different. The findings of this review suggest that it would be worthwhile to design and conduct studies that can reveal such groupings if they exist.

In neighborhoods in which violence occurs, the percentages of children who report witnessing violence increase with increases in the average age of the children. The incidence of violence in such neighborhoods also tends to increase over time and with the age of the children. Such factors suggest that the longer children reside and develop in such neighborhoods, the more likely it is that they will be repeatedly exposed to violence. This situation has led observers to characterize children's exposure to violence in such neighborhoods as chronic (Hill & Madhere, 1995).

Such observations may also have led researchers to measure exposure to violence by counting the number of different kinds of incidents of violence to which the child has been exposed, as judged by the child or the parent. Whether or not the count-the-incidents measure is valid, it has become the coin of the realm, the kind of measure obtained in most studies. However, the counts in such measures derive from different kinds of events. It is doubtful that the events are comparable and that merely adding them up provides a good measure. Events can range from seeing two strangers exchange drugs for money to seeing one's mother killed in a shooting. One count of the latter experience may be comparable to a single exposure to violence on the playground in the Pynoos study, but it is doubtful that one count of the drug-dealing exposure is comparable. Also, the events counted as the "same" may be quite different psychologically: Witnessing someone being hit might mean seeing two older children fight in one case and witnessing the beating of a family member in another case. The experience of seeing a fight between two neighbors is likely to be emotionally quite different from the experience of seeing a fight between one's father and mother. Results from the Martinez study indicated that the latter experience was more likely than the former to be associated with the expression of PTSD symptoms. Simply adding up the number of different kinds of events said to indicate violence probably does not result in a scale of magnitudes that are likely to be—or even can be—monotonically related to magnitudes of a well-scaled measure of PTSD symptomatology. Such magnitudes are not likely to be comparable from one individual to another or one study to another. Such magnitudes are also not likely to represent chronicity. A drive-by shooting is counted just once in the measure, for example, even though in one case it might represent having witbe leveled also at the "count-the-symptoms" measures of PTSD that were used in the studies reviewed. Again, it is doubtful that all symptoms are comparable and that merely counting the number provides the best possible measure. Future studies should be designed to avoid these problems of measurement. It is desirable that measurements at least have face validity. It is desirable, too, that measures be designed to have adequate psychometric properties, in particular high reliability. Variable reliabilities often were not reported in the studies reviewed. The lack of findings in some cases may have been due to the measures being too unreliable to yield correlations large enough to be significantly different from zero in samples of the size obtained. Almost all the measures of the studies reviewed could be substantially improved.

The measures of exposure to violence in the studies reviewed often did not adequately distinguish between violence in the community and violence in the home, although such a distinction was drawn in the Richters and Saltzman (1990) scale. In the measures in which a child was reported to be a victim of violence, however, it generally was clear whether the violence was perpetrated by an adult in the home or by another person (e.g., another child in the neighborhood). This distinction is important for several reasons. For one thing, violence perpetrated by adult family members is likely to be more traumatic than the same acts of violence involving nonfamily members: The former is likely to be chronic, more frequent, more intense, less controllable, more damaging to continuing relationships on which the child's development must be based, and, in particular, more damaging to the "safe haven" children must have for favorable development. The results of the Osofsky and Richters studies indeed suggest that violence committed in the home is more likely to evoke stress symptoms than comparable violence occurring outside the home. A good parent–child relationship and a family environment unsullied by violence in the home are likely to mitigate the effects of the violence the child may experience in the community outside that home. This conclusion is suggested by the results of the Martinez and Osofsky studies, although the hypothesis has yet to be pointedly and comprehensively addressed.

There is a large body of literature, both theoretical and empirical, on the family environments of children abused by parents and on the child-rearing characteristics of abusive parents (e.g., Belsky, 1993; Trickett, 1993; Wolfe, 1985). Tapping this literature could help to build theory and rationale for studies of how violence in the community affects child development and how family context mediates this impact.

Results from the studies reviewed tell little about possible effects associated with gender or ethnicity. Although all these studies had male and female participants, usually in approximately equal proportions, gender differences were analyzed in only four studies. Attar and Pynoos found no gender differences. Fitzpatrick found that victimized females had more female participants, usually in approximately equal proportions, gender differences were analyzed in only four studies. Attar and Pynoos found no gender differences. Fitzpatrick found that victimized females had more symptoms of depression than victimized males, but it is not clear whether the nature of the victimization was similar for males and females. Similarly, either there were no ethnic differences to analyze (seven studies), or no analyses of ethnic differences were carried out (one study), or no ethnic differences were found (one study).

The studies reviewed are also quite limited in what they indicate about how age or developmental stage relates to experiences of violence and the effects of violence on children's development. With one exception (Fitzpatrick's work), the samples in all the studies were of children of elementary school age. Usually, age or grade analyses were not reported, although Fitzpatrick found that older witnesses to violence reported more depression than younger witnesses, and Attar examined grade differences and found no significant relationships. There has been no systematic examination of possible differences in the effects of exposure to violence in adolescents compared with younger children. There are no empirical studies of children younger than elementary school age.

Most of the studies reviewed did not examine how violence in the community might affect children's intellectual achievement or how cognitive capabilities might help children to deal with violence. The results from two studies, however, might be interpreted as indicating only a small relationship between exposure to violence and cognitive development, a finding that is counterintuitive. Attar et al. found no strong main-effect relationships between child-report measures of exposure to violence and objective test measures of academic achievement. In the Hill study, teacher ratings of social competence correlated near zero with the witnessing, apprehension, retaliation, and global indicators of exposure to violence. To interpret such results as indicating that exposure to violence has no influence on cognitive development, however, is counter to what is known. The distractions alone produced by exposure to violence, particularly repeated exposures, would be expected to disrupt cognitive development, and the effects of stress could add to such disruption. The results indicate only static relationships, however, not cumulative relationships—the deleterious effects that could be expected to accumulate over time and with repeated exposures to violence. To examine such possible effects, longitudinal studies are needed covering substantial periods of child development. In general, longitudinal research is needed to study whether and how exposure to violence affects expectations, beliefs, self-esteem, and other major aspects of personality and cognition.

The more atrocious the violence, the more it threatens the child, and the closer it is to the child—both physically and along a continuum of relationship, as violence directed at self, parent, friend, acquaintance, someone in the community, or a stranger—the more likely it is that violence will be associated with PTSD symptoms. This correlation is largest and most likely to be detected statistically when both kinds of measurements—of exposure and of symptoms—are obtained from the child. Child-based and mother-based measures of the child's exposure to violence and child's symptoms intercorrelate near zero. But mother-based measures of the child's exposure and the child's symptoms correlate in the .10–.55 range. Such findings might point to artifact in measurement, but it is possible that they indicate that parent measures identify violence and symptoms in different children than are identified in child-based measures. Research is needed to examine this possibility.

In neighborhoods in which violence occurs, the percentages of children who report witnessing violence of one kind or another increase with an increase in the average age of the children. Research on the impact of community violence on child development is of recent origin. Only a first generation of such research has been available for review. As has been true for research on child abuse, the second generation of research in this area can build on the first and result in a considerable amount of new knowledge. Such advance in new knowledge would be aided by studies in which the research design is built on findings and theory derived from studies of child abuse and domestic violence.

Answers to these kinds of questions have been adumbrated in the extant research; new research is needed to clarify the following:

- How might violence affect children's cognitive development, and how does the child's developmental stage relate to any effects violence might produce?
- How are possible effects of exposure to violence related to the probability of being exposed, on the one hand, and to the frequency of exposure for children who continue to live in violence-prone neighborhoods, on the other hand?

Cross-sectional studies can help provide answers to these questions, but longitudinal research is critically needed to identify effects associated with repeated exposure, effects that accumulate, and effects that extend far into future development.

Future research should be based on better measurements taken along multiple dimensions. Such measurements should calibrate for the different kinds of violence to which the child has been exposed, multiple exposures to each kind of violence, and the psychological and physical nearness of the violence to the child. In addition, future research should be informed by theory and findings derived from the large body of research indicating kinds of violence to which the child has been exposed, multiple exposures to each kind of violence, and the psychological and physical nearness of the violence to the child. In addition, future research should be informed by theory and findings derived from the large body of research indicating how family environment and child-rearing characteristics relate to child development.

REFERENCES

Achenbach, T. M., & Edelbrock, C. S. (1983). *Manual for the Child Behavior Checklist and Revised Child Behavior Profile*. Burlington, VT: University of Vermont, Department of Psychiatry.

Achenbach, T. M., & Edelbrock, C. (1986). *Manual for the Teacher's Report Form and Teacher Version of the Child Behavior Profile*. Burlington, VT: University of Vermont, Department of Psychiatry.

American Psychiatric Association. (1987). *Diagnostic and statistical manual of mental disorders* (3rd ed.–revised). Washington, DC: Author.

Attar, B. K., Guerra, N. G., & Tolan, P. H. (1994). Neighborhood disadvantage, stressful life events, and adjustment in urban elementary-school children. *Journal of Clinical Psychology, 23*, 391–400.

Bell, C. C., & Jenkins, E. J. (1993). Community violence and children on Chicago's Southside. In D. Reiss, J. E. Richters, M. Radke-Yarrow, & D. Scharff (Eds.), *Children and violence* (pp. 46–54). New York: Guilford Press.

Belsky, J. (1993, November). Etiology of child maltreatment: A developmental ecological analysis. *Psychological Bulletin, 114*, 413–434.

Bodman, F. (1941). War conditions and the mental health of the child. *British Medical Journal, 2*, 286–288.

Brenitz, S. (Ed.). (1983). *Stress in Israel*. New York: Van Nostrand Reinhold.

Dubow, N., & Ulman, D. C. (1989). Assessing social support in elementary school children: The survey of children's social support. *Journal of Clinical Child Psychology, 18*, 52–64.

Eron, L. D., Walder, L. O., & Lefkowitz, M. M. (1972). *The learning of aggression in children*. Boston: Little, Brown.

Figley, R. C. (1989). *Helping traumatized families*. San Francisco: Jossey-Bass.

Fitzpatrick, K. M. (1993). Exposure to violence and presence of depression among low-income, African American youth. *Journal of Consulting and Clinical Psychology, 61*, 528–531.

Fitzpatrick, K. M., & Boldizar, J. P. (1993). The prevalence and consequences of exposure to violence among African American youth. *Journal of the American Academy of Child and Adolescent Psychiatry, 32*, 424–430.

Freeman, L. N., Mokros, H., & Poznanski, E. O. (1993). Violent events reported by normal urban school-aged children: Characteristics and depression corre-

Garmezy, N., & Rutter, M. (1985). Acute reactions to stress. In M. Rutter & L. Hersov (Eds.), *Child and adolescent psychiatry: Modern approaches* (2nd ed., pp. 152–176). Oxford, England: Blackwell Scientific.

Glover, E. (1942). Notes on the psychological effects of war conditions on the civilian population: Part III. The Blitz. *International Journal of Psychoanalysis, 29,* 17–37.

Hightower, A. D. (1986). The Teacher-Child Rating Scale: A brief objective measure of elementary school children's problem behaviors and competencies. *School Psychology Review, 15,* 393–409.

Hill, H. M., & Madhere, S. (1995). *Exposure to community violence and African American children: A multi-dimensional model.* Unpublished manuscript, Howard University, Washington, DC.

Hill, H. M., & Noblin, V. (1991). *Children's perceptions of environmental violence.* Washington, DC: Howard University.

Kovacs, M. (1981). Rating scales to assess depression in school-aged children. *Acta Paedopsychiatrica, 46,* 305–315.

Kovacs, M. (1985). The Children's Depression Inventory. *Psychopharmacology Bulletin, 21,* 995–998.

Lyons, H. A. (1973, Winter). The psychological effects of the civil disturbance on children. *Northern Teacher,* pp. 35–38.

Lyons, H. A. (1979). Civil violence: The psychological aspects. *Journal of Psychosomatic Research, 23,* 373–393.

Martinez, P., & Richters, J. E. (1993). The NIMH Community Violence Project: Children's distress symptoms associated with violence exposure. In D. Reiss, J. E. Richters, M. Radke-Yarrow, & D. Scharff (Eds.), *Children and violence* (pp. 82–95). New York: Guilford Press.

McAuley, R., & Troy, M. (1983). The impact of urban conflict and violence on children referred to a child psychiatry clinic. In J. Harbison (Ed.), *Children of the troubles* (pp. 33–43). Belfast, Ireland: Stranmillis College.

McWhirter, L. (1982, November 4). Yoked by violence together: Stress and coping in children in Northern Ireland. *Community Care,* pp. 14–17.

McWhirter, L. (1983). Growing up in Northern Ireland: From "aggression" to the "troubles." In A. P. Goldstein & M. H. Segall (Eds.), *Aggression in global perspective* (pp. 367–400). Elmsford, NY: Pergamon Press.

McWhirter, L., & Trew, K. (1981). Children in Northern Ireland: A lost generation? In. E. J. Anthony & C. Chiland (Eds.), *The child in his family. Children in turmoil: Tomorrow's children* (pp. 69–82). New York: Wiley Interscience.

Milgram & Milgram. (1976). The effect of the Yom Kippur war on anxiety level in Israeli children. *Journal of Psychology, 94,* 107–113.

Osofsky, J. D., Wewers, S., Hann, D. M., & Fick, A. C. (1993). Chronic community violence: What is happening to our children? In D. Reiss, J. E. Richters, M. Radke-Yarrow, & D. Scharff (Eds.), *Children and violence* (pp. 36–45). New York: Guilford Press.

Osofsky, J. D., Wewers, S., Hann, D. M., & Fick, A. C. (1993). Chronic community violence: What is happening to our children? In D. Reiss, J. E. Richters, M. Radke-Yarrow, & D. Scharff (Eds.), *Children and violence* (pp. 36–45). New York: Guilford Press.

Poznanski, E. O., Freeman, L., & Mokros, H. (1985). Children's depression rating scale—revised. *Psychopharmacological Bulletin, 21,* 979–989.

Pryor-Brown, L., & Cowen, E. L. (1989). Stressful life events, support, and children's school adjustment. *Journal of Clinical Child Psychology, 18,* 214–220.

Pynoos, R. S., Frederick, C., Nader, K., & Arroyo, W. (1987). Life threat and posttraumatic stress in school-age children. *Archives of General Psychiatry, 44,* 1057–1063.

Richters, J. E., & Martinez, P. (1990a). *Checklist of Child Distress Symptoms: Parent Report.* Rockville, MD: National Institute of Mental Health.

Richters, J. E., & Martinez, P. (1990b). *Things I Have Seen and Heard: A structured interview for assessing young children's violence exposure.* Rockville, MD: National Institute of Mental Health.

Richters, J. E., & Martinez, P. (1993a). The NIMH Community Violence Project: Children as victims of and witnesses to violence. In D. Reiss, J. E. Richters, M. Radke-Yarrow, & D. Scharff (Eds.), *Children and violence* (pp. 7–21). New York: Guilford Press.

Richters, J. E., & Martinez, P. (1993b). Violent communities, family choices, and children's chances: An algorithm for improving the odds. *Development and Psychopathology, 5,* 609–627.

Richters, J. E., Martinez, P., & Valla, J. P. (1990). *Levonn: A cartoon-based structured interview for assessing young children's distress symptoms.* Rockville, MD: National Institute of Mental Health.

Richters, J. E., & Saltzman, W. (1990). *Survey of children's exposure to community violence: Parent report.* Rockville, MD: National Institute of Mental Health.

Shakoor, B. H., & Chalmers, D. (1991). Co-victimization of African American children who witness violence and the theoretical implications of its effects on their cognitive, emotional, and behavioral development. *Journal of the National Medical Association, 83,* 233–238.

Spielberger, C. (1973). *STAIC Preliminary Manual: The Stait-Trait Anxiety Inventory for Children.* Palo Alto, CA: Consulting Psychologist Press.

Straus, M. A. (1979). Measuring intrafamily conflict and violence: The Conflict Tactics Scale. *Journal of Marriage and the Family, 41,* 75–88.

Terr, L. C. (1983). Chowchilla revisited: The effects of psychic trauma four years after a school-bus kidnapping. *American Journal of Psychiatry, 140,* 1543–1550.

Trickett, P. K. (1993). Maladaptive development of school-aged, physically abused children: Relationships with the child-rearing context. *Journal of Family Psychology, 7,* 134–147.

Wolfe, D. A. (1985). Child-abusive parents: An empirical review and analysis. *Psychological Bulletin, 97,* 462–482.

Ziv, & Israel, (1973). Effects of bombardment on the manifest anxiety level of children living in kibbutzim. *Journal of Consulting and Clinical Psychology, 40,* 287–291.

II

CAUSES OF DIFFERENT FORMS OF VIOLENCE AGAINST CHILDREN

6

INDIVIDUAL AND FAMILY CHARACTERISTICS ASSOCIATED WITH INTRAFAMILIAL CHILD PHYSICAL AND SEXUAL ABUSE

JOEL S. MILNER

In the past 2 decades, there has been a dramatic increase in the number of articles published on topics related to family violence. The publication increase, however, has not been evenly distributed across the different types of abuse. During recent years, there has been an increase in the proportion of articles published on child sexual abuse and a decrease in the proportion of articles published on child physical abuse. Within the child physical abuse area, there also has been a decrease in the number of publications that focus on offenders. Theory-driven studies that use clearly defined offender (or victim) groups with demographically matched comparison participants continue to represent only a small minority of all published articles. In some cases, there have been more discussions of research problems than research. For example, in one database (PsycLit-APA, 1987–1994), there were more citations of articles describing methodolog-

Preparation of this chapter was supported in part by National Institute of Mental Health Grant MH34252 to Joel S. Milner.

ical problems in child physical abuse research than citations of controlled studies investigating child physical abuse offender characteristics.

Within the purview of this book, coverage of individual and family characteristics of children who witness domestic violence or neighborhood violence is beyond the scope of this chapter. However, much has been written about the characteristics of families in which domestic violence occurs, and the reader is referred to chapter 4, this volume, for a discussion of these characteristics. In contrast, there are few data on the characteristics of families whose children witness neighborhood violence other than the confirmation that these families are likely to be poor (e.g., Martinez & Richters, 1993; Osofsky, 1995; Richters & Martinez, 1993).

Because the focus of this chapter is on research-based descriptions of parent and family characteristics associated with child abuse, specific models are not discussed. However, general organizational models of child maltreatment provide useful perspectives for guiding the understanding of child abuse. For example, Belsky (1980, 1993) pointed out that factors from different ecological levels (e.g., individual, family, community, and culture) need to be understood, and Cicchetti and Rizley (1981) indicated that both potentiating and compensatory factors of short (transient) and long (enduring) duration need to be considered at each ecological level. Therefore, despite the fact that the present chapter focuses on parent and family characteristics, the reader should be aware that multiple-level, multifactor interactional models appear to describe best the factors that contribute to child maltreatment. Community and cultural factors associated with child maltreatment are discussed elsewhere in this volume.

Descriptions of offender and family characteristics provided in this chapter are drawn from a selected review of the published literature. When possible, descriptions are based on studies that contained matched comparison groups. The research base for child physical abuse, relative to that for child sexual abuse, contains substantially more controlled studies. It is also evident that although definitional problems exist in the child physical abuse studies, definitional problems in the child sexual abuse area are more challenging. These problems include defining what constitutes sexual abuse and determining which child molesters should be grouped together in the offender groups. Additional discussion of sexual abuse definitional issues is presented in the introduction to the review of incest offender characteristics.

In the following section, the offender and family characteristics associated with intrafamilial child physical abuse are reviewed. Most of the descriptions of physical abusers are based on studies of offending mothers, because few studies have investigated offending fathers. This section is followed by a review of offender, spouse, and family characteristics associated with intrafamilial child sexual abuse. Only studies using male offenders are reviewed, because there is a paucity of data on female incest offenders.

In general, the extent to which the different offender and family characteristics are marker variables or causal factors in child abuse has not been determined, and little is known about how various potentiating and compensatory factors interact.

CHILD PHYSICAL ABUSE

Congruent with state reporting laws, most studies of child physical abusers use operational definitions requiring the presence of physical damage. A general definition that approximates definitions used in state laws and in many research projects is as follows: *Child physical abuse* is the creation, development, or active promotion of behaviors, events, or situations under the parent's or caretaker's control that result in the intentional (nonaccidental) physical injury of a child less than 18 years of age. However, exceptions to this definition exist. In some studies, assaultive behaviors (including hitting and spanking) without physical injury are included in the definition of child physical abuse.

Offender Characteristics

Demographic and Social Factors

Parental demographic risk factors include status as single parent (Gelles, 1989), adolescent parent (Gelles, 1989), and nonbiological parent (Lightcap, Kurland, & Burgess, 1982). Child physical abusers often have a childhood history of family problems, including receiving or observing maltreatment (Egeland, Jacobvitz, & Papatola, 1987; Herrenkohl, Herrenkohl, & Toedter, 1983; Hunter, Kilstrom, Kraybill, & Loda, 1978; Oates, Forrest, & Peacock, 1985; Spinetta, 1978). Although Widom (1989) indicated that the nature and strength of the relationship between an abuse history and risk for child abuse remains in question, the presence of a childhood history of physical abuse in physically abusive parents is viewed by many as support for the intergenerational-transmission-of-abuse hypothesis.

In a review of literature, Kaufman and Zigler (1987) concluded that about 30% (plus or minus 5%) of child physical abusers experienced childhood maltreatment. However, this often-cited estimate has been criticized as being too low (Belsky, 1993), in part because of the limited opportunity for abuse to occur (e.g., the follow-up period is too brief) in some of the studies used to determine the 30% rate. Irrespective of the exact prevalence of childhood abuse in physically abusive parents, many individuals who were maltreated in childhood do not abuse their children. Although the reasons some parents appear to break the cycle of abuse remain unknown, several studies have indicated that the presence of a supportive adult during childhood or a supportive relationship (spouse, friend, or therapist) during adulthood is associated with reduced risk of child abuse (Caliso & Milner, 1992; Crouch, Milner, & Caliso, 1995; Egeland, Jacobvitz, & Sroufe, 1988; Hunter et al., 1978; Litty, Kowalski, & Minor, 1996).

Lower socioeconomic status (SES) is frequently found to be a risk factor for child physical abuse. This association has been observed in reported cases (Olsen & Holmes, 1986) and in a national survey (Straus, Gelles, & Steinmetz, 1980), suggesting that the association is not simply due to a reporting bias against lower SES families. On the basis of data from another national survey, Gelles (1989) reported that child abuse was associated with lower levels of income in mothers but not in fathers. Gender effects were also observed in a study of fatal abuse cases. Jason and Andereck (1983) compared fatal and nonfatal child abuse cases occurring in Georgia during a 4.5-year period; fatal child abuse was associated with male offenders, teenaged childbirth, and lower SES. A problem with using lower SES status as a risk factor is that most lower SES parents do not physically abuse their children. It is possible, therefore, that lower SES status is important only to the extent that SES is associated with other factors such as lower levels of parental affection, poor communication, and negative parent–child interactions. This perspective is supported by Herrenkohl, Herrenkohl, Toedter, and Yanushefski (1984), who reported that covariants of lower income include single-parent status, lower intelligence, less formal education, lower levels of physical health, and higher levels of personal distress and psychopathology.

Biological Factors

Putative biological risk factors for child physical abuse include parental neuropsychological, psychophysiological, and physical health problems. Although there are few data indicating that neurological problems are risk factors for child physical abuse, Elliott (1988) proposed that some disorders (e.g., episodic dyscontrol, antisocial personality, and attention deficit disorder) that are correlated with neuropsychological deficits are associated with child abuse. Elliott (1988) suggested that cognitive deficits, such as problems in verbal processing, reduce the parent's ability to cope with family problems and increase the risk for child physical abuse. Milner and McCanne (1991) speculated that cognitive processing problems may determine whether, when, and toward whom aggression is expressed. Supporting some of Elliott's hypotheses, Nayak and Milner (1996) reported differences between demographically matched groups of high- and low-risk mothers on neuropsychological measures that assessed conceptual ability, cognitive flexibility, and problem-solving ability. Differences were also found in analyses that included IQ as a covariate, supporting Elliott's view that cognitive differences exist apart from overall differences in intelligence. However, expected differences were not found between high- and low-risk mothers on neuropsychological measures of attention, distractibility, and verbal fluency. Because the Nayak and Milner study is the only study in the field of child physical abuse that has investigated putative neuropsychological differences in a controlled design, additional research is needed before any conclusions can be drawn about putative neuropsychological impairments in physically abusive parents.

Some authors have proposed that physically abusive parents possess a hyperreactive trait (Knutson, 1978; Vasta, 1982) and are hyperresponsive to child-related stimuli (Bauer & Twentyman, 1985). Although study results are often mixed and in some cases difficult to interpret (see McCanne & Milner, 1991, for a review), investigators have generally concluded that child physical abusers (Disbrow, Doerr, & Caulfield, 1977; Friedrich, Tyler, & Clark, 1985; Frodi & Lamb, 1980; Wolfe, Fairbank, Kelly, & Bradlyn, 1983) and individuals at high risk for physical abuse (Crowe & Zeskind, 1992; Pruitt & Erickson, 1985) are more physiologically reactive to child-related stimuli (e.g., a crying child). Data also indicate that high-risk mothers, compared to low-risk mothers, are more physiologically reactive to stressful non-child-related stimuli (Casanova, Domanic, McCanne, & Milner, 1992). Although the manner in which increased physiological reactivity contributes to child physical abuse is unknown, stress-related autonomic reactivity may disrupt child-related information processing and response implementation (e.g., Milner, 1993).

Several authors have found that child physical abusers, compared to nonabusers, report more physical handicaps and physical health problems (Conger, Burgess, & Barrett, 1979; Lahey, Conger, Atkeson, & Treiber, 1984; Milner & Wimberley, 1980). Other investigators have indicated that abusers have more psychosomatic illnesses (Steele & Pollock, 1974). Although it is not known whether abusive parents have more physical health problems or simply report more physical health problems, the parent's report of frequent physical health problems appears to be a risk factor for child physical abuse.

Cognitive and Affective Factors

Cognitive and affective risk factors represent a broad array of parental personality characteristics. Controlled studies are relatively uniform in indicating that abusive parents have lower levels of self-esteem, ego strength, and feelings of personal worth (Culp, Culp, Soulis, & Letts, 1989; Evans, 1980; Melnick & Hurley, 1969; Oates & Forrest, 1985; Perry, Wells, & Doran, 1983; Rosen, 1978; Shorkey, 1980; Shorkey & Armendariz, 1985). Abusive (Wiehe, 1986) and at-risk (Stringer & LaGreca, 1985) parents also report an external locus of control that appears to include blaming others for one's problems.

Child-related cognitive risk factors include inappropriate expectations related to child development and behavior. The literature, however, is unclear as to exactly what differences in expectation exist. Although several studies have failed to find differences in child-related expectations in abusive parents, compared to nonabusive parents (Gaines, Sandgrund, Green, & Power, 1978; Kravitz & Driscoll, 1983; Starr, 1982), other studies have indicated that abusive parents have lower or higher child expectations (Oates et al., 1985; Perry et al., 1983; Spinetta, 1978; Twentyman & Plotkin, 1982). Some researchers have suggested that results may vary as a function of the questions asked. For example, Azar, Robinson, Hekimian, and Twentyman (1984) failed to find differences between abusive and matched comparison parents in their expectations regarding developmental milestones but did find differences in their expectations regarding complex child behaviors. Likewise, Chilamkurti and Milner (1993) found that expectation differences varied with the context. High-risk mothers, compared to matched low-risk mothers, had significantly lower expectations of child compliance following discipline for major transgressions and significantly higher expectations of child compliance following discipline for minor transgressions. In terms of general behavioral expectations, on a self-report questionnaire, abusers have repeatedly displayed rigid expectations regarding their children's behavior relative to matched comparison parents (e.g., a child should always be neat and clean; DePaul, Arruabarrena, & Milner, 1991; Milner, 1989; Milner & Robertson, 1990; Milner & Wimberley, 1980).

Abusive, relative to nonabusive, parents appear to perceive more negative behavior in their children, and in several cases, the reports of more negative child behaviors are not supported by the observations of other raters or observers (Mash, Johnston, & Kovitz, 1983; Reid, Kavanagh, & Baldwin, 1987; Wood-Shuman & Cone, 1986). At-risk mothers evaluate minor child transgressions as more wrong than do matched low-risk mothers (Chilamkurti & Milner, 1993). Although some authors have reported that abusive mothers, compared to matched nonabusive mothers, make different types of internal–external and stable–unstable attributions for children's positive and negative behaviors (Larrance & Twentyman, 1983), others have failed to find similar attributional differences in abusers (Rosenberg & Reppucci, 1983) and at-risk individuals (Milner & Foody, 1994). Although additional support for the existence of attributional differences has been reported, the support tends to be primarily for negative child behaviors (Bradley & Peters, 1991) or for attributions made after individuals receive mitigating information about a child's behavior (Milner & Foody, 1994). Concerning the latter instance, although overall attributional differences were not observed, low-risk individuals changed their child-related attributions (to indicate less responsibility and hostile intent) following the receipt of mitigating information, whereas high-risk individuals did not. Therefore, abusers and at-risk individuals, compared to nonabusers or independent observers, tend to view their children as being more problematic and more intentionally disruptive and disobedient. A comprehensive review of cognitive factors thought to be related to child physical abuse is available elsewhere (Milner, 1993).

The literature is relatively uniform in reporting empathy differences between abusive and comparison mothers on a variety of measures administered under different conditions (e.g., Frodi & Lamb, 1980; Letourneau, 1981; Melnick & Hurley, 1969; Wiehe, 1986). However, a recent study failed to find dispositional empathy differences between high- and low-risk females (Milner, Halsey, & Fultz, 1995). Nevertheless, the low-risk females demonstrated a significant increase in empathy when presented with a crying infant (following presentations of a smiling and quiet child), whereas the high-risk females did not show a significant change in empathy. This study indicates that context (e.g., measuring empathy in response to selected stimuli, such as a crying child) may be an important consideration in the study of empathy.

Although there have been exceptions (e.g., Starr, 1982), studies generally have found that abusive parents, compared to nonabusive parents, report more life stress (Conger et al., 1979; Gaines et al., 1978; Lawson & Hays, 1989) as well as personal distress (Lahey et al., 1984; Mash et al., 1983; Milner, 1989; Milner et al., 1995; Milner & Wimberley, 1980; Rosenberg & Reppucci, 1983). In longitudinal studies, stress and stressful conditions have been reported to be predictive of later inadequate child care and child maltreatment (Altemeier et al., 1979; Egeland, Breitenbucher, & Rosenberg, 1980). Lacking, however, are controlled studies with designs in which stress is manipulated demonstrating the impact of stress on other risk factors (e.g., attributions, evaluations).

Although most child physical abusers are not mentally ill (an often-cited figure is less than 10%), many types of psychopathology appear to increase the risk of parenting problems, and serious psychopathology may be associated with more severe types of physical assault (e.g., murder). Furthermore, emotional problems frequently have been associated with physical abuse (Conger et al., 1979; Melnick & Hurley, 1969; Oates et al., 1985; Pianta, Egeland, & Erickson, 1989; Wright, 1976). Abusers and at-risk parents tend to display a number of negative emotions that may represent general negative affectivity (Milner et al., 1995). In a variety of contexts, abusive and at-risk individuals, relative to comparison individuals, report more anxiety (Aragona, 1983; Lahey et al., 1984; Perry et al., 1983); more depression, unhappiness, and sadness (Evans, 1980; Friedrich et al., 1985; Frodi & Lamb, 1980; Lahey et al., 1984; Milner, 1989; Milner et al., 1995; Milner & Robertson, 1990; Milner & Wimberley, 1980); and, with one exception (Melnick & Hurley, 1969), more feelings of annoyance, anger, hostility, and aggression (Bauer & Twentyman, 1985; Evans, 1980; Frodi & Lamb, 1980; Lyons-Ruth, Connell, Zoll, & Stahl, 1987; Milner et al., 1995; Rosenberg & Reppucci, 1983; Susman, Trickett, Iannotti, Hollenbeck, & Zahn-Waxler, 1985).

Finally, the literature is relatively uniform in finding that abusive parents report more isolation and feelings of loneliness than comparison parents (Corse, Schmid, & Trickett, 1990; Evans, 1980; Milner, 1989; Milner & Wimberley, 1980; Shorkey, 1980; Shorkey & Armendariz, 1985; Spinetta, 1978; Trickett & Susman, 1988). Abusive, compared to nonabusive, parents report fewer friends and memberships in community organizations (Corse et al., 1990; Starr, 1988), and abusive parents appear less likely to use available resources. There is evidence that individuals who are at the greatest risk for abuse are more likely than others to drop out of treatment programs (Wolfe, Edwards, Manion, & Koverola, 1988).

Behavioral Factors

With respect to their behavior toward children, abusive parents, relative to nonabusive parents, engage in less communication and fewer interactions with their children (Bousha & Twentyman, 1984; Disbrow et al., 1977; Schmidt & Eldridge, 1986). When they do interact, abusive parents more frequently engage in negative parenting behaviors. Abusers more frequently use intrusive behaviors (Lyons-Ruth et al., 1987) and are inconsistent in their responding to children (Susman et al., 1985). It has been reported in several studies that abusive and high-risk parents, relative to comparison parents, more often used harsh disciplinary strategies, including verbal and physical assault (Chilamkurti & Milner, 1993; Lahey et al., 1984; Trickett & Kuczynski, 1986). Other studies, however, have not found different rates of negative parental behaviors in physical abusers (Burgess & Conger, 1978; Evans, 1980; Mash et al., 1983).

Compared to studies on the use of negative parenting behaviors, studies on positive parenting behaviors are more uniform. Abusers have been found to use less reasoning (Chilamkurti & Milner, 1993; Corse et al., 1990; Milner & Foody, 1994; Susman et al., 1985; Trickett & Kuczynski, 1986) and fewer positive behaviors (Bousha & Twentyman, 1984; Burgess & Conger, 1978; Lahey et al., 1984; Susman et al., 1985) with children. In addition, children of abusive and high-risk parents, relative to those of comparison parents, more frequently have attachment problems (Browne & Saqi, 1988; Egeland & Sroufe, 1981; Lyons-Ruth et al., 1987).

Although some behavioral models suggest that abusers have general coping deficits beyond child-related skill deficits, the literature on possible differences in general coping skills is mixed. Of two studies that used abusive and comparison groups, one study reported no differences in coping abilities (Gaines et al., 1978), whereas the second study found differences in problem-solving skills (Hansen, Pallotta, Tishelman, Conaway, & MacMillan, 1989). In a study that appears to provide indirect evidence for possible coping problems, Shorkey and Armendariz (1985) reported that abusive mothers, relative to comparison mothers, had more irrational thoughts. At present, additional data are needed on the extent to which child physical abusers, relative to matched comparison groups, show deficits in general coping skills.

Correlational data suggest that behavioral risk factors for child physical abuse include parental use of alcohol and drugs. It is also possible that parental use of alcohol and drugs is associated with certain types of physical abuse, such as fatal child abuse. However, the quality of the studies reporting an association between drug use (historical and current) and child abuse has been questioned (Kelleher, Chaffin, Hollenberg, & Fischer, 1994; Leonard & Jacob, 1988). Likewise, the manner in which alcohol and drug use may interact with other risk factors remains to be determined.

Family Characteristics

Family risk factors overlap with many of the aforementioned individual risk factors. Demographic characteristics, such as the lack of resources and a large number of family members, are risk factors. As the total number of stressors experienced by the family members increases, so does the risk of child maltreatment (Justice & Calvert, 1990). As noted previously, abusive parents, compared to nonabusive parents, report more conflict and less support in their family of origin. High levels of family verbal and physical conflict (including spousal abuse), parental disagreement about child discipline, social isolation of family members, and the lack of family cohesion and expressiveness in the current family are factors that are associated with risk of child physical abuse (Justice & Calvert, 1990; Mollerstrom, Patchner, & Milner, 1992; Trickett & Susman, 1989).

INTRAFAMILIAL CHILD SEXUAL ABUSE

Although child sexual abuse has received increasing attention from professionals, there is still a lack of agreement on its definition. A general definition might be as follows: *Intrafamilial child sexual abuse* is the commission of a sex act on a child under 18 years of age by an adult family member (usually over age 21). Other definitions include an upper age limit of the child that is substantially less than 18 years, and some definitions also allow for adolescent offenders as long as there is a 5-year age difference between the offender and the victim. Child sexual abuse may include both noncontact and contact behaviors. Noncontact child sexual abuse refers to the use of children in pornography and prostitution as well as noncontact sexual activities, such as exhibitionism. Contact sexual abuse includes nongenital contact, genital contact, and intercourse. Sexual behavior may be heterosexual or homosexual in nature, although most reported incest cases are heterosexual. Child sexual abuse may be situational or chronic. Case studies suggest that if the sexual abuse is chronic, the abuse may be patterned with respect to the type of sexual behavior and the type (age, gender, appearance) of the target child selected. Physical violence may or may not accompany the sexual behavior; in incest cases, physical assault is reported in a minority of the cases. Nevertheless, child physical abuse is more likely to be found in families in which incest has occurred than in families in which incest has not occurred.

Because male child molesters appear to be a heterogeneous group of offenders, several attempts have been made theoretically (e.g., Hall & Hirschman, 1992) and empirically to develop offender typologies (e.g., Knight, 1989; Knight, Carter, & Prentky, 1989; Prentky, Knight, Rosenberg, & Lee, 1989). However, the validity and usefulness of these offender subtypes remain to be determined, and the typologies have yet to be widely used in child sexual abuse research. Additional work is needed in this area, because the current state of knowledge is limited by the fact that different types (fathers vs. uncles, noncontact abusers vs. rapists) of intrafamilial child molesters are frequently grouped together, with many investigators also mixing intrafamilial and extrafamilial offenders.

Offender Characteristics

Demographic and Social Factors

Studies indicate that incest offenders are more frequently nonbiologically related caretakers. For example, in a survey (individual interviews) of 930 adult women, Russell (1984) found that 17% of the women who were raised by a stepfather and 2% of the women who were raised by a biological father reported sexual assault by the father figure. Russell also reported that the child sexual abuse by stepfathers involved more serious types of sexual assault. However, in an examination of reported incest cases, Faller (1989) found that when incest was committed by biological fathers, relative to stepfathers, the abuse occurred more frequently and over a longer period of time.

Research indicates that a substantial number of offenders report a childhood history of sexual or physical abuse or both and a lack of a nurturing family background. Although studies of incestuous fathers in prison populations have yielded high rates of reported childhood sexual abuse (e.g., 57%; Seghorn, Prentky, & Boucher, 1987), studies of nonincarcerated incestuous fathers have found lower rates. For example, across four studies of sexually abusive fathers that included mostly nonincarcerated offenders (Faller, 1989; Hanson, Lipovsky, & Saunders, 1994; Kirkland & Bauer, 1982; Langevin, Handy, Day, & Russon, 1985), approximately 25% of the offenders reported experiencing childhood sexual abuse. A relationship between negative early sexual experiences and child molestation has also been observed in a college sample (Briere & Runtz, 1989). The data are inconclusive with respect to which type of offender has experienced more childhood sexual abuse. For example, Erickson, Walbek, and Seely (1987) found that incestuous stepfathers reported more childhood sexual abuse than incestuous biological fathers, whereas Faller (1989) reported the opposite findings.

Rates of childhood sexual abuse for offenders can be compared to rates for males in the general population, which are 16% for a U.S. sample (Finkelhor, Hotaling, Lewis, & Smith, 1990) and 3%–29% for samples from 16 other countries (Finkelhor, 1994). Although data support the conclusion that a childhood history of sexual abuse is more often reported by male incest offenders than by males in the general (U.S.) population, the majority of offenders do not report childhood sexual abuse. Furthermore, although the accuracy of any group's self-report of childhood sexual abuse may be questioned, offender self-reports may contain substantial bias. For example, Hindman (1988) found that offender reports of childhood sexual abuse decreased by more than 50% when the offenders were told that they would have to submit to a lie-detector test.

With respect to sexual offenders' reports of childhood physical abuse, Williams and Finkelhor (1989) reviewed five studies and found rates ranging from 28% to 59%, with a mean of about 47%. There remains, however, a need to distinguish between incarcerated and nonincarcerated offenders to determine whether incarcerated offenders report higher rates of childhood physical abuse, as appears to be the case for childhood sexual abuse. These childhood physical abuse rates for offenders can be compared to the rate of childhood physical abuse of 19.5% reported by a male student population (Milner, Robertson, & Rogers, 1990). Although additional studies controlling for demographic factors across offender and comparison groups are needed before definitive conclusions can be made, the present data suggest that child molesters may experience more childhood physical abuse than sexual abuse, a conclusion previously reached by Williams and Finkelhor (1989). However, when abuse history is associated with offender status, the abuse history covaries with other indices of family dysfunction (Hanson et al., 1994; Parker & Parker, 1986; Seghorn et al., 1987), suggesting that the experience of childhood abuse of any type may be a marker variable for a variety of family problems.

Biological Factors

Hormonal (e.g., Lang, Flor-Henry, & Frenzel, 1990; Langevin, 1993), neurological (e.g., Langevin, Wortzman, Wright, & Handy, 1989; Wright, Nobrega, Langevin, & Wortzman, 1990), and neuropsychological (e.g.,

Langevin, Wortzman, Dickey, Wright, & Handy, 1988; Langevin et al., 1989) investigations have yielded some differences between incest offenders and other offender and comparison groups. Existing findings need to be replicated using more representative samples, however. At present, data are lacking on the possible causative and mediatory roles of hormones and neurological factors in incest offenders.

Cognitive and Affective Factors

Studies indicate that male offenders, compared to nonoffenders, report more personal distress (Milner & Robertson, 1990). Although the majority of child molesters do not display severe forms of psychopathology, it is often reported that offenders have elevated scores on measures of depression, anxiety, suspiciousness, and antisocial behavior (e.g., Kirkland & Bauer, 1982; Langevin, Paitich, Freeman, Mann, & Handy, 1978; Langevin et al., 1985; Panton, 1979; Scott & Stone, 1986). Furthermore, there may be a relationship between a childhood history of abuse, rates of molestation, and psychopathology. For example, Hunter, Childers, Gerald, and Esmaili (1990) found that male incest offenders who had been sexually abused during childhood and who molested with greater frequency had significantly more psychopathology than those offenders without a sexual abuse history and with lower frequency of assault.

Not all studies report a relationship between psychopathology and incestuous behavior. Although Serin, Malcolm, Khanna, and Barbaree (1994) reported that psychopathy was associated with deviant sexual arousal in extrafamilial offenders, psychopathy was not found to be associated with deviant sexual arousal in incest offenders. Groff and Hubble (1984) studied offender characteristics in father–daughter and stepfather–stepdaughter incest using historical, demographic, and Minnesota Multiphasic Personality Inventory (MMPI) data and found no systematic differences across types of incest. Furthermore, these authors reported that offenders appeared to have generally adequate levels of overall functioning. Walters (1987) also failed to find offender differences on the MMPI clinical scales. Following a review of MMPI studies, Milner and Murphy (1995) concluded that even when one considers studies in which offender differences were reported, the available data do not support the view that a single profile represents (and identifies) incest offenders.

Although techniques to increase victim empathy have been among the most commonly used intervention strategies with sex offenders in the United States (Knopp, Freeman-Longo, & Stevenson, 1992), Marshall, Jones, Hudson, and McDonald (1993) reported that the literature is inconclusive on whether sex offenders differ from other groups in dispositional or child-specific empathy. Marshall et al. also reported mixed results concerning empathy from two new studies. In the first study empathy differences were not found, whereas in the second study empathy differences were observed in mixed groups of intrafamilial and extrafamilial offenders. In a recent study, Hayashino, Wurtele, and Klebe (1995) failed to find differences in empathy between intra- and extrafamilial child molesters and other offender and comparison groups. Thus, the relationship between offenders' lack of empathic responsiveness and intrafamilial child sexual abuse remains unclear.

There is evidence that child sex offenders have a number of cognitive distortions related to their abusive behavior. Murphy (1990) defined *offender cognitive distortions* as self-statements that child molesters use to "minimize, justify, and rationalize their behavior." A common offender characteristic is the denial or cognitive distortion of the sexual abuse incident. Even though some offenders never admit to the behavior, other offenders attempt to justify the act (e.g., the child wanted the sex, the child enjoyed the sex, the sexual experience was educational for the child, the sex was only an expression of love). For example, Stermac and Segal (1989) reported that child molesters, relative to comparison groups, were more likely to believe that benefits result from adult–child sexual contacts. In addition to observing child-related cognitive distortions, Gudjonsson (1990) found that child molesters (a mixed group of incest and extrafamilial offenders) had cognitive distortions related to family members and relatives. In line with the view that offenders have more cognitive distortions, Abel et al. (1989) developed a measure of cognitive distortions that significantly differentiated between child molesters and controls. However, limited information is available on this measure (see Milner & Murphy, 1995, for a review). Furthermore, the degree to which cognitive distortions are present in incest offenders and the extent to which these distortions differentiate incest offenders from other offender groups remain to be determined. It is possible that cognitive distortions are not common among incest offenders; for example, Hayashino et al. (1995) reported that extrafamilial offenders had more cognitive distortions, whereas intrafamilial offenders did not differ from comparison groups on this variable.

Behavioral Factors

Research indicates that male offenders manifest a variety of interpersonal problems, including a lack of social skills and poor peer relationships (Langevin et al., 1985; Scott & Stone, 1986). With respect to the nature of offenders' relationships, some descriptive studies report that intrafamilial child sexual abusers are dominant, authoritarian, and controlling (Maisch, 1972; Mrazek & Kempe, 1981; Renshaw, 1982), whereas other studies describe offenders as shy, passive, introverted, socially withdrawn, lonely, and isolated (see Williams & Finkelhor, 1989, for a review). Herman and

Hirschman (1981) attempted to explain these divergent findings by suggesting that the offender is dominant and controlling within the family but passive and dependent outside of the family. Some of these results may be due to inaccurate descriptions of child sexual abusers, however, because some authors have observed that incest offenders are shy and lonely both inside and outside of the family (Wilson & Cox, 1983). Alternatively, what appear to be divergent findings may simply be descriptions of different subtypes of offenders. At present, this issue remains unresolved.

Perhaps related to the issues of cognitive distortions and role confusion is the finding that fathers who molest their female children report spending less time with their daughters during the first 3 years of life and engaging in fewer child care activities (Parker & Parker, 1986). The finding that intrafamilial child molesters engage in fewer early child care behaviors (e.g., dressing, reading to, and teaching their children) has been replicated by other investigators (Milner, 1994; Williams & Finkelhor, 1995). Parker and Parker (1986) proposed that familiarity and stimulus habituation resulting from the early child care behavior reduces the likelihood of incest. Taking a similar perspective, Milner (1994) suggested that the reduced experience in role-appropriate parenting behaviors that serve to define the parent–child relationship increases the likelihood of inappropriate parental behaviors such as child sexual abuse. Williams and Finkelhor (1995) concluded that the presence of caretaking behaviors affects the risk for abuse indirectly by moderating parental feelings of competence.

Data on the association between child molestation and alcohol and drug use are mixed and inconclusive (see Williams & Finkelhor, 1989, for a review). In studies in which male offenders were not found to report higher levels of drug use, the offenders may have denied drug use. Alternatively, offenders who report higher levels of drug use may desire to provide an excuse for the child molestation. There is also the possibility that drug use varies with the type of abuse. For example, on the basis of data from 17 states, Gordon (1989) found that biological father offenders, compared to stepfather offenders, had higher levels of alcohol and drug use. Although the rate of alcohol and drug use among child sex offenders is open to debate, several hypotheses have been generated to describe the nature of the relationship between alcohol and drug use and child sexual abuse. For example, in addition to the previously mentioned use of drugs as part of the offender's justification for the sexual abuse, drugs may serve as a disinhibitor of the sexual behavior or may be used to deal with negative consequences associated with the sexual assault.

Sexual Dysfunction

In addition to child sexual abuse, offenders are reported to display other deviant sexual behaviors. According to some researchers (e.g., Abel,

Becker, Cunningham-Rather, Mittelman, & Rouleau, 1988; Freund, 1990), child sexual abusers frequently have multiple paraphilias (e.g., incestuous pedophilia and exhibitionism). In a large sample study, Abel et al. (1988) reported that 84.8% and 81.0% of extrafamilial offenders who targeted a female or male child, respectively, had additional paraphilias, and 71.7% and 95.5% of intrafamilial offenders who targeted a female or male child, respectively, had additional paraphilias. In contrast, Marshall, Barbaree, and Eccles (1991) reported relatively low rates of additional paraphilias: rates of 14% and 11.8% for extrafamilial offenders against girls and boys, respectively, and a rate of 7.9% for intrafamilial offenders. The contrast between the Abel et al. and Marshall et al. findings is even more marked because Marshall et al. reported that most of the additional paraphilias identified in their study did not meet *DSM-III-R* (American Psychiatric Association, 1987) criteria for paraphilias.

Cumulative results do not show strong support for the hypothesis of deviant sexual arousal among incest offenders. For example, although Murphy, Haynes, Stalgaitis, and Flanagan (1986) found that some types of offenders showed more arousal to slide presentations of children than of adults, this pattern was not found for incest offenders. Although child sex offenders, including incest offenders, were found to respond more to audiotaped presentations of children than of adults, in other studies using audiotapes, Marshall, Barbaree, and Christophe (1986) and Lang, Black, Frenzel, and Checkley (1988) found that arousal responses of incest offenders were more like those of normals than those of extrafamilial offenders. Barbaree and Marshall (1989) observed that most incest offenders had less deviant sexual arousal than other offender groups, and Frenzel and Lang (1989) reported that intrafamilial child sexual abusers were heterogeneous in their physiological arousal to child stimuli and overlapped substantially with controls. In summarizing the literature, Milner and Murphy (1995) concluded that the existing evidence did not support the view that intrafamilial offenders display deviant arousal patterns. Although this contrasts with the relatively strong evidence that, on a group basis, extrafamilial child offenders display deviant arousal patterns, the evidence is not sufficiently uniform to conclude that deviant sexual arousal aimed at children can be used for individual classification of extrafamilial sex offenders.

Wives of Male Offenders

The wives of sex offenders have been reported to have dysfunctional families of origin (Parker & Parker, 1986) and incestuous family histories (Goodwin, McCarthy, & DiVasto, 1981). In cases involving biological father offenders, Faller (1989) found that 49.1% of the wives had experienced childhood sexual abuse. In cases involving nonbiological fathers, 69.6% of the wives had experienced childhood sexual abuse. In terms of current family functioning, Truesdell, McNeil, and Deschner (1986) reported that 22 offenders' wives out of a group of 30 experienced spousal psychological abuse and 22 wives reported spousal physical abuse, with 7 of these women reporting life-threatening spousal abuse.

Wives of male incest offenders have been reported to show evidence of dependency (Burgess, Groth, Holmstrom, & Sgroi, 1978; Spencer, 1978), dominance (Mrazek & Kempe, 1981), depression (Simari & Baskin, 1980; Wald, Archer, & Winstead, 1990), inadequacy (Herman & Hirschman, 1981), and low self-esteem (Bennett, 1980). Some authors have suggested that the female spouse often responds passively to the incest. (See Groff, 1987, for a review.)

Beginning more than 2 decades ago, however, other investigators (e.g., Maisch, 1972) indicated that personality characteristics of incest offenders' wives were generally normal. Using a standardized test and comparison groups, Scott and Stone (1986) and Groff (1987) reported that the wives of male incest offenders generally had MMPI scores in the normal range. Scott and Stone concluded that the most surprising feature of their results was that the group profile of the wives was unexpectedly normal, especially since the wives had been through substantial turmoil because of the incest. Likewise, Groff concluded that his study results did not support previous characterizations of the incest offenders' wives as being withdrawn, depressed, dependent, and inadequate. Birns and Meyer (1993) suggested that the continuing attempts to find evidence that the wife is a coperpetrator, instead of a covictim, are the result of limited and biased traditional theoretical approaches to understanding the mother's role in the family.

At present, existing data on differences between the incest offenders' wives and comparison groups are mixed and inconclusive. It is apparent, however, that extant data do not support the view that a single profile exists for the male incest offender's wife. Even if evidence is found for some personality differences (e.g., depression, low self-esteem), the high levels of childhood abuse and current spousal abuse experienced by the sex offenders' wives may produce these differences and represent victim effects. Thus, if personality differences are found, the causal contributions of the wives' characteristics to the child sexual abuse still must be demonstrated.

Family Characteristics

Historically, families of identified intrafamilial child sexual abusers have been characterized as living in overcrowded and substandard housing (Maisch, 1972; Mrazek, 1980). Offenders and family members were observed to have less education than those in a comparison group (Julian, Mohr, & Lapp, 1980). Among reported cases, lower SES has been related to child sexual abuse (e.g., Paveza, 1988), and biological father offenders, compared to stepfather offenders, have been found more frequently to have insufficient incomes (Gordon, 1989). However, epidemiological studies of sexual abuse in the general population, which include unreported cases, do not support the view that child sexual abuse rates are markedly higher among lower SES families in the United States (Finkelhor & Baron, 1986) and in Great Britain (Baker & Duncan, 1985).

Other family characteristics include family dysfunction (Brooks, 1982), family isolation (Herman & Hirschman, 1981; Justice & Justice, 1976; Renvozie, 1982), and fear of family separation (Gutheil & Avery, 1977; Lustig, Dresser, Spellman, & Murray, 1966). As part of the family dysfunction, there may be role confusion or role reversal (Justice & Justice, 1976; Spencer, 1978), and parent–child interactions may be undifferentiated from adult–adult interactions. Marital problems include marital conflicts and violence (Paveza, 1988; Truesdell et al., 1986). Biological father offenders, compared to stepfather offenders, have been reported to have more marital problems (Gordon, 1989). Offenders report a lack of support from their spouse and sexual problems with their spouse (Lang et al., 1990; Mrazek & Kempe, 1981; Renvozie, 1982; Vander May & Neff, 1982). It is also possible that as a result of marital difficulties and the previously mentioned role confusion, offenders turn to their children for fulfillment of their unmet needs. Finally, some authors have reported that other family members, including the nonabusive parent, are frequently absent from the household for substantial amounts of time (e.g., for work), which increases the opportunity for child sexual abuse by the offending parent (Maisch, 1972; Vander May & Neff, 1982).

SUMMARY OF FINDINGS

Parents who physically abuse their children are more likely to be single, young, and nonbiological parents. Physically abusive parents, compared to nonabusive parents, more often report childhood maltreatment and dysfunction in their family of origin. Although childhood maltreatment and lower SES are associated with risk for child physical abuse in both reported cases and general population surveys, most parents who have a childhood history of maltreatment or who are poor do not physically abuse their children. This suggests (and data indicate) that history of abuse and lower SES covary with other factors that are related to child physical abuse. In addition, data indicate that physically abusive parents show more physiological reactivity to child-related stimuli, with some indications that their increased reactivity extends to non-child-related stressful stimuli. It is less clear whether abusive parents have neuropsychological deficits that may disrupt processing of child-related information.

Physically abusive parents have low self-esteem, lack feelings of personal worth, and exhibit an external locus of control. They display inappropriate expectations, especially in situations involving complex child behavior. Likewise, in some contexts (e.g., everyday living situations and ambiguous situations), abusive parents perceive more negative child behaviors than do other reporters or observers. Also, in some contexts (especially negative behaviors), abusive parents make different attributions to children's behavior, with abusers, compared to nonabusers, attributing more blame and hostile intent to the child when judging the child's behavior. Fairly uniform are observations that physically abusive parents, relative to comparison parents, show less empathy in their responses to children.

Many, albeit not all, studies indicate that physically abusive parents have more life stress. More uniform are the findings that abusive parents report more personal distress. In addition, offenders, compared to matched nonoffenders, report more negative affect, such as anxiety, depression, anger, and hostility. Reports of increased negative affectivity have been associated with increased levels of physiological reactivity in abusers' responses to a crying child. Finally, abusive parents, compared to nonabusive parents, report more isolation and feelings of loneliness and appear to be less able to make use of individual and community resources. Drug use has been associated with child physical abuse and may be an important factor in severe abuse. However, drug use does not appear to be a factor in the majority of child physical abuse cases.

In terms of parenting behavior, abusive parents, compared to nonabusive parents, engage in less communication and interact less with their children. When they do interact, they are more intrusive and inconsistent. Although the data are mixed, abusive parents appear to use more harsh disciplinary techniques. What is relatively uniform are reports that physically abusive parents use fewer positive behaviors. For example, they use less reasoning and explaining and fewer rewards in the management of their children's behavior. Current family risk factors are similar to the individual risk factors already mentioned and include the lack of resources and large numbers of family stressors. In addition to the child abuse, abusive families have more verbal and physical conflict among family members. Abusive and high-risk families, relative to comparison families, also have less cohesion, less expressiveness, and more isolation.

In the case of incest, the offender tends to be a male (more likely a stepfather than a father). Many incest offenders come from families that were abusive or failed to provide a nurturing environment. Although far from conclusive, the literature suggests that childhood physical abuse may be more common than childhood sexual abuse in incest offenders. Also important is the observation that most incest offenders do not appear to have a childhood history of sexual abuse. The incest offender tends to have a variety of interpersonal problems. He has been reported to be socially withdrawn, lonely, unhappy, suspicious, low in self-esteem, distressed, antisocial, and, perhaps, a drug user. However, several controlled studies have failed to find that incest offenders differ from normals on traditional measures of psychopathology, and the degree to which drug use plays a role in incest behavior is unclear. Likewise, the degree to which incest overlaps with other paraphilias is unknown. Some researchers have reported that the majority of incest offenders have additional paraphilias, whereas others have indicated that the co-occurrence of additional clinically identifiable paraphilias in incest offenders is infrequent. In addition, although early studies suggested that incest offenders displayed deviant patterns of sexual arousal toward children, the bulk of the recent literature suggests that the sexual arousal patterns of incest offenders (unlike those of extrafamilial child molesters) are not substantially different from normal patterns (on a group basis).

Although the data are inconclusive, some studies have reported that incest offenders have cognitive distortions related to the incestuous behavior. In addition, incest offenders appear to lack early child care experiences. With respect to their feelings about their children, a popular belief has been that incest offenders lack empathy for their victims. This belief has resulted in victim empathy training becoming one of the most frequently used sex offender interventions in the United States. However, the data supporting empathy differences in incest offenders are inconclusive. Part of the lack of consistent findings may be due to the fact that empathy is a complex construct with several components (e.g., perspective taking, emotional reaction) and is measured in a variety of ways. Furthermore, apart from a consideration of dispositional empathy, situational empathy differences may be observed in one context but not in another. Given the importance placed on victim empathy training in the treatment of sex offenders, additional research is needed on this issue.

Although lower SES has been associated with incest among reported cases, surveys of incest cases in the general population have not found incest to be associated with SES. This finding suggests that a bias exists wherein cases of incest in lower SES families are more likely to be reported. With respect to the incest offender's wife, the data are mixed as to the presence of any particular personality characteristic. What is evident is that no single personality profile of incest offenders' wives has emerged, with a number of studies concluding that group data show incest offenders' wives to score in the normal range on a number of scales. In the family of the incest offender, an array of problems have been reported. Family dysfunction, including marital problems, is likely, with role reversal and role confusion reported.

CONCLUSION

Although the reader may note similarities in the characteristics of child physical and child sexual abusers, comparisons must be made with caution because the data on child physical abuse are based almost entirely on cases involving mothers and the incest data are based on male offenders. In comparing reviews of the two phenomena, it can be said that, relative to child physical abuse, the incest literature is underdeveloped, which suggests that the increase in focus on child sexual abuse that has occurred over the past decade is warranted. Furthermore, although there are problems that are generic to any study of child physical and sexual abuse, the quality of extant research in the child physical abuse area is superior. Finally, with respect to child sexual abuse, perhaps the most surprising finding of this chapter is that many commonly held beliefs about incest have not been uniformly supported by recent research, such as its relationship to lower SES status, its assumed strong relationship with a childhood history of sexual abuse (as opposed to child physical abuse), its assumed relationship to a single abuser profile (e.g., on the MMPI), its relationship to lack of empathy for the victim, and its relationship to deviant sexual arousal for children.

REFERENCES

Abel, G. G., Becker, J. V., Cunningham-Rather, J., Mittelman, M., & Rouleau, J. L. (1988). Multiple paraphilic diagnoses among sex offenders. *Bulletin of the American Academy of Psychiatry and the Law, 16*, 153–168.

Abel, G. G., Gore, D. K., Holland, C. L., Camp, N., Becker, J. V., & Rathner, J. (1989). The measurement of the cognitive distortions of child molesters. *Annals of Sex Research, 2*, 135–152.

Altemeier, W. A., III., Vietze, P. M., Sherrod, K. B., Sandler, H. M., Falsey, S., & O'Connor, S. (1979). Prediction of child maltreatment during pregnancy. *Journal of the American Academy of Child Psychiatry, 18*, 205–218.

American Psychiatric Association. (1987). *Diagnostic and statistical manual of mental disorders* (3rd ed., revised). Washington, DC: Author.

Aragona, J. A. (1983). Physical child abuse: An interactional analysis (Doctoral dissertation, University of South Florida, 1983). *Dissertation Abstracts International, 44*, 1225B.

Azar, S. T., Robinson, D. R., Hekimian, E., & Twentyman, C. T. (1984). Unrealistic expectations and problem-solving ability in maltreating and comparison mothers. *Journal of Consulting and Clinical Psychology, 52*, 687–691.

Baker, A. W., & Duncan, S. P. (1985). Child sexual abuse: A study of prevalence in Great Britain. *Child Abuse & Neglect, 9*, 457–467.

Barbaree, H. E., & Marshall, W. L. (1989). Erectile responses among heterosexual child molesters, father–daughter incest offenders, and matched nonoffenders:

5 distinct age preference profiles. *Canadian Journal of Behavioural Science, 21,* 70–82.

Bauer, W. D., & Twentyman, C. T. (1985). Abusing, neglectful, and comparison mothers' responses to child-related and non-child-related stressors. *Journal of Consulting and Clinical Psychology, 53,* 335–343.

Belsky, J. (1980). Child maltreatment: An ecological integration. *American Psychologist, 35,* 320–335.

Belsky, J. (1993). Etiology of child maltreatment: A developmental–ecological analysis. *Psychological Bulletin, 114,* 413–434.

Bennett, M. H. (1980). Father–daughter incest: A psychological study of the mother from an attachment theory perspective (Doctoral dissertation, California School of Professional Psychology, 1980). *Dissertation Abstracts International, 41,* 2381B.

Birns, B., & Meyer, S. (1993). Mothers' role in incest: Dysfunctional women or dysfunctional theories? *Journal of Child Sexual Abuse, 2*(3), 127–135.

Bousha, D. M., & Twentyman, C. T. (1984). Mother–child interactional style in abuse, neglect, and control groups: Naturalistic observations in the home. *Journal of Abnormal Psychology, 93,* 106–114.

Bradley, E. J., & Peters, R. D. (1991). Physically abusive and nonabusive mothers' perceptions of parenting and child behavior. *American Journal of Orthopsychiatry, 61,* 455–460.

Briere, J., & Runtz, M. (1989). University males' sexual interest in children: Predicting potential indices of "pedophilia" in a nonforensic sample. *Child Abuse & Neglect, 13,* 65–75.

Brooks, B. (1982). Families in treatment for incest (Doctoral dissertation, University of Massachusetts, 1981). *Dissertation Abstracts International, 42,* 3408B.

Browne, K., & Saqi, S. (1988). Mother–infant interaction and attachment in physically abusing families. *Journal of Reproductive and Infant Psychology, 6,* 163–182.

Burgess, A. W., Groth, A. N., Holmstrom, L. L., & Sgroi, S. M. (1978). *Sexual assault of children and adolescents.* Lexington, MA: Lexington Books.

Burgess, R. L., & Conger, R. D. (1978). Family interaction in abusive, neglectful, and normal families. *Child Development, 49,* 1163–1173.

Caliso, J. A., & Milner, J. S. (1992). Childhood history of abuse and child abuse screening. *Child Abuse & Neglect, 16,* 647–659.

Casanova, G. M., Domanic, J., McCanne, T. R., & Milner, J. S. (1992). Physiological responses to non-child-related stressors in mothers at risk for child abuse. *Child Abuse & Neglect, 16,* 31–44.

Chilamkurti, C., & Milner, J. S. (1993). Perceptions and evaluations of child transgressions and disciplinary techniques in high- and low-risk mothers and their children. *Child Development, 64,* 1801–1814.

Cicchetti, D., & Rizley, R. (1981). Developmental perspectives on the etiology, intergenerational transmission, and sequelae of child maltreatment. In R.

Rizley & D. Cicchetti (Eds.), *Developmental perspectives on child maltreatment* (pp. 31–55). San Francisco: Jossey-Bass.

Conger, R. D., Burgess, R. L., & Barrett, C. (1979). Child abuse related to life changes and perceptions of illness: Some preliminary findings. *Family Coordinator, 28*, 73–78.

Corse, S. C., Schmid, K., & Trickett, P. T. (1990). Social network characteristics of mothers in abusing and nonabusing families and their relationships to parenting beliefs. *Journal of Community Psychology, 18*, 44–59.

Crouch, J. L., Milner, J. S., & Caliso, J. A. (1995). Childhood physical abuse, perceived social support, and socioemotional status in adult women. *Violence and Victims, 10*, 273–283.

Crowe, H. P., & Zeskind, P. S. (1992). Psychophysiological and perceptual responses to infant cries varying in pitch: Comparisons of adults with low and high scores on the Child Abuse Potential Inventory. *Child Abuse & Neglect, 1*, 279–296.

Culp, R. E., Culp, A. M., Soulis, J., & Letts, D. (1989). Self-esteem and depression in abusive, neglecting, and nonmaltreating mothers. *Infant Mental Health Journal, 10*, 243–251.

DePaul, J., Arruabarrena, I., & Milner, J. S. (1991). Validación de una versión espanola del Child Abuse Potential Inventory para su uso en España. *Child Abuse & Neglect, 15*, 495–504.

Disbrow, M. A., Doerr, H. O., & Caulfield, C. (1977). Measuring the components of parents' potential for child abuse and neglect. *Child Abuse & Neglect, 1*, 279–296.

Egeland, B., Breitenbucher, M., & Rosenberg, D. (1980). Prospective study of the significance of life stress in the etiology of child abuse. *Journal of Consulting and Clinical Psychology, 48*, 194–205.

Egeland, B., Jacobvitz, D., & Papatola, K. (1987). Intergenerational continuity of abuse. In R. Gelles & J. Lancaster (Eds.), *Child abuse and neglect: Biosocial dimensions* (pp. 225–276). Chicago: Aldine.

Egeland, B., Jacobvitz, D., & Sroufe, L. A. (1988). Breaking the cycle of abuse. *Child Development, 59*, 1080–1088.

Egeland, B., & Sroufe, L. A. (1981). Attachment and early maltreatment. *Child Development, 52*, 44–52.

Elliott, F. A. (1988). Neurological factors. In V. B. Van Hasselt, R. L. Morrison, A. S. Bellack, & M. Hersen (Eds.), *Handbook of family violence* (pp. 359–382). New York: Plenum Press.

Erickson, W. D., Walbek, N. H., & Seely, R. K. (1987). The life histories and psychological profiles of 59 incestuous stepfathers. *Bulletin of the American Academy of Psychiatry and the Law, 15*, 349–357.

Evans, A. L. (1980). Personality characteristics and disciplinary attitudes of child-abusing mothers. *Child Abuse & Neglect, 4*, 179–187.

Faller, K. C. (1989). Why sexual abuse? An exploration of the intergenerational hypothesis. *Child Abuse & Neglect, 13*, 543–548.

Finkelhor, D. (1994). The international epidemiology of child sexual abuse. *Child Abuse & Neglect, 18*, 409–417.

Finkelhor, D., & Baron, L. (1986). Risk factors for child sexual abuse. *Journal of Interpersonal Violence, 1*, 43–71.

Finkelhor, D., Hotaling, G., Lewis, I. A., & Smith, C. (1990). Sexual abuse in a national survey of adult men and women: Prevalence, characteristics, and risk factors. *Child Abuse & Neglect, 14*, 19–28.

Frenzel, R. R., & Lang, R. A. (1989). Identifying sexual preferences in intrafamilial and extrafamilial child sexual abusers. *Annals of Sex Research, 2*, 255–275.

Freund, K. (1990). Courtship disorder. In W. L. Marshall, D. R. Laws, & H. E. Barbaree (Eds.), *Handbook of sexual assault: Issues, theories, and treatment of the offender* (pp. 195–207). New York: Plenum Press.

Friedrich, W. N., Tyler, J. D., & Clark, J. A. (1985). Personality and psychophysiological variables in abusive, neglectful, and low-income control mothers. *Journal of Nervous and Mental Disease, 173*, 449–460.

Frodi, A. M., & Lamb, M. E. (1980). Child abusers' responses to infant smiles and cries. *Child Development, 51*, 238–241.

Gaines, R., Sandgrund, A., Green, A. H., & Power, E. (1978). Etiological factors in child maltreatment: A multivariate study of abusing, neglecting, and normal mothers. *Journal of Abnormal Psychology, 87*, 531–540.

Gelles, R. J. (1989). Child abuse and violence in single-parent families: Parent absence and economic deprivation. *American Journal of Orthopsychiatry, 59*, 492–501.

Goodwin, J., McCarthy, T., & DiVasto, P. (1981). Prior incest in mothers of abused children. *Child Abuse & Neglect, 5*, 87–95.

Gordon, M. (1989). The family environment of sexual abuse: A comparison of natal and stepfather abuse. *Child Abuse & Neglect, 13*, 121–130.

Groff, M. G. (1987). Characteristics of incest offenders' wives. *Journal of Sex Research, 23*, 91–96.

Groff, M. G., & Hubble, L. M. (1984). A comparison of father–daughter and stepfather–daughter incest. *Criminal Justice and Behavior, 11*, 461–475.

Gudjonsson, G. H. (1990). Cognitive distortions and blame attributions among paedophiles. *Sexual and Marital Therapy, 5*, 183–185.

Gutheil, T. G., & Avery, N. C. (1977). Multiple overt incest as a defense against family loss. *Family Process, 16*, 105–116.

Hall, G. C. N., & Hirschman, R. (1992). Sexual aggression against children: A conceptual perspective of etiology. *Criminal Justice and Behavior, 19*, 8–23.

Hansen, D. J., Pallotta, G. M., Tishelman, A. C., Conaway, L. P., & MacMillan, V. M. (1989). Parental problem-solving skills and child behavior problems: A comparison of physically abusive, neglectful, clinic, and community families. *Journal of Family Violence, 4*, 353–368.

Hanson, R. F., Lipovsky, J. A., & Saunders, B. E. (1994). Characteristics of fathers of incest families. *Journal of Interpersonal Violence, 9*, 155–169.

Hayashino, D. S., Wurtele, S. K., & Klebe, K. J. (1995). Child molesters: An examination of cognitive factors. *Journal of Interpersonal Violence, 10,* 106–116.

Herman, J. L., & Hirschman, L. (1981). *Father–daughter incest.* Cambridge, MA: Harvard University Press.

Herrenkohl, E. C., Herrenkohl, R. C., & Toedter, L. J. (1983). Perspectives on the intergenerational transmission of abuse. In D. Finkelhor, R. J. Gelles, G. T. Hotaling, & M. A. Straus (Eds.), *The dark side of families: Current family violence research* (pp. 306–316). Beverly Hills, CA: Sage.

Herrenkohl, E. C., Herrenkohl, R. C., Toedter, L., & Yanushefski, A. M. (1984). Parent–child interaction in abusive and nonabusive families. *Journal of the American Academy of Child Psychiatry, 23,* 641–648.

Hindman, J. (1988). Research disputes assumptions about child molesters. *NDAA Bulletin, 7,* 1–3.

Hunter, J. A., Childers, S. E., Gerald, R., & Esmaili, H. (1990). An examination of variables differentiating clinical subtypes of incestuous child molesters. *International Journal of Offender Therapy and Comparative Criminology, 34,* 95–104.

Hunter, R. S., Kilstrom, N., Kraybill, E. N., & Loda, F. (1978). Antecedents of child abuse and neglect in premature infants: A prospective study in a newborn intensive care unit. *Pediatrics, 61,* 629–635.

Jason, J., & Andereck, N. D. (1983). Fatal child abuse in Georgia: The epidemiology of severe physical child abuse. *Child Abuse & Neglect, 7,* 1–9.

Julian, V., Mohr, C., & Lapp, L. (1980). Father–daughter incest. In W. Holder (Ed.), *Sexual abuse of children: Implications for treatment* (pp. 17–35). Englewood, CO: American Humane Association.

Justice, B., & Calvert, A. (1990). Family environment factors associated with child abuse. *Psychological Reports, 66,* 458.

Justice, B., & Justice, R. (1976). *The abusing family.* New York: Human Sciences Press.

Kaufman, J., & Zigler, E. (1987). Do abused children become abusive parents? *American Journal of Orthopsychiatry, 57,* 186–192.

Kelleher, K., Chaffin, M., Hollenberg, J., & Fischer, E. (1994). Alcohol and drug disorders among physically abusive and neglectful parents in a community-based sample. *American Journal of Public Health, 84,* 1586–1590.

Kirkland, K., & Bauer, C. (1982). MMPI traits of incestuous fathers. *Journal of Clinical Psychology, 38,* 645–649.

Knight, R. A. (1989). An assessment of the concurrent validity of a child molester typology. *Journal of Interpersonal Violence, 4,* 131–150.

Knight, R. A., Carter, D. L., & Prentky, R. A. (1989). A system for the classification of child molesters: Reliability and application. *Journal of Interpersonal Violence, 4,* 3–23.

Knopp, F. H., Freeman-Longo, R., & Stevenson, W. F. (1992). *Nationwide survey of juvenile & adult sex-offender treatment programs & models*. Orwell, VT: The Safer Society Program.

Knutson, J. F. (1978). Child abuse as an area of aggression research. *Journal of Pediatric Psychology, 3*, 20–27.

Kravitz, R. I., & Driscoll, J. M. (1983). Expectations for childhood development among child-abusing and nonabusing parents. *American Journal of Orthopsychiatry, 53*, 336–344.

Lahey, B. B., Conger, R. D., Atkeson, B. M., & Treiber, F. A. (1984). Parenting behavior and emotional status of physically abusive mothers. *Journal of Consulting and Clinical Psychology, 52*, 1062–1071.

Lang, R. A., Black, E. L., Frenzel, R. R., & Checkley, K. L. (1988). Aggression and erotic attraction toward children in incestuous and pedophilic men. *Annals of Sex Research, 1*, 417–441.

Lang, R. A., Flor-Henry, P., & Frenzel, R. R. (1990). Sex hormone profiles in pedophilic and incestuous men. *Annals of Sex Research, 3*, 59–74.

Langevin, R. (1993). A comparison of neuroendocrine and genetic factors in homosexuality and in pedophilia. *Annals of Sex Research, 6*, 67–76.

Langevin, R., Handy, L., Day, D., & Russon, A. (1985). Are incestuous fathers pedophilic, aggressive, and alcoholic? In R. Langevin (Ed.), *Erotic preference, gender identity, and aggression in men* (pp. 161–180). Hillsdale, NJ: Erlbaum.

Langevin, R., Paitich, D., Freeman, R., Mann, K., & Handy, L. (1978). Personality characteristics and sexual anomalies in males. *Canadian Journal of Behavioural Science, 10*, 222–237.

Langevin, R., Wortzman, G., Dickey, R., Wright, P., & Handy, L. (1988). Neuropsychological impairment of incest offenders. *Annals of Sex Research, 1*, 401–415.

Langevin, R., Wortzman, G., Wright, P., & Handy, L. (1989). Studies of brain damage and dysfunction in sex offenders. *Annals of Sex Research, 2*, 163–179.

Larrance, D. T., & Twentyman, C. T. (1983). Maternal attributions and child abuse. *Journal of Abnormal Psychology, 92*, 449–457.

Lawson, K. A., & Hays, J. R. (1989). Self-esteem and stress as factors in abuse of children. *Psychological Reports, 65*, 1259–1265.

Leonard, K. E., & Jacob, T. (1988). Alcohol, alcoholism, and family violence. In V. B. Van Hasselt, R. L. Morrison, A. S. Bellack, & M. Hersen (Eds.), *Handbook of family violence* (pp. 383–406). New York: Plenum Press.

Letourneau, C. (1981). Empathy and stress: How they affect parental aggression. *Social Work, 26*, 383–389.

Lightcap, J. L., Kurland, J. A., & Burgess, R. L. (1982). Child abuse: A test of some predictions from evolutionary theory. *Ethology and Sociobiology, 3*, 61–67.

Litty, C. G., Kowalski, R., & Minor, S. (1996). Moderating effects of physical abuse and perceived social support on the potential to abuse. *Child Abuse & Neglect, 20*, 305–314.

Lustig, N., Dresser, J., Spellman, S., & Murray, T. (1966). Incest: A family group survival pattern. *Archives of General Psychiatry, 14,* 31–40.

Lyons-Ruth, K., Connell, D. B., Zoll, D., & Stahl, J. (1987). Infants at social risk: Relations among infant maltreatment, maternal behavior, and infant attachment behavior. *Developmental Psychology, 23,* 223–232.

Maisch, H. (1972). *Incest.* New York: Stein & Day.

Marshall, W. L., Barbaree, H. E., & Christophe, D. (1986). Sexual offenders against female children: Sex preferences for age of victims and type of behavior. *Canadian Journal of Behavioural Science, 18,* 424–439.

Marshall, W. L., Barbaree, H. E., & Eccles, A. (1991). Early onset and deviant sexuality in child molesters. *Journal of Interpersonal Violence, 6,* 323–336.

Marshall, W. L., Jones, R., Hudson, S. M., & McDonald, E. (1993). Generalized empathy in child molesters. *Journal of Child Sexual Abuse, 2*(4), 61–68.

Martinez, P., & Richters, J. E. (1993). The NIMH community violence project: II. Children's distress symptoms associated with violence exposure. *Psychiatry, 56,* 22–35.

Mash, E. J., Johnston, C., & Kovitz, K. (1983). A comparison of the mother–child interactions of physically abused and non-abused children during play and task situations. *Journal of Clinical Child Psychology, 12,* 337–346.

McCanne, T. R., & Milner, J. S. (1991). Psychophysiological reactivity of physically abusive and at-risk subjects to child-related stimuli. In J. S. Milner (Ed.), *Neuropsychology of aggression* (pp. 147–166). Norwell, MA: Kluwer Academic.

Melnick, B., & Hurley, J. R. (1969). Distinctive personality attributes of child-abusing mothers. *Journal of Consulting and Clinical Psychology, 33,* 746–749.

Milner, J. S. (1989). Additional cross-validation of the Child Abuse Potential Inventory. *Psychological Assessment, 1,* 219–223.

Milner, J. S. (1993). Social information processing and physical child abuse. *Clinical Psychology Review, 13,* 275–294.

Milner, J. S. (1994, September). *Empathy and early child care behavior in intrafamilial sexual child abusers.* Poster presented at the meeting of the International Congress on Child Abuse and Neglect, Kuala Lumpur, Malaysia.

Milner, J. S., & Foody, R. (1994). The impact of mitigating information on attributions for positive and negative child behavior by adults at low- and high-risk of child abusive behavior. *Journal of Social and Clinical Psychology, 13,* 335–351.

Milner, J. S., Halsey, L. B., & Fultz, J. (1995). Empathic responsiveness and affective reactivity to infant stimuli in high- and low-risk for physical child abuse mothers. *Child Abuse & Neglect, 19,* 767–780.

Milner, J. S., & McCanne, T. R. (1991). Neuropsychological correlates of physical child abuse. In J. S. Milner (Ed.), *Neuropsychology of aggression* (pp. 131–145). Norwell, MA: Kluwer Academic.

Milner, J. S., & Murphy, W. D. (1995). Assessment of child physical and sexual abuse offenders. *Family Relations, 44,* 478–488.

Milner, J. S., & Robertson, K. R. (1990). Comparison of physical child abusers, intrafamilial sexual child abusers, and child neglecters. *Journal of Interpersonal Violence, 5,* 37–48.

Milner, J. S., Robertson, K. R., & Rogers, D. L. (1990). Childhood history of abuse and adult child abuse potential. *Journal of Family Violence, 5,* 15–34.

Milner, J. S., & Wimberley, R. C. (1980). Prediction and explanation of child abuse. *Journal of Clinical Psychology, 36,* 875–884.

Mollerstrom, W. W., Patchner, M. A., & Milner, J. S. (1992). Family functioning and child abuse potential. *Journal of Clinical Psychology, 48,* 445–454.

Mrazek, P. B. (1980). Sexual abuse of children. *Journal of Child Psychology & Psychiatry & Allied Disciplines, 21,* 91–95.

Mrazek, P. B., & Kempe, C. H. (Eds.). (1981). *Sexually abused children and their families.* New York: Pergamon Press.

Murphy, W. D. (1990). Assessment and modification of cognitive distortions in sex offenders. In W. L. Laws, D. R. Laws, & H. E. Barbaree (Eds.), *Handbook of sexual assault* (pp. 331–342). New York: Plenum Press.

Murphy, W. D., Haynes, M. R., Stalgaitis, S. J., & Flanagan, B. (1986). Differential sexual responding among four groups of sexual offenders against children. *Journal of Psychopathology and Behavioral Assessment, 8,* 339–353.

Nayak, M., & Milner, J. S. (1996). *Neuropsychological functioning: Comparison of parents at high- and low-risk for child physical abuse.* Manuscript submitted for publication.

Oates, R. K., & Forrest, D. (1985). Self-esteem and early background of abusive mothers. *Child Abuse & Neglect, 9,* 89–93.

Oates, R. K., Forrest, D., & Peacock, A. (1985). Mothers of abused children: A comparison study. *Clinical Pediatrics, 24,* 9–13.

Olsen, L. J., & Holmes, W. M. (1986). Youth at risk: Adolescents and maltreatment. *Children and Youth Services Review, 8,* 13–35.

Osofsky, J. D. (1995). The effects of exposure to violence on young children. *American Psychologist, 50,* 782–788.

Panton, J. H. (1979). MMPI profile configurations associated with incestuous families and non-incestuous child molesting. *Psychological Reports, 45,* 335–338.

Parker, H., & Parker, S. (1986). Father–daughter sexual abuse: An emerging perspective. *American Journal of Orthopsychiatry, 56,* 531–549.

Paveza, G. J. (1988). Risk factors in father–daughter child sexual abuse: A case-control study. *Journal of Interpersonal Violence, 3,* 290–306.

Perry, M. A., Wells, E. A., & Doran, L. D. (1983). Parent characteristics in abusing and non-abusing families. *Journal of Clinical Child Psychology, 12,* 329–336.

Pianta, R., Egeland, B., & Erickson, M. F. (1989). The antecedents of maltreatment: Results of the Mother–Child Interaction Research Project. In D. Cicchetti & V. Carlson (Eds.), *Child maltreatment: Theory and research on the causes and consequences of child abuse and neglect* (pp. 203–253). Cambridge, England: Cambridge University Press.

Prentky, R. A., Knight, R. A., Rosenberg, R., & Lee, A. (1989). A path analytic approach to the validation of a taxonomic system for classifying child molesters. *Journal of Quantitative Criminology, 5,* 231–257.

Pruitt, D. L., & Erickson, M. R. (1985). The Child Abuse Potential Inventory: A study of concurrent validity. *Journal of Clinical Psychology, 41,* 104–111.

PsycLIT [Database]. (1987–1994). Washington, DC.: American Psychological Association [Producer]. Available from: SilverPlatter [Distributor].

Reid, J. B., Kavanagh, K., & Baldwin, D. V. (1987). Abusive parents' perceptions of child problem behaviors: An example of parental bias. *Journal of Abnormal Child Psychology, 15,* 457–466.

Renshaw, D. C. (1982). *Incest: Understanding and treatment.* Boston: Little, Brown.

Renvozie, J. (1982). *Incest: A family pattern.* London: Routledge & Kegan Paul.

Richters, J. E., & Martinez, P. (1993). The NIMH community violence project: I. Children as victims of and witnesses to violence. *Psychiatry, 56,* 7–21.

Rosen, B. (1978). Self-concept disturbance among mothers who abuse their children. *Psychological Reports, 43,* 323–326.

Rosenberg, M. S., & Reppucci, N. D. (1983). Abusive mothers: Perceptions of their own and their children's behavior. *Journal of Consulting and Clinical Psychology, 51,* 674–682.

Russell, D. E. (1984). The prevalence and seriousness of incestuous abuse: Stepfathers vs. biological fathers. *Child Abuse & Neglect, 8,* 15–22.

Schmidt, E., & Eldridge, A. (1986). The attachment relationship and child maltreatment. *Infant Mental Health Journal, 7,* 264–273.

Scott, R. L., & Stone, D. A. (1986). MMPI profile constellations in incest families. *Journal of Consulting and Clinical Psychology, 54,* 364–368.

Seghorn, T. K., Prentky, R. A., & Boucher, R. J. (1987). Childhood sexual abuse in the lives of sexually aggressive offenders. *Journal of the American Academy of Child and Adolescent Psychiatry, 26,* 262–267.

Serin, R. C., Malcolm, P. B., Khanna, A., & Barbaree, H. E. (1994). Psychopathy and deviant sexual arousal in incarcerated sexual offenders. *Journal of Interpersonal Violence, 9,* 3–11.

Shorkey, C. T. (1980). Sense of personal worth, self-esteem, and anomia of child-abusing mothers and controls. *Journal of Clinical Psychology, 36,* 817–820.

Shorkey, C. T., & Armendariz, J. (1985). Personal worth, self-esteem, anomia, hostility and irrational thinking of abusing mothers: A multivariate approach. *Journal of Clinical Psychology, 41,* 414–421.

Simari, C., & Baskin, D. (1980). Incest: No longer a family affair. *Child Psychiatric Quarterly, 13,* 36–51.

Spencer, J. (1978). Father–daughter incest: A clinical view from the corrections field. *Child Welfare, 57,* 581–590.

Spinetta, J. J. (1978). Parental personality factors in child abuse. *Journal of Consulting and Clinical Psychology, 46,* 1409–1414.

Starr, R. H., Jr. (1982). A research-based approach to the prediction of child abuse.

In R. H. Starr, Jr. (Ed.), *Child abuse prediction: Policy implications* (pp. 105–134). Cambridge, MA: Ballinger.

Starr, R. H., Jr. (1988). Physical abuse of children. In V. B. Van Hasselt, R. L. Morrison, A. S. Bellack, & M. Hersen (Eds.), *Handbook of family violence* (pp. 119–155). New York: Plenum Press.

Steele, B. F., & Pollock, C. B. (1974). A psychiatric study of parents who abuse infants and small children. In R. E. Helfer & C. H. Kempe (Eds.), *The battered child* (2nd ed., pp. 92–139). Chicago: University of Chicago Press.

Stermac, L. E., & Segal, Z. V. (1989). Adult sexual contact with children: An examination of cognitive factors. *Behavior Therapy, 20*, 573–584.

Straus, M. A., Gelles, R. J., & Steinmetz, S. K. (1980). *Behind closed doors: Violence in the American family.* New York: Doubleday/Anchor.

Stringer, S. A., & LaGreca, A. M. (1985). Correlates of child abuse potential. *Journal of Abnormal Child Psychology, 13*, 217–226.

Susman, E. J., Trickett, P. K., Iannotti, R. J., Hollenbeck, B. E., & Zahn-Waxler, C. (1985). Child-rearing patterns in depressed, abusive, and normal mothers. *American Journal of Orthopsychiatry, 55*, 237–251.

Trickett, P. K., & Kuczynski, L. (1986). Children's misbehaviors and parental discipline strategies in abusive and nonabusive families. *Developmental Psychology, 22*, 115–123.

Trickett, P. K., & Susman, E. J. (1988). Parental perceptions of child-rearing practices in physically abusive and nonabusive families. *Developmental Psychology, 24*, 270–276.

Trickett, P. K., & Susman, E. J. (1989). Perceived similarities and disagreements about childrearing practices in abusive and nonabusive families: Intergenerational and concurrent family processes. In D. Cicchetti & V. Carlson (Eds.), *Child maltreatment: Theory and research on the causes and consequences of child abuse and neglect* (pp. 280–301). Cambridge, England: Cambridge University Press.

Truesdell, D. L., McNeil, J. S., & Deschner, J. P. (1986). Incidence of wife abuse in incestuous families. *Social Work, 31*, 138–140.

Twentyman, C. T., & Plotkin, R. C. (1982). Unrealistic expectations of parents who maltreat their children: An educational deficit that pertains to child maltreatment. *Journal of Clinical Psychology, 38*, 497–503.

Vander May, B. J., & Neff, R. L. (1982). Adult–child incest: A review of research and treatment. *Adolescence, 17*, 717–735.

Vasta, R. (1982). Physical child abuse: A dual-component analysis. *Developmental Review, 2*, 125–149.

Wald, B. K., Archer, R. P., & Winstead, B. A. (1990). Rorschach characteristics of mothers of incest victims. *Journal of Personality Assessment, 55*, 417–425.

Walters, G. D. (1987). Child sex offenders and rapists in the military prison setting. *International Journal of Offender Therapy and Comparative Criminology, 31*, 261–269.

Widom, C. S. (1989). Does violence beget violence? A critical examination of the literature. *Psychological Bulletin, 106,* 3–28.

Wiehe, V. R. (1986). Empathy and locus of control in child abusers. *Journal of Social Service Research, 9,* 17–30.

Williams, L. M., & Finkelhor, D. (1989). The characteristics of incestuous fathers: A review of recent studies. In W. L. Marshall, D. R. Laws, & H. E. Barbaree (Eds.), *Handbook of sexual assault: Issues, theories, and treatment of the offender* (pp. 231–255). New York: Plenum Press.

Williams, L. M., & Finkelhor, D. (1995). Parental caregiving and incest: Test of a biosocial model. *American Journal of Orthopsychiatry, 65,* 101–113.

Wilson, G. D., & Cox, D. N. (1983). Personality of paedophile club members. *Personality and Individual Differences, 4,* 323–329.

Wolfe, D. A., Edwards, B., Manion, I., & Koverola, C. (1988). Early interventions for parents at risk of child abuse and neglect: A preliminary investigation. *Journal of Consulting and Clinical Psychology, 56,* 40–47.

Wolfe, D. A., Fairbank, J. A., Kelly, J. A., & Bradlyn, A. S. (1983). Child abusive parents' physiological responses to stressful and non-stressful behavior in children. *Behavioral Assessment, 5,* 363–371.

Wood-Shuman, S., & Cone, J. D. (1986). Differences in abusive, at-risk for abuse, and control mothers' descriptions of normal child behavior. *Child Abuse & Neglect, 10,* 397–405.

Wright, L. (1976). The "sick but slick" syndrome as a personality component of parents of battered children. *Journal of Clinical Psychology, 32,* 41–45.

Wright, P., Nobrega, J., Langevin, R., & Wortzman, G. (1990). Brain density and symmetry in pedophilic and sexually aggressive offenders. *Annals of Sex Research, 3,* 319–328.

7

VIOLENCE WITHIN THE NEIGHBORHOOD AND COMMUNITY

SUSAN P. LIMBER AND MAURY A. NATION

Recent studies have indicated that juveniles are victims of violence in alarming numbers. The U.S. Advisory Board on Child Abuse and Neglect announced in its first report that "each year *hundreds of thousands* of [children] are ... being starved and abandoned, burned and severely beaten, raped and sodomized, berated and belittled" (1990, p. 2). Children suffer at the hands of family members, friends, and strangers; they are victimized by adults and by their own peers. In 1990, 2.4 million cases of suspected child maltreatment were recorded; by 1993, the toll had reached nearly 3 million (McCurdy & Daro, 1993). A study of first and second graders in Washington, DC, found that nearly 1 in 5 had been a victim of violence and 61% had witnessed violence within their community (Richters & Martinez, 1993). Homicide has become the fourth leading cause of death among children under the age of 15 in the United States (Sorenson & Bowie, 1994) and is the leading cause of death among African-American youths (National Research Council, 1993). Frequently, homicide or other violent crimes are perpetrated by children against other children, as evidenced in high rates (and lethality) of gang violence (Goldstein & Soriano, 1994) and other forms of youth-on-youth violence in recent years. In many communities, the barrage of threats to children's safety creates an environment that is "socially toxic" (Garbarino, 1995) for families and children. Such realizations have led researchers, policy-makers, parents, and child advocates to seek answers to questions about the causes of violence against children.

Research investigating causes of violence has followed three traditions: (a) research that focuses on individual-level risk factors, (b) research that emphasizes situational factors related to violence, and (c) research that examines ecological correlates of violence. The result of individual-level research has been the identification of several demographic and psychological characteristics (e.g., race, age, gender) that indicate a particular risk for violence perpetration and victimization (for a review, see Sampson & Lauritsen, 1993). An emerging interest in the area of situational factors includes the qualitative study of the interaction between individuals and the immediate environments that have produced violence. Research using this approach is relatively difficult to conduct owing to the complex nature of situations and lack of conceptual clarity concerning what constitutes situational factors. However, studies in this area have indicated that factors such as gun availability and the presence of alcohol and drugs have some impact on the occurrence of violence.

Researchers have identified a fairly consistent set of community characteristics that are related to the prevalence of crime and violence. In contrast to the other traditions, however, studies of community variables focus on rates of violent offenses as opposed to individual motivations or behavior. The purpose of these studies is not to suggest that communities are direct causes of individual behavior but to determine the characteristics of these geographic areas that might contribute to higher levels of violence.

In this chapter, we first discuss definitional issues related to community-level research. We then review empirical studies of the impact of neighborhood and community characteristics on violence against children, as evidenced by child maltreatment and other acts of violence within the community. Finally, we summarize several theories that attempt to explain neighborhood and community causes of violence against children and discuss methodological issues that challenge current and future macrolevel studies of this phenomenon.

DEFINITIONS OF NEIGHBORHOOD AND COMMUNITY

The terms *neighborhood* and *community* commonly are used by researchers to define boundaries of areas of study. There are numerous "objective" definitions of neighborhood and community, such as physical areas bounded by landmarks (e.g., housing complex, subdivisions), spatial areas defined by political boundaries (e.g., wards, census tracts), and catchment areas defined by economic and social behavior of residents (e.g., school districts, metropolitan statistical areas). However, none of these definitions necessarily correspond to residents' perceptions of a neighborhood or community. Phenomenological definitions, although more ecologically valid, tend to vary from person to person and therefore are less frequently studied. Often a distinction is made between the terms *community* and *neighborhood*, with *neighborhood* referring to a more intimate setting involving daily interaction (Barry, 1994). However, the lack of consensual definitions of these terms has made it difficult for community members and scientists to distinguish between them reliably. As a result, various levels of aggregation were used in the studies reviewed in this chapter (including census tracts, community areas, and cities).

EARLY STUDIES OF CAUSES OF VIOLENCE

The study of community correlates of violence is rooted in the study of delinquency rates. Although studies of the geographic distribution of crime can be traced back to the 19th century (see Levin & Lindesmith, 1937, for examples), research in the United States began in the early 20th century at the University of Chicago. One of the first significant steps toward the development of the ecological theories of crime was taken by Park and Burgess (1925), who agreed that social problems within Chicago varied systematically by neighborhood. They proposed that the highest rates of violence and other social problems were in the central business district, with rates decreasing gradually the further the neighborhood was from the center of the city.

The most significant early work on the relationship between communities and crime may be the series of studies on juvenile delinquency conducted by Shaw and McKay (1942, 1969). These studies traced the development and distribution of juvenile delinquency (on the basis of police arrest, court appearances, and convictions) in Chicago between 1900 and the 1960s. In addition to looking at the prevalence of delinquency, these authors related the rates of delinquency to development of the urban areas and population characteristics. The results of these analyses set a new standard for the study of contextual factors related to crime, and the work can be credited with several findings that drove the development of future research.

First, Shaw and McKay (1942, 1969) observed that rates of delinquency were highest in neighborhoods in the central areas of the city that served as transition areas or barriers between the inner-city areas zoned for business and industry and the suburban residential areas. Delinquency rates decreased as distance from the central business district increased. The indirect implication of these findings was that rates of delinquency were related to the ecology of the neighborhood and the overall growth processes of the cities. Second, these researchers found that higher rates of delinquency were maintained over several years, despite high turnover in the population of these areas, thus challenging the idea that individual propensity was the only factor contributing to rates of delinquency. Furthermore, they found that certain structural characteristics, particularly indices of poverty (e.g., the percentage of families receiving government assistance), rates of residential mobility, and the percentage of nonwhite residents, were linked consistently to neighborhoods with high delinquency rates, leading the authors to suggest that these might be some of the contextual factors driving rates of delinquency. Finally, Shaw and McKay (1942, 1969) argued that concentrations of poverty, high rates of residential mobility, and ethnic or racial heterogeneity caused by growth processes in urban areas contributed to social disorganization and actually hampered the ability of a community to exert control on its residents, thereby increasing the likelihood of delinquency.

Indirect consequences of the study included the refinement of methodologies, stimulation of theory, and empirical study of violence—juvenile delinquency, in particular. There were several important subsequent studies that built on these findings. For example, Bensing and Schroeder (1960) found that social problems (including delinquency, homicide, and child maltreatment) were unequally distributed across geographic areas, with high concentrations in poor communities. Schmid (1960) also confirmed a correlation between structural variables and delinquency rates. The introduction of additional variables (e.g., home ownership, unemployment), techniques, and cross-sectional methods significantly attenuated the relationships reported by Shaw and McKay (e.g., Lander, 1954). However, after reviewing these studies, both Gordon (1967) and Kornhauser (1978) concluded that the relationship between ecological variables and delinquency was strong and reliable.

RECENT STUDIES OF COMMUNITY CHARACTERISTICS AND VIOLENCE

Whereas the early research focused on the relationship between several community-level variables and rates of juvenile delinquency, the next generation of studies concentrated on neighborhood and community-level variables related to more serious acts of violence, including child maltreatment, violent offenses committed by youths against their peers, and violent offenses committed by adults against children. Although rates of child maltreatment and violent crime within the community are highly related, rather distinct literatures have developed with respect to each area. Moreover, because studies of such community- or neighborhood-level variables rarely distinguish between violent crimes committed against adults and those committed against children (with the obvious exception of studies examining causes of child maltreatment), our review is not limited to studies that examined violent crimes against children. Finally, studies of community-level causes of violence frequently include multiple structural indicators in their analyses. To help simplify the discussion of this research, we review this literature in relation to particular indicators or groups of related indicators, namely, poverty, racial composition, urbanization and population density, residential mobility, family disruption, child care burden, and social impoverishment.

Poverty

The relationship of community poverty to the level of violence against children within a community has been the source of much research and debate. A substantial body of research over the past 40 years has established links between violent crime and poverty and related phenomena such as low socioeconomic status (SES) and unemployment. For example, in early studies of violent crime in census tracts in the Houston area, Bullock (1955) reported high negative correlations (−60) between measures of SES (e.g., educational levels and employment) and the distribution of homicides. In a similar study of 42 communities in the Greater Cleveland area, Bensing and Schroeder (1960) also observed that homicide rates were significantly associated with low median income, low educational attainment, and high percentages of unskilled workers. Mladenka and Hill's (1976) study of violent crimes in 20 police districts in Houston revealed that the percentage of residents living in poverty was the strongest predictor of crime rates, explaining over 80% of the variance. More recent studies have confirmed the relationship between violence and variables related to poverty (Coulton, Korbin, Su, & Chow, 1995; Kposowa, Breault, & Harrison, 1995). For example, Coulton and colleagues (1995) observed that rates of violent crime and juvenile delinquency in Cleveland communities were highly linked with impoverishment, a factor that included the variables of family hardship, poverty rate, unemployment rate, frequency of vacant housing, population loss, percentage of black residents, and percentage of female-headed households.

Studies of gang violence also have supported the connection between community-level poverty and violence. Youth gangs are significantly more likely to emerge in poor communities than in more affluent areas (e.g., Cartwright & Howard, 1966; Thrasher, 1927) and to inflict violence against other youth (and, less frequently, adults) in these poor communities.

An analysis of gang homicides in the Chicago area by Curry and Spergel (1988) revealed that poverty was the best predictor of homicides in both black and white communities.

Not only have researchers found that absolute levels of poverty within communities are related to violence, but there is growing evidence that economic inequality between communities may be a significant contributor to violence. Perhaps the most compelling evidence for this hypothesis comes from Block (1979), who found that the proximity of poor neighborhoods to middle-class neighborhoods was the most robust predictor of homicides, robberies, and assaults. Others have found economic inequality to be related to rates of larceny and robbery (Jacobs, 1981) as well as homicide and assault (Blau & Blau, 1982). Although a number of subsequent studies have provided weaker or inconsistent support for the connection between violence and economic inequality (e.g., Harer & Steffensmeier, 1992; Patterson, 1991), a recent meta-analysis of 34 data studies by Hsieh and Pugh (1993) concluded that both absolute poverty rates and economic inequality are significantly associated with violent crime.

Not only has poverty been found to be strongly related to juvenile delinquency and violent crime within a community, but also it has been found to be associated with the frequency and severity of child maltreatment. Discussion of the link between maltreatment and poverty first emerged in early scholarly papers on child maltreatment (e.g., Gil, 1970; Kempe, Silverman, Steele, Droegemueller, & Silver, 1962; Pelton, 1978), and it has persisted throughout the last several decades of research. Recently, Pelton (1994) concluded that "no single fact about child abuse and neglect is better documented and established than its relationship to poverty and low income" (p. 131). Although child maltreatment is observed in all socioeconomic classes, there is clear evidence that it occurs significantly more frequently among poor families than among more wealthy families (e.g., Gelles, 1992; Pelton, 1989, 1994). Because poor families are likely to live in impoverished neighborhoods, it is not surprising that child maltreatment has been found to be overrepresented in economically disadvantaged neighborhoods and communities (e.g., Coulton et al., 1995; Garbarino & Crouter, 1978; Garbarino & Kostelny, 1992; Spearly & Lauderdale, 1983; Zuravin, 1989).

Several studies have suggested that income level is related not only to the presence of child maltreatment but also to its severity (e.g., Gelles, 1992; Gil, 1970). For example, in a national survey of 3,233 households with children under 18 years of age, Gelles (1992) observed that self-reports of severe violence against children were 46% more likely in households at or below the poverty level than in households above the poverty level; reports of extremely severe violence against children were 100% higher in households with income levels below the poverty level.

Moreover, child maltreatment not only is concentrated among poor families but is found disproportionately among the poorest of the poor (National Research Council, 1993; Pelton, 1989; Wolock & Horowitz, 1979). For example, Wolock and Horowitz (1979) observed that among families receiving Aid to Families with Dependent Children (AFDC) benefits, those who were involved in child maltreatment were likely to live in circumstances that were more materially (and socially) deprived than those of other AFDC recipients.

Variables related to poverty, such as unemployment, also have been analyzed in an attempt to tease out their independent contributions to rates of child maltreatment. Evidence is strong that unemployment within a community is associated with either reports or actual incidents of child maltreatment (e.g., Coulton et al., 1995; Zuravin, 1989). Researchers of several longitudinal studies have observed that increases in child abuse are preceded by high unemployment rates (e.g., Steinberg, Catalno, & Dooley, 1981); others have observed that high unemployment and high incidences of child maltreatment exist contemporaneously (Zuravin, 1989).

Racial Composition

Despite the consistency of the relationship between indicators of poverty and violence, these studies frequently are criticized for failing to account for the correlation of poverty with race. Numerous studies have found race to be a significant predictor of rates of violent offending. Block (1979) observed a high positive relationship ($r = .69$) between the percentage of black residents and personal crime rates. This relationship also was reported by Mladenka and Hill (1976), who found a correlation of .81 between the percentage of black residents and a measure of crimes against people. Numerous other researchers who reported racial composition to be a significant predictor of violence also found poverty and race to be highly correlated (see e.g., Messner and Tardiff, 1986).

When studies have employed statistical techniques that control for poverty, the evidence associating race and violence has been equivocal. In a study of 204 metropolitan statistical areas, Messner (1982) found a negative relationship between poverty and violence but a positive relationship between the percentage of black residents and rates of violence. However, 1 year later, using a reconstructed indicator of poverty, Messner (1983) found that poverty was positively related to violence and that the percentage of black residents was not significantly related to rates of violence in some regions of the country. In a study of neighborhoods in Manhattan, Messner and Tardiff (1986) observed significant relationships between poverty and homicide rates and a marginally nonsignificant relationship between race and homicide.

As a way of explaining the contradictory findings, Williams (1984) argued that there may be a nonlinear relationship among poverty, race, and violence. In one of the initial tests of this assertion, Parker (1989) found significant interactions among race and poverty variables in predicting homicide rates. Expanding these results in a study of crime data from 957 cities, Neapolitan (1992) found that violent crime rates were high only when both extreme poverty and large black populations were present. Neapolitan argued that poverty is significantly related to violence only in communities in which predominant values may be conducive to violence (as is the case when large groups of people are excluded from opportunity structures). Sampson (1985) approached the question by disaggregating crime rates by race and focusing on structural characteristics related to race-specific crime rates. He found that after controlling for structural variables, including poverty and unemployment, race was not a factor in crime rates among blacks or whites. Using a similar approach, Shihadeh and Steffensmeier (1994) found a strong positive relationship between income inequality among blacks and violence committed by blacks. Moreover, these authors reported that the percentage of black residents was largely unrelated to homicide rates for black juveniles and adults.

The relationship between race, culture, ethnicity, and child maltreatment also has been the source of much debate; studies conducted over the past 20 years have produced contradictory findings. After reviewing this extensive literature, Korbin (1994) concluded that "there is little empirical basis, at present, to indicate that any cultural, ethnic, or racial group in the United States has greater rates of child maltreatment than any other" (p. 195). Quite a few studies have failed to find significant associations between these variables. Perhaps most notably, the two national incidence studies of child abuse and neglect (National Center on Child Abuse and Neglect, 1981, 1988) revealed no relationship between race, culture, or ethnicity and the incidence of child maltreatment. Although several investigators have reported racial, cultural, or ethnic difference in maltreatment rates, interpretations of their findings are limited by a myriad of methodological difficulties, including imprecise (or inappropriate) definitions of maltreatment, race, culture, or ethnicity; a confounding of SES with racial, cultural, or ethnic factors; and bias in reporting.

Urbanization and Population Density

Although variables related to community- or neighborhood-level poverty are strong determinants of violence against children, poverty clearly is only one of several factors that contribute to such violence. Other community-level factors that have been examined by researchers include variables related to urbanization and population density. In relation to the geographic distribution of violence, one of the most consistent findings is that, in absolute numbers, more violence occurs in urban than in rural areas. As a result, most studies of the structural correlates of violence have focused on urban areas. There are a number of studies with samples sufficient to permit examination of the significance of urbanization for violence. For example, Flango and Sherbenou (1976) found that urbanization was the best predictor of serious crime and robbery in both small and large cities. Sampson and Groves (1989) also have found urbanization to be a significant factor in predicting violence.

A second line of research has examined population density within urban communities as a predictor of violence. For example, Mladenka and Hill (1976) reported a correlation of .70 between population density and crimes against people. They found a similarly high correlation between population density and overall crime rates. An often-studied variant of population density is structural density. In a study of Cleveland-area neighborhoods, Roncek (1981) found the percentage of multiunit housing structures to be a consistent predictor of violence levels. Sampson (1983) found that rates of victimization were in some cases 3 times greater in high-density versus low-density neighborhoods, even after holding other demographic variables constant. In addition, Sampson observed a positive relationship between numbers of multiunit housing structures and crime rates. Schuerman and Korbin (1986) confirmed this relationship through a longitudinal study, finding that multiplexes and rental units were robust predictors of increases in crime rates in the Los Angeles area. Recently, Shihadeh and Steffensmeier (1994) found that structural density, as measured by numbers of multifamily housing units, was significantly related to juvenile and adult robbery rates but not to homicide rates.

Like the incidence of violence generally, cases of child maltreatment are more frequent in populated urban centers than in less populated rural settings, although no community, regardless of size, is immune from such incidents. A number of researchers who have examined the relationship between residential density and incidents of child maltreatment have found crowding to be a significant contributing factor (e.g., Garbarino & Kostelny, 1992; Zuravin, 1986). For example, in her study of reported cases of child maltreatment in census tracts in Baltimore, Zuravin (1986) observed that household crowding (measured by the presence of at least 1.51 persons per room) was significantly related to reports of child abuse and neglect. However, household crowding was less strongly associated with reported child maltreatment than were social class and ethnicity.

Residential Mobility

As noted earlier, more than 50 years ago Shaw and McKay (1942) observed that one of the key predictors of juvenile delinquency was residential mobility. Since this early study, several researchers have examined the impact of high turnover of community residents on rates of violence. Block (1979) found residential instability to be a significant predictor of violence, including homicides and aggravated assaults. Using city-level data, Crutchfield, Geerken, and Gove (1982) reported that residential mobility was an important predictor of both property crime and violent crime. They argued that mobility increases anonymity, weakening informal control and leading to increases in crimes as offenders recognize decreases in surveillance. Using victimization rates from a sample of 57 neighborhoods in Rochester, New York, Tampa, and St. Louis, Smith and Jarjoura (1988) found that residential mobility was highly related to rates of violence in poor communities but not in more affluent areas. Sampson and Lauritsen (1993) argued that high mobility rates are particularly important as both precursors to and perpetuators of a transition to poverty and underclass status for a neighborhood. They found support for this thesis in Schuerman and Korbin's (1986) longitudinal study of community change, which concluded that residential mobility and family disruption were prominent indicators of the development of high-crime areas. Most recently, Coulton et al. (1995) observed a significant positive relationship between violent crime rates and residential mobility (defined by the percentage of residents who had moved within 1, 5, or 10 years).

Residential instability within a community also has been found to be related to higher rates of child maltreatment. In their studies of communities in New York, Omaha, and Chicago, Garbarino and colleagues (e.g., Garbarino, 1976; Garbarino & Crouter, 1978; Garbarino & Kostelny, 1992) identified a list of socioeconomic and demographic variables that predicted child maltreatment rates. Among the demographic variables that contributed significantly to high rates of child maltreatment within a community were measures of residential mobility, including the percentage of families who were in residence less than 1 year (Garbarino & Crouter, 1978) and the percentage of families in residence less than 5 years (Garbarino & Kostelny, 1992). Similarly, Coulton et al. (1995) observed that rates of maltreatment in Cleveland neighborhoods were positively related to the percentage of families in residence less than 10 years, those living in the community less than 5 years, and those who had lived in the community less than 1 year. Results from an ethnographic investigation by Korbin and Coulton (in press) suggested that it is not residential movement alone, but rather the composition of this movement, that is critical to communities. An influx of renters in the neighborhood was viewed as detrimental to residents of the community. Renters were viewed as uncommitted to the neighborhood and unlikely to become involved in community concerns. An influx of homeowners or a return of known individuals to a community, however, was viewed positively, because these individuals were seen as lending permanence and stability to the neighborhood.

Family Disruption

Recently, there has been increasing interest in family disruption and the related phenomenon of child care burden as predictors of violence. Typical measures of disruption have included the percentage of individuals experiencing divorce and the percentage of female-headed households. Researchers have hypothesized that elevations in these variables, combined with high levels of turnover in community residents, may indicate a breakdown in community networks and a subsequent decrease in informal social control, including adult supervision of potential juvenile perpetrators and protection of potential juvenile victims.

Several researchers have observed that divorce rates within a community are strong predictors of violent crime, including sexual assault (Blau & Blau, 1982), robbery (Sampson, 1986), and homicide (Messner & Tardiff, 1986; Sampson, 1986). In a study using racially disaggregated data, Sampson (1987) found that family disruption was a significant predictor of serious crimes for both Whites and Blacks. Others have examined additional variables associated with family disruption, including the percentage of female-headed households within a community. In a rare study using data disaggregated by race and age, Shihadeh and Steffensmeier (1994) demonstrated that the percentage of female-headed households was a strong predictor of juvenile violence and a significant (but less strong) predictor of violence among adults within a community. Coulton and colleagues (1995) found that the percentage of female-headed households was related to impoverishment, a macrostructural factor that they found to have a significant effect on drug trafficking, violent crime, and juvenile delinquency.

Family disruption also is a key correlate of analyses of community correlates of child maltreatment. The percentage of female-headed households (Coulton et al., 1995; Garbarino & Crouter, 1978; Garbarino & Kostelny, 1992; Spearly & Lauderdale, 1983) and the percentage of working mothers (Garbarino & Crouter, 1978; Spearly & Lauderdale, 1983) have been found to distinguish significantly communities with differing rates of child maltreatment.

Not only is violence against children more common in communities that are impoverished, urban, densely populated, and mobile, and in those that contain large percentages of disrupted families, but also there is evidence that violence against children occurs most frequently in communities where there are fewer adults available to supervise children. Coulton and colleagues (1995) observed that variables such as a small percentage of elderly residents, a high child:adult ratio, and a high female:male ratio contributed to higher rates of drug trafficking, violent crime, juvenile delinquency, and child maltreatment. These researchers reasoned that in communities where there are relatively few elderly and other adults to supervise children, the entire child care burden frequently rests with single females.

Social Impoverishment and Collective Efficacy

In addition to the economic, demographic, and other structural variables noted previously, there are more elusive determinants of community or neighborhood quality that have been found to be related to violence against children within a community. For example, over the last two decades many researchers have examined the extent to which maltreating families are socially more isolated than nonmaltreating families. Although this body of research suffers from numerous methodological and conceptual difficulties (e.g., Thompson, 1994, 1995), existing findings suggest that families with small social networks and infrequent contact with members of these networks are more likely to abuse (e.g., Hunter & Kilstrom, 1979; Salzinger, Kaplan, & Artemyeff, 1983; Straus, 1980) and neglect (e.g., Giovannoni & Billingsley, 1970; Polansky, Gaudin, Ammons, & Davis, 1985) their children (for reviews, see Limber & Hashima, 1993; Thompson, 1995). The presence and use of informal social networks have been viewed largely as protective factors against child maltreatment (Garbarino, 1977; National Research Council, 1993); however, researchers currently lack understanding of why maltreating families tend to be isolated and what mechanisms are most effective for building or strengthening positive support networks for these parents within communities.

In their pioneering effort to examine neighborhood determinants of child maltreatment, Garbarino and colleagues identified communities with similar economic and racial profiles that presented different risks of child maltreatment (Garbarino & Kostelny, 1992; Garbarino & Sherman, 1980). After interviewing residents in high- and low-risk communities, researchers identified a number of factors that contribute to the "social impoverishment" of high-risk communities. For example, compared to residents in a community at relatively low risk for child maltreatment, residents of the high-risk community reported less family involvement in neighborhood activities, less positive interactions among neighbors, a more negative quality of life, and overall little sense of cohesiveness or "community." In a subsequent study of high- and low-risk Chicago communities, Garbarino and Kostelny (1992) painted a similar picture of social impoverishment among neighbors in a high-risk community. Residents were not eager to talk about their community, could think of few positive characteristics, and even had difficulty identifying their neighborhood with a name. By contrast, residents in the matched low-risk community tended to describe their community as "poor but not hopeless." These residents were eager to talk about their community, reported that more services were available for families, and noted that families tended to take advantage of strong formal and informal supports.

A similar orientation was adopted by Sampson, Raudenbush, and Earls (1997) to examine neighborhoods' social controls on violent behavior. Their recent study of Chicago neighborhoods explored the impact of "collective efficacy" on ratings of violent crime. Collective efficacy was defined as the social cohesion and trust among residents (as evidenced by residents' agreements with such statements as "people around here are willing to help their neighbors," and "this is a close-knit neighborhood"), combined with their willingness to intervene for a common good (represented by respondents' ratings of the likelihood that their neighbors could be counted on to step in when children were skipping school, defacing property with graffiti, or showing disrespect to an adult; intervene when a fight broke out in front of their home; or become involved when budget cuts threatened a nearby fire station). Even after controlling for individual-level factors (e.g., age, SES, home ownership), measurement error, and prior violence, Sampson and colleagues found that the presence of collective efficacy was associated with lower rates of perceived neighborhood violence, violent victimization, and homicides.

Although research by Garbarino, Sampson, and others has raised important questions about the relationship between neighborhood quality and violence, the research community as a whole has been curiously inactive in pursuing this line of inquiry to illuminate causes of violence against children (see Melton, 1992). Much work remains to be done to identify specific factors that contribute to the social impoverishment of neighborhoods, illuminate clear connections between these factors and violence against children, and develop effective strategies to improve the quality of neighborhoods.

THEORIES OF VIOLENCE

There is no shortage of theories to explain the relationship between community characteristics and violence. Most are derived from either structural or cultural causal models. The structural model asserts that community disruption or disorganization brought on by certain structural properties is the primary causal process. One theory advanced in Shaw and McKay's study and representative of the "Chicago school" approach is the social disorganizational model. This theory posits that structural characteristics, particularly high levels of poverty, racial heterogeneity, and residential mobility, can lead to a disruption in organization of the community. This in turn results in an impairment of community processes (i.e., formal and informal social control) that might otherwise restrain deviant behavior. For example, Shaw and McKay (1969) pointed out that the influx of immigrants into a community may make it difficult for residents to agree on local standards of behavior or environmental quality. As a result, control functions of the family and neighborhood are eroded, freeing residents to commit antisocial behaviors.

A derivation of the structural model is the relative deprivation theory. Rooted in Merton's (1968) strain theory, it asserts that violence results from a sense of injustice arising from a lack of legitimate means to attain culturally prescribed goals. When this "strain" is present, it may lead to crime when certain cultural supports also are present. For example, Wilson (1987) suggested that the chances of achieving financial success through legitimate means declines for children in "underclass communities." Children in these communities may resort to illegitimate means that often involve violence, such as drug involvement or crime against property or persons, to achieve these goals, particularly if monetary success is emphasized in the culture. Therefore, crime and violence may not be related to absolute levels of poverty but to one's status and opportunities relative to culturally prescribed ideals.

Cultural models of violence posit that crime and violence ultimately originate in conformity to subcultural norms (Wolfgang & Ferracuti, 1967). Embedded in this theory is the notion that there are groupings in which the predominant culture is more conducive to violence. Therefore, conformity to this subculture is likely to result in more aggression and violence. For example, Curtis (1975) advanced the idea of a "Black counterculture" in which particular value is placed on the Black male's ability to fight, outsmart others, and sexually exploit women. Another example is Hackney's (1969) argument that Southern pride and a gun culture may explain some regional differences in violent crime rates. These subcultures may be sustained by racial inequality and structural disadvantage. However, the root causes are not racism or poverty but the adherence to the prevailing culture.

There have been several recent renditions of this theory. Jencks and Mayer (1990) suggested two mechanisms to explain the relationship between the cultural context within the community and children's behavior. The *epidemic model* suggests that children will adopt problem behaviors from peers who have set behavioral norms. Children who have not been inoculated, as to a disease, through exposure to prosocial family values or institutional norms will be susceptible to the prevailing culture (often a counterculture) advocated by peers. Conversely, *socialization models* emphasize the impact on children of norms displayed and passed on by adults. Children who are exposed only to adults who are unsuccessful or who have resorted to illegitimate methods to achieve success are likely to mimic those examples.

The theories described do not focus on the etiology of violence against children in particular, although causes of violence against children may be subsumed within their broader focus on the causes of violence within communities. Several theoretical models have been advanced to explain the etiology of child maltreatment and explore the relationship of community-level factors to the prevalence of child abuse and neglect. Belsky (1980) proposed a model of child maltreatment that provides a framework for understanding the ecology, or the broader environment, in which child maltreatment exists. According to Belsky's ecological theory, child maltreatment is influenced by forces within the individual and the family (the microsystem), as well as the community (the exosystem) and the broader society, or culture, within which a family lives (the macrosystem). Within the exosystem, Belsky recognized in particular the impact of such variables as employment status and social isolation on child maltreatment within the family.

At approximately the same time that Belsky published his ecological theory of child maltreatment, Cicchetti and Rizley (1981) proposed a *transactional model* to explain the causes, consequences, and mechanisms through which child maltreatment is perpetuated. The focus of this model is on transactions among risk factors for child abuse and neglect. According to Cicchetti and Rizley, maltreatment occurs when potentiating factors (i.e., factors that increase the probability of maltreatment) outweigh compensatory factors (i.e., factors that reduce the risk of abuse or neglect).

Drawing on both of these theories, Cicchetti and Lynch (1993) recently proposed an ecological–transactional model of child maltreatment and community violence which posits that potentiating and compensatory factors for violence occur at all levels of the family's ecology: the microsystem, exosystem, and macrosystem. The presence of these factors determines whether violence will occur at each level of the child's ecology. The authors suggested that factors at the level of the exosystem are likely to influence interfamilial child abuse "through the pressure and stress they place on families" (p. 101). For example, potentiating factors such as low cohesion among neighbors, poverty, or violence within the community may increase the chance of child maltreatment occurring in a household, particularly if they coexist with potentiating factors within the level of the microsystem itself.

LIMITATIONS OF RESEARCH ON VIOLENCE AGAINST CHILDREN

The numerous studies that test theories of violence are limited by a number of methodological issues. With a few exceptions, most of the research discussed in this chapter was conducted using data-driven approximations of structural variables and levels of aggregation. Difficulties in defining the level of analysis were discussed earlier. However, the difficulties in determining the appropriateness of the measures of some variables must be considered. For example, the significance of poverty as a predictor of violence is somewhat dependent on what measure of poverty is used. This is also the case for other variables (e.g., family disruption, relative deprivation). Unfortunately, there is little theoretical or practical consensus on what measures best approximate the variables under consideration.

Data Sources

A more troubling issue has been the potential biases that are present in the predominant data sources. Most of the sources of data pertaining to violent crimes contain one of two types of data. Most common is the FBI's uniform crime report data or similar data from local police departments. These data consist of police department reports of crime organized into standard categories. Centralization and standardization are an advantage of this approach. However, it is apparent that these data are underestimates of crime and violence in that they represent only crimes reported to police. Moreover, when analyzed by geographic area or by race, these data are vulnerable to biases across police departments, which may differ in their surveillance and arrest policies. A second source of such data is the National Crime Survey or similar surveys that focus on reports of victimization. These data tend to produce much higher rates of most crime categories. However, victimization data also are vulnerable to racial and class differences in reporting behavior. For example, Hindelang (1978) reported that blacks tend to underreport violent crimes on victimization surveys. Fortunately, with serious crimes such as homicide and robbery, data from these sources converge and display similar patterns, providing some validity for both measures.

Sources of data on the incidence of child maltreatment have similar limitations. Most investigators have used official reports of child maltreatment to estimate maltreatment rates in communities. Official reports frequently are criticized for containing underestimations of the true incidence of child maltreatment and bias against poor and minority-group families (e.g., Coulton et al., 1995; O'Toole, Turbett, & Nalpeka, 1983). Moreover, inaccuracies in the data arise from errors in record keeping, variable definitions of maltreatment, and incorrect identification of cases (Coulton et al., 1995).

Aggregation of Correlations

Perhaps the most pernicious of methodological issues that arise when aggregate data are used is the risk of contextual fallacies. Concern for this issue can be summarized in the following question: If individual-level characteristics were controlled (e.g., for race, gender, and household income), would the effects of neighborhood indicators on rates of violence disappear? In the case of income, for example, if household income is associated with violent outcomes at the individual level, this correlation would be aggregated in community-level indicators. Consequently, what is actually a correlation between poor individuals and violence may erroneously appear to be a correlation between poor communities and violence. Unfortunately, official reports rarely contain individual-level data; victimization reports contain only basic information on the perpetrator, and self-reports are usually limited to minor infractions, making it difficult to control individual characteristics in studies of community characteristics. Furthermore, it is difficult to resolve this conundrum because of the ethical implications of asking intensely personal questions about private (and often illegal) behavior without conferring the benefit of anonymity.

CONCLUSION

A truly ecological perspective for examining causes of violence against children must consider complex interactions of factors across multiple ecological levels that encompass individuals, families, neighborhoods, communities, and the larger society. To date, much research remains focused on individual- or family-level predictors of violence and fails to consider broader neighborhood, community, or societal contributors. When researchers have focused on the relationship between violence and neighborhood or community factors, they typically have identified economic, demographic, and other structural factors that contribute to rates of child maltreatment and other violent crime within the community. Factors such as poverty, unemployment, crowded housing, residential mobility, and large percentages of female-headed households clearly contribute to the creation of a climate that is ripe for violence in the community and violence against children. However, as the work of Garbarino, Sampson, and their colleagues has illustrated, there are other, more elusive (and less easily quantifiable) factors that also are critical to the creation of a climate of social impoverishment that places children at risk for violence.

Several years ago, the U.S. Advisory Board on Child Abuse and Neglect (1993) reviewed the state of knowledge with respect to causes of child maltreatment and concluded that neighborhood decline is a major cause of child maltreatment:

> In neighborhoods in which children are protected, there is friendship among neighbors, watchfulness for each other's families, physical safety of the environment, common knowledge of community resources, visible leadership, and perhaps most critically, a sense of "belonging," ownership, and collective responsibility. By contrast, some neighbor-

hoods have been so drained of these qualities that they are disastrous for children and families. (pp. 8–9)

Acknowledging the primacy of the neighborhood in supporting families, the board called for a reorientation of the nation's child protection efforts to neighborhood-based attempts to keep children safe from violence. If such efforts are to be successful, significant resources must be allotted to neighborhood-focused research to allow a better understanding of factors and strategies that can help turn around neighborhoods that are socially impoverished and dangerous for children and can support and sustain communities that are cohesive, socially rich, and safe for children.

REFERENCES

Barry, F. (1994). A neighborhood-based approach: What is it? In G. B. Melton & F. D. Barry (Eds.), *Protecting children from abuse and neglect: Foundations for a new national strategy*. New York: Guilford Press.

Belsky, J. (1980). Child maltreatment: An ecological integration. *American Psychologist, 35,* 320–355.

Bensing, R. C., & Schroeder, O. (1960). *Homicide in an urban community*. Springfield, IL: Charles C Thomas.

Blau, J., & Blau, P. M. (1982). The cost of inequality: Metropolitan structure and violent crime. *American Sociological Review, 47,* 114–129.

Block, R. (1979). Community, environment, and violent crime. *Criminology, 17,* 46–57.

Bullock, H. A. (1955). Urban homicide in theory and fact. *Journal of Criminal Law, Criminology, and Police Science, 45,* 565–575.

Bursik, R. J., Jr., & Grasmick, H. G. (1993). *Neighborhoods and crime: The dimensions of effective community control*. New York: Lexington Books.

Byrne, J., & Sampson, R. J. (1986). Key issues in the social ecology of crime. In J. Byrne & R. J. Sampson (Eds.), *The social ecology of crime* (pp. 1–22). New York: Springer-Verlag.

Cartwright, D. S., & Howard, K. J. (1966). Multivariate analysis of gang delinquency: Ecologic influences. *Multivariate Behavioral Research, 1,* 321–371.

Cicchetti, D., & Lynch, M. (1993). Toward an ecological/transactional model of community violence and child maltreatment: Consequences for children's development. *Psychiatry, 56,* 96–118.

Cicchetti, D., & Rizley, R. (1981). Developmental perspectives on the etiology, intergenerational transmission, and sequelae of child maltreatment. *New Directions for Child Development, 11,* 31–55.

Coulton, C. J., Korbin, J. E., Su, M., & Chow, J. (1995). Community level factors and child maltreatment rates. *Child Development, 66,* 1262–1276.

Crutchfield, R. M., Geerken, M., & Gove, W. (1982). Crime rate and social integration: The impact of metropolitan mobility. *Criminology, 20,* 467–478.

Curry, G. D., & Spergel, I. A. (1988). Gang homicide, delinquency and community. *Criminology, 26,* 381–405.

Curtis, L. A. (1975). *Violence, race, and culture.* Lexington, MA: Lexington Books.

Fisher, C. S. (1982). *To dwell among friends: Personal networks in town and city.* Chicago: University of Chicago Press.

Flango, E., & Sherbenou, E. (1976). Poverty, urbanization, and crime. *Criminology, 14,* 331–346.

Garbarino, J. (1976). A preliminary study of some ecological correlates of child abuse: The impact of socioeconomic stress on mothers. *Child Development, 47,* 178–185.

Garbarino, J. (1977). The human ecology of child maltreatment: A conceptual model for research. *Journal of Marriage and the Family, 39,* 721–736.

Garbarino, J. (1995). *Raising children in a socially toxic environment.* San Francisco: Jossey-Bass.

Garbarino, J., & Crouter, A. (1978). Defining the community context for parent–child relations: The correlates of child maltreatment. *Child Development, 49,* 604–616.

Garbarino, J., & Kostelny, K. (1992). Child maltreatment as a community problem. *Child Abuse and Neglect, 16,* 455–464.

Garbarino, J., & Sherman, D. (1980). High-risk neighborhoods and high-risk families: The human ecology of child maltreatment. *Child Development, 51,* 188–198.

Gelles, R. J. (1992). Poverty and violence toward children. *American Behavioral Scientist, 35,* 258–274.

Gil, D. G. (1970). *Violence against children.* Cambridge, MA: Harvard University Press.

Giovannoni, J. M., & Billingsley, A. (1970). Child neglect among the poor: A study of parental adequacy in families of three ethnic groups. *Child Welfare, 49,* 196–204.

Goldstein, A. P., & Soriano, F. I. (1994). Juvenile gangs. In L. D. Eron, J. H. Gentry, & P. Schlegel (Eds.), *Reason to hope: A psychosocial perspective on violence and youth.* Washington, DC: American Psychological Association.

Gordon, R. (1967). Issues in the ecological study of delinquency. *American Sociological Review, 32,* 927–944.

Hackney, S. (1969). Southern violence. In H. D. Graham & T. R. Gurr (Eds.), *History of violence in America* (pp. 505–528). New York: Bantam Books.

Harer, M. D., & Steffensmeier, D. (1992). The differing effects of economic inequality on Black and White rates of violence. *Social Forces, 70,* 1035–1054.

Hegedorn, J. (1988). *People and folks: Gangs, crime and the underclass in a rustbelt city.* Chicago: Lake View Press.

Hindelang, M. J. (1978). Race and involvement in common law personal crimes. *American Sociological Review, 43,* 93–109.

Hsieh, C. C., & Pugh, M. D. (1993). Poverty, income inequality, and violent crime: A meta-analysis of recent aggregate studies. *Criminal Justice Review, 18,* 182–202.

Hunter, R. S., & Kilstrom, N. (1979). Breaking the cycle in abusive families. *American Journal of Psychiatry, 136,* 1320–1322.

Jacobs, D. (1981). Inequality and economic crime. *Sociology and Social Research, 66,* 12–28.

Jencks, C., & Mayer, S. E. (1990). The social consequences of growing up in a poor neighborhood. In L. E. Lynn, Jr., & M. G. H. McGeary (Eds.), *Inner city poverty in the United States* (pp. 111–186). Washington, DC: National Academy Press.

Kempe, C. H., Silverman, F. N., Steele, B. F., Droegemueller, W., & Silver, H. K. (1962). The battered child syndrome. *Journal of the American Medical Association, 181,* 17–24.

Klein, M. (1995). *The American street gang: Its nature, prevalence, and control.* New York: Oxford University Press.

Korbin, J. (1994). Sociocultural factors in child maltreatment. In G. B. Melton & F. D. Barry (Eds.), *Protecting children from abuse and neglect* (pp. 182–223). New York: Guilford Press.

Korbin, J. E., & Coulton, C. J. (in press). Understanding the neighborhood context for children and families: Combining epidemiological and ethnographic approaches. In J. Brooks-Gunn, L. Aber, & G. Duncan (Eds.), *Neighborhood poverty: Context and consequences for children.* New York: Russell Sage Foundation.

Kornhauser, R. (1978). *Social sources of delinquency.* Chicago: University of Chicago Press.

Kposowa, A. J., Breault, K. D., & Harrison, B. M. (1995). Reassessing the structural covariates of violent and property crimes in the USA: A county level analysis. *British Journal of Sociology, 46,* 79–106.

Lander, B. (1954). *Toward an understanding of juvenile delinquency.* New York: Columbia University Press.

Levin, Y., & Lindesmith, A. (1937). English ecology and criminology of the past century. *Journal of Criminal Law and Criminology, 27,* 801–816.

Limber, S. P., & Hashima, P. Y. (1993). *The social context: What comes naturally in child protection.* Unpublished manuscript.

McCurdy, K., & Daro, D. (1993). Child maltreatment: A national survey of reports and fatalities. *Journal of Interpersonal Violence, 9,* 75–94.

Melton, G. B. (1992). It's time for neighborhood research and action. *Child Abuse and Neglect, 16,* 909–913.

Merton, R. K. (1968). *Social theory and social structure.* New York: Free Press.

Messner, S. (1982). Poverty, inequality, and the urban homicide rate. *Criminology, 20,* 103–114.

Messner, S. (1983). Regional and racial effects on the urban homicide rate: The subculture of violence revisited. *American Journal of Sociology, 88,* 997–1007.

Messner, S., & Tardiff, K. (1986). Economic inequality and levels of homicide: An analysis of urban neighborhoods. *Criminology, 24,* 297–318.

Mladenka, K., & Hill, K. (1976). A reexamination of the etiology of urban crime. *Criminology, 13,* 491–506.

National Center on Child Abuse and Neglect. (1981). *Study findings: National study of the incidence and severity of child abuse and neglect.* Washington, DC: Department of Health, Education, and Welfare.

National Center on Child Abuse and Neglect (1988). *Study of findings: Study of the national incidence and prevalence of child abuse and neglect.* Washington, DC: Author.

National Research Council. (1993). *Losing generations: Adolescents in high-risk settings.* Washington, DC: National Academy Press.

Neopolitan, J. (1992). Poverty, race, and population concentrations: Interactive associations to violent crime. *American Journal of Criminal Justice, 16,* 143–153.

O'Toole, R., Turbett, P., & Nalpeka, C. (1983). Theories, professional knowledge, and diagnosis of child abuse. In D. Finkelhor, R. Gelles, G. Hotaling, & M. Strauss (Eds.), *The dark side of families: Current family violence research* (pp. 349–362). Newbury Park, CA: Sage.

Park, R. E., Burgess, E., & McKenzie, R. (1925). *The city.* Chicago: University of Chicago Press.

Parker, R. (1989). Poverty, subculture of violence and type of homicide. *Social Forces, 67,* 983–1007.

Patterson, E. B. (1991). Poverty, income inequality, and community crime rates. *Criminology, 29,* 755–776.

Pelton, L. H. (1978). Child abuse and neglect: The myth of classlessness. *American Journal of Orthopsychiatry, 48,* 608–617.

Pelton, L. H. (1989). *For reasons of poverty: A critical analysis of the public child welfare system in the United States.* New York: Praeger.

Pelton, L. H. (1994). In G. B. Melton & F. D. Barry (Eds.), *Protecting children from abuse and neglect: Foundations for a new national strategy* (pp. 131–181). New York: Guilford Press.

Polansky, N. A., Gaudin, J. M., Ammons, P. W., & Davis, K. B. (1985). The psychological ecology of the neglectful mother. *Child Abuse and Neglect, 9,* 265–275.

Richters, J. E., & Martinez, P. (1993). The NIMH community violence project: Children as victims of and witnesses to violence, *Psychiatry, 56,* 7–21.

Roncek, D. (1981). Dangerous places: Crime and residential environment. *Social Forces, 60,* 74–96.

Salzinger, S., Kaplan, S., & Artemyeff, C. (1983). Mothers' personal social networks and child maltreatment. *Journal of Abnormal Psychology, 92,* 68–76.

Sampson, R. J. (1983). Structural density and criminal victimization. *Criminology, 21,* 276–293.

Sampson, R. J. (1985). Race and criminal violence: A demographically disaggregated analysis of urban homicide. *Crime and Delinquency, 31,* 47–82.

Sampson, R. J. (1986). Crime in cities: The effects of formal and informal social control. In A. J. Reiss Jr. & M. Tonry (Eds.), *Communities and crime* (pp. 271–311). Chicago: University of Chicago Press.

Sampson, R. J. (1987). Urban black violence: The effect of male joblessness and family disruption. *American Journal of Sociology, 93,* 348–382.

Sampson, R. J., & Groves, W. B. (1989). Community structure and crime: Testing social-disorganization theory. *American Journal of Sociology, 94,* 774–802.

Sampson, R. J., & Lauritsen, J. L. (1993). Violent victimization and offending: Individual-, situational-, and community-level risk factors. In A. J. Reiss Jr. & J. A. Roth (Eds.), *Understanding and preventing violence,* (Vol. 3, pp. 1–114). Washington, DC: National Academy Press.

Sampson, R. J., Raudenbush, S. W., & Earls, F. Neighborhoods and violent crime: A multilevel study of collective efficacy. *Science, 277,* 918–924.

Schmid, C. (1960). Urban crime areas. Part I. *American Sociological Review, 25,* 527–542.

Schuerman, L., & Korbin, S. (1986). Community careers in crime. In A. J. Reiss Jr. & M. Tonry (Eds.), *Communities and crime* (pp. 67–100). Chicago: University of Chicago Press.

Shaw, C., & McKay, H. (1942). *Juvenile delinquency in urban areas.* Chicago: University of Chicago Press.

Shaw, C., & McKay, H. (1969). *Juvenile delinquency in urban areas* (rev. ed.). Chicago: University of Chicago Press.

Shihadeh, E. S., & Steffensmeier, D. J. (1994). Economic inequality, family disruption, and urban black violence: Cities as units of stratification and social control. *Social Forces, 73,* 729–751.

Smith, D. R., & Jarjoura, G. R. (1988). Social structure and criminal victimization. *Journal of Research in Crime and Delinquency, 25,* 27–52.

Sorenson, S. B., & Bowie, P. (1994). Girls and young women. In L. D. Eron, J. H. Gentry, & P. Schlegel (Eds.), *Reason to hope: A psychosocial perspective on violence and youth.* Washington, DC: American Psychological Association.

Spearly, J. L., & Lauderdale, M. (1983). Community characteristics and ethnicity in prediction of child maltreatment rates. *Child Abuse and Neglect, 7,* 91–105.

Steinberg, L., Catalano, R., & Dooley, D. (1981). Economic antecedents of child abuse and neglect. *Child Development, 52,* 975–985.

Straus, M. A. (1980). Stress and physical abuse. *Child Abuse and Neglect, 4,* 75–88.

Thompson, R. A. (1994). Social support and the prevention of child maltreatment. In G. B. Melton & F. D. Barry (Eds.), *Protecting children from abuse and neglect* (pp. 40–130). New York: Guilford Press.

Thompson, R. A. (1995). *Preventing child maltreatment through social support: A critical analysis.* Thousand Oaks, CA: Sage.

Thrasher, F. M. (1927). *The gang.* Chicago: University of Chicago Press.

U.S. Advisory Board on Child Abuse and Neglect. (1990). *Child abuse and neglect: Critical first steps in response to a national emergency.* Washington, DC: Author.

U.S. Advisory Board on Child Abuse and Neglect. (1993). *Neighbors helping neighbors: A new national strategy for the protection of children.* Washington, DC: Author.

Williams, W. J. (1984). Economic sources of homicide: Reestimating the effects of poverty and inequality. *American Sociological Review, 49,* 283–289.

Wilson, W. J. (1987). *The truly disadvantaged: The inner city, the underclass, and public policy.* Chicago: University of Chicago Press.

Wolfgang, M., & Ferracuti, F. (1967). *The subculture of violence: Toward an integrated theory in criminology.* London: Tavistock.

Wolock, I., & Horowitz, B. (1979). Child maltreatment and material deprivation among AFDC recipient families. *Social Service Review, 53,* 175–194.

Zuravin, S. J. (1986). Residential density and urban child maltreatment: An aggregate analysis. *Journal of Family Violence, 1,* 307–322.

Zuravin, S. J. (1989). The ecology of child abuse and neglect: Review of the literature and presentation of data. *Violence and Victims, 4,* 101–120.

8

SOCIETAL CAUSES OF VIOLENCE AGAINST CHILDREN

PATRICK H. TOLAN AND NANCY GUERRA

In attempting to summarize the societal causes of violence against children, we faced two predicaments: The first was the one John Monahan mentioned in congressional testimony about the causes of violence. He noted that he had been allotted 20 minutes to tell everything that is known about the causes of such violence and that, unfortunately, it would be enough time (Monahan, 1993). As we surveyed the literature, we found a sketchy outline of implicated societal forces but few data with the power to move the reader beyond opinions. The second concern we faced was about moving to a level of discourse that is above what we refer to as "bar-stool commentary." Given the limited knowledge base and the complex array of macroforces of society that lead to violence against children, how does one comment without sounding like the local bar-stool pundit who has an opinion about everything and knows the solutions to any social problem, no matter how complex it is and how limited his or her knowledge is? The implied conclusion of this state of knowledge and opin-

The work on this manuscript was supported in part by National Institute of Mental Health Grants R18MH48034 and R01MH45936 and by the UIC Great Cities Faculty Scholar Program.

ion base seems to be that if one could remake the world and humanity, one could end violence against children; anything less would leave out major causes.

Beyond platitudes and wishes, and shy of concluding that too little is known, what are the details of the knowledge about societal causes of violence against children? Given this knowledge, what might be done to address the problem now to lessen the victimization of children? Our focus here is to indicate what is known about societal forces and to consider this knowledge in terms of prevention. We do not attempt to speculate about what should be done under ideal conditions but to delineate, with due reserve, a direction that can be inferred from the research and that we realistically expect can be followed in U.S. society at this time. To this end, we anchor our assessment of societal influences in the specifics of violence as it currently affects children in the United States. We focus on what is known about specific societal factors and how this knowledge can be incorporated into programs and policies designed to prevent or reduce violence (Tolan & Guerra, 1994).

We begin by examining violence against children in relation to the overall picture of youth violence perpetration and victimization (Tolan & Guerra, 1994). The perpetrators of violence toward children and adolescents are often other youth; whether one is a perpetrator or victim may simply depend on what day it is. Given a framework linking perpetration and victimization, we discuss four key areas of societal influence: (a) societal norms and conventions; (b) the institutionalization of violence against children; (c) the secondary status of children; and (d) social forces such as stress, poverty, and social isolation. From the perspective of sociological theory, the first two factors correspond to cultural explanations of violence, and the last two factors are related to social-structural theories of violence (Blau & Blau, 1982). However, in this chapter we intentionally avoid lengthy theoretical discussions in favor of describing how specific influences suggest direction for social action.

The approach offered here is that the societal influences we discuss act primarily as background influences on violence but can also directly influence its occurrence. These influences set the stage for the unprecedented violence in the United States involving children and youth. Also, we contend that no single factor can predict or explain much of the variance in recurrent violence or in who will be violent (Eron, Gentry, & Schlegel, 1994). Violence is a multiply determined behavior that develops and is influenced by, all levels of developmental factors as well as individual differences (Tolan, Guerra, & Kendall, 1995).

In Figure 1, we present a biopsychosocial model of influences on youth violence (Tolan & Guerra, 1994). Our approach is similar to the general developmental approach offered by Bronfenbrenner (1979); we assume that these multiple influences are best understood as levels of influ-

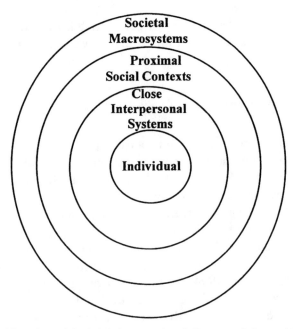

Figure 1. Multilevel model of risk factors that influence violence involving children.

ence, each nested within the less proximal influence. In this model, we differentiate among four levels of influence on violence: individual characteristics, close interpersonal relations, proximal social contexts, and societal macrosystems. Close interpersonal relations represent enduring relationships that are particularly salient environmental influences on behavior and development. Family and close friends are the primary examples of this level. Proximal social contexts represent the primary settings of development such as school, neighborhood, and work. Macrosystems are the mores, laws, policies, and general influences such as the media and the overall trends in behavior and risk in a society. The concentric circles in the figure indicate that individual characteristics are nested within close interpersonal relationships; these, in turn, are nested within proximal settings; and these are nested within societal macrosystems. We suggest, therefore, that many of the societal influences work as the base from which "smaller" and more proximal system influences occur. In other words, societal influences are likely to be less figural and their effect more diffuse, forming the background against which other, more dramatic influences occur.

This chapter focuses on aspects of violence toward and by children and youths that are at the societal macrosystem level. This is because the causes of victimization and perpetration are similar, and the segments of the population most at risk for one are also at risk for the other. The similarity may be due to societal causes in particular, although evidence suggests that the shared causes extend across all levels of influence. Another important consideration in our perspective is the emerging data that suggest that violence against children may have a different pattern from violence against older youth.

VIOLENCE PERPETRATION AND VICTIMIZATION

The basic distinction between youth and child violence that is emerging is between victimization of children under age 12 and victimization of adolescents aged 12–19. Young children are primarily assaulted by adults, and the rate of victimization is lower than during adolescence (Tolan & Guerra, 1994). During adolescence, not only does risk for victimization increase, but the most likely perpetrators become other youths (Elliott, 1994). To illustrate this distinction, we focus on the case example presented in Table 1. Using murder cases involving children under age 15 in the city of Chicago during 1994, we tabulated the age of the victim by the age of the perpetrator and the perpetrator's relationship to the victim. For victims aged 5 and under, the perpetrator was almost always an adult parent or relative. In contrast, for adolescents, 60% of the known assailants were nonrelated juveniles, and only 4 of 30 victims were murdered by a relative.

The youth victimization–perpetration relation is further detailed in Table 2. As shown, over 70% of violent crimes against youths aged 12–19 are committed by other youths. Although both age groups are harmed by violence occurring at alarming rates, these trends suggest a need to focus on youths as well as children.

The data illustrate that adolescence is the time of higher risk than any other age period for both victimization and perpetration, and the risk differential may be increasing. Rates of serious and lethal violence among juveniles have been steadily increasing in recent years (Elliott, 1994). For example, in 1992, 1.5 million crimes were committed against juveniles, representing a 23% increase from 1987. Although juveniles accounted for only 10% of the population, they represented 23% of all victims of violent crime (Office of Juvenile Justice and Delinquency Planning; OJJDP, 1994). Similar shifts have occurred in perpetration, with increases in juvenile

TABLE 1
A 1994 Case Study of 67 Homicides With Child Victims in Chicago

Age of victim (years)	Perpetrator characteristics				
	Adult parent	Adult relative	Adult nonrelative	Juvenile relative	Juvenile unknown
5 and under (n = 29)	11	2	13	0	2
6–14 (n = 38)	4	0	8	0	18

TABLE 2
Percentages of Crimes of Violence Against Children Aged 12–19 by Age of Offender

Type of crime	Age of offender (years)				
	Under 12	12–14	15–17	18–20	Total
All violent crimes	1.8	22.2	23.8	22.5	70.3
Assault	1.7	22.5	26.4	23.7	74.3

Note: For victims of 20 years or older, 16%–25% of violent crimes were by perpetrators under 20.

crime rates far exceeding those among adults, particularly for the most serious violent offenses (OJJDP, 1994). In some cases, such as forcible rape, arrest rates for juveniles have shown a steady rise from the mid-1980s through the mid-1990s. In other cases, such as murder, sharp increases have been noted in recent years. For example, the juvenile arrest rate for murder increased 84% from 1987 to 1991 (Federal Bureau of Investigation, 1992).

Childhood and adolescent violence victimization, therefore, is a complex problem consisting of both the adult abuse of children and youth-to-youth victimization, and perpetration and victimization are closely related. We discuss the societal causes as providing a context that fosters violence toward and by children and youths. The relation of victimization and perpetration to societal factors can be seen in each of the four major types of societal influences we discuss in the following sections.

SOCIETAL NORMS AND CONVENTIONS

The United States has a long-standing history of exceptionally high rates of violence, particularly lethal violence, compared to other industrialized countries (Archer & Gartner, 1984). From the Wild West to *Rambo*, violence has long played a role in the traditions of this country. Although one routinely hears pleas to "stop the violence," societal norms and conventions often stand in direct opposition to these pleas. Clearly, there are multiple examples of U.S. society's collective infatuation with violence, from the discussions about how much to use capital punishment, to the morals of popular murder mysteries, to the glory attributed to a football player who flattens an opposing player. The level of violence, the unrealistic portrayal of the effects of using violence, and the frequent use of violence by heroes to successfully solve problems in television shows and movies create a sense that violence is necessary and can solve social and personal problems. These dramatizations suggest that violence is exciting, effective, and acceptable. With the prominence of violence and its regular portrayal as effective or entertaining, an atmosphere develops that at least tolerates violence and perhaps even encourages it.

Cross-cultural and historical studies have supported the relation between societal norms concerning violence and actual levels of violence. For example, Lambert, Triandis, and Wolf (1959) reported that societies with punitive deities tend to use punitive violence more frequently. Cross-cultural studies of child-rearing attitudes and behavior also have suggested a relation between acceptance of violence in caregiving and child abuse (Solheim, 1982). Higgins and Straus (cited in Straus, Gelles, & Steinmetz, 1980) examined the use of violence in children's books from 1850 to 1970 and detected a corresponding relation between the extent of violence depicted in fiction and the concurrent violence levels in society.

The influence of norms about violence is illustrated more directly in a study by Baron, Straus, and Jaffee (1990). These authors proposed the existence of "spillover effects" of support for legitimate violence to attitudes approving the use of violence and of both of these to rates of violent acts in a society. The investigators used states of the United States as the unit of analysis and rape as the violence measure. They calculated an index of *legitimate violence* on the basis of three factors: (a) media violence level (readership rate per 100,000 of violent magazines and the Nielsen ratings of the six most violent shows in that state); (b) level of state-sponsored violence (state legislation permitting corporal punishment in schools, prisoners sentenced to death per 100,000, and executions per 100 homicide arrests over 40 years); and (c) citizen participation in legal or socially approved violent activities (hunting licenses per 100,000, state of origin of college football players, National Guard enrollment per 100,000, National Guard expenditure per capita, and lynchings per million during 1882–1927). The authors also calculated an index of *violence approval* on the basis of three factors: (a) public opinion favoring legitimate violence (percentage of respondents who support greater military spending, support the death penalty, and oppose gun permits); (b) extent of endorsement of violence in conflicts with a threatening stranger; and (c) approval of police using violence to subdue an adult male suspect. They found that the legitimate violence index and the violence approval index were highly correlated. The legitimate violence and violence approval scores did not directly correlate as highly with rates of rape as did demographic characteristics such as the proportion of the population composed of urban dwellers, blacks, or divorced males; however, these indices did relate to the demographic correlates, and they added significant variance in explanation of rape rates above that explained by the demographic predictors. Therefore, this study suggested a link between legitimate violence and attitudes that approve of violence and, ultimately, criminal violence rates.

Perhaps the strongest empirical evidence suggesting a link between societally sanctioned forms of violence and actual violence can be found in studies of the effects of media violence. Four major types of scientific studies have examined the relation between exposure to violence on television and aggression or violence: (a) experimental studies in which children's exposure to violence is manipulated and short-term changes in behavior are evaluated, (b) static observational field studies in which exposure to media violence and aggressive behavior are assessed, (c) longitudinal field studies in which children's exposure to media violence and their aggressive behavior are assessed at two or more points in their lives, and (d) community studies of changes in availability of television.

A review of this literature is beyond the scope of the chapter and can be found elsewhere (e.g., Eron & Huesmann, 1987). In short, there is clearly a convergence of evidence across all four types of studies suggesting that the current level of interpersonal violence in U.S. society has been *boosted* by the long-term effects of childhood exposure to a steady diet of dramatic media violence. This does not mean that the current level of violence is solely or even primarily due to the long-term exposure to media violence. However, it is evident that media violence is a contributing societal factor to the learning of aggression and violence in children.

It is important to realize that exposure to violence can affect risk to both populations and individuals. For instance, it has been shown that the advent of television is related to increases in general levels of aggression among children in a community (Eron & Huesmann, 1987). Additionally, within populations, children who watch more violent television are more at risk for aggression (Eron & Huesmann, 1987). Exposure to violence not only relates to aggression during childhood, but also has been shown to predict adult arrests for serious crimes as well as harshness of physical punishment toward one's children (Eron et al., 1994).

These societal macrosystem influences seem to carry cultural values that are expressed as normative influences (Wolfgang & Ferracuti, 1982). This orientation can build a "code of violence" that fosters a willingness to use violence with little reservation (Anderson, 1990). Similarly, for some men, violence toward women may be embedded in a subculture that promotes dominance of women through aggressive means (Bowker, 1983). It may be that in some segments of society men are supported in seeing violence as their province. A more insidious effect is an overall acceptance of violence that makes it easier for individuals to engage in violent acts with believed legitimacy; this acceptance may make it more likely that citizens will overstep the bounds of previous behavior regulations and engage in aggressive or violent acts because these acts are judged to be appropriate by normative comparisons. To the extent that violence is socially sanctioned, prevention and intervention efforts must compete with this normative influence.

THE INSTITUTIONALIZATION OF VIOLENCE
AGAINST CHILDREN

Consistent with a high level of societal acceptance of violence is a clear pattern of institutionalized support for violent practices against children in the United States. These practices have their roots in some of the earliest forms of child maltreatment. Although it is no longer routine to terrorize children or leave them to die, as was common throughout history, some violence against children by both parents and caregivers is seen as the prerogative of adults (Levine & Levine, 1992). The legitimacy attached to this kind of caregiving has been supported by numerous Supreme Court rulings. For example, in *Ingram v. Wright* (1977), the Supreme Court ruled that corporal punishment in school was acceptable for controlling students. The Court resorted to tautological reasoning, ruling that such violence was acceptable because it was a long-standing and commonplace practice in U.S. society. The second reason given for supporting corporal punishment was that those subjected to it were protected from misuse of the punishment because of the public nature of such actions: The Court said that because corporal punishment was publicly administered, it would not be unjustly, too extensively, or too vigorously applied. The Court concluded that corporal punishment did not constitute cruel and unusual punishment and that children in school did not need the same due-process procedural protections that are afforded adult criminals and most persons in most other public institutional settings.

Another important policy statement from the courts concerned parents' prerogative to use violence to punish children. In the *Delaney* case (1989), the Supreme Court addressed the issue of children as property of parents. This was one of a series of decisions affirming parents' rights to raise children as they see fit, growing out of their right to control their children's development and behavior in a manner akin to property owners' rights, including the use of physical punishment. The contention in *Delaney* (1989) and other cases that extreme physical punishment is an infringement on a child's civil rights and that therefore the state could intervene and regulate such behavior was put forward. By not disallowing such behavior in an earlier case, the court reasoned that the state (through its child protection services agency) had affirmed the parents' property rights over the child to do as the parent sees fit. Thus in the *Delaney* case, the court stated that an abusing parent could not be charged with violation of a child's rights because the state had not acted earlier to protect the child from the abuse. Besides employing twisted logic, the decision is also important because it focused on the idea that there is a conflict between the parent and the state with regard to the treatment of children and made the primary issue whether the state can intrude on parents' rights to manage their "chattel" as they see fit. The ruling overlooked the issue of the ways in which corporal punishment can be inflicted and how that variation can change the balance between parental rights and the states interest in protecting children from abuse. Unfortunately, in cases such as these, the rights of the victimized child are considered almost irrelevant to the legal evaluation.

Such rulings do not create attitudes supporting violence toward children. For the most part, they merely reflect current attitudes concerning parental and caregiver rights to use violence toward children. Most parents see spanking and hitting children as acceptable and appropriate behaviors (Straus et al., 1980). Corporal punishment is legal and sanctioned in schools that routinely suspend or expel students for acts of aggression. In some states, schools can invoke physical punishments that would be considered child abuse in other settings. The institutionalization of violence against children in key systems such as the family and the school further reinforces the norm that violence against children is acceptable, and it provides a context for a broad range of violent actions. The legal reinforcement of such violence by major court rulings makes its continuation more likely.

THE STATUS OF CHILDREN

In part, the acceptability of violence against children is related to the social status of children. Historians and social analysts who have traced the status of children consistently have noted that legal and social traditions have relegated children to secondary status in the United States (Levine & Levine, 1992). Although lengthy and complex descriptions of the roots of these observations could be provided, we simply note here the basis of parental rights in property law, the long delay in extending basic constitutional rights to children, and the continued discrepancy between the civil, economic, and criminal protections afforded adults and those afforded children (McCarthy & Carr, 1980).

Another indicator of the secondary status of children that may contribute to the acceptance of violence toward children is the level and nature of allocations for children's programs. For example, support services available for children often are determined by provider constituents or agency boundaries and domains rather than by the needs of children. This situation can quickly lead to an inefficient attempt by multiple agencies to address some aspect of children's problems. The agencies become bureaucracies focused on patronage employment and what are deemed "entitlement," or nonessential, services. They are labeled "money-wasting labyrinths." For example, Coughlin and Perry (1993) identified 28 offices within the federal government that administer programs for children and families, and the programs are overseen by a variety of committees within

Congress. These committees do not speak with one voice; in fact, the members may not even speak with each other. Instead, each focuses on funding programs and on establishing policies that affect its constituency. The impact on children frequently is a secondary concern at best. That their nominal purpose is to serve children may be lost in political wrangling. There is no single voice or interest group requiring that the focus on children take first place.

Administrative organizations such as these can be found at both state and local levels. They often lead to program decisions that impede due attention to the violence problems of children. For example, the Child Abuse Prevention and Treatment Act of 1974 was the first federal statute addressing the operation of child protective service agencies. It was meant to organize and elevate the quality of service rendered to abused children. However, it has had limited impact on the reporting of cases or on the strengthening of public child protective service responses (Vandeven & Newberger, 1994). In part, this is because the law was worded as a mandate rather than to indicate specific policy and practice. In addition, the level of funding has always been too small to have substantial impact on practices. The second-class status of children is reinforced by such inefficient actions.

SOCIAL FORCES

Most analyses of social forces within a society vis-à-vis violence have centered on factors related to social injustices; specific reference is made to social forces that reflect differential opportunities, rewards, and status. It is clear that racial and gender discrimination, differential access to resources, and other social inequities represent societal influences on violence; however, the mechanisms through which this effect occurs and the extent of the impact have not been determined. Researchers have placed particular emphasis on stress, poverty, and social isolation; studies indicate that these factors play a critical role in violence perpetration and victimization, although direct effects are less likely (Garbarino & Kostelny, 1993). Clearly, children as a group suffer more from these social forces than do other groups. Additionally, for children there is frequently a double effect: Children who are at high risk for violence perpetration and victimization also receive little protection and relief from the service delivery systems.

One type of social condition that can affect the risk of violence involves the transitions and stresses in children's lives (Attar, Guerra, & Tolan, 1994; Gorman-Smith, Tolan, & Henry, in press). Stressful life events have been shown to affect parental abuse of children as well as children's own interpersonal aggression, although the correlations have been neither unequivocal nor strong. A number of researchers have found that abusive families report more life stressors than do nonabusive families (Straus et al., 1980). Others have extended these findings to include mild stressors such as daily hassles (Herrenkohl & Herrenkohl, 1981). Stressful life events, including exposure to community violence, have been shown to predict children's aggression toward peers (Attar et al., 1994).

It is common to find that violence rates are related to poverty, particularly at the neighborhood level. There is more crime and violence in poor neighborhoods than wealthier neighborhoods, although relations between income and violence within a given neighborhood are relatively weak (Jencks, 1992). It is unlikely that this effect is due to income alone; it is more likely a consequence of economic inequality (Currie, 1986). Blau and Blau (1982) examined crime rates in 125 metropolitan areas in the United States. Focusing on economic inequalities, they found significantly higher murder rates in cities where the difference in income between rich and poor was extremely high and where employers discriminated against blacks. Cross-national studies of murder also have supported this influence, with the income gap between rich and poor countries accounting for as much as one sixth of the variation in countries' murder rates (Archer & Gartner, 1984).

Child abuse also appears to be significantly related to social class (Straus et al., 1980). What is less clear is the precise nature of this relation. For example, in their national survey, Straus and Gelles (1986) noted that the only difference by social class in violence toward children was that the highest income group had lower rates than other groups. Furthermore, although living in poverty related to a 75% increase in child abuse, witnessing child abuse, apart from social class considerations, had the same relative influence. The combination of poverty and witnessing child abuse related to a 400% increase in likelihood of abuse. It may be, therefore, that poverty sets the stage for increased risk for violence through increased exposure to child abuse.

Another factor associated with poverty and economic inequality is unemployment. Unemployment and part-time employment both have been shown to relate to violence against children. For instance, Steinberg, Catalano, and Dooley (1981) examined the relation between changes in employment and child abuse in two metropolitan areas. Their findings suggested that increases in abuse are related to decreases in the size of the workforce. Nonetheless, it is difficult to conclude that poverty directly influences child abuse independently of the prevailing social standards. One need only consider that the depression of the 1930s was associated with dramatic declines in murder rates, despite levels of unemployment among the highest in this century (Archer & Gartner, 1984).

Finally, social isolation, another factor often associated with poverty in urban settings, has been associated with overall levels of community violence as well as violence toward children. In one study comparing two neighborhoods matched for social class but differing in rates of child abuse, Garbarino and Sherman (1980) found that lower rates of child abuse and maltreatment were associated with more extensive social networks among families. Such networks can provide help with daily tasks, increased monitoring of children, and access to resources that help children and families cope with stressful circumstances.

There is evidence that socioeconomic influences interact with other social forces to affect violence. We have previously noted that Zuravin's (1989) review of the ecology of child maltreatment showed neighborhood economic status to be related to violence only as part of a larger array of predictive characteristics. Income level and stability, residential stability and social support, the quality of housing and business, the distribution of men and women of different age groups, economic inequalities, and job opportunities seemed to be more influential predictors. Thus, the correlates of poverty rather than poverty per se may best predict violence toward children.

CONCLUSION

The multiple influences discussed suggest that violence toward and by children and youths is dependent, at least in part, on the mores, policies, and practices of U.S. society. Any attempts to modify the alarming rates will necessitate affecting these societal factors. We have noted several societal causes of violence and have summarized data and ideas that might move the discussion "off the bar stool" to a broader social science conceptualization. We believe that it is important to consider violence against children as occurring in multiple forms and with different causes underlying those forms. We also think that consideration of child victimization in its relation to child perpetration is valuable.

The empirical understanding of these causes and of the relations among the different forms is in its infancy. In part, this is due to the difficulty in manipulating conditions or even finding comparable conditions to permit quasi-experimental evaluations to discern the important factors and processes. We have suggested that consideration of the relation of victimization to perpetration is one important advance because it is likely that the societal influences on both aspects of violence are the same. In addition, we have suggested that a useful theoretical perspective is to view the societal factors as background influences within which more proximal, and perhaps more direct, influences are nested. Finally, we have suggested that there is a need to consider how adolescent risk compares to child risk in focusing efforts toward understanding and intervention. It may be that the same societal influences are important contributors to risk for both groups, but it may also be that the greater risk for adolescents is due to the greater impact on adolescents of societal influences. Of course, these contentions need to be tested in research.

Clearly, there is need for more information—from surveys as well as correlational and intervention studies. Cross-societal studies may be a key type of research. By examining the effects of variations in policies and practices on different types of violence, researchers may gain some of the most convincing evidence about the extent of the relation between societal influences and violence in general. Also, such studies will permit the specification of which societal factors relate to violence and what the mechanisms are.

In addition to the need for more sound information, there is a need to recognize that societal causes ultimately reflect fundamental social ills. Social scientists need to consider carefully how these ills are caused and maintained, as well as how to remove some of the deleterious effects of stable societal causes, how to manage meager resources allocated to aiding children, and how to bring about the needed changes in norms, social conventions, and institutionalized supports for violence against children. Social scientists also need to consider the cost of less extensive responses or failure to recognize the basic nature of these causes. Although the effects of social ills may not be direct, they provide a background, or setting, within which more direct influences occur; addressing these societal influences is a requisite for substantial improvement.

The issues involved in the societal causes of violence against children can be summarized by the following comment by Halpern (1993):

> When we define the problem as neglect of children, we tend to look to solutions that seem immediately linked to the neglect—better health care, better child care, more investment in education, more responsive child welfare services. These obviously are critical. But the basic reasons for the lack of well-being of many children in American society are not found in schools or health clinics or social service agencies. They are found in the primacy of the marketplace in defining people's worth and entitlement, and in shaping social relations. . . . Building a reform agenda primarily on children's issues only masks the contentious issues of our common life . . . to try to protect children from the toxic effects of their society has reflected the same tendency towards denial of social reality. . . . Children's problems cannot be addressed separately from the more general problem of society. (p. 1)

REFERENCES

Anderson, E. J. (1990). *Streetwise: Race, class, and change in an urban community.* Chicago: University of Chicago Press.

Archer, D., & Gartner, R. (1984). *Violence and crime in cross-national perspective.* New Haven, CT: Yale University Press.

Attar, B. K., Guerra, N. G., & Tolan, P. H. (1994). Neighborhood disadvantage, stressful life events, and adjustment in urban elementary-school children. *Journal of Clinical Child Psychology, 23,* 391–400.

Baron, L., Straus, M. A., & Jaffee, D. (1990). Legitimate violence, violent attitudes, and rape: A test of the cultural spillover theory. *Annals of the New York Academy of Sciences,* pp. 17–110.

Blau, J., & Blau, P. (1982). The cost of inequality: Metropolitan structure and violent crime. *American Sociological Review, 47,* 114–129.

Bowker, L. H. (1983). *Beating wife-beating.* Lexington, MA: Heath.

Bronfenbrenner, U. (1979). *The ecology of human development: Experiments by nature and design.* Cambridge, MA: Harvard University Press.

Coughlin, P., & Perry, D. (1993). *National policy on children and families.* Unpublished manuscript, Georgetown University Child Development Center, Washington, DC.

Currie, E. (1986). *Confronting crime.* New York: Pantheon Books.

Elliott, D. S. (1994). Serious violent offenders: Onset, developmental course, and termination—the American Society of Criminology 1993 presidential address. *Criminology, 32,* 1–21.

Eron, L. D., Gentry, J. J., & Schlegel, P. (Eds.). (1994). *Reason to hope: A psychological perspective on violence and youth.* Washington, DC: American Psychological Association.

Eron, L. D., & Huesmann, L. R. (1987). Television as a source of maltreatment of children. *School Psychology Review, 16,* 195–202.

Federal Bureau of Investigation. (1992). *Uniform crime reports.* Washington, DC: Author.

Garbarino, J., & Kostelny, K. (1993). Neighborhood and community influences on parenting. In T. Luster & L. Okagaki (Eds.), *Parenting: An ecological perspective* (pp. 203–226). Hillsdale, NJ: Erlbaum.

Garbarino, J., & Sherman, D. (1980). High-risk neighborhoods and high-risk families: The human ecology of child maltreatment. *Child Development, 51,* 188–198.

Gorman-Smith, D., Tolan, P. H., & Henry, D. (in press). The relation of community and family to risk among urban poor adolescents. In P. Cohen, L. Robins, & C. Slomkowski (Eds.), *Where and when: Influence of historical time and place on aspects of psychopathology.* Hillsdale, NJ: Erlbaum.

Halpern, R. (1993, Fall/Winter). The meaning of child saving. *Erikson,* pp. 14–19.

Herrenkohl, R. C., & Herrenkohl, E. C. (1981). Some antecedents and developmental consequences of child maltreatment. *New Directions for Child Development, 11,* 57–76.

Ingram v. Wright, 430 U.S. 651, 97 Ct. 1401, 1977.

In re Delaney, 1989.

Jencks, C. (1992). *Rethinking social policy*. New York: Harper Perennial.

Lambert, W. W., Triandis, L. M., & Wolf, M. (1959). Some correlates of beliefs in the malevolence and benevolence of supernatural beings: A cross-societal study. *Journal of Abnormal and Social Psychology, 58,* 162–169.

Levine, M., & Levine, A. (1992). *Helping children: A social history*. New York: Oxford University Press.

McCarthy, F. B., & Carr, J. G. (1980). *Juvenile law and its processes*. New York: Bobbs-Merrill.

Monahan, J. (1993). Causes of violence. In United States Sentencing Commission (Ed.), *Drugs and violence in America*. Washington, DC: U.S. Government Printing Office.

Office of Juvenile Justice and Delinquency Planning. (1994). *Report on trends in youth crime*. Washington, DC: U.S. Government Printing Office.

Solheim, J. S. (1982). A cross-cultural examination of use of corporal punishment on children: A focus on Sweden and the United States. *Child Abuse and Neglect, 6,* 147–154.

Steinberg, L., Catalano, R., & Dooley, D. (1981). Economic antecedents of child abuse and neglect. *Child Development, 52,* 975–985.

Straus, M. A., Gelles, R. J., & Steinmetz, S. K. (1980). *Behind closed doors: Violence in the American family*. Garden City, NY: Anchor Books.

Tolan, P. H., & Guerra, N. G. (1994). *What works in reducing adolescent violence: An empirical review of the field*. Monograph prepared for the Center for the Study and Prevention of Youth Violence. Boulder: University of Colorado.

Tolan, P. H., Guerra, N. G., & Kendall, P. (1995). A developmental–ecological perspective on antisocial behavior in children and adolescents: Towards a unified risk and intervention framework. *Journal of Consulting and Clinical Psychology, 63,* 515–517.

Vandeven, A. M., & Newberger, E. H. (1994). Child abuse. *Annual Review of Public Health, 15,* 367–379.

Wolfgang, M. E., & Ferracuti, F. (1982). *The subculture of violence* (2nd ed.). Beverly Hills, CA: Sage.

Zuravin, S. J. (1989). The ecology of child abuse and neglect: Review of the literature and presentation of data. *Violence and Victims, 4,* 101–120.

III

AMELIORATING NEGATIVE DEVELOPMENTAL CONSEQUENCES: EFFECTIVE INTERVENTION STRATEGIES

9

TREATMENT AND INTERVENTION FOR CHILD VICTIMS OF VIOLENCE

DAVID KOLKO

This chapter reviews recent literature that describes and evaluates intervention techniques or programs for children who have been sexually or physically abused, neglected, psychologically or emotionally abused, or exposed to violence at home or in the community. This broad perspective on the treatment of childhood victimization is warranted owing to the accumulation of empirical evidence suggesting the adverse impact of each of these forms of maltreatment on children's development, children's subsequent experience of clinical dysfunction, and the co-occurrence of the different forms of abuse (see Toth & Cicchetti, 1993; Finkelhor, 1995). This chapter is organized by maltreatment subtype to provide an overview of salient developmental effects, treatment models or descriptions, program evaluation reports and findings from controlled studies, and clinical and research directions. Although there is clearly much overlap among these various forms of child maltreatment, separate presentation permits a clearer

This chapter was supported, in part, by Grants 90CA1459 and 90CA1547 from the National Center on Child Abuse and Neglect (NCCAN). The author appreciates the constructive comments of Cynthia Schellenbach and Elissa Brown and the technical assistance of Cathy Rich and Kathy Smith.

depiction of the progress made in developing the therapeutic and empirical underpinnings of work in each type of maltreatment.

Because the purpose of this chapter is primarily to review recent program descriptions and findings, few details are provided regarding earlier studies or reports in this area. When applicable, the reader is referred to several excellent sources to gain a more comprehensive perspective on this material (e.g., Becker et al., 1995). These sources provide additional characteristics of relevant studies, along with insightful recommendations for future work in each area. Furthermore, there are several technical and methodological developments that have been described in other sources but are relevant to the present focus on treatment models and their evaluation. For example, progress has been made in documenting the functional context and parameters of abusive interactions (e.g., frequency, severity, chronicity, situational context) using structured coding systems (Barnett, Manly, & Cicchetti, 1993) and in conducting comprehensive clinical evaluations of relevant symptoms, disorders (Chaffin, Bonner, Worley, & Lawson, 1996), and areas of individual and family resources or dysfunction (e.g., depression, aggression; Azar & Wolfe, 1989).

SEXUAL ABUSE AND SEXUAL BEHAVIOR PROBLEMS

Effects of Sexual Abuse

There is growing empirical support for the developmental consequences of sexual abuse in children and adolescents (Knutson, 1995; Letourneau, Saunders, & Kilpatrick, 1996; Putnam & Trickett, 1995), including their long-term effects (Widom & Ames, 1994) and relationship to the need for intervention (see Green, 1993). Common problems to be addressed during treatment reflect hypersexuality and sexual behavior problems; fear, anxiety, and depression; dysfunctional attributions; and social or interpersonal difficulties. Developmental concepts have been applied to a traumagenic model of child sexual abuse, highlighting the importance of understanding the developmental context of both the risks for and the effects of victimization (Finkelhor, 1995). Considerable attention in the literature has been paid to developing conceptual and therapeutic models that provide clinical guidelines for the treatment of child victims of sexual abuse who show these and other symptoms.

Models and Clinical Guidelines

Models developed from work with adult survivors bear implications for clinical work with young victims in the attempt to integrate various aspects of the treatment process, such as trauma, treatment, and recovery (Leibowitz, Harvey, & Herman, 1993). These concepts and their associated clinical strategies have been incorporated into abuse-specific treatments developed for special child populations or specific treatment methods. In terms of individual treatment, for example, Cohen and Mannarino (1993) outlined an approach based on cognitive–behavioral therapy (CBT) for preschool sexual abuse victims and their parents that is designed to be structured and brief and to target both the symptoms commonly observed in these children and the clinical issues that may predict the severity of dysfunction. Accordingly, both child issues (e.g., safety, assertion, ambivalence) and parent issues (e.g., attributions, support, child management) are addressed using several parallel procedures (e.g., imagery, contingencies, problem solving).

Because group treatment has been a primary treatment method for sexual abuse victims for some time, it is not surprising to find expansions in content and advances in clinical formulations and specific techniques. One example is the group program developed by Zaidi and Gutierrez-Kovner (1995) designed to address the traumagenic effects of sexual abuse in young girls (Finkelhor & Browne, 1985). The authors described six treatment methods within this perspective (e.g., group cohesion, discussion of abuse, coping techniques), but they also demonstrated how additional techniques (e.g., art therapy, psychodrama) can be incorporated into the program. Lindon and Nourse (1994) described a multidimensional group treatment program for adolescent girls that incorporates skills training (e.g., relaxation, assertion, social skills), psychotherapy (e.g., recognition of feelings, peer relations), and educational information (e.g., sexuality, self-protection). An advantage of this type of program is its use of specific cognitive–behavioral techniques in a structured, short-term program. Although it is less frequently reported on, family therapy for extrafamilial abuse may be needed when the child makes minimal progress following individual or group treatment (Roesler, Savin, & Grozs, 1993). Family therapy may help to provide a safe environment in which to discuss traumatic experiences; in cases of incest, there are integrated ways to conduct systemic work incorporating offenders (Greenspun, 1994). Many of these components have been integrated for use during inpatient treatment (Steinberg & Sunkenberg, 1994).

Friedrich's (1996a) integrated contextual model views the effects of abuse in children as emerging from three related domains: attachment, behavioral and emotional regulation, and self-perception/self-concept. A unique feature of this conceptualization is the delineation of treatment approaches at the levels of the individual (e.g., play treatment), group (didactics), and family (goal attainment) that are based on each of these three major aspects of functioning (see p. 116 in Friedrich, 1996). Other developments provide a clear overview of specific clinical considerations to address in understanding and treating abused adolescents, emphasizing such important issues as the initial interview, assessment of attributions, and individual, group, and educative therapies (Chaffin et al., 1996).

Empirical Reports and Studies

Much of the early research work in this area has been described in other reviews (Beutler, Williams, & Zetzer, 1994; Finkelhor & Berliner, 1995). Studies have varied on several parameters, including the age ranges of the clients (children vs. adolescents), type of treatment approach (CBT vs. psychoeducation), and format of treatment (group vs. individual therapy). Although most researchers have used quasi-experimental designs, a few have used experimental designs. When applicable, these design features are noted.

Individual Therapy

Individual therapy has been applied successfully in several uncontrolled evaluations across treatment settings. Sullivan, Scanlan, Brookhouse, Schulte, and Knutson (1992), working with deaf sexually abused children, found some improvements in self-esteem, anxiety and depression, and externalizing behavior, as well as reduced risk ratings, relative to a no-treatment group that consisted of children whose parents declined participation in treatment. Lanktree and Briere (1995) reported changes on measures of traumatic effects and depression in a large outpatient sample consisting mostly of girls and their parents for whom individual treatment was given to the girls, along with group and family therapy. Within-group repeated-measures analyses revealed several reductions in symptoms after 3 months of treatment (e.g., posttraumatic stress, dissociation, anger). At 6 months, reductions were noted for anxiety and depression, with less change evident for sexual concerns. Improvements in sexual concerns and dissociation were associated with pressing charges against the offender. The significance of the study is limited by its lack of experimental controls and of sufficient preassessment data, as well as by increased attrition over time. However, the study highlighted the different levels of improvement evidenced by different symptom clusters and the need for some children to receive treatment for more than 1 year.

In a study evaluating their CBT protocol for preschoolers, Cohen and Mannarino (1996) worked with 86 referred families with well-documented abuse histories who were randomized to treatment conditions. CBT was administered across 12 sessions, divided into individual treatment for the parent and for the child. Specialized content was delivered to each participant in this protocol. Relative to those who received a nondirective–supportive treatment, those given CBT were similar at pretreatment on all measures; after treatment, they had lower scores on measures of internalizing symptoms, home problems, and sexual behavior problems, with no differences in externalizing symptoms or social competence. A significant Group × Time interaction was observed for internalizing symptoms. A total of 13 families (15%) dropped out of treatment, and another 6 children (7%), all from the group receiving nondirective treatment, were removed from treatment by the investigators owing to clinical concerns or child deterioration. The study is noteworthy for several positive features, such as the use of a therapist-crossover design, report of client satisfaction with both protocols, inclusion of parents and children in parallel treatment, and application of abuse-specific content. A recent follow-up report found greater improvements for the CBT condition in the children's internalizing and externalizing problems, and in specific preschoolers' problem behaviors, 1 year after treatment had ended (Cohen & Mannarino, 1996), suggesting the maintenance and enhancement of treatment gains.

Structured CBT protocols have been developed for school-aged children and their parents, focusing on providing training in coping skills, attention to cognitive attributional processes, and instruction in social behavior, among other behaviors, with resulting improvements in levels of posttraumatic symptoms, anxiety (state and trait), and depression (Deblinger, McLeer, & Henry, 1990). In an extension of this study, investigators examined the relative impact of separate and combined child and parent CBT in comparison to treatment provided in the community (Deblinger, Lippmann, & Steer, 1996). Ratings of parent-reported child behavior problems were reduced only in the two conditions involving parents, whereas child-reported symptoms were reduced only in the two conditions involving children as participants. Such results may imply that improvements in self-reported symptoms are more likely if informants are included as treatment participants. The applicability of this program to sexually abused preschool children and their nonoffending mothers recently has been described (Stauffer & Deblinger, 1996). Participation in the parallel child and parent CBT protocol was associated with significant pre- to posttreatment reductions in parenting dysfunction, avoidance behavior, parent practices, and child sexual behavior, which were maintained at a 3-month follow-up. There was a high level of satisfaction with the helpfulness of treatment (95%). Such findings are favorable, especially given the brevity of treatment, but are qualified by the absence of controls, use of parent reports only, variable duration of the baseline period, and high level of disinterest or dropout (44%).

Two short-term treatments varying in degree of structure were evaluated recently in a study involving young abused girls and their offending female caretakers (Celano, Hazzard, Webb, & McCall, 1996). The structured program (Recovering from Abuse Program, or RAP) was based on the four traumagenic dynamics attributed to sexual abuse (e.g., self-blame and stigmatization, betrayal; see Finkelhor & Browne, 1985) and compared to an unstructured comparison condition (treatment as usual). Both programs resulted in significant improvements on measures of posttraumatic stress disorder (PTSD), traumagenic beliefs, and general psychosocial functioning. The structured, abuse-specific program was more effective in increasing abuse-related caretaker support of the child and in reducing caretaker self-blame and expectations of adverse consequences of the sexual abuse on the child, highlighting the impact of abuse-specific treatment on adult support of child victims and the potential value of targeting attributional processes related to abusive experiences. Of course, follow-up data are needed to document the maintenance of these improvements.

Group Therapy

Group treatment programs are commonly administered and often include diverse expressive and instructional techniques. Several uncontrolled studies have reported improvements on pre- to posttreatment outcome measures (Corder, Haizlip, & De Boer, 1990). For example, one eclectic program (including puppet and crafts work, role-playing, assertion training, sexual education, and problem solving) resulted in reduced parent reports of internalizing and externalizing symptoms but no improvements in child-rated anxiety and self-esteem measures (Hiebert-Murphy, De Luca, & Runtz, 1992). Nelki and Watters (1989) also reported fewer problems noted by caretakers following brief structured group therapy plus a parallel parent group. Work by Friedrich, Luecke, Bielke, and Place (1992) showed the benefit of integrating group treatment with individual and parent or family services for sexually abused boys. Although no change was evident in measures of depression or self-esteem following approximately 8 months of multimodal treatment, improvements were observed in aggression and social behavior, sexualized behavior, and maternal and family functioning.

Other investigators of group interventions have examined brief exposure to abuse-focused discussion and structured games or exercises; some of these authors reported improvements in self-concept, depression, and suicidal ideation (Wagner, Kilcrease-Fleming, Fowler, & Kazelskis, 1993). An article by Hack, Osachuk, and De Luca (1994) described a structured group for preadolescent boys consisting of both structured group goals and exercises (e.g., discussion of protection and feelings, writing perpetrator letters) and explicit group rules (e.g., no fighting, name calling, or touching others). Improvements were noted in self-reports (of anxiety, depression, and self-esteem) and parent reports (of internalizing and externalizing problems), which generally were maintained at a 7-month follow-up. Similar improvements were reported following an interpersonal skills training program that used role-play assessments with peers and teachers (Weist, Vannatta, Wayland, & Jackson, 1993). In some instances, however, higher levels of certain problems have been reported after intervention (loneliness, Hiebert-Murphy et al., 1992; sex play or talk, Nelki & Watters, 1989). Unfortunately, the absence of comparison groups has limited the conclusions that can be reached from these studies.

Group therapy studies that have included comparison groups in quasi-experimental designs have described similar types of improvements. One group of researchers examined the impact of a novel PTSD-oriented, 20-week CBT program with adolescents living in a group home, most of whom also received individual therapy (Sinclair et al. 1995). Both the group's participants and adult informants reported improvements on measures of PTSD and internalizing symptoms. The adolescents also acknowledged improved self-concept but no reduction in depressive symptoms. Strengths of the study included the use of a male and female cotherapy team, multivariate analyses, and both child and parent measures; however, the children were referred to treatment after variable lengths of time, and it is not clear what types of individual therapy the children received.

Rust and Troupe (1991) conducted a 6-month, multifocus group (play treatment, supportive discussion), combined with individual treatment and a parallel mother's group, and compared the results with those obtained from a nonabused, matched comparison group drawn from the same schools. Treatment was found to increase self-esteem and school achievement, although the treated group began the study with lower scores on some of these measures. Improvements also have been reported for reinforcement-oriented (vs. psychodynamic) treatment for such problems as sleep disturbances, sex play, and enuresis in young children (Downing, Jenkins, & Fisher, 1988). However, other studies have found no differences between groups having no treatment and groups having unspecified treatment (Goodman et al., 1992; Oates, O'Toole, Lynch, Stern, & Cooney, 1994).

In one of the few experimental studies of group treatment, Verleur, Hughes, and Dobkin De Rios (1986) found that psychoeducational information regarding birth control and sexually transmitted diseases resulted in increased sexual awareness scores, relative to the scores of those receiving no treatment, but the study did not include other symptom or adjustment data. The authors of two dissertations on group treatment reported improvements in self-concept and self-mastery (Perez, 1988) and negative affect (Burke, 1988), relative to no treatment. Perez (1988) also found no differences between individual and group play treatments. These two unstructured conditions differed from Burke's (1988) group treatment, which was highly structured. Using a similar design, McGain and McKinzey (1995) evaluated the impact of a treatment program involving discussions of abusive experiences, the provision of support, and suggestions regarding prevention and protection. The two groups studied were similar at pretreatment but differed at posttreatment on several scales of a behavior problem checklist (e.g., conduct problems, attention problems and immaturity, anxiety withdrawal) and on both the overall intensity and the range of problem behavior. However, the means for the experimental group fell below the clinical cutoff on the behavior problem checklist only. The use of samples matched on abuse history and demographic background and the fact that externalizing problems, especially aggression, showed improvement are notable; however, the absence of Group × Time interaction analyses, self-reports, or a discussion of attrition limits the conclusions one can draw from this study. Other comparisons of alternative interventions have revealed greater improvement in self-esteem, but in no other measures, for those given group than those given individual therapy (Baker, 1987) and no differences between the two types of therapy (Perez, 1988).

In one of the largest outcome studies reported to date, Berliner and Saunders (1996) examined the impact of structured educational groups on adolescents based on cognitive–behavioral procedures with or without an additional component of stress inoculation and gradual exposure to discussions of the abusive experience to minimize fear and anxiety. There were improvements on various measures after treatment (e.g., anxiety, fear, depression, traumatic effects, sexual behavior, internalizing symptoms) through a 2-year follow-up, but there were no significant Group × Time interactions that supported the superiority of the enhanced group program. An implication noted by the authors is the importance of documenting heightened fear and anxiety before initiating specific treatments to reduce the severity of these symptoms. This study is noteworthy for its methodological rigor and attention to monitoring of the integrity of treatment.

A recent meta-analysis of group treatment outcomes for sexually abused children extended the generally positive impression of the impact of this modality (Reeker, Ensing, & Elliott, 1997). The analysis of 15 studies evaluating the effectiveness of treatment resulted in an effect size of .79 (range: 0.00–1.63) and revealed no significant differences in the effects on different outcome measure categories. It should be noted that some of the studies were single pre- to posttreatment comparisons, potentially inflating the estimate of effect size.

Family Treatment

Family sessions and treatments have been evaluated in only a few studies. In some instances, family treatment has been integrated with instruction in normal sexual development and abuse-specific discussions to reduce risk status (Bentovim, van Elberg, & Boston, 1988; Furniss, Bingley-Miller, & Van Elberg, 1988). In one recent experimental study, the investigators evaluated the incremental benefit of child and family groups added to family–network meetings with 4- to 16-year-old child victims (Hyde, Bentovim, & Monck, 1995); the program was based on findings from a larger descriptive and treatment outcome study (Monck et al., 1994). Family–network meetings (for 4–6 weeks) allowed the family to meet with therapists and community professionals to address multiple issues (e.g., communication, protection, marital problems), whereas parallel group work (6–20 weeks) provided exposure to abuse-specific information relevant to the children (e.g., feelings, social development, self-protection information) and adults e.g., secrecy, parental response).

The full sample showed an improvement across time (pre- to post-treatment) on standardized measures of child health, behavior, and depression, but not on measures of child-reported behavior and self-concept or on teacher reports of symptoms. Mothers reported improved self-concept and behavior. Clinician ratings after treatment reflected comparable percentages of cases classified with good (33%), moderately good (36%), or little or no (31%) improvement, along with improvements over time on specific variables (e.g., child's positive self-concept, child's resolution of feelings toward mother and offender, family's perception of child's needs). There were no group differences over time on standardized measures, but clinician ratings revealed some superiority for the combined condition on several treatment aims (e.g., child sharing painful feelings and having more positive self-concept, family perception of child's needs). A high percentage of children saw group work as a positive experience (71%) and as helpful in preventing further abuse (78%). The study is noteworthy for its use of age-matched groups and inclusion of offenders in services, although it is also limited, given the number of children who lived apart from their parents or who moved during treatment, the absence of outcome data (means) reported for the primary measures used in statistical analyses, the long assessment interval (up to 12 months), and the absence of data on treatment integrity.

Other Child-Directed Services

Other forms of intervention have clinical relevance owing to their potential impact on both short- and long-term outcomes. In an interesting survey, Berliner and Conte (1995) interviewed child victims and their parents regarding the effects of disclosure and intervention. The authors reported several important findings: (a) Children most often told their mothers (rather than someone else) about the abuse (48%), and although telling was perceived as difficult for them to do, 97% said it is good to tell; (b) children's views of professional treatment were primarily positive; (c) family experiences were related to perceived impact of the experience on the child; and (d) children saw counselors as helpful if they showed understanding, concern, and sincerity. The results suggested that children are sensitive to the manner in which they are evaluated and treated and benefit from the professional contacts they receive in the aftermath of abuse. Of course, additional studies that compare the impact of specific services are needed to document the benefits and risks associated with participation in each intervention component.

Comments and Critique

A few conclusions seem warranted on the basis of this brief review. Clearly, the programs generally have different theoretical approaches and therapeutic foci, and they incorporate diverse content (e.g., support, sex education, coping, work with puppets, process group). Discussion of the abuse experience, training in some type of coping skills, and attention to the child's general safety are among the more common elements in these interventions. Moreover, the children targeted both across and within treatment programs have varied widely in age and developmental status, which may influence the degree of improvement reported for each child. Beyond the supportive results found in several reports of uncontrolled studied, the findings from recent experimental evaluations show clinical improvements following individual, group, and family treatment and, in some cases, continued improvement at follow-up. The few studies in which alternative treatments were compared revealed few group differences. Additional attention ought to be paid to the collection of follow-up reports and official child abuse records, the use of repeated-measures analyses and appropriate statistical tests, and both the expansion and comparison of alternative treatments.

PHYSICAL ABUSE

Effects of Physical Abuse

It is documented in several sources that some of the strongest effects of child physical abuse reflect problems with aggression and social or interpersonal behavior as well as negative parent–child interactions, all of which may reflect disturbances in general attachment or relationships (e.g., Knutson, 1995; Kolko, 1992, 1996a; Malinosky-Rummell & Hansen, 1993; National Academy of Sciences, 1993; Widom & Maxfield, 1996). The results of a recent national survey of adolescents suggest an array of mental health effects following physical abuse, including heightened depression, violence, and suicidal tendencies (Swenson, Saunders, & Kirkpatrick, 1996). Because fewer group differences are found when clinic or at-risk samples are used for comparison, the effects of abuse may not differ from the effects of exposure to nonabusive, but inadequate, caretaking (Wolfe & Wekerle, 1993). Although there is extensive literature in the area of child sexual abuse, more information is needed regarding the prevalence of certain types of symptoms in physically abused children (e.g., affective or cognitive symptoms, problems in family relationships) and the impact of parental functioning and practices (e.g., coercive parenting, parental psychopathology) on the development of aggressive child behavior, social incompetence, and poor parent–child (or family) relationships.

Models and Clinical Guidelines

Few specific models have been proposed to guide the application of treatment techniques for physically abused children. Instead, most studies appear to reflect a general approach to the modification of abusive behavior and its sequelae based on an interactive model of the reciprocal influences between parents and children. For example, interventions based on the social-situational model have generally emphasized parent training in the use of nonviolent disciplinary skills, anger control and stress management, and contingency management (Azar & Siegel, 1990; Kolko, 1996a; Wolfe & Wekerle, 1993), together with clinical or support services (e.g., self-help groups, provision of information on child development). Such interventions may both promote a prosocial repertoire and minimize the psychological sequelae of abusive behavior. Given the complexities inherent in most cases of abuse, it is suggested that parent-directed methods to eliminate abusive behavior be supplemented with the evaluation, education, treatment, and follow-up of abused children to promote their social-psychological development (Graziano & Mills, 1992).

Another approach, the ecological model, views physical abuse from a systemic perspective, emphasizing the interrelationships among individual, family, and social support factors (e.g., family communication, extrafamilial contacts; Belsky, 1993). Accordingly, treatment from this perspective seeks to address various child (e.g., handling feelings), parent (e.g., empathy, physical punishment), and family (e.g., role reversal) issues; however, most interventions directed toward the family system have not been formally evaluated (Parish, Myers, Brandner, & Templin, 1985; Sankey, Elmer, Halechko, & Schulberg, 1985).

One program that has both behavioral and systemic components, Parent–Child Interaction Training (PCIT; Eisenstadt, Eyberg, McNeil, Newcomb, & Funderburk, 1993), has been advocated for clinical application to the treatment of physically abused children and their parents (Urquiza & McNeil, 1996). In explaining the relevance of PCIT for these families, Urquiza and McNeil (1996) suggested that parent–child interactions in abusive families are often conflictual and problematic, that physically abused children show poor behavioral controls and heightened behavioral dysfunction, and that social learning factors influence parental use of coercive discipline. PCIT addresses these issues by providing parents with opportunities to develop more positive relationships with their children and to learn appropriate parenting techniques through ongoing coaching efforts during observed interactions. Outcome evidence has suggested the benefit of PCIT for children with behavior problems. This approach is noteworthy for its attention to various stages in the treatment process, ranging from assessment and training in behavioral play skills to training in disciplinary skills and the use of booster sessions.

Empirical Reports and Studies

Despite the widespread implementation of treatment programs for physically abused children, few studies have been reported of services both provided directly to children and designed to minimize the effects of physical abuse or minimize the child's risk for reabuse (see Kolko, 1996a; Mannarino & Cohen, 1990; Oates & Bross, 1995; Wolfe, 1994). Given children's diverse needs and characteristics, existing direct services vary along a continuum of care ranging from minimal outpatient visits to intensive treatment in different contexts.

Day and Residential Treatment

Day and residential treatment programs, primarily serving maltreated preschoolers, offer access to different therapeutic activities (e.g., recreation, learning, play) and methods (e.g., child play groups, family counseling) with trained staff (Culp, Heide, & Richardson, 1991). For example, one representative program provided children with intensive, group-based treatment programming (mean duration = 8.9 months) aimed at encouraging supportive peer relationships and identifying personal feelings, along with play therapy, speech therapy, and physical therapy (Culp, Little, Letts, & Lawrence, 1991). The program also incorporated family services such as family and individual therapy, support group counseling, parent education, and a crisis line. Relative to a control group, treated children saw themselves as having higher cognitive competence, peer acceptance, and maternal acceptance, and they received higher developmental quotients on standardized measures. Teacher ratings supported these improvements. Nevertheless, most children scored below the "normal" range in most areas.

A more recent report contained an evaluation of the effects of the Kempe Early Education Project Serving Abused Families (KEEPSAFE), which provides a therapeutic preschool program and home visitation to 3- to 6-year-old children who were sexually or physically abused or both and were judged unsuitable for public school (Oates, Gray, Schweitzer, Kempe, & Harmon, 1995). Oates et al. (1995) found improvements from intake to discharge 1 year later in general intellectual functioning for 18 of 24 children, which reflected a rate of change that was higher than that expected for normal development, with a significant difference between the scores at the two time periods. Nineteen children showed a greater-than-expected improvement in receptive language. On discharge, 8 children entered a regular classroom, 11 required special education, 3 went to residential care facilities, and 2 were too young for formal education. Although they are impressive, these improvements cannot be clearly tied to the intervention alone in the absence of a comparison or control group. Other programs for young maltreated children likewise have incorporated multiple services for the entire family (Ghuman, 1993). It should be noted that interventions that remove children from their homes, such as foster care, are beyond the scope of this review.

Behavioral Skills Training and Peer Modeling

Specific behavioral skills training and modeling procedures have been directed toward improving the preschool abused-child's peer relations and social adjustment. In a series of studies with maltreated preschoolers, Fantuzzo and his colleagues examined peer- and adult-mediated socialization techniques. Peer social initiation techniques designed to encourage social overtures to peers were found to increase prosocial interactions in two children (Fantuzzo, Stovall, Schachtel, Goins, & Hall, 1987). This intervention was found to be superior to adult initiations in improving the children's social adjustment and peer initiations (Davis & Fantuzzo, 1989; Fantuzzo, Jurecic, Stovall, Hightower, & Goins, 1988). Subsequent evidence showed that abused preschoolers may respond differentially to peer- versus adult-mediated interventions, although both interventions were somewhat limited in overall efficacy (Davis & Fantuzzo, 1989). It is interesting that withdrawn children responded better to peer sessions, whereas aggressive children showed an increase in negative behavior toward peers (Davis & Fantuzzo, 1989; Fantuzzo et al., 1987, 1988). An extension of this work confirmed that maltreated preschoolers were more socially isolative and less interactive than their nonmaltreated peers in Head Start programs, and that a multisite randomized field test of the RPT intervention was effective in increasing positive interactive peer play behavior, which was validated months later by teacher evaluations (Fantuzzo et al. 1996). This study is noteworthy for its well-developed clinical model, use of community-based settings, and attention to developmentally important outcomes for children. These excellent studies are among the few to target physically abused children directly, and their results suggest the need both to expand intervention programs targeting social behavior and to conduct long-term follow-up assessments of program maintenance. However, these studies do not include evaluations of the impact of child programs on the sequelae of physical child maltreatment or recidivism. Another cognitive–behavioral treatment study included children in parent training sessions designed to enhance the children's developmental competence (Wolfe, Edwards, Manion, & Koverola, 1988).

Family-Based Services

Some family-based interventions have included child-oriented treatment. Brunk, Henggeler, and Whelan (1987) applied a multisystemic approach to target problems in various systems affecting the family, such as peer training. Following this individualized intervention, improvements were noted in parent–child relationships and child behavior problems, relative to parent training condition, although such outcomes are qualified by the absence of follow-up data. In another treatment outcome study, family casework using behavioral techniques (modeling, reinforcement) and play therapy were compared in terms of their impact on individual behavior and family interactions (Nicol et al., 1988). Improvements were reported in family coercion but not in amount of positive behavior. Other family services have been found to be useful in improving family functioning with some at-risk families (Ayoub, Willett, & Robinson, 1992; Willett, Ayoub, & Robinson, 1991).

In-home, family-based services have also been offered to children, but the level and type of involvement for children cannot easily be determined (Whittaker, Kinney, Tracy, & Booth, 1990). In one program for abused and neglected children (Project 12-Ways; Lutzker, 1990), several individualized services were developed, including skills training procedures with children and parents (e.g., child management training, social support, assertion training, home safety training). Improvements have been reported in parent-identified goals and in reabuse rates relative to comparison cases after services ended (Lutzker & Rice, 1987). However, follow-up results have failed to demonstrate the maintenance of these treatment effects (Lutzker, 1990). Home visiting programs include some direct services to children to enhance their development, but they generally target parental functioning and competencies (see Wasik & Roberts, 1994; Wolfe, 1994).

One of the few comparisons of alternative interventions directed toward children was recently reported by Kolko (1996b). Weekly reports of high-risk indicators were obtained from physically abused, school-aged children and their parents or guardians, who were randomly assigned to either individual child and parent cognitive–behavioral treatment (CBT) or family therapy (FT). The measures were of parental anger, physical discipline or force, and family problems; they were obtained in each weekly session to monitor the course of treatment. These reports showed moderate stability over time and parent–child correspondence. The overall levels of parental anger and physical discipline or force were found to be lower in CBT than FT families, although each group showed a reduction on these items from early to late treatment sessions. It is important to note that between 20% and 23% of all children and their parents independently reported high levels of physical discipline or force during both the early and the late phases of treatment, although few incidents seemed to result in injuries; an even higher percentage of participants reported heightened parental anger and family problems. Early treatment reports from both adult and child informants predicted late reports, but only the parent reports were related to validity measures.

These findings suggest some benefit to routine monitoring of the clinical course during intervention, especially in the identification of cases at risk of reabuse; however, the study is limited by the use of a small number of self-report items to reflect high-risk behavior in the home. Nevertheless, by identifying families exhibiting high levels of coercive behavior, repeated measures throughout the treatment course may help researchers to understand the heterogeneity of abusive families, document the need for individualized interventions (Ayoub et al., 1992; Willett et al., 1991), help to target contextual problems, guide decisions about the level of protection afforded to children or priorities for additional services (Daro, 1993; Toth & Cicchetti, 1993), or identify predictors of poor prognosis. Because few studies have described the treatment course in child physical maltreatment further development of clinical measures of parent–child adjustment that can efficiently document therapeutic response seems warranted.

Treatment outcome data from this comparison study also have been reported (Kolko, 1996c). Relative to families who received routine community service (RCS), CBT and FT were associated with improvements in child-to-parent violence and child externalizing behavior, parental distress and abuse risk, and family conflict and cohesion. At the same time, there were numerous improvements across time in all three conditions (e.g., in parental anger, parental practices, and child fears). One parent participant each in CBT (5%) and FT (6%) and 3 in RCS (30%) engaged in another abuse incident on the basis of official records, with similar percentages of reabuse reported for the child victims (10%, 12%, and 30%, respectively). No differences between CBT and FT were observed in consumer satisfaction or maltreatment risk ratings at termination. The findings of this evaluation provide additional, albeit qualified, support for the continued development of individual and family treatments involving child victims of physical abuse.

Comments and Critique

Because of the limited number of studies described in this section, only a few tentative conclusions can be drawn about the role of treatment for child victims of physical abuse. Most programs have been directed toward preschoolers, and they report meaningful improvements in developmental skills or self-concept (Culp et al., 1991) and social behavior with peers (Davis & Fantuzzo, 1989; Fantuzzo et al., 1988). Of course, the incorporation of multiple therapeutic components makes it difficult to determine the specific contribution of any single component to these outcomes. Moreover, few studies have examined alternative interventions or the maintenance of improvements at follow-up, with one exception (Kolko, 1996b). In general, few services for physically abused children have been evaluated. Other studies should be carried out involving children, especially school-aged children, to examine the impact of participation in individual, group, or family therapy.

NEGLECT

Effects of Neglect

Although most of the empirical work on child neglect has been directed toward parents, the effects of neglect on children and clinical interventions directed primarily toward young children have been documented in a few sources (see Claussen & Crittenden, 1991; Crittenden, 1996). The more common developmental sequelae of child neglect include limited intellectual or adaptive functioning, social and emotional problems, various developmental delays, anxious attachment, and subsequent problems with learning and behavioral controls (see Erickson & Egeland, 1996).

Models and Clinical Guidelines

Models used to guide treatment applications have been based on social learning and behavioral principles (Lutzker & Campbell, 1994) with attention to the role of social support and social network development (DePanfilis, 1996; Gaudin, 1993). These models generally speak to the need to target multiple aspects of the family environment in an effort to enhance child, parent, and family functioning; a few of the intervention studies described next involved child work. Some of the programs described in earlier sections also target neglected children and their families (e.g., Ayoub et al., 1992; Brunk et al., 1987; Fantuzzo et al., 1988; Ghuman, 1993; Oates et al., 1995; Wasik & Roberts, 1994).

Empirical Studies and Reports

Family-Based Services

Programs for neglect generally target parental behavior and functioning and thus infrequently describe child-directed treatment strategies (see chapter 10, this volume; Wolfe, 1994). A few programs, however, are notable for their articulation of specific skills-based routines that have been taught to children. For example, the previously cited work of Lutzker with Project 12-Ways (Lutzker, 1990; Lutzker & Campbell, 1994; Wesch & Lutzker, 1991) provided collective evidence supporting the use of structured assessment and training procedures to modify individualized concerns related to abuse or neglect (e.g., environmental hazards, child illnesses). Recent applications from this project have highlighted the variability in family outcomes following training, as reflected in one case in which multiple interventions reflecting diverse parenting skills and a few child behaviors (e.g., positive and negative response, play) resulted in a positive response to specialized in-home training; however, another project was only minimally effective (Greene, Norman, Searle, Daniels, & Lubeck, 1995). A significant asset of this approach is the use of objective measures of various behaviors designed to facilitate training and evaluation.

An extension of this program, Project SafeCare, provides specific services (e.g., health and physical care, safety and accident prevention, parent–child relationships) to families with young children (birth–5 years) for whom a case has been adjudicated or who are considered at risk for abuse or neglect. Initial reports have described an evaluation of the efficacy of using videotaped training or in-home counselors to identify and modify environmental and health-related risks (Taub, Kessler, & Lutzker, 1995) and to promote positive parent–child interactions (Bigelow, Kessler, & Lutzker, 1995). These curricula are noteworthy for their analysis of content validity based on professional reports, simplified checklist of specific parental behaviors, and use of training routines that promote behavioral competency. A strong emphasis of the program is its evaluation of observations of behaviors of both children (e.g., smiling, verbalizing, imitating) and parents (e.g., looking, touch, play) that are likely to enhance the quality of family interactions.

Social Support Interventions

The promotion of social support forms the basis of several intervention approaches with neglectful families. An excellent review by Depanfilis (1996) described several types of interventions that emphasize parental functioning and involvement (e.g., Gaudin, 1993; Gaudin, Wodarski, Arkinson, & Avery, 1991). In one of the few family-based intervention studies, Gaudin et al. (1991) found that case-management and advocacy services emphasizing the mobilization of informal social networks were more effective than traditional casework according to specific (parenting attitudes) and global (worker ratings) measures, although there was a high attrition rate. Such work has suggested the importance of using just a few primary providers who work with the family for a long period of time.

Only a small number of these programs seemed to offer specific services to children, primarily through therapeutic day care, with some services available in multiservice models (e.g., support groups, behavioral skills training), similar to the format of Project 12-Ways (Crittenden, 1996). Researchers have reported that the day care programs, which include several child-oriented services as well as other parent services, have resulted in improvements for two thirds of the child participants on discharge (Miller & Whittaker, 1988; Stehno, 1984).

Comments and Critique

There is little recent literature regarding the specific impact of treatment targeting child victims of neglect, precluding any summary of findings and implications. In fact, no study was found that was directed primarily toward children. Lutzker and Campbell (1994) are unique in their attempt to implement behavioral programming with various child and parent targets. Whereas some authors working with both abused and neglected children have reported behavioral improvements, the specificity of these effects cannot be determined. Given the severity of child neglect, efforts to address these issues are certainly warranted. Unfortunately, there are difficulties in working with neglectful families that reflect their often involuntary status in seeking services and their weakened family processes (Colapinto, 1995). This area clearly deserves considerable clinical and research attention.

PSYCHOLOGICAL MALTREATMENT

Effects of Psychological Maltreatment

The effects of psychological maltreatment of children have been described in a few sources (Brassard, Germain, & Hart, 1987; Claussen & Crittenden, 1991; Hart, Brassard, & Karlson, 1996). There is evidence of problems such as limited attachment, poor social competence and social adjustment, behavioral and emotional dysfunction, limited cognitive ability and problem-solving skills, and low educational achievement. Internalizing problems seem to be somewhat more commonly studied than externalizing ones, although few studies have been conducted in this area.

Models and Clinical Guidelines

Brassard et al. (1987) ascribed to the basic human needs model, whereby psychological maltreatment is viewed as an impediment to the fulfillment of needs for physiological integrity, safety, love and belonging, and esteem. Their comprehensive treatment approach integrates components from ecological–systemic, organizational, and social learning theories, and thus it targets aspects of different systems affecting children. Other models, including the STEEP project (Erickson, 1988), emphasize parental use of prosocial verbal discussion and appropriate discipline strategies. Unfortunately, there are few reports of treatment studies directed toward children based on these approaches or on any other conceptual framework. No experimental or quasi-experimental study in this area was identified.

EXPOSURE TO FAMILY AND COMMUNITY VIOLENCE

Effects of Exposure

There is increasing evidence regarding the effects of children's exposure to violent acts committed in the family or community, revealing that children are the unintended victims of such incidents. Indeed, the adverse impact of witnessing interparental conflict or spousal abuse has been well documented; one sees many of the same types of internalizing and externalizing problems that are seen in other child victims, including the use of aggression (Fantuzzo et al., 1991; Jaffe, Wolfe, & Wilson, 1990). Children who witness such violence may learn that violence is an appropriate form of conflict resolution (Jaffe, Wilson, & Wolfe, 1986), as is suggested by empirical data comparing witnessing and nonwitnessing children (Jaffe, Wilson, & Wolfe, 1988).

Models and Clinical Guidelines

The seminal work by Jaffe et al. (1986, 1988) described the initial use of a group program (Child Witnesses of Wife Abuse) that combines psychoeducation about spousal abuse and cognitive–behavioral exercises designed to teach prosocial conflict resolution skills. The 10-week program is intended to teach children new problem-solving skills and appropriate attitudes regarding personal responsibilities and to promote a positive self-concept. Information is presented to facilitate appropriate responses to anger, development of supports and safety skills, and understanding of parental responsibilities for spousal violence.

A similar program for children is offered as part of the Domestic Violence Project (see Peled & Edleson, 1992, 1995), which provides a 10-session program for different age groups in an attempt to accomplish several outcomes (e.g., break the secret of abuse, learn protection, strengthen self-esteem) through various activities (e.g., education about feelings, conflict resolution). Of course, individual therapy may be needed to alleviate post-traumatic symptoms developed through exposure to violence. Silvern, Karyl, and Landis (1995) offered clinical recommendations for helping children to disclose such exposure and strategies to tailor this approach to meet the children's individual needs (e.g., with respect to their age or traumatic experiences).

Empirical Reports and Studies

Jaffe et al. (1988) evaluated the pre- to posttreatment changes following the aforementioned program and reported that children had a better understanding of the dynamics of wife abuse and showed improvements in safety skill development and an increase in positive impressions of their parents. Although these findings are supportive, they are limited by the absence of a control or comparison group and any symptom measures.

A more recent evaluation of this program was directed toward a group of preadolescent children who were assigned to a treatment or control group (Wagar & Rodway, 1995). The treated group showed greater improvements in attitudes about and responses to anger situations and in their understanding of responsibility for their parents' behavior and for the violence that occurred in their homes. Teachers' comments suggested other positive changes, such as increased self-confidence, friendships, and skill development. Some of the children treated were noted anecdotally to have been somewhat angry at their mothers owing to their perceived inconsistency or lack of support. Measures of child behavior or parent–family functioning would have been helpful to determine whether changes in attitudes regarding domestic violence were associated with behavior in the home. Furthermore, the absence of descriptive statistics on the attitudinal measures, independent raters, and a follow-up assessment limits the overall conclusions that can be drawn regarding the impact of the program. The authors suggested that the program could be enhanced by the addition of more specific skills training components (e.g., social skills) for the children and treatment for the parents or family. These components are consistent with those suggested for enhancing support and education groups for children of battered women (see Grunsznski, Brink, & Edleson, 1988).

Reports of small groups for child witnesses from the Domestic Violence Project have provided qualitative data regarding program process and outcome (see Peled & Edleson, 1995). Peled and Edleson (1992) conducted semistructured interviews with thirty 4- to 12-year-old children from eight different groups and several mothers, fathers, and group leaders. The content of the interviews was coded using thematic guides (e.g., feelings or thoughts about the group, special experiences, changes noticed, home influences). The authors reported changes in various domains targeted by the group, such as in their definitions of violence, expression of feelings, sharing of personal experiences, self-protection, positive experiences, and self-esteem. Reports on results with standardized measures or other scales reflecting consumer satisfaction could be a next step in extending such an evaluation.

Comments and Critique

It is plausible that the relative absence of studies in this area is related to the fact that many children of battered women have a history of physical abuse as well as exposure to parent abuse. Furthermore, there are logistic difficulties in providing services to children who reside in shelters for battered women. Limited data indicate modest effects of training on the development of appropriate attitudes and an understanding of domestic violence by children, but there are almost no data regarding the children's level of adjustment or their family environment. Clinical intervention studies should be performed to address the psychological functioning of exposed children and relate improvements to parental conflicts and violence.

OTHER FORMS OF VICTIMIZATION

Bullying

Bullying in school is a form of victimization that is not well understood and for which children may require intervention services. Child victims of bullying or peer aggression may experience many of the same symptoms and forms of distress experienced by other victimized children, including depression, helplessness, and lowered self-esteem (see American Psychological Association, 1993; Farrington, 1993). Efforts to minimize the extent and severity of bullying have been applied successfully by Olweus (1993) using a school-based program that incorporates complementary methods (e.g., teaching training, classroom management). This macrolevel program (involving a school district) has resulted in significant reductions in the incidence of bullying and an increase in victims' school adjustment. A discussion of the prevention of bullying can be found in the same sources (e.g., Farrington, 1993; Olweus, 1993). Continued development and dissemination of effective individual and group interventions for victims of bullying is warranted, provided the programs have been evaluated in controlled studies.

Ritualistic Abuse

Ritualistic abuse is another form of victimization that has not been well documented; however, a small number of studies have suggested that its effects are serious and pervasive (e.g., PTSD, depression, lowered self-esteem, behavior problems; see Faller, 1994). From a clinical perspective, ritualistic abuse may reflect the sexual abuse of children in the context of using satanic rituals, religious themes, or other symbolic practices to frighten or intimidate children, thus highlighting its potential categorization with several forms of maltreatment (sexual, physical, or psychological abuse). Because specialized intervention models or treatments have not yet been reported, there do not appear to be any formal outcome studies in this area (see Kelley, 1996).

SUMMARY AND FUTURE DIRECTIONS

Summary

The studies reviewed herein provide a modest amount of information regarding the outcomes of short-term treatments for child victims of diverse forms of maltreatment; some authors of controlled studies have reported evaluations of global changes ascertained before and after intervention. There are a few empirical studies in the area of sexual abuse, but in striking contrast, only a few direct intervention studies have been conducted with physically abused children or children exposed to family or community violence. No studies were found that have evaluated strategies directly applied to neglected or psychologically maltreated children.

Recent studies of sexually abused children have documented the benefits of abuse-specific treatment relative to clinic or community control conditions (Cohen & Mannarino, 1996; Deblinger et al., 1996; Verleur et al., 1986). In contrast, minimal support has been found for the incremental benefit of multiple components above and beyond a single component (Berliner & Saunders, 1996; Hyde et al., 1995) or for an advantage to individual or group treatment (Perez, 1988). In general, primary improvements have been demonstrated in levels of internalizing (Cohen & Mannarino, 1996) and externalizing problems (McGain & McKinzey, 1995), and modest changes have been obtained in levels of social competence and sexualized behavior (Stauffer & Deblinger, 1996), with some reports of deterioration over time (Lanktree & Briere, 1995). Unfortunately, studies that do not include actual data for inspection preclude clear interpretation of changes in primary outcomes (Hyde et al., 1995; Wagar & Rodway, 1995).

The few studies reported concerning preschool or young school-aged physically abused children have documented improvements in developmental scores (Culp et al., 1991), social competence, and peer relations (Fantuzzo et al., 1988), with comparisons showing the superiority of peer-mediated (vs. adult-mediated) intervention. One study of school-aged victims documented reductions in high-risk parental behavior at home, especially during individual (vs. family) treatment (Kolko, 1996b), and reductions in parental risk for abuse and family violence, among other family characteristics (Kolko, 1996c). The one experimental study with exposed children found changes in attitudes and knowledge regarding wife abuse (Wagar & Rodway, 1995) that were consistent with initial reports (Jaffe et al., 1988, 1990). There do not appear to be any controlled studies of treatment outcome with school-aged or adolescent child victims of forms of maltreatment other than sexual or physical abuse.

The clinical literature highlights some of the potential of psychosocial interventions to address the specific and general effects of various types of maltreatment. This work is noteworthy for its incorporation of existing empirical and clinical knowledge about these experiences in the development of abuse-specific treatments or programs. Much of the content reflects the incorporation of cognitive–behavioral techniques and PTSD formulations into such programs as Cognitive–Behavioral Therapy for Sexually Abused Preschool Children (Cohen & Mannarino, 1996), Sexually Abused Youth and Socially Aware Youth (Sinclair et al., 1995), Stuart House (Lanktree & Briere, 1995), and the Child Sexual Abuse Service of the Hospital for Sick Children (Hyde et al., 1995). A few evaluations have been reported of programs that specifically target the needs of physically abused children (Kolko, 1996b; Oates et al., 1995), psychologically maltreated children (Brassard et al., 1987), or exposed children (Jaffe et al., 1990; Peled & Edleson, 1992).

Although a common component of treatment involves encouraging children's disclosure and discussion of their perceptions of the abusive experience and helping them cope with the implications of this history (see Friedrich, 1996b), treatment often includes more general psychological methods for enhancing social or adaptive competence and minimizing individual symptoms (e.g., social skills training, relaxation, attributional training). The separate and combined effects of these complementary interventions are still in need of empirical examination. Of course, inherent in the service delivery process is the availability of a continuum of care ranging from minimal outpatient visits to intensive treatment in different contexts (e.g., day or residential treatment) involving different therapeutic activities (e.g., recreation, learning, play), modalities (e.g., child play groups, family counseling), and participants. Intensive programs that combine skills training and experiential methods may offer several advantages in addressing the various social and psychological problems of child victims (e.g., Gabel, Swanson, & Shindledecker, 1990; Mannarino & Cohen, 1990; Oates et al., 1995). Treatment of the sequelae of abuse also has been suggested as a critical ingredient in minimizing a child's risk for reabuse (Baglow, 1992); intervention services may be needed to target environmental risk factors as well as psychological reactions to an abusive experience and continued dysfunctional caretaking or family interactions (Graziano &

Mills, 1992). Potential targets for child-focused intervention could include, for example, health promotion, social and developmental stimulation, behavior management, and education (see Mannarino & Cohen, 1990). Multiple levels of intervention may be needed to ensure effectiveness in cases of abuse and neglect (see Becker et al., 1995).

Although some authors have reported positive outcomes following child-only treatment, additional benefits may accrue from the inclusion of parents or families in helping sexually and physically abused children, given evidence documenting the impact of family-oriented treatments on family relationships (Brunk et al., 1987; Hyde et al., 1995; Nicol et al., 1988). Indeed, recent studies in the areas of sexual abuse (Cohen & Mannarino, 1996; Deblinger et al., 1996; Stauffer & Deblinger, 1996) and physical abuse (Culp et al., 1991; Kolko, 1996b; Oates et al., 1995; Wolfe et al., 1988) have included parallel or combined programs for children and their parents or families, with some studies including adult offenders as well (Hyde et al., 1995; Kolko, 1996b). The participation of children and other family members may enhance treatment outcomes beyond the limits of child treatment alone, but this supposition awaits further empirical evaluation.

The outcomes reviewed herein reflect the diversity of measures and domains targeted by intervention and the need to examine children's adjustment in its developmental context. Some studies have included measures from both children and parents, among other sources such as teachers, clinicians, or archival records (Cohen & Mannarino, 1996; Hyde et al., 1995; Jaffe et al., 1988; Kolko, 1996b; Sinclair et al., 1995), whereas others would be bolstered by reports from children (Fantuzzo et al., 1988; McGain & McKinzey, 1995) or their caretakers (Oates et al., 1995; Wagar & Rodway, 1995). Measures of consumer satisfaction have described children's positive impressions of several abuse-specific services (Cohen & Mannarino, 1996; Friedrich et al., 1992; Hyde et al., 1995; Kolko, 1996c; Stauffer & Deblinger, 1996), yielding evaluation data that may be useful in identifying acceptable treatments.

Few authors have reported information about treatment integrity, attrition, and treatment removal, but most appear to devote at least some attention to enhancing engagement with the child. Treatment integrity has been established for some CBT protocols for sexually abused (Cohen & Mannarino, 1996) and physically abused (Kolko, 1996b) children, but the subject deserves greater consideration in future research because of its potential impact on clinical outcome. For studies reporting such details, low levels of attrition and removal have been found with children who were sexually abused (22%; Cohen & Mannarino, 1996), physically abused (15%; Kolko, 1996b), or exposed to spousal abuse (10%; Wagar & Rodway, 1995), which may underlie somewhat heightened consumer satisfaction. Engagement strategies have been incorporated into some studies to promote peer cohesion in group therapy (Sinclair et al., 1995; Stauffer &

Deblinger, 1996) and to enhance rapport and the therapeutic relationship during individual or family therapy (Brunk et al., 1987; Kolko, 1996b; Wolfe et al., 1988).

Efforts to enhance treatment adherence are nonetheless relevant in general clinical practice, where low rates of attendance have been found for maltreating families. In their survey of professionals, Hansen and Warner (1994) reported average rates of attendance and homework completion of 84% and 64%, respectively, and several predictors of high attendance (e.g., educational level of parent, past experience with therapy in treating maltreatment, home site) and completion of therapy (e.g., educational level and younger age of parent, home site). Certain procedures were reported to be the most effective in improving attendance (e.g., praise, tangible rewards), whereas in-session practice worked best to improve homework completion. Participation may also be encouraged by maintaining a short latency to establishing the first contact; conducting certain sessions, such as the orientation meeting, in the family's home or a local community setting; and showing sensitivity to the child's developmental level and sociocultural background. Attention to the therapeutic process is also important to evaluate, given the findings of a rare study of alliance formation suggesting that maltreated adolescents who failed to develop positive alliances with their therapists tended to show the poorest outcomes in a hospitalized sample (Eltz, Shirk, & Sarlin, 1995). Greater attention to treatment participation may enhance both acquisition and maintenance of the impact of the program.

When clients complete treatment and are discharged, the assessment of follow-up becomes an important concern, although it has been reported in few studies. The maintenance of treatment gains has been demonstrated for internalizing symptoms, avoidance, dissociation, and sexual behavior in sexually abused children (Hack et al., 1994; Lanktree & Briere, 1995; Stauffer & Deblinger, 1996) and for behavior problems in physically abused children (Kolko, 1996c; Wolfe et al., 1988). However, there is less information to indicate whether treated children continue to experience improvements in the areas that led to referral and in other clinical symptoms. Such data are necessary for documentation of the relationship between treatment outcome and both follow-up status and recidivism. Modest rates of reabuse have been reported in follow-up studies of maltreated children and youths referred to an inpatient assessment program (Levy, Markovic, Chaudhry, Ahart, & Torres, 1995) or to the court (16%; Jellinek et al., 1995), which highlights the importance of tracking children and using assessment information to guide treatment and placement decisions. Follow-up services may be warranted for certain children or parents (e.g., "checkups," or service calls). This idea gains support when one considers that the greatest risk of recidivism may occur during the first 2 years following discharge from the program (Levy et al., 1995).

Finally, one would hope that the programs discussed occur in the context of a well-coordinated service system that can efficiently and sensitively help both children and their families make contact with and profit from therapeutic resources. As outlined by Baglow (1992), a cooperative framework is needed to facilitate cross-agency collaboration in the identification of case-management priorities and the prevention of casework breakdown (regarding issues such as therapy vs. containment and monitoring of intervention).

Future Directions

Despite the accrual of findings supporting the application of abuse-specific treatments, the empirical integrity of the literature that guides current evaluations is diverse and may benefit from increasing methodological rigor. Studies that are prospective in format and that address issues of internal and external validity and experimental control are infrequently conducted. Generally, experimental and statistical methods are needed that can increase confidence in these conclusions and rule out alternative explanations of outcomes. Studies should include several positive features, such as the use of multiple measures, informants, and methods (multitrait–multimethod); multivariate analyses; repeated measures; control or comparison groups; and formal follow-up evaluations (e.g., Berliner & Saunders, 1996; Cohen & Mannarino, 1996). Becker et al. (1995) presented a useful summary of recommendations for enhancing outcome research in this area.

One general suggestion to enhance research in the area is to conduct empirical studies of treatment with children who have been exposed to physical or psychological maltreatment, domestic or family violence, and neglect, given the absence of controlled studies in these areas. Comparative evaluations could be conducted using existing programs that are conceptually defensible and therapeutically supported. Such studies should include the evaluation of treatment process and course, including patient–therapist relationships and treatment credibility, and of clinical outcomes relating to child adjustment and risk for reabuse. Such studies are needed to increase understanding of the role of child treatment and intervention.

Another important direction for evaluation efforts that may enhance the assessment–measurement process involves the selection of measures that have conceptual implications (clear ties to constructs of interest). Furthermore, measures ought to possess population sensitivity (clear ties to unique features of sample or developmental level) and therapeutic specificity (clear ties to treatment procedures), should be psychometrically sound, and should permit replication across studies. Evaluation procedures should be as objective as possible and should be monitored for integrity and reliability. The scope of assessment and follow-up could be expanded to include more information on the effects of treatment on child and family functioning (suicidality, aggression, peer relations), the development of psychiatric disorders (PTSD, major depression disorder, conduct disorder), reabuse rates, and family integrity. The lack of consistent or predictable outcomes may be as much a function of the misapplication of the measurement process as it is a reflection of the apparent randomness of findings. Suggestions for clinical assessment measures in this area can be found in an article by Rittner and Wodarski (1995).

More generally, there is minimal information about the effectiveness of treatments that differ in format, such as the manner in which children are integrated into an intervention (e.g., individual work with the child, separate child and parent training, family therapy), the specific site (community systems vs. home vs. clinic), the complexity of the program (e.g., single vs. multicomponent interventions), and the timing or sequence of intervention components (e.g., how interventions are tailored to children's developmental stages). Evaluation of these parameters may have direct implications for the development of standardized protocols and, ultimately, treatment pathways (Becker et al., 1995).

Minimal attention has been paid to the influence of the perpetrator's and other family members' level of denial of the severity of individual incidents or, alternatively, their level of support and emotional assistance offered to child victims. Much more information exists on this topic with regard to child sexual abuse than other forms of abuse. These reactions may influence the child's processing of the incident, the motivation of the perpetrator, and the likelihood of a smooth transition to service involvement. Both reactions may be antagonistic to the initiation of services and can remain as primary targets for intervention. In addition, more progress is needed in addressing salient therapeutic obstacles (e.g., cognitive limitations, chronic stress, family discord, limited resources, resistance or poor motivation, coercion, frequent attrition, positive orientation to treatment).

In addition, more progress is needed in evaluating how treatment obstacles and parameters may influence process, course, and outcome. High rates of reabuse are common both during (about one third; Cohn & Daro, 1987) and after (30%–47%; Daro, 1988) treatment, suggesting the importance of monitoring and modifying during treatment high-risk behaviors related to sexual abuse (Mannarino & Cohen, 1990) and physical abuse (Kolko, 1996b). Successful resolution of various obstacles may provide a significant challenge to practitioners. Certain variables have been found to moderate the impact of sexual abuse (e.g., sex of victim and perpetrator, relationship to victim, support following the incident, parental depression); these and other variables, such as parental functioning in cases of physical abuse (Haskett, Myers, Pirrello, & Dombalis, 1995), may affect children's subsequent adjustment. Of course, whether any of these variables mediate therapeutic outcome is difficult to ascertain at this point. Clearly, as suggested by Briere (1996), greater attention to predictors of treatment effects is warranted.

Little has been written on the subject of matching clients to interventions in this area. It would be useful, for example, to answer the following key questions about treatment impact: What is the child's risk status (how has abusive or neglectful behavior changed)? How does treatment influence the family's quality of life and adjustment (how is the child or family better off)? How are the family's natural support systems bolstered (what resources have been developed or strengthened)? These and other variables may translate into important outcomes or mediators of outcome (e.g., level of impairment, social isolation, problems getting along with others, use of mental health services, child involvement in special education). In sum, the amount of attention devoted to the evaluation of treatments for different forms of child maltreatment has been quite variable. Although several controlled studies have been conducted with sexual abuse victims, there are few recent studies with victims of physical abuse or children who are exposed to domestic violence and no studies with neglected children. Much of the existing evidence is based on program evaluations or quasi-experimental designs. Emerging controlled studies in this area highlight certain clinical benefits to the use of conceptually driven, abuse-specific treatments on primary clinical outcomes. Nevertheless, numerous gaps in knowledge exist about treatment efficacy and effectiveness with different subgroups, techniques, or settings, and the long-term impact of treatment is virtually unknown. Studies that address these and other issues raised in this chapter are needed to promote a better understanding of the sequelae of child victimization and developments in clinical practice that address the sequelae effectively. Considerable attention must be paid to improving the number and quality of intervention studies if sufficient progress is to be made toward improving the quality of life and personal welfare of child victims of abuse and neglect.

REFERENCES

American Psychological Association. (1993). *Violence and youth: Psychology's response. Vol. 1. Summary of the American Psychological Association Commission on Violence and Youth.* Washington, DC: Author.

Ayoub, C., Willett, J. B., & Robinson, D. S. (1992). Families at risk of child maltreatment: Entry-level characteristics and growth in family functioning during treatment. *Child Abuse & Neglect, 16,* 495–511.

Azar, S. T., & Siegel, B. R. (1990). Behavioral treatment of child abuse. A developmental perspective. *Behavior Modification, 14,* 279–300.

Azar, S. T., & Wolfe, D. A. (1989). Child abuse and neglect. In E. J. Marsh &

R. A. Barkley (Eds.), *Treatment of childhood disorders* (pp. 451–493). New York: Guilford Press.

Baglow, L. J. (1992). A multidimensional model for treatment of child abuse: A framework for cooperation. *Child Abuse & Neglect, 14,* 387–395.

Baker, C. R. (1987). A comparison of individual and group therapy as treatment of sexually abused adolescent females. *Dissertation Abstracts International, 47,* 4319–4320.

Barnett, D., Manly, J. T., & Cicchetti, D. (1993). Defining child maltreatment: The interface between policy and research. In D. Cicchetti & S. L. Toth (Eds.), *Child abuse, child development, and social policy* (pp. 7–74). Norwood, NJ: Ablex.

Becker, J. V., Alpert, J. L., BigFoot, D. S., Bonner, B. L., Geodie, L. F., Henggeler, S. W., Kaufman, K. L., & Walker, C. E. (1995). Empirical research on child abuse treatment: Report by the Child Abuse and Neglect Treatment Working Group, American Psychological Association. *Journal of Clinical Child Psychology, 24* (Suppl)., 23–46.

Belsky, J. (1993). Etiology of child maltreatment: A developmental–ecological analysis. *Psychological Bulletin, 114,* 413–434.

Bentovim, A., van Elberg, A., & Boston, P. (1988). The results of treatment. In A. Bentovim, A. Elton, J. Hildebrand, M. Tranter, & E. Vizard (Eds.), *Child sexual abuse within the family: Assessment and treatment* (pp. 252–268). London: Wright.

Berliner, L., & Conte, J. R. (1995). The effects of disclosure and intervention on sexually abused children. *Child Abuse & Neglect, 19,* 371–384.

Berliner, L., & Saunders, B. (1996). Treating fear and anxiety in sexually abused children: Results of a controlled 2-year follow-up study. *Child Maltreatment, 1,* 294–309.

Beutler, L. E., Williams, R. E., & Zetzer, H. A. (1994). Efficacy of treatment for victims of child sexual abuse. *Sexual Abuse of Children, 4,* 156–175.

Bigelow, K. M., Kessler, M. L., & Lutzker, J. R. (1995). Improving the parent–child relationship in abusive and neglectful families. In M. L. Kessler (Chair), *Treating physical abuse and neglect: Four approaches.* Symposium conducted at the third annual APSAC Colloquium, Tucson, AZ.

Brassard, M. R., Germain, R., & Hart, S. N. (Eds.). (1987). *Psychological maltreatment of children and youth.* Elmsford, NY: Pergamon Press.

Briere, J. (1996). Treatment outcome research with abused children: Methodological considerations in three studies. *Child Maltreatment, 1,* 348–352.

Brunk, M., Henggeler, S. W., & Whelan, J. P. (1987). Comparison of multisystemic therapy and parent training in the brief treatment of child abuse and neglect. *Journal of Consulting and Clinical Psychology, 55,* 171–178.

Burke, M. M. (1988). *Short-term group therapy for sexually abused girls: A learning theory based treatment for negative affect.* Unpublished doctoral dissertation, University of Georgia, Athens, GA.

Celano, M., Hazzard, A., Webb, C., & McCall, C. (1996). Treatment of traumagenic beliefs among sexually abused girls and their mothers: An evaluation study. *Journal of Abnormal Child Psychology, 24,* 1–17.

Chaffin, M., Bonner, B. L., Worley, K. B., & Lawson, L. (1996). Treating abused adolescents. In J. Briere, L. Berliner, J. A. Bulkley, C. Jenny, & T. Reid (Eds.), *The APSAC handbook of child maltreatment* (pp. 119–139). Thousand Oaks, CA: Sage.

Claussen, A. H., & Crittenden, P. M. (1991). Physical and psychological maltreatment: Relations among types of maltreatment. *Child Abuse & Neglect, 15,* 5–8.

Cohen, J. A., & Mannarino, A. P. (1993). A treatment model for sexually abused preschoolers. *Journal of Interpersonal Violence, 8,* 115–131.

Cohen, J. A., & Mannarino, A. P. (1996). A treatment outcome study for sexually abused preschool children: Initial findings. *Journal of the American Academy of Child and Adolescent Psychiatry, 35,* 42–50.

Cohn, A. H., & Daro, D. (1987). Is treatment too late: What ten years of evaluative research tell us. *Child Abuse and Neglect, 11,* 433–442.

Colapinto, J. A. (1995). Dilution of family process in social services: Implications for treatment of neglectful families. *Family Process, 34,* 59–74.

Corder, B. F., Haizlip, T., & De Boer, P. (1990). A pilot study for a structured, time-limited therapy group for sexually abused preadolescent victims. *Child Abuse & Neglect, 14,* 243–251.

Crittenden, P. M. (1996). Research on maltreating families: Implications for intervention. In J. Briere, L. Berliner, J. A. Bulkley, C. Jenny, & T. Reid (Eds.), *The APSAC handbook on child maltreatment* (pp. 158–174). Thousand Oaks, CA: Sage.

Culp, R. E., Heide, J., & Richardson, M. T. (1991). Maltreated children's developmental scores: Treatment versus nontreatment. *Child Abuse and Neglect, 11,* 29–34.

Culp, R. E., Little, V., Letts, D., & Lawrence, H. (1991). Maltreated children's self-concept: Effects of a comprehensive treatment program. *American Journal of Orthopsychiatry, 61,* 114–121.

Daro, D. (1988). *Confronting child abuse: Research for effective program design.* New York: Free Press.

Daro, D. (1993). Child maltreatment research: Implications for program design. In D. Cicchetti & S. L. Toth (Eds.), *Child abuse, child development, and social policy* (pp. 331–367). Norwood, NJ: Ablex.

Davis, S., & Fantuzzo, J. W. (1989). The effects of adult and peer social initiations on social behavior of withdrawn and aggressive maltreated preschool children. *Journal of Family Violence, 4,* 227–248.

Deblinger, E., Lippmann, J., & Steer, R. (1996). Sexually abused children suffering posttraumatic stress symptoms: Initial treatment outcome findings. *Child Maltreatment, 1,* 310–321.

Deblinger, E., McLeer, S. V., & Henry, D. (1990). Cognitive behavioral treatment for sexually abused children suffering post-traumatic stress: Preliminary findings. *Journal of the American Academy of Child and Adolescent Psychiatry, 29*, 747–752.

DePanfilis, D. (1996). Social isolation of neglectful families: A review of social support assessment and intervention models. *Child Maltreatment, 1*, 37–52.

Downing, J., Jenkins, S. J., & Fisher, G. L. (1988). A comparison of psychodynamic and reinforcement treatment with sexually abused children. *Elementary School Guidance and Counseling, 22*, 291–298.

Eisenstadt, T. H., Eyberg, S., McNeil, C. B., Newcomb, K., & Funderburk, B. (1993). Parent–child interaction therapy with behavior problem children: Relative effectiveness of two stages and overall treatment outcome. *Journal of Clinical Child Psychology, 22*, 42–51.

Eltz, M. J., Shirk, S. R., & Sarlin, N. (1995). Alliance formation and treatment outcome among maltreated adolescents. *Child Abuse & Neglect, 19*, 419–431.

Erickson, M. F. (1988). *School psychology in preschool settings*. Paper presented at the meeting of the National Association of School Psychologists, Chicago, IL.

Erickson, M. F., & Egeland, B. (1996). Child neglect. In J. Briere, L. Berliner, J. A. Bulkley, C. Jenny, & T. Reid (Eds.), *The APSAC handbook of child maltreatment* (pp. 4–20). Thousand Oaks, CA: Sage.

Faller, K. C. (1994). Ritual abuse: A review of research. *APSAC Advisor, 7*, 19–27.

Fantuzzo, J. W., DePaola, L. M., Lambert, L., Martino, T., Anderson, G., & Sutton, S. (1991). Effects of interparental violence on the psychological adjustment and competencies of young children. *Journal of Consulting and Clinical Psychology, 59*, 258–265.

Fantuzzo, J. W., Jurecic, L., Stovall, A., Hightower, A. D., & Goins, C. (1988). Effects of adult and peer social initiations on the social behavior of withdrawn, maltreated preschool children. *Journal of Consulting and Clinical Psychology, 56*, 34–39.

Fantuzzo, J. W., Stovall, A., Schachtel, D., Goins, C., & Hall, R. (1987). The effects of peer social initiations on the social behavior of withdrawn maltreated preschool children. *Journal of Behavior Therapy and Experimental Psychiatry, 18*, 357–363.

Fantuzzo, J. W., Sutton-Smith, B., Atkins, M., Meyers, R., Stevenson, H., Coolahan, K., Weiss, A., & Manz, P. (1996). Community-based resilient peer treatment of withdrawn maltreated preschool children. *Journal of Consulting and Clinical Psychology, 64*, 1377–1386.

Farrington, D. P. (1993). Understanding and preventing bullying. In M. Tonry (Ed.), *Crime and justice: A review of research* (pp. 381–458). Chicago: University of Chicago Press.

Finkelhor, D. (1995). The victimization of children: A developmental perspective. *American Journal of Orthopsychiatry, 65*, 177–193.

Finkelhor, D., & Berliner, L. (1995). Research on the treatment of sexually abused children: A review and recommendations. *Journal of the American Academy of Child and Adolescent Psychiatry, 34,* 1408–1423.

Finkelhor, D., & Browne, A. (1985). The traumatic impact of child sexual abuse: A conceptualization. *American Journal of Orthopsychiatry, 55,* 530–541.

Friedrich W. N. (1996a). Clinical considerations of empirical treatment studies of abused children. *Child Maltreatment, 1,* 343–347.

Friedrich, W. N. (1996b) An integrated model of psychotherapy for abused children. In J. Briere, L. Berliner, J. A. Bulkley, C. Jenny, & T. Reid (Eds.), *The APSAC handbook on child maltreatment* (pp. 104–118). Thousand Oaks, CA: Sage.

Friedrich, W. N., Luecke, W. J., Bielke, R. L., & Place, V. (1992). Psychotherapy outcome of sexually abused boys: An agency study. *Journal of Interpersonal Violence, 7,* 396–409.

Furniss, T., Bingley-Miller, L., & Van Elburg, A. (1988). Goal-oriented group treatment for sexually abused adolescent girls. *British Journal of Psychiatry, 152,* 97–106.

Gabel, S., Swanson, A. J., & Shindledecker, R. (1990). Aggressive children in a day treatment program: Changed outcome and possible explanations. *Child Abuse & Neglect, 14,* 515–523.

Gaudin, J. (1993). Effective intervention with neglectful families. *Criminal Justice and Behavior, 20,* 66–89.

Gaudin, J. M., Wodarski, J. S., Arkinson, M. K., & Avery, L. S. (1991). Remedying child neglect: Effectiveness of social network interventions. *Journal of Applied Social Sciences, 15,* 97–123.

Ghuman, J. K. (1993). An integrated model for intervention with infants, preschool children and their maltreating parents. *Infant Mental Health Journal, 14,* 147–157.

Goodman, G. S., Taub, E. P., Jones, D. P. H., Port, L. K., Ruby, L., & Prado, L. (1992). Testifying in criminal court. *Monographs of the Society for Research in Child Development, 57,* 1–142.

Graziano, A. M., & Mills, J. R. (1992). Treatment for abused children: When is a partial solution acceptable? *Child Abuse & Neglect, 16,* 217–228.

Green, A. H. (1993). Child sexual abuse: Immediate and long-term effects and intervention. *Journal of the American Academy of Child and Adolescent Psychiatry, 32,* 890–902.

Greene, B. F., Norman, K. R., Searle, M. S., Daniels, M., & Lubeck, R. C. (1995). Child abuse and neglect by parents with disabilities: A tale of two families. *Journal of Applied Behavior Analysis, 28,* 417–434.

Greenspun, W. S. (1994). Internal and interpersonal: The family transition of father–daughter incest. *Journal of Child Sexual Abuse, 3,* 1–14.

Grunsznski, R., Brink, J., & Edelson, J. (1988). Support and education groups for children of battered women. *Child Welfare, 67,* 431–444.

Hack, T. F., Osachuk, T. A., & De Luca, R. V. (1994). Group treatment of sexually abused preadolescent boys. *Families in Society: The Journal of Contemporary Human Services, 75,* 217–224.

Hansen, D. J., & Warner, J. E. (1994). Treatment adherence of maltreating families: A survey of professionals regarding prevalence and enhancement strategies. *Journal of Family Violence, 9,* 1–19.

Hart, S. N., Brassard, M. R., & Karlson, H. C. (1996). Psychological maltreatment. In J. Briere, L. Berliner, J. A. Bulkley, C. Jenny, & T. Reid (Eds.), *The APSAC handbook of child maltreatment* (pp. 72–89). Thousand Oaks, CA: Sage.

Haskett, M. E., Myers, L. W., Pirrello, V. E., & Dombalis, A. O. (1995). Parenting style as a mediating link between parental emotional health and adjustment of maltreated children. *Behavior Therapy, 26,* 625–642.

Hiebert-Murphy, D., De Luca, R., & Runtz, M. (1992). Group treatment for sexually abused girls: Evaluation outcome. *Families in Society, 73,* 205–213.

Hyde, C., Bentovim, A., & Monck, E. (1995). Some clinical and methodological implications of a treatment outcome study of sexually abused children. *Child Abuse & Neglect, 19,* 1387–1399.

Jaffe, P., Wilson, S., & Wolfe, D. A. (1986). Promoting changes in attitudes and understanding of conflict resolution among child witnesses of family violence. *Canadian Journal of Behavioral Science, 18,* 357–366.

Jaffe, P., Wilson, S., & Wolfe, D. A. (1988). Specific assessment and intervention strategies for children exposed to wife battering: Preliminary empirical investigation. *Canadian Journal of Community Mental Health, 7,* 157–163.

Jaffe, P., Wolfe, D. A., & Wilson, S. (1990). *Children of battered women.* Newbury Park, CA: Sage.

Jellinek, M. S., Little, M., Benedict, K., Murphy, J. M., Pagano, M., Poitrast, F., & Quinn, D. (1995). Placement outcomes of 206 severely maltreated children in the Boston juvenile court system: A 7.5-year follow-up study. *Child Abuse & Neglect, 19,* 1051–1064.

Kelley, S. J. (1996). Ritualistic abuse of children. In J. Briere, L. Berliner, J. A. Bulkley, C. Jenny, & T. Reid (Eds.), *The APSAC handbook on child maltreatment* (pp. 90–99). Thousand Oaks, CA: Sage.

Knutson, J. F. (1995). Psychological characteristics of maltreated children: Punitive risk factors and consequences. *Annual Review of Psychology, 46,* 401–431.

Kolko, D. J. (1992). Characteristics of child victims of physical violence: Research findings and clinical implications. *Journal of Interpersonal Violence, 7,* 244–276.

Kolko, D. J. (1996a). Child physical abuse. In J. Briere, L. Berliner, J. A. Bulkley, C. Jenny, & T. Reid (Eds.), *The APSAC handbook on child maltreatment* (pp. 21–50). Thousand Oaks, CA: Sage.

Kolko, D. J. (1996b). Clinical monitoring of treatment course in child physical abuse: Child and parent reports. *Child Abuse & Neglect, 20,* 23–43.

Kolko, D. J. (1996c). Individual cognitive–behavioral treatment and family therapy for physically abused children and their offending parents: A comparison of clinical outcomes. *Child Maltreatment, 1,* 322–342.

Lanktree, C. B., & Briere, J. (1995). Outcome of therapy for sexually abused children: A repeated measures study. *Child Abuse & Neglect, 19,* 1145–1155.

Leibowitz, L., Harvey, M. R., & Herman, J. L. (1993). A stage-by-dimension model of recovery from sexual trauma. *Journal of Interpersonal Violence, 8*, 378–391.

Letourneau, E. J., Saunders, B. E., & Kilpatrick, D. G. (1996). In B. E. Saunders (Chair), *Adolescents and abuse: Results from a national survey study*. Paper presented at the annual meeting of the San Diego Conference on Responding to Child Maltreatment, San Diego, CA.

Levy, H. B., Markovic, J., Chaudhry, U., Ahart, S., & Torres, H. (1995). Reabuse rates in a sample of children followed 5 years after discharge from a child abuse inpatient assessment program. *Child Abuse & Neglect, 19*, 1363–1377.

Lindon, J., & Nourse, C. A. (1994). A multi-dimensional model of groupwork for adolescent girls who have been sexually abused. *Child Abuse & Neglect, 18*, 341–348.

Lutzker, J. R. (1990). Project 12-Ways: Treating child abuse and neglect from an ecobehavioral perspective. In R. F. Dangel & R. F. Polster (Eds.), *Parent training: Foundations of research and practice*. New York: Guilford Press.

Lutzker, J. R., & Campbell, R. V. (1994). *Ecobehavioral family interventions in developmental disabilities*. Pacific Grove, CA: Brooks/Cole.

Lutzker, J. R., & Rice, J. M. (1987). Using recidivism data to evaluate Project 12-Ways: An ecobehavioral approach to the treatment and prevention of child abuse and neglect. *Journal of Family Violence, 2*, 283–289.

Malinosky-Rummell, R., & Hansen, D. J. (1993). Long-term consequences of child physical abuse. *Psychological Bulletin, 114*, 68–79.

Mannarino, A. P., & Cohen, J. A. (1990). Treating the abused child. In R. T. Ammerman & M. Hersen (Eds.), *Children at risk: An evaluation of factors contributing to child abuse and neglect* (pp. 249–266). New York: Plenum Press.

McGain, B., & McKinzey, R. K. (1995). The efficacy of group treatment in sexually abused girls. *Child Abuse & Neglect, 19*, 1157–1169.

Miller, J. L., & Whittaker, J. K. (1988). Social services and social support: Blended programs for families at risk of child maltreatment. *Child Welfare, 67*, 161–174.

Monck, E., Sharland, E., Bentovim, A., Goodall, G., Hyde, C., & Lewin, B. (1994). *Child sexual abuse: A descriptive and treatment outcome study*. London: HMSO.

National Academy of Sciences. (1993). *Understanding child abuse and neglect*. Washington, DC: Author.

Nelki, J. S., & Watters, J. (1989). A group for sexually abused children: Unraveling the web. *Child Abuse & Neglect, 13*, 369–375.

Nicol, A. R., Smith, J., Kay, B., Hall, D., Barlow, J., & Williams, B. (1988). A focused casework approach to the treatment of child abuse: A controlled comparison. *Journal of Child Psychology and Psychiatry, 29*, 703–711.

Oates, R. K., & Bross, D. C. (1995). What have we learned about treating child physical abuse? A literature review of the last decade. *Child Abuse & Neglect, 19*, 463–473.

Oates, R. K., Gray, J., Schweitzer, L., Kempe, R. S., & Harmon, R. J. (1995). A therapeutic preschool for abused children: The KEEPSAFE Project. *Child Abuse & Neglect, 19,* 1379–1386.

Oates, R. K., O'Toole, B. I., Lynch, D. L., Stern, A., & Cooney, G. (1994). Stability and change in outcomes for sexually abused children. *Journal of the American Academy of Child and Adolescent Psychiatry, 33,* 945–953.

Olweus, D. (1993). Bully/victim problems among schoolchildren: Long-term consequences and an effective intervention program. In S. Hodgins (Ed.), *Mental disorder and crime* (pp. 317–349). Newbury Park, CA: Sage.

Parish, R. A., Myers, P. A., Brandner, A., & Templin, K. H. (1985). Developmental milestones in abused children and their improvement with a family-oriented approach to the treatment of child abuse. *Child Abuse & Neglect, 9,* 245–250.

Peled, E., & Edleson, J. (1992). Multiple perspectives on group work with children of battered women. *Violence and Victims, 7,* 327–346.

Peled, E., & Edleson, J. L. (1995). Process and outcome in small groups for children of battered women. In E. Peled, P. G. Jaffe, & J. L. Edleson (Eds.), *Ending the cycle of violence: Community responses to children of battered women* (pp. 77–96). Thousand Oaks, CA: Sage.

Perez, C. L. (1988). A comparison of group play therapy and individual therapy for sexually abused children. *Dissertation Abstracts International, 48,* 3079.

Putnam, F. W., & Trickett, P. K. (1995). *The developmental consequences of child sexual abuse.* Paper presented at the Conference on Violence Against Children in the Family and the Community, University of Southern California, Los Angeles.

Reeker, J., Ensing, D., & Elliot, R. (1997). A meta-analytic investigation of group treatment outcomes for sexually abused children. *Child Abuse & Neglect, 21,* 669–680.

Rittner, B., & Wodarski, J. S. (1995). Clinical assessment instruments in the treatment of child abuse and neglect. *Early Child Development and Care, 106,* 43–58.

Roesler, T. A., Savin, D., & Grozs, C. (1993). Family therapy of extrafamilial sexual abuse. *Journal of the American Academy of Child and Adolescent Psychiatry, 32,* 967–970.

Runyan, D. K., Everson, M. D., Edelsohn, G. A., Hunter, W. M., & Coulter, M. L. (1988). Impact of legal intervention on sexually abused children. *Journal of Pediatrics, 113,* 647–653.

Rust, J. O., & Troupe, P. A. (1991). Relationships of treatment of child sexual abuse with school achievement and self-concept. *Journal of Early Adolescence, 11,* 420–429.

Sankey, C. C., Elmer, E., Halechko, A. D., & Schulberg, P. (1985). The development of abused and high-risk infants in different treatment modalities: Residential versus in-home care. *Child Abuse & Neglect, 9,* 237–243.

Silvern, L., Karyl, J., & Landis, T. Y. (1995). Individual psychotherapy for the traumatized children of abused women. In E. Peled, P. G. Jaffe, & J. L. Edleson

(Eds.), *Ending the cycle of violence: Community responses to children of battered women* (pp. 43–76). Thousand Oaks, CA: Sage.

Sinclair, J. J., Larzclere, R. E., Paine, M., Jones, P., Graham, K., & Jones, M. (1995). Outcome of group treatment for sexually abused adolescent females living in a group home setting. *Journal of Interpersonal Violence, 10,* 533–542.

Stauffer, L. B., & Deblinger, E. (1996). Cognitive behavioral groups for nonoffending mothers and their young sexually abused children: A preliminary treatment outcome study. *Child Maltreatment, 1,* 65–76.

Stehno, S. (1984, August). *The care and treatment program, Seattle Day Nursery.* Notes from a presentation to the American Psychological Association Convention, Atlanta.

Steinberg, R., & Sunkenberg, M. (1994). A group intervention model for sexual abuse: Treatment and education in an inpatient child psychiatric setting. *Journal of Child and Adolescent Group Therapy, 4,* 61–73.

Sullivan, P. M., Scanlan, J. M., Brookhouse, P. E., Schulte, L. E., & Knutson, J. F. (1992). The effects of psychotherapy on behavior problems of sexually abused deaf children. *Child Abuse & Neglect, 16,* 297–307.

Swenson, C. C., Saunders, B. E., & Kirkpatrick, D. G. (1996). Physical assault of adolescents: Prevalence, case characteristics, and mental health consequences. In B. E. Saunders (Chair), *Adolescents and abuse: Results from a national survey study.* Paper presented at the annual meeting of the San Diego Conference on Responding to Child Maltreatment, San Diego, CA.

Taub, H. B., Kessler, M. L., & Lutzker, J. R. (1995). Teaching neglectful families to identify and address environmental and health-related risks. In M. L. Kessler (Chair), *Treating physical abuse and neglect: Four approaches.* Symposium conducted at the third annual APSAC Colloquium, Tucson, AZ.

Toth, S. L., & Cicchetti, D. (1993). Child maltreatment: Where do we go from here in our treatment of victims? In D. Cicchetti & S. L. Toth (Eds.), *Child abuse, child development, and social policy* (pp. 399–437). Norwood, NJ: Aplex.

Urquiza, A. J., & Bodiford-McNeil, C. (1996). Parent–child interaction therapy: An intensive dyadic intervention for physically abusive families. *Child Maltreatment, 1,* 134–144.

Verleur, D., Hughes, R. E., & Dobkin De Rios, M. D. (1986). Enhancement of self-esteem among female adolescent incest victims: A controlled comparison. *Adolescence, 21,* 843–854.

Wagar, J. M., & Rodway, M. R. (1995). An evaluation of a group treatment approach for children who have witnessed wife abuse. *Journal of Family Violence, 10,* 295–306.

Wagner, W. G., Kilcrease-Fleming, D., Fowler, W. E., & Kazelskis, R. (1993). Brief-term counseling with sexually abused girls: The impact of sex of counselor on client's therapeutic involvement, self-concept, and depression. *Journal of Counseling Psychology, 40,* 490–500.

Wasik, B. H., & Roberts, R. N. (1994). Survey of home visiting programs for abused and neglected children and their families. *Child Abuse & Neglect, 18,* 271–283.

Weist, M. D., Vannatta, K., Wayland, K. K., & Jackson, C. Y. (1993). Social skills training for sexually abused girls. *Behavior Change, 10,* 244–252.

Wesch, D., & Lutzker, J. R. (1991). A comprehensive 5-year evaluation of Project 12-Ways: An ecobehavioral program for treating and preventing child abuse and neglect. *Journal of Family Violence, 6,* 17–35.

Whittaker, J., Kinney, J., Tracy, E. M., & Booth, C. (1990). *Reaching high risk families: Intensive family preservation in human services.* New York: Aldine de Gruyter.

Widom, C. S., & Ames, M. A. (1994). Criminal consequences of childhood sexual victimization. *Child Abuse & Neglect, 18,* 303–318.

Widom, C. S., & Maxfield, M. (1996, September). A prospective examination of risk for violence among abused and neglected children. In C. F. Ferris & T. Grisso (Eds.), *Understanding aggressive behavior in children. Annals of the New York Academy of Sciences* (pp. 224–237). New York: New York Academy of Sciences.

Willett, J. B., Ayoub, C. C., & Robinson, D. (1991). Using growth modeling to examine systematic differences in growth: An example of change in the functioning of families at risk of maladaptive parenting, child abuse, or neglect. *Journal of Consulting and Clinical Psychology, 59,* 38–47.

Wolfe, D. A. (1994). The role of intervention and treatment services in the prevention of child abuse and neglect. In G. B. Melton & F. D. Barry (Eds.), *Protecting children from child abuse and neglect: Foundations for a new national strategy* (pp. 224–303). New York: Guilford Press.

Wolfe, D., Edwards, B., Manion, I., & Koverola, C. (1988). Early intervention for parents at risk for child abuse and neglect: A preliminary report. *Journal of Consulting and Clinical Psychology, 56,* 40–47.

Wolfe, D. A., & Wekerle, C. (1993). Treatment strategies for child physical abuse and neglect: A critical progress report. *Clinical Psychology Review, 13,* 473–500.

Zaidi, L. Y., & Gutierrez-Kovner, V. M. (1995). Group treatment of sexually abused latency-age girls. *Journal of Interpersonal Violence, 10,* 215–227.

10

CHILD MALTREATMENT: A CRITICAL REVIEW OF RESEARCH ON TREATMENT FOR PHYSICALLY ABUSIVE PARENTS

CYNTHIA J. SCHELLENBACH

Despite impressive advances in technology and medicine to increase longevity and improve the quality of life for adults in the United States, recent data indicate that the life conditions for children in the United States are shockingly dismal. In this nation, 1 in 5 children live in poverty, infant mortality rates remain high (9 in 1,000 children), and the rate of teen pregnancy and teen parenthood is increasing (from 26 per 1,000 in 1986 to 33 per 1,000 in 1996). These trends are not limited to health care and quality of life. Disturbing facts have emerged from the data concerning social problems related to children's risk at the hands of their own parents as well. According to data released in 1995 by the National Committee for the Prevention of Child Abuse, the number of reported incidents of child abuse and neglect soared to nearly 3.1 million per year, approximately twice the number reported in 1984. Of these reported cases, about 1 million were substantiated by subsequent investigations (NCCAN, 1996).

Of serious concern to professionals is the fact that approximately 50% of these cases involve a child under the age of 7, with a majority of the serious injuries and fatalities occurring among infants and children under the age of 3 (Carnegie Corporation, 1994). According to the report of the U.S. Advisory Board on Child Abuse and Neglect (1995), 2,000 infant fatalities occurred as a result of child maltreatment in 1995. These statistics highlight the extreme physical vulnerability and isolation of these younger victims of abuse and neglect. In addition to society's concern regarding the large number of deaths to children, the nonfatal injuries to many other children have devastating effects on their lives. For example, 141,700 of the remaining child victims suffered serious injuries, and an additional 18,000 children suffered chronic disabilities as a result of maltreatment. Data from the Children's Defense League (1996) have suggested that only 75% of child victims receive any psychological treatment following this experience of trauma, and a dramatically smaller number of parents or perpetrators receive treatment. In fact, it is difficult to locate any data on the treatment needs and outcomes for perpetrators. In fact, the data on the treatment of sexual abuse perpetrators focuses primarily on male perpetrators of criminal sexual behavior rather than on parenting behavior. Despite the lack of treatment, only about 1 in 6 of these children is placed in foster care. This means that the majority of abused children remain in the care of their abusive parents, many of whom are not receiving treatment. This body of evidence presents a compelling argument for focusing scholarly and professional efforts on the development of a solid and empirically based summary of the data on programs for parents.

In this review, I describe and summarize recent research on the treatment of parents who are physically abusive. Data on the treatment of sexually abusive parents have not been included in the review because of the difference in the focus of treatment of perpetrators. The targets for intervention for physically abusive parents are more clearly understood within the context of a conceptual framework. One of the most productive conceptual frameworks assumes that the parent, the child, and the environment are transacting over time (Cicchetti & Rizley, 1981). Within this paradigm, a parent must be able to respond sensitively to the changing developmental needs of the child. Intervention for parents often involves identifying deficits related to parent characteristics (e.g., deficits in knowledge of child development), providing support for the special needs of the child, and alleviating stresses in the social environment (e.g., social isolation or violence in the neighborhood). With respect to definitional issues related to the nature of the incident, researchers have suggested that the type of maltreatment (or the experience of multiple types), the severity of abuse, the frequency and chronicity of reports, the characteristics of the perpetrator of the incident, and the occurrence of out-of-home placements all influence treatment goals (Barnett, Manly, & Cicchetti, 1993). These constructs form the basis of the criteria for outcomes of intervention programs for abusive parents. For example, many intervention programs focus on improving parents' knowledge of child development in an effort to decrease the rates of reported cases of maltreatment or the number of incidents during a specified period of time.

Two decades of previous research have provided the empirical basis for identifying targets for parental change in child abuse treatment programs. The research documents the importance of identifying the following areas of potential problems: (a) parental knowledge of child development, (b) parenting skills and behavior, (c) use of appropriate disciplinary strategies, (d) psychological adjustment of parents, (e) physical health of parents, (f) social support (from family, friends, or professionals) of parents and family, and (g) community support. Finally, it is important to consider the impact of the change in parental behavior on child outcomes or on the quality of the parent–child relationship.

Whereas many empirical studies have assessed the impact of intervention on single components, such as those components noted previously, few authors have moved beyond this unidimensional focus to a multidimensional, process-oriented focus on the impact of change on the reciprocal influences of parent and child factors in the context of the community environment. These multidimensional theoretical models have been conceptually useful in fostering understanding of the interaction of stress with cognitive and social variables in the context of parent–child interactions. For example, Cicchetti and Rizley (1981) postulated a transactional approach to understanding the interaction of risk factors that increase the probability of maltreatment. These factors are further differentiated regarding duration, as transient (e.g., situational stress) or enduring (e.g., a parent's history of abuse as a child). With this process-oriented model, one can predict that maltreatment is likely to occur when risk factors outweigh compensatory factors. The goal of the intervention process, therefore, is to decrease the level of risk and to increase the compensatory factors.

Other multidimensional process-oriented theories place increased emphasis on either the contextual determinants (Belsky, 1984) or the individual determinants (Milner, 1993) of parental behavior. As part of his ecological approach to child maltreatment, Belsky (1984) has suggested that parent behavior, demonstrated by sensitivity and responsivity to children's needs, is influenced by individual parent characteristics (e.g., temperament, developmental level, gender, and health) and by the family context (e.g., quality of the marital relationship, social support, and community resources). Parent treatment programs have often focused on parents' deficits in each of these areas (e.g., education in child development or parenting skills), but few have assessed the process by which the parent–child relationship is enhanced.

One model that emphasizes process was developed by Wolfe (1987, 1991). In his transactional model of abuse, the interaction of destabilizing factors and compensatory factors is examined in the context of the temporal development of an abusive episode of behavior. In this model, three specific stages are assumed to illustrate the development of an abusive incident of behavior. The first stage exhibits a reduced tolerance for stress, the second stage progresses to poor management of a crisis within the family, and the third stage leads to habitual patterns of arousal or coercion within the family This sequence may be buffered, over time, by the impact of stabilizing factors such as social or economic support.

The following review of treatment outcomes for parents, organized according to components, contains the salient single-component and multidimensional studies that focus on the process of behavioral interaction within a social context. The first section of the review examines alternative strategies for changing targeted components, measures of outcome, and the outcomes that resulted in change in the relationship or in the child's development. Within each section, specific interventions that address single components are identified. When possible, the implications of the research for intervention outcomes are reviewed. The second section of the review examines current studies derived from the process-oriented, comprehensive approaches to treatment. The goal of this section of the review is to link the findings from the outcome research to the theoretical models presented earlier (Belsky, 1984; Milner, 1993; Wolfe, 1987). The research is integrated with current theoretical models to determine the existing gaps in the literature and to make recommendations for a research agenda for the future. Before the presentation of the critical review, however, several methodological issues are considered.

METHODOLOGICAL ISSUES

The following survey is not an exhaustive review of treatment programs for abusive parents. Studies were included in the review if they met the following criteria: (a) inclusion of a comparison or control group in the design; (b) specification of target behaviors for change, measures of expected change, and the impact of change on parent–child relationships; and (c) discussion of the extent to which behavioral change was measured. Studies that did not meet these criteria are included in the review if they made an important contribution to a new or promising area of research. The review is organized according to type of treatment strategy, and a final section focuses on multiple-component and process-oriented strategies.

Review of the Research

Cognitive intervention strategies have targeted changes in parents' knowledge of child development, parenting skill, and behaviors related to adjustment (e.g. impulsivity, anger control), as well as stress management methods to reduce child abuse. The 11 studies reviewed (see Table 1) concerning the effectiveness of cognitive–behavioral treatment programs were generally of three types: (a) large-scale program evaluations of specific single-component treatment strategies, (b) small-scale program evaluations of specific single-component treatment strategies, and (c) reports of interventions focused on single-subject designs rather than group designs with appropriate control groups. The targets for change included child-rearing knowledge, skills, and behavior; anger and impulsivity management; stress management; and family functioning through improved parental problem-solving skills. Measures of outcome were most often written surveys of changes in knowledge base and skills, behavioral observations of reduction in aversive parent–child interactions, and tests of parenting knowledge or skills. Many studies also incorporated follow-up assessments of maintenance of gains, obtained from 2 to 15 months after the program ended. Although the measurement strategies and designs for the cognitive–behavioral studies tended to be rigorous and sound, most of the studies focused on short-terms behavioral gains in the targeted constructs. None of the studies incorporated a measure of the impact of the training on the quality of the parent–child relationship or on the long-term development of the child.

Child abuse treatment and prevention research has ranged from large-scale, family-life education models to single-subject designs with individual parents. For example, Showers (1991) implemented a large-scale family-life education program with 1,891 junior high school students. Middle school students received training in milestones of child development and nonviolent child-management strategies through the use of index cards containing printed facts. Although the study did not have a control group, results indicated that the students significantly improved their knowledge base, increasing their percentage of correct responses from 59% to 82%. This type of large-scale, single-component study focuses on measuring decreases in risk factors associated with abuse, but it has no measure of the impact of this knowledge on subsequent parenting ability of the participants.

Other studies have focused on improving parenting through the modification of individual psychological problems and behaviors of the parents (Acton & During, 1990; Resnick, 1985; Whiteman, Tanshel, & Grundy, 1987). Using a pre–post design with no control group, Acton and During (1990) trained parents in anger management, enhancement of empathy,

TABLE 1
Summary of Parent-Focused Intervention Studies

Authors	Design	Targets	Outcome
		Cognitive–behavioral strategies	
Showers (1991)	Pretest–posttest *Participants:* 1,891 students, seventh through ninth grade Written information on child rearing and child development No control group	1. Child-rearing knowledge 2. Nonviolent child-management strategies	Significant improvements in knowledge of child development (from 59% to 82%)
Acton & During (1990)	Pretest–posttest *Participants:* 24 No control group	1. Anger management 2. Enhancement of empathy 3. Decrease in physiological reactivity	Improved relationships with children (self-report) Decreased anger
Resnick (1985)	Pretest–posttest *Participants:* 54 single mothers, 10th-grade education No control group	1. Increase in self-esteem 2. Change in parenting 3. Decrease in depression arousal	1. No significant difference 2. No significant change 3. Decrease in depression arousal
Whiteman, Tanshel, & Grundy (1987)	Pretest–posttest *Participants:* 42 Control group	1. Cognitive restructuring 2. Relaxation 3. Problem solving 4. Composite	Decreased anger
Rivara (1985)	Pretest–posttest *Participants:* 71 physically abusive parents	Parent effectiveness training 6–8 weeks	33% compliance with treatment 30% reabuse (31-month follow-up)
MacMillan, Olson, & Hansen (1991)	*Participants:* Three parents Single-subject design	1. Parenting skills 2. Generalization 3. Specific skill acquisition: skill description, skill rationale, modeling, rehearsal	1. Significant decreases in target behaviors of children 2. Significant increases in parent acquisition of skills

Barth (1990)	Pretest–posttest *Participants*: 97 mothers or expectant mothers, single parents, low education, random assignment No control group	1. Increase goal attainment related to child care 2. Decrease child abuse potential 3. Decrease reported rates of child abuse and neglect	1. Significant increases in goal attainment 2. Decrease in child abuse potential 3. Not significant
Kolko (1996)	Pretest–posttest Weekly monitoring *Participants*: 38 parent–child dyads No control group	Random assignment to cognitive, behavioral, or family therapy group	Level of parental anger (and parental discipline) lower in cognitive group
Trueste, Montes, & Montes (1988)	Pretest–posttest *Participants*: 42 Control group	Home-based training in parenting strategies	Increased praise Decreased use of negative words
Wolfe, Edwards, Manion, & Koverola (1988)	Pretest–posttest, random assignment *Participants*: 30 mother–child dyads 1. Information group 2. Information and behavioral training Control group	Parenting risk, child behavior problems; improvement in home environment	Both groups showed improvement Behavioral training more positive at 1-year follow-up
Brunk, Henggeler, & Whelen (1987)	Pretest–posttest *Participants*: 33 Control group	Parent training compared with multifaceted approach (8 weeks)	Fewer symptoms Multisystem more effective in restructuring

Table continues

TABLE 1 (Continued)

Authors	Design	Targets	Outcome
		Social support strategies	
Berkeley Planning Associates (1980)	Pretest–posttest No control group	Decrease in isolation Increase in self-esteem	Increase in self-esteem and ability to cope with stress
Lovell & Richey (1995)	Nonrandom assignment Pretest–posttest *Participants:* 23 physically abusive parents Control group	16-week training in social skills	Significantly more members from community organizations Increases in satisfaction No measure of relation of social support to maltreatment
Muller, Fitzgerald, Sullivan, & Zucker (1994)	*Participants:* 200 physically abusive parents Model-testing study No control group	Social support	Fathers: Support decreased abuse Mothers: Stress mediated impact of support
		Multiple-component strategies	
Lutzker & Rice (1987)	Random assignment to 12-component intervention or comparison group *Participants:* N = 232 experimental group, N = 232 comparison group	1. Parent–child training 2. Skills training 3. Social support 4. Health maintenance 5. Job placement 6. Money management 7. Assertiveness 8. Problem solving 9. Self-concept 10. Alcoholism 11. Behavior management 12. Home management	Lower rates of recidivism

and control of physiological reactivity. According to self-report data, parents perceived improved relationships with their children and decreased feelings of anger and reactivity. Using a similar strategy, Resnick (1985) trained two groups of high-risk mothers (defined by the criteria of single-parenthood and social isolation) in parenting techniques through group discussion and behavioral rehearsal. Resnick reported a decrease in symptoms of depression for this group of parents. Parents involved in the training showed positive changes in attitudes toward children, although these changes were not maintained at follow-up. Finally, there were no significant changes in frequencies of such targeted parent behaviors as parental commands and play behaviors.

Other research has provided a model for more sophisticated parent-training designs that incorporate measures of the impact of training on parents' actual behaviors toward their children. Using a single-subject design, Macmillan, Olson, and Hansen (1991) implemented a behavioral parent-training program with the goal of training in specific skills to change inappropriate child behavior. Results indicated significant increases in parental skill acquisition and subsequent decreases in targeted negative behaviors of the children.

In a different program, researchers focused on parent training on a larger scale, examining the relationship between parent training components and process issues of training. For example, Rivara (1985) implemented a parent effectiveness training project with 71 physically abusive parents, focusing on training issues as related to outcome. On the basis of a 31-month follow-up assessment, Rivara reported that 31% of the sample demonstrated compliance with treatment, with a 30% recidivism rate. Barth (1990) worked with a high-risk group of single mothers with low levels of education in a home-based child abuse prevention program. He reported that increased goal attainment in this cognitively oriented program resulted in decreased rates of child abuse. Moreover, the program seemed to have an impact on the families who were at moderate and low risk of abuse: These families had significantly fewer legal actions taken than did high-risk families, according to child welfare reports. However, the program did not result in a decrease in reported rates of maltreatment within the extremely high-risk sample.

Kolko (1996) incorporated weekly monitoring to assess the extent to which parents changed as a result of participating in either family therapy or cognitive–behavioral therapy (see also chapter 9, this volume). Outcome data indicated that cognitive–behavioral therapy was more effective than family therapy in decreasing parents' level of anger and lowering the frequency of parents' use of discipline toward their children. Similarly, home-based training in behavioral strategies produced positive results in terms of parents' increased praise and decreased use of negative words with their children (Trueste, Montes, & Montes, 1988).

On the basis of a group of studies that compared the provision of information with combined information and behavioral training, Wolfe, Edwards, Manion, and Koverola (1988) reported that although both groups showed significant improvement, the group receiving behavioral training showed more positive results in a 1-year follow-up assessment than did the group that received information only.

Critique of Cognitive–Behavioral Research

Cognitive–behavioral programs have important limitations. First, with the exception of the program of research developed by Wolfe and his colleagues, none of the behaviorally oriented programs emphasized a need to train parents in behavioral skills that are appropriate to the developmental level of the child. Also, from a "process" view of family interaction patterns, the authors of these treatment outcome studies have failed to address other variables that may influence parents' use of newly acquired parenting skills. For example, Crittendon (1996) underscored the importance of the psychological adjustment of the parent (or the parents' own attachment history) as a determinant of the quality of parent–child interaction. Similarly, even though the behavioral programs have resulted in significant gains in behavioral skill acquisition that appear to be maintained over time, it is unclear whether and how these behaviors are supported in the context of multiple relationship problems within the abusive family. For example, the participants in all of the studies reviewed were mothers. One may ask in what ways the newly acquired behaviors of these mothers have been supported by the parenting behaviors of the fathers. It is also not known to what extent communities have supported or strained the new behavioral repertoires of the mothers. These questions underscore gaps in the literature and in the design of community-based treatment programs for abusive parents.

SOCIAL SUPPORT STRATEGIES

Review of the Research

Social support interventions for abusive parents are assumed to function in both direct and indirect ways to reduce the risk of maltreatment. According to Belsky (1984) and other adherents of the ecological model, social support from both professionals and friends functions directly as a monitor for inappropriate parenting practices. Indirectly, social support functions to provide emotional acceptance that may buffer the impact of stress on parents, which may, in turn, decrease the risk of abusive parenting practices. Although a review of the extensive literature has suggested that few controlled studies are available on the impact of social support on abusive parents, data on community support services in general are widely available. Linking families with community services and informal support groups with other parents was the most frequently provided service to parents involved in 15 national demonstration programs (Layzer & Goodson, 1992). Although outcomes based on clinical judgments of project leaders suggested that maltreatment had decreased in a majority of cases, there were cases in which ongoing maltreatment occurred. The data also suggested that services were weakly or even negatively related to family outcomes. Parents' experience of stress seemed to be the critical variable that influenced the impact of a program. According to clinical records, families who experienced a high level of stress at intake appeared to benefit less from the program.

Despite the lack of rigorous research, discussion groups or informal support groups appear to be among the most frequently used services for abusive parents. Perhaps owing to the relative ease of service delivery and the popularity of this service with parents, a self-help support group, Parents Anonymous, has been organized in many sites across the United States. The groups are sponsored by professionals who volunteer time as community consultants. A national evaluation of Parents Anonymous, using parent self-reports, indicated that participation resulted in significant decreases in parents' perceptions of abusive behavior. Parents also reported an increase in feelings of self-esteem, social contacts, and ability to deal with stress. The Parents Anonymous groups also were documented to be effective as a referral and treatment resource for abusive parents (Berkeley Planning Associates, 1980).

Few studies have evaluated the impact of social support using a well-controlled design. In one study, Lovell and Richey (1995) compared the impact of a social support skills training program to that of an informal discussion group on groups of physically abusive parents who had been reported to public agencies. The experimental group, which received the social support training, reported changes both in distribution of individuals in their network and in orientation toward these individuals; that is, following the intervention, participants in the experimental group tended to communicate with a larger number of professionals and to become more trusting of these individuals. The researchers suggested that the participants did not show even more marked changes because the crisis-oriented nature of their lives prevented them from focusing on social skills acquisition. Similarly, the standardized curriculum failed to attend to individual training needs of participants. Members of the informal social support groups also tended to benefit from the informal opportunities for social support from peers. Both groups indicated a desire to have access to a more intensive follow-up program.

In a more sophisticated study of the interaction of stress and social support in predicting maltreatment, researchers found that both social support and stress directly influenced rates of child maltreatment (Muller, Fitzgerald, Sullivan, & Zucker, 1994). Fathers' experience of increased stress increased the probability of abuse, and the direct experience of social support was associated with decreased rates of child maltreatment. Mothers, however, tended to benefit from social support only when they experienced a high level of stress; the social support, therefore, indirectly decreased the likelihood of maltreatment. It appears that for the men, social support directly enhanced feelings of self-worth and stability, leading to a decreased likelihood of abuse, whereas for the women, social support buffered the effects of stress, indirectly reducing rates of maltreatment. The data also suggested that the experience of stress may lead to rigidity and withdrawal among mothers but not among fathers. In both mothers and fathers, problems with alcohol were associated with increased rates of maltreatment. The results of this study are important because both mothers and fathers were included. Furthermore, research on the impact of social support confirms the indirect impact of support in the reduction of maltreatment and neglect.

Critique of Social Support Research

The research on the impact of social support has suggested that informal support may function in direct and indirect ways to decrease the likelihood of child maltreatment. However, outcomes of the impact of social support are often measured in terms of clinical judgments of parents' perceptions rather than standardized assessments. Moreover, the studies are limited by the failure to relate changes in social support to documented changes in reported rates of maltreatment. Finally, although the positive benefits of social support are clear on the basis of the data, research is needed to delineate the ways in which support interacts with other personal and social variables to decrease risk of maltreatment.

MULTIPLE-COMPONENT PROGRAMS

Few authors have examined the impact of multiple-component programs. One such evaluation focused on the effectiveness of a comprehensive child abuse treatment program (Project 12-Ways), between 1979 and 1985, under the leadership of Lutzker (1994). The services offered within this model included parent–child training, basic skill training, home safety, health maintenance, job placement, self-control training, money management, assertiveness training, stress reduction, single-parent services, multiple-setting behavior management and leisure counseling. A number of published reports have demonstrated the effectiveness of the program in improving home cleanliness (Watson-Perczel, Lutzker, Greene, & McGimpsey, 1988), decreasing unsafe and neglectful behaviors (Tertinger, Greene, & Lutzker, 1984), and improving meal planning and provision (Sarber, Halasz, Messmer, & Bicketter, 1983).

Data were also evaluated to determine rates of recidivism and how the services were predictive of client outcomes in comparison with a matched comparison group. The results indicated that both families who experienced Project 12-Ways and those who had access only to public services were less likely than other families to have their children placed elsewhere or adopted because of abuse or neglect. Although the differences were not statistically significant, rates of recidivism seemed consistent for participants in Project 12-Ways but 40%–50% for those who received the public services. Problems in the interpretation of the data include initial differences between the samples, the multiple-problem nature of the sample, and the limitations of outcome data.

Subsequent studies of the effectiveness of Project 12-Ways focused on the overall outcomes of the intervention in comparison to a group of matched participants who received services from a child protective agency. The target sample for Project 12-Ways consisted of 232 single mothers with a mean age of 30 and an average of three children. The matched comparison group consisted of families who were currently receiving services from the Illinois Department of Children and Family Services. The design was problematic in that the parents who were referred to Project 12-Ways had been receiving public services unsuccessfully for 2 years prior to referral to the program. Pretreatment measures indicated that 56% of the target sample had had children placed in custody owing to child abuse and neglect, compared to 42% of the comparison group. Outcome measures indicated that recidivism rates were higher for the comparison group (25%) than the Project 12-Ways group (13%). In addition, the comparison group had a gradual increase in recidivism rate up to 40% by the conclusion of the 5-year study. The results, therefore, supported the importance of the multiple-component treatment program. The study demonstrated clear group differences through the use of appropriate control groups. It might have been better if the authors had demonstrated differences in risk factors rather than limiting outcome measurement exclusively to recidivism rates. Finally, it is important to analyze specifically which components are related to positive behavioral gains for families.

HOME VISITATION PROGRAMS

Home visitation treatment programs are another example of a multiple-component strategy used in the treatment of physically abusive parents or parents at risk for abuse. Many studies of these programs have been concerned with prevention rather than treatment of abusive parents.

One of the methodological problems inherent in evaluating home visitation programs is that outcome typically is based on number of reported cases of abuse (Olds & Kitzman, 1993). These statistics either underestimate or overestimate the number of cases. Much of the research in this area focuses on indicators of outcome in several areas, including improved use of the health care system, decreased use of emergency room care, and other behavioral indicators of improved parental care for the child. The outcome studies provide a more comprehensive picture of parent–child interaction and provision of care for the child than do child abuse reports.

According to a national survey (Wasik & Roberts, 1994), more home visitation programs were affiliated with social service agencies than with health or educational institutions. It is interesting that more programs were funded by private than by public sources by a ratio of 3:2 (Keller, Cicchinelli, & Bardner, 1989).

The survey also addressed a number of process-related issues for home visitation programs, such as program goals, services, credentials of home visitors, and program evaluation. As reported in the survey, most programs have focused on training parents in child development and parenting skills, as well as in stress reduction techniques to be used in anger situations. The authors suggested that there is a need to document the ways in which programs individualize goals and measure goal achievement for specific families. Although families appeared to require direct, practical services such as transportation and homemaking help, few programs were able to provide these services.

Fewer than half of the programs included any evaluation component. Moreover, the home visitation programs that did include a research component tended to incorporate subjective assessment procedures rather than standardized tests. In addition, only 38% of the studies incorporated any kind of posttreatment assessment.

Several major evaluations of home-based child abuse prevention programs have been implemented. One of the first major studies was conducted in the state of Hawaii by the National Committee to Prevent Child Abuse. The experimental design involved random assignment of 304 high-risk families to an intensive home visitation or a control condition. Data were collected at 6-month intervals over a 1- to 2-year period. Results indicated that the mothers who participated in the treatment program significantly reduced their potential for child abuse and achieved significantly higher scores on a measure of parent–child interaction. Home visitation did not produce measurable effects in the area of social support, cognitive development, or child health outcomes.

The home visitation model implemented by Olds and his colleagues was initiated with poor, single mothers in upstate New York. This program resulted in significantly fewer cases of substantiated abuse and neglect, improved parent–child interaction, and fewer safety hazards in the home than the control group demonstrated. Significant positive changes in mental development also occurred as a result of the intervention (Olds, Henderson, Chamberlin, & Tatelbaum, 1986). In another home visitation program, Dawson (1989) reported a quite different set of outcomes. Whereas mothers in the experimental group showed significant improvement in reciprocity and in warmth and encouragement during feeding, the reports of abuse were higher in the experimental group than the control group. It may be that the home-visited group was monitored more intensively, resulting in the greater number of reports.

These studies suggest that home visitation programs are effective in improving parent–child interaction and child health outcomes and, in some cases, in decreasing rates of abuse and neglect. Several factors may account for the variable results. One is that home visitation models vary in program content and therefore in the ability to have an impact on selected outcomes. Such concerns underscore the need to document program content and process issues to illuminate the relationship between intervention and predicted outcome. Second, assessment of risk for maltreatment is a critical research issue related to targeting of clients for prevention services. There remains a need to explore standardized measures of risk for child maltreatment (as opposed to socioeconomic risk) and to relate these assessments to child maltreatment.

Most studies have emphasized individual variables rather than patterns of variables that characterize dyads or families. There is also a need for theoretical and empirical studies that articulate the role of the community in family violence and in the effects of treatment of such violence.

CONCLUSION

Theoretical Issues in Child Abuse Treatment Programs

It is necessary to use multidimensional frameworks to analyze the direct and indirect effects on the parent, the child, and the social context in evaluating treatment programs for physically abusive parents. Although much theoretical and descriptive work is advanced in the literature, few published reports use these multiple-component frameworks in empirical investigations of the efficacy of child abuse treatment programs.

This review underscores several areas in which data are not available. For example, although it is known that a large number of incidents of physical abuse involve substance abuse, little research has been conducted on the role of substance abuse in the etiology and effective treatment of physical abuse. Similarly, the role of the interaction of psychological adjustment problems and abuse has not been examined extensively. The role of fathers in the treatment process has been neglected, even when fathers are the perpetrators of the physical abuse.

Researchers have tended to focus on a myriad of specific factors within the parent, child, and social context. Empirical studies are needed that focus on the relationships among variables in the system and on the relationships of these variables to the specific developmental outcomes for children. For example, few researchers of intervention studies have measured the impact of parental changes on the quality of the parent–child relationship or on the development of the child. Moreover, the impact of the social context (e.g., other family members or the community) in supporting behavioral change is also a neglected area of research.

Methodological Issues in Research on Child Abuse Treatment

The review of the literature also underscores the need to address methodological limitations of the research on treatment outcomes for physically abusive parents. These limitations primarily involve issues of design and measurement. First, the quality of the research is dependent on the researcher's ability to use appropriate comparison groups. For example, the interpretation of a longitudinal study may be hindered by the selection of groups that have received some type of service previously or by the fact that the groups were significantly different in pretreatment characteristics. Furthermore, the ability to draw conclusions may be limited by unclear definitions of abuse and inaccuracies in reports of abuse for the treatment and comparison groups.

Second, it is critical to incorporate follow-up measures of behavioral gain, particularly with multiple-problem families. Studies that include follow-up are essential for an understanding of the overall impact of treatment programs on the family and the community. This measure is particularly relevant for the high-risk, crisis-oriented families that are likely to participate in treatment programs.

Third, outcome measures need to be broader than simple rates of reported cases of abuse and neglect. Because of problems with accuracy in such reports, measures should include assessments of changes in the quality of relationships, in the use of emergency room care, or in the potential for child abuse, in addition to rates of abuse and neglect. Similarly, multiple measurements would improve the validity of results in outcome studies. An emphasis on observational data would allow the researcher to make inferences about generalization of outcomes to long-term behavioral change. Further research is required to improve the design and measurement of the effectiveness of child abuse treatment programs for physically abusive parents.

REFERENCES

Acton, R., & During, S. (1990). The treatment of aggressive parents: An outline of a group treatment program. *Canada's Mental Health, 38*, 2–6.

Barnett, D., Manly, J. T., & Cicchetti, D. (1993). Defining child maltreatment: The interface between policy and research. In D. Cicchetti & S. L. Toth (Eds.), *Child abuse, child development, and social policy* (pp. 7–73). Norwood, NJ: Ablex.

Barth, R. P. (1990). An experimental evaluation of in-home child abuse prevention services. *Child Abuse & Neglect, 15*, 363–375.

Belsky, J. (1984). The determinants of parenting: A process model. *Child Development, 55*, 83–96.

Berkeley Planning Associates. (1980). *Child abuse and neglect treatment programs: Final report and summary of the National Demonstration Program in Child Abuse and Neglect.* Berkeley, CA: Office of Child Development.

Brunk, M., Henggeler, S. W., & Whelen, J. P. (1987). Comparison of multisystemic therapy and parent training in the brief treatment of child abuse and neglect. *Journal of Consulting and Clinical Psychology, 55*, 171–178.

Carnegie Corporation. (1994). *Starting Points: Meeting the needs of our youngest children.* New York: Author.

Children's Defense League. (1996). *The state of America's children.* Washington, DC: Children's Defense Fund.

Cicchetti, D., & Rizley, R. (1981). Developmental perspectives on the etiology, intergenerational transmission, and sequelae of child maltreatment. *New Directions for Child Development, II*, 31–55.

Kolko, D. J. (1996). Clinical monitoring of treatment course in child physical abuse: Psychometric characteristics and treatment comparisons. *Child Abuse & Neglect, 20*, 23–43.

Layzer, J. I., & Goodson, B. D. (1992). Child abuse and neglect treatment demonstrations. *Children and Youth Services Review, 14*, 67–76.

Lutzker, J. R. (1994). Project 12-Ways: Treating child abuse and neglect from an ecobehavioral perspective (pp. 260–297). In R. F. Dangel & R. A. Polster (Eds.), *Parent training: Foundations of research & practice.* New York: Guilford Press.

Lutzker, J. R., & Rice, J. M. (1987). Using recidivism data to evaluate Project 12-Ways: An ecobehavioral approach to the treatment and prevention of child abuse and neglect. *Journal of Family Violence, 2*, 283.

MacMillan, V. M., Olson, R. L., & Hansen, D. J. (1991). Low and high deviant analogue assessment of parent-training with physically abusive parents. *Journal of Family Violence, 6*, 279–301.

Milner, J. S. (1993). Social information processing and physical child abuse. *Clinical Psychology Review, 13*, 275–294.

Muller, R. T., Fitzgerald, H. E., Sullivan, S., & Zucker, R. A. (1994). Social support and stress factors in child maltreatment among alcoholic families. *Canadian Journal of Behavioral Science, 26*, 438–461.

National Center on Child Abuse and Neglect (NCCAN). (1996). *Study of national incidence and prevalence of child abuse and neglect: 1996.* Washington, DC: U.S. Department of Health and Human Services.

Olds, D. L., Henderson, C. R., Chamberlin, R., & Tatelbaum, R. (1986). Preventing child abuse and neglect: A randomized trial of nurse home visitation. *Pediatrics, 78,* 65–78.

Olds, D. L., & Kitzman, H. (1993). Review of research on home visiting for pregnant women and parents of young children. *The Future of Children: Home Visiting, 3,* 53–92.

Resnick, G. (1985). Enhancing parental competencies for high risk mothers: An evaluation of prevention effects. *Child Abuse and Neglect, 9,* 479–489.

Roberts, R. N., & Wasik, B. H. (1990). Home visiting programs for families with children from birth to three: Results of a national survey. *Journal of Early Intervention, 14,* 274–284.

Showers, J. (1991). Child behavior management cards: Prevention tools for teens. *Child Abuse and Neglect, 15,* 313–316.

Tertinger, D. A., Greene, B. F., & Lutzker, J. R. (1984). Home safety: Development and validation of one component of an ecobehavioral treatment program for abused and neglected children. *Journal of Applied Behavior Analysis, 17,* 159–177.

U.S. Advisory Board on Child Abuse and Neglect. (1995). *Creating caring communities: Blueprint for an effective federal policy on child abuse and neglect.* Washington, DC: Department of Health and Human Services, Administration for Children and Families.

Wasik, B., & Roberts, R. N. (1994). Survey of home visiting programs for abused and neglected children and their families. *Child Abuse & Neglect, 18,* 271–283.

Watson-Perczel, M., Lutzker, J. R., Greene, B. F., & McGimpsey, B. J. (1988). Assessment and modification of home cleanliness among families indicated for child neglect. *Behavior Modification, 12,* 57–81.

Whiteman, M., Tanshel, D., & Grundy, J. P. (1987). Cognitive behavioral interventions aimed at anger of parents at risk of child abuse. *Social Work, 32,* 469–474.

Wolfe, D. A. (1987). *Child abuse: Implications for child development and psychopathology.* San Diego: Sage.

Wolfe, D. A. (1991). *Preventing physical and emotional abuse of children.* New York: Guilford Press.

Wolfe, D. A., Edwards, B., Manion, I., & Koverola, C. (1988). Early interventions for parents at risk for child abuse and neglect: A preliminary investigation. *Journal of Consulting and Clinical Psychology, 56,* 40–47.

11

AGGRESSION IN THE SCHOOLS: TOWARD REDUCING ETHNIC CONFLICT AND ENHANCING ETHNIC UNDERSTANDING

NORMA D. FESHBACH AND SEYMOUR FESHBACH

Schools, once a haven to which parents could send their children with confidence regarding their safety and protection, have become an environment in which violence is a frequent visitor. In this chapter, we attempt a brief overview of the nature and scope of the problem, the factors contributing to school violence, and programs that address its reduction. After the overview, we present the essential features of a new project that we are initiating to deal with one aspect of the problem, namely, ethnic bias and ethnic conflict. In this presentation, we address issues bearing on aggression due to prejudice at the elementary, middle, and high school levels.

FREQUENCY OF AGGRESSION AND VIOLENCE IN SCHOOLS

The incidence of aggression in schools has become a matter of public concern and media interest. The *Los Angeles Times* (1994) featured a major article on the subject, headlined "Schools: Finding paths to peace amid violence." Several months before, *Time* magazine had a cover story on guns in schools and portrayed school violence as a major social issue. One wonders whether media attention to incidents of school violence exaggerates the severity of the problem and whether violence in schools is increasing. Some surveys of parents, teachers, and students indicate that the majority in each of these groups do not feel that violence is a major problem in their or their children's schools (Harris, 1993, 1994). Also, comparisons between indices of current and past frequencies of aggressive or violent school incidents do not reflect a substantial increase in school violence in the past decade (Furlong & Morrison, 1994). Schools may not be as dangerous as widely depicted in the media; however, the problem of school violence is a serious one.

A few relevant statistics can be cited. A broad survey (Harris, 1993) of a representative nationwide sample of more than 1,000 public school students, grades 3–12, and of an almost equal number of teachers indicated that only 50% of students and 77% of teachers reported feeling "very safe." A question of interpretation arises in evaluating the meaning of "somewhat safe," the response chosen by 40% of the students and 22% of the teachers. It is clear, therefore, that a significant proportion of students sampled in this survey have experienced some anxiety with regard to school violence. Twenty-two percent indicated that they were worried about being physically attacked in or around their school, and 19% reported that the use of knives or the firing of guns was a major problem. A greater percentage of teachers—46%—reported that the use of knives and guns was a major problem, with about one third of teachers stating that threats to teachers constituted a major problem at their school.

The results of other large-scale surveys of school populations are consistent with these findings, indicating that school violence is a serious social problem, not simply a figment of media exaggeration. In a 1993 survey of U.S. high school students by the University of Michigan Survey Research Center (cited by the National Center for Education Statistics, 1995b), 24% of African Americans and 14% of European Americans reported being threatened by someone with a weapon. Approximately 5% of the students reported being injured by a weapon.

School violence is by no means restricted to the inner city. In a national survey of 10,499 students aged 12–19 conducted by the Bureau of Justice in 1989 (cited in National Center for Education Statistics, 1995a), the absolute number of urban and suburban students reporting the presence of street gangs in their school was about equal, although there was a difference in percentages. A subsequent national survey of 6,800 students in grades 6 through 12, conducted in 1993 by the National Center for Education Statistics (1995b), also assessed the presence of gangs in schools. In response to one question—Do any of the students at your school belong to fighting gangs?—31% of European Americans, 42% of African Americans, and 51% of Hispanics reported the presence of gang members in their school. Although the percentage of gang membership is greater in schools with large ethnic minority-group populations, a substantial proportion of non-minority-group students also cope with fighting gangs in their schools. Because there are more nonminority-group than minority-group students in U.S. schools, the absolute number of non-minority-group students exposed to gangs at school (5.2 million) was nearly 2 million more than the number of minority-group students combined (3.2 million) who reported being exposed to fighting gangs at school.

The presence of gangs in a school significantly affects the climate of anxiety and violence that may exist in the school. The 1989 findings (see Table 1) indicated that the percentage of students fearing an attack in school nearly doubled (from 18.2% to 35.4%) when gangs were present. Both the 1989 and 1993 surveys (see Table 2) indicated that the frequency of physical attacks and other indices of violence were significantly affected by gang presence.

Formal reports from school districts of incidents of school violence offer another source of data bearing on the problem of aggression and violence in schools. Because these are crime reports, forms of aggression such as verbal threats and verbal attacks are excluded, as are most fights. In addition, the frequency of the various types of crimes is probably greater than the numbers indicate. Nevertheless, these reports provide useful information. They portray the kinds of aggression and violence that may

TABLE 1
Student Victimization and Fear at School, by Gang Presence and Students' Residence, 1989 (percentages)

Presence of gangs at school and students' residence	Victimized in last 6 months[a]	Ever feared an attack		Avoided places inside school	Brought something to school for protection in last 6 months
		At school	To or from school		
Gangs present	6.7	35.4	24.2	13.0	4.9
Urban	6.5	37.5	28.4	13.5	5.5
Suburban	6.8	32.4	19.6	13.0	5.1
Rural	6.9	38.0	25.3	13.0	1.9
No gangs	2.9	18.2	11.6	2.9	1.5
Urban	3.0	19.3	16.3	3.7	2.0
Suburban	3.0	18.1	11.0	2.6	1.4
Rural	2.6	17.5	8.9	2.9	1.1
Total	3.5	21.8	14.7	5.9	2.0

From the 1989 National Crime Victimization Survey.
[a]*Victimized* reflects a "yes" answer to either of two questions: "During the past six months, did anyone take money or things directly from you by force, weapons, or threats at school?" or "Did anyone physically attack you at school during the last six months?"

TABLE 2
Student Victimization and Fear at School, by Gang Presence and Race or Ethnicity, 1993 (percentages)

Presence of gangs at school and students' residence	Physically attacked during school year	Something taken by force	Brought weapon to school
Gangs present	5.9	2.3	6.2
White	5.5	2.3	4.6
Black	8.2	1.9	10.4
Hispanic	4.9	2.6	6.7
No gangs	2.5	0.7	1.9
White	2.5	0.5	1.5
Black	2.1	1.0	4.0
Hispanic	3.0	1.8	1.9
Total[a]	3.7	1.2	3.4

From the 1993 National Household Education Survey.
[a]Total includes racial and ethnic subgroups that are not shown separately.

beset schools, and they can be used as indicators of changes in the level of school violence.

The Los Angeles Unified School District Crime Report indicated that the level of school violence for the academic year 1993–1994 declined somewhat in comparison to the prior year (see Table 3). The cost of vandalism of school property was about $5 million for each year. Assaults with a deadly weapon against students declined from 330 reported in 1992–1993 to 255 in 1993–1994, and assaults against school personnel showed a comparable decline, down from 38 to 28. Battery of students without a deadly weapon declined from 507 in 1992–1993 to 444 in 1993–1994; battery of school personnel declined from 167 incidents to 145. There were approximately 1,300 citations for possession of weapons in 1992–1993 and about 1,000 in 1993–1994. There were two bomb incidents in 1992–1993 and, fortunately, none in 1993–1994. The modest decline in incidents of violence from 1992–1993 to 1993–1994 does not negate the fact that school violence in Los Angeles, as well as in other cities in the United States, remains a significant problem that must be addressed. It is of interest that although these incidents of violence, including possession of weapons and assault with a deadly weapon, occur with greater frequency in middle schools and high schools, they are far from rare in elementary schools.

USE OF CORPORAL PUNISHMENT IN SCHOOLS

This description of school violence would be incomplete without reference to another form of violence that occurs in our schools, namely, the use of corporal punishment directed against schoolchildren. By *corporal punishment*, we refer to the prescribed physical infliction of pain by a school

TABLE 3
Los Angeles Unified School District Crime Statistics

Description of crime	Number of incidents, 1992–1993					Number of incidents, 1993–1994				
	Grade school	Junior high school	Senior high school	Other	Total	Grade school	Junior high school	Senior high school	Other	Total
Assault										
Against students	1	1	12	1	15	1	1	4	1	7
Against adult personnel	28	42	41	6	117	37	25	38	12	112
Battery										
Against students	65	236	189	17	507	50	201	174	19	444
Against adult personnel	36	92	82	14	224	39	83	55	8	185
Assault with a deadly weapon										
Against students	38	126	149	17	330	30	119	94	12	255
Against adult personnel	12	27	22	8	69	13	17	18	5	53
Possession of weapons										
Guns	45	149	223	36	453	44	108	138	20	310
Knives	51	218	191	9	469	42	193	145	13	393
Other weapons	44	168	173	18	403	29	160	131	9	329
Vandalism of school property			$5,027,297					$4,926,988		

administrator or teacher using a paddle or related means as punishment for a major or minor infraction.

We do not imply an equivalence between the use of corporal punishment by school personnel and student acts of battery and assault with a deadly weapon; conceptually, however, the use of corporal punishment bears a similarity to student use of physical aggression. The child aggressor, no less than the school authority administering corporal punishment, feels morally justified in striking the perceived transgressor. In addition, we emphasize that in interpreting corporal punishment as a form of school violence and arguing against its use, we do not argue against the use of discipline in the training and socialization of children. We have detailed elsewhere appropriate forms of discipline that are functionally related to the infraction and that are designed, when possible, to make restitution and enhance the sensitivity and consciousness of the aggressor (Feshbach & Feshbach, 1973).

Although some forms of aggression expressed in schools may be inhibited by the use of corporal punishment, from a theoretical standpoint, the overall level of anger and violence in children who are corporally punished is likely to increase (Feshbach & Feshbach, 1973; S. Feshbach, 1970). Empirically, there are laboratory studies of the effects of punishment and data on the correlates of parental use of corporal punishment; however, there is almost no direct evidence concerning the effects of the use of corporal punishment in schools. It is of interest that an analysis of state-by-state statistics yielded a significant positive correlation between the frequency of corporal punishment administered in schools and the frequency of students dropping out of school (Maurer & Wallerstein, 1987). It has been suggested that the degree to which a school system is willing to employ corporal punishment is a reflection of the degree of violence toward children that is present in a community (Hagebak, 1973). These observations, of course, do not provide substantive empirical support for the hypothesized ineffectiveness of corporal punishment or the suggestion that it is a manifestation of aggression. Much more systematic study is required for an assessment of the effectiveness of the use of corporal punishment by school authorities.

SOME ANTECEDENTS OF AGGRESSION IN CHILDREN

Both theory and empirical research concerning children's aggressive behavior link the acquisition of dispositions to aggression and violence to experiences of frustration and to parental socialization practices that entail neglect and absence of affection, poor communication, reinforcement of aggressive behaviors, inconsistent application of discipline, frequent resort to corporal punishment, and physical abuse (Parke & Slaby, 1983). Other sources of reinforcement and modeling, such as peer norms and rewards for bullying (Olweus, 1978), also have a significant impact on the development of aggressive tendencies or behavior. Situational factors, as well as variations in aggressive response dispositions, have also been shown to have a significant influence on the manifestation of aggression. Aggression appears to be enhanced through *stimulation*, by provocation or by exposure to aggressive stimuli, or through *disinhibition*, by group participation in aggressive acts or by a context that makes likely the avoidance of punishment.

Similarly, a number of personality factors have been shown to bear on the facilitation or inhibition of aggressive acts. These include impulsiveness stemming from weakened self-monitoring or other self-control or ego factors, weakened superego factors such as minimal guilt or remorse, and cognitive dispositions to interpret ambiguous situations as provocative and misattribute intentionality and responsibility. Other relevant dispositional variables include academic problems, interpersonal difficulties, peer rejection, and low self-esteem (Parke & Slaby, 1983).

Much of the research cited is directly germane to the issues of school aggression and violence; although the aggression studied was not labeled school aggression or violence, it was often measured on the basis of teacher or classroom peer ratings of aggressive behavior. Other studies, in which the primary focus was on the school context, have yielded comparable findings. Data from the National Educational Longitudinal Study of 1988, involving administrators, teachers, eighth-grade students, and parents in more than 1,000 schools (Weishew & Peng, 1993), yielded the following correlates of the frequency of violence in a school: low socioeconomic status and single-parent families, low school achievement and low educational expectations, large school population, low teacher morale and conflicted school climate as rated by administrators, and negative student perceptions of teachers and the school atmosphere. There was a positive relationship between frequency of violence and severity of punishment for first misbehavior and an inverse relationship between frequency of violence and presence of a clearly structured school environment in which students are expected to conform to rules, carry out homework assignments, and otherwise live up to school expectations. It is noteworthy that the strongest predictor of school violence was the frequency of substance abuse problems among the students.

There is a debate in the literature concerning whether the primary source of school violence is the school and its management or the attributes of the children and their environments (Harootunian, 1986). This debate is unfortunate in that it has a "blame" connotation and tends to reduce the causes of school aggression and violence to a few independent factors. Clearly, there are individual differences in the degree to which children engage in violence within any school environment. These differences may stem from a variety of sources such as personality attributes, peer group influences, and family crises. There are also differences among schools in the incidence of violent acts, which can stem from socioeconomic and cultural factors (which can also influence within-school variations in aggression) or from variations in school personnel and administrative practices.

Moreover, it is rare that these factors operate in isolation. A child who tends to be impulsive and lash out when frustrated may display little aggression in a classroom environment that he or she finds gratifying. There may be a high incidence of student violence despite the excellence of the classroom instructor if the class size is unusually large, the students have been poorly prepared for the class, or there are few remedial opportunities available because of the lack of economic resources. School violence is a result of the interaction among individual, social, environmental, school personnel, and school management factors.

School aggression and violence represent a multidetermined phenomenon that needs to be addressed by a number of different programs operating at different levels—at the level of the school environment and atmosphere and at the level of the individual child's skills and behavioral dispositions. Ideally, these programs should be coordinated and integrated.

SCHOOL VIOLENCE AND AGGRESSION INTERVENTION PROGRAMS

Various programs have been developed to deal with particular factors in the matrix of variables influencing school violence. Violence prevention programs such as Second Step, which is directed toward younger children (Committee for Children, 1992), and the Violence Prevention Curriculum for Adolescents (Prothrow-Stith, 1987) employ a variety of methods that are largely but not exclusively drawn from established cognitive–behavioral procedures such as self-instruction, problem solving, modeling, and behavioral rehearsal. These procedures focus on the development of impulse control and anger management as well as on training in skills entailed in empathy. Other extant programs are directed toward children already identified as aggressive; for example, Lochman and his associates (Lochman, Nelson-White, & Wayland, 1991) have attempted to remedy the misperceptions, cognitive distortions, and attributions of aggressive youngsters. Goldstein's group (Goldstein, Glick, Reiner, Zimmerman, & Coultry, 1985) emphasized moral reasoning and other cognitive–behavioral procedures in their program. Patterson and his colleagues (Reid & Patterson, 1991) have established behavioral programs for training parents in more effective child-management procedures. Other researchers have developed programs in an attempt to influence the school climate and culture through consultation with administrators, teacher training, parental involvement, participation of school psychologists, modification of the physical environment, and links to community resources (Coie & Jacobs, 1993; Comer, 1988; Morrison, Furlong, & Morrison, 1994; Toby, 1993–1994). Several programs aimed at preschool-aged youngsters—the Perry Preschool Project (Schweinhart & Weikart, 1988) and the Houston Parent–Child Development Center (Johnson, 1988)—have focused on educational enrichment efforts and family supports rather than on aggression, per se. Follow-up studies (Johnson, 1988) have indicated that in addition to educational gains, significantly fewer aggressive behaviors and more prosocial behaviors were subsequently manifested.

One of the most ambitious school-based intervention projects to address the problem of aggression in inner-city youth is the Metropolitan Area Child Study implemented by Eron, Huesmann, Guerra, and their associates (Eron, Guerra, & Huesmann, 1997; Guerra, Eron, Huesmann, Tolan, & Van Acker, in press; Huesmann et al., 1996). Sixteen urban elementary schools are involved in the project, which will permit the evaluation of the effects of three different levels of intervention. One level entails a general classroom-based social cognitive and peer-relationship training program coupled with an extensive teacher-training program. A second level involves the same treatment as the first, plus small-group social cognitive and peer-relationship training for children identified to be at high risk for aggression. The third level entails the same treatment as the previous level, plus a family intervention for high-risk children and their families that focuses on improving parenting skills and family interactions. The evaluation of the treatment effects is complex, thorough, and still in progress. Initial analyses have suggested positive outcomes for the first two treatment levels but, surprisingly, not for the third, or most comprehensive, treatment (Huesmann et al., 1996).

ETHNICITY, PREJUDICE, AND SCHOOL VIOLENCE

We have developed a program that addresses issues of school violence and aggression. Our approach is not an alternative to extant programs but can be readily used in conjunction with them. It focuses on a factor that is significantly implicated in a considerable amount of school violence (Soriano & Soriano, 1994) but is infrequently addressed, namely, ethnic prejudice and ethnic conflict.

In a recent survey of a national sample of high school students, 32% of the students cited incidents of racially motivated violence that occurred in their schools; the figure increased to 40% for urban students (*Who's Who Among American High School Students*, 1992). Consistent with these data is the report of the Los Angeles County Office of Education and the Human Relations Committee that hate crimes occurred in one third of the county's junior high and middle schools (Bodinger-DeUriarte & Sancho, 1992). Modifying ethnically motivated violence and the social prejudice that underlies these aggressive acts poses an enormous challenge. Responding to this challenge requires a multiplicity of strategies.

Social prejudice is a problem that is not restricted to middle school and older children. Evidence of ethnic bias has been found in children in primary school and even in younger children (Phinney & Rotheram, 1987). Developmental changes occur in the form that ethnic prejudice takes and in the cognitive factors that mediate and mitigate social prejudice. Older elementary school children (in fourth and later grades) are better able than younger children to discriminate behaviors of different children of the same ethnicity and to integrate information bearing on social prejudice. Nevertheless, Katz and Zalk (1978) demonstrated that it is possible to modify negative racial attitudes in second as well as fifth graders. In a carefully controlled experiment, several different procedures varying from training in perceptual differentiation of minority-group faces to increased positive ethnic contact were shown to be effective in reducing ethnic prejudice. Other experimental procedures with school-aged participants that have been shown to be effective include racial discussion and racial role playing (Breckheimer & Nelson, 1976) and multiconceptual training in thinking about individuals of varying races and ethnicities (Gardiner, 1972).

At an applied level, school professionals have attempted to address issues of social prejudice through curriculum innovations that relate in varying degrees to the experimental findings that have been reviewed. Extant educational approaches pertaining to issues of ethnicity and diversity can be roughly categorized into three groups: (a) color blinds; (b) multicultural, or tourist; and (c) antibias programs (Derman-Sparks, 1989; Sleeter & Grant, 1988; Tatum, 1992). The color-blind approach predominated in the 1960s and, to a lesser extent, in the 1970s. The essence of this approach was an emphasis on the basic similarity of individuals and on the irrelevance of color, ethnicity, and related group characteristics. The multicultural approach began to take hold in the 1970s and remains the dominant method by which teachers address issues of ethnicity. The multicultural approach is sometimes referred to as the "tourist" approach because the focus of the curriculum is on the customs and holidays of different ethnic groups. Although it is useful, the approach tends to be superficial in its treatment of different ethnicities. In contrast, the antibias curriculum, which is becoming more prevalent, introduces the student to different cultures but also to the manifestations and mechanisms of prejudice. Various approaches to an antibias curriculum are presented in a recent volume edited by Hawley and Jackson (1995); these approaches, although promising, require systematization and evaluation. Our project entails the transformation of current curricula rather than the introduction of specific courses or a special curriculum. We believe this approach can have a useful, productive role among the constellation of programs that are required to ensure a significant impact on ethnic prejudice and ethnically instigated aggression.

EMPATHY, SOCIAL PREJUDICE, AND THE TRANSFORMATION OF CURRICULA

Our effort to reduce ethnically related tensions and conflicts involves a program designed to enhance an appreciation of other ethnic groups through systematic application of the mechanism of empathy. The program is intended to help children to recognize the common experiences and shared values and ideals of diverse social groups and, at the same time, to understand differences in perspectives and customs.

Although there are studies indicating that empathy is inversely related to aggression in children (N. Feshbach, 1975, 1984, 1991; Feshbach & Feshbach, 1969, 1982, 1986), there is an absence of data directly bearing on the relationship between empathy and social prejudice. From a theoretical standpoint, one would hypothesize that children who are empathic will manifest less prejudice than children who are low in empathy. There may be several processes mediating the relationship between empathy and attitudes and behavior toward people of other ethnic groups that would lead one to predict that heightened empathy will result in more positive, less prejudiced attitudes and behaviors toward individuals differing in ethnicity. The ability to understand the feelings and assume the perspective of another person, which is a major component of empathy, should mitigate conflicts and negative feelings that stem from children's misunderstandings and failure to appreciate the experience and point of view of other children from different cultural backgrounds. If conflict with a child of another ethnic background is reduced and negative appraisals of that child's behavior are modified, manifestations of aggression and prejudice directed toward that child should be reduced.

Empathy is a process that is facilitated by similarity and also functions to foster underlying similarities among individuals. Implicit in an empathic child's appreciation of another person's perspective and understanding of his or her feelings is the assumption of a basic similarity between the child and the other in the psychological processes that mediate feelings, attitudes, and behavior. Because empathy is facilitated by similarity between the perceiver and the object of empathy (Feshbach & Roe, 1968), it should help bridge the manifest differences that are the stimulus to prejudice.

Empathy can also be expected to influence prejudice through its relationship to aggression. Because the empathic person shares the pain experienced by another who is the object of aggression, aggression by an empathic individual should evoke pain in the aggressor as well as the object of the aggression. Consequently, empathy should tend to mitigate and inhibit aggression. To the extent that aggression influences prejudice or is stimulated or evoked by ethnic differences, empathy might reduce prejudice through this route.

A PROPOSAL TO TRANSFORM CURRICULA

We are in the process of developing a curriculum—more precisely, an approach to transformation of instructional procedures—that is designed to achieve the objectives of traditional curricula as well as the objectives of enhanced ethnic understanding and sensitivity and positive attitudes toward diverse ethnic groups.

Our initial efforts were guided by the notion of developing a new and separate curriculum that would entail lessons in "ethnic diversity" and that would be grade appropriate. We eventually rejected this approach. Teachers, in particular, were sensitive to the demands on classroom time and to the problems of introducing still another "subject" into the curriculum. More important, we concluded that this experience should not be isolated from the rest of the child's educational activities. We chose an alternative approach of transforming instructional strategies by incorporating empathic processes into the instruction of traditional curricula.

Norma Feshbach's three-component model of empathy (N. Feshbach, 1975) guided the proposed transformational changes. Empathy, as defined in this model, refers to an interpersonal transaction in which one individual shares the affective experience of another. The model posits three components: (a) sensitivity to, and the ability to identify feelings in, others; (b) the ability to take the perspective of another person; and (c) sensitivity to one's own feelings and the ability to express these feelings in a controlled manner.

We are in the process of developing a manual for teachers that elucidates the concept of empathy and that details general transformational principles the teacher can employ to transform the instructional approach to the curriculum. The following is an example of one of the seven general transformational principles that have been delineated.

Example of a General Transformational Principle

When the material in the curriculum involves instances of conflict, such as fighting or war; of domination, such as slavery and indentured servitude; or of negative stereotyping, such as labeling of groups as inferior and unworthy, the students should engage in group discussions and other activities that lead to an understanding of the perspectives and feelings of the different individuals or groups involved.

Because the general transformational principles are relatively abstract, we are developing more specific principles linking the transformational process and principles to particular curriculum areas such as literature and social science (see Figure 1). The following is an example of a specific principle linking the transformational process to the social science curriculum.

Example of a Specific Transformational Principle

When the curriculum material deals with the diverse populations that make up the United States (e.g., Native Americans, descendants of early settlers from England and Holland, Eastern Europeans, Scandinavians, Hispanics, and African and Asian Americans) and with the immigration of diverse groups and their changing roles in U.S. society, the particular perspectives, experiences, and feelings of these groups should be addressed. In this regard, the different ways in which prejudice and discrimination can be communicated and expressed should be discussed. Students' understanding of the painful consequences of prejudice can be heightened through assuming the role and perspective of the object of prejudice.

We are in the process of developing our manual for teachers. To make the principles more useful, concrete illustrations of the application of the principles to particular curriculum lessons are required. We plan to conduct workshops with teachers, refine the general and specific transformational principles, and carry out an appropriate evaluation of the effectiveness of this educational program. At the current time, all we can offer is a promissory note. However, we are optimistic regarding the usefulness of the approach; although it employs quite different procedures, it is theoretically related to the empathy training curriculum we implemented a number of years ago, which was shown to enhance prosocial behaviors and regulate aggressive behaviors (Feshbach, Feshbach, Fauvre, & Ballard-Campbell, 1983). A major difference between the empathy training curriculum and the proposed transformational curriculum is that the former was implemented in small groups, using precise exercises, whereas the latter is to be carried out in the classroom and makes use of the regular curriculum. However, several studies have indicated that basic features of the empathy training approach can be carried out with diverse curriculum materials and can be incorporated into instruction in a classroom setting. As part of a doctoral dissertation, Fauvre (1979) used children's stories to foster emotional understanding and empathy. Whereas in her study the children were seen individually, an empathy training program has been implemented successfully in the classroom through enrichment of the social studies, literature, and art curricula (Feshbach & Rose, 1990; Rose, 1990).

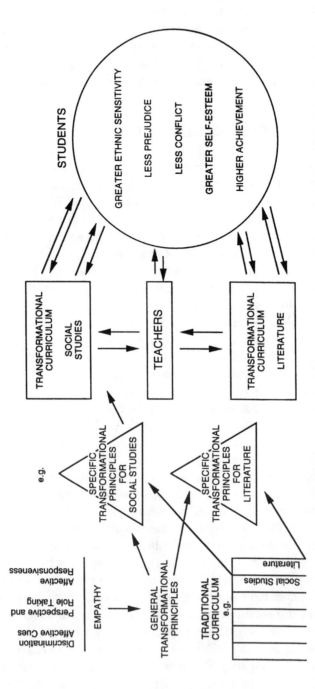

Figure 1. Working model of the application of empathy-based general and specific transformational principles to school curricula.

In addition, the curriculum exercises used in our original empathy training program, which have been partly or wholly incorporated into a number of the aggression prevention and intervention programs referred to previously, focused exclusively on the basic skills entailed in the components of empathy. In contrast, implementation of the transformational guide entails the direct application of empathy principles to classroom curricula to enhance the understanding of the perspectives and experiences of members of diverse ethnic and social groups. We anticipate that the more focused application of empathy principles will result in more substantial effects with regard to aggression reduction and prosocial behaviors, particularly in relation to interethnic interactions. Furthermore, we expect the effects of the program to generalize to a variety of situations of conflict and frustration as well as to situations involving children from different ethnic groups. In addition, in implementing this program, teachers may have to deal with their own feelings regarding different ethnic groups and modify areas of bias that they may have.

CONCLUSION

A problem as complex and pervasive as school violence, which mirrors the violence in communities, requires multilevel and sustained prevention and intervention programmatic efforts. We believe that one important facet of this complex matrix that has to be addressed is the role of ethnic bias and ethnic conflict. School violence will not be eliminated by addressing issues of racism and ethnic bias; however, its frequency, salience, and scope should be significantly reduced.

REFERENCES

Bodinger-DeUriarte, C., & Sancho, A. R. (1992). *Hate crime: A source book for schools*. Los Alamitos, CA: Southwest Center for Educational Equity, Southwest Regional Laboratory.

Breckheimer, S. E., & Nelson, R. O. (1976). Group methods for reducing racial prejudice and discrimination. *Psychological Reports, 39*, 1259–1268.

Coie, J. D., & Jacobs, M. R. (1993). The role of social context in the prevention of conduct disorder: Toward a developmental perspective on conduct disorder [Special issue]. *Development & Psychopathology, 5*, 263–275.

Comer, J. P. (1988). Educating poor minority children. *Scientific American, 256*, 42–48.

Committee for Children. (1992). *Second step: A violence prevention curriculum (preschool–kindergarten teacher's guide)*. Seattle, WA: Author.

Derman-Sparks, L. (1989). *Anti-bias curriculum: Tools for empowering young children.* Washington, DC: National Association for the Education of Young Children.

Eron, L. D., Guerra, N., & Huesmann, L. R. (1997). Poverty and violence. In S. Feshbach & J. Zagrodska (Eds.), *Aggression: Biological, developmental and social perspectives* (pp. 139–153). New York: Plenum Press.

Fauvre, M. (1979). *The development of empathy through children's literature.* Unpublished doctoral dissertation, University of California, Los Angeles.

Feshbach, N. D. (1975). Empathy in children: Some theoretical and empirical considerations. *Counseling Psychologist, 5,* 25–30.

Feshbach, N. D. (1984). Empathy, empathy training and the regulation of aggression in elementary school children. In R. M. Kaplan, V. J. Konecni, & R. Novoco (Eds.), *Aggression in children and youth* (pp. 192–208). The Hague, Netherlands: Martinus Nijhoff.

Feshbach, N. D. (1991). Studies on parental empathy: Parent and child correlates. New directions in child and family research: Shaping Head Start in the '90s. Conference Proceedings (pp. 261–264). (Eric No. ED340 473)

Feshbach, N. D., & Feshbach, S. (1969). The relationship between empathy and aggression in two age groups. *Developmental Psychology, 1,* 102–107.

Feshbach, N. D., & Feshbach, S. (1982). Empathy training and the regulation of aggression: Potentialities and limitations. *Academic Psychology Bulletin, 4,* 399–413.

Feshbach, N. D., & Feshbach, S. (1987). Affective processes and academic achievement. *Child Development, 58,* 1335–1347.

Feshbach, N. D., Feshbach, S., Fauvre, M., & Ballard-Campbell, M. (1983). *Learning to care: A curriculum for affective and social development.* Glenview, IL: Scott, Foresman.

Feshbach, N. D., & Rose, A. (1990, June 13–17). *Empathy and aggression revisited: The effects of classroom context.* Paper presented at the biennial meeting of the International Society for Research on Aggression, Banff, Canada.

Feshbach, S. (1970). Aggression. In P. H. Mussen (Ed.), *Revision of* Carmichael's manual of child psychology (Vol. II). New York: Wiley.

Feshbach, S., & Feshbach, N. D. (1973). Alternatives to corporal punishment: Implications for training and controls. *Journal of Clinical Child Psychology, 3,* 46–49.

Feshbach, S., & Feshbach, N. D. (1986). Aggression and altruism: A personality perspective. In C. Zahn-Waxler, M. Cummings, & M. Radke-Yarrow (Eds.), *Aggression and altruism: Biological and social origins.* Cambridge, England: Cambridge University Press.

Furlong, J., & Morrison, G. M. (1994). Introduction to miniseries: School violence and safety in perspective. *School Psychology Review, 23,* 139–150.

Gardiner, G. S. (1972). Complexity training and prejudice reduction. *Journal of Applied Social Psychology, 2,* 326–342.

Goldstein, A. P., Glick, B., Reiner, S., Zimmerman, D., & Coultry, B. T. M. (1985).

Aggression replacement training: A comprehensive intervention for aggressive youth. Champaign, IL: Research Press.

Guerra, N. G., Eron, L. D., Huesmann, L. R., Tolan, P., & Van Acker, R. (in press). A cognitive–ecological approach to the prevention and mitigation of violence and aggression in inner-city youth. In K. Bjorkvist & D. P. Fry (Eds.), *Styles and conflict resolution: Models and applications from around the world.* San Diego: Academic Press.

Hagebak, W. (1973). Disciplinary practices in Dallas contrasted with school systems with rules against violence against children. *Journal of Clinical Child Psychology, 2,* 14–16.

Harootunian, B. (1986). School violence and vandalism. In S. J. Apter & A. P. Goldstein (Eds.), *Youth violence: Programs and prospects* (Pergamon General Psychology Series, Vol. 135, pp. 120–139). Oxford, England: Pergamon Press.

Harris, L. (1993). *Violence in America's schools.* The Metropolitan Life Survey of the American Teacher. New York: Louis Harris.

Harris, L. (1994). *Violence in America's schools: The family perspective.* The Metropolitan Life Survey of the American Teacher. New York: Louis Harris.

Hawley, W. D., & Jackson, A. W. (Eds.). (1995). *Toward a common destiny: Improving race and ethnic relations in America.* San Francisco: Jossey-Bass.

Huesmann, L. R., Eron, L. D., Henry, C., Guerra, N. G., Tolan, P. H., & Van Acker, R. M. (1996, October). *Evaluating a cognitive–ecological approach to prevention of interpersonal violence among high risk youths.* Poster session for CDC conference, Atlanta, GA.

Johnson, D. L. (1988). Primary prevention of behavior problems in young children: The Houston Parent–Child Development Center. In R. H. Price, E. L. Cowen, R. P. Lorion, & J. Ramos (Eds.), *14 ounces of prevention: A casebook for practitioners* (pp. 44–52). Washington, DC: American Psychological Association.

Katz, P. A., & Zalk, S. R. (1978). Modification of children's racial attitudes. *Developmental Psychology, 14,* 447–461.

Larson, J. (1994). Violence prevention in the schools: A review of selected programs and procedures. *School Psychology Review, 23,* 151–164.

Lochman, J. E., Nelson-White, K. J., & Wayland, K. K. (1991). Cognitive-behavioral assessment and treatment with aggressive children. In P. C. Kendall (Ed.), *Child and adolescent therapy: Cognitive–behavioral procedures.* New York: Guilford Press.

Maurer, A., & Wallerstein, J. S. (1987). *The influence of corporal punishment on crime.* Berkeley, CA: EVAN-G.

Morrison, G. M., Furlong, M. J., & Morrison, R. L. (1994). School violence and school safety: Reframing the issue for school psychologists. *School Psychology Review, 23,* 236–256.

National Center for Education Statistics. (1995a). *Educational policy issues: Statistical perspectives. Gangs and victimization of school.* Washington, DC: U.S. Department of Education, Office of Educational Research and Improvement.

National Center for Education Statistics. (1995b). *The pocket condition of education 1995*. Washington, DC: U.S. Department of Education, Office of Educational Research and Improvement. (NCES 95-817).

Olweus, D. (1978). *Aggression in schools: Bullies and whipping boys*. Washington, DC: Hemisphere.

Parke, R. D., & Slaby, R. G. (1983). The development of aggression. In P. H. Mussen (Gen. Ed.) & E. M. Hetherington (Vol. Ed.), *Handbook of child psychology: Vol. 4. Socialization, personality, and social development* (4th ed., pp. 547–641). New York: Wiley.

Phinney, J. S., & Rotheram, M. J. (1987). *Children's ethnic socialization*. Newbury Park, CA: Sage.

Prothrow-Stith, D. (1987). *Violence prevention curriculum for adolescents*. Newton, MA: Educational Development Center.

Reid, J. B., & Patterson, G. R. (1991). Early prevention and intervention with conduct problems: A social interaction model for the integration of research and practice. In G. Stoner, M. R. Shinn, & H. M. Walker (Eds.), *Interventions for achievement and behavior problems*. Washington, DC: National Association of School Psychologists.

Rose, A. (1990, April). Empathy training in the naturalistic context of the classroom. In N. D. Feshbach (Chair), *Developmental researchers in the schools*. Symposium conducted at the annual meeting of the American Educational Research Association, Boston.

Schools: Finding paths to peace amid violence. (1994, December 8). *Los Angeles Times*, p.

Schweinhart, L. J., & Weikart, D. P. (1988). The High/Scope Perry Preschool Program. In R. H. Price, E. L. Cowen, R. P. Lorion, & J. Ramos-McKay (Eds.), *14 ounces of prevention: A casebook for practitioners* (pp. 53–65). Washington, DC: American Psychological Association.

Sleeter, C. E., & Grant, C. A. (1988). *Making choices for multicultural education: Five approaches to race, class, and gender*. Columbus, OH: Charles E. Merrill.

Soriano, M., & Soriano, F. I. (1994). School violence among culturally diverse populations: Sociocultural and institutional consideration. *School Psychology Review, 23*, 216–235.

Tatum, B. D. (1992). Talking about race, learning about racism: An application of racial identity development in the classroom. *Harvard Educational Review, 62*, 1–24.

Toby, J. (1993–1994, Winter). Everyday school violence: How disorder fuels it. *American Educator*, pp. 44–48.

Weishew, L., & Peng, S. S. (1993). Variables predicting students' problem behaviors. *Journal of Educational Research, 87*, 5–17.

Who's who among American high school students. (1992). Lake Forest, IL: Educational Communications.

12

NEIGHBORHOOD-BASED PROGRAMS

JAMES GARBARINO, KATHLEEN KOSTELNY, AND FRANK BARRY

In this chapter we evaluate research on programs that aim to reduce community violence and foster resilience. First among the topics covered is the meaning of the word *neighborhood* and of the concepts of neighboring and neighborhood-based programming. The second focus is the implications of neighborhood-based research on child maltreatment and community violence for the delivery of social services to families. Third, we examine some underlying issues concerning neighborhood-based programs aimed at child abuse prevention, and fourth, we present some general principles derived from existing programs and research regarding the creation of resilience through family and community support. We also include a review of the effectiveness of specific intervention programs.

THE MEANING OF NEIGHBORHOODS AND NEIGHBORING

Recently there has been a surging of interest in the neighborhood as a unit of analysis in responding to issues of violence. This is a natural outgrowth of two trends. The first trend involves the changing patterns of community violence. For example, in Chicago, in the last decade there has been an increase of more than 100% in the proportion of homicides com-

287

mitted in public areas, from 32% of the total in 1982 to 67% of the total in 1993. The second trend concerns the recognition that community action is an important resource in dealing with family and community violence; for example, the U.S. Advisory Board on Child Abuse and Neglect has endorsed neighborhood-based programs such as Neighbor Helping Neighbor (Barry, 1991; U.S. Advisory Board on Child Abuse and Neglect, 1990).

The concept of neighborhood has a long history as a focal point for research, theory, policy, and practice in the United States (Hawley, 1950; Warren, 1978). The U.S. Advisory Board on Child Abuse and Neglect uses the following definition of *neighborhood*: "a small geographic unit consensually identified as a single community (includes rural and urban settings)." Besides this spatial dimension, most definitions include a respect for history (the evolution of residential patterns) and psyche (some sense of shared identity among the residents, as in a common inclination to "name" the neighborhood). The result is a definition of neighborhood that has three elements: a social component, a cognitive component, and an affective component (Unger & Wandersman, 1985). Neighborhood (and neighboring) may be defined, therefore, in terms of interaction patterns, a common understanding of boundaries and identity, and a set of shared feelings of belonging.

The social component of neighborhoods includes both informal social supports (emotional, instrumental, and informational) and social networks (links to other people). This component has been central in offering support and in providing resources for coping with stressors at both an individual and a neighborhood level; however, some observers have noted a shift in the function of neighborhoods. With advances in communication, technology, and transportation, neighborhoods have lost some of the important functions that they once had (Wellman, 1979). Now, many activities and relationships take place outside a person's neighborhood. Such a view makes it necessary to consider the concept of "communities without propinquity," that is, communities that are not limited by their geographical boundaries (Wellman, 1979). People may belong to a variety of communities, depending on their interests, although they belong to only one neighborhood on the basis of where they live. Thus, a neighborhood is a geographic area where people feel physically, although not necessarily socially, close to each other (Barry, 1991).

The cognitive component of a neighborhood refers to the thoughts or ideas that individuals have about their neighborhood's social and physical environment; it can be used both to help in understanding the neighborhood and to develop ways of dealing effectively with neighborhood issues. One aspect of neighborhood cognition involves a mental mapping process resulting from repeated experiences in a neighborhood, which allows individuals to manage their neighborhood better. For example, cognitive mapping in dangerous neighborhoods determines where people feel it is safe to walk or to interact socially with others.

A neighborhood also has an affective dimension, which includes a sense of mutual help, a sense of community, and an attachment to place. The sense of mutual help involves the belief that assistance is available when needed, even though neighbors may not frequently be contacted. Indeed, heavy use of neighborhood resources may lead to a reduction in neighboring owing to overload. Neighborhood support is thus best understood in terms of confidence rather than use.

A sense of community encompasses feelings of membership and belongingness and shared socioemotional ties with others in the neighborhood. Attachment to place develops through an analysis by individuals concerning the costs and benefits of living in their neighborhood compared with other neighborhoods. It may also develop as a result of personal experiences with deep emotional dimensions, some of which occur in childhood, that cause a person to identify with a place and a community.

Neighborhood-Based Programming

However one defines *neighborhood*, it is important to understand the potential and actual impact of "neighborhood-based programming" in supporting families, preventing violence, and protecting children (Garbarino & Stocking, 1980). The premise of the neighborhood-based approach is the belief that deliberately engineered social support can do two things. First, it can override individual dynamics linked to violence. Second, it can buffer the child and family from some of the psychological and social effects of social risk factors. In this view, the neighborhood can promote personal development and psychological well-being and can stimulate health patterns of interaction both within the family and between the family and the broader environment (Weiss & Halpern, 1991).

The role of social support systems in preventing and controlling violence lies in the linking of social nurturance with social control (Garbarino & Stocking, 1980). Such support systems give people feedback about themselves and expectations about others that they otherwise might not get in the broader community context (Caplan & Killilea, 1976). Two corollary premises are embedded in neighborhood-based strategies of social support. The first premise is that the support provided can be internalized in some manner and thus have an effect beyond the period during which it is provided. The second premise is that the support provided can strengthen functioning for adults both in the community and in the family so that it also will have a significant positive effect on child health and development (Weiss & Halpern, 1991).

Two recurrent questions reverberate through all analyses of neighborhood-based programming: (a) Can family support be a "treatment," or must it be a condition of life? (b) Can neighborhood-based programming succeed amidst conditions of accumulated high risk? Beyond these fundamental issues of efficacy stand a number of issues concerning process. For example, to what extent can and should neighborhood-based social support programs for violence prevention be staffed at least in part by neighborhood volunteers or paraprofessionals? To what extent can and should efforts be aimed at assisting neighbors in helping each other? In short, to what extent is neighborhood-based programming to prevent violence inextricably tied to issues of empowerment?

Issues in Understanding Neighborhood-Based Efforts

Although community-based approaches de-emphasize "treatment" and the role of therapeutic professionals, some important questions remain to be answered by professionals in the field.

Intuitive Appeal Versus Rigorous Grounding in Theory and Research

Does existing program evaluation strongly confirm the validity of the assumptions underlying community-based family support and education programs, or has their intuitive appeal in the current political and cultural climate sustained them in the absence of conclusive empirical evidence? If forced to answer this question, one must acknowledge that neighborhood-based violence prevention and violence intervention programs rest primarily on a foundation of faith. Few researchers have addressed the validity of these approaches, particularly with high-risk families in high-risk communities.

Appropriate Matching of Services and Needs

What is the "market" for neighborhood support efforts? Weissbound (1994) has presented the assumptions of Family Focus, a neighborhood-based social support program, in this way: "A third of the families are functioning well without us; a third need and can profit from us; a third are too troubled to make good use of our program" (p. 130). Although the exact percentages in each category are open to question, the underlying analysis seems valid because it recognizes that effectiveness depends in part on an appropriate matching of services and needs. Successful participation in family-oriented social programs requires a moderate level of competence, organization, available resources, and continuing motivation. One of the early analyses of Head Start concluded that those who have the most gain the most.

The same may apply to neighborhoods. Can violence prevention and intervention programs operate from a neighborhood base if the neighborhood is socially and physically devastated? How much congruence is required among neighborhood-based institutions? Is it enough to have a school or a church? Is an active business community necessary?

These issues require one to look closely at any family-support program to see if it is reaching beyond the "easy" families and the "easy" neighborhoods. There is always the danger that the program will simply open its doors and the most functional families will walk in the door—the upper third to which Weissbound referred. The lowest functioning third are rarely able and willing to participate in such programs. This is a particularly serious concern if one seeks to employ neighborhood-based programs to prevent child maltreatment; families involved in child maltreatment and other forms of violence are often drawn from the group with the lowest levels of competence and motivation.

Consultation Versus Training

To what degree is it necessary and feasible to "train" natural helpers such as neighbors to function as violence prevention and control systems? This is a major concern in the field of neighborhood-based support programs, and it has special relevance to programs addressing violence. One approach emphasizes the need for professionals to serve as "consultants" to "natural neighbors" or "central figures." In projects conducted by Collins, Pancoast, and their colleagues (Collins & Pancoast, 1976), this approach has been adopted. In their day care information project, these researchers identified women who were already the focal point of natural helping networks in the informal day care referral "system." They saw as their goal facilitating this "natural helper" without interfering with her operations. They emphasized the existing knowledge and skills of the natural helper and the danger of disturbing her work through overt intervention. Thus, consultation rather than training was the focus of their efforts.

In contrast are training programs for preparing community members to function on behalf of mental health promotion in their community (Danish & Augelli, 1980). Because of the limitations of these natural helpers and the need to augment their skills and concepts, training rather than "merely" consultation was the focus. Using paraprofessionals has limitations, however. Halpern and Larner (1987) found that paraprofessionals encountered problems in assisting clients in areas of health care, child care, and mental health services. Other problems may arise from overidentification with the client, excessive dependency on the client, projecting one's own situation onto the client, or low expectations (Austin, 1978). Parents are also at times reluctant to reveal personal matters to workers from the community because they fear a loss of privacy.

Other professionals perceive that traditional staff education and training programs for paraprofessionals from the community are not adequate for promoting change in parents and optimal development in children, particularly when such psychically loaded issues as sexual abuse and violence are involved. For example, in addition to providing formal training, the Ounce of Prevention Fund program developed new strategies designed to change the service provider by transforming the way she viewed and understood parents, children, and parent–child relationships (Musick & Stott, 1990). The training protocol was restructured in terms of forming a relationship to model the kinds of reciprocal, interactive roles that the professional staff expected the paraprofessional staff to fulfill vis-à-vis the teen parents. Such a "chain of enablement" was intended to foster positive growth in paraprofessional staff so that they in turn could foster such growth in teenaged parents. This method of training paraprofessionals is designed to result ultimately in more enabling and nurturing parenting through a structured, well-planned trickle-down effect.

Domains of Silence

Are there topics and issues with which neighbors and indigenous paraprofessionals cannot deal because they are too personally threatening or culturally taboo. This problem extends the consultation versus training issue still further and is of special relevance to any consideration of the role of social support in preventing child maltreatment.

Two of the family issues most likely to invoke personal or cultural "domains of silence" are sexuality and aggression. Any effort that aims to prevent violence through social support systems that rely on natural helpers must contend with the fact that matters of sex and violence are least likely to be addressed (or addressed successfully). The natural helpers' own experiences of victimization, teenage sexual activity, and use of corporal punishment create powerful impediments to dealing with these issues openly, as a program's formal curriculum typically dictates (Halpern, 1990a; Musick & Stott, 1990). In the case of community violence, the issues are similar. One survey conducted in Chicago found that 60% of Head Start workers had unresolved experiences of traumatic violence (Garbarino, Dubrow, Kostelny, & Pardo, 1992). These obstacles are not insurmountable, but they need to be addressed.

In the Ounce of Prevention Fund programs, dealing with sexuality and teenaged mothers, professionals have found it possible to address issues of sexuality with community helpers, but only after an extensive program of education and "processing" (Musick & Stott, 1990). By the same token, the North Lawndale Family Support Initiative of the National Committee for Prevention of Child Abuse in Chicago was able to open a dialogue with community members about the issue of corporal punishment, a dialogue that started from the sometimes fierce unwillingness of many parents (and natural helpers from the neighborhood) to acknowledge that a problem existed in the community with respect to corporal punishment.

"Selection Effects" or "Genuine Impact"

To what extent are neighborhood effects primarily self-selection effects and the result of exclusionary policies rather than the result of the milieu represented in the neighborhood? All community and neighborhood analyses are potentially compromised on the basis of self-selection. Why are some people living in Neighborhood A and others in Neighborhood B? Rarely is random selection the answer. The systematic grouping and exclusion of families on the basis of race, ethnicity, or income militates against efforts to understand family functioning (including child maltreatment) on the basis of neighborhood characteristics.

According to a study by Freudenburg and Jones (1991), 21 of 23 communities experiencing rapid population growth had a disproportionate increase in crime. The authors suggested that changes in a community's social structure that accompany rapid growth can result in a breakdown of social control. As the "density of acquaintanceship" (i.e., the proportion of a community's residents who know each other) decreases, criminal activity increases. Another issue concerns out-migration from neighborhoods beginning to "turn bad." Such an out-migration may have debilitating effects on social networks (Fitchin, 1981) and create still more confounding self-selection effects.

Beyond these selection factors, neighborhoods differ on the basis of "ethos." Some areas are more vital and coherent than others, even when the families are of the same social class (Warren, 1978). Most neighborhoods are not very child focused. A survey in South Carolina (Melton, 1992) revealed that, on a 17-point scale, with 7 indicating *high involvement*, the average score for neighborhood residents was 2+ in response to the question "How involved are you in other people's children?" The same survey revealed that most people could not name one agency that had been particularly helpful on behalf of children.

On the other hand, if professionals recognize these analytic limitations, it may be possible to go forward with prevention programs aimed at and through neighborhoods. It has been established that context is important, as is self-selection and the content of "treatment." For example, in one recent study, Rosenbaum and Kaufman (1991) reported that youths whose families were relocated to subsidized housing in the suburbs were more than twice as likely to attend college as youths who were relocated to subsidized housing in inner-city areas—54% versus 21%. Moreover, of those relocated to the suburbs, 75% found employment vs. 41% of those relocated to the inner city (Rosenbaum & Kaufman, 1991). Because the selection of who went where was made randomly, there were no systematic differences in who was relocated where.

Rosenbaum's results suggest a powerful social support effect on important life course events. It is important to understand support as more than affirmation and noncontingent reinforcement. Rather, it is goal directed, which is why some neighborhoods support negative behavior whereas others offer prosocial support. Rosenbaum's study showed that when youths are located in a neighborhood context that provides support for occupational and educational achievement, they are more likely to pursue those life goals.

Intervening at the community level presents a significant challenge to professionals in the field of human services, because most human services in recent years have been oriented directly toward individuals. Can professionals develop the same or a higher level of proficiency in intervening at the neighborhood level than has been reached in intervening at the individual level? Can practitioners be taught to do as much to strengthen communities as they have been taught regarding strengthening individuals?

NEIGHBORHOOD-BASED RESEARCH ON CHILD MALTREATMENT AND COMMUNITY VIOLENCE

Child maltreatment and other forms of violence take place in a social as well as a psychological and cultural context. Prevention, treatment, and research should incorporate this contextual orientation (Garbarino & Stocking, 1980).

Previous research has demonstrated that low- and high-risk neighborhoods for child maltreatment are significantly different (Garbarino & Crouter, 1978; Garbarino & Kostelny, 1992a). For example, in the United States, poverty is a major link between child maltreatment and other forms of violence (Pelton, 1994). The term *high risk* may refer to areas that have high rates of child maltreatment or to neighborhoods that have higher rates of child maltreatment than would be predicted from the socioeconomic level of the residents. Two areas with similar socioeconomic profiles may have very different rates of child maltreatment; one may be high risk (having rates of child maltreatment that are higher than expected), and the other may be low risk (having rates that are lower than expected).

High-risk neighborhoods are socially impoverished as well as less socially integrated, particularly as reflected in employment and neighboring patterns (Bouchard, 1987; Deccio, Horner, & Wilson, 1991; Garbarino & Kostelny, 1992b; Sattin & Miller, 1971). Factors include instability of residence, high number of vacant housing units in the neighborhood, and absence of telephones (Deccio et al., 1991). In a study of two socioeconomically similar Chicago neighborhoods, one high risk and the other low risk for child maltreatment, clear differences were found in the climate of the two communities. For example, whereas residents of the low-risk community described themselves as a community of the working poor, the high-risk neighborhood had only an 18% employment rate. Employment, even at low wages, is a social indicator of prosocial orientation and of functionality, apart from the financial implications of being employed. Furthermore, the general tone of the high-risk neighborhood was depressed; people had a hard time thinking of anything good to say about their neighborhood. In contrast, in the low-risk community, people were eager to talk about their community; although they listed serious problems, most of them felt that their community was poor but a decent place to live.

Escalation of Social Impoverishment

Researchers who are familiar with the history of low-income urban neighborhoods have tracked a deterioration of social structure and an escalation of social impoverishment (Halpern, 1990b; Wilson, 1987). For example, until the 1960s, the social organization of many inner-city black neighborhoods was enhanced by the presence of working- and middle-class families. These neighborhoods featured a vertical integration of different income groups: Lower class, working-class, and middle-class professional black families lived in the same neighborhoods (Wilson, 1987). However, by the 1980s, most of the middle- and working-class population had moved from these neighborhoods, leaving behind an underclass with few mainstream role models to maintain the traditional values of education, work, and family stability. This pattern is evident in data from Cleveland (Coulton et al., 1992) showing that the likelihood of poor families living in neighborhoods that were predominantly poor increased from 23% in 1960 to 60% in 1990.

Moreover, there is often a breakdown in social control among members of these neighborhoods. For example, DuBow and Emmons (1981) suggested that for informal social control to be effective, a neighborhood must have a consensus on values or norms, be able to monitor behavior, and be willing to intervene when behavior is not acceptable. In socially impoverished neighborhoods, both a consensus on values and the ability to monitor behavior are often lacking (DuBow & Emmons, 1981).

Efforts at intervention must include an approach to the psychosocial factors in the community that influence the ability and willingness of both professionals and residents to make a public commitment to social support programs. Of particular concern regarding social support programs in socially impoverished neighborhoods is the impact of community violence on the public behavior of community resource people.

Effect of Violence on Professionals Who Serve Children

Although the effects of community violence and social deterioration are often noted as social problems, rarely are these issues considered in relation to the stresses they place on those providing services, especially in the context of pervasive violence. Human service workers increasingly find themselves serving children and families who live in community environments that are chronically violent. These include some large public housing developments and socially deteriorated, low-income neighborhoods in cities across the nation. For example, over 100,000 children live in public housing projects in Chicago, where the rate of "serious assault" has increased more than 400% since the mid-1970s.

Current research is now focusing on the effects of routine exposure to community violence on children living in public housing. In one study of children living in a public housing project in Chicago, every child in the sample had had firsthand encounters with a shooting by age 5 (Garbarino et al., 1992). Additionally, in a survey of 1,000 elementary and high school students on Chicago's south side, 40% had witnessed a shooting, more than 33% had seen a stabbing, and 25% had seen a murder (Bell, 1991). In Alabama, 43% of a sample of inner-city children (between the ages of 7 and 19) had witnessed a homicide (Growing up afraid, 1992). Growing up in a highly stressful environment can lead to long-term mental health problems, even when children have access to parental protection in the short term (cf. Garbarino et al., 1992).

In addition to their exposure to community violence, children living in these areas are more likely to be victims of child abuse and neglect. In Chicago, areas having high crime rates have child maltreatment rates up to 4 times higher than the city average (Garbarino & Kostelny, 1992a). These incidents of domestic violence interact dynamically with the incidents of community violence. Some of the incidents outside the homes are in fact related to domestic conflicts; children and parents are exposed to violence in other families indirectly as part of their life experience as neighbors and friends. Professionals often struggle with their own fears in seeking to respond to the needs of these children.

Implications for Social Services to Families

The fact that high-risk families live in high-risk neighborhoods is not the only issue of concern in considering a commitment to prevent child maltreatment through the use of social support mechanisms. The people who provide services to families in high-risk communities are also at risk for experiencing violence in the course of their day-to-day work. For example, one of the regional directors of the Department of Children and Family Services in Chicago reported that at any given time at least 2 of his 40 caseworkers are unable to work because of injuries sustained while going to or coming from the homes of the families they serve. Many more have had significant traumas and experienced fear when asked to investigate cases in high-crime communities. In a survey of Head Start staff working in communities with high levels of community violence, over 60% had witnessed shootings and gang-related activities. Such experiences undermine the ability of neighborhood-based programs to support families.

Professionals who deal with children who are regularly exposed to violence are often at a loss as to how to respond to them. For example, in six training sessions involving Head Start staff from four major Chicago public housing complexes, the majority of the staff participating expressed their feelings of inadequacy in being unable to help their students deal with the violence they encountered in their daily lives. Many of these staff members were indigenous to the communities they served.

Successful child abuse prevention and child protective services must address the issues of powerlessness, traumatization, and immobilizing fear that impede effective family life and social development for a significant and growing proportion of children living in violent communities. Part of this task involves understanding the needs of professionals working in these environments, who often feel powerless, traumatized, and afraid. How do they make sense of prevention and protection missions in neighborhoods so violent that they fear for their personal safety? How are they to bring messages of family safety? Does everyone concerned accept lower standards for child protection in such environments? Do professionals fall silent when confronted with harsh, even violent, child rearing?

There has been little research conducted on the immediate and long-term consequences of exposure to community violence for service providers. Clarifying the stresses these workers face and illuminating the support they need will be an important addition to efforts to improve and inform services.

UNDERLYING ISSUES CONCERNING NEIGHBORHOOD-BASED SOCIAL SUPPORT PROGRAMS

To understand how to address violence at the community level, it is necessary to consider issues facing neighborhood-focused social support programs regardless of their setting. We include in our analysis, therefore, the broad range of settings in which U.S. children grow up, including suburban neighborhoods, and in which professionals seek to employ social support approaches to prevent child maltreatment (Halpern, 1990a).

The first of these issues speaks to the different orientations we refer to as "categorical" approaches (e.g., programs aimed at drug use, parent education, or some other specific "problem") and "generic" approaches (e.g., programs aimed at general improvement in family functioning, child development, or community well-being). One way to address this issue is to focus on the generic role of social support in childhood resilience. Social support outside the family is a source of resilience for children. This bolsters the argument that general efforts to increase neighborhood activities in support of children can help prevent the most deleterious consequences of child maltreatment.

Factors Leading to Resilience and Coping

Convergent findings from several studies of life course responses to stressful early experiences have suggested the following ameliorating factors that lead to prosocial and healthy adaptability (Lösel & Bliesener, 1990):

- Active attempts to cope with stress (rather than just reacting)
- Cognitive competence (at least an average level of intelligence)
- Experiences of self-efficacy, with corresponding self-confidence and positive self-esteem
- Temperamental characteristics that favor active coping attempts and positive relationships with others (e.g., activity, goal orientation, sociability) rather than passive withdrawal
- A stable emotional relationship with at least one parent or other reference person
- An open, supportive educational climate and parental model of behavior that encourages constructive coping with problems
- Social support from persons outside the family

These factors have been identified as important when the stresses involved are in the "normal" range found in the mainstream of modern industrial societies (e.g., poverty, family conflict, childhood physical disability, and parental involvement in substance abuse). They provide a starting point for efforts to understand the impact of programs intended to enhance family coping and reduce child maltreatment.

Of the seven factors identified in the research on resilience and coping, several are particularly relevant to our concerns: social support from persons outside the family; an open, supportive educational climate and parental model of behavior that encourages constructive coping with problems; and a stable emotional relationship with at least one parent or other reference person. Although most of the research on social support is correlational, lacking the dynamic and experimental design factors needed for researchers to be certain about paths of causality, these three factors among the seven cited by Lösel and Bliesener provide the beginning of an agenda for developing neighborhood-support programs to prevent child maltreatment and for broader interventions as well (Thompson, 1992).

The last factor in the resilience list is at the heart of our concern: social support from persons outside the family. We see this finding as a generic affirmation of the validity of a social support approach. The implication is that the importance of social support increases inversely with the resources of the family: The poorer need more help. However, a catch-22 often operates in such situations: The more troubled and impoverished a family system is *inside* its boundaries, the less effective it will be in identifying, soliciting, and making effective use of resources *outside* its boundaries (Gaudin & Polansky, 1985). Neglectful mothers are less ready, willing, and able to see and make use of social support in their neighborhoods and more in need of such support than other mothers. This vicious cycle has been evident repeatedly in results of studies of child maltreatment (Garbarino & Eckenrode, 1997).

The second resilience factor, a stable emotional relationship with at least one parent or other reference person, translates into our model of generic social support through repeated findings that depth, as opposed to simply breadth, is an important feature of social support (and one often neglected in programmatic approaches). In addition to needing social support from friends, neighbors, coworkers, and professionals, parents and children need social support in its most intensive form. Children need someone who is absolutely crazy about them. This is clear from research on parenting (children must have *someone* in this role), but it is also important in the functioning and development of youths and adults, including those in parenting roles.

The implications are important. For example, in efforts to prevent child maltreatment among malfunctioning parent–child dyads, clinicians found that the effects of their programmatic intervention were attenuated to the point of being negligible for mothers who supported revisions in parenting style and practices but who had no close allies. For poor mothers, this person is likely to be neighborhood based. Only by identifying such a maternal ally and incorporating her into the preventive intervention was Wahler able to ensure that the preventive strategies he was teaching the mother would endure. This finding parallels those of other studies in emphasizing the importance of social support for the goals of professional intervention.

The third factor (the sixth and seventh of Lösel and Bliesener's resilience factors) explicitly targets the community's institutions. It is schools, religious institutions, civic organizations, and other social entities that operationalize the concept of "an open, supportive educational climate." Programs and role models that teach and reward the reflective "processing" of experience are an essential feature of social support at the neighborhood and community level.

It is important to remember that social support has at least two distinct dimensions. The first is its role in making the individual feel connected, which is important in its own right. The second is its role in promoting prosocial behavior (e.g., avoiding child maltreatment even under stressful conditions). This may explain the finding that, under conditions of social stress, families whose only social network is composed of kin are more likely to abuse children than families whose network includes nonkin (Gelles & Straus, 1988). Kin-only networks are more likely than more diverse networks to offer consensual support for a negative interpretation of child behavior and a corresponding rationale for maladaptive parent behavior. Considering the structure of social support without regard to its value and cultural content is insufficient. One can see further evidence of this point by explicitly focusing on socially maladaptive methods of coping.

Maladaptive Coping

Some families are forced to cope with highly stressful situations, such as the chronic danger and social impoverishment of many low-income neighborhoods or the unstable and alienated neighborhoods that reflect community disruption even in the absence of poverty. These families may adapt in ways that are dysfunctional. Families may cope with highly stressful conditions by adopting a worldview or personae that may be dysfunctional in the "normal" situations in which they are expected to participate, such as in school and other settings of the larger community. For example, aggressive behavior may appear to be adaptive in the abnormal context of chronic violence. However, such aggressive behavior may be maladaptive to school success, as it stimulates rejection at school.

Moreover, some adaptations to chronic threat and social impoverishment, such as emotional withdrawal, may be socially adaptive in the short run but become a danger to the next generation, when the individual who has withdrawn becomes a parent. This phenomenon has been observed in families of Holocaust survivors (Danieli, 1988). A family's inability to be a good neighbor and to make use of social support (let alone to serve as a source of social support to others) may be one of the casualties of the developmental process that results from exposure to constant violence.

Even in the absence of this intergenerational process, however, the links between threat, stress, and social support may directly affect families. Parents' adaptations to socially impoverished and threatening environments may produce child-rearing strategies that impede normal development. For example, the parent who prohibits a child from playing outside in an effort to protect the child from gun violence may be denying the child a chance to engage in social and athletic play.

Similarly, the fear felt by parents in high-crime environments may be manifest as a restrictive and punitive style of discipline (including physical assault), which may reflect an effort to protect the child from falling under the influence of negative forces such as gangs in the neighborhood. This "adaptive" strategy, which may be socially supported in the neighborhood, can be a significant impediment to efforts aimed at preventing child maltreatment.

Furthermore, punitive child rearing is likely to have the result of heightening aggression on the child's part, with one consequence being a difficulty in succeeding in social contexts that provide alternatives to the "culture" of the highly stressed and socially impoverished neighborhood environment. In addition, this style of parenting can lead to the child's endorsing and accepting violence as the modus operandi for social control, which in turn rationalizes the "culture of aggression" that further impedes efforts to prevent child maltreatment. However, holding the child back from negative forces through punitive restrictiveness is generally much less successful as a strategy than promoting positive alternatives to the negative subculture feared by the parent (Scheinfeld, 1983). This finding parallels more generic conceptions of social influence that emphasize the need to communicate empowerment as a resource in coping, as is evident in the following items from the list of resources for resilience noted previously: experiences of self-efficacy, with a corresponding self-confidence and positive self-esteem, and temperamental characteristics that favor active coping attempts and positive relationships with others (e.g., activity, goal orientation, sociability) rather than passive withdrawal.

This discussion highlights an important dilemma. Over time, negative neighborhoods stimulate and reinforce negative individual behavior (on the part of newcomers or children growing up), and one eventually sees negative individual behavior and attitudes as both the cause and the effect of negative neighborhoods. Therefore, attempting to change neighborhoods without changing individuals may be foolhardy; one must design and implement programs that restructure the social and physical environment of the neighborhood in ways that induce and reinforce changed individual behavior. Such efforts are necessary to create a climate in which more conventional educational and therapeutic innovations can take root. A strategy that incorporates economic initiatives with social and psychological interventions seems most suitable for meeting these objectives.

Origins of Participation

Participation and the ethos that supports it are major components of social support interventions. Research identifying the factors that enhance participation in neighborhood organizations, particularly "block organizations," is highly relevant to the concern of this chapter. Any effort to stimulate social support through neighborhood organization must accommodate to these factors. Through a community development project, Wandersman, Florin, Friedmann, & Meir (1987) found that participation in block organizations is related to being "rooted" in place demographically:

Members tended to be older, married, homeowners, female, and long-term residents. This finding confirms the observations that Collins and Pancoast (1976) made concerning "natural helping networks." It is primarily older women (whose children are grown) who have a long history in the neighborhood who serve as "central figures" and "natural helpers."

Beyond these demographic factors, Wandersman and his colleagues identified some "psychological variables" that predict participation. These include a sense of civic duty and political efficacy, a perception that existing problems are within the realm of local control, a stronger-than-average sense of community, and a high level of self-esteem. Once again, there is a congruence between these findings and what Collins and Pancoast observed: that demographic position alone is insufficient; an individual must have attributes that translate opportunity into participation.

The preceding findings are important in a consideration of the role of neighborhood social support in preventing child maltreatment. Such programs must seek out self-confident, public-spirited older married women who are long-term residents of the neighborhood. In the high-risk neighborhoods, these women are often already carrying a heavy load of family responsibility. For example, they are often caring for their grandchildren and sometimes providing a home and financial support for their adult children. In some areas, these women may be overwhelmed with their responsibilities rather than "free from drain," as are the usual candidates for leadership roles in social support networks identified by Collins and Pancoast. However, the neighborhoods most in need of preventive intervention are those in which the attributes cited by Wandersman are in shortest supply. These attributes are by no means absent, but any effort must begin with the recognition that special pains and investment will be required to identify existing resources for participation and to enhance these resources. One must keep this fact in mind when reading the following examination of specific programs.

Program Reviews

The Elmira, New York, Home Health Visiting Program

Olds and his colleagues (1989) conducted a family-support program that combined significant intervention with a sophisticated research design. Home health visitors (registered nurses) were assigned to a family during the mother's pregnancy and for the first 2 years of the child's life. These nurse-practitioners provided parent education regarding fetal and infant development to 400 first-time mothers in a small county of 100,000 residents in the Appalachian region of New York State. They also involved family members and friends in child care and support of the mother and linked family members with other health and human services. The mothers were either teenagers, unmarried, or of low socioeconomic status. Visits to the mothers were initially made weekly and then tapered off to monthly. Two other, less intense forms of intervention—free transportation to health clinics, and screening and diagnostic testing—were examined. There was a significant preventive effect for poor, unmarried mothers 19 years of age or younger (child maltreatment rates of 4% for the longer, health visitor treatment vs. 19% for the other intervention conditions). The young mothers receiving home health visiting also punished their children less frequently, and their babies were seen in the emergency room less often as well as seen by physicians less frequently for accidents and poisonings. Olds speculated that the long-term health visitors developed a relationship characterized by both nurturance and feedback with their young clients.

North Lawndale Family Support Initiative

The Chicago-based North Lawndale Family Support Initiative (NLFSI), sponsored by the National Committee to Prevent Child Abuse (Lauderdale & Savage, 1991), highlights the strengths and limitations of neighborhood-oriented programming aimed at preventing child maltreatment. In 1989, out of 77 Chicago communities, the community of North Lawndale had the second highest rate of child fatalities over a 7-year period. The total number of reported cases of child abuse had also risen 65% in an 18-month period from June 1986 to December 1987. Although North Lawndale's population is only 0.5% of the state of Illinois, it experienced 13% of all substantiated child abuse fatalities in Illinois during that period.

The NLFSI, a 5-year demonstration project begun in 1989 to establish a community-based prevention strategy, first identified neighborhood leaders and secured their cooperation to support child abuse prevention efforts. These community leaders then identified individuals and groups (e.g., civic groups, elected officials, religious officials, professionals, schools, organized labor) that also could be enlisted in their efforts at child abuse prevention. The leaders provided valuable perspectives on the causes of child abuse and neglect in the community, opened doors to needed human resources in the community, and sanctioned the planning and implementation of prevention programs and activities. After the needs of the neighborhood were assessed, strategies were developed to address the preventive educational needs of school-aged children, educational and support needs of parents, treatment programs for victims of abuse, substance abuse treatment, and perinatal support.

Outcome data revealed that the most effective strategies for engaging the community in child abuse prevention included establishing an advisory council, conducting a comprehensive needs assessment, carrying out a public awareness campaign, and establishing life skills training in the schools.

The parent education and parent support groups were the least effective strategies, owing to inadequate program design and implementation difficulties.

As a result of the findings, recommendations were made that aimed at increasing community impact, enhancing public awareness activities, increasing services, and identifying appropriate staff requirements. To increase community impact, it was recommended that child abuse prevention efforts include an advisory council composed of respected representatives from a range of social service agencies, as well as parents in the community and professionals from the schools. Sensitivity to the particular characteristics of the community was also found to be a necessary component for greater community impact because it increased the sense among community members that the program was their own (as opposed to it being imposed on them).

To enhance public awareness, it was recommended that activities be established that provide an opportunity for interaction between community residents and child abuse professionals. Furthermore, community residents were more receptive when child abuse prevention messages were presented in a positive, nonaccusatory way, when they were responsive to the needs of different groups (such as children or youths), and when community residents and organizations were given the opportunity and responsibility to be involved in the public awareness campaigns.

Increasing child abuse prevention services through community-based agencies such as schools was found to be an effective way to educate and involve the community. It was found that spending time meeting and enlisting the support of senior staff at the agencies providing the services was crucial to the success of the prevention services. Finally, identifying key staff persons who had a track record and commitment to community outreach and community organizing helped build trust with community residents and was crucial in developing community-based programs.

The Neighborhood Parenting Support Project

The Neighborhood Parenting Support Project was developed in 1988 in two neighborhoods in Winnipeg, Canada, that had 3 to 4 times the city average of child maltreatment cases (cf. Garbarino & Kostelny, 1992b). The premise of the program was that if social support for parenting was strengthened at the neighborhood level, the risk of child maltreatment would be reduced.

After identifying and mapping neighborhood and parent social networks, project staff initiated a social network intervention that consisted of consulting, connecting, convening, constructing, and coaching. Through a neighborhood parenting support worker, parents were helped to change their personal social networks, reinforcing positive connections and weakening destructive connections. For example, parents were helped to weaken stressful ties with family members and reinforce ties with neighbors who might be less critical of the parent and better able to help by providing child care support in emergencies or emotional support in a crisis.

The neighborhood parenting support worker provided social support in identifying and solving problems, as well as in networking skills, parenting skills, support- and help-seeking skills, communication skills, and support-giving skills. The neighborhood parenting support worker joined with and supported neighborhood central figures, natural helpers, and network "connectors" in an effort to develop a referral network and neighborhood parenting support network structures. She "connected" with people in settings frequented by parents and children, such as family centers, day care centers, playgrounds, self-service laundries, and churches.

William Penn Prevention Initiative

The William Penn Prevention Initiative was designed to achieve a reduction in the risk for child abuse and neglect among families residing in some of the most at-risk communities in the Greater Philadelphia area (cf. Garbarino & Kostelny, 1992b). Fourteen demonstration projects representing different types of service (e.g., home health visits, parent education, parent support) were evaluated across services by the National Committee to Prevent Child Abuse.

Issues evaluated were the extent to which the initiative changed specific parenting practices, personal functioning, and parent–child interactions. The group of the 14 demonstration projects significantly reduced their clients' levels of risk for maltreatment as measured by the Child Abuse Potential Inventory and staff assessments. Overall, participants showed a decrease in their risk for child abuse. Moreover, the staff rated nearly 70% of all participants as having benefited from services. In terms of specific at-risk behaviors, clients were significantly less likely to use corporal punishment, inadequately supervise their children, or ignore their children's emotional needs.

Additionally, these gains were retained and enhanced over time. Participants reported continued changes in their methods of discipline and an increase in positive interactions with their children; a significant decrease in the likelihood for maltreatment was observed. The most powerful predictor of client outcomes was the intensity with which services were provided. The greater the number of weekly contacts clients had with a program, the less likely they were to engage in child maltreatment. Moreover, the high-risk clients who received multiple types of interventions were more likely than similar clients who received a single intervention to have a reduced risk for maltreatment.

GENERAL PRINCIPLES DERIVED FROM PROGRAMS AND RESEARCH: THE RELATIONSHIP BETWEEN FAMILY SUPPORT AND COMMUNITY SUPPORT IN CREATING RESILIENCE

Children at developmental risk, such as that associated with the conditions that produce violence, need relationships with adults—"teaching" relationships—to help them process their experiences in a way that prevents developmental harm. Vygotsky (1986) referred to this developmental space between what the child can do alone and what the child can do with the help of a teacher as the "zone of proximal development." Developmentalists have come to recognize that it is the dynamic relationship between the child's competence alone and the child's competence in the company of a guiding teacher that leads to forward movement. This competence is an important characteristic of the social environment for children.

Children who experience maltreatment are generally denied processing within the family (Garbarino & Eckenrode, 1997). Indeed, they receive the opposite of what they need, particularly in conditions of social risk derived from the social environment outside the home. This is one reason that the problem of child maltreatment in the context of high-stress–low-support social environments deserves the highest priority as a matter of social policy. It seems likely that these are the children who can least tolerate maltreatment, because they face the risk of child maltreatment in the context of accumulated risks. Sameroff and Fiese (1990) reported that it is the accumulation of risks, rather than the presence of any single risk, that is generally associated with developmental harm. Poor children who live in a nonsupportive social environment are most vulnerable to developmental damage as a result of being abused or neglected. Likewise, victims of family violence are least able to tolerate violence in the community (Garbarino & Kostelny, 1996).

The critical function of mediation and processing seems particularly important in the case of prosocial socialization, which is inextricably linked to the problem of child maltreatment both as an interpersonal issue within families and as a social issue in communities. The key is whether or not the child's "teachers" in the community (be they adults or peers) lead the child toward prosocial thinking.

When children develop in the context of a nurturing affective system—a warm family, for example—the result is ever-advancing moral development and the development of a principled ethic of caring (Gilligan, 1982). Even if the parents create a rigid, noninteractive "authoritarian" family context (and thus block moral development), the larger community may compensate: "The child of authoritarian parents may function in a larger more democratic society whose varied patterns provide the requisite experiences for conceptualizing an egalitarian model of distributive justice"

(Fields, 1987, p. 5). Without this intervention, the "natural" socialization of the depleted community proceeds, with its consequences in intergenerational aggression, neighborhood deterioration, and family malfunction.

Families can provide the emotional context for the necessary "processing" to make positive moral sense of social experience outside the home, but to do so, they must be functioning well to start with. This is hardly the case when there is child maltreatment; in such cases, neighbors and professionals in communities can stimulate higher order moral development and compensatory socialization. They may accomplish this by presenting a supportive and democratic milieu in such places as schools, churches, neighborhood associations, and local political parties. Without these efforts, the result is likely to be impaired social and moral development, particularly among boys, who are more vulnerable to this risk, as they are to most other risks (Werner, 1990). This analysis leads to the following four principles.

Principle 1. Poor Families Need Neighborhood Resources More Than Others

There appears to be an inverse relationship between social class and the relevance of neighborhood (Lewis, 1978). Poor families and individuals are more dependent on local resources than are affluent families. This principle has at least two important implications. The first implication is that middle-class professionals and policymakers are likely to underestimate the importance of neighborhood factors because they depend less on such factors in their personal lives. Results of a survey in South Carolina (Melton, 1992) indicated that, when facing a problem with their child, middle-class families were particularly likely to go directly to professional specialists rather than rely on the social network. This finding implies the need for special training and sensitization for professionals, including on-site "walk-arounds," to emphasize the salience of neighborhood geography in family life.

The second implication is that advocacy efforts will be needed to preserve and enhance not just neighborhoods in general, but neighborhoods for poor families in particular. One facet of this intervention is financial. Part of the process of neighborhood decline derives from the deterioration or departure of banks and other financially stabilizing influences (e.g., the net outflow of insurance premiums starves investment).

Principle 2. Negative Social Momentum Can Be Reversed

Community differences are evident in the positive and negative "social momentum" occurring within neighborhoods. Some neighborhoods engender negative social momentum, which attracts antisocial and deteriorating individuals and families while at the same time discouraging and displacing prosocial and functional families (Rutter, 1989). Reversing such a downward spiral, termed *neighborhood revitalization*, may require outside intervention to initiate a process of positive social momentum that attracts functional families and improves the social environment for children.

The mechanics and logistics of such efforts require the coordination of economic investment, social services, political mobilization, and law enforcement; jobs, housing, and safety are the basics of community well-being. Efforts to promote community cooperation to produce community self-reliance are essential (Stokes, 1981). Programs such as Adopt a School and I Have a Dream can serve as vehicles to involve private philanthropy as part of this effort. Although their impact is largely unevaluated in this context, neighborhood watches and "block parents" programs seem likely to contribute to this process.

Principle 3. Homogeneity Increases Positive and Negative Cohesiveness

Social class homogeneity promotes higher levels of neighborhood interaction and integration (Unger & Wandersman, 1985). Similarity increases integration (in the sense of raising group cohesiveness rather than combining different groups). This process works for the socially rich neighborhood and against the socially impoverished neighborhood. The principle parallels the finding by Straus and his colleagues (Gelles & Straus, 1988) at the individual level that if the only social network an individual has is family, that individual is more likely to react to stress with abuse than a similar individual who has a network that combines kin and friends. Diversity is a prosocial force despite the fact that homogeneity promotes interaction and cohesion; interaction and cohesion can either inhibit or facilitate positive treatment of children, depending on the content of the interaction and the direction of the coherence.

In some economically and socially impoverished neighborhoods, therefore, the facilitating effects of homogeneity may be exceeded in importance by the negative momentum present. In neighborhoods that are poor, are highly stressed, and have little support, homogeneity may facilitate intensive neighboring that leads to *greater* social pathology. Support can enhance negative rather than positive child outcomes; the key is *prosocial* support.

The process has an important bearing on the role of schools in promoting neighborhood-based family support and violence prevention. The local school (most notably, the elementary school) can serve as a focal point for family support and violence prevention systems, particularly if its social mission is defined broadly. However, policies that dilute the neighborhood character of schools (e.g., busing to achieve racial balance or serve other social goals) dilute this role. Local school councils, such as have been instituted in Chicago, may serve to energize the school as a center for family-support systems and neighborhood mobilization. However, simple bureaucratic reform is insufficient. The communities most in need often lack the organizational resources and motivation to seize this opportunity effectively.

Principle 4. Correlates of Participation Must Be Addressed

Factors such as perceived connection to the issue, problem-focused coping style, and family consensus serve as motivation to participate in neighborhood groups (Wandersman et al., 1987). Research on neighborhood organization illuminates the individual decision-making process that governs participation and involvement in formal groups. These factors are relevant in assessing the potential of neighborhood social support to affect the problem of child maltreatment. The strong themes of "family autonomy" and "privacy" evident in U.S. culture militate against recognition of a connection between oneself and the dynamics of violence. There is a need to promote definitions of child maltreatment and other forms of violence that suggest they are a collective problem of the neighborhood, not simply a problem of individual parents or families. Demonstration projects are needed to field-test alternative approaches to accomplishing this goal.

By the same token, it is necessary to understand how individual coping styles affect the likelihood of participation in neighborhood-based family support and violence prevention programs. In general, the more "empowered" neighbors are in their lives as workers, citizens, and parents, the more likely they are to bring an assumption of effectiveness and potency to neighborhood activities. Once again, one is faced with a dilemma: The neighborhoods most in need of social support programs aimed at violence prevention and control are generally composed of individuals least likely to define themselves in ways that facilitate participation in such efforts. Generally, programming of this sort works best in areas least in need of it; the greatest potency is required for success in the areas most in need.

The role of family consensus in facilitating neighborhood participation reveals a parallel dilemma. Families involved in child maltreatment are not good candidates for family consensus on issues related to social support in the neighborhood (at least not in terms of facilitating such support, given that their orientation is likely to be "isolated and distancing"). On the other hand, the best-functioning families in the neighborhood are good candidates for neighborhood activity because they are likely to have family consensus concerning the "normal" needs and processes of families.

This review of factors that affect neighboring, therefore, highlights the need for special investments in high-stress–low-resource neighborhoods to reverse negative social momentum, which is a precondition for relying on neighborhood-based social support efforts to deal with the problem of violence. In well-functioning (i.e., high-resource–low-stress) environments, however, it should prove easier to turn the neighborhood's focus toward dealing with violence in all forms as long as organizers can deal successfully with the issues of family autonomy and privacy. Of course, such neighborhoods account for relatively little of the total violence problem, so that the net effect on the overall problem will be small.

The plight of neighborhoods at risk for child maltreatment owing to a deterioration of economic and social supports bears a relationship to situations of "acute disaster," in which there is a dramatic destruction of the infrastructure of daily life. However, the neighborhoods most at risk for violence usually have experienced a chronic deterioration rather than an abrupt calamity. Young children are confronted with vivid and concrete evidence of their vulnerability; their parents may be demoralized and appear socially powerless.

The plight of families in some high-risk areas might well be termed a social catastrophe, and violence serves as a special risk factor for children in such situations. These children have access neither to the buffering of parents through their positive attachments nor to the ameliorating and compensating influences of the community. The quality of life for young children and their reservoirs of resilience thus become "social indicators" of the balance of social supports for parents and the parental capacity to buffer social stress in the lives of children (Garbarino, 1992).

After reviewing a large body of research dealing with violence and aggression, Goldstein concluded that "aggressive behavior used to achieve a personal goal, such as wealth and power, and that may be perceived by the actor as justified (or even as nonaggressive) is a primary cause of the aggressive and criminal behavior of others" (Goldstein, 1986, p. ix). The social deterioration of many neighborhoods raises troubling questions about the existence of sufficient positive social identity to provide a meaningful context for any assertion of power and authority. Without such a framework of collective meaning, all actions and goals become personal, in the sense intended by Goldstein in the preceding quotation.

This analysis reveals that families and communities may be threats to socialization. As a "personal" use of violence, child maltreatment is a prime stimulator of aggression; it resonates and conspires with the extrafamilial experiences of the child living in a dangerous environment. At present, little is known about how this conspiracy works against the child's development and against child protection efforts. Clearly, those mechanisms should become the focus of research and policy initiatives.

CONCLUSION

This analysis of neighborhood-based social support programs and policies calls attention to an important reality about neighborhood life, that social momentum is a powerful force. When things are going badly, the tendency is for all the social systems to be pulled down together. It takes extraordinary energy and effort to resist such negative social momentum (e.g., a political leader of special talent, commitment, and resources or a powerful social program that creates its own positive momentum in the neighborhood).

Violence is a symptom not only of individual or family trouble but also of neighborhood and community trouble. It may well "conspire" with negative community forces to jeopardize still further the development of children. Although many children can absorb and overcome an experience with one or two risk factors, when the risk factors add up, they may well precipitate developmental crisis and impairment (Sameroff & Fiese, 1990). This, we believe, is the situation faced by abused and neglected children living amidst violence in the most devastated neighborhoods.

The challenge is to deal with the conspiracy of negative social indicators; social indicators can be responsive to social change, such as through the energizing effect of community mobilization. The task of implementing violence prevention initiatives is not easy and will require powerful efforts to reverse negative social momentum, with an appreciation for the compounding of problems engendered by community violence in the lives of victimized children.

Translating this broad conclusion into specific policy and programming is a challenge. One appealing approach for research and demonstration projects is to identify "prevention zones," which can become the target for comprehensive, sustained intervention by a wide range of public and private agencies. As families in the group most at risk for exposure to violence deteriorate, the relevance of "easy" neighborhood-based approaches to social support may diminish while the need for a powerful neighborhood-based approach increases (Halpern, 1990a). This circumstance both encourages further efforts at exploring the implementation of neighborhood-based family support and warns professionals that superficial investments and commitments are unlikely to resolve the issues faced by high-risk families in multiproblem neighborhoods.

REFERENCES

Austin, M. (1978). *Professionals and paraprofessionals*. New York: Human Sciences Press.

Barry, F. (1991). *Neighborhoodbased approach: What is it?* Background paper for the

U.S. Advisory Board on Child Abuse and Neglect. Ithaca, NY: Family Life Development Center, Cornell University.

Bell, C. (1991). Traumatic stress and children in danger. *Journal of Health Care for the Poor and Underserved, 2,* 178–188.

Bouchard, C. (1987). *Child maltreatment in Montreal.* Montreal, Canada: University of Quebec.

Caplan, G., & Killilea, M. (Eds.). (1976). *Support systems and mutual help: Multi-disciplinary explorations.* Philadelphia: Grune & Stratton.

Collins, A., & Pancoast, D. (1976). *Natural helping networks.* Washington, DC: National Association of Social Workers.

Coulton, J., Korbin, J., Su, M., & Chow, J. (1995). Community level factors and child maltreatment rates. *Child Development, 65,* 1262–1276.

Danieli, Y. (1988). Treating survivors and children of survivors of the Nazi holo-caust. In F. Ochberg (Ed.), *Posttraumatic therapy and victims of violence.* New York: Brunner/Mazel.

Danish, S., & Augelli, D. (1980). *Helping Skills: A basic training program.* New York: Human Sciences Press.

Deccio, G., Horner, B., & Wilson, D. (1991). *Highrisk neighborhoods and highrisk families: Replication research related to the human ecology of child maltreatment.* Cheney, WA: Eastern Washington University Press.

DuBow, F., & Emmons, D. (1981). Reactions to crime: The political contest. *Sage Criminal Justice Annals, 16,* 167–181.

Fields, R. (1987). *Terrorized into terrorist: Sequelae of PTSD in young victims.* Paper presented at the meeting of the Society for Traumatic Stress Studies, New York.

Fitchin, J. (1981). *Poverty in rural America: A case study.* Boulder, CO: Westview Press.

Freudenburg, W., & Jones, J. (1991). Attitudes and stress in the presence of tech-nological risk. *Social Forces, 69,* 1143–1168.

Garbarino, J. (1992). *Children and families in the social environment* (2nd ed.). Haw-thorne, New York: Aldine de Gruyter.

Garbarino, J., & Crouter, A. (1978). Defining the community context of parent–child relations. *Child Development, 49,* 604–616.

Garbarino, J., Dubrow, N., Kostelny, K., & Pardo, C. (1992). *Children in danger: Coping with the consequences of community violence.* San Francisco: Jossey-Bass.

Garbarino, J., & Eckenrode, J. (1997). *Understanding abusive families.* San Fran-cisco: Jossey-Bass.

Garbarino, J., & Kostelny, K. (1992a). Child maltreatment as a community problem. *International Journal of Child Abuse and Neglect, 16,* 455–464.

Garbarino, J., & Kostelny, K. (1992b). *Neighborhood-based programs.* Prepared for the U.S. Advisory Board on Child Abuse and Neglect. Washington, DC: National Center on Child Abuse and Neglect.

Garbarino, J., & Stocking, H. (1980). *Protecting children from abuse and neglect.* San Francisco: Jossey-Bass.

Gaudin, J., & Polansky, N. (1985). Social distancing of the neglectful family: Sex, race, and social class influences. *Social Service Review, 58*, 245–253.

Gelles, R., & Straus, M. (1988). *Intimate violence: The causes and consequences of abuse in the American Family.* New York: Simon & Schuster.

Gilligan, C. (1982). *In a different voice.* New York: Cambridge University Press.

Goldstein, J. (1986). *Aggression and crimes of violence.* New York: Oxford Press.

Growing up afraid. (1992, March 9). *Newsweek,* p. 29.

Halpern, R. (1990a). Community-based early intervention. In S. J. Meisels & J. P. Shonkoff (Eds.), *Handbook of early childhood intervention* (pp. 469–498). New York: Cambridge University Press.

Halpern, R. (1990b). Parent support and education programs. *Children and Youth Services Review, 12*, 285–308.

Halpern, R., & Larner, M. (1987). Lay family support during pregnancy and infancy: The Child Survival/Fair Start Initiative. *Infant Mental Health Journal, 8*, 130–143.

Hawley, A. (1950). *Human ecology: A theory of community structure.* New York: Ronald Press.

Lauderdale, M., & Savage, K. (1991, June). *Prevention strategies in the neighborhood environment.* Paper presented at the NCCAN Prevention Conference, Washington, DC.

Lewis, M. (1978). Nearest neighbor analysis of epidemiological and community variables. *Psychological Bulletin, 85*, 1302–1308.

Lösel, F., & Bliesener, T. (1990). Resilience in adolescence. In K. Hurelmann & F. Lösel (Eds.), *Health hazards in adolescence* (pp. 101–136). New York: de Gruyter.

Melton, G. (1992). It's time for neighborhood research and action. *Child Abuse and Neglect, 6*, 909–913.

Musick, J. S., & Stott, F. (1990). Paraprofessionals, parenting and child development: Understanding the problems and seeking solutions. In S. J. Meisels & J. P. Shonkoff (Eds.), *Handbook of early childhood intervention* (pp. 651–667). New York: Cambridge University Press.

Olds, D., Henderson, C., Tatelbaum, R., & Chamberlain, R. (1989). The prevention of maltreatment. In D. Cicchetti & V. Carlson (Eds.), *Child maltreatment: Theory and research on the causes and consequences of child abuse and neglect* (pp. 722–763). New York: Cambridge University Press.

Pelton, L. (1994). The role of material factors in child abuse and neglect. In G. Melton & F. Barry (Eds.), *Protecting children from abuse and neglect* (pp. 131–181). New York: Guilford Press.

Reardon, P. (1988, June 22). CHA violent crimes up 9% for year. *Chicago Tribune,* sec. 1, p. 1.

Rosenbaum, J., & Kaufman, J. (1991, August). *Educational and occupational achieve-*

ments of low income black youth in white suburbs. Paper presented at the annual meetings of the American Sociological Association, Cincinnati, OH.

Rutter, M. (1989). Pathways from childhood to adult life. *Journal of Child Psychology and Psychiatry, 4,* 91–115.

Sameroff, A. J., & Fiese, B. H. (1990). Transactional regulation and early intervention. In S. J. Meisels & J. P. Shonkoff (Eds.), *Handbook of early childhood intervention.* New York: Cambridge University Press.

Sattin, D., & Miller, J. (1971). The ecology of child abuse within a military community. *American Journal of Orthopsychiatry, 41,* 675–678.

Scheinfeld, D. (1983). Family relationships and school achievement among boys of lower-income urban black families. *American Journal of Orthopsychiatry, 53,* 127–143.

Stokes, B. (1981). *Helping ourselves: Local solutions to global problems.* New York: Norton.

Thompson, R. (1992). *Social support and the prevention of child maltreatment.* Washington, DC: U.S. Advisory Board on Child Abuse and Neglect.

Unger, D., & Wandersman, A. (1985). The importance of neighbors: The social, cognitive, and affective components of neighboring. *American Journal of Community Psychology, 13,* 139–169.

Vygotsky, L. (1986). *Thought and language.* Cambridge, MA: MIT Press.

Wandersman, A., Florin, P., Friedmann, R., & Meir, R. (1987). Who participates, who does not, and why? *Sociological forum, 2,* 534–555.

Warren, R. (1978). *The community in America.* Boston: Houghton Mifflin.

Weiss, H., & Halpern, R. (1991). *Community-based family support and educational programs: Something old or something new?* New York: National Center for Children in Poverty, Columbia University.

Weissbound, B. (1994). The evolution of the family resource movement. In L. Kagan & B. Weissbound (Eds.), *Putting families first.* San Francisco: Jossey-Bass.

Wellman, B. (1979). The community question: The intimate networks of East Yonkers. *American Journal of Sociology, 84,* 1201–1231.

Werner, E. (1990). Protective factors and individual resilience. In R. Meisells & J. Shonkoff (Eds.), *Handbook of early intervention.* Cambridge, England: Cambridge University Press.

Wilson, W. J. (1987). *The truly disadvantaged.* Chicago: University of Chicago Press.

IV

PREVENTING THE DIFFERENT FORMS OF VIOLENCE AGAINST CHILDREN

13

CHILD SEXUAL ABUSE PREVENTION PROGRAMS THAT TARGET YOUNG CHILDREN

N. DICKON REPPUCCI, DEBORAH LAND,
AND JEFFREY J. HAUGAARD

This chapter focuses almost exclusively on child sexual abuse prevention programs because they have primarily targeted children as the program recipients.[1] This orientation contrasts dramatically with physical abuse and neglect prevention programs, which primarily have targeted parents (Olsen & Widom, 1993). In the realm of physical abuse, most programs that target children are school based, often a part of family-life curricula; the goal is to inform children that they can report abuse by telling their teachers or by calling a special telephone number. In addition, there are public service announcements that are carried by the mass media, mainly television, again providing a telephone number that a child can call. Clearly, the latter are aimed at children old enough to be watching television and mature enough to (a) understand the message, (b) write down the necessary information, and (c) make the telephone call, thus eliminating most preschool children

---

[1]Several of the basic assumptions and arguments presented in this chapter have been highlighted previously by Reppucci and Haugaard (1989, 1993). The current chapter updates the literature and fine-tunes several of the arguments.

and many younger elementary school children. Olsen and Widom (1993) have noted that the effectiveness of these two types of programs has not been systematically investigated, even in the most rudimentary fashion. Therefore, the remainder of this chapter is focused on child sexual abuse prevention, for which most of the programs have been aimed at children and some systematic evaluation has taken place.

DEFINITION

The term *child sexual abuse* has been defined variously in legal statutes, by researchers, and by mental health professionals (Haugaard & Reppucci, 1988). The use of a broad and encompassing definition dramatically increases the number of children who can be categorized as having been abused and has been valuable in alerting professionals and the public to the widespread nature of these abusive experiences. However, broad definitions have yielded such heterogeneous groups that research findings can be meaningless. For example, the effects on a diverse group of sexually abused children might appear to be minimal because the meaningful negative effects on a small group of children who experienced intercourse were masked by the minimal effect on a larger group who saw an exhibitionist.

EXTENT OF THE PROBLEM

Most research findings about the prevalence of child sexual abuse are based on large-scale surveys, surveys of special samples, or studies of identified sexual abuse victims. The following summary provides an overview of these findings (for details and extensive referencing, see Haugaard & Reppucci, 1988). Large-scale surveys have indicated that prevalence rates range from about 10% to 60%, that most victims are girls with a modal age of 10 (although many cases occur at younger ages), and that many victims are abused once by a male whom they know. The form of abuse is most often fondling. Older children are abused more often by non–family members who are usually known to the victims than are younger children, and they experience more force to gain compliance. Yet younger children often show more physical trauma. Special samples have included prostitutes, runaway children, incarcerated delinquents, psychiatric patients, and mothers receiving counseling after coming to the attention of child protection agencies for physical abuse or neglect. The rates of sexual abuse, including incestuous experiences, are generally higher for these special samples than for college samples but similar to the rates for samples of urban women. Children from samples of identified sexual abuse victims (generally, clients at clinics or child protective service agencies) are most often girls and almost always have been abused by someone they know. The average

age of these victims is about 9 or 10 years, and the average age is frequently lower for boys than for girls. The abuser is more often the father than is the case in general surveys, although there are also a significant number of teenage perpetrators. The type of sexual activity is more often some form of intercourse than in other samples.

Because the prevalence of sexual abuse is not strongly linked to demographic factors, there is limited usefulness in identifying risk groups as targets of intervention (Melton, 1992). Although high-risk communities are unlikely to be identified, there is some indication that it might be possible to identify high-risk families. An elevated risk of sexual abuse for girls occurs in families that are troubled or in transition, such as when a parent is absent, a mother is unavailable because of high mother–daughter conflict or disability, parents are in conflict, the mother's educational status is markedly inferior to the father's, or a stepfather is present (Melton, 1992). The fact that children at high risk for sexual abuse can be identified does not necessarily suggest that interventions should be targeted directly at those children; because the family situation may be placing them at risk, the family may be the more appropriate focus of intervention.

THE OFFENDERS

Little is known about offenders except that most are male. Few researchers have investigated how offenders target children and conduct the process of victimization. The investigators who have examined offenders' behavior and perceptions usually have had limited sample sizes, have studied a specific category of offender (e.g., incarcerated offenders), or have restricted their scope to offenders of children of one gender or a specific age range (Elliott, Browne, & Kilcoyne, 1995). Although Budin and Johnson (1989) found that over 90% of 72 incarcerated perpetrators endorsed teaching children to say no to assailants, their additional findings, and findings from studies of offenders by Conte, Wolf, and Smith (1989), Kaufman, Harbeck-Weber, and Rudy (1994), and Elliott et al. (1995), have suggested that neither self-defense techniques nor a child's saying no would effectively deter many assailants and could lead to greater injury. Offenders in the study by Kaufman et al. (1994) rated both child strategies (e.g., don't keep secrets from your parents) and parental strategies (e.g., let child know that he or she is loved) as very important in making female adolescents from 12 to 17 years of age less vulnerable to abuse. In a study of 91 child sex offenders from a variety of treatment programs, including those located in the community, special hospitals, and prisons, Elliott et al. (1995) found that teaching a child to say no may be effective when the child is first approached or when he or she is not alone. Instructing the child to say no or to threaten to tell once he or she is alone with the offender or after first being approached, however, could place the child at greater risk; 39% of abusers reported that they were willing to use force or threats of violence to ensure the child's compliance once the abuse had begun. When asked in a forced-choice question what they had done when their victims exhibited distress, 25% of the offenders reported that they continued with the abuse, 49% responded that they saw no distress in their victims, and only 26% indicated that they stopped the abuse.

Many offenders described a process of gradual desensitization of a child to abuse, which may make it difficult for the child to determine exactly when the abuse is about to take place or actually has taken place and more difficult for the child to know when to tell or say no (Budin & Johnson, 1989; Conte et al., 1989; Elliott et al., 1995). Once the child realizes that abuse has occurred, the child may feel she or he already has consented to the abuse (Conte et al., 1989). Further elucidation of the specific knowledge and behaviors that enable children of various ages to avoid abuse is needed, along with similar solicitation of offenders' perceptions of successful prevention strategies for children of all ages and both genders.

PREVENTION PROGRAMS

The documented high incidence of child sexual abuse during the past 15 years has highlighted the pressing need for effective prevention programs (Reppucci & Haugaard, 1989). The response has been the development of various programs largely focused on young children (aged 4–12 years) and typically implemented in day care centers and elementary schools throughout the country. Although programs for middle and high school youth are widespread, usually part of family-life curricula, systematic evaluation is rare (Wurtele & Miller-Perrin, 1992). Therefore, our comments in this chapter are directed exclusively at prevention programs for children aged 12 and younger. The vast majority of these programs focus on empowering these young children by teaching them concepts and actions for understanding and repelling sexual abuse. Two goals are emphasized: (a) *primary prevention* (keeping the abuse from ever occurring) and (b) *detection* (encouraging disclosure of past and ongoing abuse so that children can receive intervention and protection). Programs vary in content, length, format, and type of instructor. They usually are presented to every child in a particular school or grade. Specific topics commonly addressed include educating children about what sexual abuse is; broadening children's awareness of possible abusers to include people they know and like; teaching that each child has the right to control access to his or her body; describing a variety of "touches" that a child can experience; stressing actions that a child can take in a potentially abusive situation, such as saying no, leaving, or running away; teaching that some secrets should not be kept and that a child is never at fault for sexual abuse; and stressing that a child should keep telling a trusted adult if he or she is touched in an inappropriate manner until something is done to protect the child. Most programs emphasize the importance of parental involvement, but there is little indication that this occurs with more than a small minority of parents (Berrick, 1988; Kohl, 1993). Few programs devote the resources necessary to ensure parental participation (Reppucci, Jones, & Cook, 1994).

OUTCOME RESEARCH

The most common and consistent finding among the few programs that have been evaluated is a statistically significant, yet often slight (e.g., a 1- to 2-point gain on a 10- to 40-item questionnaire) and therefore relatively meaningless, increase in knowledge about sexual abuse following a prevention program (Berrick & Gilbert, 1991; Carroll, Miltenberger, & O'Neill, 1992; Harvey, Forehand, Brown, & Holmes, 1988; Hazzard, Webb, Kleemeier, Angert, & Pohl, 1988; MacMillan, MacMillan, Offord, Griffith, & MacMillan, 1994; Saslawsky & Wurtele, 1986; Swan, Press, & Briggs, 1985; Tutty, 1992, 1994; Wurtele, Marrs, & Miller-Perrin, 1987). Some authors have suggested that review sessions are necessary to maintain what gains are made (Plummer, 1984; Tutty, 1994). It is not surprising that older children tend to learn more than younger children (Hazzard et al., 1988a; Nemerofsky, Carran, & Rosenberg, 1994; Tutty, 1992, 1994). In addition, many children answer a high percentage of the questions accurately before they participate in a prevention program (Berrick & Gilbert, 1991; Swan et al., 1985; Tutty, 1992, 1994), suggesting that either children know more than prevention educators think they do or that better assessment instruments are needed to demonstrate the full increase in learning. These results do not justify Finkelhor and Strapko's (1992) conclusion that "the most clearly established finding is that children do indeed learn the concepts that the programs teach" (p. 164).

Some authors have suggested that behavioral skills training programs that encourage children's active participation through role playing result in better retention than does typical passive observing (Fryer, Kraizer, & Myoshi, 1987; Harvey et al., 1988; Kraizer, Witte, & Fryer, 1989; Miltenberger, Thiesse-Duffy, Suda, Kozak, & Bruellman, 1990; Poche, Yoder, & Miltenberger, 1988; Wurtele et al., 1987; Wurtele, Saslawsky, Miller, Marrs, & Britcher, 1986). Kraizer et al. (1989), for example, used scripted role play to measure children's ability and willingness to terminate unwanted touch effectively and appropriately in the face of flattery, emotional coercion, rejection, bribery, and secrecy, all of which are behaviors used by sexual offenders (Conte et al., 1989). Children who participated in a sexual abuse prevention program incorporating role play exhibited some behavioral change in their ability to resist victimization, which was correlated with measures of knowledge and self-esteem (Kraizer et al., 1989). Offenders also endorsed the use of role play in prevention efforts (Elliott et al., 1995).

Most evaluations of sexual abuse prevention programs have basic design problems (for extensive reviews, see Kolko, 1988; Reppucci & Haugaard, 1993; Wurtele & Miller-Perrin, 1992). Although a few researchers have used a repeated measures design and nonintervention control groups matched for variables such as age, gender, and socioeconomic status (SES), most have not. Other design flaws include the use of small samples, lack of attention to the reliability and validity of the measuring instruments, lack of pretesting to establish a baseline of knowledge, and short-term assessments, usually after 3 months or less. In a survey of school-based prevention programs across the country, Kohl (1993) found that although 114 of 126 respondents from individual programs reported that their program was evaluated, 54 respondents did not specify an evaluation design, and 51 used only a pre–post design.

With the preceding information as background, we delineate seven critical assumptions on which the vast majority of the child sexual abuse prevention programs are based, provide a brief statement of the existing knowledge in the field regarding each assumption, and sketch a research agenda for each. We then conclude the chapter with four general recommendations for increasing knowledge concerning child sexual abuse prevention, adapted from one of the author's [N.D.R.] contributions to the American Psychological Association's Task Force on Child Abuse Prevention (Wolfe, Reppucci, & Hart, 1995).

KEY PROGRAM ASSUMPTIONS

Assumption 1

Assumption: A link between children's knowledge and their behavior exists such that increasing their knowledge about sexual abuse will increase their use of preventive behaviors.

Knowledge: This assumption largely is untested. Some investigators have incorporated behavioral measures into their evaluations, ranging from hypothetical vignettes to role-play situations to in vivo stranger-abduction scenarios. Their results have been equivocal. Hazzard et al. (1988b) found a significant increase in knowledge about child sexual abuse in their experimental group relative to their control group yet failed to find a significant difference between the two groups in knowledge of prevention skills in response to videotaped vignettes. Kraizer et al. (1989), however, found a correlation between knowledge and behavioral change in scripted role-play situations. Which behavioral measures are most valid is not known.

Research Agenda: Investigations to determine the critical components of programs that facilitate the link between knowledge and behavior should be undertaken. The preliminary findings on the importance of active participation by children provide one avenue of investigation. Sensitive and valid measuring instruments need to be developed. The correspondence between children's knowledge of prevention concepts, their responses to vignettes, their behaviors in role-play situations, and their responses in situ should be investigated when ethically possible.

Assumption 2

Assumption: It is known what types of knowledge and skills will make a child less susceptible to sexual abuse, and these are being taught.

Knowledge: Although information in this area is increasing (e.g., Conte et al., 1989; Elliott et al., 1995), it is still quite limited. Finkelhor, Asdigian, and Dziuba-Leatherman (1995), in a survey of 2,000 children, found that children who had participated in more comprehensive prevention programs reported significantly more use of prevention strategies than children who had participated in less comprehensive or no prevention programs. However, there were no significant differences across groups in the number of completed incidents of sexual abuse as a percentage of all attempted and completed incidents.

Skills useful for preventing one type of sexual abuse might not be useful for preventing another type, and some skills may be useful for children of one age but not for children of another. Although developmentally sensitive curricula appear to be imperative. Melton (1992) has concluded that current sexual abuse prevention programs "generally have failed to consider cognitive-developmental factors" and "look remarkably similar across age groups" (p. 182). Tutty (1994) took an important step in investigating whether young children have more difficulty than older children learning specific prevention concepts commonly included in sexual abuse prevention programs. She compared the responses of first, third, and sixth graders on each of 35 items of the Children's Knowledge of Abuse Questionnaire administered both before and after participation in a prevention program. She found that although even first graders received high scores on many core abuse-prevention concepts at pretest, the first graders had considerably more difficulty than the older children in learning some core prevention concepts, such as those related to saying no to authority figures, trusting familiar adults, and not blaming themselves if they allowed adults to touch them in uncomfortable ways. The specific items the youngest children found most difficult were as follows:

> A stranger is someone you don't know, even though they say they know you.

If a grown-up tells you to do something you always have to do it.
You can always tell who's a stranger—they look mean.
You have to let grown-ups touch you whether you like it or not.
Even someone in your family might want to touch your private parts
    in a way that feels confusing.

Research Agenda: Development and evaluation of educational programs must be sensitive to the development status of the program recipients. Basic research focused on understanding how decision-making and action-taking processes are developed and used at various levels of cognitive and emotional development in varying contexts should be a priority. Without these evaluations, there is a risk of developing programs that make adults feel better but do not protect children (e.g., Pelcovitz, Adler, Kaplan, Packman, & Krieger, 1992).

Assumption 3

Assumption: Children can be empowered to prevent their own sexual abuse.

Knowledge: Programs for women to combat rape that focus on awareness and self-defense techniques provide the theoretical basis for sexual abuse prevention programs for children. No evidence exists, however, to suggest that what might be an appropriate strategy to reduce assaults on adult women and, perhaps, adolescents is equally appropriate for younger children. For example, two 10-year-old female abuse victims who had participated in a prevention program prior to their abuse were surprised that adults would think that advice to tell somebody about abuse had any relevance to the abusive situation in which they felt overpowered by an adult in authority who made threats. One of them said, "I was just too afraid to make decisions" (Pelcovitz et al., 1992, p. 890). Clearly, the extent to which strategies to make children feel empowered will result in reduced risk for sexual abuse is unclear. Recently, Dziuba-Leatherman and Finkelhor (1994) studied boys' perceptions of their risk for sexual abuse and found that prevention programs may make the children feel empowered and in control. However, they acknowledged that it is not known whether the programs actually increase children's control and that, therefore, the programs may instill in children a false sense of security.

We agree with Wurtele and Miller-Perrin (1992) that "children and adolescents have a right to be enlightened about sexuality and sexual abuse and to know about their right to live free from such abuse. The more pertinent question is not *whether* to educate children about sexual abuse but rather *how* to do so in an effective, sensitive manner" (p. 89). We also think that the question of *when* to educate them needs to be addressed.

We have no qualms about educating adolescents directly (although the issue of how to do it remains), because we believe that adolescents are cognitively competent to understand the material presented; however, a much better understanding of younger children's competence and judgment is needed before we can agree that the current methods advocated for empowerment have the potential to be effective strategies.

Research Agenda: The specific effectiveness and possible negative consequences of empowerment strategies need to be tested. Also, prevention programs based on other theories, with other targets (e.g., parents), should be developed and their effectiveness compared to that of child-targeted empowerment-based prevention programs.

Assumption 4

Assumption: Prevention programs have no negative effects, or negative effects are insignificant when compared to the positive effects.

Knowledge: Although this issue has received increased attention in the past decade, the results are mixed; some investigators have reported no evidence of negative effects as measured by increased anxieties and fears (Binder & McNeil, 1987; Hazzard, Webb, & Kleemeier, 1988; Miltenberger & Thiesse-Duffy, 1988; Wurtele & Miller-Perrin, 1987), whereas others have reported such effects for at least a small proportion of program participants (Finkelhor & Dziuba-Leatherman, 1995; Garbarino, 1987; Gilbert, Berrick, LeProhn, & Nyman, 1989; Kleemeier & Webb, 1986; Swan et al., 1985; Wurtele, Kast, Miller-Perrin, & Kondrick, 1989). Finkelhor and Dziuba-Leatherman's (1995) survey findings have suggested that 8% of children who were exposed to prevention programs worried a lot, and 53% worried a little, about being abused. These investigators interpreted these results as positive and adaptive, which may be the case considering that some anxiety, as long as it is not too extreme, often results in positive outcomes. However, there have been no systematic follow-up assessments to determine the amount of anxiety that is helpful versus harmful. More alarming is the finding that children who participated in more comprehensive prevention programs suffered more injuries while being sexually abused than did other children. Finkelhor et al. (1995) attributed this finding to these children's greater tendency to fight back during their victimization.

Furthermore, few researchers have examined other possible types of negative consequences. One exception is the examination of generalized fear or discomfort with respect to appropriate physical affection and discernment of safe versus unsafe situations, which some investigators have included in their evaluations (e.g., Hazzard et al., 1988a; Wurtele & Miller-Perrin, 1987). For example, Hazzard et al. (1988b) surveyed parents regarding their observations of child noncompliance and changes in their child's responses to appropriate physical affection following his or her participation in a prevention program and found no differences between experimental and control group parents' responses. Another exception, although the effect was not noted as a negative one, is Nibert, Cooper, Ford, Fitch, and Robinson's (1989) finding of a 12% decrease (from 64% to 52%) in discussions about sexual abuse between parents and children after the children had participated in a prevention program. If a goal is to increase parent–child communication about these matters, these results are surely negative!

Research Agenda: An increasing number of investigators are considering evaluation studies to provide information about the negative consequences of prevention programs (Carroll et al., 1992). Studies may show that certain program components are associated with the development of fear and anxiety, and an understanding of the outcomes of this anxiety may aid in the debate about the value of anxiety in reducing sexual abuse (e.g., Finkelhor & Dziuba-Leatherman, 1995). In addition, other issues warrant investigation such as the effects on sexuality. (See Krivacska, 1992; Wurtele, 1993.) For example, will the programs that teach the incorrectness of some forms of touching adversely affect children's long-term comfort with nonsexual physical contact with their parents and significant others, exploratory sexual play with peers, or even sexual behavior as adults, and is increased physical violence to the child likely in situations where the child actively attempts to resist victimization by fighting back?

Assumption 5

Assumption: Parental involvement is valuable but not crucial to the success of child abuse prevention efforts.

Knowledge: Many researchers have advocated the inclusion of parents in child abuse prevention program efforts. Only a few studies, however, have examined what role, if any, parents want to play in prevention; parents' knowledge about child sexual abuse; and how parents would like to obtain prevention information or training (Elrod & Rubin, 1993). In their survey of 101 parents of children attending either preschool or day care centers, Elrod and Rubin (1993) found that over 90% rated themselves or their spouse as the person they most preferred to educate their child about sexual abuse; however, 78% also approved of a required school sexual abuse prevention curriculum. In Wurtele, Kvaternick, and Franklin's (1992) survey of 375 parents of preschoolers, 72.5% of parents supported the inclusion of sexual abuse prevention programs in all preschools and day care centers, and 94.1% of parents endorsed the teaching of prevention concepts both at home and at school. However, only 56% of Elrod and Rubin's (1993) parents knew that abusers are more likely to be familiar people than strangers, and Wurtele et al. (1992) similarly found that the majority of parents discussing sexual abuse with their children focused on danger from strangers, not from acquaintances or intimates.

Most of the parents in Elrod and Rubin's (1993) sample indicated that they did not plan to discuss certain core concepts with their children, such as who the abusers are, the likelihood of abuse happening to the child, and why abuse happens. In addition, over 50% of these parents rated the aforementioned topics as too threatening to be part of a school prevention curriculum. Over 50% of fathers rated the topics of self-protection, consequences of telling, and abuse not being the child's fault as unacceptable for inclusion in a school prevention curriculum. It appears that although the majority of these parents supported school-based child sexual abuse prevention programs, they did not approve of the inclusion of several concepts judged by prevention educators to be essential; however, many parents appeared to be uncomfortable discussing key prevention concepts at home. Furthermore, Elrod and Rubin (1993) reported that about one third of their sample were fatalistic about the current prevalence of child sexual abuse, did not care for any more information, or did not believe that child sexual abuse would intrude on their lives. Although such attitudes have fueled many prevention educators' beliefs that they must deal directly with the children, an alternative strategy is to focus additionally on the parents in an attempt to provide them with more information and techniques for dealing with their children.

It is not known how parents' lack of knowledge, discomfort, disinterest, and disapproval affect children's mastery and use of prevention concepts. Wurtele et al. (1992) cautioned, however, that if prevention educators do not coordinate what is taught in school-based prevention programs with what is believed and taught at home, children could become confused, and conflict between children and parents could result. Tutty (1993) argued that children learn personal boundaries primarily through family interaction and that therefore it should be expected that family norms and beliefs affect children's learning of prevention concepts. Finkelhor et al. (1995) found that children who had received prevention instruction from parents were more likely to have disclosed sexual victimization. Preparing parents to handle disclosures of attempted or completed abuse, however, largely has been neglected in sexual abuse prevention programs (Berrick, 1989). Of the 126 programs surveyed by Kohl (1993), only 12 were reported to address the issue of the "adult responding to disclosure." It does not seem ethical to instruct young children to disclose abuse and not teach their families how to handle such disclosures in ways that do not exacerbate the effects of the abuse.

Furthermore, prevention programs have not addressed the issue of parents, in addition to other caretakers, as perpetrators (Olsen & Widom, 1993). Durfee (1989) called for perinatal programs focused on families, including support programs for all caretakers and older siblings; support systems to help all caretakers, including men, become competent in caring for infants and toddlers; and educational forums to help caretakers, children, and families learn to read each other's cues more accurately and to negotiate reasonable intimacy. He also stated the following:

> The basic issues of respect, empathy, reciprocity, vicarious enjoyment in the pleasures of others, intimacy, and boundaries are integral to positive relationships of all forms. Child sexual abuse as an act of violence and perversion involves a lack of these qualities in that particular relationship. Prevention of that violence and perversion would logically include the encouragement of those positive qualities in relationships. (Durfee, 1989, p. 451)

Although an attempt to teach adults to be competent caregivers probably would not eradicate abuse, it might decrease the incidence by improving the bonds between trusted nonabusive caretakers and children. Theoretically, this effort might help more children feel secure and loved, thereby making them less vulnerable.

Research Agenda: The relatively exclusive focus on educating the child to prevent his or her victimization may have kept professionals from considering alternative approaches to prevention of child sexual abuse. Researchers and prevention educators should consider programs that focus on parents and other adults, rather than continuing to focus solely on children. Inclusion of parents in child sexual abuse prevention programs should not be limited to training parents to teach children prevention concepts. Parents should not rely on children to evaluate whether external situations feel good or bad; parents should be taught to evaluate external situations on the basis of their child's description (rather than evaluation) of the situations and their own observations, so that they may protect their child from relatives, neighbors, baby-sitters, and others who come in contact with the child (Berrick, 1989). In sum, we agree with Wurtele and Miller-Perrin's (1992) conclusion as it pertains to elementary school and younger children that "classroom-based programs should only be supported when they operate in the context of multilevel preventive efforts (e.g., parent, community, and population-centered approaches), each of which should be viewed as making a contribution toward CSA [child sexual abuse] prevention" (p. 90).

Assumption 6

Assumption: Primary prevention has been achieved by the existing programs.

Knowledge: No evidence exists, not even one published case study, that primary prevention of sexual abuse has ever been achieved with young children, nor is there any evidence to support the notion that the programs may deter potential abusers because of fear of detection. MacMillan et al. (1994), through a search of six databases (Medline, ERIC, PsycINFO, Criminal Justice Periodical Index, and Child Abuse and Neglect), identified and reviewed 19 program evaluations published between January 1979 and May 1993 that met the following criteria: a targeted population of children up to and including 18 years of age; a primary prevention intervention, an outcome of, or associated with, sexual abuse prevention; and a prospective, controlled trial. They found that no researcher examined whether the targeted intervention prevented the outcome of sexual abuse directly, and therefore, they concluded that "there is no evidence to support or refute the hypothesis that educating children, parents or teachers with regard to abduction and sexual victimization of children actually reduced the occurrence of such offenses" (MacMillan et al., 1994, p. 874).

Some case examples raise concerns about prevention programs. For example, Pelcovitz et al. (1992) reported that 22 kindergarteners through third graders from upper SES homes were systematically abused over a 2-year period by an auxiliary school employee before accidental disclosure of the abuse occurred. At least 19 of the children had been enrolled previously in classes in which the 40-minute Disney Home Video child abuse prevention film *Too Smart for Strangers* (1985; cited by Pelcovitz et al., 1992) had been shown; some of the children had seen the film in more than one class. It is revealing that a boy who was approximately 6 years old at the time the abuse began reported that the film had not been helpful to him because his abuser had not appeared in the movie. Of course, a more comprehensive prevention program may have had a more positive impact on the children.

Although the survey by Finkelhor et al. (1995) provided retrospective data that suggested that some children used what they learned, the previously mentioned increase in injury from sexual assault by the children who may have used what they learned is troubling. Moreover, these data may have little relevance to the 10-and-under age group (the focus of this critique) because the large majority of the respondents were 12 years or older, and no child surveyed was under 10 years of age.

Research Agenda: Although demonstrating the effectiveness of primary prevention programs is a time-consuming and expensive undertaking, longitudinal studies should be initiated using large sample sizes, appropriate control groups, and ample time periods (e.g., 5–10 years). Studies including follow-up beyond a few weeks generally track only the experimental group owing to the conviction that it is unethical to withhold the intervention from the control group (MacMillan et al., 1994). Given the compelling need for conclusive evidence of program effectiveness, maintaining the control group through an extended follow-up period seems warranted.

Assumption 7

Assumption: Detection of ongoing sexual abuse as a primary goal has been achieved.

Knowledge: Although many case examples and findings from evaluation studies have supported this assumption, and Finkelhor and Strapko (1992) claimed that detection is the "most important unambiguous finding" (p. 160) of the prevention programs, no careful investigation of this claim exists; for example, no systematic information is available regarding what percentage of youths are likely to disclose abuse in response to prevention programs or how many of the disclosures of abuse are confirmed. Most evaluations of sexual abuse prevention programs do not include documentation of the number of confirmed disclosures in an experimental group in comparison to a control group. Of the 19 published evaluations of prevention programs included in the review by MacMillan et al. (1994), only 3 included disclosure data. Analysis of these data, however, was limited in one study by lack of information about the timing of disclosure (e.g., before, during, or after the program) and in the other two by the size of the control group and nonrandom assignment to groups.

Research Agenda: A systematic large-scale investigation of the impact of disclosure should be undertaken that examines the percentage of disclosure, confirmation of the abuse, impact of the disclosure on the family and child, and the changes that occur as a result of the disclosure. Finkelhor and Strapko (1992) suggested that the current prevention programs should be renamed "disclosure" programs. If the programs are primarily useful for detection, then the search for alternative means of preventing child sexual abuse takes on even more urgency.

RECOMMENDATIONS FOR SEXUAL ABUSE PREVENTION

The aforementioned research agenda guidelines correspond to specific assumptions of child-focused sexual abuse prevention programs. These guidelines convey our belief that current child-focused efforts are insufficient to prevent child sexual abuse. Not enough is known about the process and context of victimization to warrant the almost exclusive focus on the child as the preventive agent. At the risk of being redundant, we include the following recommendations (adapted from Wolfe et al., 1995) to emphasize the need to expand beyond child-focused programs and suggest how to begin to do so.

Recommendation 1

Sophisticated research studies should be launched with the goals of understanding the process that a child must go through to repel or report abuse and determining how this process is experienced by children at various levels of cognitive and emotional development in varying ecological contexts (Reppucci & Herman, 1991). Such efforts should be more closely linked to basic theories of child development, sexuality, and family dynamics. Investigators should compare children who successfully avert victimization to those who do not, to determine whether empowerment is a key factor in avoiding abuse. In longitudinal studies of the effectiveness of prevention efforts, the following could be measured: child knowledge, skills, and empowerment; parental knowledge, attitudes, and skills; family structure and conflict; community resources; and tolerance of sexual abuse. Models could be created to determine what the critical variables are in preventing child sexual abuse.

Recommendation 2

The focus of prevention programs should be expanded beyond the potential child victim (Reppucci & Haugaard, 1993). Although many professionals have suggested that it is necessary to involve parents, few have expended resources on this endeavor (Reppucci et al., 1994), and participation rates have been disappointing (Berrick, 1988). Moreover, there is a conspicuous absence of programs that target adults other than parents, even though these adults are the most likely recipients of children's reports of abuse. Reppucci and Haugaard (1993) stressed the potential of targeting parents and other adults through places of employment, churches, and community service groups, as well as through small discussion groups in local homes. In addition, Reppucci and Herman (1991) emphasized the importance of using the mass media to provide information. Of the 101 parents surveyed by Elrod and Rubin (1993), 99% identified the media as their most frequent source of information on child sexual abuse. Mass media innovations might also reach more men, who are the major perpetrators and the parents least likely to attend a typical evening session in schools, churches, or other community centers.

Recommendation 3

Melton (1992) argued that efforts to increase supports to families in transition or under stress are likely to have the most significant impact on prevention, a conclusion that ties in well with the experience of various family-support programs. Moreover, public awareness programs aimed at strengthening adult awareness and vigilance of potential abuse situations hold promise, such as programs that provide information about ways to interview and select a baby-sitter (Institute for the Prevention of Child Abuse, 1991). In general, strategies that rely on improving adult supervision and reducing children's exposure to possible risk situations deserve greater attention.

Recommendation 4

Professionals involved in child sexual abuse prevention must turn their attention toward some of the underlying social and cultural issues that are suspected to be at the root of such exploitation and abuse. To date, relatively little research has been conducted on the motivating factors involved in child sexual abuse. Because almost all of the offenders are male, a long-term strategy should be developed that addresses some of the suspected roots of such behavior from a socialization perspective. More responsibility for prevention should be directed at socialization agents (e.g., schools, parents, churches, service groups) in an effort to heighten society's awareness of the problem.

Finally, even though prevention programs focusing on environmental change have not yet been developed, attention should be paid to such approaches (Holman & Stokols, 1994). The history of public health strongly suggests that prevention programs designed to change an individual's risky behavior are not very successful (Melton, 1992). Eliminating or reducing the opportunities for risky behaviors has produced greater increases in safety in other areas (e.g., childproof caps and lead-free paint prevent poisoning more effectively than programs to increase parental vigilance to diminish children's risk-taking), and this tactic might well be effective in preventing child sexual abuse.

CONCLUSIONS

We do not mean to be unduly critical regarding efforts to empower young children to recognize and cope with the dangers of sexual abuse. However, we believe it is reasonable to question whether this relatively exclusive focus on children as their own protectors is appropriate, to emphasize that children's developmental capacities must be considered, and to encourage more rigorous evaluations of both positive and negative effects of every prevention program. We are aware of the difficulties in completing such research. Clearly, there are several ethical and legal hurdles. For example, assessing whether children have developed the skills to repel a sexual approach is likely to involve placing children in the stressful situation of being confronted by a potential abuser. It is unlikely that current ethical standards would allow this type of research to occur. Although behavioral assessments have been used to evaluate a stranger-abduction prevention program (Fryer et al., 1987), the behaviors of the mock abductor were less anxiety provoking than would be the repeated attempts of a potential molester whom a child would need to repel. It might be possible to ask children about their responses to potentially abusive situations, but this would require parental permission (possibly missing some children whose abuse was known to, or suspected by, a parent) and would place the researchers in the difficult position of having to determine whether to report the experiences of some children to legal authorities. A second issue to note is that even if ethical and legal difficulties could be overcome, evaluation of prevention programs requires large initial populations for both intervention and control groups and a period of at least several years for collecting follow-up data. Research of the necessary magnitude cannot be accomplished without a considerable amount of time and funding. Unfortunately, most private and public agencies interested in preventing child abuse are primarily focused on implementing and disseminating their programs to as wide an audience as possible. To use funds otherwise is viewed as ethically inappropriate, given the goal of protecting children. This means that funds for evaluation are usually minimal or absent.

Advocates of current approaches that target young children (e.g., Plummer, 1994) must recognize that only by questioning these interventions can one sharpen them and develop new and more effective ones. As children grow to maturity, they experience various ecological contexts, including family, school, peer group, neighborhood, and society as a whole. Each context influences children, and each may be an appropriate context for intervention. It is crucial that educators and researchers be open to these contexts as foci for intervention and supportive of rigorous evaluation, even if it means diverting some funding from intervention. Given the enormity of the problem and the large number of youths affected, innovative programs must be developed, implemented, and evaluated.

REFERENCES

Berrick, J. D. (1988). Parental involvement in child abuse prevention training: What do they learn? *Child Abuse & Neglect, 12,* 543–553.

Berrick, J. D. (1989). Sexual abuse prevention education: Is it appropriate for the preschool child? *Children and Youth Services Review, 11,* 145–158.

Berrick, J. D., & Gilbert, N. (1991). *With the best of intentions: The child sexual abuse prevention movement.* New York: Guilford Press.

Binder, R. L., & McNeil, D. E. (1987). Evaluation of a school-based sexual abuse prevention program: Cognitive and emotional effects. *Child Abuse & Neglect, 11,* 497–506.

Budin, L. E., & Johnson, C. F. (1989). Sex abuse prevention programs: Offenders' attitudes about their efficacy. *Child Abuse & Neglect, 13,* 77–87.

Carroll, L. A., Miltenberger, R. G., & O'Neill, H. K. (1992). A review and critique of research evaluating child sexual abuse prevention programs. *Education and Treatment of Children, 15,* 335–354.

Conte, J. R., Wolf, S., & Smith, T. (1989). What sexual offenders tell us about prevention strategies. *Child Abuse & Neglect, 13,* 293–301.

Durfee, M. (1989). Prevention of child sexual abuse. *Psychiatric Clinics of North America, 12,* 445–453.

Dziuba-Leatherman, J., & Finkelhor, D. (1994). How does receiving information about sexual abuse influence boys' perceptions of their risk? *Child Abuse & Neglect, 18,* 557–568.

Elliott, M., Browne, K., & Kilcoyne, J. (1995). Child sexual abuse prevention: What offenders tell us. *Child Abuse & Neglect, 19,* 579–594.

Elrod, J. M., & Rubin, R. H. (1993). Parental involvement in sexual abuse prevention education. *Child Abuse & Neglect, 17,* 527–538.

Finkelhor, D., Asdigian, N., & Dziuba-Leatherman, J. (1995). The effectiveness of victimization prevention instruction: An evaluation of children's responses to actual threats and assaults. *Child Abuse & Neglect, 19,* 137–149.

Finkelhor, D., & Dziuba-Leatherman, J. (1995). Victimization prevention programs: A national survey of children's exposure and reactions. *Child Abuse & Neglect, 19,* 125–135.

Finkelhor, D., & Strapko, N. (1992). Sexual abuse prevention education: A review of evaluation studies. In D. J. Willis, E. Holden, & M. Rosenberg (Eds.), *Prevention of child maltreatment: Developmental and ecological perspectives* (pp. 150–167). New York: Wiley.

Fryer, G. E., Kraizer, S. K., & Miyoshi, T. (1987). Measuring actual reduction of risk to child abuse: A new approach. *Child Abuse & Neglect, 11,* 173–179.

Garbarino, J. (1987). Children's response to a sexual abuse prevention program: A study of the *Spiderman* comic. *Child Abuse & Neglect, 11,* 143–148.

Gilbert, N., Berrick, J., LeProhn, N., & Nyman, N. (1989). *Protecting young children from sexual abuse: Does preschool training work?* Lexington, MA: Lexington Books.

Harvey, P., Forehand, R., Brown, C., & Holmes, T. (1988). The prevention of sexual abuse: Examination of the effectiveness of a program with kindergarten-age children. *Behavior Therapy, 19,* 429–435.

Haugaard, J. J., & Reppucci, N. D. (1988). *The sexual abuse of children: A comprehensive guide to current knowledge and intervention strategies.* San Francisco: Jossey-Bass.

Hazzard, A. P., Webb, C., & Kleemeier, C. (1988). *Child sexual assault prevention programs: Helpful or harmful?* Unpublished manuscript, Emory University School of Medicine, Atlanta, GA.

Hazzard, A. P., Webb, C., Kleemeier, C., Angert, L., & Pohl, J. (1988). Child sexual abuse prevention: Evaluation and one-year follow-up. *Child Abuse & Neglect, 15,* 123–138.

Holman, E. A., & Stokols, D. (1994). The environmental psychology of child sexual abuse. *Journal of Environmental Psychology, 14,* 237–252.

Institute for the Prevention of Child Abuse. (1991). *Choosing a babysitter.* (Available from IPCA, 25 Spadina Rd., Toronto, Ontario, Canada)

Kaufman, K. L., Harbeck-Weber, C., & Rudy, L. (1994). Re-examining the efficacy of child sexual abuse prevention strategies: Victims' and offenders' attitudes. *Child Abuse & Neglect, 18,* 349–356.

Kleemeier, C., & Webb, C. (1986, August). *Evaluation of a school-based prevention program.* Paper presented at the annual meeting of the American Psychological Association, Washington, DC.

Kohl, J. (1993). School-based child sexual abuse prevention programs. *Journal of Family Violence, 8,* 137–150.

Kolko, D. J. (1988). Educational programs to promote awareness and prevention of child sexual victimization: A review and methodological critique. *Clinical Psychology Review, 8,* 195–209.

Kraizer, S., Witte, S. S., & Fryer, G. E., Jr. (1989, September–October). Child sexual abuse prevention programs: What makes them effective in protecting children? *Children Today,* pp. 23–27.

Krivacska, J. J. (1992). Child sexual abuse prevention programs: The prevention of childhood sexuality? *Journal of Child Sexual Abuse, 1,* 83–112.

MacMillan, H. L., MacMillan, J. H., Offord, D. R., Griffith, L., & MacMillan, A. (1994). Primary prevention of child sexual abuse: A critical review: Part II. *Journal of Child Psychology and Psychiatry, 35,* 857–876.

Melton, G. (1992). The improbability of prevention of sexual abuse. In D. J. Willis, E. Holden, & M. Rosenberg (Eds.), *Prevention of child maltreatment: Developmental and ecological perspectives* (pp. 168–189). New York: Wiley.

Miltenberger, R. G., & Thiesse-Duffy, E. (1988). Evaluation of home-based programs for teaching personal safety skills to children. *Journal of Applied Behavior Analysis, 21,* 81–87.

Miltenberger, R. G., Thiesse-Duffy, E., Suda, K. T., Kozak, C., & Bruellman, J. (1990). Teaching prevention skills to children: The use of multiple measures to evaluate parent versus expert instruction. *Child and Behavior Therapy, 12*(4), 65–86.

Nemerofsky, A. G., Carran, D. T., & Rosenberg, L. A. (1994). Age variation in performance among preschool children in a sexual abuse prevention program. *Journal of Child Sexual Abuse, 3,* 85–102.

Nibert, D., Cooper, S., Ford, J., Fitch, L. K., & Robinson, J. (1989). The ability of young children to learn abuse prevention. *Response to the Victimization of Women and Children, 12*(4), 14–21.

Olsen, J. L., & Widom, C. S. (1993). Prevention of child abuse and neglect. *Applied and Preventive Psychology, 2,* 217–229.

Pelcovitz, D., Adler, N. A., Kaplan, S., Packman, L., & Krieger, R. (1992). The failure of a school-based child sexual abuse prevention program. *Journal of the American Academy of Child and Adolescent Psychiatry, 31,* 887–892.

Plummer, C. A. (1984, August). *Preventing sexual abuse: What in-school programs teach children.* Second National Conference for Family Violence Researchers. (Available from C. Plummer, P.O. Box 421, Kalamazoo, MI 49005-0421)

Plummer, C. A. (1994). Prevention is appropriate, prevention is successful. In R. J. Gelles & D. R. Loseke (Eds.), *Current controversies on family violence* (pp. 288–305). Newbury Park, CA: Sage.

Poche, C., Yoder, P., & Miltenberger, R. (1988). Teaching self-protection to children using television techniques. *Journal of Applied Behavioral Analysis, 21,* 253–261.

Reppucci, N. D., & Haugaard, J. J. (1989). Prevention of child sexual abuse: Myth or reality? *American Psychologist, 44,* 266–275.

Reppucci, N. D., & Haugaard, J. J. (1993). Problems with child sexual abuse prevention programs. In R. J. Gelles & D. R. Loseke (Eds.), *Current controversies on family violence* (pp. 306–322). Newbury Park, CA: Sage.

Reppucci, N. D., & Herman, J. (1991). Sexuality education and child sexual abuse prevention programs in the schools. In G. Grant (Ed.), *Review of research in education* (pp. 127–166). Washington, DC: American Education Research Association.

Reppucci, N. D., Jones, L. M., & Cook, S. L. (1994). Involving parents in child sexual abuse prevention programs. *Journal of Child and Family Studies, 3,* 137–142.

Saslawsky, D. A., & Wurtele, S. K. (1986). Educating children about sexual abuse: Implications for pediatric intervention and possible prevention. *Journal of Pediatric Psychology, 11,* 235–245.

Swan, H. L., Press, A. N., & Briggs, S. L. (1985). Child sexual abuse prevention: Does it work? *Child Welfare, 64,* 667–674.

Tutty, L. M. (1992). The ability of elementary school children to learn child sexual abuse prevention concepts. *Child Abuse & Neglect, 16,* 369–384.

Tutty, L. M. (1993). Parents' perceptions of their child's knowledge of sexual abuse prevention concepts. *Journal of Child Sexual Abuse, 2*(1), 83–103.

Tutty, L. M. (1994). Developmental issues in young children's learning of sexual abuse prevention concepts. *Child Abuse & Neglect, 18,* 179–192.

Wolfe, D. A., Reppucci, N. D., & Hart, S. (1995). Child abuse prevention: Knowledge and priorities. *Journal of Clinical Child Psychology, 24*(Suppl.), 5–22.

Wurtele, S. K. (1993). Enhancing children's sexual development through child sexual abuse prevention programs. *Journal of Sex Education and Therapy, 19,* 37–46.

Wurtele, S. K., Kast, L., Miller-Perrin, C. L., & Kondrick, P. (1989). Comparison of programs for teaching personal safety skills to preschoolers. *Journal of Consulting and Clinical Psychology, 57,* 505–511.

Wurtele, S. K., Kvaternick, M., & Franklin, C. F. (1992). Sexual abuse prevention for preschoolers: A survey of parents' behaviors, attitudes, and beliefs. *Journal of Child Sexual Abuse, 1*(1), 113–128.

Wurtele, S. K., Marrs, S. K., & Miller-Perrin, C. L. (1987). Practice makes perfect?

The role of participant modelling in sexual abuse prevention programs. *Journal of Consulting and Clinical Psychology, 55,* 599–602.

Wurtele, S. K., & Miller-Perrin, C. L. (1987). An evaluation of side effects associated with participation in a child sexual abuse prevention program. *Journal of School Health, 57,* 228–231.

Wurtele, S. K., & Miller-Perrin, C. L. (1992). *Preventing child sexual abuse: Sharing the responsibility.* Lincoln, NE: University of Nebraska Press.

Wurtele, S. K., Saslawsky, D. A., Miller, C. L., Marrs, S. R., & Britcher, J. C. (1986). Teaching personal safety skills for potential prevention of sexual abuse: A comparison of treatments. *Journal of Consulting and Clinical Psychology, 54,* 688–692.

14

WINDOWS FOR PREVENTING CHILD AND PARTNER ABUSE: EARLY CHILDHOOD AND ADOLESCENCE

CHRISTINE WEKERLE AND DAVID A. WOLFE

Adequate definitions of both child maltreatment and the converse—healthy, nonviolent parent–child relationships—are essential for research on the causes and effects of maltreatment and for the entire system of detection, prevention, and delivery of service to problem families. Workers in communities must identify children and families in need of help, while simultaneously educating all community members concerning the currently acceptable and unacceptable forms of child rearing. Practical strategies to reduce the incidence of child maltreatment depend, in part, on the way a society defines inappropriate child-rearing methods, as reflected in community standards for tolerating familial violence and assisting families before the fact.

This work was supported in part by a research grant to both authors from the National Health Research and Development Program (Health Canada) and by a senior research fellowship (D. Wolfe) and a new investigator fellowship (C. Wekerle) from the Ontario Mental Health Foundation. We also thank Ms. Anna-Lee Pittman and Ms. Consiglia Novielli for their considerable assistance.

339

The reality and complexity of child abuse have created a definitional conundrum. Different definitions of maltreatment have emerged over the past 20 years, primarily in response to the particular purpose of an organization, government legislation, a community agency, or a researcher. Municipalities and states, for example, often adopt a definition that focuses largely on evidentiary criteria for prosecuting or acting on behalf of children, whereas treatment providers may weigh other discretionary criteria more heavily in determining what they consider to be an act of abuse or neglect. This problem exists in large part because child abuse most often is "discovered" as a single, dramatic, visible event. However, research and clinical experience clearly indicate that abuse is embedded in a pattern of ongoing negative, harsh, and abusive behaviors that precede a more serious act of violence (Wolfe, 1985), as well as in a larger community context that at worst encourages such behavior or at best tolerates it. To be prevention focused, therefore, definitions of child maltreatment must focus on what is inappropriate not only at the individual level (i.e., discrete abuse events) but also at the dyadic level (e.g., hostile parent–child interactions). Furthermore, professionals concerned with prevention must consider both sides of the relationship equation to include the *determinants of healthy parent–child relationships*, along with those of unhealthy relationships. Social policies must encourage early assistance and health promotion rather than rely so heavily on detection and limited intervention after the fact. This argument for prevention is augmented by the limited success of treatment programs to prevent recidivism with abusive parents (Wolfe & Wekerle, 1993).

The view of child maltreatment as part of an ongoing problem in the parent–child relationship raises an important question for prevention: Does prevention aim to reduce single incidents of child abuse, or does it aim to prevent the abusive pattern from becoming established (or both)? By adopting a wider net for prevention, in which abusive acts and the interpersonal patterns that support them are targeted, prevention efforts are better matched with the reality of child abuse: offenses committed within dysfunctional relationships. By implication, the wide array of negative relationship factors become targets for prevention, and positive relationship factors become targets for promotion. Given this relationship emphasis, child abuse prevention can be conceptualized as any effort designed to decrease interpersonal dysfunction and increase interpersonal competence, such as community development programs, parent training, job training, and proper medical services.

More specifically, child abuse prevention incorporates methods developed to eliminate any form of violence (verbal, physical, or sexual) against a child or another family member, as well as efforts to promote a strong, healthy parent–child relationship. Therefore, an innovative strategy is to extend child abuse prevention efforts to include interventions that are intended to promote healthy, nonviolent relationships (targeting beliefs about self, partners, and relationships, as well as related affective, cognitive, and behavioral skills) and to ameliorate violence-promoting relationships. The overall goal is to facilitate a positive, nonaversive interactional style across salient partners (i.e., parent to child, parent to parent, partner to partner). In keeping with this expanded view of child abuse prevention, we present an overview of prevention programs, followed by a theoretical discussion supporting a relational focus to prevention. We then profile two specific prevention programs that use relationship-based timing for initiating interventions, one directed at the onset of parenting status (the Prenatal/Early Infancy Project) and the other directed at the onset of romantic partnerships, a precursor to achieving parenting status (the Youth Relationships Project).

OVERVIEW OF PREVENTION PROGRAMS

The importance of the parent–child relationship and its context has evolved in recent years to a position of primacy in the promotion of healthy relationships and the prevention of child abuse and neglect (Cicchetti, Toth, & Bush, 1988; Martin, 1990). Simultaneously, the view of abuse and neglect has shifted gradually away from a deviance–disease orientation toward a recognition of the vast number of stress factors that impinge on the developing parent–child relationship. This shift toward a more process-oriented, contextual approach to child abuse and neglect places greater emphasis on the importance of promoting parental competence and reducing the burden of stress on families (Melton & Barry, 1994).

Key factors for determining healthy parent–child relationships have been identified. Although many of the following factors occur naturally in some families, other families require early assistance and additional resources to achieve the desired goal (Wekerle & Wolfe, 1993):

- Adequate parental knowledge of child development and the demands of parenting
- Adequate parental skill in coping with the stress related to caring for small children and in enhancing child development through proper stimulation and attention
- Opportunities to form secure parent–child attachment and adaptive early patterns of communication
- Adequate parental knowledge of home management, including knowledge of basic financial planning, maintaining a proper shelter, and meal planning
- Opportunities to reduce and share the burden of child care among men and women
- Increased access to social and health services

On the basis of these factors, important strides have been made in reducing child abuse and neglect among parents and children at high risk of abuse. The literature reveals the following effects (Wekerle & Wolfe, 1993; Wolfe & Wekerle, 1993):

- For families with clear risk markers (single-parent status, at least one child under 5 years, socioeconomic disadvantage, child behavior problem), fairly intensive (1–3 years) group or home-visit interventions or both, providing parental support and instruction in child management or child cognitive stimulation, have benefited parental attitudes and behavior and overall maternal adjustment.
- For low-risk samples (i.e., general risk marker of first-time parent), brief (less than 1 month) home-visit interventions have produced gains in positive knowledge, attitudes, and parenting behavior; very brief interventions (in-hospital only, following delivery) have not emerged as effective.
- Positive improvements in both child cognitive ability and behavioral adjustment have emerged from studies involving consistent (but not necessarily lengthy) delivery of child development–focused interventions.
- Family-support programs have improved general maternal functioning, rather than specific dimensions of personal adjustment.
- Multilevel programs (i.e., offering additional services as parents required them over a longer period of time) were worth the additional effort and expense, compared to less intensive services, for higher risk families.

Accordingly, important prevention targets are those that reduce relationship vulnerabilities and build on strengths. Targets may be at the individual level (e.g., employing intervention "graduates" as therapists) and the contextual level (e.g., facilitating the mother in her role as a worker). Both levels offer a route to improved conceptualizations of self, other, and the relationship.

Most abuse-prevention work reviewed to date (Wekerle & Wolfe, 1993) has been embedded in the ecological approach (e.g., Belsky, 1980; Bronfenbrenner, 1979; Garbarino, 1977), in which the environmental context has been emphasized to the detriment of the potential mediating role of individual cognitive and emotional processes (Emery, 1989). The remainder of this chapter considers prevention programs and prevention aims that address some of the *psychological processes that underlie parenting behav-*

iors. These targets differ from the traditional prevention targets, such as increasing knowledge of child development or of specific parenting strategies. Instead, the purpose of this type of prevention is to alter abuse-facilitating cognitive and affective models of relationships in favor of healthier relationship conceptualizations. In short, we advocate addressing directly how parents "learn" to parent.

In reviewing recent prevention efforts with an emphasis on the relational context and developmentally relevant opportunities for intervention, we focus on two groups that provide opportunities for intervention: (a) new and expectant parents and (b) at-risk youths beginning the dating process. In both groups, one sees the importance of the dyad and dyadic "fit" for prevention efforts. In this discussion, we detail psychological processes contributing to the dyadic fit and how these components are becoming the focus of prevention programs.

THE RELATIONAL CONTEXT

Child maltreatment has been conceptualized as a "relational psychopathology": a poor fit between the child, parent, and environmental characteristics (Cicchetti & Olsen, 1990). A key focus of the relational pathology is provided by the cognitive and affective relationship "templates" developed from infancy in caretaking relationships. Attachment theory (Bowlby, 1980; Sroufe, 1989) holds that information about relationships—attitudes toward, expectations for, and emotions about the self and other in relationships—tends to be coherent across time, signaling which interactants and situations will be gravitated to and which will be avoided (Waters, Posada, Crowell, & Lay, 1993). Secure attachment models are believed to emerge from satisfying and generally positive relationship experiences, in which the other is seen as loving, consistently responsive, and sensitive, enabling the self to be viewed as worthy of love and stable. In contrast, insecure attachment emerges from inconsistent, unresponsive, hostile, and insensitive caretaking, in which relationships are unfulfilling or painful, the other is viewed negatively (e.g., as all powerful, all important, untrustworthy, aversive), and the self is experienced as a negative (e.g., as unlovable, unstable, powerless). It has been suggested that insecure attachments in childhood set the stage for abuse because rejection, role reversal, and fear are familiar territory for the parent with unresolved loss or a history of maltreatment (Alexander, 1992). That is, insecure attachment may reduce the psychological barriers to abuse, possibly by weakening the protective orientation in parenting and strengthening a negative characterological view of the child. Although the mechanisms are unclear, considerable research supports the cycle-of-violence hypothesis (Widom, 1989).

The attachment literature confirms that the vast majority of maltreated infants are classified as insecurely attached to their caregivers (70%–100% across studies; Cicchetti et al., 1988), suggesting that the child lacks confidence in the mother as an available and responsive provider and the mother has difficulty in providing sensitive, nurturant, and responsive care. The disorganized–disoriented attachment of many maltreated children (Carlson, Cicchetti, Barnett, & Brunwald, 1989) suggests that no single, clear approach to relationships exists. Instead, the maltreated child must flexibly deploy proximity seeking, avoidance, and resistance toward the primary caregiver, as the winds of caregiver change appear to dictate (Crittenden, 1988).

Once abuse occurs, relationships may become cognitively and affectively dichotomized into a victim–victimizer interpersonal stance (Cicchetti & Howes, 1991; Crittenden & Ainsworth, 1989; Dodge, Pettit, & Bates, 1994). Maltreatment in the context of already dysfunctional relationships presents the potential for a violent, not merely conflictual, *dynamic*. Therefore, child abuse can be recast as relationship violence, and prevention efforts may profit from related theoretical and empirical work. Indeed, the overlap among areas of relationship violence is becoming part of public consciousness; Daro and Gelles (1992) reported on survey findings that indicate that the public sees domestic violence as a major contributor to child abuse. Studies have supported the large overlap (between 40% and 60%; Straus & Gelles, 1990); a partner-assaultive man is likely to aggress against his children, and an assaulted woman may turn aggressively toward her children. Abusive adults have been found to be aversive with their children, partners, social network members, and professionals (Crittenden, 1988). These aversive exchanges across interactions contribute to the maintenance of abusive behavior in the abusive perpetrator (Jaffe, Wolfe, & Wilson, 1990).

In a similar fashion, abused children are more aggressive and less empathic toward their preschool (Main & George, 1985), school-aged (Dodge et al., 1994), and adolescent (Widom, 1989) peers than are other children. Childhood abuse is also predictive of violence in adolescent (Wolfe, Wekerle, Reitzel-Jaffe, & Lefebvre, in press) and adult (Dutton, 1995) partnerships. The intergenerational transmission of abuse is, at its core, the transmission of a propensity toward an insecure and hostile interactional style (e.g., Aber & Allen, 1987; Erickson, Sroufe, & Egeland, 1985; Kaufman & Zigler, 1987, 1989), dominated by power and control issues (Crittenden, 1988). Accumulating research has emphasized the role of attachment models; for example, correspondence in attachment classification has been shown across three generations, that is, in grandmother–mother–infant triads (Benoit & Parker, 1994).

Targeting Dyadic "Fit"

A Focus on Changing Negative Processes

A common theme across the research on domestic violence (Hotaling & Sugarman, 1986) and child abuse (Milner, 1993; Wekerle & Wolfe, 1993) is the notion of the abuser, as opposed to the victim, "driving" the violent system. Consistently, attachment behavior is considered the property of an individual rather than a relationship (Bowlby, 1982); the individual engages with and responds to others in a way that is consistent with their mental models of relating, and this aspect of model-consistent choice in behavior clearly identifies a violent response as a *selected* response, albeit one that may fall into the domain of automatic rather than effortful cognitive processing (Milner, 1993). Neither partner nor child can be construed as having "provoked" a violent response from another. Although victims need to increase their awareness of danger signals, safety skills, and abuse-facilitating behaviors, offenders are responsible for committing the grievous acts. Child abuse and domestic violence are adult actions.

However, this orientation does not indicate that the offending behavior occurs in a vacuum. The majority of child abuse incidents occur in the context of parental punishment for perceived child misbehavior (Wolfe, 1985). Furthermore, not all children in an abusive environment receive the same level of abusive parenting (Wolfe, 1987). A poor fit among the parent, child, and environmental characteristics (Cicchetti & Olsen, 1990) may be the critical element in the realization of an adult's already existing propensity toward abusiveness.

For the at-risk and abusive person, the very fact of a relationship (as when a child is born or when a partnership is begun) is a "fit" challenge, given that the at-risk and abusive person has mixed, angry, or no feelings about the value of relationships (Benoit, Zeanah, & Barton, 1989). Another factor limiting the at-risk and abusive individual's relatedness potential is the chronic psychological distress that is often present. Male batterers have been found to report early abusive experiences more frequently, to identify greater current posttraumatic stress and symptoms of depression, and to direct associated rage and abuse at their partners (Dutton, 1994, 1995). Chronic depressive symptoms have also been identified in abusive mothers (Wolfe, 1985, 1987), linked to a history of early trauma that may include loss and child abuse (Blatt & Homann, 1992). Research with maltreated children has highlighted the difficult situation of having a sense of inner badness (Schneider-Rosen & Cicchetti, 1991) yet having few words to articulate this feeling (Beeghly & Cicchetti, 1994; Cicchetti & Beeghly, 1987). When such early training in suffering silently becomes intolerable, this aversive affect style may be acted out and attributed (mistakenly) to others who would take it. Physical communication of frustration may be the prime means, given the reduced ability to express feelings, especially negative feelings, verbally (Dutton, 1994).

To date, prevention programs for child abuse and neglect have targeted maternal adjustment variables. For example, of the 34 studies reviewed (Wekerle & Wolfe, 1993), 16 targeted maternal adjustment, with positive gains reported in 13. Measures of maternal adjustment included depression, anxiety, parenting stress, and social support as well as lifestyle variables such as employment, reduced family size, and educational achievement. What have not been targeted are the processes implicated in maternal distress.

The empirical work on information processing in the context of negative mood states (e.g., depression) indicates that whereas automatic processing (i.e., processing that is rapid, unconscious, or difficult to interrupt) may not be compromised, effortful processing (i.e., conscious, reflective processing; Hartlage, Alloy, Vazquez, & Dykman, 1993) is likely reduced. Furthermore, mood-congruent effortful processing may be less affected, which suggests that distress is consistent with the selection of negative and punitive parental behaviors, such as threats, punishment, and disapproval. Researchers in the areas of motivation and attention have shown that affectively unpleasant states, like depression and trauma-related distress, facilitate defensive reflexes when the person is focused on avoiding harm, which may be achieved through either withdrawal or approach–attack responses (Lang, 1995). In this regard, abusive parents operate under an attentional deficit (Wahler & Dumas, 1989), disproportionately processing negative child behavior (Mash, Johnston, & Kovitz, 1983) that serves to reinforce their victim–victimizer view of relationships (i.e., the child as an aversion, threat, or "abuser"). Researchers have suggested that this tendency may factor into a dyadic, mutually reinforced negative bias (MacKinnon, Lamb, Belsky, & Baum, 1990), given the work showing that maltreated children also demonstrated greater attention to aggressive (Rieder & Cicchetti, 1989) and anger-related (Cummings, Hennessy, Rabideau, & Cicchetti, 1994) stimuli.

The misattributions, misperceptions, and missed information that are consistent with relationship models may not be facilitating positive relating. The notion, is, then, to prevent selective attention and cognitive distortion, for both parent and child, that is a function of fitting mental models of relationships to situations that do not inherently fit well. One intervention that challenges such negative biases while inducing effortful processing of positive interpersonal information is called "synthesis teaching," a method developed for use with depressed, socially isolated mothers whose children have behavior problems (Wahler & Dumas, 1989).

Although difficult child behaviors can catch most parents off guard, model-consistent child behavior is considered to "derail" parents who are prone to abusiveness into acts of child abuse. For example, whereas every child says no to parental commands, various child characteristics may be related to a greater frequency and duration of noncompliance, such as verbal assertiveness, aggression, or emotional intensity. Similarly, whereas every parent feels upset with child noncompliance, abusive parents appear to become more upset, more quickly (Vasta, 1982; Wolfe, 1985, 1987). In other words, an idiosyncratic child expression of normative child behavior may be responded to with an exaggerated, but normative, parental response in some situations of child abuse. A consideration of how the child's temperament matches the parent's personality has been given impetus in recent research suggesting the long-term consistency of inhibited (withdrawing) and uninhibited (approaching) child temperament until adolescence (e.g., Schwartz, Snidman, & Kagan, 1996). An innately active child can be expected to respond to parental aggression differently from an innately passive child. For instance, in mother–child dyads in which the child is classified as aggressive, children make regular use of coercive control and mothers set limits inconsistently, failing to oppose extreme forms of coercion (Dumas, LaFreniere, & Serketich, 1995). Children classified as anxious were found to be both resistant and coercive, and their mothers tended to exhibit both unresponsiveness and coercion (Dumas et al., 1995).

For parents who are prone to abuse and have a low felt sense of personal power (Bugental, 1993), any extended conflict situation may be experienced as a direct assault on their fragile parental authority. This situation may be particularly toxic for the intense, aggressive, or persistent child, leaving the child vulnerable to the parent's effort to achieve "counterpower." In this scenario, the abusive parent is reinforced in his or her self-view as victim (i.e., of particularly noxious child behavior), thereby feeling "just cause" in responding to the child's "provocation" with harsh and abusive parental behavior. A similar process is suggested in abusive adult relationships, in which power abuses are often precipitated by distorted perceptions of threat and vulnerability; that is, batterers are most likely to respond abusively when they believe their partner is abandoning them or in some manner leaving them feeling vulnerable (Dutton, 1994).

To date, prevention programs have targeted parental behavior, with positive gains reported in making mothers less aversive, less abusive, and more positive (Wekerle & Wolfe, 1993); child behavior has not been directly targeted as much (as it is in the case of compliance training), nor has the behavior of fathers or male partners. Such strategies as errorless learning to build in child success while fading parental structure and support over time have begun to be included in prevention programs (Peterson, 1996). Unfortunately, the way in which the dyadic fit can be meaningfully incorporated into child abuse prevention has been underarticulated, particularly because the children are not selected in advance. To date, prevention programs have not targeted "fit-oriented" interventions, such as child temperament–parenting strategy matching.

One exception is described in a recent report on an insecure attachment prevention program in the Netherlands with low-risk parents (first-time parents, mostly intact couples, full-term infants; van den Boom, 1994, 1995). Selection criteria focused on child temperament, with irritability determined in the weeks following birth. Child irritability was a key inclusion criterion on the basis of preliminary research that revealed that parents of such infants displayed a predictable behavioral pattern of dysfunctional interaction—approaching the child during child fussiness, but withdrawing and ceasing interaction once child fussiness ended or was curtailed. In other words, these parents of irritable infants were reducing the possibility for positive rather than negative reinforcement to guide their interactions with their child. The timing of this intervention was empirically determined and developmentally sensitive; that is, the evidence showed that by 5 months of age, interactions with irritable infants had become negatively focused in a patterned way. A maternal-sensitivity skills training intervention with irritable infants (6 months at study entry) was delivered over 3 months (three 2-hour sessions) in an attempt to promote secure attachment by improving the mother's ability to monitor infant signals attentively and accurately and to respond appropriately and contingently. A home visitor focused on individualized interactional feedback to assist mothers in adjusting to their infant's unique cues, with consideration for maternal stylistic tendencies.

Mothers in the intervention group were found to be more responsive, stimulating, visually attentive, and positively controlling of their infant's behavior, and their infants were more sociable, self-soothing, and exploratory, and they cried less, compared to mothers and infants in the control group. Additionally, children in the intervention group were more likely to be classified as securely attached at 12 months (van den Boom, 1994) and at 18 months (van den Boom, 1995). Positive interactional gains for both parent (including interactions with fathers) and child (including interactions with peers) were found for the intervention group in the child's 2nd and 3rd years. An important feature of this program evaluation was that the system of relational partners was broadened to include fathers, siblings, and peers, to allow assessment of the transmission and generalizability of intervention-related, relationship-based change.

The efficacy of such brief, but individualized, behavior-based interventions for preventing insecure child attachment, particularly when the timing of intervention is developmentally informed, is supported by a recent meta-analytic study (van Ijzendoorn, Juffer, & Duyvesteyn, 1995). Interventions that are individualized, in-depth, in vivo, and within the context of a supportive therapeutic relationship may be among the most effective. Preventions based on a notion of dyadic fit would reasonably select on a dyadic risk marker, that is, on the basis of intake assessment interactions, and would include individual risk markers such as parental history of maltreatment (but not yet maltreating), difficult child temperament, and child behavior problems.

A Focus on Enhancing Positive Processes

One of the important developmental domains in which positive growth is compromised by a history of child abuse is the development of self and social functioning (Cole & Putnam, 1992). The implication of a parental "damaged self" is that the true focus of parent–child interactions is on the parent's cognitive and emotional preoccupation with self-injury and related needs, at the expense of the child's emotional state and related needs (Crittenden, 1993). Applying these findings to the at-risk mother would require that the negative self-referential set be directly targeted, either concurrently with or preceding parenting-related interventions, to make a maximal impact in child abuse prevention.

Berkowitz (1990) identified emotional self-awareness as a critical first step in the self-regulation of aggression. This process would also include awareness of abuse-preventing emotions such as empathy, concern, worry, and pride, which support positive motivation in parenting and a child-based orientation (Dix, 1991). We submit that a capable, stable, loving, lovable, and responsible self-image is a necessary precursor to sensitive and competent parenting, although it is an ideal that is rarely met. Abuse-prevention programs are beginning to target maternal self-concept directly, particularly self-concept as a mother and parent, with teaching of "affective reprogramming" (changing the child from an aversive to a positive stimulus) and perspective taking (building in empathy and a child orientation; e.g., Heineman, 1992; Peterson, 1996); empirical validation, however, remains to be accomplished. Prevention programs that target parental self-improvement, particularly in relationships, should demonstrate positive change in attachment-related measures that are self-reported (e.g., Relationship Satisfaction Questionnaire; Griffin & Bartholomew, 1994), interviewer rated (e.g., Adult Attachment Interview; George, Kaplan, & Main, 1985), or observed (e.g., dyadic interactions; see Wekerle & Wolfe, 1993, for a discussion). With the exception of studies in which observational coding schemes were used, the focus of measurement has been on only one participant in the relational dyad (or system), with assessments of individual perceptions of, and reported responses to, attachment figures rather than of the process of interaction.

In sum, relational change requires (a) involving additional relational partners to open up new ways of relating and (b) reorganizing the mental representations of relationships, involving cognitive, affective, and behavioral components (Lyons-Ruth & Zeanah, 1993). The process of attachment has been applied to relationships other than caretaking ones, such as with peers and romantic partners (Hazan & Shaver, 1994). This notion may be applied to child abuse prevention; the psychological processes supporting a violent relationship dynamic *across key interactants* represent a viable target for prevention. Positive relationship change in one domain (e.g., partnerships) may generalize to other domains (e.g., relationships with children, coworkers, or community members). Intervention includes assistance in making more effortful and planful the negatively biased cognitive and emotional processes that seem primarily automatic but are not yet crystallized (Milner, 1993). The hope is that the parent who is at risk for abuse or reflexive in responding to his or her child can become a reflective, nonabusive parent. In consolidating this skill, the parent may become more adaptive in other salient relationships at home, at work, and in the community. The task is to build in and on positive alternatives to such a degree that they become overlearned and more automatic.

Within this relationship focus, the twin goals of violence prevention and health promotion continue to be paramount. In concert with the notion of dyadic fit, the timing of an intervention is of considerable importance. In considering child abuse, two main windows of opportunity for prevention emerge. First, teenage dating relationships—when intimacy is being actively pursued with an *individual of choice*—seem to present a prime opportunity to intervene proactively with regard to relationship beliefs and skills. Although such an intervention may not appear useful as a child abuse prevention strategy, we propose that enhancing the youth's relationship view and behaviors by directly addressing violence in dating relationships should bode well for functioning in future relationships. One would hope that gains in the sphere of dating relationships would generalize to the parent–child relationship (when parenting status has been achieved), the partner coparenting relationship, and the partner relationship in general. Second, the birth of a first child also highlights an opportunity for intervening in the family system, especially in the context of the *particular child*. The next section explores the transition from theory to practice, highlighting the importance of intervention timing, relationship-based targets for change, and the objectives of health promotion as well as violence prevention.

TIMING FOR PREVENTION: NEW AND EXPECTANT PARENTS

The negotiation of new relationships marks a point of leverage for intervention to alter the mental representations of relationships. For this reason, new parenthood emerges as a prime intervention window. In fact, some of the most promising prevention efforts have been reported for this target population (Daro & McCurdy, 1994; Olds & Kitzman, 1993; Wekerle & Wolfe, 1993). The most consistent gains have been reported in the parent–child interactional domain, in parental reports of child behavior problems, and in overall parental adjustment (e.g., measures of stress-related symptoms, feelings of depression and dysphoria). Community-based home visiting programs have been shown to be efficacious in reducing both child abuse specifically and abuse-related indices; for example, fewer accidents and emergency room visits and lower rates of corporal punishment have been reported. These findings across parent, child, and interactional domains are consistent with the view that critical relationship factors (i.e., the dyadic fit, the model of the other, and the model of the self) may have been favorably altered. Although parenting behavior has been clearly associated with adult attachment models (e.g., Crowell, O'Connor, Wollmers, Sprafkin, & Rao, 1991), prevention programs have not assessed change in attachment models as a function of intervention per se.

In an effort to avoid either underservicing or overproviding, a consultation model that is client focused and flexible has shown effectiveness across parent, child, and relationship domains (Wekerle & Wolfe, 1993). On the basis of a prevention philosophy and an emphasis on parent–child relationships, several researchers over the past decade and a half have designed programs to assist new parents in their challenging role with the goal of strengthening the parent–infant relationship from the beginning. Most of these projects involved medical professionals, hospital services, or both in implementing the expanded services provided to participants in the experimental conditions, and many entailed home visits that began either prenatally (generally in the third trimester) or in the early postpartum period. Parents' needs for support, parenting instruction, and resource linkage seem to be fulfilled best by the more personalized, "outreach" nature of the home visitor approach. An example of this approach is the Prenatal/Early Infancy Project (PEIP) of David Olds and colleagues.

The Prenatal/Early Infancy Project

A prominent "success story" regarding child maltreatment prevention is found in the ongoing work of David Olds (Olds, Henderson, Chamberlin, & Tatelbaum, 1986; Olds, Henderson, & Kitzman, 1994; Olds, Kitzman, Cole, & Robinson, 1997). His research team began in the late 1970s in upstate New York by targeting first-time parents who also possessed one or more child abuse risk factors, for example, status as teenaged or single parent or low income. The program offers varying degrees of child care services to participants, as well as pre- and postnatal home visits by nurses who provide resource linkages and education in child development. At-risk individuals who receive this intervention are viewed in terms of their strengths and abilities rather than deficits alone. This view translates into an empowerment strategy; women are assisted in understanding and meeting their own needs and those of their newborn child and are taught the skills necessary to enhance their relationship with their child as well as their own self-development.

Two major psychological determinants of health have been demonstrated to change through (a) helping mothers to develop or change their understanding of child health and development as well as expectations for their own development and (b) enhancing self-efficacy in the mothers by developing their strengths and confidence. Interventions concerning the social determinants of health involve the formation of close, therapeutic alliances with the mother and other family members during pregnancy. Visitors build effective relationships by focusing on mothers' and family members' strengths and by addressing issues of concern to them. The economic determinants of health are also addressed. Family stressors are identified, and families are linked with needed health and human services. For example, families are helped to obtain needed financial assistance, subsidized housing, family counseling, nutritional supplementation, assistance in finding clothing and furniture, and medical care.

This program has been replicated in three sites in the United States, and a variation of the program is being tested at the present time through a research study being conducted in Hamilton, Ontario, Canada. The evidence to date suggests that success in one geographic setting can be achieved in others, although variations in local environments must first be carefully considered. The program developers have emphasized that understanding better how to manage variations in local environments to ensure that the essential elements of the program are reproduced is an important consideration in the dissemination of this method.

Tailoring Intervention Needs

Because prevention studies to date have shown little specificity in matching participants with treatments (Wekerle & Wolfe, 1993), an important future direction is tailoring interventions to participant characteristics. Daro and Gelles (1992) suggested that at-risk families can be classified into three categories in terms of openness to intervention. In "consumer" families, parents are receptive, show initiative in seeking intervention, and are at least somewhat aware of their need for parent education and support. In "dependent" families, parents are more hesitant and isolated, may or may not be aware of their needs for parenting assistance, and are unskilled at accessing intervention services. These families are thought to require more outreach, more intensive services, more follow-up, and greater "selling" of the programs. "Resistant" families often have the greatest needs and the most urgency to respond. They consist of parents with multiple problems who are the least responsive to services and are considered the poorest candidates for success, even though they are often in crisis and create the largest cost to the child welfare system.

Other attempts to classify families have focused on vulnerabilities. Poverty is associated with physical abuse and, in particular, neglect (Jones & McCurdy, 1992). Within the disadvantaged class, certain groups have been found to display greater vulnerability for physical violence, including single parents, young caregivers, and caregivers with young children (Gelles, 1992); these factors converge in many single-parent, female-headed families. Research has supported the view that socioeconomically disadvantaged mothers are at risk for maltreatment because of their tendency to rely on aversive parenting strategies and that the circumstances of disadvantage directly interfere with their ability to base parenting on child behavior (e.g., Dumas & Wekerle, 1995). More intensive and comprehensive services must be effectively provided for those in greatest need in a way that is empowering to the individual, is validating to the caretaking role, and simultaneously reflects and challenges the context of a patriarchal ideal (Febbraro, 1994). Such power-conscious interventions would provide a more comprehensive approach by simultaneously targeting power dynamics in the intimate relationships of at-risk individuals and targeting power relations within society and the prevailing culture.

TIMING FOR PREVENTION: ADOLESCENT DATING RELATIONSHIPS

Adolescence marks the stage when primary affective ties are being moved from the family to the peer network and romantic partnerships. In parallel, adolescents' increased capacity for abstract thought and their motivation to achieve an autonomous identity propel them toward exploration of self within the relational domain, including such psychological processes as heightened social comparison and self-reflection (Crockett & Petersen, 1993). It is precisely the "in flux" nature of adolescence that identifies the stage as a window for changes in relationships. Although Hazan and Shaver (1987, 1994) specified adult romantic love as the targets for change, it seems logical to include adolescent partnerships, which also are guided by internal models of relationships.

Hazan and Shaver (1994) identified early adolescence as an important period of developmental shift in attachment behaviors. With the onset of adolescence, attachment needs gradually shift from parents to peers, such that searching for a "safe haven" (i.e., provision of support) becomes an important motivator underlying the adolescent's "need" to be with peers. Furman and Wehner (1992) drew a distinction in the relationship motivators between early and mid-to-late adolescent romantic partnerships. The fact that most early romantic liaisons are short lived and casual and overlap with peerships suggests that affiliative and sexual needs predominate, whereas with later adolescent partnerships, attachment and caregiving behavioral systems become important as well. However, Hazan and Shaver (1987) argued that the continuity in attachment models between childhood and adolescence should be greater than with adulthood, given the lack of opportunity to revise such models with an increasing number of important relationships. Consequently, adolescence may be an opportune time to reorganize the mental representations of relationships of those who are at risk for abusiveness (e.g., adolescents with a history of child maltreatment) through teaching new ways of relating within the new relationships that are being experienced.

In adolescence, specific relationship goals such as intimacy, companionship, nurturance, and assistance have the opportunity to be fulfilled by the adolescents' exploration of peerships and partnerships (Furman & Buhrmester, 1985, 1992). Also, important relationship skills are being acquired, reinforced, and refined, including methods of handling interpersonal conflict. For example, adolescent girls tend to use more prosocial means of compromise, whereas boys tend to rely on power assertion and submission as a means to resolve disputes with friends (Laursen & Collins, 1994). For these and similar reasons, adolescence may be an important window of opportunity for altering negative relationship variables while enhancing positive ones. However, attempting to explore the parent–child relationship as an exemplar of relationships when an adolescent has not yet achieved parenting status is a poor stage–environment fit (Eccles et al., 1993) on which to base prevention efforts. Instead, teenagers would be expected to show a readiness to explore relationship-based issues for current concerns, such as in relationships with family-of-origin members, peers, and dating partners.

Not all adolescents are vulnerable to becoming interpersonally violent, and a critical factor may be the experience of such violence while growing up (see Wekerle & Wolfe, 1996, for a discussion of child maltreatment sequelae). Research has shown that childhood victimization increases the likelihood that adolescents will be both violent toward others (Widom, 1989; Wolfe et al., in press) and the recipients of violence (Wolfe, Wekerle, Reitzel-Jaffe, & Gough, 1995). An increased risk of intimate violence, including violence toward close peers, partners, and future children, can be anticipated for such youths, given that the foundations for such violence are organized in childhood but are often activated in adolescence (Earls, Cairns, & Mercy, 1993), perhaps as a function of the grouping together of similar adolescents (i.e., the "assortative pairing" phenomenon; Quinton, Pickles, Maughan, & Rutter, 1993). Dating violence during adolescence, combined with a past history of violence in the family of origin (i.e., child physical abuse or wife abuse), is a significant predictor of intimate violence in early adulthood and marriage (Murphy, Meyer, & O'Leary,

1994; O'Leary, Malone, & Tyree, 1994). The predictive importance of adolescent relationship violence and the formative nature of relationships in adolescence direct a prevention focus on relationship issues, such as the constructs of self and other, the value and expectations of relationships, and particular relationship dynamics associated with violence (e.g., victim–victimizer conceptualizations).

The Emergence of Patterns of Intimate Violence During Midadolescence

The teenage years have been identified as important for the understanding of the pathways to violence because adolescent dating relationships may represent a transition point between childhood experiences of maltreatment or negative learning experiences and the increased likelihood of personal violence or victimization in adulthood (Bethke & DeJoy, 1993). Adolescence may be a developmental period in which some teenagers begin to adjust to an unhealthy pattern of intimate interaction that extends into adulthood and includes parenthood.

Adolescence has been virtually ignored in terms of its dynamic importance in establishing a pattern of relationships with intimate partners and future family members; however, studies have suggested that emotional and physical abuse among teenage dating partners is as widespread and frequent as in adult relationships (Marx, Van Wie, & Gross, 1996; Suderman & Jaffe, 1993) and that patterns of abusive teenage relationships resemble adult patterns and cycles of violence: There is a building of tension, an explosion of anger, and a honeymoon period of making up (Walker, 1989). It is disturbing that teenagers appear to be poorly informed concerning what constitutes normative dating behavior. Youths already involved in an abusive dating relationship or who grew up in a violent home may accept abusive behavior as a normal part of intimate relationships (O'Leary et al., 1994). For these reasons, dating violence may represent a bridge between experiencing maltreatment and witnessing wife assault in childhood and the occurrence of similar relationship patterns of violence or victimization in adulthood (Malamuth, Sockloskie, Koss, & Tanaka, 1991).

Intimate Violence Among Maltreated Youths

Our research team investigated the degree of abusive behavior in dating relationships among an at-risk sample of youths: those who were under the supervision or care of child protective services owing to present or past maltreatment. We discovered that both girls and boys are at risk for becoming both offenders and victims of violent and abusive behavior toward or by an intimate partner. Our sample of 168 youths served by a child protective service agency (aged 14–16; 79 males, 89 females) illustrated the at-risk status of these youths for relationship violence. The majority of the youths (96%) indicated that they had begun dating. Victimization by dating partners among girls included sexual touching against their will (25%), being kissed against their will (22%), and being forced to have sex (10%). Furthermore, 23% reported being kicked, hit, or punched by dating partners, and 17% reported being pushed, shoved, or shaken. Although males reported low levels of forced sexual contact, they reported physical violence in the form of being slapped or having hair pulled (16%) and being kicked, hit, or punched (19%) by their dating partner. In terms of offending behaviors, these males reported most frequently kissing their partner against their will (14%), whereas females endorsed kicking, hitting, or punching their partner (26%); slapping or pulling their partner's hair (22%); and pushing, shoving, or shaking their partner (18%).

As we expected, these adolescents perceived their attachment style to be predominantly insecure. Only 7.6% of the youths identified themselves as highly secure (on the basis of a median split), using Hazan and Shaver's approach (1987, 1994). In contrast, using the same measure with a high school sample (Wekerle & Wolfe, in press) we found 40% of youths endorsing themselves as more likely to approach partners with a secure style (i.e., "I find it pretty easy to get close to others and I am comfortable depending on them. I rarely worry about being abandoned or about someone getting too close to me"). These data encourage a prevention approach that addresses an individual's attachment style and other relationship variables.

Testing a Model of Adolescent Relationship Violence

The preceding data support developmentally sensitive timing for positioning a dating violence prevention program in the midadolescent years when dating violence is emerging; however, it is critical that a specific theoretical model that incorporates important factors that mediate the relationship between antecedents and subsequent relationship abuse be directly connected to the measurement and intervention model (Wekerle & Wolfe, 1993). Our model (Wolfe et al., 1995) concerning the development of relationship violence consists of three theoretical constructs composed of risk factors associated with relationship-based violence: (a) *family background* (including maltreatment as well as alcohol abuse and other family factors); (b) *psychological adjustment* (including trauma-related symptoms, attachment ratings, and interpersonal sensitivity); and (c) *personal resources* (such as social competence and peer relations). High school students completed measures related to these constructs, along with a criterion measure, the Conflict in Relationships Questionnaire (CIRQ; Wolfe, Reitzel-Jaffe, Gough, & Wekerle, 1994), which we developed specifically to assess the nature and extent of coercive (i.e., involving physical, sexual, and emotional abuse) and positive (i.e., involving problem-solving communication) conflict resolution among teenaged dating partners.

We tested this model first with a sample of 359 average high school students to determine the degree of association between these three variables and current offender- or victim-related experiences with dating partners. The results supported the hypothesis that a history of maltreatment is associated with relationship violence during adolescence, especially for boys. For instance, correlations between a history of child maltreatment and *coercive behavior toward a dating partner* were significant for males ($r = .37$; $p < .001$) but not for females ($r = .11$) in the sample. Histories of maltreatment were significantly associated with experiences of physical and emotional abuse *by a dating partner toward the respondent* for both genders, however ($r = .40$, $p < .001$; $r = .25$, $p < .01$, for males and females, respectively).

Overall, for high school boys, simply knowing the general nature of their childhood maltreatment experiences, coupled with either their problem-solving skills or their feelings of interpersonal hostility, allowed us to predict whether they were engaging in some degree of physically, sexually, or emotionally coercive behavior *toward a dating partner* (i.e., offender experiences; $r = .21$, $p < .01$; Wolfe et al., in press). Furthermore, adolescent males who represented the greatest risk for being both victims and offenders in relationship violence were those with elevated maltreatment histories *and* an insecure attachment style (Wekerle & Wolfe, in press).

For high school girls, on the other hand, knowing their history of maltreatment, coupled with their feelings of interpersonal hostility, allowed us to predict the extent to which their dating partners engaged in some degree of physically, sexually, or emotionally coercive behavior *toward them* (i.e., victim experiences; $r = .25$, $p < .001$). Although maltreatment history and insecure attachment style each uniquely predicted relationship violence among females, a high-risk group (high maltreatment and high insecure attachment style) was not found, as was the case with adolescent males (Wekerle & Wolfe, in press). We recently replicated these findings with a second sample of high school students ($N = 450$) who were currently or recently involved in a steady dating relationship, confirming the stable nature of these associations.

The Youth Relationships Project

The Youth Relationships Project (YRP) program and curriculum manual (Wolfe et al., 1996) was developed to help at-risk youths understand the critical importance of the abuse of power and control to relationship violence (Pence & Paymar, 1993) and relate these concepts to their own relationships. We found that when youths were offered opportunities to explore the richness and rewards of relationships, they were eager to learn about choices and responsibilities. The "initiation phase" of social dating presents a prime opportunity to become aware of the ways in which violent and abusive behavior toward intimate partners may occur, often without purpose or intention. This premise holds true not only for individuals from violent and abusive family backgrounds, in which negative experiences were prominent, but for other adolescents as well.

Encouraged by the tremendous gains reported in prevention activity focusing predominantly on health-related behaviors (e.g., smoking, weight loss, high-risk sexual behavior; Prochaska, DiClemente, & Norcross, 1992), we formulated an early intervention–prevention model that made use of the various stages of behavioral change identified and the methods that have been successful with youths. Again, a major theme that emerged in our prevention model was the importance of *gender dynamics*, which we defined in terms of power in relationships as well as attitudes and values regarding gender roles (Amaro, 1995). Understanding the importance of gender issues was a crucial factor in the formation of this prevention model.

Our intervention approach relies heavily on the strength of empowerment in the context of adolescent development and social dating. Empowerment involves "personal power" that is built through personal connections with others, which in turn creates the freedom to be open and receptive with others. The principles of participatory education, in particular, have been well adapted to health education and disease prevention. Educational programs designed to promote social change and individual or group empowerment are active by nature. Accordingly, we assist young people in achieving control over their lives through their own efforts and critical thinking about relationships. Such control, in turn, assists them in recognizing some of the underlying determinants of their dissatisfaction or interpersonal problems, in describing alternatives, and in taking action that leads to changes in their personal relationship situation. Empowerment strategies, by design, encourage people *to act on the system*, rather than *to be acted on by the system* (Wallerstein, 1992).

Rather than attempting to address historical factors directly (such as child maltreatment), this strategy focuses on building on current strengths and identifying and replacing negative relationship factors at a point in time when people are motivated to learn about intimate relationships. Although some level of abusive or violent behavior may be emergent, we assumed that no pattern or violent dynamic had been established as yet. Our goal was to prevent violence in close relationships and to promote positive, egalitarian relationships. By directly targeting the youth's understanding of relationships, of his or her personal inventory of relationship-related factors, and of the partner's role in relationships, we proposed to promote a more positive, less aversive interactional style with salient others—in particular, with dating partners. This opportunity to learn about relationships occurs in the context of forming new peerships (the YRP is a coeducational group intervention), witnessing and observing new partnership role models (the YRP is cofacilitated by a male and a female mental health professional), and experiencing dating partnerships outside the YRP group. It was anticipated that relationship gains made within the dating context would be extended to later partnering and parenting contexts.

On the basis of our understanding of change and our model of vulnerability, we designed a prevention program focusing on the following three specific aims that (a) defined the learning objectives for both the psychological (i.e., cognitive, affective, and behavioral) and the interpersonal growth of each participant and (b) incorporated information, skills, and social action learning components (Wolfe, Wekerle, & Scott, 1997; Wolfe et al., 1997).

Aims of the Program

To help youths understand the critical issues related to healthy relationships. Youths begin the YRP program by discussing and debating issues related to healthy versus unhealthy relationships (e.g., dating violence, wife assault, proaggression attitudes and beliefs, conflict resolution skills, and the building of healthy relationships). Films of dating violence are presented, and the teenagers discuss the impact and extent of personal violence. To increase interest and participation, the teenagers construct a collage of positive and negative images of men and women taken from magazines as a way to explore the nature of male and female stereotypes. To impart accurate information, we provide the youths with technical information concerning the prevalence of violence, the typical victims of violence, and the myths associated with violence in families and in relationships. Information about the effects of abuse is personalized in that the films include men and women talking about their experiences in violent relationships.

To help youths develop skills for building healthy relationships and to recognize and respond to abuse in their own and their peers' relationships. Youths need to observe how others handle conflict, arousal, or debate appropriately, without resorting to power-based solutions or ineffective forms of communication. A series of exercises dealing with communication and conflict resolution skills combines the educational strategies of discussion, modeling, and role-play, and the youths are taught to apply these skills to everyday experiences.

To consolidate learning of new attitudes and skills and to increase competency through community involvement and social action. To accomplish this aim, participants are provided with information about resources in the community that can assist them in managing unfamiliar, stressful issues in their relationships and are given opportunities to access community services. Young people benefit most from prevention programs that build in ample opportunity for their own personal commitment and action. Furthermore, the social action component of the YRP extends the supportive function of relationships from the peer group to a male–female peer coupling and the community at large. Accordingly, we developed community-based, hands-on experiences in which male and female participants are paired and given an opportunity to practice solving hypothetical problems by involving their peer and community resources. They are presented with hypothetical problem situations and go about finding ways in the community to receive help and advice. Cofacilitators act as consultants and make their approach to community persons as realistic, yet successful, as possible. Finally, participants organize and carry out a community project or activity that involves a violence prevention theme. Through social action, they reaffirm their personal and group commitment to end intimate abuse, and they have the opportunity to demonstrate this commitment to nonviolence to others.

Current Evaluation Progress

The long-term evaluation of the YRP is ongoing; it involves repeated follow-ups of 400 participants for 2 years. Preliminary findings, described subsequently, have provided an initial indication of the degree of change emerging from the program. Participating youths (aged 14–16) from child protective service agencies and local high schools volunteer to take part; they are not referred or selected on the basis of any current relationship problems (our research inclusionary criteria focus primarily on youths who experienced violence and abuse while growing up). Participants are randomly assigned either to receive the YRP 18-week program or to a no-intervention control condition. The emphasis is placed on health promotion rather than violence prevention, which avoids stigmatization and accurately reflects the approach of the program.

A self-report measurement package (i.e., measures of peer relations, trauma experiences, dating background, and conflict experiences during dating relationships) is completed by participants at the beginning, middle, and end of the 18-week program (or control period) and every 6 months thereafter for a period of 2 years. Brief telephone interviews are held with the participants on a bimonthly basis to gather dating information. If a participant is in a dating relationship, a videotaped interaction is obtained of the couple during a problem-solving exercise and coded for an analysis of their interactions. Current dating partners are asked to complete the same questionnaires, which allows for cross-informant data on the target participant and the relationship.

We explored the degree of interest, motivation, and understanding shown by 30 group participants across the 18 weeks of the program using hierarchical linear modeling (HLM; Bryk & Raudenbush, 1987). On the basis of weekly cofacilitator 7-point ratings (1 = *lowest level of attainment*, 7 = *highest level of attainment*), we found growth in several areas indicative of group process, such as self-expression skills, involvement and participation, listening, and interest and support given and received. For example, positive growth across 18 assessment waves was shown for support given to others, $\beta_1 = 0.12$, $t = 4.22$, $p < .001$, an indication that participants expressed statements of support to other members of the group increasingly more often as the weeks progressed. A tau correlation of -0.46 for these data indicates that teens who had limited supportive skills at entry tended to gain at a faster rate.

We also compared rates of growth between the intervention ($n = 30$) and control ($n = 28$) groups during the first 6 months of follow-up (four time points), as shown in Table 1. Level 2 HLM analyses are presented to illustrate how these growth curves are compared for participants in each condition on one of our primary outcome measures: the use of coercive tactics toward a dating partner. Table 1 indicates a trend ($p < .20$) for the mean growth rate for the intervention group to exceed that of controls on this measure. The significant χ^2 for variance in growth rate suggests significant variation in the participants' changes in coercive behavior; as expected, some changed at a faster rate than others. Finally, 12.5% of the variance in rate of change on the conflicts-in-relationships measure of co-

TABLE 1
HLM Linear Model of Change (Decline) on the CIRQ Measure of Coercion (Physical or Sexual) Toward a Dating Partner

Final Estimation of Fixed Effects				
Fixed effect	Coefficient	SE	t	p
Mean initial status, β_0				
Initial status, G_{00}	0.78	0.26	3.00	<.01
Initial group difference, G_{01}	−0.15	0.11	−1.31	<.20
Mean growth rate, (slope, β_1)				
Control group, G_{10}	0.00	0.10	0.03	<.40
Treatment effect, G_{11} [a]	−0.06	0.04	1.32	<.20

Final Estimation of Variance Components				
Random effect	Variance component	df	χ^2	p
Initial status, U_0	0.05	47	61.38	<.10
Growth rate, U_1	0.01	47	64.64	<.05
Level 1 error, R	0.05			

Variance explained by experimental condition	Initial status	Growth
	47.5%	12.5%

Note: The CIR scale ranges from 0 (*never*) to 3 (*more than three times*) since the last assessment. HLM = hierarchical linear modeling; CIR = Conflict in Relationships.
[a] Our hypothesis was that this parameter would be negative and significant, to indicate greater rate of decline in use of coercion among treatment participants relative to controls.

ercion (the CIRQ) was accounted for by intervention status. The addition of more participants across several more time points will result in adequate power to detect between-group differences in growth. Ultimately, the true test of whether intervening to improve adolescent partnerships and alter relationship representations is a viable child abuse prevention strategy will occur when YRP youths have achieved parenting status. To date, too few YRP graduates are parents (less than 10%) to allow meaningful results as to whether child abuse and aversive and punitive parenting exist to a lesser extent in intervention versus control participants. Therefore, the efficacy of the YRP as a child abuse prevention strategy remains an empirical question.

CONCLUSION

Children who are at developmental risk owing to conditions that produce child maltreatment need relationships with adults. These relationships provide the teaching opportunities that prevent developmental harm and promote healthy adaptation. Children who experience maltreatment are generally denied opportunities for guidance that produce forward movement and, in fact, receive just the opposite (e.g., high stress and few resources). Such high-stress–low-support social environments deserve the highest priority in terms of social policy; these children are least likely to tolerate maltreatment or any further developmental interference.

The vision for prevention of child abuse and neglect captured by this analysis is one of inclusion and support (as opposed to interception and protection alone). This perspective further implies that primary needs of children, youth, and families (and, by direct implication, reduction in the incidence of child abuse and neglect) are well served through supportive neighborhoods as well as through educational efforts in schools and communities to promote healthy, nonviolent relationships. Such a radical yet sensible approach to the widespread problems related to violence in the home involves diligent planning and action to ensure that communities and families receive needed support at a point in time that allows maximum benefit. The fulfillment of this kind of strategy will not be easy and clearly will involve a reversal of powerful social trends that perpetuate the high incidence of violent behavior toward intimate partners and children.

REFERENCES

Aber, J. L., & Allen, J. P. (1987). Effects of maltreatment on young children's socioemotional development: An attachment theory perspective. *Developmental Psychology, 23*, 406–414.

Alexander, P. C. (1992). Application of attachment theory to the study of sexual abuse. *Journal of Consulting and Clinical Psychology, 60,* 185–195.

Amaro, H. (1995). Love, sex, and power: Considering women's realities in HIV prevention. *American Psychologist, 50,* 437–447.

Beeghly, M., & Cicchetti, D. (1994). Child maltreatment, attachment, and the self system: Emergence of an internal state lexicon in toddlers at high social risk. *Development and Psychopathology, 6,* 5–30.

Belsky, J. (1980). Child maltreatment: An ecological integration. *American Psychologist, 35,* 320–335.

Benoit, D., & Parker, K. C. H. (1994). Stability and transmission of attachment across three generations. *Child Development, 65,* 1444–1456.

Benoit, D., Zeanah, C. H., & Barton, M. L. (1989). Maternal attachment disturbances in failure to thrive. *Infant Mental Health Journal, 10,* 185–202.

Berkowitz, L. (1990). On the formation and regulation of anger and aggression: A cognitive–neoassociationistic analysis. *American Psychologist, 45,* 494–503.

Bethke, T. M., & DeJoy, D. M. (1993). An experimental study of factors influencing the acceptability of dating violence. *Journal of Interpersonal Violence, 8,* 36–51.

Blatt, S. J., & Homann, E. (1992). Parent–child interaction in the etiology of dependent and self-critical depression. *Clinical Psychology Review, 12,* 47–91.

Bowlby, J. (1980). *Attachment and loss.* New York: Basic Books.

Bowlby, J. (1982). *Attachment and loss: Vol. 1. Attachment* (2nd ed.). New York: Basic Books. (Original work published 1969)

Bronfenbrenner, U. (1979). *The ecology of human development: Experiments by nature and design.* Cambridge, MA: Harvard University Press.

Bryk, A. S., & Raudenbush, S. W. (1987). Application of hierarchical linear models to assessing change. *Psychological Bulletin, 101,* 147–158.

Bugental, D. B. (1993). Communication in abusive relationships: Cognitive constructions of interpersonal power. *American Behavioral Scientist, 36,* 288–308.

Carlson, V., Cicchetti, D., Barnett, D., & Brunwald, K. (1989). Disorganized/disoriented attachment relationships in maltreated infants. *Developmental Psychology, 25,* 525–531.

Cicchetti, D., & Beeghly, M. (1987). Symbolic development in maltreated youngsters: An organizational perspective. *New Directions for Child Development, 36,* 5–29.

Cicchetti, D., & Howes, P. W. (1991). Developmental psychopathology in the context of the family: Illustrations from the study of child maltreatment. *Canadian Journal of Behavioral Science, 23,* 257–281.

Cicchetti, D., & Olsen, K. (1990). The developmental psychopathology of child maltreatment. In M. Lewis & S. M. Miller (Eds.), *Handbook of developmental psychopathology* (pp. 261–279). New York: Plenum Press.

Cicchetti, D., Toth, S., & Bush, M. (1988). Developmental psychopathology and incompetence in childhood: Suggestions for intervention. In B. B. Lahey &

A. E. Kazdin (Eds.), *Advances in clinical child psychology* (Vol. 11, pp. 1–77). New York: Plenum Press.

Cole, P. M., & Putnam, F. W. (1992). Effect of incest on self and social functioning: A developmental psychopathology perspective. *Journal of Consulting and Clinical Psychology, 60*, 174–184.

Crittenden, P. M. (1988). Distorted patterns of relationship in maltreating families: The role of internal representation models. *Journal of Reproductive and Infant Psychology, 6*, 183–199.

Crittenden, P. M. (1993). An information-processing perspective on the behavior of neglectful parents. *Criminal Justice and Behavior, 20*, 27–48.

Crittenden, P. M., & Ainsworth, M. D. S. (1989). Attachment and child abuse. In D. Cicchetti & V. Carlson (Eds.), *Child maltreatment: Theory and research on the causes and consequences of child abuse and neglect* (pp. 432–463). New York: Cambridge University Press.

Crockett, L. J., & Petersen, A. C. (1993). Adolescent development: Health risks and opportunities for health promotion. In S. G. Millstein, A. C. Petersen, & E. O. Nightingale (Eds.), *Promoting the health of adolescents: New directions for the twenty-first century* (pp. 13–37). New York: Oxford University Press.

Crowell, J. A., O'Connor, E., Wollmers, G., Sprafkin, J., and Rao, U. (1991). Mothers' conceptualizations of parent–child relationships: Relation to mother–child interaction and child behavior problems. *Development and Psychopathology, 6*, 31–42.

Cummings, E. M., Hennessy, K. D., Rabideau, G. J., & Cicchetti, D. (1994). Responses of physically abused boys to interadult anger involving their mothers. *Development and Psychopathology, 6*, 31–42.

Daro, D., & Gelles, R. J. (1992). Public attitudes and behaviors with respect to child abuse prevention. *Journal of Interpersonal Violence, 7*, 517–531.

Daro, D., & McCurdy, K. (1994). Preventing child abuse and neglect: Programmatic interventions. *Child Welfare, 73*, 405–430.

Dix, T. (1991). The adaptive organization of parenting: Adaptive and maladaptive processes. *Psychological Bulletin, 110*, 3–25.

Dodge, K. A., Pettit, G. S., & Bates, J. E. (1994). Effects of physical maltreatment on the development of peer relations. *Development and Psychopathology, 6*, 43–55.

Dumas, J. E., LaFreniere, P. J., & Serketich, W. J. (1995). "Balance of power": A transactional analysis of control in mother–child dyads involving socially competent, aggressive, and anxious children. *Journal of Abnormal Psychology, 104*, 104–113.

Dumas, J. E., & Wekerle, C. (1995). Maternal reports of child behavior problems and personal distress as predictors of dysfunctional parenting. *Development and Psychopathology, 7*, 465–479.

Dutton, D. G. (1994). *The domestic assault of women: Psychological and criminal justice perspectives.* Vancouver, Canada: UBC Press.

Dutton, D. G. (1995). Trauma-symptoms and PTSD-like profiles in perpetrators of intimate abuse. *Journal of Traumatic Stress, 8*, 299–316.

Earls, F., Cairns, R. B., & Mercy, J. A. (1993). The control of violence and the promotion of nonviolence in adolescents. In S. G. Millstein, A. C. Petersen & E. O. Nightingale (Eds.), *Promoting the health of adolescents: New directions for the twenty-first century* (pp. 285–304). New York: Oxford University Press.

Eccles, J. S., Midgley, C., Wigfield, A., Buchanan, C. M., Reuman, D., Flanagan, C., & MacIver, D. (1993). Development during adolescence: The impact of stage–environment fit on young adolescents' experiences in the schools and in families. *American Psychologist, 48*, 90–101.

Emery, R. E. (1989). Family violence. *American Psychologist, 44*, 321–328.

Erickson, M. F., Sroufe, L. A., & Egeland, B. (1985). The relationship between quality of attachment and relationship problems in preschool in a high-risk sample. *Monographs of the Society for Research in Child Development, 50* (Serial No. 209).

Febbraro, A. R. (1994). Single mothers "at risk" for child maltreatment: An appraisal of person-centred interventions and a call for emancipatory action. *Canadian Journal of Community Mental Health, 13*, 47–60.

Furman, W., & Buhrmester, D. (1985). Children's perceptions of the personal relationships in their social networks. *Developmental Psychology, 21*, 1014–1024.

Furman, W., & Buhrmester, D. (1992). Age and sex differences in perceptions of networks of personal relationships. *Child Development, 63*, 103–115.

Furman, W., & Wehner, E. A. (1992). Romantic views: Toward a theory of adolescent romantic relationships. In R. Montemayor (Ed.), *Advances in adolescent development: Vol. 3. Relationships in adolescence.* Beverly Hills, CA: Sage.

Garbarino, J. (1977). The human ecology of child maltreatment: A conceptual model for research. *Journal of Marriage and the Family, 39*, 721–735.

Gelles, R. J. (1992). Poverty and violence towards children. *American Behavioral Scientist, 35*, 258–274.

George, C., Kaplan, N., & Main, M. (1985). *The Adult Attachment Interview.* Unpublished manuscript, University of California at Berkeley, Department of Psychology.

Griffin, D., & Bartholomew, K. (1994). Models of the self and other: Fundamental dimensions underlying measures of adult attachment. *Journal of Personality and Social Psychology, 67*, 430–445.

Hartlage, S., Alloy, L. B., Vazquez, C., & Dykman, B. (1993). Automatic and effortful processing in depression. *Psychological Bulletin, 113*, 247–278.

Hazan, C., & Shaver, P. (1987). Romantic love conceptualized as an attachment process. *Journal of Personality and Social Psychology, 52*, 511–524.

Hazan, C., & Shaver, P. R. (1994). Attachment as an organizational framework for research on close relationships. *Psychological Inquiry, 5*, 1–22.

Heineman, L. (1992). Seeking a good enough mirror: Art therapy and mirroring in a prevention program's parent training group. *Pratt Institute Creative Arts Therapy Review, 13*, 23–30.

Hotaling, G. T., & Sugarman, D. B. (1986). An analysis of risk markers in husband to wife violence: The current state of knowledge. *Violence and Victims, 1,* 101–124.

Jaffe, P., Wolfe, D. A., & Wilson, S. (1990). *Children of battered women.* Thousand Oaks, CA: Sage.

Jones, E. D., & McCurdy, K. (1992). The links between types of maltreatment and demographic characteristics of children. *Child Abuse & Neglect, 16,* 201–215.

Kaufman, J., & Zigler, E. (1987). Do abused children become abusive parents? *American Journal of Orthopsychiatry, 57,* 186–192.

Kaufman, J., & Zigler, E. (1989). The intergenerational transmission of child abuse and the prospect of predicting future abusers. In D. Cicchetti & V. Carlson (Eds.), *Child maltreatment: Research and theory on the causes and consequences of child abuse and neglect* (pp. 129–150). New York: Cambridge University Press.

Lang, P. J. (1995). The emotion probe: Studies of motivation and attention. *American Psychologist, 50,* 372–385.

Laursen, B., & Collins, W. A. (1994). Interpersonal conflict during adolescence. *Psychological Bulletin, 115,* 197–209.

Lyons-Ruth, K., & Zeanah, C. H., Jr. (1993). The family context of infant mental health: I. Affective development in the primary caregiving relationship. In C. H. Zeanah, Jr. (Ed.), *Handbook of infant mental health* (pp. 14–37). New York: Guilford Press.

MacKinnon, C. E., Lamb, M. E., Belsky, J., & Baum, C. (1990). An affective–cognitive model of mother–child aggression. *Development and Psychopathology, 2,* 1–13.

Main, M., & George, C. (1985). Responses of abused and disadvantaged toddlers to distress in agemates: A study in the day care setting. *Developmental Psychology, 21,* 407–412.

Malamuth, N. M., Sockloskie, R. J., Koss, M. P., & Tanaka, J. S. (1991). Characteristics of aggressors against women: Testing a model using a national sample of college students. *Journal of Consulting and Clinical Psychology, 59,* 670–681.

Martin, B. (1990). The transmission of relationship difficulties from one generation to the next. *Journal of Youth and Adolescence, 19,* 181–199.

Marx, B. P., Van Wie, V., & Gross, A. M. (1996). Date rape risk factors: A review and methodological critique of the literature. *Aggression and Violent Behavior, 1,* 27–45.

Mash, E. J., Johnston, C., & Kovitz, K. (1983). A comparison of the mother–child interactions of physically abused and non-abused children during play and task situations. *Journal of Clinical Child Psychology, 12,* 337–346.

Melton, G. B., & Barry, F. D. (1994). Neighbors helping neighbors: The vision of the U.S. Advisory Board on Child Abuse and Neglect. In G. B. Melton & F. D. Barry (Eds.), *Protecting children from abuse and neglect: Foundations for a new national strategy* (pp. 1–13). New York: Guilford Press.

Milner, J. S. (1993). Social information processing and physical child abuse. *Clinical Psychology Review, 13*, 275–294.

Murphy, C. M., Meyer, S., & O'Leary, K. D. (1994). Dependency characteristics of partner assaultive men. *Journal of Abnormal Psychology, 103*, 729–735.

Olds, D., Henderson, C., Chamberlin, R., & Tatelbaum, R. (1986). Preventing child abuse and neglect: A randomized trial of nurse home visitation. *Pediatrics, 78*, 65–78.

Olds, D., Henderson, C. R., & Kitzman, H. (1994). Does prenatal and infancy nurse home visitation have enduring effects on qualities of parental care giving and child health at 25 to 50 months of life? *Pediatrics, 93*, 89–98.

Olds, D., & Kitzman, H. (1993). Review of research on home visiting for pregnant women and parents of young children. *The Future of Children, 3*, 53–92.

Olds, D., Kitzman, H., Cole, B., & Robinson, J. (1997). Theoretical foundations of a program of home visitation for pregnant women and parents of young children. *Journal of Community Psychology, 25*, 9–25.

O'Leary, K. D., Malone, J., & Tyree, A. (1994). Physical aggression in early marriage: Prerelationship and relationship effects. *Journal of Consulting and Clinical Psychology, 62*, 594–602.

Pence, E., & Paymar, M. (1993). *Education groups for men who batter: The Duluth model.* New York: Springer.

Peterson, L. (1996, November). *Prevention and treatment of child abuse and neglect: In-depth intervention for parental vulnerability.* Workshop presented at the annual meeting of the Association for the Advancement of Behavior Therapy, New York.

Prochaska, J., DiClemente, C., & Norcross, J. (1992). In search of how people change. *American Psychologist, 47*, 1102–1114.

Quinton, D., Pickles, A., Maughan, B., & Rutter, M. (1993). Partners, peers, and pathways: Assortative pairing and continuities in conduct disorder. *Development and Psychopathology, 5*, 763–783.

Rieder, C., & Cicchetti, D. (1989). Organizational perspective on cognitive control functioning and cognitive–affective balance in maltreated children. *Developmental Psychology, 25*, 382–393.

Schneider-Rosen, K., & Cicchetti, D. (1991). Early self-knowledge and emotional development: Visual self-recognition and affective reactions to mirror self-image in maltreated and nonmaltreated toddlers. *Developmental Psychology, 27*, 471–478.

Schwartz, C. E., Snidman, N., & Kagan, J. (1996). Early childhood temperament as a determinant of externalizing behavior in adolescence. *Development and Psychopathology, 8*, 527–537.

Sroufe, L. A. (1989). Pathways to adaptation and maladaptation: Psychopathology as developmental deviation. In D. Cicchetti (Ed.), *Rochester Symposium on Developmental Psychopathology: Vol. 1. The emergence of a discipline* (pp. 13–40). Hillsdale, NJ: Erlbaum.

Straus, M. A., & Gelles, R. J. (Eds.). (1990). *Physical violence in American families*. New Brunswick, NJ: Transaction Books.

Suderman, M., & Jaffe, P. (1993, August). Dating violence among a sample of 1567 high school students. In D. Wolfe (Chair), *Violence in adolescent relationships: Identifying risk factors and prevention methods*. Symposium conducted at the annual convention of the American Psychological Association, Toronto, Canada.

Van den Boom, D. C. (1994). The influence of temperament and mothering on attachment and exploration: An experimental manipulation of sensitive responsiveness among lower-class mothers with irritable infants. *Child Development, 65*, 1457–1477.

Van den Boom, D. C. (1995). Do first-year intervention effects endure? Follow-up during toddlerhood of a sample of Dutch irritable infants. *Child Development, 66*, 1798–1816.

Van Ijzendoorn, M. H., Juffer, F., & Duyvesteyn, M. G. C. (1995). Breaking the intergenerational cycle of insecure attachment: A review of the effects of attachment-based interventions on maternal sensitivity and infant security. *Journal of Child Psychology and Psychiatry, 36*, 225–248.

Vasta, R. (1982). Physical child abuse: A dual-component analysis. *Developmental Review, 2*, 125–149.

Wahler, R. G., & Dumas, J. E. (1989). Attentional problems in dysfunctional mother–child interactions: An interbehavioral model. *Psychological Bulletin, 105*, 116–130.

Walker, L. E. A. (1989). Psychology and violence against women. *American Psychologist, 44*, 695–702.

Wallerstein, N. (1992). Powerlessness, empowerment, and health: Implications for health promotion programs. *American Journal of Health Promotion, 6*, 197–205.

Waters, E., Posada, G., Crowell, J., & Lay, K. (1993). Is attachment theory ready to contribute to our understanding of disruptive behavior problems? *Development and Psychopathology, 5*, 215–224.

Wekerle, C., & Wolfe, D. A. (1993). Prevention of child physical abuse and neglect: Promising new directions. *Clinical Psychology Review, 13*, 501–540.

Wekerle, C., & Wolfe, D. A. (1996). Child abuse and neglect. In E. J. Mash & R. A. Barclay (Eds.), *Child psychopathology*. New York: Guilford Press.

Wekerle, C., & Wolfe, D. A. (in press). The role of child maltreatment and attachment style in adolescent relationship violence. *Development and Psychopathology*.

Widom, C. S. (1989). Does violence beget violence? A critical examination of the literature. *Psychological Bulletin, 106*, 3–28.

Wolfe, D. A. (1985). Child abusive parents: An empirical review and analysis. *Psychological Bulletin, 97*, 462–482.

Wolfe, D. A. (1987). *Child abuse: Implications for child development and psychopathology*. Newbury Park, CA: Sage.

Wolfe, D. A., Reitzel-Jaffe, D., Gough, R., & Wekerle, C. (1994). *The conflicts in relationships: Measuring physical and sexual coercion among youth.* Available from the Youth Relationships Project, Department of Psychology, University of Western Ontario, London, Canada, N6A 5C2.

Wolfe, D. A., & Wekerle, C. (1993). Treatment strategies for child physical abuse and neglect: A critical progress report. *Clinical Psychology Review, 13,* 473–500.

Wolfe, D. A., Wekerle, C., Gough, R., Reitzel-Jaffe, D., Grasley, C., & Pittman, A. (1996). *The youth relationships manual: A group approach to ending woman abuse and promoting healthy relationships.* Newbury Park, CA: Sage.

Wolfe, D. A., Wekerle, C., Reitzel-Jaffe, D., & Gough, R. (1995). Strategies to address violence in the lives of high-risk youth. In E. Peled, P. G. Jaffe, & J. L. Edelson (Eds.), *Ending the cycle of violence: Community responses to children of battered women* (pp. 255–274). Newbury Park, CA: Sage.

Wolfe, D. A., Wekerle, C., Reitzel-Jaffe, D., Grasley, C., Pittman, A., & McEachran, A. (1997). Interrupting the cycle of violence: Empowering youth to promote healthy relationships. In D. Wolfe, R. McMahon, & R. Dev. Peters (Eds.), *Child abuse: New directions in prevention and treatment across the life span.* Newbury Park, CA: Sage.

Wolfe, D. A., Wekerle, C., Reitzel-Jaffe, D., & Lefebvre, L. (in press). Factors associated with abusive relationships among maltreated and non-maltreated youth. *Development and Psychopathology.*

Wolfe, D. A., Wekerle, C., & Scott, K. (1997). *Alternatives to violence: Empowering youth to develop healthy relationships.* Newburg Park, CA: Sage.

15

PREVENTING YOUTH VIOLENCE THROUGH RESEARCH-GUIDED INTERVENTION

RONALD G. SLABY

After more than 50 years of behavioral science research on the development and regulation of aggressive and violent behavior, we know that violence does not simply appear mysteriously and full blown in adolescence. Rather, the social habits and internal resources that children develop in the early years often set them on a pathway either toward greater involvement with violence or toward nonviolent and socially constructive behavior. If left untreated, these pathways may guide children for years to come.

Although involvement with violence is currently a common and repeated pattern for many U.S. children, this pattern can be changed or prevented. Violence can be largely prevented through the early, systematic, and coordinated application of violence prevention interventions that are guided by research. In this chapter, I will describe (a) an emerging discipline focused on violence prevention, (b) a national plan for preventing violence, (c) a central strategy for organizing violence prevention initiatives, and (d) a variety of specific research-guided interventions designed to reduce or prevent violence and aimed at juvenile offenders, middle school children, young children, families, media users, student athletes, and communities.

CREATING A NEW DISCIPLINE

To generate a strategic national plan for the prevention of violence in the United States, the Centers for Disease Control and Prevention (CDC) in 1990 assembled a cross-disciplinary panel of 20 professionals, of which I was a member. In facing this daunting task, the members of this panel envisioned the creation of a new discipline of violence prevention. This new discipline would unite the best research and practice from the fields of behavioral science, public health, criminal justice, and education, integrating each of these individual disciplines to create a superordinate discipline that would be greater than the sum of its parts. To create the new discipline of violence prevention, researchers and investigators from each area would need to develop and implement solutions to the problem of violence by building a bridge between the two most important kinds of knowledge: *evidence* derived from scientific research and *wisdom* derived from innovative practice. Either type of knowledge alone would be inadequate for solving the problem of violence. Research evidence uninformed by the wisdom of practitioners is often inapplicable, and personal wisdom not grounded in scientific evidence and objective evaluation is often misguided. Only by linking evidence with wisdom across fields of expertise could this panel develop a promising national plan for the prevention of violence.

The panel, chaired by Felton J. Earls, proceeded to develop the national plan in several steps. First, the panel integrated the two background papers that had been specially written for it on the prevention of self-destructive violence (e.g., attempted and completed suicide; Spirito, 1990) and the prevention of interpersonal violence (e.g., assault, homicide, and other violent behaviors directed toward others; Slaby, 1990). Next, the panel members repeatedly revised the preliminary plan, on the basis of input from panel members and from the staffs of 14 federal agencies. The revised plan was presented to the Third National Injury Control Conference in Denver in the form of a preconference position paper. Finally, the members further revised this national plan on the basis of conference feedback and input solicited from hundreds of expert reviewers from a wide range of related fields. The final plan for preventing "intentional" injury and death from violence in the United States (Earls, Slaby, & Spirito, 1992) was presented, together with plans for preventing six forms of "unintentional" injury (injuries related to motor vehicles, injuries related to home and leisure activities, occupational injuries, and injuries associated with trauma care systems, acute care, and rehabilitation), in *Injury Control:*

Position Papers From the Third National Injury Control Conference: Setting the National Agenda for Injury Control in the 1990's. Summaries of, and excerpts from, these papers have also been published in a wide variety of journals and in various forms (e.g., Centers for Disease Control; CDC, 1993; Rosenberg, O'Carroll, & Powell, 1992).

In presenting this national plan for the prevention of violence to the Senate Committee on Governmental Affairs, chaired by Senator John Glenn, the panel members deliberately focused on explicit solutions to the problem of violence (Slaby, 1992). The plan was further supported at these hearings by testimony from the Government Accounting Office (GAO), in which it was estimated that $6–$8 could be saved for every dollar spent investing in violence prevention programs with accountability (McDonald, 1992). This estimate was based on results of the moderately effective violence prevention programs that already existed. Even greater savings would be possible if the effectiveness of current programs were improved through research.

Despite the financial arguments in support of violence prevention programs with accountability, the United States spends an estimated 94% of federal funds for violence not on prevention but on waiting for violence to happen and then reacting to it (McDonald, 1992), primarily by attempting to apprehend, convict, sentence, place on probation, imprison, and parole perpetrators of violence. Little of the money spent after violence occurs is spent on treatment for violent offenders, and most treatment programs deal only with problems of drug abuse and not with violence. Since the 1980s, the prison population in the United States has nearly tripled and the problem of violence continues to plague U.S. society. It is not surprising that the recidivism rate for violent offenders is high. In addition to the enormous human costs (e.g., fear, injury, loss of life, suffering, grief) of this ineffective, reactive approach to violence, the financial cost per individual exceeds that of sending someone to Harvard or Yale each year. Clearly, changing priorities in spending regarding violence would result in a "smart money" policy, and it would serve the vital interests of the country.

Within a year after the CDC national plan called for the formation of a new discipline of violence prevention, former U.S. surgeon general C. Everett Koop declared the prevention of violence a public health emergency, and key presidential cabinet members echoed and advanced the CDC summons. Attorney General Janet Reno, Secretary of Health and Human Services Donna Shalala, Secretary of Education Richard Riley, and drug czar Lee Brown shared a stage with prominent behavioral scientists in a national town meeting broadcast on satellite television in July of 1993. They called for the creation of a new discipline with a shared strategy based on a reprioritization of federal spending to prevent violence.

Not all individuals in policymaking positions are in favor of implementing programs to prevent violence, however. Many politicians are prepared instead to serve an alternative agenda based on fear, punishment, and ineffective political strategies. For example, one Senate staff member summed up this political agenda by declaring that "the war on drugs is over—the war on violence has begun." This statement is misleading in several ways. The "war on drugs" is not over. The war on drugs, as it has been carried out, has directly added to the problem of violence. The concept of a "war on violence" is an irony that defines the problem in a way that defies solution.

If U.S. citizens permit political representatives to define national strategy as a "war on violence," it is likely that millions of dollars and many years will be spent generating more heat than light on this issue, until someone finally proposes the ultimate simplistic and ineffective solution: "Just say no to violence." Instead, it is necessary to reject political agendas and quick fixes in favor of building a sound and effective educational agenda for treating and preventing violence that will provide a lasting solution.

DEVELOPING A NATIONAL PLAN

The CDC panel's recommendations focused on four tasks that could have a major impact on the prevention of death and injury from violence: (a) building an infrastructure, (b) reducing violence from firearms, (c) reducing violence associated with alcohol and other drugs, and (d) providing childhood experiences that help to prevent violence (Earls et al., 1992). Overall, this national plan directly challenges psychologists to use research formulations, methods, and findings to develop and implement effective initiatives to help prevent youth violence. To contribute most effectively to the emerging discipline of violence prevention, psychologists will need to work together with members of other disciplines to develop new definitions, partnerships, perspectives, applications, and roles that can advance the understanding, treatment, and prevention of violence (Slaby & Eron, 1994).

Building an Infrastructure

Building an infrastructure for the prevention of violence means making prevention a funding priority; connecting disciplines; working collaboratively to generate prevention programs; improving recognition, referral, and treatment of high-risk individuals; and developing better professional training, surveillance methods and data, and accountability. The process of building such an infrastructure has already begun, although political appeals to public fear and quick fixes often retard or undermine this process.

Reducing Violence From Firearms

A reduction in gun violence would save many lives and substantially reduce injuries. Research suggests that firearms violence may be reduced through a variety of interventions, including limiting access of youths to guns, establishing and enforcing registration and restrictive licensing of gun owners, educating the public about the risks of gun ownership, promoting safe storage and removal of guns from homes, imposing special excise taxes on guns and ammunition, developing better techniques for enforcing existing legislation and regulations, creating safety standards for domestically manufactured and imported guns and ammunition, and promoting technological advances in providing security without firearms (e.g., Earls et al., 1992; National Committee for Injury Prevention & Control, 1989; O'Carroll et al., 1991).

Increases in the access to, and use of, firearms (particularly handguns) have contributed to major increases in violent death and injury among U.S. youths. Guns were used in 8 out of 10 homicides committed by juveniles, and the number of gun-related murders rose threefold between 1984 and 1991 (Snyder & Sickmund, 1995). The use of firearms turns ordinary altercations into fatal or severely injurious incidents. For example, U.S. citizens are no more likely to get into fights than are Canadians living in comparable urban settings that differ primarily in their gun-control policies. However, people in the United States are much more likely to die or be severely injured during those fights, owing almost entirely to the greater use of guns (Sloan et al., 1988). In stark contrast to policies of other developed countries in the world, U.S. legislative, regulatory, and enforcement policies fail to prevent guns from being readily accessible to children and youths as well as to adults. Absent are adequate manufacturing standards, safety features, regulatory oversight, law enforcement, licensing requirements, user education, and corrective treatment for violators. Under these circumstances, a gun in the hands of a youth is a formula for a violent death or injury.

Reducing Violence Associated With Drugs

Reducing violence associated with alcohol and other drugs is an important part of a national plan to reduce injuries and deaths. The phrase "alcohol and other drugs" (AOD) begins with alcohol and explicitly includes alcohol in the category of drugs because alcohol is probably the drug that makes the greatest contribution to the problem of violence. Alcohol consumption is associated with an increased risk of becoming either a victim or a perpetrator of violence. The second greatest drug contribution to violence may come from the trafficking of illegal drugs, usually by youths who carry guns and serve as "enemy" on the front lines in U.S. society's "war on drugs." The third greatest drug contribution comes from illegal drug users, whose clouded judgment, impulsive behavior, and need to support their addictions may lead to violence (National Committee for Injury Prevention and Control, 1989). Violence associated with AOD can be reduced through education of the public and professionals about the association between AOD and violence, conducting research to clarify further the mechanisms underlying the observed association between AOD and violence, decreasing the initial and experimental use of alcohol and other drugs by youth, identifying and treating chronic users of AOD who are at high risk for violent behavior, and changing the environmental factors that contribute to violence through the sale and trafficking of AOD.

Providing Childhood Experiences That Help to Prevent Violence

Providing such experiences may be the key to building an effective and lasting national strategy. Patterns of involvement with violence—or, alternatively, nonviolent, socially constructive patterns of behavior—are acquired by children through specific and alterable processes of socialization and development. A key to preventing violence lies in reducing social experiences that serve as "violence toxins" while building the internal resources that strengthen children's "immune system" against violence. This part of the national plan presents an educational challenge to those who deal with children and their families. It challenges educators to teach, parents to socialize, professionals to guide, the media to serve, and policymakers to support children and their families in developing the skills, beliefs, and behaviors that can provide them with effective alternatives to violence. In addition, it challenges socializing agents to help children develop the patterns of thought and action that will equip them to become the violence preventers of the next generation (Slaby, 1993a, 1997).

SYNTHESIZING PSYCHOLOGICAL RESEARCH AND PRACTICE

Because psychology was the first discipline to bring the study of violence and injury into the realm of science—more than 50 years ago—it was appropriate that the American Psychological Association (APA) took an early initiative to address the national problem of violence involving youths. In 1991 the APA established the Commission on Violence and Youth, chaired by Leonard D. Eron, for the purpose of reviewing and synthesizing the research formulations, findings, and applications that could help professionals to deal effectively with the problems of youth violence. The 12-member commission was strongly supported by a 130-member cadre of experts and by an experienced group of contributing authors, staff members, and consultants. The commission also sought input and feedback on early formulations and draft reports through open hearings, plenary sessions, conference presentations, and meetings with representatives of a variety of federal agencies and APA working groups. The commission's work is available in the form of a summary report, entitled *Violence and Youth: Psychology's Response* (APA, 1993), and in a book presenting scholarly review chapters, entitled *Reason to Hope: A Psychosocial Perspective on Violence and Youth* (Eron, Gentry, & Schlegel, 1994). More recently, a report entitled *Violence in the Family* was produced by an APA presidential task force established to address this problem (APA, 1996).

Together, these documents overwhelmingly affirm a message of hope—that the knowledge and the means are available for beginning to deliver to the youths of the nation both the social experiences and the internal resources that can prepare them to deal effectively with the violence they face today and to become effective violence preventers in the future (Slaby, 1993b). A central conclusion of these APA commission's reports is that

> violence is learned. Therefore, it can be unlearned or conditions can be changed so that it is not learned in the first place. The earlier we intervene, the easier it is to prevent or change learned patterns of violence—but it's never too late. (APA, 1993, p. x)

This conclusion has become a central organizing theme for a wide variety of interventions designed to prevent or treat violence. It provides a focal point—learning—from which to understand the problem and generate effective remedies. It also identifies developmental pathways leading to violence that may be redirected through early preventive intervention or later corrective treatment.

FORMULATING A CENTRAL STRATEGY

As a response to the creation of a new discipline, the development of a national plan for preventing violence, and the synthesis of psychological research and practice, a central strategy for the prevention of youth violence is beginning to emerge. This strategy is guided by several principles, formulated here as prescriptions: (a) Intervene early and preventively, (b) reduce social experiences that contribute to violence, (c) strengthen internal resources that protect against violence, and (d) coordinate strategies across social domains.

Intervene Early and Preventively

Patterns of violence develop early and last a long time. Violence does not simply appear, mysteriously and full blown, in an adolescent. Rather, children's patterns of involvement with violence often become established early and, if left untreated, guide them for years to come (APA, 1993; Pepler & Slaby, 1994). Although patterns of violence can be effectively altered through corrective treatment during adolescence and adulthood, intervention with children before adolescence may be particularly important for the following reasons:

First, *young children often become involved in severe levels of violence as victims, witnesses, and even perpetrators.* In 1992, 902 children 9 years of age or younger were murdered in the United States, representing a rate of 2.27 per 100,000 (Baker, Fingerhut, Higgins, Chen, & Braver, 1996). Homicides among young children have steadily increased each year from 1990 to 1994 (Federal Bureau of Investigation, 1996). Young children suffer more victimization than do adults (with the exception of homicide), when one considers physical punishments, sibling assaults, and bullying (Finkelhor & Dziuba-Leatherman, 1994). One recent finding of the National Institute of Mental Health Community Violence Project was that among children in the fifth and sixth grades in a high-risk community in Washington, D.C., 32% had been victimized by some form of violence, and 72% had witnessed violence to someone else or had viewed a dead body outside the home. Also, 45% of first and second graders in this community had witnessed muggings, 31% had witnessed shootings, and 39% had seen dead bodies (Richters & Martinez, 1993). In two separate studies performed in neighborhoods at high risk for violence, one in Denver (Huizinga, Loeber, & Thornberry, 1993) and the other in Pittsburgh (Huizinga, Loeber, & Thornberry, 1994), 10% of boys reported having committed at least one street crime (e.g., fighting, purse snatching, burglary, bicycle theft, theft from school) by age 7.

Second, *young children often show immediate debilitating effects of violence.* Victims of nonfatal violent attacks frequently suffer the immediate consequences of psychological injury, pain, and physical injury. Young children who witness violence may suffer similar consequences affecting the domains of cognitive, social, emotional, and psychological functioning. For example, children who witness violence may suffer a form of posttraumatic stress syndrome, and they often manifest symptoms associated with depression and anxiety, including withdrawal, extreme fear, affect dysregulation, blunted affect, dissociative reactions, difficulty in concentrating, intrusive thoughts, and flashbacks (Richters, 1993). Children who witness violence may also display other maladaptive social behaviors, such as tantrums, defiance, difficulty in cooperating with others, and increased aggression. These symptoms and behaviors, in turn, can diminish children's ability to form relationships and can lower their tolerance for violence as they grow to adulthood (Groves, 1994). Indeed, it is not only the reality, but also the fear, of violence that weighs heavily on children at a very early age. In one recent survey of children aged 7–10, consisting of 120 one-to-one interviews, the majority reported that their biggest worry was being shot or stabbed when they got older (Fairbank, Maslin, & Maulin, 1995).

Third, *young children's experience with violence, if left untreated, often has serious long-term effects.* Children who are victims of repeated physical punishment or abuse by parents or repeated bullying by peers often suffer long-term consequences, including depression, impaired self-esteem, and suicidal ideation (Olweus, 1993b; Straus, 1996). Persistent patterns of aggressive behavior among peers often leave both the repeat aggressor and the repeat victim with few or no positive, stable peer relationships, resulting in loneliness and lack of peer support for changing those patterns (Slaby, Roedell, Arezzo, & Hendrix, 1995; Slaby, Wilson-Brewer, & DeVos, 1994). Victims of peer aggression in early childhood are also likely to be repeatedly bullied or victimized by their peers, often throughout childhood (Olweus, 1993a; Patterson, Littman, & Bricker, 1967; Schwartz, Dodge, & Coie, 1994). Young victims of violence sometimes learn to become perpetrators of violence by responding to perceived threats with preemptive violent attacks, by retaliating against their victimizer, or by learning to use violence against others (McCord, 1983; Straus, 1991).

Indeed, physical abuse and neglect in early childhood have been found to lead to an increased risk of violent criminal behavior in adulthood (Widom, 1989a, 1989b). If left untreated, young children's early patterns of aggressive behavior are likely to (a) persist with increasing predictability from childhood into adulthood (Farrington, 1992; Huesmann, Eron, Lefkowitz, & Walder, 1984; Olweus, 1979), (b) broaden into a wider range of aggressive and violent behaviors (Patterson, Reid, & Dishion, 1992), and (c) escalate in level of severity (Loeber et al., 1993). Studies of violent youths have revealed a developmental sequence of escalating aggressive behaviors toward peers. Typically, violence-prone children progress from the first step of verbally harassing or bullying others; to the second step of fighting with individuals or gangs; to the third step of attacking, strong-arming, or forcing sex on someone (Loeber et al., 1993). As children develop into adolescents, they become more able and more likely to commit serious delinquent and violent acts, owing to their increased physical ability and mobility as well as their greater access to weapons, drugs, and delinquent peers (Snyder & Sickmund, 1995).

Fourth, *intervention with young children holds the promise of clear and lasting effects.* Although it is never too late to intervene to change a child's patterns of behavior, it appears to be easier to change these patterns by intervening early. The early years may present the greatest opportunity to coordinate a child's social domains, reduce the social experiences that contribute to violence, and build internal resources that protect against violence. Because children's patterns of involvement with violence often are learned at an early age and persist into later years, intervention in the early years may be particularly effective both for nonviolent, well-functioning children and for children who are becoming involved with violence as aggressors, victims, or bystanders who passively support or actively encourage violence. Although long-term research evidence is limited, it appears that systematic and consistent intervention, beginning in the early years when children are most malleable and continuing into adolescence, holds great promise for preventing violence by guiding children along a developmental pathway toward healthy and nonviolent life choices (APA, 1993; Grossman et al., 1997; Hendrix & Molloy, 1990; Olweus, 1993a; Pepler & Slaby, 1994; Slaby et al., 1995; Yoshikawa, 1994).

Reduce Social Experiences That Contribute to Violence

A number of social experiences may contribute to children's risk of becoming involved with violence, either as aggressors, as victims, or as bystanders who support and contribute to violence. Although each risk factor can be seen as a "violence toxin" that contributes to an individual's involvement with violence, none leads inevitably to violence. The relationship is analogous to that of smoking and cancer: Many smokers will not get lung cancer, and many lung cancer victims have not smoked. However, it is known that the risk factors are clear contributing causes of the disease, and each risk factor may combine with other causal risk factors to multiply the effects. Therefore, one way to prevent violence is to reduce children's exposure to risk factors. In addition to the factors of access to firearms and to AOD, a variety of other risk factors serve as "violence toxins," including (a) experiencing violence; (b) witnessing violence; (c) viewing or interacting with media violence; (d) experiencing socioeconomic inequality; and (e) experiencing discrimination, verbal abuse, or harassment.

Experiencing violence through child abuse, bullying, assault, rape, or battering elevates the risk that a child will become involved in violence as a repeat victim or perpetrator. The experience of early physical abuse and neglect is a predictor of violent criminal behavior in adulthood, even though the effects are not inevitable. In a study that directly tested this relationship, it was found that most individuals (89%) who had court records of abuse or neglect in childhood did not have criminal records for violence as adults but that individuals who experienced abuse or neglect in childhood were 42% more likely than others to have such criminal records as adults (Widom, 1989a).

Witnessing violence in one's home or community, apart from experiencing it directly, is also a risk factor for becoming a perpetrator or a victim of violence. Effects of exposure to violence include increased aggressive behavior, poor achievement, anxiety, fearfulness, social isolation, depression, and emotional distress (Bell & Jenkins, 1991). In some homes and communities, children's risk of exposure to violence is enormous (e.g., Richters & Martinez, 1993). Some programs have focused on reducing children's exposure to real-life violence and helping them deal more effectively with the psychological effects of the violence they have witnessed.

Viewing or interacting with media violence is an important risk factor for involvement with real-life violence, particularly because the media generally portray violence in unrealistic, misleading, and glorified ways. Media violence contributes to several different effects, including (a) increased meanness, aggression, and even serious violent behavior; (b) increased fear, mistrust, and self-protective behavior, such as carrying a gun; (c) increased emotional desensitization, cognitive callousness, and behavioral apathy toward victims of violence; and (d) increased appetite for further exposure to violence (Donnerstein, Slaby, & Eron, 1994). Despite the pervasiveness of media violence, its effects can be reduced by controlling exposure and by teaching the critical skills needed to "see through" the unrealistic and glorified portrayals of violence (Slaby et al., 1995).

Experiencing socioeconomic inequality (e.g., living under survival conditions while others have plenty) is a more precise risk factor for involvement with violence than poverty alone. In the 1980s the United States underwent the largest shift of wealth during any decade in its history, a shift of resources from the middle class and the poor to the wealthy, thereby further widening the enormous gap representing socioeconomic inequality. When social conditions of poverty (e.g., crowded housing) combine with social disorganization (e.g., inadequate security and law enforcement) and social injustice (e.g., lack of opportunity to change one's circumstances), the conditions are particularly volatile for violence (APA, 1993; Hill et al., 1994).

Experiencing discrimination, verbal abuse, or harassment because of membership in a social group (discriminatory practices on the basis of race, religion, ethnic group, gender, or sexual orientation) is a risk factor for involvement with violence. If children are permitted or encouraged to develop prejudices and use hate speech, violent hate crimes often follow (APA, 1993; Hill, Soriano, Chen, & La Fromboise, 1994).

Strengthen Internal Resources That Protect Against Violence

Beyond reducing children's exposure to risk factors, educators and parents can help to prevent violence by strengthening children's psychological immunity and resilience. Each child's susceptibility to risk factors is related to the strength of this "immune system." Children develop patterns of thought about how to solve social problems and about what role violent and nonviolent alternatives may play in solving those problems. These patterns of thought often become nonmindful, habitual, and rather automatic—used as an individual's "default mode"—particularly in highly arousing and ambiguous situations. Through various phases of development, highly aggressive children have been found to differ dramatically from their less aggressive peers in their patterns of thought (Dodge & Frame, 1982; Guerra & Slaby, 1989; Perry, Perry, & Rasmussen, 1986; Slaby & Guerra, 1988). These patterns are measurable, and they become increasingly individualized and stable with development. However, researchers have shown that habits of thought can be altered through direct intervention (e.g., Slaby & Guerra, 1988) and that such changes may lead to corresponding reductions in subsequent violent behavior (Kazdin, 1987; Guerra & Slaby, 1990).

For example, learned "habits of thought" have been found to differ markedly for aggressive and nonaggressive children (Guerra & Slaby, 1989), as well as for violent juvenile offenders and their nonviolent peers (Slaby & Guerra, 1988). Aggressive and violent individuals usually lack skills in solving social problems effectively (cognitive process), hold beliefs that support the use of violence (cognitive content), and respond to situations impulsively (cognitive style; Slaby, 1996). Although these habits of thought leave violent individuals highly vulnerable to the "violence toxins," these individuals can be taught through structured interventions to change their patterns of thought, leading to reductions in their subsequent aggressive behaviors (Guerra & Slaby, 1990; Slaby, Wilson-Brewer, & DeVos, 1994).

Some 5-year-old children who experienced physical abuse at home were found to violently attack other children in the kindergarten classroom, whereas others who also experienced physical abuse at home did not (Dodge, Bates, & Pettit, 1990). What differentiates the individuals who succumb to the "violence toxin" of physical abuse from those who do not? The children who broke the cycle of violence and did not turn their own victimization experience into an attack on others were those who had acquired the cognitive skills needed to solve problems in alternative, nonviolent ways: those who had developed a strong "immune system" with which to neutralize the "violence toxins."

The successful bully or batterer may coerce the victim into adopting habits of thought that are as psychologically destructive for the victim as the physical harm that the victim endures. For example, although in almost every difficult situation there may be dozens of options that can solve the problem nonviolently and effectively, the victim may come to believe that there are only two responses to the threat or use of violence: to submit or attack first. Unless potential victims learn to think of and use the many nonviolent and effective ways to respond to an aggressor, they risk being repeatedly victimized or becoming perpetrators of violence.

An individual's learned patterns of thought and emotional response enable him or her to succumb to, neutralize, or even counteract the impact of the social experiences that generally act as "violence toxins." This means that educators and parents can play a major role in preventing violence not only by reducing children's exposure to risk factors, but also by strengthening children's "immume system"—by teaching them the cognitive and emotional skills, beliefs, and behavioral strategies they can use to solve problems effectively and nonviolently (e.g., Hill et al., 1994; Pepler & Slaby, 1994; Slaby, 1997).

Coordinate Social Domains

Children learn their patterns of involvement with violence within the social domains of their families, the media, their schools, their peer groups, and their community groups. Each day children may interact with family members, view television, interact with teachers and classmates in school, play with their peers after school, and perhaps engage in community-based organizations such as boys' and girls' clubs. Because children typically navigate daily among each of these social domains, what they learn about violence within any one domain often carries over in their patterns of behavior to the other domains. Indeed, children's patterns of aggressive behavior have been found to be quite consistent from one social domain to another (Parke & Slaby, 1983).

Interventions are usually designed to affect children's experiences within one social domain, with little attention paid to the coordination of children's experiences across domains. However, the effectiveness of an intervention within any one domain of a child's daily life may depend on the extent to which other domains provide supportive or contradictory social experiences. For example, parents' violence prevention efforts are often undercut when these efforts are not supported or are directly contradicted by their children's experiences with media, peer groups, community groups, or schools (Anderson, 1997). Similarly, school-based or youth organization–based interventions may be less effective in changing the violence-supporting patterns of behavior for children who face daily violence in their families, media experiences, or peer groups. Therefore, an important aspect of effective violence prevention involves coordinating and interconnecting to help children make meaningful connections among their violence prevention experiences across the domains of family, media, school, peers, and community organizations.

INTERVENING TO PREVENT OR TREAT VIOLENCE

Guided by the preceding principles for effective intervention, researchers have developed a variety of interventions to prevent or treat violence among youths. The following sections provide examples.

Violent Juvenile Offenders: Viewpoints

Nancy Guerra, Ann Moore, and I developed an assessment-based treatment program for violent juvenile offenders with funds from California's Center for Law-Related Education. Our first step was to assess cognitive skills and beliefs supporting violence that were hypothesized to differentiate among three groups of adolescents: (a) juvenile offenders incarcerated in a maximum-security correctional facility for violent criminal acts (including assault and battery, robbery, rape, attempted murder, and murder); (b) high school students (with demographic characteristics similar to those of the offenders) who were rated by their teachers as high in their display of aggressive behavior; and (c) high school students rated as low in aggression. Findings indicated that the three groups differed substantially in both their specific skills in solving social problems and their generalized beliefs supporting the use of aggression. Violent offenders were most likely (and less aggressive students were least likely) to solve social problems by (a) defining problems in hostile ways, (b) adopting hostile goals, (c) seeking few additional facts, (d) generating alternative solutions, (e) anticipating few consequences of aggression, and (f) choosing few "best" and "second best" solutions that were rated as effective. Violent offenders were also most likely to hold beliefs supporting the use of violence, including the beliefs that (g) violence is a legitimate response, (h) violence increases one's self-esteem, (i) violence helps avoid a negative image, and (j) violence does not lead to suffering by the victim (Slaby & Guerra, 1988).

On the basis of these findings, my coworkers and I developed a cognitive mediation training program to address each of the cognitive factors found to differentiate the violent offenders from their nonoffender peers in high school. The curriculum and teacher guide, *Viewpoints: A Guide to Conflict Resolution and Decision Making for Adolescents* (Guerra, Moore, & Slaby, 1995), consists of 10 sessions designed to help violent offenders in small-group settings develop their skills in solving social problems and question their beliefs that support the use of aggression. Pilot research permitted a preliminary version of this program to be refined to enhance its relevance and ease of implementation.

To assess the effectiveness of this cognitive mediation training program in reducing violence-supporting cognitions and subsequent aggressive behavior, my associates and I carried out an intervention and outcome evaluation. Male and female violent offenders within the correctional facility were randomly assigned either to participate in the cognitive mediation training group, to participate in an attention control group (offering similar professional attention and group participation in a basic career skills–building program that did not involve cognitive mediation training), or to participate in a no-treatment control group. Compared to violent offenders in both control groups, those in the treatment group showed improvements in cognitive skills and beliefs, as well as directly related decreases in aggressive, impulsive, and inflexible behaviors within the institution, as rated by residential counselors who were blind to the treatment condition (Guerra & Slaby, 1990). We also found a tendency for violent offenders to delay violations of parole during the 2-year period following their release from the institution. The Viewpoints treatment program for violent juvenile offenders was presented to the U.S. Congress in a congressional briefing (Slaby, 1993b), and it was described in the public television series entitled *What Should We Do About Violence?* which first aired nationally in January of 1995 (Moyers, 1995).

Middle School Students: Aggressors, Victims, and Bystanders

A curricular intervention for middle school students entitled *Aggressors, Victims, and Bystanders: Thinking and Acting to Prevent Violence* was developed and evaluated over a 5-year period by the Education Development Center with funds from the Centers for Disease Control and Prevention (Slaby, Wilson-Brewer, & Dash, 1994). The primary aim of this project was to develop a violence prevention curriculum for broad use with middle school students in communities at high risk for violence. The strategy integrated a public health approach to primary prevention with behavioral science research on the development and control of aggression. The curriculum was designed to reduce violence by altering patterns of thought that support an individual's involvement with violence in the roles of aggressor, victim, and bystander. Unlike most other violence prevention curricula and strategies, which have traditionally focused exclusively on the aggressor, this intervention also addresses the separate but interrelated roles of victims and bystanders and suggests that all three players can build skills of thinking and acting to resolve problems nonviolently.

Aggressive children commonly show a tendency to act impulsively, hold beliefs that support the use of violence, and lack skills in solving social problems in thorough and effective ways. Although these habits of thought provide a strong and enduring basis for predicting an individual's risk for violence throughout his or her lifetime, they can be changed through curricular intervention. It also is known that aggressive children carefully and repeatedly select certain children as victims. Children who are repeatedly victimized also may develop habits of thought that put them at risk for involvement with violence. Because violent behaviors commonly occur in the presence of onlookers, the majority of children, who are neither aggressors nor victims, play an important bystander role that often influences whether violence will occur. Some bystanders support violence through their passive acceptance, instigation, or active encouragement, whereas others help to prevent violence through their withdrawal of support or preventive action.

The curriculum was developed and evaluated in three steps, each involving a specific method of research, supplemented by active and intense collaboration of expert advisors, teachers, and students. First, my colleagues and I conducted *basic research* to assess each student's cognitive skills, beliefs, and behavioral intents in relation to his or her peer-nominated tendency to become involved in conflict as an aggressor (e.g., pick fights), a victim (e.g., get picked on), or a bystander who supports aggression (e.g., encourages fights). Second, we developed a preliminary curriculum on the basis of our findings of key cognitive factors supporting violence, as well as on an extensive review of 33 related curricula. We then revised the preliminary curriculum on the basis of *formative research* designed to obtain specific feedback from teachers and students on factors such as its clarity, relevance, age-appropriateness, engagement, and practical usefulness. Finally, we conducted *outcome research* by implementing the preliminary curriculum with over 300 high-risk, inner-city early adolescents and evaluating its effectiveness, in comparison with a no-treatment control group, in reducing violence-enhancing patterns of thought and behavior. Findings provided limited support for the hypothesized effects of intervention. The curricular intervention led to changes in students' belief that violence is not a desirable response; their behavioral intent to resolve conflict without aggression, to seek relevant information, and to avoid conflict; and their self-rated behavior indicating withdrawal of bystander acceptance and encouragement of aggression.

The final report of this project (including its curriculum, measures, and findings) is available from the National Technical Information Service (Slaby, Wilson-Brewer, & DeVos, 1994). The *Aggressors, Victims, and Bystanders* curriculum is currently being used broadly. In Illinois, where the teaching of violence prevention in public high school and middle school is now required by law, this curriculum has been approved for use by the Commission for the Prevention of Violence. Training in the use of the curriculum is currently offered by the Education Development Center in Newton, Massachusetts, and by the Rocky Mountain Center for Health Promotion and Education in Denver, Colorado. The implementation of the curriculum in a junior high school classroom is the subject of a documentary entitled *Peaceful Solutions* currently airing on public television stations (Peters, 1997). This program is also available for teacher training in video format, accompanied by a teachers guide (Thirteen/WNET, 1997).

Young Children: Early Violence Prevention

A teacher's handbook for reducing aggression in young children was developed through a project at the Education Development Center that was jointly funded by the Florence V. Burden Foundation and the A. L. Mailman Family Foundations. The purpose of the handbook was to provide teachers of children 2–7 years of age with practical and effective strategies for reducing aggression among young children in groups and for preparing young children with the skills and strategies they need to prevent violence in their later lives.

To ensure that the violence prevention strategies derived from research were presented in a way that was most useful to teachers, a stepwise process involving formative evaluations was developed. First, several hundred research studies were identified, gathered, and reviewed. Second, a board of advisors reviewed the preliminary scope, organization, and strategy for developing the book and recommended additions and changes. Third, two panels of reviewers (located in Boston and Seattle), each composed of preschool or Head Start teachers, education coordinators, and early childhood development specialists, reviewed, rated, and critically evaluated a preliminary draft of the handbook. The preliminary handbook was then revised on the basis of feedback regarding its clarity, age-appropriateness, relevance, engagement, tone, and practical usefulness. Finally, the revised handbook was reviewed by a variety of expert researchers and practitioners in the field of early childhood education, and final revisions were made.

This handbook served as a starting point for the development of the book *Early Violence Prevention: Tools for Teachers of Young Children* (Slaby et al., 1995), published by the National Association for the Education of Young Children. This book presents preschool teachers, Head Start teachers, and other child care providers with practical and effective strategies for reducing aggression and preventing violence in a format that is broadly useful. These strategies, derived from research-based teaching techniques are known to be useful in early childhood programs to reduce violence, promote positive social interactions, and promote the resilience of children. Rather than developing a specific and delimited violence prevention curriculum for young children, my colleagues and I provided teachers with a set of practical tools that are based on solid research evidence supporting their effectiveness. In addition, an annotated resource list that includes curriculum materials was provided. Because not all the techniques will work well in every situation or with every child, each teacher needs to learn how to determine which technique to choose for a given purpose, how to apply it, how to adapt it to fit the needs and interests of a particular child or class, and how to modify the technique as circumstances change. In short, teachers are provided with the resources they need to infuse the best practices in early violence prevention into their daily interactions with young children.

Early Violence Prevention presents teachers with research findings and related teaching applications with which to address issues of violence in the following six major areas:

1. Teachers can prepare children to deal with the violence they may face in the outside world through a combination of strat-

egies. They can help children recognize violence and its consequences and provide them with a safe place to express their feelings and their fears. They can also address safety and self-protection issues with children and learn how to recognize and respond effectively to children's traumatic reactions to violence or abuse.

2. Teachers can organize their school environment to minimize violence. They can structure the physical and programmatic environment by arranging and reorganizing their physical space in the classroom and the playground, their materials, and their activities, with the goal of minimizing aggression.

3. Teachers can establish sound procedures to respond to violence in the classroom. They can respond effectively to aggressive behavior when facing routine incidents of conflict and aggression as well as when working with children who show repeated and severe problems with aggressive behavior.

4. Teachers can teach children the skills they need to solve their conflicts constructively. They can directly teach early violence prevention skills that children need for solving social problems, sharing, and interacting assertively and thoughtfully with others.

5. Teachers can help children learn nonviolent strategies from others. They can help children use their developing abilities to see connections between themselves and others and to learn from role models in the classroom and in the media.

6. Teachers can take steps to enhance the effectiveness of their violence prevention activities in the classroom by building partnerships with parents and with representatives from public schools, community organizations, and professional organizations. After reviewing the teaching tools presented throughout this book, teachers can use the tools to develop and implement a broad violence prevention plan for their school and community.

The fact that Early Violence Prevention provides teachers with a variety of potentially effective violence prevention tools to apply in the clasroom does not imply that teachers are automatons who implement new procedures simply because they read about them in print. Instead, teachers bring their own experiences, skills, and beliefs to the topic of violence prevention, some of which may interfere with the effective implementation of violence prevention programs. To address these potential obstacles to effective intervention, researchers initiated a project entitled Violence Prevention for Very Young Children, in which they developed and evaluated the effectiveness of a teacher-training video to motivate teachers to use research-guided violence prevention strategies (Doepel, 1995). Funded by the National Institute of Mental Health, the project of Echo Bridge Productions will assess the separate and combined effects of video and print methods of teacher training on preschool and Head Start teachers' "violence prevention efficacy" (e.g., generalized beliefs that they can help to prevent violence by applying sound research-guided procedures). The preliminary version of the teacher-training video was recently presented at the annual meeting of the National Association for the Education of Young Children (Slaby, Roedell, Doepel, Connell, & Healy, 1996).

Families: Pediatric Violence Prevention

Pediatricians and other health care providers can help parents and their children develop the habits of thought they need to protect themselves from violence and to take active measures to prevent future involvement with violence. Over the last 20 years, a violence prevention and treatment program has been developed in the pediatrics department of the East Boston Neighborhood Health Center. This facility is the major source of pediatric and adolescent health care for an inner-city island community of 35,000 mainly working-class white and Hispanic residents. The program was initiated by Dr. Peter Stringham after he reviewed city records and discovered that the single most frequent cause of early death among residents served by the health center was interpersonal violence. Over time, he developed a variety of practical methods for preventing violence for children and their families (Stringham & Weitzman, 1988).

In 1987, Stringham and I began to collaborate, using the "habits of thought" model of cognitive mediation and research-guided strategies to organize and further develop a variety of individual interventions and to incorporate them into the pediatric department's health supervision program (Slaby & Stringham, 1994). Guided by a developmental framework for addressing age-appropriate issues for the child and the family, the program focuses on such issues as access to firearms in the home, witnessing violence in the home and community, viewing media violence, using consistent and nonpunitive discipline, bullying, access to alcohol and other drugs, street fighting, partner abuse, and rape. To implement this program, pediatricians are trained to (a) take a thorough history of children's involvement with violence as aggressors, victims, bystanders, or nonviolent problem solvers; (b) educate parents about ways to help their children develop habits of thought and behavioral patterns that lead to nonviolent problem solving; and (c) provide follow-up visits to support the changes children and their parents make to help prevent violence.

Today, a staff of 8 doctors, 4 nurses, 2 nurse practitioners, and 12 support personnel administer the program in the health center, which processes 7,000 scheduled visits and 16,000 walk-in visits annually. By applying the "habits of thought" model and related role-playing techniques, staff members have increased their skills in providing violence prevention and treatment for children and their families. Building on the health center's central role in the community, the staff have also helped to make violence prevention a priority in neighborhood youth programs and in the schools.

In a related revision of health care training in the Boston area, curricula at Boston University Medical School, Tufts Medical School, and Harvard Medical School are currently being revised to provide students with extensive training and experience in dealing with issues of violence prevention and treatment (e.g., Boston Teaching Hospitals, 1996). For example, administrators at Harvard Medical School are currently attempting to integrate into the curriculum the recommendations from task force reports addressing the topics of weapons and gangs, teen dating and adolescent violence, elder abuse, batterers and their treatment, violence in the media, child abuse, sexual assault, domestic violence, hate crimes, and neurobiological contributions to violence (Harvard Medical School, 1996).

Media Users: Remedies for Media Violence

The Massachusetts Medical Society and its alliance, in cooperation with the Harvard Community Health Plan Foundation, the Education Development Center, and the National Foundation to Improve Television, organized a strategic planning conference in November of 1995 entitled Remedies for Media Violence. The purpose of this initiative was to provide a forum for 110 health professionals, educators, parents, community leaders, and members of the media to generate, disseminate, and advance specific remedies for media violence. Participants were divided into the following five strategic planning groups, each of which generated their top three remedies, rationales for these remedies, and action steps by which to accomplish the remedies: (a) media and business, (b) policy and regulation, (c) public health and education, (d) parent and teacher, and (e) community groups. Perhaps the most important aspect of this initiative was that it "brought together a diverse group of people and organizations to develop a concrete plan of action," according to Jeanne Gaz, president of the Massachusetts Medical Society Alliance ("Tackling TV Violence," 1996, p. 5).

To further the development of community partnerships and advance community education on media violence effects and remedies, the Massachusetts Medical Society and its alliance, together with the United Nations Children's Emergency Fund (UNICEF), the Children's Hospital, the Massachusetts Department of Public Health, the Education Development Center, the National Foundation to Improve Television, and Wheelock College, developed a community-wide educational campaign entitled Seeing Through Media Violence. This educational campaign focused on

December 15, 1996, UNICEF's International Children's Day of Broadcasting, which Carol Bellamy, executive director of UNICEF, had declared as a day for the television industry to institute a major worldwide campaign against violence (Bellamy, 1995). In addition to receiving cooperation from representatives of several stations in the Boston area, the group sent the following message to executives at several thousand television stations worldwide who were involved in the International Children's Day of Broadcasting:

> Television is a persistent and effective teacher—whether the lessons are taught by design or default. Television can continue to teach our children the unrealistic, misleading, and deadly lessons that have for decades fostered violence, fear, and desensitization—as research evidence has clearly confirmed. Or this teacher can design a new lesson plan that will serve the educational and informational needs of children throughout the world by teaching a broad variety of accurate, effective, and life-saving solutions to the problems of violence. Which television teacher will we choose to teach our children? The time to decide is upon us. (Slaby, 1996)

Student Athletes: Mentors in Violence Prevention

The Mentors in Violence Prevention (MVP) program was developed in 1993 by Northeastern University's Center for the Study of Sport in Society with funding from the Funds for Post Secondary Education program of the U.S. Department of Education. It has grown to become a major part of an AmeriCorp project entitled Athletes in Service to America. The purpose of the MVP program is to inspire and prepare student athletes to provide leadership in reducing men's violence against women (Katz, 1995). The program defines men's violence against women primarily as a men's issue, rather than a women's issue, and it provides the athletes with the cognitive preparation they need to respond effectively from the position of bystander to instances of other men's violence against women.

The primary version of this program is delivered by prominent male athletes to other male athletes on their university teams, although alternative versions of the program have also been developed for female athletes and for younger students. Training begins with the facilitator asking the young men to personalize this issue by raising their hand if they have a sister, girlfriend, mother, grandmother, or female friend that they care about. They are then reminded that men's and women's lives are intertwined, so that every time a man is violent against a woman, the victim is some man's sister, girlfriend, mother, grandmother, or female friend. To make this issue concrete, the athletes are then asked to close their eyes and imagine the particular girl or woman they care about being brutally beaten while another man is standing idly by and doing nothing to stop the beating; as the beating continues, the other man still passively watches and does nothing to stop the beating. When the athletes are asked to open their eyes and describe the other man who did nothing to stop the assault, they typically label him a "loser," "punk," "wimp," or "coward." What the athletes may not yet anticipate is that the program will induce them to deal with the ultimate questions, Are you that man? What would you need to do to *not* be that man? How can you prepare yourself to stand up against men's violence against women? and How can you prepare yourself to become an MVP who prepares and inspires other young males in high schools and middle schools to stand up against men's violence against women?

After completing these initial exercises, the athletes work through the MVP *Playbook*. The *Playbook* consists of series of common scenarios involving men's violence against women (e.g., incidents of assault, sexist behavior, female objectification, harassment of lesbians, rape, battering) that each athlete might experience as a bystander (or, in several scenarios, as a potential perpetrator). After reading each scenario, participants read and discuss the related "train of thought," which consists of a checklist of thoughts that men in this situation may experience. Finally, athletes choose their own personal response option from a list that includes the possibility of creating one's own option. One option that is always included but strongly discouraged is to do nothing. The discussions related to choosing one's own "best" personal option are always highly interactive and raise discussions of similar situations that most men have experienced or heard about from family, friends, or members of their communities. These exercises provide a structured opportunity for men to talk with other men about issues of masculinity, violence, and sexism. They also help athletes to prepare themselves to respond in a way they can be proud of "when their play is called" (i.e., when they face a similar situation in life). Rather than casting athletes in a presumed blameful position, this program calls on them to serve as leaders and mentors for others.

Inspired by the MVP program's goal to reposition violence against women as a men's issue and to make bystanders to such violence take responsibility to stop it, the Liz Claiborne Foundation funded the creation of a public service announcement to be aired nationally, usually during football games. The 30-second spot delivers the following powerful message:

> Set in a packed stadium various items—a happy birthday message, notification that a car has its lights on—flash on a scoreboard. Suddenly, fans look up in disgust as a message reveals that the man sitting in "Sec. 829, seat 12, beat up his girlfriend last night." A football player appears on the screen, takes off his helmet and talks to the camera. "If you think hitting a woman makes you a big man, you won't mind if we let 70,000 see just how big you are." (Huebner, 1996, p. E9)

This spot presents an athlete, as well as 70,000 fans with whom the viewers can readily identify, taking an important stand against men's violence against women.

Communities: Empowering Parents Through Community Support

The effectiveness of violence prevention interventions within the domains of family, media, school, peers, and community organizations may depend in large measure on the extent to which these interventions are coordinated across domains in ways that help children make consistent meaning of their various social experiences (Parke & Slaby, 1983). However, community-based programs designed to coordinate violence prevention interventions across social domains are rare. With sufficient skills, resources, and community support, parents can be empowered to play a key role in helping to coordinate their children's violence prevention experiences across domains.

Parents may play a number of important violence prevention roles, including teacher, disciplinarian, role model, supervisor, community leader, and "meaning maker." Parents can help to prevent violence for their own children and for other children in the community by (a) directly teaching their young children healthy, nonviolent patterns of behavior; (b) learning and applying effective, nonviolent means of disciplining and correcting children when they misbehave; (c) presenting themselves and others as effective role models for resolving conflict nonviolently; (d) supervising children's involvement with media, schools, peer groups, and community organizations; (e) leading community efforts to develop, coordinate, and effectively implement community-based support services; and (f) helping children in their community to make effective meaning out of their various violence prevention experiences and to carve out a safe developmental pathway into adulthood. Far too often, however, parents do not have the resources, skills, or community support to fill these roles effectively.

In a recently initiated project, titled "Securing a Future for our Children," Education Development Center has identified three communities (located within Hartford, CT; Philadelphia, PA; and Baltimore, MD) that have significant potential to deliver coordinated community-based violence prevention experiences designed to reduce or prevent harm to children 3 to 10 years of age who have witnessed violence (Brilliant, 1996). Funded for 3 to 6 years by the Bernard van Leer Foundation, located in The Hague, Netherlands, these three American communities have begun to implement their plans for empowing parents and paraprofessionals to help surround young children with the support they need to overcome the problems associated with violence and to lead lives free from violence. It is hoped that the community-based programs not only will deliver effective and coordinated interventions but also will serve as a model for other communities.

CONCLUSION

The diverse research-guided interventions described in this chapter target a broad set of groups (juvenile offenders, students, young children, families, media users, athletes, and children in high-risk communities), and they employ a broad set of delivery systems (correctional facilities, schools, day care centers, health centers, television stations, athletic teams, and community-based organizations). However, each of the interventions is guided by research as well as a central strategy based on several key principles, or prescriptions, for the prevention of youth violence: (a) Intervene early and preventively, (b) reduce social experiences that contribute to violence, (c) strengthen internal resources that protect against violence, and (d) coordinate strategies across social domains. Together, these research-guided interventions offer a concrete foundation for psychology's message of hope—that the knowledge and the means are available with which to begin to deliver to the youths of the nation both the social experiences and the internal resources that will prepare them to deal effectively with the violence they face today and to become effective violence preventers in the future.

REFERENCES

American Psychological Association. (1993). *Violence and youth: Psychology's response. Vol. I: Summary of the American Psychological Association Commission on Violence and Youth.* Washington, DC: Author.

American Psychological Association. (1996). *Violence and the family: Report of the American Psychological Association Presidential Task Force on Violence and the Family.* Washington, DC: Author.

Anderson, E. (1997). The code of violence in the inner city. In J. McCord (Ed.), *Violence and children in the inner city.* New York: Cambridge University Press.

Baker, S. P., Fingerhut, L. A., Higgins, L., Chen, L., & Braver, E. R. (1996). *Injury to children and teenagers: State-by-state mortality facts.* Richmond, VA: The Maternal and Child Health Bureau.

Bell, C. C., & Jenkins, E. J. (1991). Traumatic stress and children. *Journal of Health Care for the Poor and Underserved, 2,* 175–185.

Bellamy, C. (1995, September 26). Address to the International Conference on Violence on the Screen and the Rights of Children, Lund, Sweden.

Boston Teaching Hospitals. (1996). *Domestic Violence Task Force Report and Recommendations.* Deaconess Hospital, One Deaconess Road, Boston, MA 02215. (617-632-8003).

Brilliant, K. (1996). *Securing the future for young children: Parents and para-professionals develop community-based approaches to violence prevention and trauma re-*

duction. Grant proposal from Education Development Center to the Bernard van Leer Foundation. Newton, MA: Education Development Center.

Centers for Disease Control (CDC). (1993, May). *Injury control in the 1990s: A national plan for action.* Report to the Second World Conference on Injury Control, Washington, DC. (Available from CDC at 770-488-4362)

Dodge, K. A., Bates, J. E., & Pettit, G. S. (1990). Mechanisms in the cycle of violence. *Science, 250,* 1678–1683.

Dodge, K. A., & Frame, C. L. (1982). Social cognitive biases and deficits in aggressive boys. *Child Development, 53,* 629–635.

Doepel, D. G. (1995). *Violence prevention for very young children.* Grant proposal submitted by Echo Bridge Productions to the National Institute of Mental Health, Small Business Innovative Research.

Donnerstein, E., Slaby, R. G., & Eron, L. D. (1994). The mass media and youth aggression. In L. D. Eron, J. Gentry, & P. Schlegel (Eds.), *Reason to hope: A psychosocial perspective on violence and youth* (pp. 219–250). Washington, DC: American Psychological Association.

Earls, F. J., Slaby, R. G., & Spirito, A. (1992). Prevention of violence and injuries due to violence. In *Injury control: Position papers from the Third National Injury Control Conference, setting the national agenda for injury control in the 1990s* (pp. 159–254). Atlanta: Centers for Disease Control, U.S. Department of Health and Human Services. (Available from CDC at 770-488-4362)

Eron, L. D., Gentry, J., & Schlegel, P. (Eds.). (1994). *Reason to hope: A psychosocial perspective on violence and youth.* Washington, DC: American Psychological Association. (Available from APA at 800-374-2721)

Fairbank, Maslin, & Maulin. (1995). *National health and safety study: Summary of results.* Opinion research and public policy analysis. San Francisco, CA: Author.

Farrington, D. P. (1992). The need for longitudinal experimental research in offending and antisocial behavior. In J. McCord & R. E. Tremblay (Eds.), *Preventing antisocial behavior.* New York: Guilford Press.

Federal Bureau of Investigation. (1996). *Crime in the United States, 1990–1994.* Washington, DC: Author.

Grossman, D. C., Neckerman, H. J., Koepsell, T. D., Lui, P., Asher, K. N., Beland, K., Frey, K., & Rivara, F. P. (1997). Effectiveness of a violence prevention curriculum among children in elementary school. *Journal of the American Medical Association, 277,* 1605–1611.

Groves, B. M. (1994). Interventions with parents and caregivers in the community: Lessons from the Child Witness to Violence project. In *Caring for infants and toddlers in violent environments: Hurt, healing, and hope.* Arlington, VA: Zero to Three/National Center for Clinical Infant Programs.

Guerra, N. G., Moore, A., & Slaby, R. G. (1995). *Viewpoints: A guide to conflict resolution and decision making for adolescents* (curriculum). Champaign, IL: Research Press.

Guerra, N. G., & Slaby, R. G. (1989). Evaluative factors in social problem solving by aggressive boys. *Journal of Abnormal Child Psychology, 17,* 277–289.

Guerra, N. G., & Slaby, R. G. (1990). Cognitive mediators of aggression in adolescent offenders: 2. Intervention. *Developmental Psychology, 26,* 269–277.

Harvard Medical School. (1996). Violence Education Steering Committee Meeting. Office of Educational Development, Harvard Medical School. (unpublished)

Hendrix, K., & Molloy, P. J. (1990). *Interventions in early childhood.* Background paper prepared for the Forum on Youth Violence in Minority Communities: Setting the Agenda for Prevention. Atlanta: Centers for Disease Control and the Minority Health Professions Foundations with the Morehouse School of Medicine.

Hill, H. M., Soriano, F. I., Chen, S. A., & La Fromboise, T. (1994). Sociocultural factors in the etiology and prevention of violence among ethnic minority youth. In L. D. Eron, J. Gentry, & P. Schlegel (Eds.), *Reason to hope: A psychosocial perspective on violence and youth* (pp. 59–97). Washington, DC: American Psychological Association.

Huebner, B. (1996, November 15). NU is spreading message on abuse of women. *The Boston Globe,* p. E9.

Huesmann, L. R., Eron, L. D., Lefkowitz, M. M., & Walder, L. O. (1984). The stability of aggression over time and generations. *Developmental Psychology, 20,* 1120–1134.

Huizinga, D., Loeber, R., & Thornberry, T. (1993). *Urban delinquency and substance abuse: Initial findings.* Washington, DC: Office of Juvenile Justice and Delinquency Prevention.

Huizinga, D., Loeber, R., & Thornberry, T. (1994). *Urban delinquency and substance abuse: Technical appendix.* Washington, DC: Office of Juvenile Justice and Delinquency Prevention.

Katz, J. (1995). The mentors in violence prevention (MVP project: Inspiring male student athletes to provide leadership in reducing men's violence against women). *Harvard Education Review, 50,* 384–396.

Kazdin, A. E. (1987). Treatment of antisocial behavior in children: Current status and future directions. *Psychological Bulletin, 102,* 187–203.

Loeber, R., Wung, P., Keenan, K., Giroux, B., Stouthamer-Loeber, M., Van-Kammen, W. B., & Maugham, B. (1993). Developmental pathways in disruptive child behavior. *Developmental Psychopathology, 5,* 103–133.

McCord, J. (1983). A forty percent perspective on effects of child abuse and neglect. *Child Abuse & Neglect, 7,* 265–270.

McDonald, G. J. (1992, March 31). Testimony presented to the U.S. Senate Committee on Governmental Affairs. *Congressional Record.*

Moyers, W. (1995). *What can we do about violence?* Public Television Service, television documentary. New York: Public Affairs Television/WNET. (Aired nationally in January 1995)

National Committee for Injury Prevention and Control. (1989). *Injury prevention: Meeting the challenge*. New York: Oxford University Press.

O'Carroll, P. W., Lofton, C., Waller, J. B., McDowall, D., Bukoff, A., & Scott, R. O. (1991). Preventing homicides: An evaluation of the efficacy of a Detroit gun ordinance. *American Journal of Public Health, 81,* 576–581.

Olweus, D. (1979). Stability and aggressive patterns in males: A review. *Psychological Bulletin, 86,* 852–875.

Olweus, D. (1993a). *Bullying at school: What we know and what we can do.* Cambridge, MA: Basil Blackwell.

Olweus, D. (1993b). Victimization by peers: Antecedents and long-term outcomes. In K. H. Rubin & J. B. Asendorf (Eds.), *Social withdrawal, inhibition, and shyness in childhood* (pp. 315–341). Hillsdale, NJ: Erlbaum.

Parke, R. D., & Slaby, R. G. (1983). The development of aggression. In P. H. Mussen (Series Ed.), *Handbook of child psychology* (Vol. IV, 4th ed., pp. 547–641). New York: Wiley.

Patterson, G. R., Littman, R. A., & Bricker, W. (1967). Assertive behavior in children: A step toward a theory of aggression. *Monographs of the Society for Research in Child Development, 32* (5, Serial No. 113).

Patterson, G. R., Reid, J. B., & Dishion, T. J. (1992). *Antisocial boys.* Eugene, OR: Castilia Press.

Pepler, D. J., & Slaby, R. G. (1994). Theoretical and developmental perspectives on violence and youth. In L. D. Eron, J. Gentry, & P. Schlegel (Eds.), *Reason to hope: A psychosocial perspective on violence and youth* (pp. 27–58). Washington, DC: American Psychological Association.

Perry, D. G., Perry, L. C., & Rasmussen, P. (1986). Cognitive social learning mediators of aggression. *Child Development, 57,* 700–711.

Peters, J. (1997). *Peaceful solutions.* Public Television Service, television documentary. New York: WNET.

Richters, J. E. (1993). Community violence and children's development: Toward a research agenda for the 1990's. *Psychiatry, 56,* 3–6.

Richters, J. E., & Martinez, P. (1993). The NIMH Community Violence Project: I. Children as victims of and witnesses to violence. *Psychiatry, 56,* 7–21.

Rosenberg, M. L., O'Carroll, P. W., & Powell, K. E. (1992). Let's be clear: Violence is a public health problem. *Journal of the American Medical Association, 267,* 3071–3072.

Schwartz, D., Dodge, K. A., & Coie, J. D. (1994). The emergence of chronic peer victimization in boys' play groups. *Child Development, 64,* 1755–1772.

Slaby, R. G. (1990). *Prevention of interpersonal violence.* Background paper for the national panel on the prevention of violence and injuries due to violence. Unpublished manuscript.

Slaby, R. G. (1992, March 31). The prevention of youth violence. Testimony presented to the U.S. Senate Committee on Governmental Affairs. *Congressional Record.* (Reprinted by National Criminal Justice Reference Service, Document 147960)

Slaby, R. G. (1993a, December). *Preventing youth violence: What works.* Invited briefing to the U.S. Congress, Washington, DC.

Slaby, R. G. (1993b, August). *Violence and youth: Psychology's message of hope.* Invited address on behalf of the American Psychological Association Commission on Violence and Youth, National Press Club, Edward R. Murrow Room, Washington, DC.

Slaby, R. G. (1996). *Statement to UNICEF, International Children's Day of Broadcasting.* Newton, MA: Education Development Center.

Slaby, R. G. (1997). Psychological mediators of violence in inner city youth. In J. McCord (Ed.), *Violence and children in the inner city.* New York: Cambridge University Press.

Slaby, R. G., & Eron, L. D. (1994). Afterword. In L. D. Eron, J. Gentry, & P. Schlegel (Eds.), *Reason to hope: A psychosocial perspective on violence and youth* (pp. 457–461). Washington, DC: American Psychological Association.

Slaby, R. G., & Guerra, N. G. (1988). Cognitive mediators of aggression in adolescent offenders. 1. Assessment. *Developmental Psychology, 24,* 580–588.

Slaby, R. G., Roedell, W. C., Arezzo, D. A., & Hendrix, K. (1995). *Early violence prevention: Tools for teachers of young children.* Washington, DC: National Association for the Education of Young Children.

Slaby, R. G., Roedell, W. C., Doepel, D. G., Connell, B., & Healy, L. (1996, November). *Early violence prevention: It's never too early and it's not too late.* Invited symposium at the annual meeting of the National Association for the Education of Young Children, Dallas, TX.

Slaby, R. G., & Stringham, P. (1994). Prevention of peer and community violence: The pediatrician's role. *Pediatrics, 94*(Suppl.), 608–616.

Slaby, R. G., Wilson-Brewer, R., & Dash, K. (1994). *Aggressors, victims, and bystanders: Thinking and acting to prevent violence* (a violence prevention curriculum for grades 6–9). Newton, MA: Education Development Center. (Available from Education Development Center, 55 Chapel Street, Newton, MA 02158, 617-969-7100, extension 2215)

Slaby, R. G., Wilson-Brewer, R., & DeVos, E. (1994). *Aggressors, victims, & bystanders: An assessment-based middle school violence prevention curriculum.* Final report concerning Grant 103559 to Education Development Center from the Centers for Disease Control and Prevention, Atlanta, GA. (Available from National Technical Information Service, 5285 Port Royal Road, Springfield, VA 22161, 703-487-4660)

Sloan, J. H., Kellerman, A. L., Reay, D. T., Ferris, J. A., Koepsell, T., Rivara, F. P., Rice, C., Gray, L., & Logerfo, J. (1988). Handgun regulations, crime, assaults and homicide: A tale of two cities. *New England Journal of Medicine, 319,* 1256–1262.

Snyder, H., & Sickmund, M. (1995). *Juvenile offenders and victims: A national report.* Rockville, MD: Office of Juvenile Justice and Delinquency Prevention. (Available from OJJDP Clearinghouse, Box 6000, Rockville, MD 20857, 800-638-8736)

Spirito, A. (1990). *Prevention of self-directed violence*. Background paper for the national panel on the prevention of violence and injuries due to violence. Unpublished manuscript.

Straus, M. A. (1991). Discipline and deviance: Physical punishment of children and violence and other crime in adulthood. *Social Problems, 38,* 133–154.

Straus, M. A. (1996). Corporal punishment of children and adult depression and suicidal ideation. In J. McCord (Ed.), *Coercion and punishment in long-term perspectives*. New York: Cambridge University Press.

Stringham, P., & Weitzman, M. (1988). Violence counseling in the routine health care of adolescents. *Journal of Adolescent Health Care, 9,* 389–393.

Tackling TV violence. (1996, March/April). *AMA Alliance Today*, pp. 4–7.

Thirteen/WNET. (1997). *Peaceful solutions: Conflict resolution and violence prevention strategies* [Video and teacher's guide]. New York: Author.

Widom, C. S. (1989a). The cycle of violence. *Science, 244,* 160–166.

Widom, C. S. (1989b). Does violence beget violence? A critical examination of the literature. *Psychological Bulletin, 106,* 3–28.

Yoshikawa, H. (1994). Prevention as cumulative protection: Effects of early family support and education on chronic delinquency and its risks. *Psychological Bulletin, 115,* 28–54.

16

PREVENTION OF VIOLENCE AT THE SOCIETAL LEVEL

DIANE J. WILLIS AND JANE SILOVSKY

Violence in the United States has reached such great proportions that it now constitutes a public health problem. Child maltreatment, family violence, youth gangs, and violence by guns have cost the nation a great deal not only in terms of human misery and nonproductivity, but also financially. Greater amounts of money are being diverted to the building of prisons and maintenance of prisoners; provision of foster care; and supplying of legal, medical, and mental health services than ever before, leaving little money for prevention programs.

What causes violence at the societal level, and what can be done to prevent it? In this chapter, we address only four of the many risk factors contributing to violence and propose ways in which violence might be prevented. Poverty, substance abuse, and youth violence are tearing at the fabric of U.S. society, and media violence (e.g., television, movies, video games) unquestionably affects the children. These risk factors are discussed in the following sections.

POVERTY

The number of children living in poverty in the United States today is staggering. In 1991, over 5 million children below the age of 6 years were reported to live in poverty (Knitzer & Aber, 1995; National Center for Children in Poverty, 1993). More than 4 of every 10 children under the age of 6 years lived in poverty or in families who were "near poor," with incomes under 185% of the poverty line (National Center for Children in Poverty, 1993). The situation is even worse for many children from minority-group cultures. For example, it is estimated that over half of African American children live below the federal poverty line (Knitzer & Aber, 1995).

Poverty can have significant ramifications for multiple aspects of children's health and well-being, and these ramifications, in turn, can influence the progress and strength of the society at large. The United States does not appear to be fostering and nurturing its "future"; for example, the medical care and health of children in poverty are sorely lacking. Over a third of the children living in poverty do not have their required immunizations at age 2 years; 9–12 million children have no health insurance; often, children living in poverty are provided little preventive care, receiving expensive emergency medical care instead; and Medicare reimbursement is so low that private-practice physicians often cannot afford to see these patients (Maurer, 1991). The rates of infant mortality and low-birth-weight babies are inexcusably high, and these rates would likely be dramatically lowered if adequate prenatal care were provided (Maurer, 1991). Children from families with low incomes have been found to be at greater risk for childhood death from disease, accidents, and homicides (Nersesian, Petit, Shaper, Lemieux, & Naor, 1985). Unfortunately, examination of provisions currently before the U.S. Congress reveals that these conditions are sure to worsen (Singer, 1996).

The adverse impact of poverty on children's psychological adjustment has been demonstrated (McLeod & Shanahan, 1993). Previous research also has documented a link between poverty and child maltreatment (Garbarino, 1976; Jones & McCurdy, 1992; National Center on Child Abuse and Neglect [NCCAN], 1981). Conditions of poverty have been found to be most clearly related to physical abuse and neglect; there is much less evidence linking poverty to child sexual abuse (Jones & McCurdy, 1992). Although some have suggested that, owing to reporting biases and disparate patterns of health care use, poor families are disproportionately reported for suspected child maltreatment, the accumulation of research appears to demonstrate that poverty is a risk factor for child maltreatment. For example, Steinberg, Catalano, and Dooley (1981) followed families in a longitudinal study and found an increase in child abuse after job losses.

The current trend of research is to elucidate the etiological factors (e.g., parental stress, social isolation) and potential protective factors (e.g., community support) that help to explain the relationship between poverty and child maltreatment (Culbertson & Schellenbach, 1992). Many researchers examining poverty as a risk factor for child maltreatment have not examined child neglect separately from abuse in their maltreatment groups. In the following overview of the research, differential risk factors related to neglect or abuse are noted.

Poverty and single-parenthood have been found to be related to increased risk of family violence against children. Gelles (1992) examined the relationship between poverty and self-reported violence by parents toward children using large, nationally representative samples from the 1976 and 1985 National Family Violence Surveys. Mothers living in poverty were found to be at greater risk of maltreating children with severe violence than mothers living above the poverty line. Fathers did not show an increased risk with poverty, except for single fathers, who demonstrated a strikingly high rate of severely violent behavior toward their children. Overall, the increased risk of violence by single parents was heightened for families living in poverty. Single-parenthood and poverty have also been found to be risk factors for child neglect. Giovannoni and Billingsley (1970) investigated families living in poverty who differed in history of neglect (i.e., no history, potential neglect, and confirmed history of neglect) and ethnicity (i.e., families of European descent, African American families, and Spanish-speaking families). Neither the mother's history of family structure (one- or two-parent family) nor family stability (number of changes in family composition) were related to current parental adequacy. However, current single-parent status and marital disruptions did relate to child-neglect status. The number of children was also related, with neglectful families having more children. Poverty was a significant factor even within this truncated range of income. Those living at the lowest level of poverty were more likely to have neglected their children. Kotch et al. (1995) also found that more children in the home and extremely low income were significant risk factors for child maltreatment.

Numerous factors associated with poverty have been considered to be as critical in causing child maltreatment as lack of material commodities. It is important to learn how low income, single-parenthood, and having a larger number of children lead to greater risk of child maltreatment. The heightened level of stressful life events has been suggested as a mediating factor causing increased child maltreatment in poor families. However, Gelles (1992) found that stressful events had the strongest relationship with severe violence against children in middle-income families with incomes in the range of $6,000 to $19,999 rather than in poor or higher income families. The relationship between stressful life events and child maltreatment has remained unclear: Some researchers have found an increased risk of child maltreatment with greater daily stressors (Oates, Davis, & Ryan, 1980), and others have found no relationship between negative events and child maltreatment but have found a protective effect of positive life events for low-income families with limited social support (Kotch et al., 1995).

The relationship between poverty and parenting beliefs and behaviors has been examined as a potential mediating factor in predicting child maltreatment. Trickett, Aber, Carlson, and Cicchetti (1991) combined data from two studies and examined the relations among child-rearing attitudes, poverty, and child physical abuse. Families with a history of child abuse reported more conflict and controlling parental behavior and less cohesion, expressiveness, achievement orientation, intellectual orientation, and religious emphasis than did the comparison sample. It is interesting that socioeconomic status (SES) was negatively correlated with authoritarian parenting style for the comparison group only. The parents with a history of abuse reported a relatively equal level (although elevated) of authoritarian parent behavior across the levels of SES.

McLeod and Shanahan (1993) astutely noted that because families move in and out of poverty, the length of time in poverty should be examined for any differential effects on parenting, risk for child maltreatment, and children's adjustment. These authors examined the relations between length of time in poverty, parenting behaviors, and children's mental health. Maternal behaviors mediated the relationship between current poverty status and children's mental health but did not affect the relationship between persistent poverty and children's adjustment. Persistent poverty had a direct relation to internalizing symptoms in the children. Current poverty status, however, had an indirect relation to externalizing symptoms, mediated by lower maternal responsiveness and harsher punishment. Corporal punishment was associated with both internalizing and externalizing symptoms in the child, as reported by the parent. It is interesting that persistent poverty was associated with less frequent use of corporal punishment.

Domestic violence and maternal mental health have been found to be associated with child maltreatment in poor families. Zuravin and Greif (1989) investigated families in the Aid for Families With Dependent Children (AFDC) program, comparing mothers with a history of maltreating their children to mothers with no history of child abuse. Differences in level of violence in partner relationships and in mother's psychological adjustment were found. Mothers who had a history of maltreating their children were more likely to report experiencing violence in their relationship with their male partner. In addition, mothers who had maltreated their children reported greater depression, more alcohol binges, and poorer self-esteem than mothers without a history of child maltreatment.

Substance abuse and family psychiatric history, particularly depression, have been considered risk factors for child maltreatment. A survey of child protective service agencies in all 50 states found that in a vast majority of states substance abuse is a major presenting problem of clients (Daro & McCurdy, 1992). Some substances, such as crack cocaine, have been blamed for the increase in child abuse cases in the last decade and the devastation of children living in low-income communities (Koppelman & Jones, 1989).

Chaffin, Kelleher, and Hollenberg (1996) examined the potential risk factors of substance abuse, parental psychiatric history, and social risk factors (including socioeconomic status) in predicting physical abuse and neglect. These factors were evaluated in a large sample (7,103 parents) in two waves separated by 1 year. Factors were elucidated that predicted self-report of abusive or neglectful behavior in the second wave in families that did not report maltreatment during the first assessment. Substance abuse, obsessive–compulsive disorder, and low SES predicted self-reported neglectful behavior at the second assessment. Substance abuse, depression, and number of people in the household predicted self-reported physical abuse at this assessment. It is interesting that SES had minimal predictive value for child neglect after substance abuse was controlled for, and SES did not significantly predict physical abuse. Participants who reported abusive or neglectful behaviors at the first wave were excluded from the analysis, and SES may have a stronger effect on pervasive child maltreatment.

Zuravin and Greif (1989) found a relatively high level of depression overall in their sample of families in the AFDC program, with 47% of the mothers without a history of maltreating their children reporting significant depressive symptoms. These results are similar to those of Hall, Williams, and Greenberg (1985), who found that 48% of their sample of low-income mothers reported depressive symptoms. Many of the other risk factors, such as being a single parent, are more prevalent in poor families than in families that are better off financially. All these findings lead to the most challenging questions in risk assessment research: Given the high prevalence of risk factors, what combination of factors leads to child maltreatment? Does the accumulation of risk factors lead to child maltreatment? Is a certain combination of risk factors needed, such as substance abuse along with the trigger of a significant life event? Do different combinations of risk factors lead to different types of child maltreatment, such as chronic versus acute abuse or neglect versus physical abuse? Should researchers focus more on protective factors that allow families at great risk for child maltreatment to maintain control and provide for their children?

One protective factor that has been investigated is social support. Giovannoni and Billingsley (1970) found that informal and formal social support differentiated adequate from neglectful families, with adequate families having more frequent contact with relatives, receiving greater supportive aid (e.g., baby-sitting) from relatives, and attending church regularly. The latter two were particularly common for African American families.

Searching for community-level protective factors, Garbarino and Kostelny (1992) investigated communities that had a large number of the factors that are known to place children at risk for child maltreatment, such as high concentrations of families living at or below the poverty level. Within these communities, they compared those that had a lower-than-expected rate of child maltreatment (low risk) to those with a higher-than-expected level (high risk). Demographic and socioeconomic similarity was a requirement for selection. Members of the low-risk communities were found to have a more positive view of their community, to be more active in community projects, and to have more involvement in community agencies. Coulton and Pandey (1992) found that areas with high concentrations of poverty, with substandard housing and higher crime rates, were at higher risk for poor outcomes for children. These factors can be viewed as undermining community involvement and support.

Broad-based interventions that assist families at the community level may have the best likelihood of significantly affecting rates of child maltreatment (Garbarino & Kostelny, 1992). Researchers have reported the best results from programs focused on empowering the community, providing treatment for substance abuse, providing positive parenting interventions, and assisting families in providing all the basic needs for their children (Willis, Holden, & Rosenberg, 1992).

SUBSTANCE ABUSE AND VIOLENCE

The link between substance abuse, especially of alcohol, and violence has been clearly established (Roth, 1994). It has been reported that alcohol drinking precedes half of all violent crimes, including murder, and that chronic drinkers are more likely than others to have a history of violent behavior (Roth, 1994). Also, it has been estimated that one half of the murders in New York in 1988 were drug related (Roth, 1994). As far back as the 1960s, professionals familiar with child maltreatment believed that substance abuse was a risk factor. In Young's (1964) study of child maltreatment, 62% of 300 families were found to have members with severe and chronic drinking problems.

More recently, Famularo, Kinscherff, and Fenton (1992) reviewed 190 randomly selected records of a large juvenile court and found that "67% of the cases involved parents who were classified as substance abusers" (p. 475). There was a clear association between (a) cocaine abuse and sexual maltreatment and (b) alcohol abuse and physical maltreatment. The association of drugs and alcohol with violence is further demonstrated by the tremendous increase in placements of children into foster care. In a 3-year period (1986–1989), approximately 80,000 children were added to the existing foster care population (Besharov, 1990).

States hit hardest by drugs such as crack (New York and California) had enormous increases in their foster care system. During the 3-year period from 1986 to 1989, California's foster care population rose from 47,327 to

66,763. New York had a 98% increase in children in foster care, from 27,504 to 54,326. The impact of substance abuse on criminal activity associated with violence has increased as well. Bays (1990) reported that there are approximately 10 million adult alcoholics, 500,000 heroin addicts, and between 5 and 8 million cocaine users in the United States, making cocaine one of the costliest additions to affect the country.

Other studies have also found a strong relationship between parental substance abuse and child maltreatment (Kelley, 1992; Murphy et al., 1991; U.S. Department of Health and Human Services, 1994).

Numerous efforts have been directed at the prevention of substance abuse, with only marginal success. The incidence of substance use and abuse among children, youths, and adults continues to increase, and the recidivism rate after treatment is quite high, suggesting that intervention programs have not been successful (Pagliaro & Pagliaro, 1996). Research has indicated that children and youths with "problematic patterns of substance use respond differently to different treatment approaches—what works best for one child or adolescent may not work best" for another (Pagliaro & Pagliaro, 1996, p. 266). If professionals are to intervene before these youngsters become parents or before they commit some form of violence, they must develop better intervention, prevention, assessment, and treatment methods. Parents generally begin drinking in their youth, suggesting that early and appropriate intervention and education about the harmful effects of drugs is critical.

Prevention of alcoholism has not been a top priority in this country, unlike prevention of cigarette smoking. Broad-scale alcohol and drug education programs should be incorporated into curricula. The U.S. Department of Education (1986, 1992) has developed school-based prevention programs tailored to specific characteristics of children and schools (such as ethnicity and type of community). Although the programs require a great deal of time and considerable assessment of needs within each community that plans to use them, they are unquestionably more effective than standard programs, which lack relevance to the community (Pagliaro & Pagliaro, 1996). Another useful prevention model developed for teachers, principals, and administrators and geared for children in kindergarten through the 12th grade was developed by Flatter and McCormick (1992). This program presents drug education using a developmental format, with lesson plans and activities in an expandable form, whereby new information can be inserted; it also provides suggestions for educators on working with parents and the community.

Prevention efforts must have multiple components, for example, strengthening families through education and job opportunities; providing effective community-based substance abuse treatment programs; introducing prevention programs in earlier grades in the schools; disallowing substances in schools, including tobacco; and facilitating more proactive involvement of the community in enacting programs and solutions to this serious problem. At the societal level, Norman and Turner (1993) suggested increasing the price of legal substances, raising the legal drinking age, and banning advertising of cigarettes and alcohol. DiFranza (1992) noted that communities and schools with a *resolve* and *commitment* to reduce the incidence of tobacco use have been successful in their endeavor. This same resolve and commitment to reduce alcohol and drug abuse must be encouraged and developed at the community level if the incidence of violence is to be reduced at the societal level.

TELEVISION VIOLENCE

Television violence and its influence on aggressive behavior have been studied since the early 1970s. The early studies established such a strong causal relationship between televised violence and aggression that additional research on this topic seemed moot. In the more recent reviews (American Psychological Association, 1993; Comstock & Paik, 1990; Rosenthal, 1986), it was concluded again that the effect of televised violence on aggression is long lasting. Such results should alert everyone to this serious impact. In testimony before the U.S. Senate Subcommittee on the Judiciary on Television Violence, Wilcox (1993) discussed the nature of the effects on children and youths of viewing televised violence. Wilcox discussed "copycat violence," whereby children and youths imitate violent or aggressive acts they have viewed. Second, he reported that viewing violence tends to remove inhibitions concerning aggression; that is, after viewing antisocial and violent behaviors day in and day out, children who are predisposed to aggressive behavior are less inhibited in acting out these behaviors. Third, he stated that witnessing violence on a daily basis has a harmful effect on the attitudes and values of everyone, including the developing child; that is, the public becomes desensitized to violence.

Wilcox (1993) testified before the Senate Subcommittee as follows:

> Children who watch repeated acts of violence on television become desensitized to the effects of violence when they witness it in the real world beyond television. They become less likely to empathize with or help victims of actual violence. A steady diet of televised violence cultivates antisocial values and attitudes (Liebert & Sprafkin, 1988). These children believe that aggression is an appropriate means of settling disagreements and responding to frustration in general. This value-shaping effect of televised violence is especially pervasive, and holds true for persons of all ages, not just children. (p. 4)

Donnerstein (1993), in his testimony before Congress, reported that school-age children watch about 2–4 hours of television per day and that by the time they are out of elementary school they have seen approximately

8,000 murders and over 100,000 violent acts. Huston et al. (1992) estimated that a person has viewed over 200,000 violent acts on television by the time he or she has reached the late teens. Is it any wonder that children and youths become desensitized to violence and that this has a major impact on society? In the American Psychological Association (APA) publication, *Violence and Youth* (1993), there is a clear statement of the effects on children and youths of exposure to violence in the mass media; the authors concluded that exposure to violence has harmful lifelong consequences for children and that continual exposure changes attitudes and behavior toward violence and increases acceptance of aggressive attitudes and behavior. In a recent work, the National Television Violence Study Council (1996) reported that the perpetrator of violence often engages in repeated acts of violence and that he or she goes unpunished about three fourths of the time. The perpetrator learns that violent behavior is useful, successful, and desirable, and therefore it is rewarded.

All of the researchers and writers discussed so far have offered suggestions for decreasing violence in the media with the anticipated effect of reducing violence at the societal level. The National Television Violence Study Council (1996) offered a number of recommendations for the television industry, public policymakers, and parents. The group suggested that continued pressure be exerted on the television industry to produce more programs that avoid violence or at least attempt to keep the incidence of violent acts low. The public could be sensitized to a different message if the industry would begin to (a) show programs that portray the negative consequences of violence; (b) punish instead of reward these acts; (c) air programs that show ways of solving problems that are alternatives to the use of violence; and (d) feature programs with a strong antiviolence theme, thus helping the audience learn that there are consequences to violence and that violence can lead to pain and suffering. Parents need to be discriminating about what their children view, and they must consider a child's developmental level in making these decisions. In this manner, also, policymakers can monitor the nature and extent of violence shown on television.

The APA (1993) made even stronger recommendations for preventing violence at the societal level. These included calling on the Federal Communications Commission (FCC) to establish rules that mandate broadcasters and other telecasters to show programs with excessive violence after 10:00 p.m. to avoid the height of children's viewing. The FCC could make additional requirements a condition of license renewal to encourage television stations to help solve the problem of youth violence. "Congress could also expect a national educational violence prevention campaign involving television programming to address the need for public education to help prevent youth violence in America" (APA, 1993, p. 78).

VIOLENCE BY YOUTHS

The National Research Council (NRC; 1993) published its findings from a study of high-risk youths in a book entitled *Losing Generations: Adolescents in High-Risk Settings*. To no one's surprise, family income and employment status were found to "contribute to and shape the settings in which adolescents live" (p. 2). Because of the economic deterioration of children and youths in the United States, reflected in the increase in single-parent households, residential stratification, easy access to drugs and alcohol, increased school failure of low-income, high-risk adolescents, the isolation of vocational education from the academic curriculum, and insufficient access to neighborhood-based health and mental health services, a large number of adolescents come in contact with the child welfare system and the juvenile justice system (NRC, 1993). The authors of the NRC study reported that crime is concentrated in low-income urban neighborhoods largely owing to economic and residential stratification and that the "power of settings on adolescent development has been underappreciated" (p. 11). Neighborhood disadvantage contributes to higher levels of aggression, according to Duncan, Brooks-Gunn, and Klebanov (1994), who examined economic deprivation and early childhood development and found that family income and poverty status correlated not only with IQ but with behavior of children. These investigators found that, in settings with a mix of affluent and nonaffluent neighbors, children tended to have higher IQs than children in largely poor neighborhoods; they also found that children reared with mostly low-income neighbors experienced an increase in externalizing behavior problems.

Children living in violent neighborhoods can be subjected to great trauma and horror and often are exposed to atrocities that others cannot even imagine. During the 1950s in Chicago's largest housing project, murder and aggravated assault occurred 20 times more often than in the rest of the city (Garbarino, Dubrow, Kostelny, & Pardo, 1992). Public housing projects are home to about 1.6 million children (National Association of Housing Redevelopment Officials, 1989). In high-risk, low-income urban neighborhoods, many 5-year-old children have witnessed shootings, and by adolescence they have seen stabbings, shootings, and homicides (Bell, 1991).

Owing to the drug problem, increased gang activity, and the proliferation of lethal weapons, whole neighborhoods can become dangerous, and youth are at greater risk of engaging in violence. Garbarino et al. (1992), in their book *Children in Danger*, discussed at length the consequences of community violence and the developmental toll of inner-city life.

School-based interventions must be relevant to the psychological needs of youths, and vocational training should be coordinated with labor market needs. Unfortunately, as the NRC (1993) pointed out, "funding for higher education is regarded as a vital national economic investment, while support for labor market transitions, particularly for youths most at risk of failing to make the school-to-work transition, is viewed as a social, rather than an economic, responsibility" (p. 145). Too few programs serve 14- and 15-year-old youths, and vocational education programs need to offer "a more sequenced series of courses throughout high school" (p. 146) and not solely when a youth reaches the age of 16 years.

Efforts are needed at the city and state levels to rebuild and strengthen low-income neighborhoods, support families through the provision of jobs and safe neighborhoods, provide easily accessible educational programs for parents and youths to obtain their general education diploma (GED), and perhaps offer vouchers to enable parents to move out of deteriorating neighborhoods.

PREVENTION OF VIOLENCE AT THE SOCIETAL LEVEL

The U.S. Advisory Board on Child Abuse and Neglect (U.S. ABCAN; 1990, 1991, 1993) has recognized the serious nature of child maltreatment (citing poverty and substance abuse as contributing factors) as well as the serious nature of violence at the societal level. The 1990 and 1993 reports of this board set forth recommendations to Congress of ways to strengthen families and thus reduce violence at the societal and community levels. First and foremost, it must be recognized that the level of violence toward children and youths in the United States constitutes a national emergency and that leadership is required from the highest officials at the national and state levels to address this problem. Second, national and local efforts to combat violence and, in particular, child maltreatment must be coordinated. At both levels, human resources need to be increased or expanded; for example, child protection workers need better training and manageable caseloads, state-of-the art substance abuse treatment programs need to be available, and legal system personnel need better training. The states and the federal government need to improve coordination among federal, state, tribal, and private sectors to improve the material and social supports for families and to reduce societal influences such as media violence and violence in the schools (U.S. ABCAN, 1993).

Third, efforts to strengthen families should occur early on, when children are infants and toddlers, by such means as increasing funding for the program Early Head Start. Increased funding for family preservation services, coupled with a trial of universal, voluntary neonatal home visitation (funded at the federal level), needs to be supported and implemented. The United States rarely plans a coordinated strategy for reducing problems. Rather, money is appropriated and laws are passed to mandate programs without a systematic, coordinated, and integrated effort to mobilize resources and people to combat problems in an organized fashion. Therefore, a fourth recommendation might be the implementation of a planned, systematic, and coordinated approach to the reduction of violence and of the ingredients creating violence.

Fifth, poverty and economic instability have had a devastating effect on children and families, and as reported, the incidence of maltreatment or violence is high among this population. The National Commission on Children (1991) urged Congress to create a $1,000 refundable tax credit for all children through age 18; provide the earned income tax credit as an incentive for low-income parents to enter the job force; continue providing a social safety net for families moving from welfare to work; offer community employment opportunities to poor parents who are willing and able to work; and reorient AFDC as short-term income support primarily for families who are experiencing disability, unemployment, or other hardship (National Commission on Children, 1991 pp. 80–81).

Sixth, a research panel urged that Congress and the states fund additional research on violence; strengthen research resources in the fields of law, psychology, social services, criminal justice, sociology, medicine, and public health; create a corps of research practitioners in the area of violence and violence prevention; and fund more collaborative, interdisciplinary research into the causes of violence and the development of effective training protocols (Panel on Research on Child Abuse and Neglect, 1993). This group of investigators also offered many other research directions.

Seventh, the United States has sufficient resources to revitalize urban neighborhoods to provide new economic opportunities. Housing policies that reverse geographic concentrations of low-income families would enhance the prospects of children and families. Community-based programs may need to be initiated or strengthened so that prosocial values in families are promoted. Coupled with these policies, stronger community police programs need to be instituted, and violence prevention needs to be stressed (Roth, 1994). Cracking down on alcohol excesses, illegal drugs, and firearms would also help to reduce the incidence of violence.

Ultimately, to prevent violence at the societal level, it would be helpful to have flexible work schedules and improved benefits in jobs, educational and support programs offered at work, parental leave policies, employer-supported child care, and family-oriented policies (Massachusetts Committee for Children and Youth, 1987, p. 83). After violence has erupted, effective treatment resources are needed at the community level, including treatment for substance abuse, dysfunctional parenting, and child abuse. If services were school based, parents could more easily enroll in literacy classes or obtain job training, parenting assistance, vouchers for the Women, Infants, and Children (WIC) food supplementation program, health screening, and a host of other services provided at the local level.

CONCLUSION

This chapter contains a review of the effects of poverty, substance abuse, youth risk factors, and television violence on the escalating incidence of violence in U.S. society. Recognizing that solutions are not simple, we advocate broad prevention strategies at the federal, state, and local levels. These strategies need to be planned, systematic, coordinated, integrated at the level of the community, and based on the needs of the community. Reducing the incidence of poverty and substance abuse would curtail the high child maltreatment rate, and the deglamorizing of violence and promotion of more positive avenues of settling disputes on television programs would teach children prosocial ways of handling conflict.

REFERENCES

American Psychological Association. (1993). *Violence and youth: Psychology's response*. Washington, DC: Author.

Bays, J. (1990). Substance abuse and child abuse: Impact of addiction on the child. *Pediatric Clinics of North America, 37*, 881–904.

Bell, C. (1991). Traumatic stress and children in danger. *Journal of Health Care for the Poor and Underserved, 2*, 175–188.

Besharov, D. J. (1990). Crack children in foster care. *Children Today, 35*, 21–25.

Chaffin, M., Kelleher, K., & Hollenberg, J. (1996). Onset of physical abuse and neglect: Psychiatric, substance abuse, and social risk factors from prospective community data. *Child Abuse and Neglect, 20*, 191–203.

Comstock, G., & Paik, H. (1990). *The effects of television violence on aggressive behavior: A meta-analysis*. A preliminary report to the National Research Council for the Panel on the Understanding and Control of Violent Behavior. Syracuse, NY: S. I. Newhouse School of Public Communications, Syracuse University.

Coulton, C. J., & Pandey, S. (1992). Geographic concentration of poverty and risk to children in urban neighborhoods. *American Behavioral Scientists, 35*, 238–257.

Culbertson, J. L., & Schellenbach, C. J. (1992). Prevention of maltreatment in infants and young children. In D. J. Willis, E. W. Holden, & M. Rosenberg (Eds.), *Prevention of child maltreatment* (pp. 47–77). New York: Wiley.

Daro, D., & McCurdy, K. (1992). *Current trends in child abuse reporting and fatalities: NCPCA's 1991 annual fifty state survey*. Chicago: National Committee for the Prevention of Child Abuse.

DiFranza, J. R. (1992). Preventing teenage tobacco addiction. *Journal of Family Practice, 34*, 753–756.

Donnerstein, E. (1993). *Testimony before the Committee on Commerce, Science, and*

Transportation on Media Violence. Washington, DC: American Psychological Association.

Duncan, G. J., Brooks-Gunn, J., & Klebanov, P. K. (1994). Economic deprivation and early childhood development. *Child Development, 65,* 296–318.

Famularo, R., Kinscherff, R., & Fenton, T. (1992). Parental substance abuse and the nature of child maltreatment. *Child Abuse & Neglect, 16,* 475–483.

Flatter, C. H., & McCormick, K. (1992). *Learning to live drug free: A curriculum for prevention* (Ed/OESE 92-36R). Washington, DC: U.S. Department of Education.

Garbarino, J. (1976). A preliminary study of some ecological correlates of child abuse: The impact of socioeconomic stress on mothers. *Child Development, 74,* 178–185.

Garbarino, J., Dubrow, N., Kostelny, K., & Pardo, C. (1992). *Children in danger: Coping with the consequences of community violence.* San Francisco: Jossey-Bass.

Garbarino, J., & Kostelny, K. (1992). Child maltreatment as a community problem. *Child Abuse and Neglect, 16,* 455–464.

Gelles, R. J. (1992). Poverty and violence toward children. *American Behavioral Scientist, 35,* 258–274.

Giovannoni, J. M., & Billingsley, A. (1970). Child neglect among the poor: A study of parental adequacy in families of three ethnic groups. *Child Welfare, 49,* 196–204.

Hall, L. A., Williams, C. A., & Greenberg, R. S. (1985). Supports, stressors, and depressive symptoms in low-income mothers of young children. *American Journal of Public Health, 75,* 518–522.

Huston, A. C., Donnerstein, E., Fairchild, H., Feshbach, N. D., Katz, P. A., Murray, J. P., Rubinstein, E. A., Wilcox, B. L., & Zuckerman, D. (1992). *Big world, small screen: The role of television in American society.* Lincoln, NB: University of Nebraska Press.

Jones, E. D., & McCurdy, K. (1992). The links between types of maltreatment and demographic characteristics of children. *Child Abuse and Neglect, 16,* 201–215.

Kelley, S. J. (1992). Parenting stress and child maltreatment in drug-exposed children. *Child Abuse and Neglect, 16,* 317–328.

Knitzer, J., & Aber, J. L. (1995). Young children in poverty: Facing the facts. *American Journal of Orthopsychiatry, 65,* 174–176.

Koppelman, J., & Jones, J. M. (1989, Fall). Crack: It's destroying fragile low-income families. *Public Welfare,* pp. 13–15.

Kotch, J. B., Browne, D. C., Ringwalt, C., Stewart, P. W., Ruina, E., Holt, K., Lowman, B., & Jung, J. (1995). Risk of child abuse or neglect in a cohort of low-income children. *Child Abuse and Neglect, 19,* 1115–1130.

Liebert, R. M., & Sprafkin, J. (1988). *The early window.* New York: Pergamon Press.

Massachusetts Committee for Children and Youth. (1987). *Preventing child abuse: A resource for policymakers and advocates*. Boston: Author.

Maurer, H. M. (1991). The growing neglect of American children. *American Journal of Diseases in Children, 145*, 540–541.

McLeod, J. D., & Shanahan, M. J. (1993). Poverty, parenting, and children's mental health. *American Sociological Review, 58*, 351–366.

Murphy, J. M., Jellinek, M., Quinn, D., Smith, G., Poitrast, F. G., & Goshko, M. (1991). Substance abuse and serious child mistreatment: Prevalence, risk, and outcome in a court sample. *Child Abuse and Neglect, 15*, 197–211.

National Association of Housing Redevelopment Officials. (1989). *The many faces of public housing*. Washington, DC: Author.

National Center for Children in Poverty. (1993). *Five million children: 1993 update*. New York: Columbia University School of Public Health.

National Center on Child Abuse and Neglect (NCCAN). (1981). *The national incidence study of child abuse and neglect: Report of findings*. Washington, DC: Author.

National Commission on Children. (1991). *Beyond rhetoric: A new American agenda for children and families*. Washington, DC: Author.

National Research Council (NRC). (1993). *Losing generations: Adolescents in high-risk settings*. Washington, DC: National Academy Press.

National Television Violence Study Council. (1996). *National Television Violence Study: Executive Summary, 1994–1995*. Studio City, CA: Mediascope.

Nersesian, W. S., Petit, M. R., Shaper, R., Lemieux, D., & Naor, E. (1985). Childhood death and poverty: A study of all childhood deaths in Maine, 1976–1980. *Pediatrics, 75*, 41–50.

Norman, E., & Turner, S. (1993). Adolescent substance abuse prevention programs: Theories, models, and research in the encourging '80s. *Journal of Primary Prevention, 14*, 3–20.

Oates, R. K., Davis, A. A., & Ryan, M. G. (1980). Predictive factors for child abuse. *Australian Pediatric Journal, 16*, 239–243.

Pagliaro, A. M., & Pagliaro, L. A. (1996). *Substance use among children and adolescents*. New York: Wiley.

Panel on Research on Child Abuse and Neglect. (1993). *Understanding child abuse and neglect*. Washington, DC: National Academy Press.

Rosenthal, R. (1986). Media violence, antisocial behavior, and the social consequences of small effects. *Journal of Social Issues, 42*, 141–154.

Roth, J. A. (1994). Psychoactive substances and violence. *National Institute of Justice*. Washington, DC: U.S. Government Printing Office.

Singer, J. (1996). Homeless children and their health care providers. *The Child, Youth, and Family Services Quarterly, 19*, 9–11.

Steinberg, L. D., Catalano, R., & Dooley, D. (1981). Economic antecedents of child abuse and neglect. *Child Development, 52*, 975–985.

Trickett, P. K., Aber, J. L., Carlson, V., & Cicchetti, D. (1991). Relationship of socioeconomic status to the etiology and developmental sequelae of physical child abuse. *Developmental Psychology, 27,* 148–158.

U.S. Advisory Board on Child Abuse and Neglect (U.S. ABCAN). (1990). *Child abuse and neglect: Critical first steps in response to a national emergency.* Washington, DC: U.S. Department of Health and Human Services.

U.S. Advisory Board on Child Abuse and Neglect (U.S. ABCAN). (1991). *Creating caring communities: Blueprint for an effective federal policy on child abuse and neglect.* Washington, DC: U.S. Department of Health and Human Services.

U.S. Advisory Board on Child Abuse and Neglect (U.S. ABCAN). (1993). *Neighbors helping neighbors: A new strategy for the protection of children.* Washington, DC: U.S. Department of Health and Human Services.

U.S. Department of Education. (1986). *Schools without drugs.* Washington, DC: Author.

U.S. Department of Education. (1992). *Success stories from drug-free schools: A guide for educators, parents, and policymakers* (ED/OESE 92-47R). Washington, DC: Author.

U.S. Department of Health and Human Services. (1994). *Protecting children in substance abusing families.* Washington, DC: The Clearinghouse on Child Abuse and Neglect Information.

Wilcox, B. (1993). *Hearings before the Subcommittee on Constitution of the Committee on the Judiciary on Television Violence.* Testimony on behalf of the American Psychological Association.

Willis, D. J., Holden, E. W., & Rosenberg, M. (1992). *Prevention of child maltreatment: Developmental and ecological perspectives.* New York: Wiley.

Young, L. (1964). *Wednesday's children: A study of child neglect values.* New York: McGraw-Hill.

Zuravin, S., & Greif, G. L. (1989, February). Normative and child-maltreating AFDC mothers. *Social Casework: The Journal of Contemporary Social Work,* pp. 76–84.

V

ADVANCING KNOWLEDGE
AND EFFECTIVENESS

17

INTEGRATING AND ADVANCING THE KNOWLEDGE BASE ABOUT VIOLENCE AGAINST CHILDREN: IMPLICATIONS FOR INTERVENTION AND PREVENTION

PENELOPE K. TRICKETT, LARUE ALLEN,
CYNTHIA J. SCHELLENBACH, AND
EDWARD F. ZIGLER

If there is one goal that virtually everyone in the United States—rich and poor, Democrat and Republican, every ethnic background—can agree on, it is that of preventing the horror of child abuse and other forms of violence perpetrated on children. Unfortunately, the current status of prevention efforts does not measure up to the strength of the desire to protect children from intentional harm. Prevention can only be as effective as the basic knowledge and theory that guide it. This chapter begins with a summary and integration of the basic knowledge and theory concerning the causes and consequences of child abuse and other forms of violence; the focus is on the contribution of this information to current and future prevention programs and other intervention efforts.

DEVELOPMENTAL CONSEQUENCES OF ABUSE AND VIOLENCE

Research knowledge of the consequences of child abuse and other forms of violence for children's development is essential for the design of appropriate and specific interventions and secondary prevention efforts. It is clear from chapters 2, 3, and 4, this volume, that much research has been performed over the last several decades on the impact of physical abuse, sexual abuse, and exposure to marital violence. At present, there is less research knowledge about the impact of exposure to community violence, but this information is beginning to accrue. It is plain that a lot has been learned but that a lot more needs to be learned for this knowledge to be maximally useful for prevention and intervention efforts.

What facts are known? First, it is quite evident that all the forms of violence under consideration here often result in adverse effects on the development and adjustment of children and adolescents. These effects include problems of aggression and undercontrol as well as problems of depression and social withdrawal. They include problems with relationships with parents, other adults, and peers. Academic performance is often adversely affected as well. These forms of violence are associated with behavior problems and psychopathology from early childhood through adolescence and, in some cases, adulthood, as well as with social deviancy (e.g., delinquency) beginning in early adolescence. The current knowledge about the nature of these problems remains at what might be called a "generic" level. That is, the different forms of violence have all been found to result in any of the problems listed. The only "specific" relationship yet identified is that sexually abused children, unlike victims of other types of violence, tend to exhibit problems involving sexual acting out (see chapter 3, this volume).

It is also evident that there is a considerable amount of variability in response to these forms of violence. Some of this variability seems to be tied to the type of violence experienced (e.g., sexual abuse versus community violence), and some occurs within types and even within samples. Margolin (see chapter 4, this volume) has provided, in Table 1 of her chapter, a clear illustration of the critical similarities and differences of the experiences of physical abuse, sexual abuse, and exposure to marital or community violence. The most critical features seem to be (a) whether the parent or parent figure is the perpetrator and, if so, whether other features of the family environment buffer or further exacerbate the negative impact of the violence on the child, and (b) the degree of personal threat imposed by the violence, including how much pain, fear, and violation of bodily integrity are involved and how often that threat occurs—that is, the recurring or chronic nature of the violence.

For both physical abuse and exposure to marital violence, the parent or parent figure is usually the perpetrator of the violence. For sexual abuse, this feature varies. In some sexual abuse samples, extrafamilial abuse is included, and even when the sample is limited to intrafamilial abuse, non-parental adults (e.g., uncles, cousins) often are perpetrators. Research is beginning to accrue indicating that sexual abuse has especially deleterious effects when the father figure, especially the biological father, is the perpetrator (e.g., see Trickett, Reiffman, Horowitz, & Putnam, 1997). In community violence studies, the parent is usually not a perpetrator; however, Horn and Trickett (chapter 5, this volume) point out that in some studies exposure to community violence is measured in such a way that it is unclear whether it includes exposure to, or even being the victim of, family violence. The relevance of this point is that, to the degree that the parent is involved in the commission of the abuse or violence, there is a betrayal of the parental role as protector, nurturer, and supporter and a violation of the home as a safe haven.

There is considerable evidence that the child-rearing environments of families in which there is physical abuse are less than optimal and tend to contribute to the maladaptive development of abused children. Less is known about these characteristics in homes in which sexual abuse or marital violence occurs. Although this subject has not yet been the focus of community violence studies, there are hints that the family environment can be an important mediator buffering the bad effects of community violence. Learning more about child-rearing characteristics and home environments of families of victims in all these types of environments would provide important knowledge for designing effective interventions.

The second critical feature of these forms of violence is the degree of personal threat experienced by the child. All these forms of violence generally produce fear and anxiety. Physical abuse alone always includes pain. Sexual abuse can be, but is not always, accompanied by physical violence, threats of violence, or pain. Furthermore, sexual abuse almost always involves body contact, which probably increases the level of personal threat experienced by the child. Exposure to violence, whether in the family or community, may produce less fear than experiencing abuse, because it does not involve pain or body contact; these effects vary a lot, however, as Pynoos, Frederick, Nader, and Arroyo (1987) showed in their study of schoolchildren who experienced a school-yard sniper attack (see chapter 5, this volume).

In short, to understand more clearly how child abuse and other forms of violence affect children, one has to attend carefully to the issues of research definitions. This is an area that has plagued the child abuse field for years (National Research Council, 1993). It is clearly not sufficient to say only that a research participant was "physically abused" or "exposed to community violence." In addition, Horn and Trickett (chapter 5, this volume) point out that a "count" measure of exposure to community violence that does not take into account the nature of the incident obfuscates more than it clarifies. A much more detailed description of the nature and severity of the abuse or violence is required, including the identity of the perpetrator, the duration, and the chronicity, if researchers are ever to understand the variability of outcomes for children experiencing abuse and violence.

Additionally, although research on the psychological consequences of abuse and violence usually identifies samples as victims of one form of violence or another, it is becoming increasingly clear that many children experience multiple forms of maltreatment across multiple contexts (Rossman & Rosenberg, 1997). For example, children exposed to marital violence are at high risk of physical abuse as well (see chapter 4, this volume), and neighborhoods with high rates of child maltreatment often also have high rates of community violence (Coulton, Korbin, Su, & Chow, 1995). Again, a full understanding of children's experiences with these different forms of violence is necessary for appropriate intervention and prevention efforts to be designed and implemented.

Another of the apparent causes of variability of impact of child abuse and violence concerns the characteristics of the victims, including gender, age or developmental stage, and ethnicity or other cultural or subcultural factors. Although the research findings are inconsistent, it may be that, regardless of the type of abuse or violence, boys are more likely to exhibit externalizing problems (e.g., problems with aggression, undercontrol, acting-out behaviors) and girls are more likely to show internalizing problems (e.g., depression, anxiety, social withdrawal). This sex difference pattern has been described frequently with regard to other domains (Zahn-Waxler, 1993). It appears, however, that both boys and girls who are victims of different forms of abuse and violence are likely to exhibit both externalizing and internalizing forms of psychopathology and behavior problems; this also needs to be clarified by future research so that more appropriate interventions can be designed. For example, designers of prevention programs for female victims of sexual abuse should target amelioration or prevention not only of depression or anxiety but also of conduct disorder or delinquency. Similarly, programs for boys should focus not only on antisocial behavior or conduct problems but on depression or anxiety as well.

Another point about gender concerns the lack of studies of boys who have been sexually abused. Although most of the studies of physical abuse and of marital or community violence have included samples of both males and females, most samples of child victims of sexual abuse are all female or have too few males to allow examination of gender differences (see chapter 3, this volume). Most prevalence and incidence studies have indicated that about 20% of reported cases of sexual abuse involve males (National Center for Child Abuse and Neglect; NCCAN, 1996). There is some reason to think that proportionately fewer male than female victims are known to authorities, but even if the 20% rate is correct, according to the latest incidence study of NCCAN (1996), that would mean that over 60,000 boys are victims of sexual abuse each year in the United States. This large group should not be ignored either in the research or in the intervention or prevention efforts.

Concerning age or developmental stage differences, most knowledge about the consequences of child abuse and violence has come from research with samples of school-aged children, and the studies have shown the pattern of "generic" problems described previously. In very young children, both sexual abuse and exposure to marital violence have been shown to result in emotional distress, immature or regressive behavior, and somatic complaints such as headaches and stomachaches. The research on the very young victims of physical abuse has focused on parent–child attachment, and the results have consistently indicated problems in this domain, with implications for later peer relationship problems, among other deleterious outcomes. There are currently no empirical studies of the impact of community violence on children younger than elementary school age. The research on these very young victims is scant and should be expanded so that interventions can be appropriate to the age level of the children.

The adolescent period has been virtually ignored by researchers of community violence, even though there is reason to believe that adolescents are in the age group most likely to be exposed to this form of violence. Investigators of physical abuse, sexual abuse, and marital violence all have reported that the problems in adolescence are similar to those found in middle childhood, although these problems may manifest themselves somewhat differently at different ages (e.g., initiation of sexual activity, running away, and delinquent acts are reported in early adolescence).

Another area that has received scant attention as a mediator or moderator of the impact of abuse and violence is that of race, ethnicity, or other cultural or subcultural differences. Although national incidence studies have indicated no overall ethnic group differences in rates of abuse (NCCAN, 1996), there are some indications of more subtle differences in the abuse experiences of children from different racial and ethnic groups. For example, in a sample of 6- to 16-year-old sexually abused girls, the African American girls were, on average, abused at an older age and for a shorter period of time than were the Caucasian girls (Trickett et al., 1997). Differences in the characteristics of sexual abuse in Latina samples have been reported (Huston, Parra, Prihoda, & Foulds, 1995; Mennen, 1994, 1995). Exposure to community violence may well differ on this basis from the other forms of violence in that minority-group youths, who are more likely to grow up in poverty and in urban areas, are more often exposed to violence than are other youths. It also seems likely that the nature of the exposure (e.g., the severity and chronicity) may vary by ethnic group. These and other possible ethnic-group variations in abuse and violence experiences have implications for developmental outcomes and thus for the design of interventions.

In sum, although there is still a lot to learn about the specific nature and mediators of the psychological consequences of child abuse and violence, it is clear that psychological distress and behavior problems are a frequent and often long-lasting consequence and that interventions designed to ameliorate the symptoms should be available to victims of abuse and violence. Kolko (chapter 9, this volume) indicates that research knowledge is beginning to accrue about effective interventions with child sexual abuse victims and, to a much lesser degree, physical abuse victims. There is apparently no empirical evidence about effective interventions for children exposed to marital, school, or community violence.

The studies Kolko summarizes have indicated that effective therapeutic models are beginning to be identified for sexual abuse victims. The best programs, to date, have included (a) both a child component and a parent component (involving the nonabusing parent), (b) a cognitive–behavioral therapy approach focused on specific behavior problems (see also Pithers, 1997), and (c) a component of treatment encouraging the child's disclosure and discussion of perceptions of the abusive experience. Whether these models are effective for victims of other types of abuse and violence and whether other approaches might be preferable for some groups, such as school-based programs for victims of community violence, await further intervention research.

CAUSES OF VIOLENCE AGAINST CHILDREN: HOW SHALL WE ADDRESS THE QUESTION?

Each of the chapters in this volume on causes of violence against children makes it clear that from whatever level of analysis one approaches the question of causes, one must inevitably refer to additional levels for a complete understanding. The societal level discussed by Tolan and Guerra (chapter 8), subsumes the neighborhood and community levels, presented by Limber and Nation (chapter 7). These encompass the school and other settings where children receive care, discussed by Feshbach and Feshbach (chapter 11), which is a larger unit than the family, the focus of Milner's presentation (chapter 6). However, there are significant causal questions that cross levels of analysis.

What is notable from all the chapters is that the best, most complete causal knowledge across these levels of interest is in the area of physical abuse. This is, in fact, the only area in which research has been conducted at all these levels, from individual to societal. Professionals know next to nothing about causal factors at the neighborhood, community, or societal level of sexual abuse or marital violence and are ignorant of familial factors that may be associated with exposure of children to community violence or that may serve as mediators (i.e., they tend to protect the exposed child from negative outcomes). The discussion that follows is limited by these large gaps in knowledge about the causes across levels of all the forms of abuse and violence. The same gaps in knowledge are also reflected in the discussion of prevention research later in this chapter. Perhaps because there is more of a knowledge base, however incomplete, most of the prevention research reviewed in this book has focused on the prevention of physical child abuse.

For every level, the themes of continuity and change are important ones. Longitudinal research is important for determining which of the children who are abused become child abusers and under what circumstances and for uncovering the factors related to the decline or resurrection of a school or community into or out of a state that elicits or facilitates violence against children. Although it usually is not necessary to detail every causal factor before attempting to prevent problems, it is particularly difficult to alter the course of events regarding violence against children by focusing on correlates alone. Longitudinal studies that illuminate the paths by which these behaviors develop and grow are needed to permit pinpointing of the levers for preventive intervention.

For neighborhoods, communities, and societies, if not for all levels at which one can examine the problem of violence against children, both historical and cross-national comparative analyses can serve the same purpose: identifying, by following the course of development of the phenomenon, levers for preventive intervention. France, for example, has experienced a dramatic increase in violence against children in schools over the last decade or so (Bachmann, 1996). Some argue that the course of events there mimics the trajectory of events as they unfolded in the United States perhaps a quarter century ago. If there is any truth in this argument, researchers, policymakers, and practitioners in both these and other countries could learn from a comparison of the two case histories. Similarly, an overview of the historical, economic, political, demographic, and cultural changes in a set of communities or schools, selected perhaps because they vary in their experience of violence against children, could reveal some of the precipitating, enabling, and sustaining conditions of this violence. Such analyses can help researchers to address the question of why two communities (or two families or two schools) that might appear to be similar on several indicators nonetheless vary greatly in their rates of violence against children.

Cross-level questions demand operationalization of constructs with care to avoid addressing at the individual level a question better addressed at the community level. In investigating the impact of community cohesion on the rates of child victimization, for example, it is important not to derive information on both cohesion and victimization from the same individual sources. If one decides to create a neighborhood measure by aggregating responses from the individual level, it should be a conscious decision over which one can exercise control to avoid having a mixed-level mess with results that are difficult to interpret.

Research questions that draw attention to more than one level of analysis can also be multilevel (Shinn, 1990). That is, one might ask the same question at the individual, the family, and the neighborhood level to see whether the causal process and relationships among variables are similar. Research questions for which developmental hypotheses are relevant, such as those involving children or adolescents, challenge the investigator to consider both the vertical dimension, or levels of analysis (whether cross-level or multilevel), and the horizontal dimension, or change across time (Allen, 1990).

The three chapters of this volume on causes of violence against children pose questions that illustrate clearly the value of both the horizontal and vertical approaches to addressing the problem. Milner, in chapter 6, discusses individual and familial factors associated with intrafamilial child physical and sexual abuse. The degree to which reporting problems complicate the ability to understand the causes of the problem is outstanding. If lower socioeconomic status (SES) is associated with incest among reported cases but not among surveys of the general population, one must wonder whether the truth lies with either of these samples or with neither. Studying the stability of findings over time and sampling from several groups at once are both helpful in getting such questions answered. If one is looking for levers for change, it is more important to understand the roles of variables such as parental stress or parental self-esteem. Milner (chapter 6) suggests that these variables are often associated with more physical abuse, although the findings for stress are less consistent. The interaction of these factors with factors at other levels, such as the neighborhood or community level, might further explain why some individuals with a given profile of risk avoid the expression of violence against children whereas others succumb.

The issue of violence against youths in schools, discussed by Feshbach and Feshbach (chapter 11, this volume), presents another example of the need for horizontal and vertical analyses. Schools have characteristics that are independent of the individuals who inhabit them, and the inhabitants have their own characteristics. Somewhere in the interaction of the schools and their inhabitants (perhaps dependent on another contextual variable, such as the neighborhood in which the school is embedded) lies the cause of the recent increase in assaults and shootings committed by youths against other youths in school. The blame has been laid on a lapse in school discipline, the availability of drugs, the existence of gangs, and the presence of guns (Glazer, 1992). None of these alone explains why the increase in school violence is occurring unevenly, without attacking every school with a similar student body, in similar neighborhoods. Data from the National Crime Survey (Garofalo, Siegel, & Laub, 1987) have indicated that many school victimization scenarios unfold because peer interactions that occur in routine daily activities have escalated into situations of harm. Once again, without an analysis of the history of a set of schools and of the interaction of the settings and their inhabitants over time, one cannot imagine a complete understanding of why school violence is currently escalating both here and abroad.

Both Limber and Nation (chapter 7, this volume) and Tolan and Guerra (chapter 8), focusing on "higher" levels of analysis, draw attention to pressing questions that involve the interaction of these levels with others. Both sets of authors note that the majority of research focuses on either the individual or the family level, often invoking variables at other levels without measuring them at those levels. No one doubts that poverty is a bad thing, with many correlates that compromise the quality of life of those who are poor; however, at every level, simply measuring income is inadequate. What is it about poverty *at the neighborhood level* that increases the chances of child abuse? What factors in poor neighborhoods, again measured at the neighborhood level, protect some families in the neighborhood from high rates of child abuse? The frequent invocation of poverty as "the answer" occurs at every level and lends itself to a multilevel analysis that would reveal whether processes at each level are similar. Individual poverty can be measured, as can neighborhood poverty, and societal poverty can be operationalized as well. Will similar protective factors operate in the relationship between risk and violence outcomes at all of these levels?

Tolan and Guerra (chapter 8) underline another significant issue. They suggest that it is important to consider the relationship between child victimization and child perpetration and whether the causes of both are similar. They specifically refer to the degree to which this question lends itself to an examination of societal influences, arguing that societal influences on both aspects of violence are likely to be the same. We add that an understanding of the predictors of victimization at virtually any level of analysis could help researchers, in a similar way, to understand whether victimization and perpetration have the same causal pathways and whether any similarities are replicated across levels. It is known that community violence victimization rates are higher among middle school teenagers than among older youths (Sullivan, 1996), although the middle school age group seems to be the least studied. This intriguing finding could be contextualized with a consideration of the settings in which this violence occurs, the various societies in which this trajectory has been documented, and even the evolution of this trend over time. As we noted earlier in this chapter, a more complete understanding of the long-term consequences for children of experiencing violence in the family and in the community can help to clarify the victim-to-victimizer question. The victimization side of the violence problem is an overlooked and potentially valuable facet of a comprehensive approach to research on uncovering the causes of violence against children.

PROTECTING CHILDREN FROM ABUSE AND OTHER VIOLENCE

As we discussed earlier in this chapter, the knowledge on which prevention efforts should be based is fragmented and filled with conflicting evidence, and theories are still not well enunciated or validated. It is therefore not surprising that most existing prevention programs are unproved at best and ineffective at worst. Much of the responsibility for this sorry state of affairs rests with woefully inadequate evaluation research. Although there are some notable exceptions, evaluations of prevention programs often defy the most basic empirical rules: Treatments are incomparable, control groups are lacking, samples are too small for meaningful differences to be discerned, inappropriate statistical analyses are used, pretests are absent, and "longitudinal" follow-up is completed within a few weeks of treatment (see chapter 18, this volume, as well as critiques of research by Melton et al., 1995; National Research Council, 1993; Wekerle & Wolfe, 1993). Although there is no excuse for bad research, program planners can be forgiven their lack of attention to evaluation, because the problem of child abuse is so immediate and dangerous that there is no luxury of time to study, analyze, refine, and reassess their efforts thoroughly. As Reppucci, Land, and Haugaard (chapter 13) point out, funders give short shrift to research in favor of supporting programs for real children to prevent real harm and disseminating the programs to benefit more children.

Not only is the effectiveness of current programs uncertain, but it is unknown if such programs could achieve the prevention goals for which they were designed. Plummer (1993) described the way that prevention efforts are kindled by public indignation and demand—by the desire "to do something." Such pressure leads to programs based on "good intentions and high hopes" rather than clear theoretical direction (Gelles & Loseke, 1993, p. 254). To be sure, the rudimentary level of research does not promote theory building or even establish the framework in which to weave current threads of understanding. Scholars have therefore turned to more established areas of developmental theory to help them conceptualize the problem of child abuse and to suggest solutions. The predominant model in developmental psychology today is the ecological approach originated by Bronfenbrenner (1979). The model envisions the child's course of development as a complex process that is primarily influenced by the family; the family in turn is affected by the social and economic structures of the community; and the community is shaped by the state, nation, and larger world order.

On the surface, ecological theory appears to be an adequate explanatory edifice for the phenomenon of violence against children. For example, in the area of physical abuse, the child's traits and level of development are expressed within the context of the family; the family's ability to meet the child's developmental needs is shaped by the stresses and supports it derives from the community (where each member's own developmental level was achieved); and the community's capacity to meet family needs is affected by economic events and government policies filtered to the locality through national and global circumstances.

When global economics directs the marketplace and national policies promote individual responsibility by withdrawing safety nets, there is a diminution in the jobs, social services, and human networks that support families. Isolated in a cultural environment that glorifies violence and aggression, family members become more inclined to behave aggressively and to accept aggressive behavior as normative. Similarly, when children are exposed in schools to peers who carry guns and other deadly weapons, the school staff's ability to protect children is influenced by the stresses that they endure from working in a dangerous environment and teaching a population whose needs seem greater every year. These stresses may be mitigated by support from the surrounding community and from local and national policies that shore up teachers' and administrators' abilities to deal with both the victimizers and the victims. The principal point is that violence against and protection for children arise from a complex, mutual interaction among an individual's ontogenetic development and the micro-, exo-, and macrosystems (Belsky, 1980).

The ecological model offers a credible explanation of the causes of child abuse, but what can it contribute to the area of prevention? If the sources of child abuse arise from the child, the family, and the proximal and distal ecologies, the guiding principle for prevention is to target all of these areas for change. This in fact is the recommendation of the working group on prevention of the American Psychological Association (APA) Coordinating Committee on Child Abuse and Neglect: "Research has shown that prevention programs that target single risk factors are not nearly as effective as prevention programs that assume an ecological model and examine risk factors in the context of the individual, the family, community, and society" (Willis, 1995, p. 3). In the same vein, the U.S. Advisory Board on Child Abuse and Neglect (1993b), which entitled its fourth annual report *Neighbors Helping Neighbors*, called for a community-based system that provides a network of services responsive to the myriad needs of families and casting a wide safety net for children.

Members of the APA Coordinating Committee (Wolfe, Reppucci, & Hart, 1995) argued that because abuse is tightly interwoven with other social ills, a piecemeal approach to prevention might not significantly reduce the prevalence of abuse. In line with this thinking, Willis and

Silovsky (chapter 16, this volume) recommended that city and state governments need to rebuild and strengthen low-income neighborhoods; support families by providing jobs and safe environments; improve schools and housing; bolster health and child care benefits; expand parental leave policies; and reduce televised violence, substance abuse, access to firearms, and the incidence of poverty. Although pursuing these ideas may not prevent the abuse of a child born today, it is nonetheless imperative that researchers, practitioners, and policymakers keep an eye on the future. For now, any plans to revamp society are simply too long term to offer a viable solution to the immediate crisis of child abuse. Such plans also depend on a national commitment to provide resources to purge society of the conditions that lead to maltreatment and to develop an atmosphere that values children. It is not sufficient to wait for such major alterations of the social fabric that is life in the United States.

Smaller social solutions may not work either, even if they could be implemented, without better knowledge about the causes of abuse. For example, televised violence is commonly cited as a contributor to maltreatment. When people become accustomed to violent acts taking place in their living room many times a day, they become desensitized to victims' pain and suffering and begin to accept violence into their own behavioral repertoire. Although a strong correlation between televised violence and aggression has been reported (see chapter 16, this volume), the current knowledge base is not adequate to determine whether the same correlation exists with child abuse.

Another suggestion common in the prevention literature is to attack the national problem of substance abuse, a problem Willis and Silovsky (chapter 16) cite as a major contribution to the risk of child maltreatment. Slaby (chapter 15) notes that the national "war on drugs," at least as it is currently being waged, has helped to create a culture of violence. This culture is frequently mentioned as conducive to an array of forms of violence against children in the family, the school, and the community at large.

Reppucci, Land, and Haugaard (chapter 13) argue that prevention programs focusing on environmental change should receive more attention, but such programs have not yet been developed. Efforts to prevent violence against children by changing smaller chunks of society, such as the neighborhood and school, are hampered by the same lack of guidance and overabundance of optimism, although here there are some causes for the optimism. A scattering of local programs have succeeded in changing undesirable behavior that may be related to violence against children, small successes that are reminiscent of George Bush's "points of light." Boston, for example, has become the envy of the nation for its extraordinary record for an inner city: Not a single youth was killed by firearms in well over a year (Lamb, 1987). Willis and Silovsky (chapter 16, this volume) note the parallel success of many schools in eliminating drugs and weapons from their campuses. If a school can do it, so can a neighborhood and beyond. These authors draw encouragement from public health experiences suggesting that prevention programs designed to reduce opportunities for risk can increase safety in other areas.

The present discussion highlights a drawback of local prevention efforts. When resources and hopes are expended on a program, a false sense of security can be generated. One example is found in school-based antidelinquency programs. Peer mediation, conflict resolution, coping strategies, and other techniques are typically presented in some combination for one class period a week for 6 weeks or so—about the equivalent of 1 school day. It is ridiculous to think that such brief training can extinguish antisocial behavior. Clearly, programs need to be long and intensive for successful change to be possible. In terms of child abuse prevention, change at the local level is a more promising approach than "changing the universe," but local workers need to know what to do to effect change, and research has provided them with few answers. The result is that people try token programs and hope that their children will be safer.

The mandate for research is clear. At the same time that researchers design programs that can capitalize on the knowledge available, they must continue to work to fill the gaps in the knowledge regarding causes of and ways to prevent violence against children. Children are exposed to violence at multiple levels and in multiple contexts (e.g., the home, school, and neighborhood). To stem this tide of abuse—and exposing children to any form of violence is indeed abuse—one must understand interrelationships among the violent events at varying levels of analysis, including the relationships among their causes and their consequences. Interventions arising from this understanding must be evaluated, using the best scientific practices, to determine and enhance their success.

A false sense of security is also engendered by programs that target children as agents of prevention. Using the example of sexual abuse prevention, Reppucci, Land, and Haugaard (chapter 13, this volume) expose the flaws in the assumptions underlying such programs and conclude that there is absolutely no evidence that they work and some evidence that they can cause harm. The APA Coordinating Committee drew the same conclusion concerning programs aimed at preschoolers. The committee cited Finkelhor and Strapko's suggestion to rename them child sexual abuse "detection facilitation," rather then "prevention," programs, although there is not much evidence that they are good at detection either (Wolfe et al., 1995).

The truth of the matter is that children are not responsible for their abuse at the hands of adults whom they must trust to nurture and protect them. It is absurd to think that children can be trained to change the behavior of their caregivers (Finkelhor, 1995). The emptiness of child-focused prevention programs is made most apparent by a consideration of the ages when children are at the highest risk for abuse. Children under 2 years are among those at greatest risk, especially risk of serious injury (NCCAN, 1996; Gelles, 1996). What kind of program could possibly be devised to teach a 6-month-old to stop her parents from throwing her against the wall or out the window? The burden of change is unquestionably on the parents.

Adults are the ones who abuse children, and they are the most logical focus of efforts to prevent physical or sexual abuse. Indeed, the most promising results in programs that target physical abuse have been obtained with programs that focus on parents (U.S. Advisory Board on Child Abuse and Neglect, 1991; Wolfe et al., 1995). A number of lines of thinking converge to support this conclusion. From the perspective of ecological theory, stressors arise from the workplace or lack of one; struggles to meet basic economic and psychological needs; isolation from social supports; problems with the available health, education, and child care systems; and lack of knowledge about child development and effective parenting. This model accounts for the higher prevalence of child abuse in the lower socioeconomic classes as well as the fact that child abuse also appears among wealthier groups, who are not immune to such stressors. A related model emphasizes the abuser's developmental level, with lower levels implying a higher burden of stressors, more impulsivity and externalizing behaviors, and a greater likelihood of parenting that is authoritarian and relies on corporal punishment (Polansky, Chalmers, Buttenweiser, & Williams, 1981; Ross & Zigler, 1983).

It is important to note that almost all parent-focused programs and most of the research on the characteristics of abusive parents have involved mothers only—not fathers. The chapters by Milner (chapter 6) and Schellenbach (chapter 10) contain discussions of this issue; researchers have avoided trying to understand, intervene in, or prevent child abuse by fathers. All the studies reviewed by Milner on the characteristics of physically abusive parents involved samples of mothers; none were of fathers. Furthermore, none of the studies on sexually abusive males have examined the *parenting* characteristics of sexually abusive men. Similarly, Schellenbach's review of interventions with parents includes none in which abusive fathers were the targets of change. It is as if professionals have thrown up their hands at the task of understanding and preventing fathers and other men from sexually abusing or physically attacking children and instead hope to teach children to protect themselves from these incomprehensible and uncontrollable individuals.

Wekerle and Wolfe (chapter 14) present the unusual approach of focusing on both females and males and on attempting to prevent abuse by dealing with teenagers who are not yet parents. Noting that the field has moved beyond the earlier emphasis on psychological disease to one of psychological process, these authors explain abusive parenting as a core relationship problem. Beginning with interpersonal relations that foster insecure parent–child attachment, both the adult's and child's views of relationships and of themselves develop in a manner that promotes dysfunctional social interactions. Negative relationship factors thus become the appropriate targets for prevention, and positive relationship factors are targeted for promotion. Wekerle and Wolfe see a "window of opportunity" for prevention during the periods when new relationships are being formed. These periods include adolescence, when dating relationships are begun, and birth, when baby and parents get to know one another.

Promoting healthy parent–child relationships is the goal of some of the most effective abuse prevention efforts. For example, the Healthy Start Program begun in Hawaii provides home visitation services to new parents in high-risk groups. Initial evaluations have suggested that the program reduced the incidence of abuse and neglect and possibly alleviated other risks associated with poor developmental outcomes (Center on Child Abuse Prevention Research, 1996). These results were so well received that the Healthy Start model (Healthy Families America) has been adopted in 31 states (Daro, 1996), and the U.S. Advisory Board on Child Abuse and Neglect (1991) has strongly recommended home visitation as a solution of choice for abuse prevention planning.

The appeal of this approach is that it is consistent with much of the collective wisdom accrued in the fields of developmental psychology, clinical practice, family support, and related areas. Home visiting embodies primary prevention, which is more effective and more cost effective than remedial efforts and spares a child from pain or death. Visitation programs can avoid stigmatizing parents as "at risk" by being available to all, which is the practice in some states' versions of Healthy Start and in the successful Parents as Teachers program. When workers enter a home, services can be individualized to meet each family's unique needs and to bolster its strengths. These elements show promise as components of a multiservice approach to enhancing parents' child-rearing knowledge and skills, alleviating stresses on family functioning, promoting healthy child development, and quite likely preventing child maltreatment. However, more rigorous evaluation of the programs is required; later reports of Healthy Start, for example, have shown few longitudinal benefits (Center on Child Abuse Prevention Research, 1996).

There are other promising approaches at the community level. For example, the New Haven Child Development–Community Policing Program puts mental health professionals into partnerships with the police to collaborate on strategies for early intervention and prevention of violence against youth (Berkowitz, 1997). Children who are victims of, witnesses to, and perpetrators of violence are often noticed first by police; however, officers typically do not have the skills, time, and other resources required to meet these children's psychological needs. Although mental health professionals have those skills, children who are acutely traumatized by violence usually do not appear for services until long after the event, if at all. Through the New Haven program, clinicians and police learn more about each other's roles; a 24-hour-a-day consultation service has been set up for officers so that they always have access to mental health advice; and an ongoing case conference allows both sides to discuss their interventions and learn how better to help victims, as well as perpetrators, of violence. The program is now being replicated in seven cities, with enthusiasm expressed as these new collaborations begin.

All of the authors of the chapters in this volume dealing with prevention allude to the need for social policies that will allow effective prevention programs to be developed now and in the future. An immediate policy change called for by these contributors and many others (e.g., Gelles, 1996; U.S. Advisory Board on Child Abuse and Neglect, 1995) is the reorientation of protective service agencies toward child safety as opposed to family preservation. Gelles went so far as to argue that because past behavior is the best predictor of future behavior, efforts to preserve families preserve a child's risk of abuse. He has criticized federal policies that have channeled funds into preservation programs at the expense of support for primary prevention. Wekerle and Wolfe (chapter 14, this volume) likewise press for policies that encourage early assistance and the promotion of healthy families in place of those that emphasize detection and limited postmortem intervention, a plea repeated by Slaby (chapter 15) in the context of youth violence. Willis and Silovsky (chapter 16) summarize the confusion in the policy arena by arguing that the national government and the states rarely coordinate their efforts and resources, internally or externally, to develop planned strategies for remediating shared problems such as child abuse. The titles of the reports of the U.S. Advisory Board on Child Abuse and Neglect (e.g., *The Continuing Child Protection Emergency*, 1993a; *A Nation's Shame*, 1995) should serve as a wake-up call to legislators at all levels of government to rally around the policy recommendations contained therein.

CONCLUSION

There are thousands of scholarly books and papers on the topic of child abuse and other forms of violence, indicating that professional interest is high. The fact that this interest has not translated into a more established science is unquestionably due to inadequate support for research to bolster knowledge and spawn viable theories. As recently as 1989, the National Center on Child Abuse and Neglect adopted a policy to ban support for basic research contributing to theory, as opposed to practice, and balked at developing research training programs (see Melton et al., 1995). These policies have since been reversed, and in 1993 the National Research Council called for a doubling of research funds at the federal level and a pooling of state research efforts. The U.S. Advisory Board on Child Abuse and Neglect (1995) recently recommended specific types of research in need of support, including basic studies as well as program evaluation.

These developments ignite hope for the eventual prevention of all forms of violence against children. However, hopeful anticipation must not serve as an excuse to avoid the immediate need for prevention activities. At the First National Conference on Child Abuse and Neglect, a paper entitled "Controlling Child Abuse in America: An Effort Doomed to Failure?" was presented (Zigler, 1976). Twenty years later, the title remains appropriate. It should not be. Professionals already know where to begin. They are realistic enough to admit that they cannot change the universe but that they can reduce risks by strengthening families. They have ideas about how to help children who have experienced abuse. They know what policies are needed to increase insights, develop more effective services, and put a dent in the prevalence of violence against children. Action has to occur on the basis of what is known, and researchers have to pursue knowledge actively about the complex causes of all forms of violence against children. Today's child deserves the best that can be offered with current knowledge; tomorrow's child deserves even better.

REFERENCES

Allen, L. (1990). A developmental perspective on multiple levels of analysis in community research. In P. Tolan, C. Keys, F. Chertok, & L. Jason (Eds.), *Researching community psychology: Issues of theory and methods*. Washington, DC: American Psychological Association.

Bachmann, C. (1996). *Violences urbaines* [Urban violence.] Paris: Albin Michel.

Belsky, J. (1980). Child maltreatment: An ecological integration. *American Psychologist, 35,* 320–335.

Berkowitz, S. (1997, April). *From victim to perpetrator: Breaking the cycle of violence.* Paper presented at the meeting of the Society for Research in Child Development, Washington, DC.

Bronfenbrenner, U. (1979). *The ecology of human development.* Cambridge, MA: Harvard University Press.

Center on Child Abuse Prevention Research. (1996). *Intensive home visitation: A randomized trial, follow-up and risk assessment study of Hawaii's Healthy Start Program.* Chicago: Author.

Coulton, C. J., Korbin, J. E., Su, M., & Chow, J. (1995). Community level factors and child maltreatment rates. *Child Development, 66,* 1262–1276.

Daro, D. (1996). Preventing child abuse: A new national initiative. *Child, Youth, and Family Services Quarterly, 19*(2), 9–11.

Finkelhor, D. (1995). The victimization of children: A developmental perspective. *American Journal of Orthopsychiatry, 65*, 177–193.

Garofalo, J., Siegel, L., & Laub, J. (1987). School-related victimizations among adolescents: An analysis of National Crime Survey (NCS) narratives. Lifestyle and routine activity theories of crime. *Journal of Quantitative Criminology, 3*, 321–338.

Gelles, R. J. (1996). *The book of David: How preserving families can cost children's lives.* New York: Basic Books.

Gelles, R. J., & Loseke, D. R. (1993). Issues in social intervention. In R. J. Gelles & D. R. Loseke (Eds.), *Current controversies on family violence* (pp. 251–255). Newbury Park, CA: Sage.

Glazer, S. (1992). Violence in schools. *Congressional Quarterly Researcher, 2*, 785–808.

Huston, R. L., Parra, J. M., Prihoda, T. J., & Foulds, D. M. (1995). Characteristics of childhood sexual abuse in a predominantly Mexican-American population. *Child Abuse & Neglect, 19*, 165–176.

Lamb, D. (1987, April 8). New approach cripples Boston's gang network: Putting probation officers on the streets. *Los Angeles Times*, p. A1.

Melton, G. B., Goodman, G. S., Kalichman, S. C., Levine, M., Saywitz, K. J., & Koocher, G. P. (1995). Empirical research on children and the law. *Journal of Clinical Child Psychology, 24*, 47–77.

Mennen, F. E. (1994). Sexual abuse in Latina girls: Their functioning and a comparison with white and African American girls. *Hispanic Journal of Behavioral Sciences, 16*, 475–486.

Mennen, F. E. (1995). The relationship of race/ethnicity to symptoms in childhood sexual abuse. *Child Abuse & Neglect, 19*, 115–124.

National Center for Child Abuse and Neglect (NCCAN). (1996). *Third study of national incidence and prevalence of child abuse and neglect.* Washington, DC: U.S. Department of Health and Human Services.

National Research Council. (1993). *Understanding child abuse and neglect.* Washington, DC: National Academy of Sciences.

Pithers, W. (1997, March). *Does treatment work? Myths and facts.* Poster session presented at the Research Grantees meeting of the National Center on Child Abuse and Neglect, Bethesda, MD.

Plummer, C. A. (1993). Prevention is appropriate, prevention is successful. In R. J. Gelles & D. R. Loseke (Eds.), *Current controversies on family violence.* Newbury Park, CA: Sage.

Polansky, N. A., Chalmers, M., Buttenweiser, E., & Williams, D. (1981). *Damaged parents: An anatomy of child neglect.* Chicago: University of Chicago Press.

Pynoos, R. S., Frederick, C., Nader, K., & Arroyo, W. (1987). Life threat and posttraumatic stress in school-age children. *Archives of General Psychiatry, 44*, 1057–1063.

Ross, C. J., & Zigler, E. (1983). Treatment issues in child abuse. *Journal of the American Academy of Child Psychiatry, 22*, 305–308.

Rossman, B. B. R., & Rosenberg, M. S. (1997). *The multiple victimization of children: Conceptual, developmental, research, and clinical issues.* Binghamton, NY: Haworth Press.

Shinn, M. (1990). Mixing and matching: Levels of conceptualization, measurement, and statistical analysis in community research. In P. Tolan, C. Keys, F. Chertok, & L. Jason (Eds.), *Researching community psychology: Issues of theory and methods.* Washington, DC: American Psychological Association.

Sullivan, M. (1996, November). *Violence in early adolescence: Events and development.* Poster session presented at the meeting of the American Society of Criminology, Chicago, IL.

Trickett, P. K., Reiffman, A., Horowitz, L., & Putnam, F. (1997). Characteristics of sexual abuse and trauma and the prediction of developmental outcomes. In D. Cicchetti & S. L. Toth (Eds.), *Rochester Symposium on Developmental Psychopathology: Volume VIII. The effects of trauma on the developmental process.* Rochester, NY: University of Rochester Press.

U.S. Advisory Board on Child Abuse and Neglect. (1991). *Creating caring communities: Blueprint for an effective federal policy on child abuse and neglect.* Washington, DC: U.S. Government Printing Office.

U.S. Advisory Board on Child Abuse and Neglect. (1993a). *The continuing child protection emergency: A challenge to the nation.* Washington, DC: U.S. Government Printing Office.

U.S. Advisory Board on Child Abuse and Neglect. (1993b). *Neighbors helping neighbors: A new national strategy for the protection of children.* Washington, DC: U.S. Government Printing Office.

U.S. Advisory Board on Child Abuse and Neglect. (1995). *A nation's shame: Fatal child abuse and neglect in the United States.* Washington, DC: U.S. Government Printing Office.

Wekerle, C., & Wolfe, D. A. (1993). Prevention of child physical abuse and neglect: Promising new directions. *Clinical Psychology Review, 13*, 501–540.

Willis, D. J. (1995). Psychological impact of child abuse and neglect. *Journal of Clinical Child Psychology, 24*, 2–4.

Wolfe, D. A., Reppucci, N. D., & Hart, S. (1995). Child abuse prevention: Knowledge and priorities. *Journal of Clinical Child Psychology, 24*, 5–22.

Zahn-Waxler, C. (1993). Warriors and worriers: Gender and psychopathology. *Development and Psychopathology, 5*, 79–89.

Zigler, E. (1976). Controlling child abuse in America: An effort doomed to failure? In *Proceedings of the First National Conference on Child Abuse and Neglect* (pp. 29–35; DHEW Publication No. OHD 77-30094). Washington, DC: U.S. Department of Health, Education, and Welfare.

18

EVALUATION RESEARCH ON VIOLENCE INTERVENTIONS: ISSUES AND STRATEGIES FOR DESIGN

PATRICK H. TOLAN AND C. HENDRICKS BROWN

A reading of the other chapters in this volume and the related research suggests that the field is at a "weigh station" in its methodological and substantive development related to intervention. Much has been accomplished, but these accomplishments must be qualified in several ways. The power and reliability of measures and empirical tests are improving. Also, the rate of publication of such studies is increasing. There is growing consensus about the need for empirical studies to guide risk, intervention, and policy, and in some areas, there is relative certainty about what investigations are needed next. However, there are still substantial gaps in the knowledge about violence and children, and the literature is thin at many points.

In many cases, researchers have used methods that limit confidence in the results, which strains the confidence with which the findings can be used to argue for the value of violence prevention and intervention and to guide policy. The existing literature is composed mostly of efficacy studies that have questionable external validity and generalization across populations. Also, the existing studies have tended to focus on risk apart from its relevance to intervention. Although there is evidence that some interventions can aid perpetrators, victims, and families and other significant persons closely related to direct victims (Tolan & Guerra, 1994), the robustness of the findings and their general usefulness for practice are not clear. The existing empirical evidence provides a tenuous connection across studies, although the existing findings may be promising.

This chapter provides a framework and some guidelines for evaluation research on interventions to prevent violence affecting children. We hope to facilitate empirical investigations of key questions concerning the causes of and solutions to violence affecting children and to deepen and broaden the knowledge base needed for sound and effective policy in this area (Brown & Liao, 1996). Because violence interventions, like many prevention or other large-scale interventions, do not readily fit the intervention design and analysis templates used for small, tightly controlled, laboratory studies, it is difficult to ascertain what evaluations should be done (Cohen, 1990; Wicker, 1985). In this chapter, we summarize some of the issues involved in designing violence interventions and suggest some design and analytical approaches that can be applied to improve the strength and sensitivity of evaluations. In doing so, we do not emphasize as much the general principles of evaluation (see Rossi & Freeman, 1985, for such a guide) but instead attempt to identify the issues that may arise in instances of evaluation within the focus of this book. At the end of this chapter, we provide an example of how alternative strategies for evaluation can work in interventions for domestic abusers.

We do not limit our discussion of evaluation to instances in which the most stringent design criteria can be met (i.e., a design with a sizable number of units that are balanced and randomly assigned to the intervention condition, with periodic follow-up throughout a developmentally appropriate range). Instead, we emphasize evaluations that are appropriate when such optimally designed studies cannot be realized (Brown & Liao, 1996). This approach has a corollary contention: Scientifically useful evaluation almost always can and should be applied to intervention programs designed to lessen the harm from violence to children.

In this chapter, we use the term *scientific evaluation* to refer to any process of evaluation that first takes into account all of the following in obtaining inferences about the impact of an intervention: the design of the study; the means by which participants were assigned to, offered, or exposed to the intervention conditions; the methods of collecting data on participants and their environments; and the follow-up or attrition of participants (Kraemer & Kraemer, 1994). Second, a scientific evaluation must follow generally accepted statistical guidelines for making quantitative conclusions; for example, in the presence of low statistical power, one cannot conclude that there are no differences in treatment (Cohen, 1990; Fisher, 1935). Third, scientific evaluations can and should allow for explicit testing of theories or hypotheses that lend support to or argue against these explanations (Koepsell et al., 1992; Lorion, Price, & Eaton, 1989). For example, the hypothesis that the impact of an intervention is dependent on the amount of exposure to the intervention can be tested by looking for a "dose response" relationship between the implementation and the outcome.

A scientific evaluation according to this definition need not be built around a randomized trial. Indeed, even randomized trials, which provide the most rigid examination of impact, can at best supply an indirect measure of the impact of the intervention at an individual level (Brown, 1993b, Holland, 1986; Rubin, 1974), for no study can measure each participant's response simultaneously under intervention and control conditions. The most important strength of randomized trials is that they can limit the effects of variables or conditions that are not under the direct control of the researcher, and therefore they eliminate many of the alternative explanations that could be offered to explain observed differences in interventions (Brown & Liao, 1996).

Nonrandomized trials have an important place in research on violence. An example from medical research helps point this out. Despite the major advances that controlled clinical trials have made in improving health, the first step in learning about medical interventions has typically been careful observation under conditions of nonrandomized experimentation, that is, case studies of new surgical procedures such as heart transplants, which may or may not be followed later by a rigorous, randomized trial. It is through the following four steps that the scientific evaluation of nonrandomized trials will likely provide the most knowledge (Cohen & McSweeny, 1982): (a) selecting potentially valuable interventions to reduce violence, (b) providing suggestions as to how an intervention program can be improved on the basis of data, (c) combining the results of a number of trials to provide overall estimates of impact, and (d) identifying environmental conditions under which an intervention's effectiveness varies.

THE IMPORTANCE AND NECESSITY OF EVALUATION

Scientific evaluation is important not only for quantifying the impact of an intervention to allow objective comparisons with alternative intervention strategies, but also because both funders and policymakers are demanding data-based evidence of effects on target behaviors as well as costs. In the current political climate, in which juvenile and adult violent crime are of great concern to the public, emotions, perception of blame, and a desire to apply quick solutions to complex problems all play large roles in determining which strategies are selected to deal with these problems. A case in point is California's "three strikes and you're out" law, which provides mandatory long-term prison sentencing for multiple offenders. Although the law may have the effect of reducing crime in the short run, its enormous cost and lack of a prevention effort aimed at the next generations of offenders will make reliance on this sole strategy one of the least cost-effective choices for policymakers (Greenwood, Model, Rydell, & Chiesa, 1996; Reid & Eddy, 1996a, 1996b). It is unfortunate that the current policies toward violence and crime are little influenced by the results of careful studies. The most promising ways to alter this situation are to design and analyze evaluations carefully and to synthesize the results. Also, violence prevention proponents have a social responsibility to provide the soundest information to those directly in need of intervention as well as to the public. We believe that the scientific evaluation of interventions to reduce violence provides one of the best methods of meeting this social responsibility both to the communities directly affected and to the broader public. Without such an approach, based on carefully analyzed data, it is unlikely that improvements in violence prevention programs will flourish and that a sound public health strategy can be implemented (Tolan & Guerra, in press).

For efficiency, we frame our discussion around comparisons of a single intervention program with one or more control conditions, such as no treatment, treatment as usual, or some lesser level of treatment. In most cases, the issues we raise and the potential value of the suggested approaches are applicable to more complex multiple-group comparisons or to component comparisons, albeit with some modifications. Discussion and useful modifications for multigroup or multicomponent intervention comparisons can be found elsewhere (see Tolan, Kendall, & Beidel, 1996; West, Aiken, & Todd, 1993).

IMPEDIMENTS AND COMPLICATING CHARACTERISTICS

The concerns that limit interest in the evaluation of intervention processes and effects are numerous and in many cases represent a substantial number of potential problems (Rossi & Freeman, 1985). It would be shortsighted to fail to acknowledge that these may be formidable impediments to the evaluation of violence interventions. These impediments can usually be addressed or overcome, often more readily than it seems at first consideration (Koepsell et al., 1992); their due consideration, however, is an important step in evaluation design for interpretation of results. The most common and important impediments are discussed in the following sections.

Evaluation Will Not Be Sensitive and Refined Enough

Evaluations may fail to capture the intervention effects that the program providers are sure exist on the basis of clinical experience. A derivative of this general concern is the worry that the evaluation will lead to embarrassing results—that the program is not substantially positive. This finding could lead to the end of funding and perhaps to the very existence of a social agency. The failure to have positive results can sully the reputation of a theoretician, program developer, or agency and can become a political liability when one is competing for funding.

Evaluation Will Focus on Some Statistical Judgment at the Cost of Undermining Clinical Effects

A policymaker or program staff person may justify an intervention because of reports of benefits by individuals or a sentiment that "helping one child" is enough to justify a violence program, rather than on the basis of scientific statistical criteria. In contrast, an evaluator may be more focused on the change in scores on the evaluation scale than on the validity of that scale in representing meaningful program effects. With the current lack of knowledge concerning how to measure the effects of violence, and with even less knowledge about empirically validated measures for violence interventions, program staff can readily question the wisdom of depending on quantitative evaluation to judge effects over their experience or the judgment of consumers and advocates.

The Requirements for a Sound Evaluation Will Constrain the Intervention Activity

Desirable evaluation design features such as random assignment and consistency in services delivered to each participant can conflict with human interests of serving all who are in need and matching services to clients' needs. A related concern is the need to divide limited resources between the program and the evaluation. The cost of evaluation may be seen as draining off precious funds that could be used to help more persons. A scientific study may seem to be a luxury that does not justify taking money away from programming, especially to those who are not evaluators.

Evaluation Will Be Developed Apart From the Community Base of the Intervention

Evaluators often come from universities or corporate cultures and may not appreciate the importance of community involvement in violence intervention. Communities and community-oriented agencies may resist evaluation because of the fear that there will not be due consideration of the importance of who decides what is to be evaluated and how process and outcome effects are defined. Many workers in social agencies appreciate the ethnic, gender, and class politics that are incumbent in violence intervention and its evaluation. The actual as well as perceived differences between the evaluators' characterization of these concerns and those held by program staff and administration can lead to skepticism about the benefits of evaluation (Shadish, 1990). If the evaluation team is not from the agency or does not have substantive and technical knowledge about the specific community or violence issue that is the focus of the intervention, the members of the team are likely to be seen as lacking adequate understanding by those carrying out the program. Related to this issue is the inevitable variation in perspectives among those involved and the need for careful deliberation of what is critical to evaluate, how that evaluation effort is to be conceived, and how the measurement and analysis approach reflects such conceptions and the varied perspectives (Mitroff, 1983).

It Is Unclear How and by Whom the Information Will Be Used

There may be a lack of appreciation for what evaluation results can and cannot explain. If the program managers and funders are unclear about how to use evaluation information, they may prefer not to have such studies done. For example, they may fear that the results will be presented as overly definitive concerning the usefulness of the program and the next steps in program refinement, undermining the prerogative they presume as program managers. Who owns the evaluation data and how that data should be disseminated are issues that need discussion before the evaluation is done (Rossi & Freeman, 1985).

These concerns are often based on realistic worry, bad prior experiences, or a lack of information to counter skepticism or mistrust. In some cases the potential loss from evaluation compared to the potential gain may seem too great to justify evaluation. In fact, in almost all cases this is not accurate. The type of evaluation and its purpose may need careful consideration and articulation, and the planned dissemination may require careful regulation. However, in most instances, evaluation addresses and helps to overcome the problems and worries listed here. Most of the time the more pertinent issue is how to evaluate the program in a manner that incorporates these viewpoints, considers these concerns, and serves its intended purposes, all within the given constraints.

Other Substantial Impediments

In addition to the aforementioned practical concerns, most violence intervention evaluations present formidable methodological challenges. Probably most daunting and common is having to demonstrate measurable short-term effects for an intervention of limited duration and intensity (Brown & Liao, 1996; Kraemer & Kraemer, 1994). Funding for demonstrations and their evaluations is often provided at a level and for a duration that make longer intervention and follow-up impossible. However, the prevailing evidence is that most effects are likely to be modest and may not be fully determinable for some time after completion (Lipsey & Wilson, 1993; Tolan & Guerra, 1994). Similarly, most theories guiding the programs do not predict a sudden curative effect. It is important, therefore, that evaluators balance a realistic response to these practical limitations with a sound evaluation method that fits the theoretical model of the intervention.

THE NEED FOR ACCUMULATING SCIENTIFICALLY EVALUATED INTERVENTIONS

Given the preceding list of substantial and often vexing concerns, one can see why empirical evaluation may not be chosen. However, evaluation is needed to provide sound and systematic advancement of the knowledge base. Also, it can be argued there is an ethical imperative to apply empirical evaluation to any program until the soundness of findings about its effects, predictable benefits, and potential risks can be clearly determined (Lorion, Tolan, & Wahler, 1987).

The current status of the field is analogous to that of pharmacology in the early 1900s. At that time, most medicines were patented; they were developed and sold on the basis of endorsements, hearsay, and their claimed use by many persons. The formulations were not based on clinical trials to establish the benefits, safety, and potential complications of the medicines. Similarly, at this point in time there is a critical need to advance violence intervention from a set of "patented programs," in which many remain untested, to a set of tested programs with known benefits for specific populations and problems.

DEPENDING ON META-ANALYTIC JUDGMENT TO DETERMINE EFFICACY AND EFFECTIVENESS[1]

A major requisite for the field to move forward is to combine results from multiple studies of similar and dissimilar interventions with similar and dissimilar communities. Judgments about the value of an intervention that are based on a single or few studies can be misleading. Single studies or even a small set of studies of an efficacious intervention cannot discriminate which components or processes were the "active ingredients" of the project. Many programs that are planned and implemented are not effective

---

[1]*Efficacy* refers to demonstrated effects in a carefully controlled demonstration project. *Effectiveness* refers to demonstrated effects in a field trial with conditions comparable to those of normal delivery of service.

(Tolan & Guerra, in press); however, the lack of effects from a single intervention should not be taken as definitive evidence of effectiveness. Instead, efficacy and effectiveness trials should function as the building blocks for meta-analysis, which can provide estimates across studies of the relative effects of different approaches and different service delivery methods for different populations.

The value of combining the results from multiple studies rather than inferring definitive meaning from a single trial can be demonstrated by a simple example. Suppose 20 separate studies are performed to examine the impact of one intervention. In each study, one community is assigned to intervention and one to control, and the population-level change in violent behavior is evaluated after the intervention period ends. Because there are no replications of the intervention condition in any of the separate studies, each study provides limited information about the effectiveness of the intervention. After all, a beneficial result in any one study may be due to any of a myriad of reasons the community that happened to receive the intervention turned in better results. In contrast, combining these 20 results may overcome the limited statistical power in any single study and permit identification of robust patterns.

There are a small number of conditions that must hold for there to be benefit from combining information. First, there can be no systematic bias in all of the separate trials that favors one condition over another. Such bias can enter if communities are selected preferentially for intervention; for example, if all the researchers first singled out highly motivated or mobilized communities to receive the intervention and then selected a control community from within all neighboring communities, there would be a systematic difference in community motivation across the studies. Such a systematic difference is far more important in the analysis of a large number of studies than in the analysis of a small number, because bias begins to dominate in the former case.

Second, there cannot be any systematic exclusion of studies on the basis of negative results. This problem, often referred to as *publication bias* because it appears when negative studies fail to be published, can also make interventions appear better than they really are (Lipsey & Wilson, 1993). Therefore, a subtle but also important issue for evaluation for building the knowledge base is that allowing only effective program evaluations to be released, considered, and disseminated can lead to serious bias in the estimation of relative effects, particularly if the failure to find results reflects underpowered analyses (too few participants for the size of the effect). Such shortsighted emphases are misleading concerning the important purpose of evaluations, which is to provide reliable information for decision making. The supposition that failure in one test of a program's effectiveness should discourage further research on that approach can systematically and prematurely exclude some valuable interventions. This type of judgment is analogous to dropping a line of research on cures for cancer simply because one clinical trial fails to show benefits. This reasoning could lead to a public health disaster with a substantially harmful impact on morbidity and mortality rates.

The value of the scientific evaluation of violence programs is in the progression in knowledge about what strategies can be effective and the limitations of that effect. The analytical goal is to sort through systematic attempts to affect violence and, from the patterns of results across studies, to construct an understanding of the most apt approaches, determine how to build on those that work, and identify needed modifications of what did not work. Building these databases depends on scientific evaluation. However, the scientific methods used for evaluation need to be differentiated from scientific goals.

DIFFERENTIATING BETWEEN SCIENTIFIC METHODS AND SCIENTIFIC GOALS

Evaluation applies scientific designs to build useful knowledge for decision making, but it differs from scientific experiments in its purpose. Science has a central concern with replication based on the belief that one can discover fundamental truths that can become generalized rules. Evaluation is characterized by the same interest in methods that permit replication and generalizability, but it differs in its goal. The purpose of evaluation is to answer questions and provide direction for stakeholders in a given situation rather than to establish elemental determinants (Shadish, 1990; Tolan, Keys, Chertok, & Jason, 1990). Researchers in evaluation focus on establishing conventions and noting trends that suggest advisable actions.

There is a subtle but important difference, therefore, between the goals of evaluation and those of scientific experiments. Confusion can lead to the valuing of scientific experiments and devaluing of evaluations, which cannot provide clear and generalizable determinations of the source of effects (i.e., rule out all other possible hypotheses). Evaluation requires the use of scientific methods to maximize reliability and validity but does not have the scientific goal of establishing a clear and specific causal link. This confusion seems to represent a too literal assumption of common goals (Cronbach, 1975; Mitroff, 1983) and may lead evaluators to be too constrained to engage violence programmers in a productive discussion during evaluation planning. For example, the pros and cons of random assignment or the value of standardized instruments may not be discussed but rather treated as absolutes by evaluators. Failure to consider and directly discuss these issues may hinder their incorporation by programmers or the adherence of programmers to other important scientific concerns such as program integrity and the necessity of obtaining complete evaluation data.

We discuss in the following sections two critical differences between the scientific methods used for evaluation and the more general scientific goals of building theory and providing causal links. These are (a) the standardization of instruments and criteria to measure outcome and (b) the standard of proof.

Interest in Standardizing Instruments

In evaluation, studies may rely on generally available data and methods rather than on the collection of detailed data with prescriptively designed instruments, as is ordinarily required in scientific studies. As an example, reported rates of violence within a community or school are much easier to collect than are individual-level data on victimization. The use of standard, readily available measures permits an efficiency of understanding and a comparability across program evaluations that is important for enabling meta-analytic summarizing and for facilitating program design and policy decisions (Koepsell et al., 1992). There needs to be balance between refined calibration of each instrument and the specificity of the instrument for a given program and the comparability of findings across studies. For example, once standards are established concerning the domains that must be assessed to determine the effects of a violence prevention program for children, and the instruments are developed and validated to measure such domains adequately, criterion scores can be established to determine whether statistically significant effects are clinically meaningful and have substantial public health benefits. Also, derivative programs and cross-validation tests of programs can be compared directly to previous results for determining generality to other populations and contexts. This is not to deny that the empirical establishment of validity is a requisite; however, reliance on common instruments and criteria can be vital to efficient knowledge building and advancement of the field.

The Standard of Proof

Traditionally, in most scientific inquiry in the social sciences, a level of probability equivalent to the .05 level (adjusted for multiple comparisons) is commonly used to permit rejection of the null hypothesis or hypotheses. Recently, the authority ascribed to this standard has been prominently questioned (Cohen, 1990; Maltz, 1994). Most statisticians take the view that the sizes of effects or other similar measures, along with confidence intervals, provide more information than does simple significance at a specified level such as .05. In evaluating violence programs, this perspective of including confidence intervals becomes especially important, because most studies do not have sufficient power to offer much hope of reaching significance at the .05 level. It is primarily in the combination of results that one can expect statistical power to be sufficiently high.

DESIGNING EVALUATION STUDIES OF VIOLENCE PROGRAMS

Evaluations of violence programs must be sensitive to multiple practical concerns. Because of this, it is critical to distinguish between the issues of scientific evaluation and the use of similar methods for large-scale community-based randomized trials (Brown & Liao, 1996; Kraemer & Kraemer, 1994). With such due consideration, it is almost always possible to design a scientifically valuable evaluation of a violence program targeting children. In the next section, we outline several major characteristics of, and decision points in, designing such evaluations and suggest some strategies.

The Benefits of Random Assignment

Evaluations in which there is random assignment have many advantages, and securing random assignment is one of the most desirable features for any evaluation design (Cohen, 1990; Hsu, 1989). Because random assignment to an intervention condition minimizes confounding of other characteristics, especially unmeasured ones, randomization makes interpretation of results more straightforward than it is in designs that rely on statistical controls or other qualifiers of conclusions to determine effects (Brown & Liao, 1996). However, random assignment at times is difficult to institute. Service sponsors may see it as depriving those in need of potential benefits or may believe it connotes a dehumanizing perspective about participants (e.g., treating participants as "guinea pigs"). A funder may not permit random assignment, or administrators may prefer to offer the program on the basis of perceived risk or need. The alternative view of randomization, however, may be just as compelling. It can be viewed as a way to provide a level playing field, with equal chances for everyone to be offered an intervention that potentially could be of benefit but must be evaluated. It has been our experience that both program staff and evaluators benefit from a direct discussion of whether random assignment is feasible or appropriate in a study. Usually this discussion uncovers hidden assumptions about the program that may not be realistic, for example, that no one could possibly be harmed by it or that one can tell which participants are going to do worse if they do not receive the intervention. In many cases, this discussion can lead to an understanding of these incorrect presumptions and to support of random assignment.

The Role of the Unit in Assignment

It is important to recognize that random assignment does not guarantee adequate control for systematic variation (Cornfield, 1978). Randomization tests were specifically introduced to evaluate how unusual a particular outcome of a study was compared to all other outcomes derived from reassignments of intervention conditions (Fisher, 1935). Indeed, in a recent trial conducted at Johns Hopkins University (Dolan et al., 1993), 15 schools were matched and divided into five groups of 3, and the 3 schools in each group were randomly assigned to intervention and control conditions. Although this method of assignment of schools to intervention did minimize their differences on 12 measures of catchment-area sociodemographic conditions and school-level data, no possible assignment could provide exact matches of all pertinent community characteristics. In fact, when the investigators examined the combination of 12 community variables that were the least balanced across groups, they found that intervention conditions differed by more than 1 standard deviation on these variables. In this study, in which the design was optimally balanced, there were some combinations of sociodemographic variables that still could not be balanced perfectly.

The issue of random assignment failing to ensure equality across conditions most commonly occurs when a demonstration project has small numbers of participants owing to funding constraints. Even in the largest evaluations, there may be systematic variation within the sample by condition in important characteristics, such as school attended, family socioeconomic status, or prior risk for violence. If participants in differing conditions are also differentiated by larger ecological units, such as classroom, school, or neighborhood, then the extent of randomness by assignment may be limited because it depends on the number of these larger units, which are the units of assignment. When the unit of assignment has relatively few cases, systematic variations are quite plausible (Gibbons et al., 1993). Random assignment that ignores ecological units such as schools, families, or neighborhoods does not overcome this problem but merely obscures it. In addition to obscuring potential confounds, failure to consider these larger units may lead to grossly incorrect inferences regarding the impact of the intervention (Brown, 1993b; Brown & Liao, 1996; Laird & Ware, 1982).

Setting characteristics can vary and settings that impede implementation of the program constrain impact enough that a program that is effective in some settings but not others may appear, on average, to have no effect, causing a misleading conclusion about the intervention. For example, the likelihood that a conflict-management program will lessen the risk of violence in a school is probably dependent on the overall school norms about violence and the commitment to the program of the school personnel. Change in individual children who happen to attend that school will depend on these larger unit characteristics. This fact needs to be taken into account in evaluation designs and through the use of appropriate statistical methods in analyses (Bryk & Raudenbush, 1992; Gibbons et al., 1993; Laird & Ware, 1982).

For successful evaluation of an intervention, it is important to assign units at the appropriate level. Brown and Liao (1996) introduced the concept of the unit of intervention, which pertains to the operating level on which the intervention is likely to have its impact. For example, in an intervention that is limited to training elementary school teachers to manage aggressive and violent behavior in the classroom, the classroom would serve as the unit of intervention. On the other hand, a comprehensive school-based program with the aim of reducing aggressive acts in all the classrooms as well as in the playground and halls would have the school as its unit of intervention. Great savings in power can occur when the unit of assignment is the same as the unit of intervention (Shinn, 1990).

When Random Assignment to Treatment Is Not Possible

It is a general principle that analysis and interpretation are more difficult in a nonrandomized study than in a randomized one. Even though randomization is sometimes held up as the primary standard of a scientific study, balance (i.e., equivalence among the intervention groups) at the start of the study is as important as, if not more important than, random assignment. In the example we mentioned previously, the investigator may want to balance the communities so that the members have the same level of motivation to reduce violence, which may require hand matching of communities.

If random assignment from the same population to the intervention and control or comparison groups is not possible, it may be possible to randomize some aspect of the treatment. For example, one can randomize the training of service providers as to training methods within the intervention condition; controls imposed on the implementation of service; or the level, dosage, duration, or extent of service offered. All these strategies permit more confident evaluation of some aspect of the program's effects, which can be useful in understanding how much confidence should be extended to comparisons of basic effects that were based on nonrandom assignment. For example, if after randomly assigning participants to a modest versus a high level of intervention, the outcomes turn out to be virtually the same, one could justify limiting confidence in the need for the longer or more involved program.

There are several other design strategies one can apply. The two most common are (a) a wait-listed procedure, or some variant of it, applied in a randomized fashion, and (b) a propensity score method to reduce the bias in nonrandomized studies. Wait-listed designs rely on a randomly defined subset of the sample being assigned to immediate versus delayed intervention (with no intervention if resources are depleted). They can be applied usefully not only at the individual level, such as for a family treatment program for violent offenders, but also at the community level (Hsu, 1989). This design was used recently in a child abuse program for all 10,000 third graders in a large metropolitan city. The curriculum was presented both at the classroom and at the school level, but its evaluation was based on reports of child abuse, which, because of confidentiality, could not easily be matched to individual children within each elementary school. Because the program was being offered at all of the nearly 100 elementary schools, it was decided to assign schools randomly, by geographic location (region), to different times when the program would begin. By doing this, the evaluators could compare rates of child abuse reports before and after the curriculum was started in each region. Data from previous years could be used to adjust for varying seasonal rates of reporting (such as higher rates when school begins), and random assignment throughout the year allowed for comparisons to be made between areas that had and had not been exposed to the intervention, even during times when a report in the media about child abuse heightened awareness. The primary result of not having randomized intervention, however, is that the analysis becomes more complicated because it has to correct statistically for outside events that can be handled in a randomized study.

The second method used as an alternative to randomization is an analytical method—the use of propensity scores—that generally reduces bias coming from self-selection of those who obtain the intervention (Rosenbaum & Rubin, 1983). In a propensity score analysis, two separate models are built, one to assess what characteristics of the data are related to intervention assignment (which should be none if the assignment is random) and the other to evaluate the outcome after adjusting for characteristics related to intervention assignment. The first model of intervention assignment often involves logistic regression, and from such a model, one can obtain, for each participant, an estimated probability, or propensity, of being assigned to the intervention. This propensity, which is built on the factors that empirically predict who would receive the intervention, serves as a way to adjust for the baseline differences between the intervention and control groups that matter in terms of intervention assignment. The second model examines intervention impact after adjustment for these propensity scores. The method of propensity score adjustment has been shown to be beneficial in reducing bias, and it should be used whenever assignment is not random. A key requirement of this method, however, is to have comparable baseline data for all intervention and control conditions. When it is desirable to combine evidence from different trials, a propensity score analysis requires that comparable baseline information have been collected in all the studies.

Between- or Within-Group Comparison

In deciding what nonrandomized design for evaluation is plausible, one needs to decide whether between-group comparisons are feasible or whether the study will be limited to within-intervention-group comparisons. We strongly recommend that some well-matched control or comparison group be identified and included in every evaluation. Without this, one is severely hampered in drawing conclusions about program effects. Sometimes, combinations of controls can be used to advantage. For example, choosing a control from the same cohort, as well as using the prior cohort to serve as control, allows one to juxtapose comparisons for evaluating interventions and begin to identify what factors pertain to cohort and period effects. If archival data can be used for evaluation, such comparison groups can be added with minimal costs. Of course, the key issue for matched controls is the extent to which one can determine any systematic differences and then statistically control for them in evaluation analyses.

If within-group comparison is the only available method, a key question is whether or not one can get multiple measures over time (Francis, Fletcher, Stuebing, Davidson, & Thompson, 1991). In particular, it is important to obtain enough data points prior to intervention to have a reliable and stable estimate of baseline conditions (Rogosa & Willett, 1985). A minimum of two, and preferably three, preintervention data points are useful. Similarly, multiple data points beyond the intervention period aid the reliability of estimation of effects. Multiple data points during intervention, in these repeated-measures evaluations, can provide rich information on the process of change during intervention, not only to single groups but also within the context of a randomized trial (Muthen & Curran, 1996).

An Alternative Strategy: Defining Risk and Its Relation to Program Effects

Another general alternative when random assignment is not plausible is to assign participants according to risk status and to use statistical methods to evaluate the extent to which treated groups approximate an untreated low-risk group. For example, one can compare outcomes of treated participants with more severe risk levels and risk-defining characteristics (and with poorer prognosis), with outcomes of a low-risk or normal population as the criterion. The ability to do so depends on the soundness of the epidemiological and risk data available for guiding these comparisons (Tolan, Guerra, & Kendall, 1995). The strength of such evaluations also depends on the strength of the predictor model for poor outcomes (Tolan,

1996). Finally, the power and specificity of such evaluations are bolstered by the extent to which the relation between the intervention activity and risk reduction is specified and measured (Lorion et al., 1989). The more one can show that intervention activities specifically relate to better outcomes, systematically and as predicted, the more confidence one can have in the value of the program.

An Example of a Case in Which One Cannot Match or Randomize

A common intervention for violence to or by children centers on parent training (Tolan & Guerra, 1994). Training in parenting for child abuse offenders represents a strategy used in many communities. Frequently, assignment to such services is based on an individual judgment of an administrator, most often a judge, rather than on any objective criterion. This assignment may be done with much wisdom but may not be articulated in a manner that allows an evaluator to match participants across conditions. The criterion may be as vague as a judgment of "severity."

In this case, one cannot randomly assign and match treatment and comparisons. A major limitation is that the classification variable is poorly and perhaps unreliably defined. If the judge's decision is completely unreliable, the evaluation assignment may approximate random assignment, but this "benefit" cannot be depended on for interpretation. More likely, there will be some level of reliability in the decision, and although it may be related to some of the baseline data on the participants, the judgment may also be based on information that is not coded or available to evaluators.

However, one may still be able to obtain enough information about the participants to determine statistically whether or not they differ systematically from whose who were not offered the intervention. In particular, it may be important to find indicators of "severity" to determine how much this variable affects inclusion. The evaluator can then compare the participants in the intervention group with those who are not in the group using propensity scores to remove some of the bias in uncorrected differences between the intervention and control groups. Propensity scores can be used also to assess whether the intervention appears to have a greater impact on those with greater severity than on those with less severity. Such analyses begin to address the extent of fit between the individual and the available intervention. There are analytical techniques that can be used to examine the differential impact of interventions without the assumption of an overly simplistic linear relationship (Brown, 1993a).

Although the administrative structure of a program may seem to proscribe random assignment, random assignment of dosage or form of treatment, through a wait-list control or other service delivery features, may be palatable to the programmers (Brown & Liao, 1996). Also, as part of an extended series of evaluations, one could compare those assigned to the intervention who participated to those who did not participate and also to the entire control group. In addition, one could compare participating persons among those assigned to the intervention to those in the control group who, in more sophisticated analyses, would be projected to participate had they been offered the intervention (Bloom, 1984; Little & Yau, 1996). Such analyses of participation can help identify important subgroups of persons who are positively affected by an intervention and what effects the program has. As part of a series of comparisons, such information can bolster confidence in the value of the program.

When one cannot employ random assignment, another strategy is to use existing data to improve the reliability of assignment and therefore the ability to consider covariates of assignment in analyses. For example, by first collecting historical information from a previous preintervention cohort regarding each offender's case and matching these data with rearrest history, one can build an empirical predictive model of recidivism in the absence of a readily available intervention program. Using these historical data, one could objectively classify offenders in this historical cohort as either high or low risk for reoffending and use the same model to predict high- or low-risk status in a concurrent cohort, one that can be referred to the intervention program to be tested. If assignment to treatment is based on a person's judgment (e.g., the judge), it would also be valuable to have those judging review the same historical cases and provide their own risk categorization. This step may articulate the system of classification used, and it also permits comparison of these markers with more objective indicators. By comparing the predictive validity of the judge's assessment and a data-based version, as well as combining the information in an integrated risk assessment, the researchers can more clearly define the low-risk group and can have confidence in its use as a comparison group for the recidivism rate in the concurrent severe group, whose members have been assigned to the treatment by the judge. Also, by comparing the outcome of the high-risk group, which received the treatment program, to that of the concurrent, untreated low-risk group, a relative reduction in the recidivism rate can be assessed. Differences in the recidivism rate, or more generally, differences in the complete distribution of the time to rearrest, provide an assessment of the reduction in recidivism in the high-risk group compared to that in the low-risk group. Because of the different lengths of follow-up of participants, the preferred methods of analyzing such data involve survival analysis techniques (Kalbfleisch & Prentice, 1980; Lee, 1992).

One can draw conclusions about the intervention program's beneficial effects on the basis of evidence that all of the following occurred: (a) The historical high-risk group experienced higher recidivism than the historical lower risk group; (b) the concurrent high-risk group, which was exposed to the intervention, had a lower recidivism rate than the historically high-risk group, which did not have the intervention; and (c) the difference in recidivism decreased in the concurrent cohort compared to the preintervention historical cohort. Of course, even if all these points were supported by the data, explanations other than the effectiveness of the treatment could account for the findings. Although the conclusions have some veracity, they are not absolute. If the risk status measure had less validity concurrently than historically, for example, if police policies about reporting domestic violence changed between the two periods, thereby making recidivism rates noncomparable, the conclusion of a beneficial intervention effect on the high-risk population would be misleading. Like all nonrandomized studies, this one contains numerous threats to validity.

Evaluating Outcomes With Longitudinal Data

A major consideration in the evaluation of violence programs involves the use of multiple measures to assess the extent to which an intervention program affects outcomes. With multiple measures come more complex analytical techniques. Four characteristics of particular importance in evaluating impact using longitudinal data are (a) the autocorrelation of error across time, (b) the interaction of risk with intervention effects, (c) participant attrition and accretion, and (d) the distributional characteristics of the measures of change.

Autocorrelated Errors

Studies of violence and aggression that track individuals over time always include notation of the stability of such behaviors across time (Coie & Dodge, 1996). This stability shows up in longitudinal data as positive correlations across time. One consequence of these correlations is that summary results at different points in time are not independent of one another; therefore, part of the reason for intervention differences at 1-year outcome assessments could be the existing differences at 6-month outcome assessments. If one reported the results at each time point only, one would not know what proportion of the differences found was due to autocorrelation in the data. One strategy used in evaluation is to make explicit use of the autocorrelation structure across time to increase the statistical power in detecting differences. Specifically, one can model the outcomes in growth models in which each participant has his or her own growth trajectory, which can be described by a few individual-level parameters. These individual-level growth parameters, such as the initial level and the participant's mean growth rate across time, can be analyzed in a second-stage analysis to assess differences in these distributions across intervention groups. When growth curve models do an adequate job of describing individual-level growth, they provide an increase in statistical power over analyses that treat only one outcome at a time (Curran & Muthen, 1996; Muthen & Curran, 1996)

Risk Intervention Effect Interactions

Most interventions, particularly preventive ones, are applied to persons with differential risk whose response to a given intervention is likely to vary (Smith & Sechrest, 1991). However, it has been common practice to assume that the best indicator of a program's value is its average effect across all persons receiving it. In fact, it may be more likely for low-risk participants to show little change because they do not have much room for diminishment in risk, whereas those with greater risk can show greater benefit (Brown & Liao, 1996). In contrast, it may be that some violence prevention programs (e.g., conflict resolution) work better for the portion of the population with moderate risk (Tolan & Guerra, 1995). Therefore, it is important to consider how much change that is not due to maturity and measurement error is plausible with the target group (Francis et al., 1991). For more intensive programs targeting selectively high-risk individuals, one might expect more change per participant, leading to more substantial effect sizes for those able to show much change (Lorion et al., 1989). Similarly, in a large universally applied intervention, the extent of change may vary substantially as a function of initial risk (Brown, 1993a, 1993b). In both cases, mean effects for a given population may be misleading with regard to the merit of the program. One often wants to evaluate how risk status prior to the intervention interacted with the benefits of the program. These questions call for analyses that consider conditional effects on preintervention-level data. It may also be useful to evaluate impact variation by initial status at different times postintervention, because impact may evidence at different points post-intervention, depending on initial risk level. Some repeated measures analyses do not explicitly indicate conditional effects on the level of the individual before intervention started, and these analyses cannot reveal a complete picture of who benefited from an intervention.

Attrition and Accretion

In any longitudinal study, a major concern is loss for follow-up of participants from the initial assessment (Brown, 1990; Brown & Liao, 1996; Little & Rubin, 1987). If there is differential attrition by intervention group across time (e.g., more initially violent participants in the control group who are less likely to agree to reinterview, compared to the intervention group), one could observe poorer outcomes in the intervention group despite an overall benefit to that group (Tolan et al., 1996). There are statistical methods that can be applied to help differentiate the impact of a program from differential attrition effects; although they work well in a large number of theoretical cases (Little & Rubin, 1987), in studies with substantial amounts of missing data nonrandom missing data may lead to erroneous conclusions. The standard we recommend that evaluators follow in dealing with missing data on outcomes is to fit models under a non-ignorable missing-data mechanism, which often requires iterative solutions, such as the EM algorithm (Dempster, Laird, & Rubin, 1977; Schafer, 1996). It is then useful to follow up with sensitivity analyses of this non-ignorable assumption (Rubin, 1977).

A practical decision to address is how to handle participants who receive less than the full dose of intervention, whether they come into or move out of the communities involved during the period when the intervention is going on. Accretion, or the entry of participants into the intervention condition, can hinder evaluation in several ways. If participants cross conditions, one would expect to find an attenuated result in analyses that use their assignment to the initial condition. Dropping these participants may be more practical, but the analysis will lose credibility to those who believe that only "intent to treat" analyses are appropriate. Our suggestion is to perform both analyses: classifying all participants by individual intervention assignment as well as removing those who do not participate or receive an insignificant portion of the intervention. The preferred result is to find effects for both analyses, with larger effects for analyses of participants only. If there are no meaningful differences in these analyses, the value of the program needs to be questioned, particularly as attrition and accretion increase. If there are differences in the significance or size of the comparisons, careful consideration of covariates of benefit among those who receive a portion of the intervention can reveal potential explanations useful for future programming.

Another unexpected impact occurs when the intervention is over a long period of time and has a highly mobile or shifting population, such as occurs in the inner-city schools of the Metropolitan Area Child Study (Guerra, Eron, Huesmann, Tolan, & Van Acker, in press). Owing to yearly mobility rates of up to 40% in this population, an intervention that started with a classroom of 30 children contained only 18 of the original children at the end and an additional 12 children who entered at various points in the intervention! In schools with high turnover rates, an intervention may be a strong enough incentive for a family to stay in the same area so that the child may be provided services, thus causing a beneficial intervention effect but making the analysis problematic. The detection of effects and the distinction of these effects from those of limited involvement require careful analysis and examination of effects across multiple analyses (e.g., randomly assigned groups, minimal-dosage groups, stable vs. mobile classrooms). Because accretion is common to most violence prevention and treatment programs, its effects on analyses must be considered in evaluation research.

Distributional Characteristics of Indicators of Change

In addition to the commonly noted problems of unreliability of measurement and autocorrelation affecting the interpretation of change scores, evaluators of violence intervention programs should give careful attention to distributional characteristics of measures, particularly those related to measuring change in target characteristics (e.g., dependent variables). Most of the characteristics are low base-rate problems, and many of the scales used to measure change in such behaviors transform the scales to reduce skewness and improve linearity (Tukey, 1970). A more useful alternative may be to model such behavior using skewed distributions such as the Poisson distribution or to model the data as a mixture distribution (Muthen, Brown, Khoo, Yang, & Jo, 1996). If they are not considered, these distributional characteristics can undermine the validity of the usual normal distribution–based analyses and act to either underestimate or overestimate a program's impact.

CONCLUSION

We have demonstrated that scientific evaluations of intervention programs are possible under a wide set of circumstances that include designs with a formal randomization to intervention assignment as well as designs in which assignment is subject to conditions, only some of which can be modeled. The development of scientifically useful evaluation designs rests not only on precision and control, but also on due consideration of stakeholders' reservations and interests and on the use of newer and alternative analysis strategies. When these approaches are used, program evaluation can aid program design and make sound decision making more likely. Also, the evaluation of specific programs needs to be subsumed into the development of databases for meta-analytic and trend analyses that can build strategies. The result will be less focus on ensuring that only successful program results are published or on judging program benefits on the basis of one or a few tests. The most demanding designs—for example, those that randomize not only classrooms to intervention but also children to classrooms—can be easier to analyze than designs that do not have such randomization (Ialongo et al., 1996). Even when a study has only a tiny number of units to assign, random assignment can be a major benefit when the results of a number of such studies are combined.

The "real world" often places major limitations on the design of an intervention. It may seem that random assignment or other features of strong evaluation are often impossible or have political consequences that would sacrifice the integrity of the program. We have suggested that there are few instances in which this is the case and a number of alternative methods of randomizing and otherwise strengthening evaluation. The general principle is to reduce some of the bias inherent in the evaluation and to measure bias as much as possible. The scientific methods serve a practical aim.

Taking a broad view of each evaluation of a violence program—that each contributes to the overall knowledge of which programs work and for whom they work—we recommend that all researchers report how the assignment to intervention was done and collect baseline data that can be used to build a predictive model of intervention choice. In addition, reporting baseline differences by condition, outcome distributions after adjusting for baseline differences, and interaction effects of intervention by baseline characteristics will enhance the base of knowledge and allow investigators to combine results from separate studies. It will be possible then to have substantial influence on programmers and policy.

REFERENCES

Bloom, H. S. (1984). Accounting for no-shows in experimental evaluation designs. *Evaluation Review, 8*, 225–246.

Brown, C. H. (1990). Protecting against nonrandomly missing data in longitudinal studies. *Biometrics, 46*, 143–155.

Brown, C. H. (1993a). Analyzing preventive trials with generalized additive models. *American Journal of Community Psychology, 21*, 635–664.

Brown, C. H. (1993b). Statistical methods for preventive trials in mental health. *Statistics in Medicine, 12*, 289–300.

Brown, C. H., & Liao, J. (1996). *Principles for designing randomized preventive trials in mental health*. Manuscript submitted for publication.

Bryk, A. S., & Raudenbush, S. W. (1992). *Hierarchical linear models: Applications and data analysis methods*. Newbury Park, CA: Sage.

Cohen, J. (1990). Things I have learned (so far). *American Psychologist, 45*, 1304–1312.

Cohen, S. H., & McSweeny, A. J. (1982). Designs for evaluation of youth treatment programs. In A. J. McSweeny, W. J. Fremouw, & R. P. Hawkins (Eds.), *Practical program evaluation in youth treatment* (pp. 61–95). Springfield, IL: Charles C Thomas.

Coie, J. D., & Dodge, K. A. (1996). Aggression and antisocial behavior. In W. Damon (Series Ed.) & N. Eisenberg (Vol. Ed.), *Handbook of Child Psychology: Vol. 3. Social, emotional, and personality development* (5th ed.). New York: Wiley.

Cornfield, J. (1978). Randomization by group: A formal analysis. *American Journal of Epidemiology, 108,* 100–102.

Cronbach, L. J. (1975). Beyond the two disciplines of scientific psychology. *American Psychologist, 30,* 116–126.

Curran, P., & Muthen, B. O. (1996). *Testing developmental theories in intervention research: Latent growth analysis and power estimation.* Manuscript submitted for publication.

Dempster, A. P., Laird, N. M., & Rubin, D. B. (1977). Maximum likelihood estimation from incomplete data via the EM algorithm (with discussion). *Journal of the Royal Statistical Society Series B, 39,* 1–38.

Dolan, L. J., Kellam, S. G., Brown, C. H., Werthamer-Larsson, L., Rebok, G. W., Mayer, L. S., Laudolff, J., Turkkan, J. S., Ford, C., & Wheeler, L. (1993). The short-term impact of two classroom-based preventive interventions on aggressive and shy behaviors and poor achievement. *Journal of Applied Developmental Psychology, 14,* 317–345.

Fisher, R. A. (1935). *The design of experiments.* Edinburgh, Scotland: Oliver & Boyd.

Francis, D. J., Fletcher, J. M., Stuebing, K. K., Davidson, K. C., & Thompson, N. M. (1991). Analysis of change: Modeling individual growth. *Journal of Consulting and Clinical Psychology, 59,* 27–37.

Gibbons, R. D., Hedeker, D. R., Elkin, I., Waternaux, C., Kraemer, H. C., Greenhouse, J. B., Shea, M. T., Imber, S. D., Sotsky, S. N., & Watkins, J. D. (1993). Some conceptual and statistical issues in analysis of longitudinal psychiatric data. *Archives of General Psychiatry, 50,* 739–750.

Greenwood, P. W., Model, K. E., Rydell, C. P., & Chiesa, J. (1996). *Diverting children from a life of crime: Measuring costs and benefits* (Report 17, RAND Corporation). Santa Monica, CA: RAND.

Guerra, N. G., Eron, L. D., Huesmann, L. R., Tolan, P. H., & Van Acker, R. (in press). A cognitive/ecological approach to the prevention and mitigation of violence and aggression in inner-city youth. In K. Bjorkquist & D. P. Fry (Eds.), *Styles of conflict resolution: Models and applications from around the world.* New York: Academic Press.

Holland, P. W. (1986). Statistics and causal inference. *Journal of the American Statistical Association, 81,* 945–960.

Hsu, L. M. (1989). Random sampling, randomization, and equivalence of contrasted groups in psychotherapy outcome research. *Journal of Consulting and Clinical Psychology, 57,* 131–137.

Ialongo, N., Werthamer, L., Kellam, S. G., Brown, C. H., Wang, S., & Lin, Y. (1996). *Proximal impact of classroom and family preventive interventions on early risk behaviors for later aggression, depression, and drug use* (technical report, Johns Hopkins University Prevention Research Center). Baltimore: Johns Hopkins Press.

Kalbfleisch, J. D., & Prentice, R. L. (1980). *The statistical analysis of failure time data.* New York: Wiley.

Koepsell, T. D., Wagner, E. H., Cheadle, A. C., Patrick, D. C., Martin, P. H., & Diehr, P. (1992). Selected methodological issues in evaluating community-based health promotion and disease prevention programs. *Annual Review of Public Health, 13,* 31–57.

Kraemer, H. C., & Kraemer, K. L. (1994). Design and analysis issues for trials of prevention programs in mental health research. In institute of Medicine, *Reducing risks for mental disorders: Frontiers for preventive intervention research* (pp. 129–156). Washington, DC: Institute of Medicine.

Laird, N. M., & Ware, J. H. (1982). Random effects models for longitudinal data. *Biometrics, 38,* 963–974.

Lee, E. T. (1992). *Statistical methods for survival data analysis* (2nd ed.). New York: Wiley.

Lipsey, M. W., & Wilson, D. B. (1993). The efficacy of psychological, educational and behavioral treatment: Confirmation from meta-analysis. *American Psychologist, 48,* 1181–1209.

Little, R. J. A., & Rubin, D. B. (1987). *Statistical analysis with missing data.* New York: Wiley.

Little, R. J. A., & Yau, L. H-Y. (1996). *Statistical analysis of longitudinal data with drop-outs.* Manuscript submitted for publication.

Lorion, R. P., Price, R. H., & Eaton, W. W. (1989). The prevention of child and adolescent disorders: From theory to research. In D. Shaffer, I. Philips, & M. M. Silverman (Eds.), *Prevention of mental disorders, alcohol and other drug use in children and adolescents* (pp. 55–96). Rockville, MD: Office for Substance Abuse Prevention.

Lorion, R. P., Tolan, P. H., & Wahler, R. G. (1987). Prevention. In H. C. Quay (Ed.), *The handbook of juvenile delinquency* (pp. 383–416). New York: Wiley.

Maltz, M. (1994). Deviating from the mean: The declining significance of significance. *Journal of Research in Crime and Delinquency, 31,* 408–437.

Mitroff, I. I. (1983). Beyond experimentation: New methods for a new age. In E. Seidman (Ed.), *Handbook of social intervention* (pp. 163–177). Beverly Hills, CA: Sage.

Muthen, B. O., Brown, C. H., Khoo, S-T., Yang, C-C., & Jo, B. (1996). *General growth mixture modeling of latent trajectory classes: Perspectives and prospects* (technical report, UCLA College of Education). Los Angeles: UCLA Press.

Muthen, B. O., & Curran, P. (1996). *General growth modelling in experimental designs: A latent variable framework for analysis and power estimation.* Manuscript submitted for publication.

Reid, J. R., & Eddy, J. M. (1996a). *Can we afford to prevent violence? Can we afford not to? Comments on Peter W. Greenwood's "The cost-effectiveness of early intervention as a strategy for reducing violent crime"* (technical report, Oregon Social Learning Center). Portland, OR: Oregon Social Learning Center.

Reid, J. R., & Eddy, J. M. (1996b). The prevention of antisocial behavior: Some considerations in the search for effective interventions. In D. M. Stoff, J. Breiling, & J. D. Maser (Eds.), *The handbook of antisocial behavior.* New York: Wiley.

Rogosa, D. R., & Willett, J. B. (1985). Understanding correlates of change by modeling individual differences in growth. *Psychometrika, 50,* 203–228.

Rosenbaum, P. R., & Rubin, D. B. (1983). The central role of the propensity score in observational studies for causal effects. *Biometrika, 70,* 41–55.

Rossi, P. H., & Freeman, H. E. (1985). *Evaluation: A systematic approach.* Beverly Hills, CA: Sage.

Rubin, D. B. (1974). Estimating causal effects of treatments in randomized and nonrandomized studies. *Journal of Educational Psychology, 66,* 688–701.

Rubin, D. B. (1977). Formalizing subjective notions about the effect of nonrespondents in sample surveys. *Journal of the American Statistical Association, 72,* 538–543.

Schafer, J. L. (1996). *Analysis of incomplete multivariate data.* New York: Chapman & Hall.

Shadish, W. R. (1990). Defining excellence criteria in community research. In P. Tolan, C. Keys, F. Chertok, & L. Jason (Eds.), *Researching community psychology: Issues of theory and methods* (pp. 9–20). Washington, DC: American Psychological Association.

Shinn, M. (1990). Mixing and matching: Levels of conceptualization, measurement, and statistical analysis in community research. In P. H. Tolan, C. Keys, F. Chertok, & L. Jason (Eds.), *Researching community psychology: Issues of theory and methods* (pp. 111–126). Washington, DC: American Psychological Association.

Smith, B., & Sechrest, L. (1991). Treatment of Aptitude × Treatment interactions. *Journal of Consulting and Clinical Psychology, 59,* 233–244.

Tolan, P. H. (1996). Characteristics shared by exemplary child clinical interventions for indicated populations. In M. C. Roberts (Ed.), *Model programs in child and family mental health* (pp. 91–107). Hillsdale, NJ: Erlbaum.

Tolan, P. H., & Guerra, N. G. (1994). *What works in reducing adolescent violence: An empirical review of the field.* Monograph prepared for the Center for the Study and Prevention of Youth Violence. Boulder: University of Colorado.

Tolan, P. H., & Guerra, N. G. (1995). Progress and prospects in youth violence-prevention evaluation. *American Journal of Preventive Medicine, 12,* 129–131.

Tolan, P. H., & Guerra, N. G. (in press). Societal causes of violence towards children. In P. K. Trickett & C. Schellenbach (Eds.), *Violence against children in the family and the community.* Washington, DC: American Psychological Association.

Tolan, P. H., Guerra, N. G., & Kendall, P. C. (1995). A developmental–ecological perspective on antisocial behavior in children and adolescents: Towards a unified risk and intervention framework. *Journal of Consulting and Clinical Psychology, 63,* 579–584.

Tolan, P. H., Kendall, P. C., & Beidel, D. C. (1996). *A case for treatment comparison studies of child and adolescent interventions.* Manuscript submitted for publication.

Tolan, P. H., Keys, C., Chertok, F., & Jason, L. (1990). *Researching community* psychology: *Issues of theory and methods*. Washington, DC: American Psychological Association.

Tukey, J. W. (1970). *Exploratory data analysis* (Vol. 1, limited preliminary edition). Reading, MA: Addison-Wesley.

West, S. G., Aiken, L. S., & Todd, M. (1993). Probing the effects of individual components in multiple component prevention programs. *American Journal of Community Psychology, 21*, 571–605.

Wicker, A. W. (1985). Getting out of our conceptual ruts: Strategies for expanding conceptual frameworks. *American Psychologist, 40*, 1094–1103.

19

PUBLIC POLICY APPLICATIONS OF RESEARCH ON VIOLENCE AND CHILDREN

JUDITH C. MEYERS AND BRIAN L. WILCOX

Although a great deal of research is summarized in the preceding chapters of this volume, few of the findings point directly to specific policy responses. To understand why this is true, it is necessary to examine both the nature of public policy and the limits of what public policy can do (both in general and in the specific context of the current political environment) to prevent violence against children, as well as the nature and limitation of research with regard to its usefulness in policymaking.

HOW PUBLIC POLICY CAN WORK TO PREVENT VIOLENCE AGAINST CHILDREN

Public policy can be used to prevent or reduce violence in a number of ways, 11 of which are outlined in this section. These actions can occur at the federal, state, or local level of policymaking.

1. Government can regulate the production, sale, or use of products that are the instruments of violence, so that those who

465

are prone to use them for criminal purposes have less access to them. Examples include banning various types of assault weapons; restricting or controlling who can have a license or permit to buy or own firearms, such as by adding conviction on a domestic violence charge to the list of items that disqualify a person from obtaining a handgun permit; and requiring a waiting period and background check for buying a handgun, as imposed by the Brady Handgun Violence Prevention Act. Regulations can also be applied to the sale and use of alcohol or drugs, which are associated secondarily with increases in violence. Providing V-chips for television (an electronic feature designed to allow parents to block the display of programs with certain ratings) and requiring a set minimum number of hours for children's programming are additional product regulations that can influence children's exposure to violence in the media.

2. Government can regulate the behavior of people who are in groups at high risk of perpetrating violence, either because of their own past records or because of the group to which they belong. Youth curfews are one example. A survey conducted in 1995 by the U.S. Conference of Mayors indicated that 70.2% of cities currently have a youth curfew in place and another 6% are considering one (Burke, 1996). Another example is the 1996 amendment to the Federal Violent Crime Control and Law Enforcement Act, commonly referred to as Megan's Law (P.L. 104-145), which requires the release of relevant information to protect the public from sexually violent offenders. Although this type of regulation does not directly focus on the perpetrator's behavior, it certainly has direct consequences.

3. Government can impose stiffer criminal sanctions on those who violate the laws meant to protect the public. For example, in some bills proposed in the 104th Congress to reauthorize the Office of Juvenile Justice and Delinquency Prevention, there were mandates requiring adult prosecution for juveniles 14 years or older who commit violent federal crimes or major drug trafficking offenses. Many states already have lowered the age at which juveniles can be tried, convicted, and sentenced as adults. Another example is legislation that imposes criminal penalties for adult gun owners whose unsafe firearm storage methods result in death or injury or legislation that imposes severe penalties for those who take firearms to schools.

4. Government can impose higher taxes on dangerous products

and substances as a disincentive for people to buy and therefore use them, for example, on alcohol, ammunition, or firearms.

5. Government can fund community prevention efforts and services as well as evaluations of these programs. The 1994 Violent Crime Control and Law Enforcement Act authorized $7 billion for an array of initiatives in crime prevention, with an emphasis on comprehensive, prevention-focused, community–government partnerships. Many federal executive agencies have provided grant funds for such efforts.

6. Individual states can expand and further define mandates on professional groups related to training and reporting. Policies can require training in domestic violence, child abuse, and conflict resolution for all police, medical and nursing students, teachers, and others in the helping professions as well as require additional professionals, such as teachers, to report suspicion of child abuse.

7. Government can fund research, evaluation, and curriculum development. For instance, the National Center for Injury Prevention and Control's Division of Violence Prevention at the Center for Disease Control and Prevention provided $1.6 million in 1996 to develop, implement, and evaluate community-based intervention programs to prevent violent injury. Among the organization's listed priorities were programs that create prosocial environments for child development and opportunities for youths at risk.

8. Government can educate the public, disseminate information, and provide technical assistance to communities trying to eradicate violence. This can be done in various ways. The bully pulpit of the president or a governor provides an officeholder the opportunity to use his or her position to educate the public and keep an issue on the public agenda. President Clinton has been outspoken concerning the need to reduce violence among youths through such means as school uniforms, curfews, V-chips, and educational programming to reduce children's exposure to violence on television. The Center for Disease Control and Prevention has held forums on youth violence geared toward helping to establish frameworks for community action. The Office of Juvenile Justice and Delinquency Prevention broadcast a free national satellite teleconference on promising approaches to youth gun violence prevention and intervention.

9. States can reform their child protection systems to maximize the safety of the 1 million children for whom child abuse or

neglect is documented each year and work to keep these children in the environments that are most supportive of healthy growth and development. As recommended by the National Advisory Committee on Child Abuse and Neglect and with the support of the Edna McConnell Clark Foundation, many communities are moving toward neighborhood-based child protection service systems that build community ownership of the problem and connect formal and informal supports and services, so that child protection is no longer seen as a task only for the government.

The nine categories of interventions outlined so far are for the most part directly related to issues for which violence is the central focus. Public policy can also affect the risk factors associated with violence, as discussed throughout this volume, thus secondarily working to reduce the incidence of violence, as in the final two items.

10. Government can intervene to alter conditions that lead to violent behavior through providing prevention and early intervention services and supports for families and by reforming the way that services are organized and delivered, particularly in poorer communities. Examples of enhanced services include increased prenatal care, early childhood education, family resource centers, and mental health and drug treatment. Service systems can be reformed so that they are comprehensive, concerned with prevention, and neighborhood based. Changing the design and control of public housing is another approach that might alter the rate of violence in a community.

11. Government can affect broader quality-of-life issues, largely through economic interventions. Some would argue that welfare reform and increasing the minimum wage are intended to do this; both actions were taken by the 104th Congress.

THE ROLE OF RESEARCH IN POLICYMAKING

Although there is much that can be done through the policy process to prevent violence and mediate its effects on children and families, there are also severe limits in the capacity of public policy to induce change. Researchers have to understand the public policy process if they want their policy recommendations based on research findings to be taken seriously. When researchers consider the potential role their research can play in formulating policy that will result in preventing or mitigating the effects of violence on children, a commonly held assumption must first be examined: that policymakers will make the right decisions—*right* defined by the scientist as decisions that are informed by and reflective of the findings of scientific research—if they have sufficient information about the nature and extent of the problem and identify possible solutions. With strong research findings as an underpinning, they will then accommodate to the political, economic, and social realities of effecting change. Experience suggests that this assumption is too often wrong. Policymakers operate in a political environment where political realities often determine how they use and interpret research findings. What may represent good policy may not be good politics, and the reverse may be true as well: What is good for political gain may not reflect sound policy. The best scenario occurs when good policy and good politics converge, but that scenario does not often occur, particularly when it comes to such emotionally laden issues as violence and crime.

For example, crime has moved to the top of the political agenda over the past few years at both the state and national levels. During this time, many states have proposed or passed laws enabling them to build more detention facilities and boot camps; to lower the ages at which juveniles can be tried, convicted, and sentenced (and in some cases executed) as adults; and to create safe school zones with expulsion of students for gun possession and increased penalties for crimes committed at or near schools. Some states have passed stiffer truancy laws that require handcuffing of truants. These laws were passed in response to public fears and pressure to reduce crime and make the streets safe. These laws were, and continue to be, good politics, but are they good policy, based on informed decisions? There is no evidence in the research literature that demonstrates the efficacy of some of these stricter sanctions in reducing the crime problem significantly among juveniles. Prosecuting today's teenaged criminals as adults may satisfy current political pressures, but it may do little to prevent their younger brothers or sisters from following in their footsteps (Torbet et al., 1996).

The words of the former governor of Arizona exemplify this political position. In his 1994 state-of-the-state message, he said the following: "I was not hired to be Arizona's chief social theorist. I was not sent here to sit meditating on Freud or the latest 'root causes' of criminal behavior. The criminal law deals not with theories but with thugs." He stated in the same speech that he had just read an article that concluded that money spent on corrections is wasted. "The author's cause suffered in my case from bad timing. I had just finished reading an article about Polly Klaas" (Berke, 1994, p. A8). (Polly Klaas was a 12-year-old who was abducted from her home in California and murdered by a man previously convicted twice for violent crimes, who had been released on parole.)

Politicians act to minimize their exposure to risks of public failure, and failures, when it comes to violence, are quickly embedded in the collective conscience, in part because of media coverage. The names Willy Horton and Polly Klaas immediately bring these failures to mind. The stories associated with their names (one a perpetrator, the other a victim) generally have a greater bearing on the policy process than all the research literature cited throughout this volume. This effect is perhaps most evident in the area of child abuse: One false positive—one child who is returned home from foster care or not removed from home after a child abuse investigation who subsequently dies because of abuse or neglect at the hands of a parent—is a much more powerful force in shaping public policy than are thousands of nameless, faceless false negatives—children who languish in foster care or juvenile detention because it was wrongly determined that they could not safely live at home even with the proper supports and services.

This line of thinking has been dramatically evident in New York City, where the death of two children in the recent past, both of whose families had been investigated by the Administration for Children's Services, yet the children were not removed from the home, resulted in a significant change in a policy approach that up to that time had strongly funded and supported family preservation services (cf. Gelles, 1996).

These situations illustrate that knowledge derived from research is not sufficient for, and sometimes perceived as not relevant to, the policy process. Elected officials usually react to crises, media attention on issues, and political forces. The policymaking process is rarely a rational, linear one. Politics is a series of trade-offs, and research-based knowledge is but one of many influences on that process. The following was noted in the National Research Council's report on *Understanding and Preventing Violence* (Reiss & Roth, 1993):

> Research findings, policy choices for the control of violence, and public values are inevitably intertwined. Policy advocates can be expected to selectively publicize findings that support their positions and the methodological flaws in studies that produce contradictory findings. So long as the policy-making arena resembles a free market of ideas, all perspectives are represented and the accumulation of evidence and resolution of scientific disputes at least raise the level of public policy debate. (p. 38)

This last point is important. Scientific research can play a vital role in the policy formation process, but it is only one of many ingredients in the mix that produces policy. This process can prove frustrating to scientists, but it remains essential that researchers oversee the ways in which their research is used or misused by policymakers and advocates (Wilcox, 1987).

There are a number of factors that either increase or decrease the likelihood that any research findings might be used by policymakers.

Policymakers seldom read *Child Development* or *Child Abuse and Neglect.* In the final section of this chapter, we offer suggestions that can enhance the probability of appropriate use of research findings.

THE CURRENT POLICY ENVIRONMENT AND VIOLENCE PREVENTION

We have alluded to a number of characteristics in the current policy environment that are shaping policy related to violence and youth. Policy responses built on rehabilitation concepts have fallen into disfavor in recent years, as witnessed by efforts at the state and federal levels to direct crime dollars into prison construction and to prosecute more youths as adults. Likewise, efforts to build a more comprehensive violence prevention effort have met with a mixed response. During the consideration of anticrime legislation by the 103rd and 104th Congresses, proposals to create a variety of crime prevention programs for youths were frequently loudly dismissed by legislators as an ineffectual response reflecting their proponents' tendencies to be "soft on crime." Most of the youth crime prevention components of the legislation were eventually removed from the bill.

Beyond the ideological forces allied against some youth violence prevention efforts, there are a number of characteristics in the current policy context that are shaping policy responses to the problems of youth violence. The two factors having the most significant effects on likely policy actions, which we address in turn, are the federal fiscal crisis and the growing devolution movement.

The Fiscal Crisis

It is an axiom among those who study the making of social policy that understanding policy means understanding the flow of funding. Dollars drive policy. Less knowledgeable observers tend to focus on the passage of legislation as the end point of the policy process, but it is not uncommon for legislative bodies, both federal and state, to pass legislation only to let it die of starvation. Many a program has been authorized but never funded.

The current fiscal climate is unique in the challenges it presents to policymakers. Heclo (1996) has provided a succinct analysis of three broad factors precipitating the fiscal dilemma that will confront federal (and to a lesser extent, state) policymakers. First, old sources of "fiscal slack" have dried up, making it far more difficult for policymakers to find revenue for new social programs. The "peace dividend"—money saved by the ending of the cold war—was consumed by growth in other government sectors such as health care. The domestic portion of the budget grew parallel to the defense shrinkage, but the dollars were eaten up by entitlements and other mandatory spending. The economy is still slow relative to pre-1973 rates of growth. While the market has grown, the growth in the gross national product is nowhere near what it was in the 1960s, and growth of personal income and wealth, although showing a small upturn in the past two years, is still relatively flat overall, especially compared to the postwar economy up until the early 1970s. Finally, the result of the 1981 legislation that indexed tax brackets to inflation has been that increases in income below the rate of inflation no longer push one into a higher tax bracket. "Bracket creep," which was once a steady source of rising federal revenues, is now a thing of the past and a major reason for the decline in fiscal slack.

Second, deficits racked up in prior years, along with policy decisions obligating federal funds in future years, have placed strains on present and future spending choices. The deficits and resulting debt, which grew most rapidly during the 1980s, require that a growing portion of federal revenues be devoted to interest payments on the national debt. These interest payment obligations became the fastest growing portion of the federal budget in the late 1980s, and they used dollars that might have been spent on various discretionary programs, including social programs serving children and youths. In addition to the growing interest payments on the debt, increasing middle-class entitlement spending has put tremendous pressures on the federal budget. By the mid-1990s, federal spending for retirement, disability, and health benefits alone equaled approximately 55% of federal revenues. The growth in entitlement spending, particularly for the most broad-based entitlement programs, has already forced significant reductions in other budget categories, especially in the nondefense discretionary arena.

Finally, Heclo (1996) noted that the worst news is yet to come. Over the next few decades, the baby boom generation will enter retirement in enormous numbers. As its members retire, they will begin claiming the various entitlement benefits due them. Entitlement spending will expand rapidly and, in the absence of changes in the tax rate or the entitlement benefits themselves, will consume more than 100% of federal revenues.

The federal budgetary crisis has already had significant effects on social spending. Not surprisingly, Congress has thus far focused its budget cutting on defense spending and programs serving low-income citizens and immigrants. Most programs that address youth violence have so far been spared significant cuts, but the increasing pressures on the budget make such cuts more likely unless dramatic steps are taken to increase federal revenues or reduce entitlement obligations.

It is important to recognize that at the same time, but for somewhat different reasons, many states are experiencing increased budgetary pressures. Slowed economic growth coupled with pressures to reduce taxes have reduced fiscal slack. Virtually all states are required by law to produce balanced budgets, so the option of running a deficit when revenue shortfalls occur is not available to most states. An additional, increasingly important source of fiscal strain on state budgets is described in the next section.

Devolution of Responsibility for Policy

One response of policymakers to the current fiscal crisis has been a reevaluation of the responsibilities of federal, state, and local governments. Among the many programs funded in whole or in part by the federal government, some were once primarily or wholly the responsibility of state or local governments. For a variety of reasons, over time the federal government assumed significant responsibility in areas such as foster care, child care, income security (cash welfare), child support enforcement, and drug abuse prevention. In recent years, however, this trend has been reversed.

The term *devolution* has been used by policymakers to describe the process of moving authority and responsibility for a variety of federal programs to the states. Many states are also engaging in a devolution process in which responsibility for programs is being shifted from states to localities.

The devolution revolution stems in part from a shift in political ideology and administrative theory. Proponents of devolution argue that many "federal" programs are in fact administered by state and local governments. State grant programs administered by the Office of Juvenile Justice and Delinquency Prevention and the National Center on Child Abuse and Neglect, for example, are directed at state or local governments that implement programs within the guidelines of the legislation authorizing the grant programs. Devolution proponents suggest that the federal government's involvement results in programs that are insensitive to state and local needs and conditions, are weighted down with unnecessary bureaucracy and regulation, and, as a consequence, waste valuable resources. Devolution is proposed as a means of streamlining government and putting program responsibility, authority, and resources closer to people they are intended to serve. Governors, state legislators, mayors, and members of city councils are more attuned to the needs of their constituents than are federal legislators and bureaucrats, it is argued.

There are other forces driving the devolution process, however. One of the principal tools used by devolution proponents is the block grant. Although these grants take many forms, they generally result in the consolidation of a variety of categorical programs into a single "block," thereby giving state or local officials greater flexibility in the use of funds. Typically, there are fewer restrictions on the use of the block grant funds and fewer reporting requirements than would have been the case with the separate categorical programs. In the current fiscal environment, however, block grants and other consolidation proposals are being used principally as a means of reducing the federal government's financial burden by shifting costs (as well as program authority) to state and local governments. One former governor described the current block grant initiatives as a huge shell game being played by Washington, in which program authority and responsibility are being handed to the states while the funding is being used for other federal purposes, such as deficit reduction.

There is little doubt that the block grants proposed over the last few years have been offered primarily as budget-cutting tools. It is not uncommon for block grants to have their funding frozen at a particular level—usually below the level of the combined funding for the consolidated categorical programs they replace—and thus be immune to inflationary pressures. This tactic shifts to the states the costs associated with inflation, as well as the risk that demand for program services (and resulting costs) might increase dramatically in response to a recession.

These two factors—the fiscal crisis and the devolution response—may have dramatic effects on policy responses to the issue of violence and children. As we have noted, the federal government maintains a wide variety of programs that touch on this issue. Deep cuts in federal funding can be expected to affect many of these programs directly, especially research programs, which lack an organized constituency. The absence of fiscal flexibility rules out all but the most politically popular new spending initiatives, and in the current federal political environment, prevention initiatives that do not rely on deterrence have not proved popular. Although looking to the states for leadership in this arena might be the best option in the short run, over the long run states will encounter fiscal problems of their own, which are likely to be exacerbated as states begin to experience the long-term effects of the new welfare reform. Creativity will be required to design prevention and service programs in this new climate.

WHAT RESEARCHERS CAN DO TO PROMOTE CONSTRUCTIVE POLICY

In light of the preceding discussion of the role of public policy and the current policy environment, we next consider the nature and limitations of research with regard to its usefulness in policymaking and what researchers can do to maximize their impact.

These are not easy times, politically speaking, for researchers to have a strong voice in promoting policy at the federal level. At a June 1996 hearing before the Senate Judiciary Committee on the topic of youth violence, a spokesperson for the American Psychological Association (APA), testifying on effective and ineffective approaches to the prevention of youth violence, was criticized by a representative of the Heritage Foundation, a conservative think tank, who at one point dismissed the role of the social sciences in policy applications, particularly when conclusions drawn from the research counter those of "common sense." At another point the critic turned around and argued that reliance on social science research is a very expensive way of confirming what we "already know."

Researchers do not have to be apologists for validating common sense, as Sechrest and Bootzin (1996) stated in the following quotation:

> Some of scientific psychology may sound like no more than common sense, and, indeed, one of the missions of the discipline should be to verify common sense and derive an explanation for those things that seem obvious to us. That is no more absurd than the expectation that physics should be able to explain why, for example, iron is hard. But not all of the knowledge of psychology is self-evident. The field has important things to say to policy makers, and we must learn how to help them to listen and understand. (p. 389)

Following are some steps that researchers can take to maximize the influence of their findings:

1. *Communicate findings clearly to policymakers*, in language that is simple, brief, straightforward, and devoid of jargon. There are examples of findings throughout this volume that would have to be translated into straightforward language if they were to be of use to people who are not familiar with the research process, with psychological theory, or with psychological terms.

2. *Do not neglect state and local policymakers*, because the action will increasingly take place at those levels as the federal government devolves responsibility for budget and policy to states, which will in turn pass responsibility to local governments. Relevant local government entities include not only city and county legislators and executives, but also such groups as school boards and boards that govern the use of other public facilities such as parks or libraries.

3. *Determine what information is most useful and for what purpose.* Researchers should talk to policymakers and find out what information they need. The types of research most often needed include accurate statistical data, particularly epidemiological reports on the incidence and prevalence of violence involving children and youth that describe the extent of the problem and create a baseline for comparison; program evaluations that contain reports of outcomes and long-term follow-up studies of interventions; and cost–benefit analyses of the consequences of violence and proposed interventions. Policymakers are interested in practical information about what works for whom at what cost.

4. *Be realistic and cautious about what research can offer to inform*

policy. According to committee reports and compendiums examining the research base for interventions to prevent violence, the scientific basis for developing effective prevention policies and programs remains rudimentary (Mercy, Rosenberg, Powell, Broome, and Roper, 1993; Reiss & Roth, 1993). The National Research Council, in a report of the Panel on the Understanding and Control of Violent Behavior (Reiss & Roth, 1993) titled *Understanding and Preventing Violence*, wrote the following:

> The panel found that a substantial knowledge base exists regarding some aspects of violent events and behaviors and that certain areas of knowledge are expanding rapidly. However, we were frustrated to realize that it was still not possible to link these fields of knowledge together in a manner that would provide a strong theoretical base on which to build prevention and intervention programs. (p. 21)

Authors throughout this volume make similar statements that serve to limit the applications of the research, statements that indicate that the knowledge base is limited, statistical relationships are relatively weak or unclear, and the results are equivocal. They also state that the interpretation of their findings are limited by a myriad of methodological difficulties, including imprecise definitions of terms, inadequate measures, bias in reporting that affects the quality of the data sources, and confounding of variables.

5. *Beware of what Campbell called the "overadvocacy trap,"* which is speaking with a certainty unjustified by the validity of the findings, and of Meehl's notion of "fireside injunctions," which refers to using the imprimatur of research to pass along commonsense, anecdotal, and culturally transmitted beliefs about human behavior (Sechrest & Bootzin, 1996, p. 388). Throughout this book, there is evidence that research has illuminated relationships but not specific factors that contribute to the conditions and not clear connections between factors and violence against children that can be translated to effective strategies. There are numerous statements of opinion, belief, and presumption that are based as much on common sense and values as on research findings. Although none of these caveats or qualifications are particularly unusual in the research domain, communicating them to policymakers serves to limit confidence in using social science research as the basis for policy decisions; the critic from the Heritage Foundation cited earlier demonstrated this lack of confidence.

6. *Be clear about the theories underlying one's research and the evidence to support them,* but also understand the underpinnings of the beliefs of the policymakers. Belief in individual responsibility versus social responsibility or individually oriented theory versus family systems theory can affect one's preferred policy response.
7. *Disseminate the findings of research in places where policymakers are likely to find them.* In a recent *New York Times* article summarizing findings concerning the effectiveness of drug abuse education programs, it was pointed out that the DARE program, with little scientific evidence to support its effectiveness, was much more widely implemented in the nation's school systems than were alternative programs that studies had found to be effective. Officials at the National Institute of Drug Abuse attributed this difference to the fact that officials in school systems did not know about the competing programs because the social scientists who designed them had failed to market them (Kolata, 1996).
8. *Use the research findings in the domain of teaching.* Most researchers are teachers as well. There is a great need for help in designing training curricula for workers at all levels of government, from agency directors to frontline workers. Researchers can have great influence by participating in the development of both the content and the process of that training. There is also a great need to change the way psychologists train their own professional and preprofessional students so that the students are prepared to work in the new types of integrated neighborhood-based systems envisioned.

CONCLUSION

Even with better efforts to communicate and disseminate the findings of research in ways that respond to the needs of policymakers, it is important to recognize that there are limits to what policy can do to affect the problem of violence. Public policy is a "blunt tool" when it comes to changing human behavior, and alone it cannot change social values, legislate violence out of existence, or revolutionize society's relationship to violence in the media. Policy is an essential tool, however, for communicating prosocial values and encouraging innovation at the local, grassroots level, where concrete change takes place. Research has a central role to play in framing realistic policy approaches and encouraging innovation grounded in scientific knowledge.

REFERENCES

Berke, R. (1994, January 24). Governors' '94 message: Crime, crime and crime. *The New York Times.* p. A8.

Burke, T. (1996). When the clock strikes ten: Youth curfews cut crime. *Youth Today, 5*(3), 1.

Gelles, R. J. (1996). *The book of Daniel.* New York: Basic Books.

Heclo, H. (1996). Coming into a new land: The changing context of American social policy. In S. B. Kamerman & A. J. Kahn (Eds.), *Confronting the new politics of child and family policy in the United States: Report I. Whither American social policy?* (pp. 1–42). New York: Columbia University School of Social Work.

Kolata, G. (1996, September 18). Experts are at odds on how best to tackle rise in teen-agers' drug use. *The New York Times.* p. B7.

Mercy, J., Rosenberg, M., Powell, K., Broome, C., & Roper, W. (1993). Public health policy for preventing violence. *Health Affairs, 12,* 7–29.

Reiss, A. J., & Roth, J. A. (Eds.). (1993). *Understanding and preventing violence.* Washington, DC: National Academy Press.

Sechrest, L., & Bootzin, R. (1996). Psychology and inferences about public policy. *Psychology, Public Policy, and Law, 2,* 377–392.

Torbet, P., Gable, R., Hurst, H., Montgomery, I., Szymanski, L., & Thomas, D. (1996). State responses to serious and violent juvenile crime. Washington, DC: Office of Juvenile Justice and Delinquency Prevention.

Wilcox, B. L. (1987). Pornography, social science, and politics: When research and ideology collide. *American Psychologist, 42,* 941–943.

AUTHOR INDEX

Numbers in italics indicate names that appear in the reference sections.

479

van Ijzendoorn, M. H., 348, 368
VanKammen, W. B., 396
Vannatta, K., 218, 249
van Wie, V., 355, 366
Vargo, M., 60, 96
Vargo, M. C., 65, 96
Vasta, R., 145, 169, 347, 368
Vazquez, C., 346, 365
Verleur, D., 219, 234, 248
Vermetten, E., 44, 46, 50, 52
Vietze, P. M., 160
Villeponteaux, L. A., 55
Vivian, D., 77, 98
Vogel, D., 74, 93
Vondra, J., 82, 100
Vondra, J. I., 23, 38
Vygotsky, L., 306, 314

Wagar, J. M., 232, 234, 235, 236, 248
Wagner, E. H., 461
Wagner, W. G., 218, 248
Wahler, R. G., 346, 368, 445, 462
Walbek, N. H., 151, 162
Wald, B. K., 156, 169
Walder, L. O., 118, 135, 379, 396
Walker, C. E., 241
Walker, L. E., 82, 100
Walker, L. E. A., 355, 368
Waller, J. B., 397
Wallerstein, J. S., 274, 285
Wallerstein, N., 358, 368
Walters, G. D., 152, 169
Walton, V. A., 47, 54
Wandersman, A., 288, 301, 308, 309, 314
Wang, S., 461
Ware, J. H., 450, 451, 462
Warner, J. E., 237, 245
Warren, R., 288, 293, 314
Wasik, B., 264, 268
Wasik, B. H., 226, 228, 248
Waterman, J., 25, 33
Waternaux, C., 461
Waters, E., 25, 38, 343, 368
Watkins, J. D., 461
Watson-Perczel, M., 263, 268
Watters, J., 218, 219, 246
Wauchope, B. A., 13, 16, 38
Wayland, K. K., 218, 249, 276, 285
Webb, C., 217, 241, 321, 325, 334, 335
Wehner, E. A., 353, 365
Weikart, D. P., 277, 286
Weishew, L., 275, 286
Weiss, A., 225, 243
Weiss, H., 289, 314
Weissbourd, B., 290, 314
Weist, M. D., 218, 249

Weitzman, M., 389, 399
Wekerle, C., 88, 101, 222, 223, 249, 340, 341,
    342, 344, 345, 346, 347, 349, 350,
    351, 352, 353, 354, 356, 357, 359,
    364, 368, 369, 428, 437
Weldy, S. R., 23, 36, 45, 54
Wellman, B., 288, 314
Wells, E. A., 145, 167
Werner, E., 307, 314
Werthamer, L., 461
Werthamer-Larsson, L., 461
Wesch, D., 229, 249
West, S. G., 442, 463
Westerman, M. A., 85, 100
Westra, B. L., 65, 100
Wewers, S. 61, 98, 109, 126, 136
Wheeler, L., 461
Whelan, J. P., 226, 241, 257, 267
White, K. M., 12, 37
White, S., 43, 45, 56
Whiteman, M., 255, 256, 268
Whittaker, J., 226, 249
Whittaker, J. K., 230, 246
Who's Who Among American High School Stu-
    dents, 277, 286
Wicker, A. W., 440, 464
Widom, C. S., 64, 88, 100, 143, 170, 222,
    249, 317, 318, 327, 335, 344, 354,
    368, 379, 380, 399
Wiehe, V. R., 145, 147, 170
Wierson, M., 85, 94
Wigfield, A., 365
Wilcox, B., 408, 416
Wilcox, B. L., 414, 470, 478
Will, B., 31, 37
Willett, J. B., 226, 227, 240, 249, 453, 462
Willey, R., 40, 54
Williams, B., 246
Williams, C. A., 405, 414
Williams, D., 432, 436
Williams, L. M., 40, 41, 54, 56, 90, 97, 151,
    153, 154, 170
Williams, R. E., 216, 241
Williams, W. J., 178, 193
Willis, D. J., 406, 416, 429, 437
Wills, G. D., 82, 100
Wilson, D., 294, 312
Wilson, D. B., 445, 446, 462
Wilson, G. D., 154, 170
Wilson, L., 21, 36
Wilson, M., 13, 34
Wilson, S., 61, 65, 96, 101, 231, 245, 366
Wilson, S. K., 59, 60, 65, 96, 100
Wilson, W. J., 184, 193, 295, 314
Wilson-Brewer, R., 379, 382, 385, 386, 398
Wimberley, R. C., 145, 146, 147, 148, 167
Winstead, B. A., 156, 169

SUBJECT INDEX

Behavioral skills training
  physically abused children, 225–226
  sexual abuse prevention, 218–219, 321–322
Beliefs about violence, juvenile offenders, 384–385
Between-group comparison, 453
Bias, meta-analytic studies, 446
Biological risk factors
  physical abuse offenders, 144–145
  sexual abuse offenders, 151–152
Biopsychosocial model, 196–197
Block grants, 473–474
Block organizations, 301–302
Boys
  maltreatment impact, 422
  marital violence exposure effects, 79–80
  sexual abuse effect, 422–423
  vulnerability, 80
Brain structure/function
  experience-dependent organization, 22, 31
  and parental behavior, 31
Bullying
  effects of, 233, 379
  reinforcement of, 275
  school intervention programs, 233
Bystanders
  curriculum intervention, 385–386
  violence role, 385

Capital punishment, 200
Caseworkers, exposure to violence, 296–297
Catecholamines, sexually abused children, 45
Causal factors
  horizontal and vertical analyses, 426–427
  knowledge base, 424–428
Change indicators, distribution of, 459
Checklist of Child Distress Symptoms, 121–127
"Chicago school" approach, 183
Child abuse. See Physical abuse; Sexual abuse, childhood
Child Abuse Prevention and Treatment Act of 1974, 204
Child based measures. See Children's reports
Child Behavior Checklist, 72, 122
Child Behavior Checklist-Teacher Report Form, 117–118
Child development. See Developmental effects
Child molesters. See Sexual abuse offenders
Child neglect
  developmental sequelae, 228
  family-based services, 228–229
  poverty role, 401–406
  social support interventions, 229–230
  treatment models, 228

Child-only treatment, 236
Child-rearing attitudes
  adults abused as children, 47
  child abuse link, 200, 404
  poverty interaction, 404
Child sexual abuse. See Sexual abuse, childhood
Children's books, violent content, 200
Children's Depression Inventory, 115
Children's Depression Rating Scale, 119
Children's Knowledge of Abuse Questionnaire, 323
Children's Perception of Environmental Violence Scale, 120
Children's programs, 203–204
Children's reports
  community violence exposure, 121–130
    mother-based report correlation, 128–130
  domestic violence exposure, 81–82
  treatment program evaluation, 236
Chowchilla kidnapping, 111–112
Cocaine abuse, 406
"Code of violence," 201
Coercive behavior
  in adolescent dating relationships, 357, 361–362
    prevention program effect, 361–362
  in children, abuse response, 25–27
  and mother–child dyad, 347
Cognitive–behavioral therapy
  physically abused children, 225–226
  physically abusive parents, 255–260
  sexual abuse victims, 215–217, 220, 424
Cognitive deficits, physical abuse offenders, 144–145
Cognitive development
  and community violence exposure, 133
  prevention program consideration, 323
  sexual abuse effects, 43–48
Cognitive distortions
  child molesters, 153
  in parent–child relationship, prevention, 346
Cognitive-mediation training
  outcome evaluation, 384–385
  pediatric violence prevention program, 389–390
  violent juvenile offenders, 384–385
Cognitive processes, biases, 346–347
Cohesiveness, neighborhoods, 308–309
"Collective efficacy," 183
Colorblind curriculum, 278
Commission on Violence and Youth (APA), 376–377
Community helpers
  characteristics of, 301–302
  consultation versus training issue, 291–292

"domains of silence," 292
Community support programs
  parent empowerment role, 393
  police partnership approach, 433–434
  poverty protection factor, 405–406
  resilience role, general principles, 306–310
  research evaluation impediments, 443–444
Community violence, 103–137, 171–193
  and academic achievement, 133
  "adaptation failure score," 127
  aggregate data limitations, 186–187
  child exposure to, 103–137, 421–422
    outcome studies, 105–137
    reporter effects, 121–129
    treatment, 231–233
  child-reports, 121–129
    mother-report correlation, 128–129
  count-the-incidents measures, 131, 421
  cultural causal models, 183–185
  data source limitations, 186
  definitions, 172–173
  determinants, 175–183, 294–295
  developmental effects, 133, 231
  domestic violence relationship, 60–61, 296
  ecological factors, 173–174, 185
  family disruption role, 181–182
  frequency of exposure to, 4, 103–104,
      171–172, 296
  in high- versus low-risk neighborhoods,
      294–295
  home violence exposure distinction, 132
  measurement limitations, 131–132
  neighborhood-based intervention programs,
      287–314
  and poverty, 175–178
  racial factors, 177–178
  structural causal models, 183–185
Compliant behavior, 24–27
Compulsive compliance, 24–25
Conduct disorder, 65, 71
Confidence intervals, 448
Conflict in Relationships Questionnaire,
    356
Conflict reactions, 74–76
Conflict sensitization, 87–88
Conflict Tactics Scale, 122, 124
"Consumer" families, 352
Consumer satisfaction, 236
Control beliefs, and marital conflict coping,
    88–89
Coping ability
  physical abuse offender deficits, 148–149
  in socially impoverished neighborhoods,
      300–301
  underlying factors, 298–299
"Copycat violence," 408
Corporal punishment

community natural helpers issue, 292
  institutionalization of, 202–203
  poverty relationship, 404, 432
  in schools, 202, 272–274
Correlational data, 186–187
Cortisol levels
  mental disorders association, 50
  sexually abused children, 45, 50
Cost savings, prevention programs, 373
Count-the-incidents measures, 131
Coy behavior displays, 25
Crack cocaine, 406
Criminal behavior, predictors, 380
Cross-sectional designs, 40–41
Crowding effects, 179
Cultural models
  community violence, 183–185
  and societal norm of violence, 201
Curfew policies, 466
Curriculum interventions
  aggressive children, 385–386
  drawbacks, 431
  empathic process instruction, 280–283
  in health care training, 390
  racial prejudice reduction, 278–283
  substance abuse, 407
Cycle-of-violence hypothesis, 344

Daily hassles
  abusive families, 205, 403
  poverty interaction, 403
Dangerous contexts, 14–38
  evolutionary processes, 29
  and hypervigilance, 23–24
  learned responses, 19–20, 31–32
  and maltreated children's behavior, 26
  neurobiology of response to, 19–23
  physical abuse critical component, 14–38
  variation in perception of, 27–28
DARE program, 477
Dating violence, 353–362
  adulthood intimate violence predictor, 354–
      355
  in at-risk youth, 355–357
  empowerment role in prevention of, 358
  gender dynamics, 358
  and insecure attachment style, 356–357
  marital violence exposure effects, 64
  predictors of, 356–357
  prevention program, 356–362
Day treatment programs
  child neglect victims, 230
  physically abused children, 224–225
Death penalty, 200
Delaney case, 202
Delinquency. See Juvenile delinquency

Habits of thought
  juvenile offenders, 382
  pediatric violence prevention program, 389–
    390
Handgun violence reduction, 375
Hate crimes, 381
Head Start teachers
  training video, 388–389
  violence prevention training, 386–389
Health problems, physical abuse offenders, 145
Health promotion
  and adolescent dating relationships, 359–
    360
  and dyadic fit programs, 340–342, 350
  home visitation programs, 433
  new and expectant parents, 350–353
Health services, and poverty, 402
Healthy Start program, 433
Hippocampal density, and sexual abuse, 46
Hispanic children, violence exposure, 82
Historical cohort data, 455–456
Home visitation programs
  child neglect intervention, 228–229
  evaluation of, 264–265
  physical abuse intervention, 226, 259, 263–
    265, 302–303, 433
  Prenatal/Early Infancy Project, 350–353
  research evaluation, 433
  violence prevention recommendations, 411
Homework completion, enhancement of, 237
Homicide
  juvenile perpetration–victimization relation-
    ship, 198–199
  and poverty, 175–178, 205
  racial factors, 177–178
Hormones, sexual abuse offenders, 151–152
Hospital for Sick Children program, 235
Household crowding, 179
Houston Parent–Child Development Center,
  277
Hyperreactivity, abusive parents, 145
Hypervigilance
  abusive parents, 23–24
  maltreated children, 23
  neurobiology, 19, 21–23

"Immune system" strategies, 381–382
Impulse control, intervention programs, 276
In-home services. See Home visitation pro-
    grams
Incest offenders, 149–155. See also Sexual
    abuse offenders
  behavioral factors, 153–154
  biological factors, 151–152
  characteristics, 150–155
  cognitive distortions, 153

  deviant sexual arousal, 155
  family factors, 156–157
  paraphilias, 154–155
  wives' characteristics, 155–156
Incidence data, limitations, 186
Income inequality. See Economic inequality
Income level. See also Poverty
  child maltreatment factor, 175–177
  and physical abuse risk, 144
Income support programs, 412
Indigenous helpers
  characteristics of, 301–302
  consultation versus training issue, 291–292
  "domains of silence," 292
Individual therapy, sexual abuse victims, 216–
    218
Infant fatalities, 252
Infants
  child maltreatment rates, 252
  first-time parents prevention program, 350–
    353
Information processing biases
  negative mood state effects, 346
  and punitive parental behavior, 346–347
Ingram v. Wright, 202
Inhibited children, 347
Insecure attachment
  child maltreatment dynamics, 343–344
  and youth dating violence, 356
Intelligence. See IQ
Intergenerational transmission
  attachment theory, 343–344
  maladaptive coping strategies, 300
  and marital violence exposure, 63–64
  parent–child interactional style, 344
  physical abuse, 143–144, 343–344
  sexual abuse, 150–151
Internalizing problems
  cognitive–behavioral therapy, 217
  gender differences, 80, 422
  and marital violence exposure, 65, 71–72
    boys versus girls, 80, 422
  sexual abuse effects, 45
Intervention programs. See also Prevention
    programs
  child neglect, 228–230
  consumer satisfaction measures, 236
  domestic violence exposure, 231–233
  effectiveness and efficacy evaluation, 445–
    447
  evaluation research, 428, 439–460
  integrity of, 236–237
  maintenance of gains, 237
  meta-analysis, 445–447
  physical abuse victims, 222–228
  physically abusive parents, 251–268
  and reabuse, 237, 239

sexual abuse victims, 214–222, 424
Intimate relationship violence. *See* Dating violence
IQ (Intelligence Quotient)
    physical abuse offenders, 144
    and poor neighborhoods, 410
Irritable temperament, 348

Juvenile delinquency. *See also* Youth violence
    ecological variables, 173–174
    learned "habits of thought," 382–383
    and poverty, 175–176
    public policy, 469
    school-based interventions, 431
    in sexual abuse victims, 46

KEEPSAFE program, 224–225
Kempe program, 224–225
Kidnapping violence, 111–112
Kinship networks, 300
Knowledge-oriented programs
    evaluation of, 323
    sexual abuse prevention, 321–323

Latina sexual abuse, 423
Learned responses, and danger, 19–20, 31–32
Legitimate violence index, 200
Lethal violence, juveniles, 198–199
Levonn test, 122–123
Life Events & Circumstances Scale, 119
Life stress
    child maltreatment relationship, 204–205
    physical abuse offenders, 147, 403
    poverty interaction, 403
Limbic system, 21
Local government policy
    devolution effects on, 473–474
    research findings influence, 475
Locomotor development, 27
Loneliness
    child sexual abusers, 153–154
    physical abuse offenders, 148
Longitudinal data
    accretion effect, 458
    autocorrelation errors, 456–457
    differential attrition problem, 457–458
    risk status effects on, 457
Losing Generations, 410
Love, as abuse risk factor, 16–17

Macrosystems, 197
Maintenance of treatment gains, 237
Marital conflict exposure, 76–77

Marital violence, 57–91
    child physical abuse link, 60, 344
    as child psychological abuse, 86
    child witnesses, 57–91
        developmental effects, 77–79
        intervention programs, 231–233
    data collection problems, 59–60
    developmental effects of exposure to, 77–79, 420–424
    ethnicity role, 82
    fear of abandonment link, 17
    gender differences in effects of, 79–80
    modeling of, 88
    versus nonviolent conflict effects, 65, 76–77
    protective factors, 89
    rates of children's exposure to, 58–60
    teenage dating violence link, 355
    as traumatic stressor, 86–87
Mass media. *See also* Television violence
    remedies for violent content, 390–391
    sexual abuse information source, 331
    violent content effects, 201, 381
Matching clients to intervention, 240
Maternal alcoholism, 82–83
Maternal depression
    child maltreatment dynamic, 345–347
    and negative cognitive bias, 346–347
    poverty interaction, 404–405
    prevention program target, 346–347
Maternal stress, 82–83
Media effects. *See* Mass media
Megan's Law, 466
Memory of sexual abuse, 41
Memory problems
    adults abused as children, 46, 51
    and cortisol elevation, 50
Mental processes
    in dangerous contexts, neurobiology, 19–20
    negative mood state effects, 346
    physical abuse effects, 18–25
    and punitive parental behavior, 346–347
Mentors in Violence Prevention program, 391–393
Meta-analysis
    bias conditions, 446
    intervention program evaluation, 445–447
Metropolitan Area Child Study, 277, 458
Missing data analysis, 457–458
MMPI, incest offenders, 152
Modeling hypothesis, 74–76, 88
Money-wasting labyrinths, 203
Moral development, 306–307
Moralistic policy approach, 31–32
Mother absence or presence, 116–117
Mothers. *See also* Maternal depression
    child dyadic "fit" targeting, 345–349

Mothers (*continued*)
    insecure attachment prevention program, 348
    marital aggression, 72, 80
    negative information processing bias, 346–347
    poverty effect, 403
    self-concept targeted intervention, 349
    social support importance, 299
Mothers' reports
    community violence exposure effects, 121–130
        child report correlations, 128–130
        underestimation, 125
    marital violence exposure effects, 59–60, 81
    treatment program evaluation, 236
Motor development
    and physical abuse, 27
    and sexual abuse, 43–48
Multicultural curriculum, 278

National Crime Survey, 186
National plan, violence prevention, 374–376
Negative affectivity
    and effortful information processing, 346
    in parent–child dyads, 346–347
    physical abuse offenders, 147
    prevention program target, 346–347, 349–350
Negative social momentum, 307–308
Neglect. *See* Child neglect
Neighbor Helping Neighbor program, 288
Neighborhood, definition of, 172–173, 287–289
Neighborhood-based programs, 287–314
    consultation versus training issue, 291–292
    general issues, 290–291
    human service worker stress, 295–297
    "natural helpers" in, 291–292
    paraprofessional training, 291–292
    participation factors, 301–302, 309
    poor families need, 307
    premise of, 289
    resilience role, general principles, 306–310
    reviews of, 302–305
    social support role, 289, 297–310
Neighborhood disadvantage
    child maltreatment cause, 187–188
    and community violence exposure, 118
    protective factors, 427
The Neighborhood Parenting Support Project, 304–305
Neighborhood revitalization, 308
Neighborhood violence. *See* Community violence
Neighboring, 287–289

Neonatal home visitation, 411
Neuropsychological deficits
    physically abuse mothers, 144–145
    and verbal processing, parents, 144
New Haven Child Development–Community Policing Program, 433–434
Nonrandomized trials
    examples of, 454–456
    propensity score analysis in, 452–453
    in scientific evaluation, 441
    wait-listed procedure in, 451–452
Normative parenting, 16
North Lawndale Family Support Initiative, 292, 303–304
Novelty response, neurobiology, 19

Offender characteristics. *See* Physically abusive parents; Sexual abuse offenders
Ounce of Prevention Fund programs, 292
"Outreach" programs. *See* Home visitation programs

Paraphilias, in child sexual abusers, 154–155
Paraprofessionals
    consultation versus training issue, 292
    "domains of silence," 292
    in neighborhood-based programs, 291–292
Parent-based treatment
    child neglect, 228–229
    ecological model, 253
    physical abuse, 226–227, 251–268, 432–433
    sexual abuse, 326–328, 331
    transaction model, 253–254
Parent–Child Interaction Training, 223–224
Parent–child relationship
    child maltreatment link, 340, 344
    dyadic "fit" targeting, 345–350
    intergenerational effects, 344
    positive processes intervention focus, 349–350
    prevention program targeting, 345–353, 432–433
    promotion of healthy form of, 340–342, 350
    psychological processes, 342–343
Parent training
    evaluation research designs, 454
    physical abuse intervention, 259–260
Parental empowerment, 393
Parental involvement, prevention programs, 326–328
Parental report. *See also* Mothers' reports
    marital violence exposure effects, 59–60
    treatment program evaluation, 236

504   *SUBJECT INDEX*

Parenting
 in abusive couples, 84–86
 child sexual abusers, 154
 dyadic "fit" interventions, 345–350
 physical abuse offenders, 148
 positive behaviors, 148
 prevention program model, 342–343
 and stress, 82–83
Parents. *See* Physically abusive parents; Sexual
  abuse offenders
Parents Anonymous groups, 261
Parents as Teachers program, 433
Parents' educational level, 124
Parents' rights, 202–203
"Patented programs," 445
Paternal alcoholism, 82–83
Peaceful Solutions, 386
Pediatric violence prevention program, 389–
  390
Peer aggression. *See* Bullying
Peer modeling, 225–226
Peer-Nominated Aggression Scale, 118
Peer relationships, and violence prevention,
  358–359
Perry Preschool Project, 277
Personality
 aggressive behavior correlation, 275
 wives of incest offenders, 156
Physical abuse, 11–38, 222–228. *See also*
  Physically abusive parents
 attachment relationship link, 343–344
 causal theories, 12–15
 and child aggression, individual differences,
  382
 child behavioral adaptation, 26–27
 criminal behavior predictor, 380
 danger perception as critical cause, 11–32
 day and residential treatment, 224–225
 developmental effects, 11–38, 222–223,
  379, 420–424
 domestic violence correlation, 60
 evolutionary theory, 19, 26, 29
 family-based interventions, 226–227
 family characteristics, 149
 incidence, 3–4, 378
 intergenerational transmission, 143–144,
  343–344
 mental processing effects of, 18–25
 moralistic policy counterproductive aspects,
  31–32
 neurobiological perspective, 19–23
 as normative parenting extreme, 16
 offender characteristics, 143–149
 parent–child dyadic "fit" targeting,
  345–349
 personal threat effect, 421
 poverty role, 401–406

protective behavior relationship, 16–18,
  28–32, 300–301
research definition issue, 421–422
treatment and intervention, 222–228
 models and clinical guidelines, 223–224
violence dynamic of, 344
Physically abusive parents, 143–149, 251–268
 affective risk factors, 147–148
 attributions, 146–147
 behavioral factors, 148–149
 and child-related expectations, 146
 cognitive–behavioral interventions, 255–
  260
  research critique, 260
 demographic and social factors, 143–144
 dyadic "fit" targeting, 345–349
 family risk factors, 149
 home visitation programs, 263–265
 intergenerational transmission, 143–144,
  343–344
 intervention programs, 251–268, 432
 multiple-component programs, 262–265
 neuropsychological risk factors, 144–145
 physiological reactivity, 23–24, 145
 psychopathology, 147
 social support interventions, 260–262
 violence dynamics, 344
Physical development, and sexual abuse, 43–
  48
Physical punishment. *See* Corporal punishment
Physiological reactivity, 145
Police partnerships, 433–434
Policy issues. *See* Public policy
Political conflicts, policymaking, 469–470
Population density
 child maltreatment role, 179
 and violent crime, 178–179
Positive affect, falsification of, 24
Posttraumatic stress disorder
 and community violence exposure, 111–130
 "count the incidents" measures, 131
 "count the symptoms" measures, 132
 group treatment, 219
 and marital violence exposure, 86–87
 symptoms, 87
Poverty, 401–406
 child maltreatment relationship, 175–177,
  205, 401–406
 community protection factors, 405–406,
  427
 length of time in, 404
 life event stress interaction, 403
 maternal depression interaction, 404–405
 policy recommendations, 412
 protective factors, 405–406
 social support as buffer, 307, 405
 statistics for children, 402
 substance abuse interaction, 404–405

Poverty (*continued*)
  tailored family intervention, 353
Power conflicts
  dating violence dynamics, 358
  mother-child dyad, 347
  targeted interventions, 353
Preconscious processing, 19–21
Pregnancy, and spousal violence, 79
Prejudice. *See* Ethnic prejudice
Prenatal/Early Infancy Project, 350–353
Preschool children
  child maltreatment rates, 251–252
  marital violence exposure, 78–79
  sexual abuse effects, 45
  treatment effects, 234
  violence prevention, teacher training, 386–
    389
Preschool teachers
  training video, 388–389
  violence prevention training, 386–389
Prevention programs
  adolescent dating violence, 356–362
  and attachment theory, 343–344
  central strategy, 377–383
  child empowerment strategies, 324–325
  child sexual abuse, 317–337
  cognitive-developmental considerations, 323
  environmental change focus, 332, 430
  ethical aspects, sexual abuse, 332–333
  evaluation research, 428, 439–460
  federal policy, 373–374
  financial savings, 373
  "habits of thought" model, 382, 389–390
  knowledge base overview, 428–435
  knowledge-oriented approach, 321–324
  national plan, 372–376
  outcome research, sexual abuse, 321–322
  overview, 341–343, 428–434
  parent-child dyadic fit approach, 342–350
  parental involvement issue, 326–328
  political agenda, 374
  Prenatal/Early Infancy Project, 350–353
  recommendations, 330–332
  research-guided methods, 371–399
  sexual abuse, 317–337, 431
    negative consequences possibility, 325–
      326, 431
  tailoring of, 352–353
  teacher training, young children, 386–389
  youth violence, 371–399
"Prevention zones," 311
Primary prevention
  child sexual abuse, 320, 328–329
  home visitation programs, 433
Priming, danger response, 21–22
Problem-solving skills, 148–149
Process-oriented approach

models, 253–254
  parent–child relationship, 342–343
Project SafeCare, 229
Project 12-Ways, 229, 262–263
Propensity score analysis, 452–454
Prosocial behavior
  neighborhood homogeneity role, 308
  social support link, 299–300, 306–307
Protective behavior
  and anger, 16–18
  child abuse as, 16–18, 28–32
Protective factors
  marital violence exposure, 89
  and poverty, 405–406
  social support role, 297–299, 306–310
Psychoeducational information, 219–220
Psychological maltreatment
  effects of, 230
  treatment approaches, 230–231
Psychopathology
  incest offenders, 152
  physical abuse offenders, 147
Psychopathy, incest offenders, 152
Psychotherapy, sexual abuse victims, 216–
    218
Public housing
  and violence exposure, 296, 410
  youth violence role, 410
Public policy, 465–477
  applications, 465–468
  devolution effects on, 473–474
  fiscal constraints, 471–474
  moralistic emphasis problem, 30–32
  political conflicts, 469–470
  research role in, 468–471
Publication bias, 446
Punishment, protective function, 29–31
Punitive discipline
  and child aggression, 301
  protective function, 29–31, 300–301
Purdue PTSD scale, 115

Random assignment, 449–456
  alternatives to, 451–456
  benefits, 441, 449
  in program evaluation, 449–456
RAP program, 217–218
Reabuse. *See* Recidivism
Recidivism
  rates of, 239
    multiple-component programs, 263
    treatment follow-up studies, 237
Recovering from Abuse Program, 217–218
Relationship Satisfaction Questionnaire, 349
Relative deprivation theory, 184
Repeated trauma, 40

national policy recommendations, 409
remedies, 390–391, 409
Temperament, 347–348
Temporally ordered information, 19–20
Therapeutic alliance, 237
Too Smart for Strangers, 329
"Tourist" curriculum, 278
Transactional model
child maltreatment, 185, 253–254
and family treatment, 254
Treatment adherence, 237
Treatment programs. *See* Intervention programs

Unemployment, 177, 205
Uniform crime report data, 186
Unit of intervention concept, 451
Urbanization
child maltreatment frequency, 179
violent crime rates, 178–179

Vagal tone, 89
Verbal abuse, children's exposure to, 65
Victim-to-victimizer question, 198–199, 427
Victimization
children versus juveniles, 198–199, 427
intergenerational data, 63
and marital violence exposure, 61–62
predictors, 198–199, 427–428
Videos, teacher training, 388–389
Viewpoints treatment program, 384–385
Vigilance. *See* Hypervigilance

Violence approval index, 200
Violence Prevention Curriculum for Adolescents, 276
"Violence toxins," 376, 382
Violent sexual abuse, 49–50
Vocational training, 410–411

Wait-listed designs, 451–452, 454–455
"War on Drugs," 374, 430
Wartime violence exposure, 104–105
William Penn Prevention Initiative, 305
Within-group comparison, 453
Witness to violence. *See* Exposure to violence
Wives of sex offenders, 155–156
Working mothers, 181

Youth curfews, 466
Youth Relationships Project, 357–362
evaluation of, 360–362
goals, 359–360
Youth violence
in dating relationships, prevention, 353–362
learned "habits of thought" in, 382
national plan for prevention, 372–376
and neighborhood disadvantage, 410
perpetration-victimization relationship, 198–199
public policy, 469
research-guided intervention, 371–399
school-based interventions, 410–411
Viewpoints treatment program, 384–385

ABOUT THE EDITORS

Penelope K. Trickett, PhD, is an Associate Professor of Social Work and Psychology at the University of Southern California. She is a developmental psychologist whose research, for almost the last 20 years, has focused on the developmental consequences of physical or sexual abuse on children and adolescents and on the characteristics of families in which such abuse occurs. She has an Independent Scientist Award from the National Institute of Mental Health, titled "The Developmental Consequences of Child Abuse and Violence." In addition, Dr. Trickett is conducting a longitudinal study, now in its 10th year, of the psychological impact of familial sexual abuse on girls and female adolescents. She served as member, and then Chair, of the American Psychological Association's Committee on Children, Youth, and Families from 1992 to 1995. She is currently member-at-large of the Executive Committee of the Section on Child Maltreatment of APA's Division of Child, Youth, and Family Services.

Cynthia J. Schellenbach, PhD, earned her doctoral degree in Human Development from the Pennsylvania State University in University Park. She has published research on adolescent parenting and child abuse prevention for the past 12 years. Dr. Schellenbach is currently conducting a longitudinal research project on the process and impact of community-based child abuse prevention initiatives. She works actively in these areas within the American Psychological Association and is currently President-elect of Division 37, the Division of Child, Youth, and Family Services. She is also a liaison to the Committee on Children, Youth, and Families of the American Psychological Association.